Expertise in Context

Human and Machine

Expertise in Context

Human and Machine

Edited by

Paul J. Feltovich
Kenneth M. Ford
&
Robert R. Hoffman

AAAI Press / The MIT Press
Menlo Park, California / Cambridge, Massachusetts / London, England

Copublished and distributed by The MIT Press, Massachusetts Institute of Technology, Cambridge, Massachusetts and London, England.

Portions of Chapter 1 by K. A. Ericsson & N. Charness originally appeared in *American Psychologist* 49(8), copyright, American Psychological Association. It is reprinted with permission.

Chapter 6 by R. J. Sternberg, Chapter 10 by N. M. Agnew, K. M. Ford & P. J. Hayes, and Chapter 22 by M. Minsky originally appeared in *ESRA* 7(1), copyright, JAI Press. They are reprinted here with permission.

Library of Congress Cataloging in Publication
    Expertise in context : human and machine / edited by Paul J. Feltovich, Kenneth M. Ford, and Robert R. Hoffman.
        p. cm.
    Includes bibliographical references and index.
    ISBN 0-262-56110-7 (pbk.: alk. paper)
    1. Expert systems (Computer science). I. Feltovich, Paul J., 1947– .
II. Ford, Kenneth M. III. Hoffman, Robert R.
QA76.76E95E9893   1997
153—dc21   96-51805
                                                        CIP

Printed on acid-free paper in the United States of America.

Contents

Section V. Pushing the Envelope

Section VI. Recapitulation and Synthesis

Preface

Several disciplines share an interest in understanding the concept of expertise. In particular, the nature of intelligence and expertise are matters of significant concern to psychologists, philosophers, and various kinds of cognitive scientists. Computerized "expert systems" form the best known applications of artificial intelligence (AI). But what is the expertise that experts (human or otherwise) can be said to have? This issue raises many other questions, and has lately given rise to considerable controversy. Some of this discussion reaches to the very foundations of cognitive theory, with new perspectives contributed by the social sciences.

Some interpret the history, philosophy, and sociology of science as challenging the confidence we have placed in our traditional methods of generating knowledge. For example, history informs us that knowledge is highly fragile, that it is at the mercy of shifts in historical context, and that yesterday's experts are today's museum pieces. So how can we have high confidence in modern expertise? Expertise develops, and is labeled as such, in a social context. Nevertheless, we all act as if we believe that some expert knowledge is more than merely social construction. What is the relation between the individual and group processes involved in knowledge in general and expertise in particular? What is the relation between the development of individual expertise and the development of group expertise, for example, by a firm or industry?

Recent work in psychology has focused on the cognitive strategies that distinguish novices from experts, and the mechanisms by which expertise is acquired. Fundamental debates in statistics and psychology have been concerned with the measurement and assessment of expertise. What (if anything) do the empirical tools of psychology and the observational skills of ethnomethodology tell us about expertise and how it is acquired? How does "expertise" differ from mere "knowledge?" Does the distinction between "being an expert" and "being knowledgeable" have to do with skill level? With domain? Or is "being an expert" primarily a role that some are selected to play? If so, what are the selectors and how do we account for individual differences amongst experts? What role do social practices concerning deference, respect or authority play? How can expertise be assessed and compared? Can experts be calibrated? What is required for a domain to admit expertise at all?

And finally, what are the specific implications of various theories of expertise for those engaged in the design and construction of knowledge-based systems? Many have noted that expert reasoning seems to differ qualitatively from novice reasoning. What are the representational ramifications for the knowledge engineer of this observation? How are the computer instantiations of expertise related to human expertise and knowledge? Some work in machine learning is aimed at developing systems that independently acquire expertise by use of statistical or inductive methods—can this be said to be expertise?

The nature of knowledge is central to AI. The large number of successful applications of conventional AI technology, utilizing knowledge obtained by careful conversations with human experts, has already begun to put a strain on the classical idea that knowledge can simply be written down (perhaps with a little effort and guided introspection). It is becoming clear, for example, that while coherent bodies of useful information can be incorporated into working software, these are often inconsistent with one another, or mutually inexpressible. To build larger knowledge bases, or establish reliable channels of communication between several knowledge bases, seems to require more than simply seeking to achieve consistency among various human experts. Recent "knowledge interchange" initiatives are converging on general-purpose expressive languages; but these, while valuable, by their nature do not address the issues of conceptual analysis which are at the root of this problem. We believe that there is a timely need to try to ask, *what is the essential nature of expert knowledge?*

The chapters in this book have evolved from talks originally presented at the Third International Workshop on Human & Machine Cognition held at Seaside, Florida during May 13-15, 1993. The special focus of that workshop was "Expertise in Context." It should be noted that although the workshop took place in 1993, the papers that appear here are actually of much more recent vintage. They were completed some time after the workshop (in some cases *far* after) and have benefited both from the spontaneous exchanges that happened in that halcyon setting and a subsequent extensive review process.

We did not get answers to all the pertinent questions in a few days, but we did focus discussion in some new directions which may provide the beginnings of some real insight into challenging new areas. To some extent the workshop (like this resulting volume) was motivated by the need to build bridges. Much of the recent work in situated cognition has sought its roots in very different intellectual soil than that traditionally occupied by AI and cognitive science. Several authors have perceived their work, which emphasizes social embeddings rather than mental constructions, as an alternative to, and replacement for the mainstream AI tradition. We believe that much of the acrimony in the resulting debates arise from mutual misunderstanding, and that vehicles such as this workshop and book comprise important means by which we can all come to better understand what one another are saying.

The International Workshop on Human & Machine Cognition convenes every other year to address a central interdisciplinary topic bearing on artificial intelligence and cognitive science. The other workshops in the series have been about the Frame Problem (1989), Android Epistemology (1991) and Smart Machines in Education & Training (1995). This workshop series has become known for its operating scheme: first, find an exciting interdisciplinary topic; next, select a small group (about forty) of the most interesting participants; and finally, plop them down in a spectacular location conducive to a free exchange of ideas (and sometimes argument) that often continues informally late into the night. Thus far this recipe seems to have worked well.

Kenneth Ford
Pensacola, Florida, August, 1996

Acknowledgments

We wish to thank the many people who contributed their time and talents to the success of this book. We must especially thank the program committee of the workshop from which it sprang and our indefatigable "workshop referees" for their invaluable service. The most essential contribution was, of course, from the authors of the papers themselves. Mike Hamilton of AAAI Press and Robert Prior of MIT Press helped make the process of editing this volume a pleasant one. We would like to thank Jeff Yerkes, without whom the volume would barely have seen the light of day. We especially would like to thank Emily Fuller and Jackie Gibson of Seaside Group Services for their amazing cooperation and patience during the workshop.

Workshops of this scope and ambition require sponsors. The workshop's primary benefactors were: The National Science Foundation, American Association for Artificial Intelligence (AAAI), and The University of West Florida. In addition the workshop enjoyed generous corporate donations from Taylor & Francis Publishing, John Wiley & Sons, and The West Florida Regional Medical Center.

A Preliminary Tour of Human and Machine Expertise in Context

Paul J. Feltovich, Kenneth M. Ford & Robert R. Hoffman

The aims of this introduction are modest—to portray the basic organization of the volume and to give brief sketches of the contents of the chapters, especially as the chapters relate most directly to expertise in context. The main reason the introduction is lean is that the hard work of analysis and integration is reserved for the concluding chapter (Chapter 24: "A General Framework for Conceiving of Expertise and Expert Systems"). Much that might otherwise be included in an introduction may be found there. We now proceed with an overview of the contents of this volume.

Findings from some of the earliest work on expertise, conducted in the area of chess, were both striking and perhaps counterintuitive for their time (de Groot 1965; Simon and Chase 1973). The findings were striking in the sense that they indicated that experts see and know the world (but only that limited part of it where they are expert) in ways fundamentally different from ordinary people. The results were counterintuitive in that they implicated differences in perception, knowledge, and knowledge organization as the basic source of expert capability and not fundamental differences in reasoning. The knowledge-based foundation of expertise also imputed to *experience* a critical role in the development of expertise; that is, a newcomer to a field who is a particularly astute "reasoner" is not likely to rank among the experts. In many studies following the chess studies, the primary source of the enhanced capability of the expert has been shown to be specialized knowledge and its organization, and the appropriate coupling of these to situations of use. This research has also demonstrated consistently that the fundamental cognitive changes characteristic of expertise require many years of practice for their development.

The chess work involved the study of individuals and adhered to the basic notion that expertise is a fundamentally cognitive thing, a set of cognitive changes that occur over long periods of practicing some skill—for example, playing chess, working problems in physics, diagnosing patients in medicine, and so forth. For many years, much (but not all) of research on the nature of expertise and its development has shared this basic belief. The work has been fruitful, many findings beyond the early ones have been established, and much about the cognition of expertise can now be characterized fairly well (see, e.g., Chi, Glaser and Farr 1988; Ericsson 1996; Ericsson and Smith 1991; Hoffman 1992).

More recently however, there has been a growing recognition that expertise is more complicated. Why can some people work at something for many years and still not be very adept? Something about the particular person, in interaction with the conditions of practice (including perhaps other people), is clearly important. Does the nature of the skill or endeavor itself matter in attributing expertise? For instance, most of us, from many years of doing it, are highly accomplished at tying our shoes. Is this expertise? Is this the kind of thing that is viewed as expertise in our society (or maybe in some other society)? To what kind of endeavors is expertise attributed? Are there experts if nobody recognizes them as such? Who gets the chance to practice—including getting a chance to work on the special cases (e.g., the tricky medical cases or the odd automobile transmission problems) that push the edges past the common? How often do people, especially those doing highly complex and valued tasks in a society, actually work completely alone? How *do* they work? How do they interact with and depend on other people and institutions? Who gets to be a medical doctor (or renowned chicken sexer), and how, and in interaction with whom and what—and who, once trained, acquires and retains the challenging patient (or chicken) base? Are the conditions in which people work and practice themselves changing? Do people stay in the same line of work as long as they used to? If the world changes substantially over relatively short periods of time, can there be expertise at all?

These many questions pertain to context. What is increasingly being recognized is that, well, "no one is an island." All human activity takes place in a complex setting. All parts of context affect, indeed co-constitute, all the others. Even though recognizing this, we trust that there are degrees of influence and that in science (and in everyday life) we can partition people and events *at least somewhat* without losing the phenomena we are trying to understand (or perhaps the phenomena we are trying to *transport* in the case of expert systems). But, how far can we go in compartmentalizing? At what gain, or loss? To what extent and how do we need to deal with the context of expertise for the various purposes that we consider expertise at all? One of the major themes of this volume involves addressing this last question—and related ones such as those noted above.

Reflecting the history of the study of expertise, the major sections of the volume start with the individual and then spread outward. Hence, the first section for the most part addresses expertise from the point of view of the individual and individual cognition (even though some of the chapters branch beyond the individual). We have titled this section "The Cognitivist Perspective." The section serves both to review and extend what is known about expertise and its development from the classic point of view.

The first chapter ("Cognitive and Developmental Factors in Expert Performance"), by Ericsson and Charness, stands as a fairly comprehensive review of research on expertise from the cognitivist perspective, focusing on exceptional human performance. Experts' abstracted, relational, "deep" representation of situations is one of the best established phenomena of expertise. Less understood is how this kind of representation benefits the expert, what it does in enabling more proficient problem solving or decision making. This benefit is addressed by Zeitz in the second chapter ("Some Concrete Advantages of Abstraction: How Experts' Representations Facilitate Reasoning"). An emerging finding with regard to experts is that they frequently reason from what is given overtly in a problem to possible solutions, rather than first proposing potential solutions and testing these out deliberately. Results from a program of research focused on directionality in expert reasoning are presented by Patel and Ramoni (Chapter 3, "Cognitive Models of Directional Inference in Expert Medical Reasoning"). Abstractions, such as generalizations, that experts glean over time from their experiences are one vehicle by which they can take advantage of the extended practice required for the development of expertise. However, another vehicle is the *particular* instances, cases of practice, that have made up this experience. The role of such particularized knowledge in expertise is addressed by Seifert, Patalano, Hammond and Converse in the fourth chapter ("Experience and Expertise: The Role of Memory in Planning for Opportunities"). Much of the research on expert cognition has been conducted in domains (e.g., chess, physics, and medical diagnosis) where the fundamental structure and rules of procedure are relatively stable. What does it imply for expertise when, as seems to be more and more the case recently, work environments become much more labile? This question is taken up in the last chapter of the first section (Chapter 5, "Issues of Expert Flexibility in Contexts Characterized by Complexity and Change") by Feltovich, Spiro and Coulson.

The chapters of Section II ("Expertise in Context") extend expertise in various ways beyond the individual. Sternberg (Chapter 6, "Cognitive Conceptions of Expertise"), proposes a framework, which includes factors that are social and organizational, for broadening our concept of expertise. LaFrance (Chapter 7, "Metaphors for Expertise: How Knowledge Engineers Picture Human Expertise") also presents a framework for helping to understand the nature of expertise. This scheme expresses a number of metaphors that at various times have been used to characterize expertise and the process of "knowledge acquisition" (the process of discerning an expert's knowledge so that it can be replicated in computers). Some of these metaphors emphasize the individual, while others stress more cooperative, model-construction kinds of processes. Stein (Chapter 8, "A Look at Expertise from a Social Perspective") takes a distinctly social and organizational perspective on expertise. He presents a methodology for identifying the individuals within an organization who serve as the greatest sources for consultation on matters of importance to the organization and its day-to-day function. The research reported by Shalin, Geddes, Bertram, Szczepkowski and DuBois (Chapter 9, "Expertise in Dynamic, Physical Task Domains") takes context into account in at least two ways. First, the research is conducted in actual settings of work, in their natural complexity. Second, some of the research explores the nature of working groups, individuals involved in achieving a common goal. Considering these aspects of context has enabled the investigators both to solidify some findings from more individualistic studies of expertise and also to extend and augment them. The last chapter in Section II (Chapter 10, "Expertise in Context: Personally Constructed, Socially Selected, and Reality-Relevant?") by Agnew, Ford and Hayes, takes a comprehensive approach to expertise, interleaving the individual, the contextual, and the relationship of both of these to the "real."

The two chapters of Section III ("Socially Situated Expertise") investigate the situated nature of human activity and, hence, expertise. Clancey (Chapter 11, "The Conceptual Nature of Knowledge, Situations, and Activity") emphasizes the complexity, dynamic nature, and social constitution of the contexts of human activity. Collins (Chapter 12, "Rat Tale: Sociology's Contribution to Understanding Human and Machine Cognition"), while sharing some views similar to Clancey, focuses on the "repairs" people are able to make to what he considers the deficiencies of machines, by virtue of the people having been socialized. The arguments of both Collins and Clancey point to a role for smart machines as helpers, decision aides, human collaboration aides, and the like, rather than as stand-alone intelligent agents.

Section IV ("Expert Systems in Context") focuses on computer-based expert systems to a greater extent than on human expertise. The chapter by Shadbolt and O'Hara (Chapter 13, "Model-Based Expert Systems and the Explanation of Expertise") has two main aims. One is to present a brief history of expert systems. A theme of progressive accommodation to the particulars of context can be seen in this history. The second aim is to explore ways that the development of expert systems can inform about the nature of human expertise. Hayes (Chapter 14, "A Study of Solution Quality in Expert and Knowledge-Based System Reasoning") presents a method for evaluating the quality of an expert system by comparing products from the system to the same products made by humans. Chapter 15, by Stern and Luger, ("Abduction and Abstraction in Diagnosis: A Schema-Based Account") presents a computer system for analyzing semiconductor component failures. Such analysis is highly specialized to the particular features of the situation of failure. Hexmoor and Shapiro (Chapter 16, "Integrating Skill and Knowledge in Expert Agents") propose an analog in expert systems to the development of automaticity in human skill development. In Chapter 17 ("Toward Automated Expert Reasoning and Expert-Novice Communication"), Miller and Perlis explore adjustment of default expectations in an expert system as a means for achieving context-sensitivity. This process mirrors a similar one in humans. Lerch, Prietula and Kulik (Chapter 18, "The Turing Effect: The Nature of Trust in Expert Systems Advice") explore the important interface between expert systems and human users. In particular, their chapter investigates the characteristics of an expert system that contribute to confidence in the advice given by the system. In the final chapter of Section IV (Chapter 19, "Interpreting Generic Structures: Expert Systems, Expertise, and Context"), O'Hara and Shadbolt address directly the problem of accounting for context in the development of expert systems. The approach they propose involves the utilization of vast, highly differentiated variants of basic component models for constructing expert systems, each tailored to the specifics of circumstances. The trick, then, becomes one of finding and matching models to particular contexts.

Section V ("Pushing the Envelope") contains four chapters somewhat different from the others. These discuss aspects of expertise that are unusual. Bringsjord (Chapter 20, "An Argument for the Uncomputability of Infinitary Mathematical Expertise") presents an argument that a certain kind of expertise, the expert mathematician's understanding of infinities, is not amenable to representation in computers. The next chapter by Kyburg (Chapter 21, "Expertise and Context in Uncertain Inference") presents a formalism that takes into account both generalizations and particulars (context) of a situation to capture how experts can improve their capability based on experience. Minsky (Chapter 22, "Negative Expertise") argues that much of expertise consists of knowing what *not* to think or do in a situation, in addition to knowing how to act in a more positive way. In the last chapter of the section (Chapter 23, "Context, Cognition, and Intelligent Interactive Information Infrastructures), Rappaport first discusses how the functional context of human thinking and decision making is a constructive process and then goes on to address how new kinds of information systems can be built so that they participate actively in these context construction processes of their users. This participation should make such systems more valuable and effective.

Section VI ("Recapitulation and Synthesis") contains one chapter. In this chapter (Chapter 24, "A General Conceptual Framework for Conceiving of Expertise and Expert Systems"), Hoffman, Feltovich and Ford address the significance and themes of the previous chapters, provide integration, and present a framework through which the chapters can be related.

Acknowledgments

Joan Feltovich and Rand Spiro, as readers who had not yet read the chapters, made considerable contributions to this introduction.

References

Chi, M.T.H., Glaser, R. & Farr, M.J. (Eds.). (1988). *The Nature of Expertise.* Hillsdale, NJ: Lawrence Erlbaum.

de Groot, A.D. (1965). *Thought and Choice in Chess.* The Hague, Netherlands: Mouton.

Ericsson, K.A. & Smith, J. (Eds.). (1991). *Toward a General Theory of Expertise.* Cambridge, UK: Cambridge University Press.

Ericsson, K.A. (1996). *The Road to Excellence: The Acquisition of Expert Performance in the Arts and Sciences, Sports and Games.* Mahwah, NJ: Lawrence Erlbaum Associates.

Hoffman, R.R. (Ed.). (1992). *The Psychology of Expertise: Cognitive Research and Empirical AI.* New York: Springer-Verlag.

Simon, H.A. & Chase, W.G. (1973). Skill in chess. *American Scientist, 61,* 394-403.

The Cognitivist Perspective

CHAPTER 1

Cognitive and Developmental Factors in Expert Performance

K. Anders Ericsson & Neil Charness

Introduction

In nearly every field of human endeavor, the performance of the best practitioners is so outstanding, so superior even to the performance of other highly experienced individuals in the field, that most people believe a unique, qualitative attribute, commonly called innate talent, must be invoked to account for this highest level of performance. Although these differences in performance are by far the largest psychologists have been able to reliably measure among healthy adults, exceptional performance has not, until recently, been extensively studied by scientists.

In the last decade, interest in outstanding and exceptional achievements and performance has increased dramatically. Many books have been recently published on the topic of genius (e.g., Gardner 1993a; Murray 1989a; Simonton 1984, 1988b; Weisberg 1986, 1993), exceptionally creative individuals (e.g., Wallace and Gruber 1989), prodigies (e.g., Feldman 1986; Wallace 1986), and exceptional performance and performers (e.g., Howe 1990; Radford 1990; Smith 1983). Of particular interest to the general public has been the remarkable ability of idiot savants or savants, who in spite of a very low general intellectual functioning display superior performance in specific tasks and domains, such as mental multiplication and recall of music (Howe 1990; Treffert 1989). The pioneering research comparing the performance of experts and beginners (novices) by de Groot (1946/1978) and Chase and Simon (1973) has spawned a great deal of research (Chi, Glaser, and Farr 1988; Ericsson and Smith 1991a). A parallel development in computer science has sought to extract the knowledge of experts by interviews (Hoffman

1992) to build expert systems, which are computer models that are designed to duplicate the performance of these experts and make their expertise generally available. These efforts at artificial intelligence seem to have been most successful in domains that have established symbolic representations, such as mathematical calculation, chess, and music (Barr and Feigenbaum 1981-2; Cohen and Feigenbaum 1982), which incidentally are the main domains in which prodigies and savants have been able to display clearly superior performance (Feldman 1980, 1986).[1]

The recent advances in our understanding of exceptional performance have had little impact on general theories in psychology. The new knowledge has not fulfilled the humanistic goals of gaining insights from the lives of outstanding people about how people might improve their lives. Maslow long ago eloquently expressed these goals:

> If we want to know how fast a human being can run, then it is no use to average out the speed of a 'good sample' of the population; it is far better to collect Olympic gold medal winners and see how well they can do. If we want to know the possibilities for spiritual growth, value growth, or moral development in a human being, then I maintain that we can learn most by studying our moral, ethical, or saintly people....Even when 'good specimens,' the saints and sages and great leaders of history, have been available for study, the temptation too often has been to consider them not human but supernaturally endowed (1971, p. 7).

The reasons for the lack of impact become clear if we consider the two most dominant approaches and their respective goals. The human information-processing approach, or the skills approach, has attempted to explain exceptional performance in terms of knowledge and skills acquired through experience. This approach, originally developed by Newell and Simon (1972), has tried to show that the basic information-processing system with its elementary information processes and basic capacities remains intact during skill acquisition and that outstanding performance results from incremental increases in knowledge and skill due to the extended effects of experience. By constraining the changes to acquired knowledge and skill, this approach has been able to account for exceptional performance within existing general theories of human cognition. According to this approach, the mechanisms identified in laboratory studies of learning can be extrapolated to account for expertise and expert performance by an incremental accumulation of knowledge and skill over a decade of intense experience in the domain. The long duration of the necessary period of experience and the presumed vast complexity of the accumulated knowledge has discouraged investigators from empirically studying the acquisition of expert performance. Similarly, individual differences in expert performance, when the amount of experience is controlled, have not been of major interest and have been typically assumed to reflect differences in the original structure of basic processes, capacities, and abilities.

The other major approach focuses on the individual differences of exceptional performers that would allow them to succeed in a specific domain. One of the most influential representatives of this approach is Howard Gardner, who in 1983 presented his theory of multiple intelligence in his book *Frames of Mind: The Theory of Multiple Intelligence*. Gardner (1983, 1993a, 1993b) draws on the recent advances in biology and brain physiology about neural mechanisms and localization of brain activity to propose an account of the achievements of savants, prodigies, and geniuses in specific domains. He argued that exceptional performance results from a close match between the individual's intelligence profile and the demands of the particular domain. A major concern in this approach is the early identification and nurturing of children with high levels of the required intelligence for a specific domain. Findings within this approach have limited implications for the lives of the vast majority of children and adults of average abilities and talents.

In this chapter we propose a different approach to the study of exceptional performance and achievement, which we refer to as *the study of expert performance*. Drawing on our earlier published research, we focus on reproducible, empirical phenomena of superior performance. We will thus not seriously consider anecdotes or unique events, including major artistic and scientific innovations, because they cannot be repeatedly reproduced on demand and hence fall outside the class of phenomena that can be studied by experimental methods. Our approach involves the identification of reproducible superior performance in the everyday life of exceptional performers and the capture of this performance under laboratory conditions. First, we show that it is possible to study and analyze the mechanisms that mediate expert performance. We also show that the critical mechanisms reflect complex, domain-specific cognitive structures and skills that performers have acquired over extended periods of time. Hence, individuals do not achieve expert performance by gradually refining and extrapolating the performance they exhibited before starting to practice but instead by restructuring the performance and acquiring new methods and skills. In the final section, we will show that individuals improve their performance and attain an expert level, not merely as an automatic consequence of more experience with an activity but rather through structured learning and effortful adaptation.

The Study of Expert Performance

The conceptions of expert performance as primarily an acquired skill versus a reflection of innate talents have influenced how expert performance and expert performers are studied. When the goal is to identify critical talents and capacities, investigators have located experts and then compared measurements of their abilities with those of control subjects on standard laboratory tests. Tests involve simple stimuli and tasks in order to minimize any effects of previously acquired knowledge and skill. Given the lack of success of this line of research (see Ericsson and Charness 1994), we advocate a different approach that identifies the crucial aspects of experts' performance that these experts exhibit regularly at a superior level in their domain. If experts have acquired their superior performance by extended adaptation to the specific constraints in their domains, we need to identify representative tasks that incorporate these constraints to be able to reproduce the natural performance of experts under controlled conditions in the laboratory. We will illustrate this method of designing representative test situations with several examples later in this section.

Once the superior performance of experts can be reliably reproduced in a test situation, this performance can then be analyzed to assess its mediating acquired mechanisms. Following Ericsson and Smith (1991b), we define expert performance as consistently superior performance on a specified set of *representative tasks* for the domain that can be administered to any subject. The virtue of defining expert performance in this restricted sense is that the definition both meets all the criteria of laboratory studies of performance and comes close to meeting those for evaluating performance by public competitions and open tournaments in many domains of expertise.

Perceived Experts Versus Consistent Expert Performance

In many domains, rules and standardized conditions have evolved, and fair methods have been designed for measuring performance. The conditions of testing in many sports and other activities, such as typing competitions, are the same for all participating individuals. In other domains, the criteria for expert performance cannot be easily translated into a set of standardized tasks that captures and measures that performance. In some domains, expert performance is determined by judges or the results of competitive tournaments. Psychometric methods based on tournament results, most notably in chess (Elo 1986), have successfully derived latent measures of performance on an interval scale. In the arts and sciences, selected individuals are awarded prizes and honors by their peers, typically on the basis of significant achievements such as published books and research articles and specific artistic performances.

Some type of metric is of course required to identify *superior performance*. The statistical term *outlier* may be a useful heuristic for judging superior performance. If someone is performing at least two standard deviations above the mean level in the population, that individual could be said to be performing at an expert level. In the domain of chess (Elo 1986), the term *expert* is defined as a range of chess ratings (2000-2199) approximately two or three standard deviations (200 rating points) above the mean (1600 rating points) and five or six standard deviations above the mean of chess players starting to play in chess tournaments.

In most domains it is easier to identify individuals who are socially recognized as experts than it would be to specify observable performance at which these individuals excel. The distinction between the perception of expertise and actual expert performance has become increasingly important since research has shown that the performance of some individuals who are nominated as experts is not measurably superior. For example, studies have found that financial experts' stock investments yield returns that are not consistently better than the average of the stock market, that is, financial experts' performance does not differ from the result of essentially random selection of stocks. When successful investors are identified and their subsequent investments are tracked, there is no evidence for sustained superiority (McClosky 1990). A large body of evidence has been accumulated showing that experts frequently do not outperform other people in many relevant tasks in their domains of expertise (Camerer and Johnson 1991). Experts may have much more knowledge and experience than others, yet their performance on critical tasks may not be reliably better than that of nonexperts (Ericsson and Lehmann 1996). In summary, researchers cannot seek out experts and simply assume that their performance on relevant tasks is superior; they must instead demonstrate this superior performance.

Identifying and Capturing Expert Performance

For most domains of expertise, people have at least an intuitive conception of the kind of activities at which an expert should excel. In everyday life, however, these activities rarely have clearly defined starting and end points, nor do the exact external conditions of a specific activity reoccur. The main challenge is thus to identify particular well-defined tasks that frequently occur and that capture the essence of expert performance in a specific domain. It is then possible to determine the contexts in which each task naturally occurs and to present these tasks in a controlled context to a larger group of other experts.

De Groot's (1946/1978) research on expertise in chess is generally considered the pioneering effort to capture expert performance. Ability in chess playing is determined by the outcomes of chess games between opponents competing in tournaments. Each game is different and is rarely repeated exactly except for the case of moves in the opening phase of the game. De Groot, who was himself a chess master, determined that the ability to play chess is best captured in the task of selecting the next move for a given chess position taken from the middle of the game between two chess masters. Consistently superior performance on this task for arbitrary chess positions logically implies a very high level of skill. Researchers can therefore elicit experts' superiority in performing a critical task by presenting the same unfamiliar chess position to any number of chess players and asking them to find the best next move. De Groot (1946/1978) demonstrated that performance on this task discriminates well between chess players at different levels of skill and thus captures the essential phenomenon of ability to play this game.

In numerous subsequent studies, researchers have used a similar approach to study the highest levels of thinking in accepted experts in various domains of expertise (Chi *et al.* 1988; Ericsson and Smith 1991b). If expert performance reflects extended adaptation to the demands of naturally occurring situations, it is important that researchers capture the structure of these situations in order to elicit maximal performance from the experts. Furthermore, if the tasks designed for research are sufficiently similar to normal situations, experts can rely on their existing skills, and no experiment-specific changes are necessary. How similar these situations have to be to real-life situations is an empirical question. In general, researchers should strive to define the simplest situation in which experts' superior performance can still be reliably reproduced.

Description and Analysis of Expert Performance

The mere fact that it is possible to identify a set of representative tasks that can elicit superior performance from experts under standardized conditions is important. It dramatically reduces the number of contextual factors that can logically be essential for reproducing that superior performance. More important, it allows researchers to reproduce the phenomenon of expert performance under controlled conditions and in a reliable fashion. Researchers can thus precisely describe the tasks and stimuli and can theoretically determine which mechanisms are capable of reliably producing accurate performance across the set of tasks. Part of the standard methodology in cognitive psychology is to analyze the possible methods subjects could use to generate the correct response to a specific task, given their knowledge about procedures and facts in the domain. The same methodology can be applied to tasks that capture expert performance. Because, however, the knowledge experts may apply to a specific task is quite extensive and complex, it is virtually impossible for nonexperts to understand an analysis of such a task. Instead of describing such a case, we will illustrate the methodology and related issues with a relatively simple skill, mental multiplication.

Mental Multiplication: An Illustration of Task Analysis. In a study of mental multiplication, the experimenter typically reads a problem to a subject: What is the result of multiplying 24 by 36? The subject then reports the correct answer—864. It may be possible that highly experienced subjects recognize that particular problem and retrieve the answer immediately from memory. That possibility is remote for normal subjects, and one can surmise that they must calculate the answer by relying on their knowledge of the multiplication table and familiar methods for complex multiplication. The most likely method is the paper-and-pencil method taught in the schools, where 24*36 is broken down into 24*6 and 24*30 and the products are added together, illustrated as Case B in Table 1.

Often students are told to put the highest number first. By this rule, the first step in solving 24*36 is to rearrange it as 36*24 and then to break it down as 36*4 and 36*20 (Method A). More sophisticated subjects may recognize that 24*36 is equivalent to (30–6)*(30+6) and use the formula (a–b)*(a+b) = a**2–b**2, thus calculating 24*36 as 30**2–6**2 = 900–36 = 864 (Method C). Other subjects may recognize other shortcuts, such as 24*36 = (2*12)*(3*12) = 6*12**2 = 6*144 (Method D). Skilled mental calculators often prefer to calculate the answer in the reverse order, as is illustrated in Method E. Especially for more complex problems this procedure allows them to report the first digit of the final result long before they have completed the calculation of the remaining digits. Because most people expect that the entire answer has to be available before the first digit can be announced, the last method gives the appearance of faster calculation speeds.

Based on observations of the speed and accuracy of performance, an investigator cannot determine which of the methods in Table 1 a subject relied on for solving a specific multiplication problem. However, if the subject was instructed to think aloud (see Ericsson and Simon 1993, for the detailed procedure) while completing the mental multiplication, the investigator could record in detail the mediating sequences of the subject's thoughts, as is illustrated in the right hand column of Table 1. Although methodologically rigorous methods for encoding and evaluating think-aloud protocols are available (Ericsson and Simon 1993), the visual match between Method B and the protocol in Table 1 is sufficiently clear for the purposes of our illustration. Even with a less detailed record of the verbalized intermediate products in the calculation, it is possible to reject most of the alternative methods as being inconsistent with a recorded protocol.

Think-Aloud Protocols and Task Analysis in Research on Expert Performance

Since the demise of classic introspective analysis of consciousness around the turn of the century, investigators have been reluctant to consider any type of verbal report as valid data on subjects' cognitive processes. More recently investigators have been particularly concerned that having subjects generate verbal reports changes the underlying processes. In a recent review of more than 40 experimental studies comparing performance with and without verbalization, Ericsson and Simon (1993) showed that the structure of cognitive processes can change if subjects are required to explain their cognitive processes. In contrast, if subjects were asked simply to verbalize the thoughts that come

Method A:	24		36 times 24
	36		4
	144		carry the—no wait
	72		4
	864		carry the 2
			14
Method B:	36		144
	24		0
	144		36 times 2 is
	72		12
	864		6
			72
Method C:	$24*36 = (30-6)*(30+6) =$		720 plus 144
	$30**2-6**2 = 900-36 = 864$		4
			uh, uh
Method D:	AB	24	6
	CD	36	8
	$100*A*C$	600	uh, 864
	$10*A*D$	120	
	$10*C*B$	120	
	$B*D$	24	
		864	
Method E:	$24*36 = 4*6*6*6 = 4*6**3 = 4*216 = 864$		

Table 1. Examples of five different possible methods of mentally multiplying 24
with 36 (left panel) and a transcribed think-aloud protocol
from a subject generating the correct answer (right panel).

to their attention (think aloud), Ericsson and Simon (1993) found no reliable evidence that structural changes to cognitive processing occurred. Thinking aloud appears only to require additional time for subjects to complete verbalization and therefore leads to somewhat longer solution times in some cases.

A critical concern in applying this methodology to expert performance is how much information the think-aloud protocols of experts contain about the mediating cognitive processes. Obviously many forms of skilled perceptual-motor performance are so rapid that concurrent verbalization of thought would seem impossible. We will later consider alternative methodologies for such cases; but for a wide range of expert performance, think-aloud protocols have provided a rich source of information on expert performance. In his work on chess masters, de Groot (1946/1978) instructed his subjects to think aloud as they identified the best move for chess positions. From an analysis of the verbal reports, de Groot was able to describe how his subjects selected their moves. First they familiarized themselves with the position and extracted the strengths and weaknesses of its structure. Then they systematically explored the consequences of promising moves and the opponent's like-

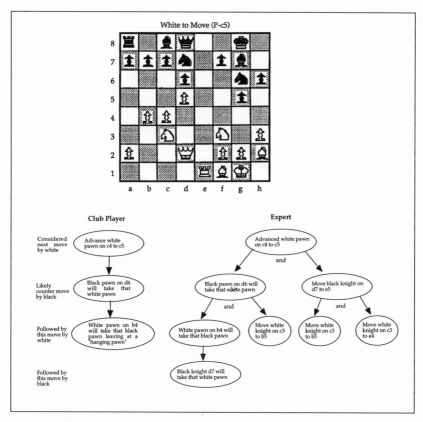

Figure 1. Chess position presented to chess players with the instruction to select the best next move by white (top panel).

Note. The think aloud protocols of a good club player (chess rating=1657) and a chess expert (chess rating=2004) collected by Charness (1981a) are shown in bottom panel to illustrate differences in evaluation and planning for one specific move, P-c5 (white pawn from c4 to c5), the best move for this position. Reported considerations for other potential moves have been omitted. The chess expert considers more alternative move sequences and some of them to a greater depth than the club player does. (From "Search in Chess: Age and Skill Differences" by N. Charness 1981, *Journal of Experimental Psychology: Human Perception and Performance, 7,* p. 469. Copyright 1981 by American Psychological Association.)

ly countermoves by planning several moves ahead. From subjects' verbalizations, de Groot and subsequent investigators (Charness 1981a) have been able to represent the sequences of moves subjects explored as search trees and to measure the amount and depth of planning for chess players at different levels of expertise. This is illustrated in figure 1.

The results of these analyses show that the amount and depth of search increase as a function of chess expertise to a given point (the level of chess experts); thereafter, no further systematic differences were found (Charness 1989). That the very best chess players still differ in their ability to find and selectively explore the most promising moves suggests that the structure of their internal representation of chess positions differs from that of nonexperts.

The central importance of experts' representation of solutions is revealed by verbal reports in other domains such as physics and medical diagnosis. When novices in physics solve a problem, they typically start with the question that asks for, say, a velocity; then they try to recall formulas for calculating velocities and then construct step by step a sequence of formulas by reasoning backward from the goal to the information given in the problem. In contrast, more experienced subjects proceed by forward reasoning. As they read the description of the problem situation an integrated representation is generated and updated, so when they finally encounter the question in the problem text, they retrieve a solution plan from memory (Larkin, McDermott, Simon, and Simon 1980). This finding suggests that experts form an immediate representation of the problem that systematically cues their knowledge, whereas novices do not have this kind of orderly and efficient access to their knowledge (see also Zeitz, this volume). Similarly, medical experts comprehend and integrate the information they receive about patients to find the correct diagnosis by reasoning forward, whereas less accomplished practitioners tend to generate plausible diagnoses that aid their search for confirming and disconfirming evidence (Patel and Groen 1991).

Experts' representation of the relevant information about the situation is critical to their ability to reason, to plan out, and to evaluate consequences of possible actions. Approximately 100 years ago Binet was intrigued by some chess players' claims that they could visualize chess positions clearly when they played chess games without a visible chessboard (blindfold chess). Binet (1894) and subsequently Luria (1968) studied individuals with exceptional memory abilities, who claimed to visualize the information presented to them as a mental image. These claims, if substantiated, would imply that some individuals have a sensory-based memory akin to a photographic memory, making them qualitatively different from the vast majority of human adults. To gain understanding of these processes and capacities, investigators have turned to tests of perception and memory.

Immediate Memory of Perceived Situations

To study subjects' immediate perception of chess positions, de Groot (1946/1978) restricted the presentation to 2–15 seconds and then removed the chess position from view. Even after such a brief exposure, the best chess players were able to describe the structure of the chess position and could reproduce the locations of the chess pieces almost perfectly. Weaker chess players' memory was much worse, and generally the amount of information chess players could recall was found to be a function of skill. In a classic study, Chase and Simon (1973) studied subjects' memory for briefly presented chess positions and replicated de Groot's findings under controlled conditions. To the same subjects Chase and Simon also presented chess positions with randomly rearranged chess pieces. Memory for these scrambled positions was uniformly poor and did not differ reliably as a function of skill. This finding has been frequently replicated and shows that the superior memory for briefly presented chess positions is not due to any general memory ability, such as photographic memory, but depends critically on subjects' ability to perceive meaningful patterns and relations between chess pieces. Although a recent review (Gobet and Simon, in press) has shown that there is a reliable advantage for the best chess players even for scrambled positions, the size of this advantage is very small for brief visual presentations. The largest expertise advantage for scrambled positions has been observed for chess positions presented auditorily with a verbal description of the location of one piece at a time for all pieces of the scrambled chess configuration (Saariluoma 1989). In this memory task the mediation of experts' superior memory by photographic memory would seem very unlikely. Furthermore, Ericsson and Kintsch (1995) have recently proposed an alternative skill-based mechanism for the observed superiority of chess masters on that task.

Originally Chase and Simon (1973) proposed that experts' superior short-term memory for chess positions was due to their ability to recognize configurations of chess pieces on the basis of their knowledge of vast numbers of specific patterns of pieces. With greater knowledge of more complex and larger configurations of chess pieces (chunks), an expert could recall more individual chess pieces with the same number of chunks. Hence, Chase and Simon could account for very large individual differences in memory for chess positions within the limits of the capacity of normal short-term memory (STM), which is approximately seven chunks (Miller 1956).

The Chase-Simon theory has been very influential. It gives an elegant account of experts' superior memory only for representative stimuli from their domain, and not even for randomly rearranged versions of the same stimuli (see Ericsson and Smith 1991b for a summary of the various domains of expertise in which this finding has been demonstrated). At that time, Chase and Simon (1973) believed that storage of new information in long-term memory (LTM) was quite time consuming and that memory for briefly presented information could be maintained only in STM for experts and nonexperts alike. However, subsequent research by Chase and Ericsson (1982) on the effects of practice on a specific task measuring the capacity of STM has shown that through extended practice (more than 200 hours), it is possible for subjects to improve performance by more than 1000%. These improvements are not mediated by increasingly larger chunks in STM but reflect the acquisition of memory skills that enable subjects to store information in LTM and thereby circumvent the capacity constraint of STM. Hence, with extensive practice it is possible to attain skills that lead to qualitative, not simply quantitative, differences in memory performance for a specific type of presented information.

From experimental analyses of their trained subjects and from a review of data on other individuals with exceptional memory, Chase and Ericsson (1982; Ericsson 1985) extracted several general findings of skilled memory that apply to all subjects. Exceptional memory is nearly always restricted to one type of material, frequently random sequences of digits. The convergence of acquired memory skills and alleged exceptional memory was demonstrated when the trained subjects performed tasks given previously to "exceptional" subjects. Figure 2 (middle panel) shows a matrix that Binet presented visually to his subjects. Below the matrix are several orders in which the same subjects were asked to recall the numbers from the matrix that they memorized.

Ericsson and Chase (1982) found that their subjects matched or surpassed the exceptional subjects both in the speed of initial memorization and in the speed of subsequent recall. A detailed analysis contrasting the speed for different orders of recall showed the same pattern in trained and exceptional subjects, both of whom recalled by rows faster than by columns. Consistent with their acquired memory skill, the trained subjects encoded each row of the matrix as a group by relying on their extensive knowledge of facts relevant to numbers. They then associated a cue corresponding to the spatial location of each row with a retrieval structure illustrated in the top panel of figure 2. To recall numbers in flexible order, subjects retrieved the relevant row using the corresponding retrieval cue and then extracted the desired next digit or digits. The high correlation between the recall times predicted from this method and the recall times observed for both exceptional and trained subjects imply that these groups have a similar memory representation. When the biographical background of individuals exhibiting exceptional memory performance was examined, Ericsson (1985, 1988) found evidence for extended experience and practice with related memory tasks. Hence, these exceptional individuals and the trained college students should be viewed as expert performers on these laboratory tasks, where the same type of memory skills has been acquired during extended prior experience.

Acquired memory skill (long-term working memory [Ericsson and Kintsch 1995]) accounts well even for the superior memory of experts. In many types of expert performance, research has shown that working memory is essentially unaffected by interruptions, during which the experts are forced to engage in an unrelated activity designed to eliminate any continued storage of information in STM. After the interruption and after a brief delay involving recall and reactivation of relevant information stored in LTM, experts can

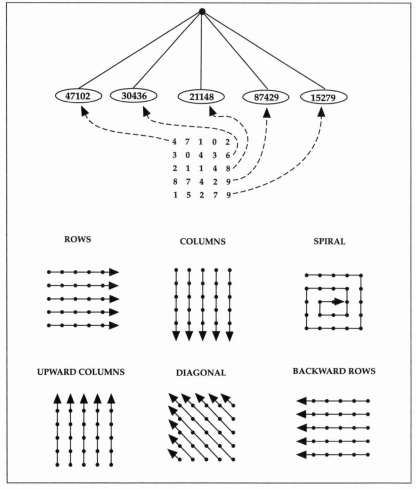

Figure 2. 25-digit matrix used by Binet to test his memory experts.

Note. Binet asked subjects to repeat the entire matrix in various orders shown at bottom, or to repeat individual rows as five-digit numbers. Top shows trained subjects' representation of matrix as a sequence of rows, with all digits in a row stored together in an integrated memory encoding.

resume activity without decrements in performance. Storage in LTM is further evidenced by experts' ability to recall relevant information about the task even when they are unexpectedly asked for recall after the task has been completed. The amount recalled is found to increase as a function of the level of expert performance (Charness 1991).

The critical aspect of experts' working memory is not the amount of information stored, per se, but rather how the information is stored and indexed in LTM. In support of this claim, several cases have been reported in which nonexperts have been able to match the amount of domain-specific information recalled by experts, but without attaining the expert's sophisticated representation of the information. After 50 hours of training on memory for presented chess positions, a college student with minimal knowledge of chess was able to match the performance of chess masters. However, an analysis of how the chess position was encoded revealed that the trained subject focused on perceptually salient patterns in the periphery of the chessboard, whereas the chess master attended to the central aspects critical to the selection of the next moves (Ericsson and Harris 1990). When told explicitly to memorize presented medical information, medical students match or even surpass medical experts (Patel and Groen 1991; Schmidt and Boshuizen 1993). However, the medical experts are more able than medical students to identify and recall the important pieces of presented information. Medical experts also encode more general clinical findings, which are sufficient for reasoning about the case but not specific enough to recall or reconstruct the detailed facts presented about the medical patient (Boshuizen and Schmidt 1992; Groen and Patel 1988).

Experts acquire skill in memory to meet specific demands of encoding and accessibility in specific activities in a given domain. For this reason their skill is unlikely to transfer from one domain to another. The demands for storage of intermediate products in mental calculation differ from the demands of blindfold chess, wherein the chess master must be able not simply to access the current position but also to plan and accurately select the best chess moves. The acquisition of memory skill in a domain is integrated with the acquisition of skill in organizing acquired knowledge and refining of procedures and strategies, and it allows experts to circumvent limits on working memory imposed by the limited capacity of STM.

Perceptual-Motor Skill in Expert Performance

In many domains it is critical that experts respond not just accurately but also rapidly in dynamically changing situations. A skilled performer needs to be able to perceive and encode the current situation as well as to select and execute an action or a series of actions rapidly. In laboratory studies of skill acquisition, investigators have been able to demonstrate an increase in the speed of perceptual-motor reactions as a direct function of practice. With extensive amounts of practice, subjects are able to evoke automatically the correct reaction to familiar stimulus situations. This analysis of perceived situations and automatically evoked responses is central to our understanding of skilled performance, yet it seems to be insufficient to account for the speeds observed in many types of expert performance. The time it takes to respond to a stimulus even after extensive training is often between 0.5 and 1.0 seconds, which is too slow to account for a return of a hard tennis serve, a goalie's catching a hockey puck, or fluent motor activities in typing and music.

The standard paradigm in laboratory psychology relies on independent trials in which the occurrence of the presented stimulus, which the subject does not control, defines the beginning of a trial. In contrast, in the perceptual environment in everyday life, expert performance is continuous and changing, and experts must be able to recognize if and when a particular action is required. Most important, it is possible for the expert to analyze the current situation and thereby anticipate future events. Research on the return of a tennis serve shows that experts do not wait until they can see the ball approaching them. Instead they carefully study the action of the server's racquet and are able to predict approximately where in the service area the tennis ball will land even before the server has hit the ball. Abernethy (1991) has recently reviewed the critical role of anticipation in expert performance in many racquet sports. Similarly, expert typists are looking well ahead at the text they are typing in any particular instant. The difference between the text visually fixated and the letters typed in a given instant (eye-hand span) increases with the typists' typing speed. High-speed filming of the movements of expert typists' fingers shows that their fingers are simultaneously moved toward the relevant keys well ahead of when they are actually struck. The largest differences in speed between expert and novice typists are found for successive keystrokes made with fingers of different hands because the corresponding movements can overlap completely after extended typing practice. When the typing situation is artificially changed to eliminate looking ahead at the text to be typed, the speed advantage of expert typists is virtually eliminated (Salthouse 1991a). Similar findings relating the amount of looking ahead and speed of performance have been obtained for reading aloud (Levin and Addis 1979) and sight-reading of music (Sloboda 1985).

In summary, by successfully anticipating future events and skillfully coordinating overlapping movements, the expert performer is able to circumvent potential limits on basic elements of serial reactions.

General Comments on the Structure of Expert Performance

Recent studies of expert performance have questioned the talent-based view that expert performance becomes increasingly dependent on unmodifiable innate components. Although these studies have revealed how beginners acquire complex cognitive structures and skills that circumvent the basic limits confronting them, researchers have not uncovered some set of simple strategies that would allow nonexperts to rapidly acquire expert performance, except in a few isolated cases, such as the sexing of chickens (Biederman and Shiffrar 1987). Analyses of exceptional performance, such as exceptional memory and absolute pitch, have shown how it differs from the performance of beginners and how beginners can acquire skill through instruction in the correct general strategy and corresponding training procedures (Howe 1990). However, to attain exceptional levels of performance, subjects must in addition undergo a very long period of active learning, during which they refine and improve their skill, ideally under the supervision of a teacher or coach.

By acquiring new methods and skills, expert performers are able to circumvent basic, most likely physiological, limits imposed on serial reactions and working memory. The traditional distinction between physiological (unmodifiable physical) and cognitive (modifiable mental) factors that influence performance does not seem valid in studies of expert performance. For the purposes of the typical one-hour experiment in psychology, changes in physiological factors might be negligible; but once we consider extended activities, physiological adaptations and changes are not just likely but virtually inevitable. Hence we will also consider the possibility that most of the physiological attributes that distinguish experts are not innately determined characteristics but rather the results of extended, intense practice. In the following section we will describe the particular activities (deliberate practice) that appear to be necessary to attain these improvements (Ericsson, Krampe, and Tesch-Römer 1993).

Acquisition of Expert Performance

A relatively uncontroversial assertion is that attaining an expert level of performance in a domain requires mastery of all of the relevant knowledge and prerequisite skills. Our analysis has shown that the central mechanisms mediating the superior performance of experts are acquired; therefore acquisition of relevant knowledge and skills may be the major limiting factor in attaining expert performance. Some of the strongest evidence for this claim comes from a historical description of how domains of expertise evolved with increased specialization within each domain. To measure the duration of the acquisition process, we will analyze the length of time it takes for the best individuals to attain the highest levels of performance within a domain. Finally we will specify the type of practice that seems to be necessary to acquire expert performance in a domain.

Evolution of Domains of Expertise and the Emergence of Specialization

Most domains of expertise today have a fairly long history of continued development. The knowledge in natural science and calculus that represented the cutting edge of mathematics a few centuries ago, and that only the experts of that time were able to master, is today taught in high school and college (Feldman 1980). Many experts today are struggling to master the developments in a small subarea of one of the many natural sciences. Before the 20th century it was common for musicians to compose and play their own music; since then, distinct career patterns have emerged for composers, solo performers, accompanists, teachers, and conductors. When Tchaikovsky asked two of the greatest violinists of his day to play his violin concerto, they refused, deeming the score unplayable (Platt 1966). Today, elite violinists consider the concerto part of their standard repertory. The improvement in music training has been so considerable that according to Roth (1982), the virtuoso Paganini "would indeed cut a sorry figure if placed upon the modern concert stage" (p. 23). Paganini's techniques and Tchaikovsky's concerto were deemed impossible until other musicians figured out how to master and describe them so that students could learn them as well. Almost 100 years ago the first Olympic Games were held, and results on standardized events were recorded. Since then records for events have been continuously broken and improved. For example, the winning time for the first Olympic Marathon is comparable to the current qualifying time for the Boston Marathon, attained by many thousands of amateur runners every year. Today amateur athletes cannot successfully compete with individuals training full time, and training methods for specific events are continuously refined by professional coaches and trainers.

In all major domains there has been a steady accumulation of knowledge about the domain and about the skills and techniques that mediate superior performance. This accumulated experience is documented and regularly updated in books, encyclopedias, and instructional material written by masters and professional teachers in the domain. During the last centuries the levels of performance have increased, in some domains dramatically so. To attain the highest level of performance possible in this decade, it is necessary both to specialize and to engage in the activity full time.

Minimum Period of Attainment of Expert Performance

Another measure of the complexity of a domain is the length of time it takes an individual to master it and attain a very high level of performance or make outstanding achievements. Of particular interest is how fast the most "talented" or best performers can attain an international level of performance. In their classic study on chess, Simon and Chase (1973) argued that a 10-year period of intense preparation is necessary to reach the level of an international chess master and suggested similar requirements in other domains. In a review of subsequent research, Ericsson, Krampe, and Tesch-Römer (1993) showed that the 10-year rule is remarkably accurate, although there are at least some exceptions. However, even those exceptions, such as Bobby

Fischer, who started playing chess very early and attained an international level at age 15, are only about a year shy of the 10 year requirement. Winning international competitions in sports, arts, and science appears to require at least 10 years of preparation and typically substantially longer. In the sciences and some of the arts, such as literature, the necessary preparation overlaps so much with regular education that it is often difficult to determine a precise starting point. However, when the time interval between scientists' and authors' first accepted publication and their most valued publication is measured, it averages more than 10 years and implies an even longer preparation period (Raskin 1936). Even for the most successful ("talented") individuals, the major domains of expertise are sufficiently complex that mastery of them requires approximately 10 years of essentially full-time preparation, which corresponds to several thousands of hours of practice.

Practice Activities to Attain Expert Performance

In almost every domain, methods for instruction and efficient training have developed in parallel with the accumulation of relevant knowledge and techniques. For many sports and performance arts in particular, professional teachers and coaches monitor training programs tailored to the needs of individuals ranging from beginners to experts. The training activities are designed to improve specific aspects of performance through repetition and successive refinement. To receive maximal benefit from feedback, individuals have to monitor their training with full concentration, which is effortful and limits the duration of daily training. Ericsson, Krampe, and Tesch-Römer (1993) refer to individualized training on tasks selected by a qualified teacher as *deliberate practice*. They argue that the amount of this type of practice should be closely related to the level of acquired performance.

From surveys of the kinds of activities individuals engage in for the popular domains, such as tennis and golf, it is clear that the vast majority of active individuals spend very little if any time on deliberate practice. Once amateurs have attained an acceptable level of performance, their primary goal becomes inherent enjoyment of the activity, and most of their time is spent on playful interaction. The most enjoyable states of play are characterized as flow (Csikszentmihalyi 1990), when the individual is absorbed in effortless engagement in a continuously changing situation. During play even individuals who desire to improve their performance do not encounter the same or similar situations on a frequent and predictable basis. For example, a tennis player wanting to improve a weakness, such as a backhand volley, might encounter a relevant situation only once per game. In contrast, a tennis coach would give that individual many hundreds of opportunities to improve and refine that type of shot during a training session.

Work, another type of activity, refers to public performances, competitions, and other performances motivated by external social and monetary rewards. Although work activities offer some opportunities for learning, they are far from optimal. In work activities, the goal is to generate a quality product reliably and efficiently. In several domains, such as performance arts and sports, there is a clear distinction between training before a performance and the performance itself. During the performance itself, opportunities for learning and improvements are minimal, although the problems encountered can be addressed during training following the performance. Most occupations and professional domains pay individuals to generate efficiently services and products of consistently high quality. To give their best performance in work activities, individuals rely on previously well-entrenched methods rather than exploring new methods with unknown reliability. In summary, deliberate practice is an effortful activity motivated by the goal of improving performance. Unlike play, deliberate practice is not necessarily inherently motivating; and unlike work, it does not necessarily lead to immediate social and monetary rewards (Ericsson, Krampe, and Tesch-Römer 1993).

Individualized training of students, who begin as very young children under the supervision of professional teachers and coaches, is a relatively recent trend. It was only in 1756, for example, that Wolfgang Amadeus Mozart's father published the first book in German on teaching students to play the violin. Before organized education became the norm, people acquired skill through apprenticeship, working as adolescents with skilled performers, frequently one of their parents. Recently there has been a lot of interest in this type of learning environment within the framework of situated cognition (Lave 1988; Lave and Wenger 1991). A significant element of apprenticeship is the imitation of skilled performers and careful study and copying of their work. In the arts the study and imitation of masterpieces has a long history. For example, Benjamin Franklin (1788/1986) described in his autobiography how he tried to learn to write in a clear and logical fashion. He would read through a passage in a good book to understand it rather than memorize it and then try to reproduce its structure and content. Then he would compare his reproduction with the original to identify differences. By repeated application of this cycle of study, reproduction, and comparison with a well-structured original, Franklin argued that he acquired his skill in organizing thoughts for speaking and writing.

With the advent of audio and video recording, which have opened new possibilities for repeated study of master artists' performance, reproduction and comparison have been extended to allow individualized study and improvement of performance. This general method is central to achieving expert performance in chess. Advanced chess players spend as many as four hours a day studying published games between international chess masters (Forbes 1992). The effective component of this type of study is predicting the chess master's next move without looking ahead. If the prediction is wrong, the advanced player examines the chess position more deeply to identify the reasons for the chess master's move. The activity of planning and extended evaluation of chess games is likely to improve a player's ability to internally represent chess positions, a memory skill that we have already discussed. This form of self-directed study has most of the characteristics of deliberate practice, but it is probably not as effective as individualized study guided by a skilled teacher. It is interesting to note that most of the recent world champions in chess were at one time tutored by chess masters (Ericsson, Krampe, and Tesch-Römer 1993).

Deliberate practice differs from other domain-related activities because it provides optimal opportunities for learning and skill acquisition. If the regular activities in a domain did not offer accurate and preferably immediate feedback or opportunities for corrected repetitions, improvements in performance with further experience would not be expected from traditional learning theory (Ericsson, Krampe, and Tesch-Römer 1993). Most amateurs and employees spend a very small amount of time on deliberate efforts to improve their performance, once it has reached an acceptable level. Under these conditions only weak relations between amount of experience and performance would be predicted, which is consistent with the empirical data. Recent research has explored the question whether deliberate practice can account for the attainment of elite performance levels and for individual differences among expert-level performers. According to the framework proposed by Ericsson, Krampe, and Tesch-Römer, the primary mechanism creating expert-level performance in a domain is deliberate practice.

Acquiring Elite Performance

Why do individuals even begin to engage in deliberate practice, when this activity is not inherently enjoyable? From many interviews with international-level performers and their parents and teachers, Bloom and his colleagues (1985a) found that international-level performers in several domains start out as children by engaging in playful activities in the domain (see Phase I in figure 3).

After a period of playful and enjoyable experience they reveal "talent" or promise. At this point parents typically suggest that their children take lessons from a teacher and engage in, at least initially, limited amounts of deliberate practice in order to realize their potential for expert performance in the domain. The parents help their children acquire regular habits of practice and teach them that this activity has instrumental value by noticing improvements in performance. The next phase (Bloom 1985b) is an extended period of preparation and ends with the individual's commitment to pursue activities in the domain on a full-time basis. During this period the daily amounts of deliberate practice are increased, and more advanced teachers and training facilities are sought out. Occasionally parents even move to a different region of

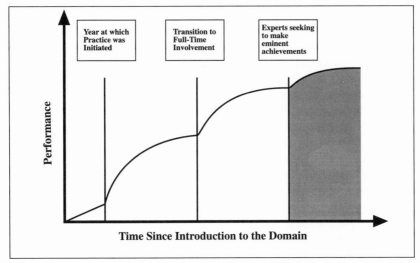

*Figure 3. Three phases of development of expert performance followed by a
qualitatively different fourth phase of efforts to attain eminent achievements.*

Note. From "Can We Create Gifted People?" by K.A. Ericsson, R. Th. Krampe & S. Heizmann in *The Origins and Development of High Ability* (pp. 222-249), 1993, Chichester, England: Wiley. Copyright by Ciba Foundation. Adapted by permission.

the country to provide their children with the best training environment. In
the next phase, the individual makes a full-time commitment to improving
performance. This phase ends when the individual either can make a living as
a professional performer in the domain or terminates full-time engagement in
the activity. Bloom found that during this phase nearly all of the individuals
who ultimately reach an international level performance work with master
teachers who either themselves had reached that level or had previously
trained other individuals to that level. All through their development, international-level performers are provided with the best teachers for their current
level of performance and engage in a great amount of deliberate practice.

The dilemma in most domains of expertise is that millions of young individuals enter these domains with aspirations to reach the highest levels of
performance, but almost by definition only a very small number can succeed.
Given the low probability of ultimate success, parents and coaches have been
very much interested in identifying these select individuals as early as possible and giving them encouragement, support, and the best learning opportunities. The consistent failures to identify specific "talents" in children is not
surprising when one considers the qualitative changes occurring during the
long period of development. In many performance domains, international
performers start practice at age 4 to 6, when it is unclear what kind of objec-

tive evidence of talent and promise they could possibly display. Available descriptions suggest that children this young display interest and motivation to practice rather than exceptional performance. Once deliberate practice has begun, the primary measure of acquired skill and talent is the current level of performance compared with that of other children of comparable ages in the community. Only later at about age 10 to 12 do the children typically start participating in competitions, where their performance is compared with that of other successful children from a larger geographical area. As performance level and age increase, the criteria for evaluating performance also change. In the arts and sciences, technical proficiency is no longer enough, and adult criteria of abstract understanding and artistic expression are applied.

During the first three phases of development, individuals master the knowledge and skills that master teachers and coaches know how to convey. To achieve the highest level (eminent performance), individuals must enter a fourth phase, going beyond the available knowledge in the domain to produce a unique contribution to the domain. Eminent scientists make major discoveries and propose new theories that permanently change the concepts and knowledge in the domain. Similarly eminent artists generate new techniques and interpretations that extend the boundaries for future art. The process of generating innovations differs from the acquisition of expertise and mastery. Major innovations by definition go beyond anything even the master teachers know and could possibly teach. Furthermore, innovations are rare, and it is unusual that eminent individuals make more than a single major innovation during their entire lives. Unlike consistently superior expert performance, innovation occurs so infrequently and unpredictably that the likelihood of its ever being captured in the laboratory is small. However, it is still possible through retrospective analysis of concurrent records, such as notebooks and diaries (Gruber 1981; Wallace and Gruber 1989), to reconstruct the processes leading up to major discoveries. Once the context of a particular discovery has been identified, it is possible to reconstruct the situation and study how other naive subjects with the necessary knowledge can uncover the original discovery (Qin and Simon 1990). Let us now turn back to expert performance, which we consider both reproducible and instructable.

Individual Differences in Expert Performance

Biographies of international-level performers indicate that a long period of intense, supervised practice preceded their achievements. The simple assumption that these levels of deliberate practice are necessary accounts for the fact that the vast majority of active individuals who prematurely stop practicing never reach the highest levels of performance. However, in most domains of expert performance a relatively large number of individuals continue deliberate practice and thus meet the criterion of necessity. Within this group striking individual differences in adult performance nonetheless remain.

Ericsson, Krampe, and Tesch-Römer (1993) hypothesized that differences in the amount of deliberate practice could account for even the individual differences among the select group of people who continue a regimen of deliberate practice. The main assumption, which they call the *monotonic-benefits assumption,* is that individuals' performances are a monotonic function of the amount of deliberate practice accumulated since these individuals began deliberate practice in a domain. The accumulated amount of deliberate practice and the level of performance an individual achieves at a given age is thus a function of the starting age for practice and the weekly amount of practice during the intervening years. This function is illustrated in figure 4. The second curve has been simply moved horizontally to reflect a later starting age, and the third curve reflects in addition a lower weekly rate of practice.

To evaluate these predictions empirically, it is necessary to measure the amount of time individuals spend on various activities, in particular deliberate practice. One way of doing so, which is to have them keep detailed diaries, has a fairly long tradition in studies of time budgeting in sociology (Juster and Stafford 1985). In most domains with teachers and coaches, deliberate practice is regularly scheduled on a daily basis, and advanced performers can accurately estimate their current and past amounts of practice as well as their starting ages and other characteristics of their practice history.

In a comprehensive review of studies comparing starting ages and amount of weekly practice for international, national, and regional-level performers in many different domains, Ericsson, Krampe, and Tesch-Römer (1993) found that performers who reached higher levels tended to start practicing as many as two to five years earlier than did less accomplished performers. Individuals who attained higher levels of performance often spent more time on deliberate practice than did less accomplished individuals, even when there was no difference in the total time both groups spent on domain-related activities. Differences in the amount of deliberate practice accumulated during their development differentiated groups of expert performers at various current level of performance. The three functions in figure 4 illustrate how simple differences in starting ages and weekly amounts of practice can yield very stable differences in amounts of training and performance levels.

Everyone recognizes that maturational factors affect performance. For this reason competitions are nearly always structured by groups of contestants with the same ages. By the time individuals approach their middle to late teens (the shaded area in figure 4) and are applying for scholarships, and admission to the studios of master teachers and the best training environments, large differences in past practice and acquired skill are already present. Ericsson, Krampe, and Tesch-Römer found that by age 20, the top-level violinists in their study had practiced an average of more than 10,000 hours, approximately 2,500 hours more than the next most accomplished group of expert

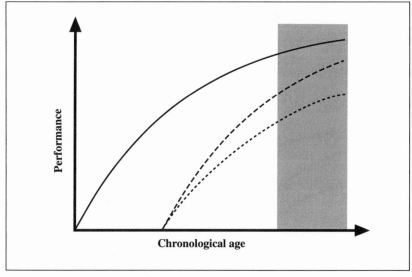

Figure 4. Relations between age and performance.

Note. The late period involving selection to the best music academies has been shaded. Solid line: performance associated with an early starting age and a high level of practice. Dashed line: performance for equally high level of practice but later starting age. Dotted line: performance associated with same late starting age but lower level of practice. From "Can We Create Gifted People?" by K.A. Ericsson, R. Th. Krampe & S. Heizmann in *The Origins and Development of High Ability* (pp. 222-249), 1993, Chichester, England: Wiley. Copyright by Ciba Foundation. Adapted by permission.

violinists and 5,000 hours more than the group who performed at the "lowest expert" level.

In summary, evidence from many domains (Ericsson 1996; Ericsson, Krampe, and Tesch-Römer 1993) shows that the top-level experts have spent a very large amount of time improving their performance and that the total amount accumulated during development is several years of additional full-time practice more than that of other less accomplished performers. This difference is roughly equivalent to the difference between freshmen and seniors in a highly competitive college. In these environments, where the best opportunities for further development are offered only to the individuals with the best current performance, it may be difficult for individuals with less prior practice and lower levels of performance even to secure situations in which they can practice full time. It is virtually impossible for them to catch up with the best performers because those performers maintain their lead through continuous practice at optimal levels.

The Structure of Practice in the Daily Lives of Elite Performers

From analyses of diaries and other sources of biographical material, Ericsson, Krampe, and Tesch-Römer (1993) concluded that expert performers design their lives to optimize their engagement in deliberate practice. Expert musicians spent approximately four hours a day—every day including weekends—on deliberate practice. Practice sessions were approximately one hour long, followed by a period of rest. Performers practiced most frequently during the morning, when some research indicates that individuals have the highest capacity for complex, demanding activity during the day (Folkard and Monks 1985). All the expert musicians reported on the importance of sleep and rest in maintaining their high levels of daily practice. The expert musicians in the two best groups, who practiced longer each day, slept more than those in the least accomplished group and also slept more than other reference groups of subjects of comparable age. The additional sleep was primarily from an afternoon nap. Expert subjects maximize the amount of time they can spend on deliberate practice when they can fully focus on their training goals without fatigue. Many master teachers and coaches consider practice while fatigued and unfocused not only wasteful but even harmful to sustained improvements.

Focused, effortful practice of limited duration has been found to be important in many domains of expert performance (Ericsson 1996). Interestingly the estimated amount of deliberate practice that individuals can sustain for extended periods of time does not seem to vary across domains and is close to four hours a day (Ericsson, Krampe, and Tesch-Römer 1993).

The effort and intensity of deliberate practice is most readily observable for perceptual-motor behavior in sports and performance arts. One goal of most of the practice activities is to push the limits of performance to higher levels by, for example, stretching in ballet, or repeated maximal efforts until exhaustion during interval training in running and weight lifting. It is well known that intense exercise increases endurance and the size of muscles. However, recent research in sports physiology has shown that anatomical changes in response to extended intense exercise are more far-reaching than commonly believed. Within a few weeks of vigorous training, the number of capillaries supplying blood to the trained muscles increases. Longitudinal studies show that after years of "elite-level" endurance training, the heart adapts and increases in size to values outside the normal range for healthy adults. The metabolism and general characteristics of muscle fibers also change—from slow-twitch to fast-twitch or vice versa. Most interestingly these changes are limited only to those muscles that are trained and critical to the particular sports event for which the athlete is preparing. Many of these changes appear to increase when practice overlaps with the body's development during childhood and adolescence. For example, the flexibility required for elite performance in ballet requires that dancers begin practicing before age 10 or 11. With the exception of height, the characteristics that differentiate elite athletes and performance artists from less accomplished performers in the same domains appear to reflect the successful adaptations of the body to intense practice activities extended over many years (Ericsson, Krampe, and Tesch-Römer 1993).

These physiological adaptations are not unique to expert performers. Similar but smaller changes are found for individuals who train at less intense levels. Similar extreme adaptations are seen in individuals living under extreme environmental conditions, such as at very high altitudes, or coping with diseases, such as partial blockages of the blood supply to the heart. Many occupation-specific problems that expert performers experience in middle age also seem to result from related types of (mal)adaptive processes.

It is becoming increasingly clear that maximizing the intensity and duration of training is not necessarily good. Expert performers have a constant problem with avoiding strains and injuries and allowing the body enough time to adapt and recuperate. Even in the absence of physical injuries, an increasing number of athletes and musicians overtrain and do not allow themselves enough rest to maintain a stable equilibrium from day to day. Sustained overtraining leads to burnout, for which the only known remedy is to terminate practice completely for long periods. It appears that top-level adult experts practice at the highest possible level that can be sustained for extended periods without burnout or injury. Hence, it may be extremely difficult to consistently practice harder and improve faster than these individuals already do.

Expert Performance from a Life Span Perspective

Elite performers in most domains are engaged essentially full-time from childhood and adolescence to late adulthood. The study of expert performers therefore offers a unique perspective on life span development and especially on the effects of aging. Many studies have examined the performance of experts as a function of age or of the ages when experts attained their best performance or their highest achievement. It is extremely rare for performers to attain their best performance before reaching adulthood, but it is not necessarily the case that performance continues to improve in those who keep exercising their skills across the life span. Rather, a peak age for performance seems to fall in the 20s, 30s, and 40s, as Lehman (1953) first noted. The age distributions for peak performance in vigorous sports are remarkably narrow and centered in the 20s with systematic differences between different types of sports (Schulz and Curnow 1988). In vigorous sports it is rare for elite athletes above age 30 to reach their personal best or even in many cases remain competitive with younger colleagues. Although less pronounced, similar age distributions centered somewhere in the 30s are found for fine motor skills and even predominantly cognitive activities, such as chess, science, and the arts. Simonton (1988a) has argued that the relative decline with age may be slight and may be attributable to the fact that total creative output for artists and scientists declines, although the probability of achieving an outstanding performance remains constant. Thus the frequency of producing an outstanding work declines with age. Perhaps the best evidence for decline with age is Elo's (1965) analysis of the careers of grand master chess players. As seen in figure 5 (from Charness and Bosman 1990), there is a peak for chess players in their 30s, although performance at 63 years of age is no worse than that at 21 years.

The peak age for creative achievement differs considerably between domains. In pure mathematics, theoretical physics, and lyric poetry, the peak ages for contributions occur in the late 20s and early 30s. In novel writing, history, and philosophy, the peaks are less pronounced and occur in the 40s and early 50s (Simonton 1988a). Even within domains the peak age for performance seems to vary systematically with the types of demands placed on the performer. In international-level tournament chess, individuals typically play chess games for four to five hours daily for more than a week. Furthermore, tournament chess makes strong demands on working memory and, to some extent, on speed of processing, when players attempt to choose the best move by searching through the problem space of possible moves. On average, a tournament chess player has approximately three minutes to consider each move (when normal time controls are used). In "postal chess," players have several days to make a move. Because deliberation times are longer and the players can use external memory to maintain the results of analysis, ascension to the world postal chess championship occurs much later, near 46 years of age as compared with 30 years of age for tournament chess (Charness and Bosman 1990).

To researchers on aging, the decline in expert performance in old age, which in many domains is often relatively slight, is less interesting than expert performers' ability to maintain a very high level of performance during ages when beginners and less accomplished performers display clear effects of aging. A common hypothesis related to the notion of innate talent is that experts generally age more slowly than other performers and thus no observable impairments would be expected. However, this hypothesis is not consistent with recent research on expert performance in chess (Charness 1981b), typing (Bosman 1993; Salthouse 1984), and music (Krampe and Ericsson, in press). The superior performance of older experts is found to be restricted to relevant tasks in their domains of expertise. For unrelated psychometric tasks and some tasks related to occupational activities, normal age-related decline is observed (Salthouse 1991b).

The mediating mechanisms in younger and older experts' performance have been examined in laboratory studies developed under the expert perfor-

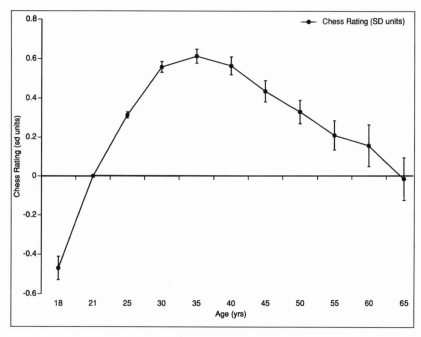

Figure 5. Grand master performance by age.

Note. Chess ratings scaled in standard deviation units, with performance at age 21 for each individual set to zero (data from Elo 1986). Averaged scores across grand masters shown with standard error bars. From "Expertise and Aging: Life in the Lab" (p. 358) by N. Charness & E.A. Bosman in *Aging and Cognition: Knowledge Organization and Utilization,* T. H. Hess (Ed.), 1990, Amsterdam: Elsevier. Copyright by Elsevier. Adapted by permission.

mance approach. In typing, older experts who type at the same speed as younger experts are found to have larger eye-hand spans that permit older experts to compensate through advance preparation (Bosman 1993; Salthouse 1984). Older chess experts' ability to select the best chess move is associated with less planning than that of younger experts at an equivalent skill level. This suggests that older chess experts compensate through more extensive knowledge of chess (Charness 1981a). Comparisons of older and younger expert pianists' ability to perform simple and complex sequences of key strokes requiring bimanual coordination reveal no or small differences, whereas the same comparisons between older and younger amateur pianists reveal clear decrements with age that increase with the complexity of the tasks (Krampe and Ericsson, in press). Such age effects require greater diversity in the models proposed to explain expertise. It is now evident that at least in typing and chess, two individuals at the same level of skill can achieve their performance through mechanisms with different structure. Although it is convenient to collapse a measure of expertise onto a unidimensional scale (such as chess rating or net words per minute for typing), this is an oversimplification that may obscure individual differences in the underlying processes that mediate same-level performance.

The Role of Deliberate Practice. In the previous sections we described the evidence for the necessity of deliberate practice for initially acquiring expert performance. The maintenance of expert performance could be due to the unique structure of the mechanisms acquired in expert performance or to a level of deliberate practice maintained during adulthood or both.

The most marked age-related decline is generally observed in perceptual-motor performance displayed in many types of sports. High levels of practice are necessary to attain the physiological adaptations that are found in expert performers, and the effects of practice appear to be particularly large when intense practice overlaps with physical development during childhood and adolescence. Most of these adaptations require that practice is maintained; if not, the changes revert to normal values, although for some anatomical changes many years of no practice appear necessary before the reversion is completed. Hence, much of the age-related decline in performance may reflect the reduction or termination of practice. Studies of master athletes show that older athletes do not practice at the same intensity as the best young athletes. When older master athletes are compared with young athletes training at a similar level, many physiological measurements do not differ between them. However, at least some physiological functions, such as maximal heart rate, show an age-related decline independent of past or current practice. In summary, the ability to retain superior performance in sports appears to depend critically on maintaining practice during adulthood (Ericsson 1990).

Evidence on the role of early and maintained practice in retaining cognitive aspects of expertise is much less extensive. Takeuchi and Hulse's (1993) recent review of absolute (perfect) pitch shows that children can easily acquire this ability at around the ages of three to five. Acquisition of the same ability during adulthood is very difficult and time consuming. Some other abilities, such as the acquisition of second languages (especially accents and pronunciation), appear easier to acquire at young rather than adult ages. Whether early acquisition of abilities, per se, translates into better retention into old age is currently not known.

Virtually by definition expert performers remain highly active in their domains of expertise. With increasing age, they typically reduce their intensive work schedules, a change in life style that is consistent with the decrease observed in their productivity (Simonton 1988a). Roe (1953) found that eminent scientists reduce their level of work during evenings and weekends. Information about the distribution of time among different types of activities and especially the amount of time spent on maintaining and improving performance is essentially lacking. However, Krampe and Ericsson (in press) collected both diaries and retrospective estimates of past practice for older expert pianists. Consistent with the lack of performance differences between younger and older pianists in tasks relevant to piano playing, Krampe found that the older experts still practiced approximately 10 hours a week and spent more than 40 additional hours a week on other music-related activities. In addition he found that individual differences in performance among older pianists could be predicted well by the amount of practice during the past 10 years. Whether a reduction in practice by older chess players and typists accounts for the differences between younger and older experts in these fields cannot currently be answered, given the lack of longitudinal data on performance and practice.

The study of expert performance over the life span of the performers is needed. This perspective is quite likely to provide new insights into the plasticity of the structure of human performance as a function of different developmental phases. Through investigation of focused sustained practice, it may be possible to determine which aspects can and, at least with the current training methods, cannot be modified to enhance current and future performance. Of particular practical and theoretical interest are those factors that enable experts to retain and maintain superior performance into old age.

Summary and Conclusion

The differences in performance between experts and beginners are the largest that have been reliably reproduced with healthy, normal adults under controlled test conditions. From the life-long efforts of expert performers who continuously strive to improve and reach their best performance, one can infer that expert performance represents the highest performance possible, given current knowledge and training methods in the domain. Individuals' acquisition of expert performance is thus a naturally occurring experiment for identifying the limits of human performance. It is hard to imagine better empirical evidence on maximal performance except for one critical flaw. As children, future international level performers are not randomly assigned to their training condition. Hence one cannot rule out the possibility that there is something different about those individuals who ultimately reach expert-level performance.

Nevertheless, the traditional view of talent, which concludes that successful individuals have special innate abilities and basic capacities, is not consistent with the reviewed evidence. Efforts to specify and measure characteristics of talent that allow early identification and successful prediction of adult performance have failed. Differences between expert and less accomplished performers reflect acquired knowledge and skills or physiological adaptations effected by training, with the only confirmed exception being height.

More plausible loci of individual differences are factors that predispose individuals toward engaging in deliberate practice and enable them to sustain high levels of practice for many years. Differences in these factors clearly have, in part, an environmental origin and can be modified as the level of practice is slowly increased with further experience. However, some of these factors, such as preferred activity level and temperament, may have a genetic component. Furthermore, there may need to be a good fit between such predisposing factors and the task environment (along the lines of Thomas and Chess's temperament-environment fit model; 1984) for expert-level performance to develop.

For some time, the study of exceptional and expert performance has been considered outside the scope of general psychology because such performance has been attributed to innate characteristics possessed by outstanding individuals. A better explanation is that expert performance reflects extreme adaptations, accomplished through life-long effort, to demands in restricted, well-defined domains. By capturing and examining the performance of experts in a given domain, researchers have identified adaptive changes with physiological components as well as the acquisition of domain-specific skills that circumvent basic limits on speed and memory. Experts with different teachers and training histories attain their superior performance after many years of continued effort by acquiring skills and making adaptations with the same general structure. These findings imply that in each domain, there is only a limited number of ways in which individuals can make large improvements in performance. When mediating mechanisms of the same general type are found in experts in very different domains that have evolved independently from each other, an account of this structure based on shared instruction is highly unlikely.

There is no reason to believe that changes in the structure of human performance and skill are restricted to the traditional domains of expertise. Similar changes should be expected in many everyday activities, such as thinking, comprehension, and problem solving, studied in general psychology. However, people acquire everyday skills under less structured conditions that lack strict and generalizable criteria for evaluation. These conditions also vary among individuals because of their specific living situations. In contrast, stable expert performance is typically restricted to standardized situations in a domain. Hence, the criteria for expert performance offer a shared goal for individuals in a domain that directs and constrains their life-long efforts to attain their maximal performance. Even when psychologists' ultimate goal is to describe and understand everyday skills, they are more likely to succeed by studying expert performance, than by examining everyday skills because the former is acquired under much more controlled and better understood conditions and achieved at higher levels of proficiency in a specific domain.

We believe that studies of the acquisition and structure of expert performance offer unique evidence on many general theoretical and applied issues in psychology. Extended deliberate practice gives near maximal values on the possible effects of environmental variables (in interaction with developmental variables) relevant to theoretical claims for invariant cognitive capacities and general laws of performance. We will significantly advance our knowledge of the interaction between environment and development by observing the effects of training during the early development of expert performers and the effects of maintaining training for older experts in late adulthood. The study of expert performance complements cross-cultural studies of environmental influences on thinking and cognition. The relation between language and thinking, traditionally restricted to comparisons between different languages (Hunt and Agnoli 1991), should be particularly suitable for study in the context of expertise, where domain-specific names, concepts, and knowledge are explicated in training manuals and books and subjects with differing levels of mastery of the vocabulary and where "language" of the domain can be easily found.

For applied psychologists, the study of expert performers and their master teachers and coaches offers a nearly untapped reservoir of knowledge about optimal training and specific training methods that has been accumulated in many domains for a long time. Across very different domains of expert performance, Ericsson, Krampe, and Tesch-Römer (1993) uncovered evidence for intriguing invariances in the duration and daily scheduling of practice activities. Further efforts to investigate training and development of training methods and to derive principles that generalize across domains should be particularly fruitful. Most important, a better understanding of social and other factors that motivate and sustain future expert performers at an optimal level of deliberate practice should have direct relevance to motivational problems in education, especially in our school system.

In sum, an analysis of the acquired characteristics and skills of expert performers, as well as their developmental history and training methods, will provide us with general insights into the structure and limits of human adaptations.

Implications for Designers of AI Systems

What lessons can designers of expert systems take from the study of human experts? We will have to be somewhat speculative here. Think of human acquisition of expertise as involving two complementary processes: high motivation to put in the hours of deliberate practice necessary to acquire the mechanisms to by-pass human physical and cognitive limitations, and to acquire the knowledge base necessary to respond accurately and flexibly to the tens of thousands of unique cases that the expert may encounter. First, on the positive side, designers need not be concerned, as are humans, with by-passing the basic limitations of human memory systems. Either as a direct by-product of practice, or as a deliberate strategy of skill acquisition, human experts spend many hours to develop retrieval structures that enable them to access information from their nearly unlimited long-term memories nearly as quickly as from short-term memory. Second, designers need not be concerned with refinement of the representations of motor programs needed to carry out tasks such as the skillful playing of poly-rhythms. They can always develop two coordinated processors to manage the counterpoint. Nonetheless, when it comes to refining programs to do real-time motor programming to produce musical interpretations rather than mechanical renditions, some attention is needed to the processes that humans have adopted. Generally, though, hardware limitations that work against the human are easily by-passed within computer architectures. Third, designers need not be concerned with motivation, unless it is in the context of knowledge elicitation techniques with humans.

On the negative side, the mere fact that even the most able experts instructed by the best teachers require around a decade of study and deliberate practice to reach an international level of performance raises some intriguing questions for the design of expert systems. One might infer from this fact that the necessary knowledge for this level of performance is simply more extensive than commonly believed, but there are a couple of arguments suggesting that the problem of identifying the critical domain-specific knowledge and rules is more fundamental. First, teachers directly instruct students about some of the knowledge and rules, but such instruction constitute only a small fraction of the acquisition process. The main core of the acquisition process is based on deliberate practice where future expert performers engage in representative tasks that provide immediate feedback and opportunities for error correction and/or gradual refinement. These performers acquire skills and representations to allow them to plan, evaluate and reason about past and future actions, and they serve a dual role: to mediate the already-attained superior performance and to facilitate continued improvement and maintenance of expert performance (Ericsson and Lehmann 1996). Hence, the principal learning in experts occurs in response to feedback of errors and inferior actions in encountered representative situations. In these situations the experts can then rely on their mental representation used for planning and reasoning to diagnose the source of the problem and make specific adjustments that are consistent and integrated with all of their knowledge and skills. Such a complex monitoring process of learning virtually assures gradual improvement of performance. However, this view of expert performance and learning raises problems for eliciting experts' knowledge. Experts have typically been shown to have difficulty in explicating verbal rules that generalize across different contexts and situations, yet the same experts are able to provide informative concurrent and retrospective reports on their specific thoughts while confronting particular representative tasks (Ericsson and Simon 1993). In addition, the same level of expert performance could be mediated by skills and representations that differ considerably in content and structure across different experts. Hence it may not be possible to mix pieces of domain-specific knowledge obtained from different experts without causing a wide range of undesirable interactions in the associated expert system.

Let's consider in more detail the case of chess programs, which at this point are better than all but a few hundred humans of the estimated 5 or 6 million who play the game seriously. It took about 100 years for humans to assemble the information about good opening lines of play in the *Encyclopedia of Chess Openings* and perhaps 10 years to put together databases for endgame play. Programmers can capitalize on these knowledge bases to embed the opening wisdom of grandmasters in their programs in a matter of weeks or months. Whether the programs truly benefit from this mass of knowledge without a refined integration of the knowledge in the opening book to suit their particular strengths (tactics) and weaknesses (strategy) is very unlikely, however. Things are far rosier when it comes to using endgame databases where programs can easily outplay the best humans. Similarly, programs do not have to wrestle with the problem of managing working memory resources the way humans do when they resort to progressive deepening to manage search processes. Finally, programs can substitute extensive search for extensive knowledge (Newell 1989) and still reach very high levels of performance. So, Grandmaster-level chess programs have become a reality with little or no need to elicit knowledge from human experts.

Not every domain will have the knowledge base so well catalogued, nor be so open to the substitution of search for knowledge. In those domains, learning programs that mimic human experts' complex learning and deliberate practice seem to be a promising possibility.

Author Notes

This chapter is for the most part a shortened version of K.A. Ericsson and N. Charness's "Expert performance: Its structure and acquisition," published in *American Psychologist, 49(8),* 725-747 (Copyright 1994 by American Psychological Association). However, the text has been adapted to the goals of this book and updated with recent references. Furthermore, original sections have been added to address new issues.

Note

1. The field of visual art may offer at least one recent exception (Feldman, 1986). The Chinese girl, Yani, produced some acclaimed paintings between the ages of three and six (Ho, 1989), but matters are complicated by the fact that these paintings were selected by her father (a professional painter) from more than 4,000 paintings completed by Yani during this three-year period (Feng, 1984).

References

Abernethy, B. (1991). Visual search strategies and decision-making in sport. *International Journal of Sport Psychology, 22,* 189-210.

Barr, A. & Feigenbaum, E.A. (Eds.). (1981-2). *The Handbook of Artificial Intelligence.* Vols. 1-2. Stanford, CA: HeurisTech Press.

Biederman, I. & Shiffrar, M.M. (1987). Sexing day-old chicks: A case study and expert systems analysis of a difficult perceptual-learning task. *Journal of Experimental Psychology: Learning, Memory and Cognition, 13,* 640-645.

Binet, A. (1894). *Psychologie des grands calculateurs et joueurs d'echecs.* [Psychology of great mental calculators and chess players.] Paris: Libraire Hachette.

Bloom, B.S. (Ed.). (1985a). *Developing Talent in Young People.* New York: Ballantine Books.

Bloom, B.S. (1985b). Generalizations about talent development. In B. S. Bloom (Ed.), *Developing Talent in Young People* (pp. 507-549). New York: Ballantine Books.

Boshuizen, H.P.A. & Schmidt, H.G. (1992). On the role of biomedical knowledge in clinical reasoning by experts, intermediates and novices. *Cognitive Science, 16,* 153-184.

Bosman, E.A. (1993). Age-related differences in motoric aspects of transcription typing skill. *Psychology and Aging, 8,* 87-102.

Camerer, C.F. & Johnson, E.J. (1991). The process-performance paradox in expert judgment: How can the experts know so much and predict so badly? In K.A. Ericsson & J. Smith (Eds.), *Towards a General Theory of Expertise: Prospects and Limits* (pp. 195-217). Cambridge, England: Cambridge University Press.

Charness, N. (1981a). Search in chess: Age and skill differences. *Journal of Experimental Psychology: Human Perception and Performance, 7,* 467-476.

Charness, N. (1981b). Visual short-term memory and aging in chess players. *Journal of Gerontology, 36,* 615-619.

Charness, N. (1989). Expertise in chess and bridge. In D. Klahr & K. Kotovsky (Eds.), *Complex Information Processing: The Impact of Herbert A. Simon* (pp. 183-208). Hillsdale, NJ: Erlbaum.

Charness, N. (1991). Expertise in chess: The balance between knowledge and search. In K.A. Ericsson & J. Smith (Eds.), *Towards a General Theory of Expertise: Prospects and Limits* (pp. 195-217). Cambridge, England: Cambridge University Press.

Charness, N. & Bosman, E.A. (1990). Expertise and aging: Life in the lab. In T.H. Hess (Ed.), *Aging and Cognition: Knowledge Organization and Utilization* (pp. 343-385). Amsterdam: Elsevier.

Chase, W.G. & Ericsson, K.A. (1982). Skill and working memory. In G.H. Bower (Ed.), *The Psychology of Learning and Motivation* (Vol. 16, pp. 1-58). New York: Academic Press.

Chase, W.G. & Simon, H.A. (1973). The mind's eye in chess. In W.G. Chase (Ed.), *Visual Information Processing* (pp. 215-281). New York: Academic Press.

Chi, M.T.H., Glaser, R. & Farr, M.J. (Eds.). (1988). *The Nature of Expertise.* Hillsdale, NJ: Erlbaum.

Cohen, P.R. & Feigenbaum, E.A. (Eds.). (1982). *The Handbook of Artificial Intelligence.* Vol. 3. Stanford, CA: HeurisTech Press.

Csikszentmihalyi, M. (1990). *Flow: The Psychology of Optimal Experience.* New York: Harper & Row.

de Groot, A. (1978). *Thought and Choice and Chess.* [Original work published 1946.] The Hague, The Netherlands: Mouton.

Elo, A.E. (1965). Age changes in master chess performances. *Journal of Gerontology, 20,* 289-299.

Elo, A.E. (1986). *The Rating of Chessplayers, Past and Present* (2nd ed.). New York: Arco.

Ericsson, K.A. (1985). Memory skill. *Canadian Journal of Psychology, 39(2),* 188-231.

Ericsson, K.A. (1988). Analysis of memory performance in terms of memory skill. In R.J. Sternberg (Ed.), *Advances in the Psychology of Human Intelligence* (Vol. 4, pp. 137-179). Hillsdale, NJ: Erlbaum.

Ericsson, K.A. (1990). Peak performance and age: An examination of peak performance in sports. In P.B. Baltes & M.M. Baltes (Eds.), *Successful Aging: Perspectives from the Behavioral Sciences* (pp. 164-195). New York: Cambridge University Press.

Ericsson, K.A. (Ed.). (1996). The acquisition of expert performance: An introduction to some of the issues. In *The Road to Excellence: The Acquisition of Expert Performance in the Arts and Sciences, Sports, and Games* (pp 1-50). Mahweh, NJ: Erlbaum.

Ericsson, K.A. & Charness, N. (1994). Expert performance: Its structure and acquisition. *American Psychologist, 49(8),* 725-747.

Ericsson, K.A. & Chase, W.G. (1982). Exceptional memory. *American Scientist, 70,* 607-615.

Ericsson, K.A. & Harris, M.S. (1990). *Expert chess memory without chess knowledge: A training study.* Poster presented at the 31st Annual Meeting of the Psychonomic Society, New Orleans, LA.

Ericsson, K.A. & Kintsch, W. (1995). Long-term working memory. *Psychological Review, 102(2),* 211-245.

Ericsson, K.A., Krampe, R.T. & Heizmann, S. (1993). Can we create gifted people? In CIBA Foundation Symposium 178 *The Origin and Development of High Ability* (pp. 222-249). Chichester, England: Wiley.

Ericsson, K.A., Krampe, R.T. & Tesch-Römer, C. (1993). The role of deliberate practice in the acquisition of expert performance. *Psychological Review, 100,* 363-406.

Ericsson, K.A. & Lehmann, A.C. (1996). Expert and exceptional performance: Evidence on maximal adaptations on task constraints. *Annual Review of Psychology, 47,* 273-305.

Ericsson, K.A. & Simon, H.A. (1993). *Protocol Analysis: Verbal Reports as Data* (rev. ed.). Cambridge, MA: MIT Press.

Ericsson, K.A. & Smith, J. (Eds.). (1991a). *Toward a General Theory of Expertise: Prospects and Limits.* Cambridge, England: Cambridge University Press.

Ericsson, K.A. & Smith, J. (Eds.). (1991b). Prospects and limits of the empirical study of expertise: An introduction. In K. A. Ericsson & J. Smith (Eds.) *Toward a General Theory of Expertise: Prospects and Limits* (pp. 195-217). Cambridge, England: Cambridge University Press.

Feldman, D.H. (1980). *Beyond Universals in Cognitive Development.* Norwood, NJ: Ablex.

Feldman, D.H. (1986). *Nature's Gambit: Child Prodigies and the Development of Human Potential*. New York: Basic Books.

Feng, J. (1984). Foreword. In L. Shufen & J. Cheng'an (Eds.), *Yani's Monkeys* (pp. 1-2). Beijing, China: Foreign Languages Press.

Folkard, S. & Monk, T.H. (Eds.). (1985). Circadian performance rhythms. In *Hours of Work* (pp. 37-52). Chichester, England: Wiley.

Forbes, C. (1992). *The Polgar Sisters: Training or Genius?* New York: Henry Holt.

Franklin, B. (1986). *The Autobiography and Other Writings*. [Autobiography was originally published in 1788.] New York: Penguin Books.

Gardner, H. (1983). *Frames of Mind: The Theory of Multiple Intelligences*. New York: Basic Books.

Gardner, H. (1993a). *Creating Minds*. New York: Basic Books.

Gardner, H. (1993b). *Multiple Intelligences: The Theory in Practice*. New York: Basic Books.

Gobet, F. & Simon, H.A. (in press). Recall of rapidly presented random chess positions as a function of chess skill. *Psychonomic Bulletin & Review*.

Groen, G.J. & Patel, V.L. (1988). The relationship between comprehension and reasoning in medical expertise. In M.T.H. Chi, R. Glaser & M.J. Farr (Eds.), *The Nature of Expertise* (pp. 287-310). Hillsdale, NJ: Erlbaum.

Gruber, H.E. (1981). *Darwin on Man: A Psychological Study of Scientific Creativity* (2nd ed.). Chicago: University of Chicago Press.

Ho, W.-C. (Ed.). (1989). *Yani: The Brush of Innocence*. New York: Hudson Hills.

Hoffman, R.R. (Ed.). (1992). *The Psychology of Expertise: Cognitive Research and Empirical AI*. New York: Springer-Verlag.

Howe, M.J.A. (1990). *The Origins of Exceptional Abilities*. Oxford, England: Basil Blackwell.

Hunt, E. & Agnoli, F. (1991). The Whorfian hypothesis: A cognitive psychology perspective. *Psychological Review, 98,* 377-389.

Juster, F.T. & Stafford, F.P. (Eds.). (1985). *Time, Goods and Well-Being*. Ann Arbor: University of Michigan, Institute for Social Research.

Krampe. R. Th., & Ericsson, K. A. (in press). Maintaining excellence: Deliberate practice and elite performance in young and older pianists. *Journal of Experimental Psychology: General*.

Larkin, J.H., McDermott, J., Simon, D.P. & Simon, H.A. (1980). Models of competence in solving physics problems. *Cognitive Science, 4,* 317-345.

Lave, J. (1988). *Cognition in Practice*. Cambridge, England: Cambridge University Press.

Lave, J. & Wenger, E. (1991). *Situated Learning: Legitimate Peripheral Participation*. Cambridge, England: Cambridge University Press.

Lehman, H.C. (1953). *Age and Achievement*. Princeton, NJ: Princeton University Press.

Levin, H. & Addis, A.B. (1979). *The Eye-Voice Span*. Cambridge, MA: MIT Press.

Luria, A.R. (1968). *The Mind of a Mnemonist*. New York: Avon.

Maslow, A.H. (1971). *The Farther Reaches of Human Nature*. New York: Viking.

McClosky, D.N. (1990). *If You're So Smart: The Narrative of Economic Expertise*. Chicago: University of Chicago Press.

Miller, G.A. (1956). The magical number seven, plus or minus two: Some limits on our capacity for processing information. *Psychological Review, 63*, 81-97.

Murray, P. (Ed.). (1989a). *Genius: The History of an Idea.* Oxford, England: Basil Blackwell.

Newell, A. (1989). Putting it all together. In D. Klahr & K. Kotovsky (Eds.), *Complex Information Processing: The Impact of Herbert A. Simon* (pp. 399-440). Hillsdale, NJ: Lawrence Erlbaum.

Newell, A. & Simon, H.A. (1972). *Human Problem Solving.* Englewood Cliffs, NJ: Prentice-Hall.

Patel, V.L. & Groen, G.J. (1991). The general and specific nature of medical expertise: A critical look. In K.A. Ericsson & J. Smith (Eds.), *Towards a General Theory of Expertise: Prospects and Limits* (pp. 195-217). Cambridge, England: Cambridge University Press.

Platt, R. (1966). General introduction. In J.E. Meade & A.S. Parkes (Eds.), *Genetic and Environmental Factors in Human Ability* (pp. ix-xi). Edinburgh, Scotland: Oliver & Boyd.

Qin, Y. & Simon, H.A. (1990). Laboratory replication of scientific discovery processes. *Cognitive Science, 14,* 281-312.

Radford, J. (1990). *Child Prodigies and Exceptional Early Achievers.* New York: Free Press.

Raskin, E. (1936). Comparison of scientific and literary ability: A biographical study of eminent scientists and letters of the nineteenth century. *Journal of Abnormal and Social Psychology, 31,* 20-35.

Roe, A. (1953). A psychological study of eminent psychologists and anthropologists, and a comparison with biological and physical scientists. *Psychological Monographs: General and Applied, 67,* (Whole No. 352), 1-55.

Roth, H. (1982). *Master Violinists in Performance.* Neptune City, NJ: Paganinia.

Salthouse, T.A. (1984). Effects of age and skill in typing. *Journal of Experimental Psychology: General, 13,* 345-371.

Salthouse, T.A. (1991a). Expertise as the circumvention of human processing limitations. In K.A. Ericsson & J. Smith (Eds.), *Towards a General Theory of Expertise: Prospects and Limits* (pp. 195-217). Cambridge, England: Cambridge University Press.

Salthouse, T.A. (1991b). *Theoretical Perspectives on Cognitive Aging.* Hillsdale, NJ: Erlbaum.

Saariluoma, P. (1989). Chess players' recall of auditorily presented chess positions. *European Journal of Cognitive Psychology, 1,* 309-320.

Schmidt, H.G. & Boshuizen, H.P.A. (1993). On the origin of intermediate effects in clinical case recall. *Memory & Cognition, 21,* 338-351.

Schulz, R. & Curnow, C. (1988). Peak performance and age among superathletes: Track and field, swimming, baseball, tennis, and golf. *Journal of Gerontology: Psychological Sciences, 43,* 113-120.

Simon, H.A. & Chase, W.G. (1973). Skill in chess. *American Scientist, 61,* 394-403.

Simonton, D.K. (1984). *Genius, Creativity, and Leadership: Historiometric Inquiries.* Cambridge, MA: Harvard University Press.

Simonton, D.K. (1988a). Age and outstanding achievement: What do we know after a century of research? *Psychological Bulletin, 104,* 251-267.

Simonton, D.K. (1988b). *Scientific Genius: A Psychology of Science.* Cambridge, England: Cambridge University Press.

Sloboda, J.A. (1985). *The Musical Mind: The Cognitive Psychology of Music.* Oxford, England: Oxford University Press.

Smith, S.B. (1983). *The Great Mental Calculators.* New York: Columbia University Press.

Takeuchi, A.H. & Hulse, S.H. (1993). Absolute pitch. *Psychological Bulletin, 113,* 345-361.

Thomas, A. & Chess, S. (1984). Genesis and evolution of behavioral disorders: From infancy to early adult life. *American Journal of Psychiatry, 141,* 1-9.

Treffert, D.A. (1989). *Extraordinary People: Understanding "Idiot Savants."* New York: Harper & Row.

Wallace, A. (1986). *The Prodigy.* New York: Dutton.

Wallace, D.B. & Gruber, H.E. (Eds.). (1989). *Creative People at Work.* New York: Oxford University Press.

Weisberg, R.W. (1986). *Creativity: Genius and Other Myths.* New York: Freeman.

Weisberg, R.W. (1993). *Creativity: Beyond the Myth of Genius.* New York: Freeman.

CHAPTER 2

Some Concrete Advantages of Abstraction: How Experts' Representations Facilitate Reasoning

Colleen M. Zeitz

Introduction

Available evidence suggests that experts reason at a more abstract or principled level than novices. Like novices, experts form a mundane, literal level of mental representation. Yet, unlike novices, experts also appear able to create more complex, abstract representations. In addition, experts' knowledge bases are said to be organized around more abstract concepts. For example, a mechanics problem for a physics expert is characterized by the relevant implicit physics concepts: the forces involved, the relationships among them, and the principles that pertain to these interrelationships. Experts derive these features, which are not mentioned in problem descriptions, and use them in classifying problems.

Much evidence exists of abstractness in representation and good reasoning co-occurring in experts [e.g., physics (Chi, Feltovich, and Glaser 1981), computer science (Adelson 1981), literature (Zeitz 1994), clinical psychology (Dawson, Zeitz and Wright 1989), painting (Schmidt, McLaughlin and Leighton 1989), and political science (Voss, Green, Post and Penner 1983)]. However, little progress has been made in explaining the connection between abstract representations and reasoning. This chapter examines experts' representations across a variety of domains in an attempt to characterize a systematic pattern in the usage of abstraction. Two specific questions are addressed:

1) How does abstraction confer advantages? and 2) What is the connection between abstraction and superior reasoning?

Abstraction is commonly accepted as beneficial, having a long and strong association with expertise. But on reflection, it is not obvious that rejecting the most detailed and precise level of information representation in order to concentrate on a less distinct representation should lead to superior performance. This chapter attempts to specify some of the reasons why abstraction yields superior reasoning. I propose that experts' preferred level for processing is actually a "moderately abstract level" of representation. This intermediate level of representation consists of a comfortable, efficient compromise between the two extremes of the highest level of abstraction possible (e.g., formulas, such as $F=MA$ in physics) and a concrete, highly detailed representation (e.g., a specific pulley problem in physics). The functional requirements of the tasks of a particular field determine the exact degree of abstraction (within the intermediate range) that is optimal for that domain. It is suggested that a moderately abstract conceptual representation (MACR) is formed through the encoding of the current situation in relation to the categories that are functional in the domain. Thus, an important part of becoming an expert in a domain is becoming facile at processing information at the appropriate level of abstraction for that domain.

This chapter is organized in the following way. The next section examines the relationship between the development of experts' representations and the ways children's representations change as they develop reasoning skills. Four reasons why moderately abstract representations facilitate children's reasoning are presented. In the next four sections, findings from numerous domains of expertise are used to illustrate how each of the four benefits of MACRs support expert reasoning. I then present evidence that the reliance on MACRs has certain defined costs that are reflected in experts' performances. Next, I relate how MACRs are formed. Finally, I specify the instructional usefulness of this kind of representation.

Abstraction in Child Development

This section presents the argument that in the development of expertise, the shift from a literal, surface-based system of representation to a more abstract one, parallels a shift that occurs in child development, from verbatim representations to gist representations. The surface form of inputs is preserved in verbatim traces, whereas gist traces are patternlike and preserve the meaning of inputs (Brainerd and Reyna 1993). For example, for the task of transitive inference it has been shown that children do not operate on verbatim premises of the form "The red stick is longer than the blue stick" and "The blue stick is longer than the yellow stick." Instead, they encode the gist of the incoming pattern of information, such as that sticks were laid down so that "things get bigger to the left" and use this level of representation to solve problems (Reyna and Brainerd 1991; Reyna and Ellis 1994).

Brainerd and Reyna argue that the development of reasoning and remembering in children is governed by changes in the ability to store each of these types of representations and to process them with different types of operations. Verbatim-oriented processing shows little change over the preschool and elementary school years and deteriorates thereafter, whereas gist-oriented memory performance improves throughout childhood and adolescence for a broad range of stimuli (Brainerd and Reyna 1993). Brainerd and Reyna offer a number of reasons why a verbatim representation may be less useful than gist for some purposes. An analogy can be made between the advantages of gist and the benefits of MACRs. The specific consequences of these representation properties for experts' reasoning ability will be discussed below.

In this discussion it will be argued that a MACR provides a better foundation for expert reasoning than a more detailed representation because (following Brainerd and Reyna 1993): 1) Detailed representations become rapidly inaccessible because of their sensitivity to retroactive interference from subsequent encoding and processing. Abstractions are more stable and reasoning cannot be effective if it operates on a form of information that tends to become inaccessible. 2) A MACR can be retrieved by a broader range of retrieval cues and therefore is more accessible. 3) A MACR is an easier memory form to manipulate because of its schematic nature. 4) Processing nonessential details in a concrete representation may produce no accuracy gains and may actually interfere with successful reasoning.

In this framework, the development of expertise amounts to becoming facile at processing information at the level of abstraction appropriate for use in a given domain. Experts' representations develop in directions that enable effective application of knowledge to the solution of the problems of a field (Feltovich 1983; Feltovich and Barrows 1984). According to fuzzy trace theory, reasoning processes prefer to ignore distinctions that have few or limited consequences for target tasks (Brainerd and Reyna 1993; Reyna and Brainerd 1991). When memory options at various levels of abstraction are available, reasoning gravitates toward representations that are as thematic, streamlined and global as possible. By this argument, the reasoning of novices is nonoptimal because novices can only form detailed, surface-level representations of specialized domain information.

Table 1 includes a list of the properties of MACRs along with a method by which each property could facilitate the reasoning of experts. (For a review of the relevant empirical evidence, see Brainerd and Reyna 1990). By analyzing experts' representations across a variety of domains, the next four sections of this chapter offer an explanation of how each of these properties may affect experts' reasoning abilities.

Properties	Consequences
Stability	Superior memory performance
Accessibility	Bridge between detailed and highly abstra representations
	Efficient retrieval
Schematic Nature	Argument construction is facilitated
	Interpretation is enhanced
	Analogical reasoning is possible
Elimination of irrelevant details	Recognition of principled relationships

Table 1. Properties and Consequences of MACRs.

Stability of MACRs

Processing can erode detailed representations, while more abstract representations appear to be less vulnerable to the effects of retroactive interference (Brainerd and Reyna 1993). It is unlikely that experts' reasoning would be accurate if it were based on a form of representation that rapidly became inaccessible. The stability of MACRs should manifest itself in the accuracy of experts' memory performance relative to novices, and the qualities of the materials for which superior memory is demonstrated, as well as materials for which experts' memory is not exceptional. In their fields of knowledge, experts' memory is superior to novices' and exceeds what is generally accepted as the capacity of human working memory (Miller 1956). [While short term memory is limited in the number of meaningful units or chunks that it can hold simultaneously, an expert's chunk contains a much larger amount of information (Chase and Ericsson 1981; Chase and Simon 1973)]. Experts' exceptional memory performance has been demonstrated in such diverse domains of knowledge as bridge (Engle and Bukstel 1978), chess (Chase and Simon 1973), computer programming (Adelson 1981), baseball (Spilich, Vesonder, Chiesi and Voss 1979), problem solving in physics (Dee-Lucas and Larkin 1988), clinical psychology (Dawson et al. 1989), and electronic troubleshooting (Egan and Schwartz 1979). Superior memory has even been demonstrated by experts who are children (Chi 1978).

Because experts' memory performance relies on a conceptual level of representation, experts' memory is superior to novices' only in limited circumstances. Three constraints on experts' superior memory abilities are suggested. First, this ability holds only for content that is specific to their domain of expertise (e.g., Hatano and Osawa 1983; Zeitz 1994) because experts can form MACRs only for the kinds of information they regularly use in their field.

Second, experts' special representation abilities are not engaged by stimuli that violate the conventions which permit meaning in a domain. In a classic experiment (De Groot 1966; Chase and Simon 1973), when chess pieces were arranged as they might be in the midst of an actual game, experts recalled, after a very brief exposure, the positions of many more pieces than novices. However, the experts' recall-superiority was disrupted when they were presented with configurations that were impossible or meaningless, given the rules of chess. Apparently experts' knowledge bases allow them to recode stimuli in their domain, that is, to encode information in a reorganized form that reflects the structure of the domain. Chess experts chunk a number of pieces together into a meaningful pattern, whereas novices' basic unit of recall is a single or few game pieces. When chess pieces are placed randomly on a board, experts' performance deteriorates because they cannot perceive familiar, meaningful patterns.

A similar pattern holds for medical expertise (Patel and Groen 1991). When the temporal progression of the symptoms of a medical problem was intact, experts' recall and diagnoses were significantly more accurate than novices'. However, experts' performance was equivalent to novices' for a temporally distorted presentation, whereas the performance of novices was not affected by this manipulation.

Third, available research indicates that experts' display superior memory at the conceptual rather than surface level. A study of expertise in literature (Zeitz 1994) showed that literary experts were superior to novices in gist-level recall, but not verbatim recall of literary texts. It is particularly striking that expert-novice differences in verbatim-level recall do not obtain in this domain, because in the field of literature how ideas are expressed is clearly important. In addition, experts' and novices' memories did not differ for plot statements, which consist of simple accounts of actions and are intended to be taken literally. Sentences containing similes, metaphors, references to symbols, and irony are considered to contain multiple levels. Experts did surpass novices in recognition memory for multi-level sentences. Because these sentences have resonances beyond their literal meaning, they are central to literary texts, and experts in literature are more sensitive to changes in them. In general, experts do not excel at memory tasks that tap a surface level representation, such as verbatim recall, because experts do not have any special abilities with regard to such representations.[1] Experts' memory performance exceeds novices' only when memory is measured at the level of abstraction most useful for the tasks of that domain (which is generally not the verbatim level).

A meta-analysis of developmental studies has shown that reasoning accuracy is independent of memory accuracy in studies where memory is tested at a verbatim level, but dependent on memory accuracy when it is measured at the gist level (Brainerd and Reyna 1992). The fact that the representations that are correlated with successful reasoning are those at the gist level suggests that experts' superior memory for domain-relevant information at an intermediate level of abstraction should contribute to superior reasoning performance within their domain of expertise.

Experts can impose an organizational framework onto unstructured stimuli when they are allowed multiple exposures of sufficient duration. Memory performance in two studies of experts in computer science appears to reflect the construction of a MACR for disjointed stimuli. Adelson (1981) found that computer programming experts were able to perceive the structure inherent in unsequenced lines of computer code. In contrast, novice programmers were able to perceive only superficial similarities between the lines of code, which resulted in their recalling fewer of these lines than the experts did. Similarly, McKeithen, Reitman, Rueter and Hirtle (1981) presented programming experts and novices with an unordered list of key programming words. The experts tended to organize their recalls according to the words' purposes in programming, whereas the novices used a variety of strategies, such as stringing the words into sentences or organizing them according to phonetic features. For the experts, the concepts the keywords represented were organized in a specialized, meaningful way, and this conceptual organization was manifested in their recall orders.

In fact, because of their use of MACRs, experts can sometimes process a larger, more complex unit of information more effectively than a simpler one—as demonstrated in a study of baseball expertise (Chiesi, Spilich and Voss 1979). Experts and novices were asked to memorize sentences about baseball that were presented along with zero, one, or two context sentences which were not to be memorized. While novices were most successful at recalling target sentences that lacked context sentences, experts best recalled stimuli that were presented with two context sentences. Thus, experts had superior recall when they were presented with more information, presumably because the additional information enabled the experts to form a more meaningful and coherent representation of the target sentences.

In the work of Adelson; McKeithen *et al.*; and Chiesi *et al.*; it is clear that novices' memory performance relies on a detailed, surface-oriented representation that is strongly influenced by the original format of the stimuli. In contrast, experts' memory performance reflects an interpretation and organization that has been imposed upon the raw stimuli. The fact that this processing aids memory performance indicates that the expert is able to integrate high-level abstract knowledge of the domain with the concrete, detailed stimuli to form a hybrid representation that is neither so general as to lose contact with the material to be remembered nor so concrete and detailed as to be strongly influenced by the original formatting of the material.

Ericsson and Staszewski (1989) have examined studies of expertise (in memorizing series of digits and dinner orders, and in mental calculation) and have concluded that experts can accurately store and access large amounts of information in long-term memory at the speed with which short-term memory is normally used. They view this skilled memory effect as "a natural by-product of experts' use of LTM to maintain information in an easily accessible state for processing in complex tasks" (p. 238). The authors conclude that experts' superior memory performance is an epiphenomenon of the optimization of representation structures to facilitate reasoning.

It is somewhat difficult to prove that the lack of stability of novices' representations is the cause of their reasoning difficulties, partially because reasoning is such a complex process. The strongest evidence comes from consideration of experts in mental calculation. In this domain the individual component processes are extremely simple: the vast majority of adults can compute (or, more likely, retrieve) the product or sum of two digits. However, most adults can calculate the product of multi-digit numbers (e.g., 536 x 74) only when they have access to external memory aids. In contrast, experts at mental calculation are able to maintain accurate representations of the operands and intermediate results leading to the reliably accurate calculation of the product of multi-digit numbers (e.g., 76 x 96,842) (Staszewski 1988). Experts in mental calculation acquire domain-specific skills that enable them to circumvent the limited storage capacity of short-term memory (Staszewski 1988). It seems likely that in other domains, where the reasoning tasks of experts are more complex and the component processes remain opaque, expert-novice differences in representation stability have direct and dramatic effects on experts' and novices' information processing as well.

In summary, experts form representations that are conceptually-based and moderately abstract. Representations with these properties tend to be more stable and result in experts' superior performance for memory tasks where recall for coherent domain-relevant materials is measured at an appropriate level, and an increased likelihood of successful completion of reasoning processes that rely on these representations. The next section examines how MACRs may enhance the accessibility of additional information needed to move reasoning processes forward.

MACR's Facilitation of Retrieval

The focus on abstract representation was initiated with work on expertise in physics (Chi *et al.* 1981; Larkin 1981; Larkin, McDermott, Simon and Simon 1980). In general, novices' knowledge enables only a surface level problem representation that consists mostly of the objects and features explicitly presented in the situation. Novices classify introductory mechanics problems as, for example, inclined plane problems or pulley problems. Their ability to address problems follows from this representation based on elements of the problem statement. Their solution procedures are syntactic and specific—they often attempt to translate given problem statements directly into equations for solution.

In contrast, experts' knowledge organization enables them to represent problems in a deeper way. Experts' categorizations are based on principles, such as conservation of energy or Newton's second law of motion (Chi *et al.* 1981). In solving textbook mechanics problems, experts translate problem statements into spatial, abstract representations that may be explicitly manifested in the drawing of a "free-body diagram" (Larkin *et al.* 1980). In attacking a problem, experts qualitatively assess its nature, building a mental model or representation from which they can make inferences and add constraints to reduce the size of the set of possible solutions which need to be considered (Gentner and Gentner 1983).

In physics there is great agreement as to the nature of the useful abstractions for solving problems in the domain. The theoretical language of physics is accepted as an appropriate and useful level of abstraction, and there is agreement across experts, as evidenced by their common categorizations (Chi *et al.* 1981) and diagrams which relate theoretical entities (such as force and velocity). It is not difficult to postulate why a working familiarity with these abstractions supports superior reasoning. The moderately abstract concepts serve as a bridge between the concrete and detailed physical situations and the highly abstract formulas that yield mathematical solutions. Chi *et al.* (1981) provide compelling evidence that access to this critical bridging level of representation differentiates experts' and novices' reasoning. When asked to explain the basic approach they would take to solve a particular problem, novices did not seem to be able to comply. They either suggested strategies general enough that they could apply to any problem (e.g., figure out what is happening, see relationships, think of formulas) or they gave the specific equations they would use to combine quantities in the problem statement. In contrast, experts could provide solution plans at an intermediate level of abstraction, and, like their categorizations, these plans were based on the major physics principle that was most relevant for the problem.

Distilling a problem to its MACR is advantageous for experts and difficult for novices because it amounts to moving to a principle-based level of analysis. It is only at this deeper level of analysis that the physicist's body of knowledge can be brought to bear on the problem. The MACR of a physics problem can be manipulated until it matches up with a category of problem the physicist knows how to solve (cf. Clancey 1985). Thus, the ability to form MACRs of problem situations seems to be one requirement for successful reasoning in physics. Because MACRs consist of the essential components of complex entities, they also make novel, meaningful combinations and interpretations possible, as will be discussed in the next section.

Schematic Nature of MACR

MACRs are also advantageous in domains that involve tasks that are not as well defined as physics problems. Phelps and Shanteau (1978) have shown that expert livestock judges are able to integrate a large number of dimensions of animal quality into three aggregate categories of information. Expert judges are able to use these more abstract categories of information as the basis of their overall evaluations.

Schmidt *et al.* (1989) compared expert and novice strategies for understanding paintings. The analyses of paintings by experts were at a more abstract level, which subsumed both formal elements and painting subject matter. Novices emphasized the discernible semantic features or content of paintings more than the formal elements (e.g., line, color, shape) when viewing realist paintings. Schmidt *et al.* also noted expert-novice differences in the degree of integration of mentioned features. Novices tended to make simple observations regarding individual features, such as color or mood, but rarely combined them, for instance, to attempt to explain how the particular colors contributed to the mood. In contrast:

> Commenting on the Seurat painting, one expert noted that 'the work is naturalistic in colour, yet the abstract quality of forms and flatness of space rendered the naturalism ironic.' This subtle analysis contrasts sharply with that by novices, who by and large found the painting pleasing to look at and reminiscent of some past picnic or outing they enjoyed. (Schmidt *et al.* 1989, p. 70)

Where novices may have just noticed a feature, experts suggested a reason for it, analyzing it in the context of the entire work. Experts tended to combine observations in complex patterns to derive further interpretations.

This result is echoed in other ill-structured domains. In the domain of political science, Voss *et al.* (1983) found that experts' descriptions of problem situations were more abstract than novices.' For example, in addressing the problem of increasing crop productivity in the former Soviet Union, novices suggested the need for specific items, such as tractors, whereas experts suggested the need for infrastructure development. In addition, experts perceived the lack of fertilizer, repair parts and infrastructure as elements related to a more abstract concept of the lack of capital investment. Voss *et al.* also found that experts provided more extensive arguments to support their solutions to problems. The evidence from the domains of livestock judging, painting, and political science suggests that because a MACR is easier to maintain and manipulate, its formation may be a necessary predecessor to the integration of information and the perception of coherent patterns. In addition, the MACR's enhanced access to prior knowledge may be required in the construction of cohesive interpretations and arguments.

Similar findings come from a study in which experts and novices expressed their understanding of works of literature (Zeitz 1994). Literary experts surpassed novices in reasoning about literary texts: they generated arguments with greater hierarchical depth and made more complex comparisons between texts. Experts were able to get beyond the surface level of the texts' characters and events to derive interpretations. Novices tended to be limited to the surface level and their attempts at analysis often included only the repetition of factual information. The experts' performance on low-level tasks such as verbatim recall, as well as their analyses of nonliterary texts, which would not be expected to be affected by MACRs, were not superior to those of novices. As in other ill-structured domains, MACR enhances the reasoning of literary experts because it facilitates the integration of information, the access to relevant prior knowledge, and argument construction.

The Analogical Reasoning Ability of Experts

In the process of forming a MACR, literary experts move beyond the surface level of texts to identify critical aspects of the texts and to perceive patterns that can be related to the texts' overall themes. Empirical support can be derived from the order of the relations expert and novice subjects mapped when asked to generate a specific comparison between a short story and a poem. Subjects were instructed to compare and contrast the relationship between inside (e.g., inside Louisa's house, inside the child's room) and outside in *A New England Nun* and "The World and the Child." To analyze these essays, coders classified each relation that subjects described into one of three categories: zero-order relations, which are simple object attributes; first-order relations, which connect two or more entities; or second-order relations, which entail relations between relations (Gentner 1983). For example, one expert wrote, "Louisa's relationship with the outside world is much *more harmonious.*" This contains a simple first-order relation between Louisa and the world. There is also a second-order relation, namely that Louisa's relationship to the outside world is more harmonious than the relationship of the child to the outside world.

Figures 1 and 2 are graphical representations of each of these analogical mappings. The circles represent the entities that subjects mentioned and lines are used to represent relations between them (thick for second order, medium for first-order, and thin lines connected to only one entity for first-order relations). The top half of each figure contains relations and entities from the short story, and the bottom half concerns the poem. The novice's mapping in figure 1 reflects a basic level representation and includes only the bare bones of the texts. In contrast, the expert's mapping in figure 2 contains extra nodes and more connections, and these connections are qualitatively different from those generated by novices. The more abstract nature of the experts' representations is illustrated by their generation of the largest num-

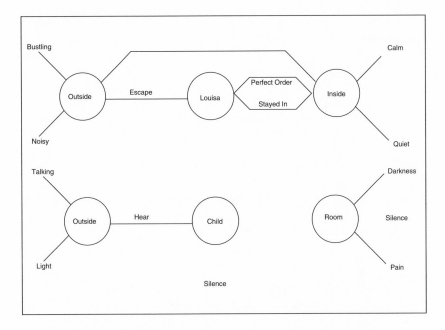

Figure 1. Graphic representation of one novice's analogy mapping.

ber of second-order relations in their mappings. The ability to find and describe a correspondence between relations requires a substantial degree of abstraction from the literal features of the texts. In fact, these graphical representations (i.e., figures 1 and 2) could be viewed as partial illustrations of the networks of nodes and relations that make up subjects' representations.

Once again a parallel with child development can be drawn, to what Gentner terms the "relational shift." Children tend to focus on the surface level and map lower-order relations when interpreting analogies and metaphors. A 5 year old, given the figural comparison "A cloud is like a sponge" produces an attributional interpretation, such as "Both are round and fluffy." A typical adult response is "Both can hold water for some time and then later give it back." Thus there is evidence for a developmental shift from a focus on common object attributes to a focus on common relations in analogical processing (Gentner 1988), just as adults seem to shift their attention to more abstract relations with the development of expertise.

Another demonstration of the superior analogical reasoning skills of experts can be seen in the domain of algebra. Novick (1988) found that expert problem solvers demonstrated successful positive transfer of solution procedures to new analogous problems. They were also less likely to be fooled by solution procedures from a problem with only surface level similarities.

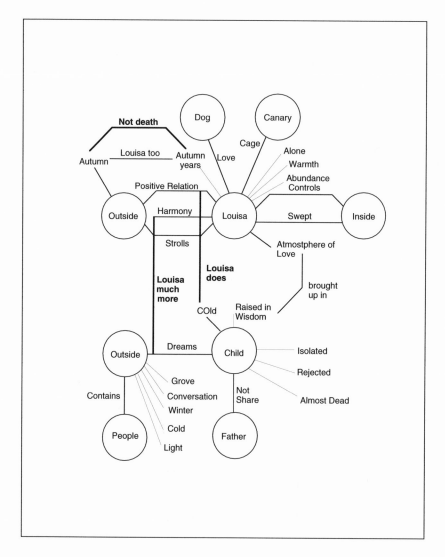

Figure 2. Graphic representation of one expert's analogy mapping.

Gick and Holyoak (1983) have shown that the abstraction of a schema facilitates analogical problem solving. When subjects were asked to generate the underlying similarities among a set of isomorphic story problems and their solutions, they were more likely to be able to apply the generalized solution to a new problem. Those subjects who wrote summaries that highlighted the common abstract structure of the instances were able to retrieve and apply the prior solution to the superficially dissimilar problem. By this argument, it is experts' formation of MACRs that facilitates their more complex analogical mappings between entities. In analogical reasoning, it is necessary to abstract away from the details in order to detect more global patterns. MACRs allow the detection of high-order relationships despite differences in surface features. The following section addresses how MACRs facilitate the recognition of patterns and relationships by filtering out unnecessary information.

Elimination of Irrelevant Details in MACRs

Experts' superior ability to construct arguments and analogies requires the perception of implicit patterns. The sensitivity of experts to implicit regularities was the focus of an investigation in the domain of clinical psychology. In this field it is necessary to be able to reason about patterns in large, unstructured bodies of behavioral data, and MACRs appear to play a key role in this ability. Dawson *et al.* (1989) presented clinical psychology experts and novices with sentence pairs describing antecedent situations and children's behavioral responses. These stimuli represented observations of events involving hypothetical children: a prototypical aggressive child whose behavior patterns corresponded to those displayed by actual aggressive children, as well as a "random" child whose behavior did not vary systematically across situations. For example, one sentence pair presented concerning the aggressive child (Greg) was "A boy complains to Greg for using the last of the green paint. Greg points to the child's work and says it all stinks anyway."

Novices and experts performed equally well when recall of the individual sentences was measured. However, experts' estimates of the probability of a certain category of response behavior given a particular type of antecedent were much more accurate than novices' for the aggressive child. In this case, the experts' superior memory for behavior patterns was based on their ability to abstract away from the original detailed scenarios. However, they were only able to do so for the case in which there was a coherent pattern in the information. Just as chess experts' performance approximated that of novices for the recall of random chessboards, clinical experts did not excel in summarizing the random child's behavior. In both cases, experts could not form MACRs because the meaningful relationships in the stimuli were distorted.

Patterns of antecedent-consequent behavior linkages are the basis of MACRs that transcend the experts' detailed representations of individual actions. More generally, categorization on a moderately abstract level provides an efficient means of summarizing information that cannot be retained at the surface level because of memory limitations. Such categorization may also facilitate the combination of many individual observations into meaningful patterns. This formation of an accurate representation at an appropriate level of abstraction may provide a useful framework that facilitates experts' reasoning about large bodies of complex information that may appear unwieldy, feature-less and even overwhelming to novices. Thus, novices "fail to see the forest for the trees" because they tend to form concrete, detailed representations.

In medical diagnosis, experts have to integrate many different pieces of in-formation that are not available simultaneously (e.g., preconditions, system malfunctions and consequences). Thus, it is necessary for medical experts to perform some kind of feature consolidation in order to make use of com-monalities across different problems (Feltovich and Barrows 1984). Patel and Groen (1991) suggest that experts use abstract representation structures to filter out unnecessary information. Because novices lack these structures, they are forced to remember information in a raw form.

Studies of medical expertise reveal a strong connection between forward reasoning and accuracy of performance (Patel and Groen 1991). Expert problem-solvers tend to work forward from the given information to the un-known (or diagnosis). Less knowledgeable problem solvers tend to use back-ward reasoning, which entails working from a hypothesis regarding a diagno-sis back to the given information. Without a filtering mechanism, forward reasoning can yield a profusion of irrelevant chains of inference. One study found that physicians tended to operate more on the highly relevant infor-mation in a problem by making selective inferences. In contrast, intermedi-ates appeared unable to discriminate between high- and low-relevance infor-mation and therefore operated on both (Patel and Groen 1991). More generally, since novices are unable to focus on relevant material, they can ini-tiate many unsuccessful searches which result in the access of irrelevant prior knowledge. In contrast, experts' reliance on an intermediate level of repre-sentation allows them to use the most efficient reasoning method (i.e., for-ward reasoning) while shielding them from its potential pitfalls (i.e., informa-tion explosion) (Larkin 1981). The next section considers the downside of experts' reliance on a MACR.

Limitations Imposed by MACRs

Abstraction can have costs as well as benefits. In some experimental situa-tions, experts' reliance on MACRs has been shown to detract from their per-formance. Frensch and Sternberg (1989) elegantly demonstrated that ex-perts' and novices' reliance on different levels of representation can lead to different kinds of vulnerabilities. They tested the response of bridge experts and novices to modifications in the rules of the game. They found that novices' performance was more negatively affected by surface structure changes, such as changing the names given to the suits and face cards, or re-arranging the ordering of face cards and suits. Experts, on the other hand, were more strongly affected by changes in the deeper structure, that is, the rules of play (e.g., when the rules for who leads each round were changed, the experts' performance decreased dramatically.) Thus, because experts represent information on a deeper, more principled level, this is the level to which they are most vulnerable to changes. They can overcome surface structure changes and still apply their knowledge effectively.

Arkes and Freedman (1984) have shown that experts in the domains of baseball and Ohio geography are more liable than novices to falsely recognize sentences which could be inferred from presented text. They explained this finding in terms of the idea that experts store the gist of the situations, whereas novices remember the sentences verbatim. This suggests that the formation of a MACR (which is neither as specific as the verbatim sentences nor as abstract as a general summary or theme) may be so efficient at facilitating access to the knowledge base that it may be impossible for experts to distinguish their representations from their prior knowledge in a subsequent memory test.

Likewise, Adelson (1984) has shown novices to be at an advantage in answering concrete questions about how a program functions compared to computer science experts, whose representations no longer included the details of the programs. These findings are informative because they provide another kind of evidence for abstraction and help to characterize the nature of its costs. (See Sternberg and Frensch 1992, for a discussion of other costs of expertise.)

Novices appear to perform well in tasks such as adjusting to changes in the rules of bridge, distinguishing presented from inferable sentences, and recalling the particular commands used in a program because they are using a verbatim representation that preserves the details of the presented material. Experts' interpretation and integration of information requires abstracting away from the facts to some degree. Above, I illustrated the potential value for reasoning performance of the loss of detail, but the studies discussed here highlight the negative consequences (which are rarely problematic in normal situations) of the loss of the details of surface form. Thus, experts performed poorly in these carefully engineered artificial situations because their MACRs have evolved to maximize benefits and minimize costs for the tasks most often encountered in the experts' respective domains. (See Feltovich 1983, for a discussion of the functional basis of experts' representations.)

The Question of Flexibility

MACRs can shed light on the controversial issue of the degree of experts' flexibility. Many studies claim that experts are flexible whereas novices are inflexible. A comparable number of studies appear to show the reverse, with some researchers specifically stating that inflexibility is a cost of expertise (Sternberg and Frensch 1992).

The research supporting experts' flexibility usually examines experts' reasoning about typical problems naturally occurring within their domain. For example, expert radiologists have been shown to be able to tune their perception of features in x-ray pictures to the specific case with which they are working, leading to more accurate diagnoses. As they encounter new problem features regarding a patient's condition, they can flexibly change their problem representation. Thus, experts can avoid prematurely committing themselves to a specific diagnosis before all the data are available (Lesgold *et al.* 1988).

Expert physicians have also been shown to use knowledge flexibly in understanding patients' illnesses. For less difficult problems, they can skip inference steps (e.g., directly linking patient findings and clinical concepts without invoking any biomedical concepts) due to knowledge encapsulation. When a problem is complicated enough to demand it, expert physicians' encapsulated knowledge can be "unpacked" and applied (Boshuizen and Schmidt 1995). Voss *et al.* offer an explanation for the observed flexibility in experts' reasoning.

> The experiences that enhance expert's knowledge organization no doubt cover a wide range of issues and problems, and the expert thus develops a highly flexible information-processing system. It is flexible in the sense that domain-related information, whatever it is, may be readily interpreted in terms of existing structures, and new information may be assimilated into the appropriate structures. (1983, pp. 207-208)

Sternberg and Frensch have allowed that experts' knowledge structures are sufficiently abstract to permit application to novel instances of familiar types of problems. They also state that the automaticity of some aspects of experts' problem solving in the domain means that when these routines are applicable to a problem, resources are freed up for dealing with novel aspects of the problem. In contrast, novices are overwhelmed by all the facets of a problem because no portion can be processed automatically. Thus novices are apt to get bogged down in local details. However, automaticity has associated costs, the foremost of these being the lack of control, in that individuals are unable to stop ongoing automatic processes, even when they are inappropriate to the task at hand. For this reason, problem solvers who have automatized their solution strategies can be less flexible than ones who have not (Sternberg and Frensch 1992).

On the side of inflexibility, experts in a number of domains do not appear to be able to shift from the MACR level to a detailed level of representation, as evidenced by their inability to recall items at the verbatim level (Dawson *et al.* 1989; Zeitz 1994) and their inability to answer questions about the surface level of learned material (Adelson 1984; Arkes and Freedman 1984; Zeitz 1994). There may be domains in which more importance is placed on details, but generally, depending on the experimental task and its similarity to the sorts of tasks usually conducted in a domain, experts may be unable to reproduce many of the details of a situation. In addition, experts respond poorly to conceptual changes to the domain, such as changing the rules of play or in processing stimuli which violate the principles of the domain (Chase and Simon 1973; Dawson *et al.* 1989; Frensch and Sternberg 1989).

If we restrict our consideration to the performance of tasks that do not violate the conceptual rules of the domain and that do not require the use of concrete, detailed representations, we find that within their domain of expertise experts' reasoning is generally far more flexible than that of novices. In summary, experts display flexible application of MACRs to problems within the domain, but experts can be inflexible in performing tasks that require total reconfiguration of their conceptually-organized representations or switching to a nonpreferred level of abstraction. The next section considers how MACRs are formed.

The Formation of MACRs

Experts in both ill-structured and well-structured domains rely on integrative, conceptual representations that subsume the surface level features that novices focus on. Upon encountering a problem, an expert uses the methods of analysis available to him or her to identify what is important about the situation given the task at hand. For example, in medical diagnosis, a clinician attempts to understand a patient's problem by constructing an illness script. An illness script consists of abstract categories of illness features which recur across different illnesses, specifically 1) the enabling conditions or how the patient's condition came to be, 2) faults or the major points of malfunction and 3) the consequences or symptoms (Feltovich and Barrows 1984; Schmidt, Norman and Boshuizen 1990). The classification system prevalent in the domain enables the expert to distill the essence of the situation and discard the inconsequential. The classification system of the domain is important because the expert needs to relate the current instance to a previously stored category so that this category can be used as an entry point to the relevant subsection of the expert's knowledge base. Thus, the MACR serves as the link between the particulars of the problem in question and the experts' extensive body of knowledge. The connection to a category provides guidance for the access and application of not only principles, but specific solution procedures, and it enhances the ability to establish analogies to previously stored cases. The next section considers how conceptual models at an intermediate level of abstraction can be used to support instruction.

Moderately Abstract Conceptual Models in Instruction

The crucial importance of principled representations in experts' performances suggests that the moderately abstract conceptual level may be a promising focus in instruction. Providing learners with a framework to which they can attach more detailed levels of new information in order to form a coherent, fleshed-out structure can enhance both knowledge organization and proceduralization (Kieras and Bovair 1984). In introducing a domain of knowledge, first a meaningful framework can be provided in the form of an explanation of a key aspect of expert domain knowledge, such as a principled description of a physics problem or a derived theme of a piece of literature. This explanation can then be elaborated upon, one level at a time, until the details have been described.

The degree of hierarchical structure present in explanatory material strongly influences the knowledge representation of the learner. In the domain of plastic extrusion machine operation, novices who initially received training in the abstract, conceptual relationships among domain concepts acquired better developed knowledge structures, as measured by the number of hierarchical levels in their knowledge bases, than novices who were initially exposed to lower level aspects of the domain (Koubek, Clarkston and Calvez 1994).

Training-induced differences in representation have been shown to affect reasoning performance as well. Novice learners who were initially presented with a breadth-first overview of the subsystems and then the components of a complex troubleshooting domain were able to use it as a scaffolding to organize information during their acquisition of later declarative knowledge and problem-solving procedures. These novices' knowledge bases were more hierarchically organized, their problem-solving efforts were faster and more successful, and their performances were more automatic than those of novices who learn the same material in a bottom-up sequence (Zeitz and Spoehr 1989).

White's (1993) research has also supported the instructional usefulness of conceptual models at an intermediate level of abstraction. In contrast to more traditional "top-down" approaches to science education that use abstract formulas as a starting point, or "bottom-up" approaches that start with the manipulation of physical objects, in this "middle-out" approach, students are introduced to new domains via causal models represented at an intermediate level of abstraction. MACRs create a coherent link between real-world phenomena and computational formalisms.

One model that White's tutoring system employs concerns a generic transport mechanism that can represent a number of physical processes, such as the distribution of electrical charge, the diffusion of gases, and the flow of heat. In this model, if two objects are connected and they contain different amounts of "stuff," then "stuff" will flow from one to the other. The model is at an intermediate level because it is more abstract than a model of the movement of individual particles and less abstract than a model based on specific principles such as $\Delta V=IR$.

White's program of research illustrates that for a given domain, it is possible to define a useful moderately abstract level of representation. Sixth graders who worked with these models for eight weeks solved notoriously difficult problems involving physics concepts that are often misunderstood, and solved them more successfully than high school students who had completed the relevant section of a physics course (White 1993).

Summary and Conclusions

In summary, this chapter has described how MACRs support the reasoning of experts. A number of parallels between the development of reasoning and representation abilities in children have been exploited in order to coordinate experimental findings concerning experts' representation and reasoning performance. MACRs have been proposed to: 1) lead to enhanced memory performance, 2) serve as a bridge between concrete, detailed problem information and the expert's more general knowledge base, 3) enhance the selection and coordination of evidence in argumentation and 4) allow a broader view of individual instances, permitting the perception of patterns. MACRs aid reasoning in these ways because they have properties which enhance information processing. That is, they tend to remain longer in memory and tend to be more easily and accurately accessed and manipulated than more concrete, detailed levels of representation. There are specific costs associated with the reliance on this level of representation because the details of the surface form of the material are clouded. Finally, there are a number of educational implications regarding the best way to introduce information to novices in order to facilitate their acquisition of the ability to represent this knowledge on the MACR level.

The value of positing MACRs with the qualities described is that they provide a coherent account that accommodates the most prevalent findings concerning the memory and reasoning of experts. This permits integration of research on a wide variety of domains of expertise, including both well- and ill-structured domains. Of course, knowing that experts rely on a MACR does not amount to an a priori detailed and specific characterization of the nature of experts' representations in a particular domain. A careful analysis of the experts' performance in a given domain is required in order to discern the system of categorization that is most useful and meaningful in *that* domain.

The most important practical implication of this chapter is that the level of abstraction of representation must be considered as a crucial factor in simulating and training expertise. Establishing the MACR level that is appropriate for a given domain (i.e., the level that is used by experts in the domain) is a promising starting point for designing an expert system. The psychologist's manipulative techniques, such as asking experts to recall stimuli at various levels of abstraction and contrasting situations which disrupt the expert's superior performance with those that do not, may be a more successful approach than trying to elicit information about levels of representation from the expert directly. It is suggested that knowledge bases of expert systems should be organized around the principles of the given domain. It is also likely to prove profitable to search for techniques for forming an appropriately abstract representation of problems input to an expert system as a precursor to applying solution procedures. Finally, the moderately abstract conceptual level has been demonstrated to be an effective basis for introducing novices to a domain. Future research in expertise might profit from attempts to specify the precise nature of MACRs for particular domains. In addition, it will be important to research how experts' ability to form this type of representation develops.

Author Notes

This chapter is based in part on a talk given at the Third International Workshop on Human and Machine Cognition, Special Topic: Expertise in Context, Seaside, FL, May 1993, for which Micki Chi was the second author. This research was supported by the Andrew W. Mellon Foundation. Correspondence should be sent to Colleen Zeitz, 93 Arlington Avenue, Providence, RI 02906.

Note

1. Although chess experts are able to place individual game pieces correctly on a board, they are not relying on a literally-based representation. If they were, a randomly arranged board would be no more challenging than a coherently arranged one. In the domain of chess, however, each piece's function is unique and thus a necessary part of understanding the interrelationships that make up an entire board position. Although chess experts are able to "unpack" their conceptual representations of boards to identify the locations of individual game pieces, literature experts do not appear to be able to perform this operation on text representations. The explanation may lie in the fact that a word may be replaced with one of several synonyms or a given statement may be stated in active or passive voice without a significant change in meaning (not to mention that texts contain many more words than there are pieces in a chess set). There are likely to be exceptions to this generalization, such as key phrases or a critical metaphor in a text, but in most

cases it appears that the exact phrasing used is not a necessary part of a conceptual representation of a text and for this reason the verbatim text cannot be recovered from the literary expert's representation.

References

Adelson, B. (1981). Problem solving and the development of abstract categories in programming languages. *Memory and Cognition, 9,* 422-433.

Adelson, B. (1984). When novices surpass experts: The difficulty of the task may increase with expertise. *Journal of Experimental Psychology: Learning, Memory, and Cognition, 10,* 483-495.

Arkes, H.R. & Freedman, M.R. (1984). A demonstration of the costs and benefits of expertise in recognition memory. *Memory & Cognition, 12,* 84-89.

Boshuizen, H.P.A. & Schmidt, H.G. (1995). The development of clinical reasoning expertise. In J. Higgs & M. Jones (Eds.), *Clinical Reasoning in the Health Professions* (pp. 24-34). Oxford: Butterworth Heinemann.

Brainerd, C.J. & Reyna, V.F. (1990). Gist is the grist: Fuzzy-trace theory and perceptual salience effects in cognitive development. *Developmental Review, 10,* 3-47.

Brainerd, C.J. & Reyna, V.F. (1992). Explaining "memory free" reasoning. *Psychological Science, 3,* 332-339.

Brainerd, C.J. & Reyna, V.F. (1993). Memory independence and memory interference in cognitive development. *Psychological Review, 100,* 42-67.

Chase, W.G. & Ericsson, K.A. (1981). Skilled memory. In J.R. Anderson (Ed.), *Cognitive Skills and Their Acquisition* (pp. 141-190). Hillsdale, NJ: Erlbaum.

Chase, W.G. & Simon, H.A. (1973). Perception in chess. *Cognitive Psychology, 4,* 55-81.

Chi, M.T.H. (1978). Knowledge structures and memory development. In R. Siegler (Ed.), *Children's Thinking: What Develops?* (pp. 73-96). Hillsdale, NJ: Erlbaum.

Chi, M.T.H., Feltovich, P.J. & Glaser, R. (1981). Categorization and representation of physics problems by experts and novices. *Cognitive Science, 5,* 121-152.

Chiesi, H.L., Spilich, G.J. & Voss, J.F. (1979). Acquisition of domain-related information in relation to high and low domain knowledge. *Journal of Verbal Learning and Verbal Behavior, 18,* 257-273.

Clancey, W.J. (1985). Heuristic classification. *Artificial Intelligence, 27,* 289-350.

Dawson, V.L., Zeitz, C.M. & Wright, J.C. (1989). Expert-novice differences in person perception: Evidence of experts' sensitivities to the organization of behavior. *Social Cognition, 7,* 1-30.

De Groot, A. (1966). Perception and memory versus thought: Some old ideas and recent findings. In B. Kleinmuntz (Ed.), *Problem Solving* (pp. 19-50). New York: Wiley.

Dee-Lucas, D. & Larkin, J.H. (1988). Attentional strategies for studying scientific texts. *Memory and Cognition, 16,* 469-479.

Egan, D. & Schwartz, B. (1979). Chunking in recall of symbolic drawings. *Memory & Cognition, 7,* 149-158.

Engle, R.W. & Bukstel, L. (1978). Memory processes among bridge players of differing expertise. *American Journal of Psychology, 91,* 673-689.

Ericsson, K.A. & Staszewski, J.J. (1989). Skilled memory and expertise: Mechanisms of exceptional performance. In D. Klahr & K. Kotovsky (Eds.), *Complex Information Processing: The Impact of Herbert A. Simon* (pp. 235-267). Hillsdale, NJ: Erlbaum.

Feltovich, P.J. (1983). Expertise: Reorganizing and refining knowledge for use. *Profession's Education Researcher Notes (A.E.R.A., Division I), 4,* 5-9.

Feltovich, P.J. & Barrows, H.S. (1984). Issues of generality in medical problem solving. In H.G. Schmidt & M.L. DeVolder (Eds.), *Tutorials in Problem-Based Learning* (pp. 128-142) Van Gorcum, Assen: Maastrict, The Netherlands.

Frensch, P.A. & Sternberg, R.J. (1989). Expertise and intelligent thinking: When is it worse to know better? In R.J. Sternberg (Ed.), *Advances in the Psychology of Human Intelligence* (Vol. 5, pp. 157-188). Hillsdale, NJ: Erlbaum.

Gentner, D. (1983). Structure-mapping: A theoretical framework for analogy. *Cognitive Science, 7,* 155-170

Gentner, D. (1988). Metaphor as structure-mapping: The relational shift. *Child Development, 59,* 47-59.

Gentner, D. & Gentner, D.R. (1983). Flowing waters or teeming crowds: Mental models of electricity. In D. Gentner & A.L. Stevens (Eds.), *Mental Models* (pp. 99-129). Hillsdale, NJ: Erlbaum.

Gick, M.L. & Holyoak, K.J. (1983). Schema induction and analogical transfer. *Cognitive Psychology, 15,* 1-38.

Hatano, G. & Osawa, K. (1983). Digit memory of grand experts in abacus-derived mental calculation. *Cognition, 15,* 95-110.

Kieras, D.E. & Bovair, S. (1984). The role of a mental model in learning to operate a device. *Cognitive Science, 8,* 255-273.

Koubek, R.J., Clarkston, T.P. & Calvez, V. (1994). The training of knowledge structures for manufacturing tasks: An empirical study. *Ergonomics, 37,* 765-780.

Larkin, J.H. (1981). Enriching formal knowledge: A model for learning to solve problems in physics. In J.R. Anderson (Ed.), *Cognitive Skills and Their Acquisition* (pp. 311-335). Hillsdale, NJ: Erlbaum.

Larkin, J.H., McDermott, J., Simon, D.P. & Simon, H.A. (1980). Expert and novice performance in solving physics problems. *Science, 208,* 1335-1342.

Lesgold, A., Rubinson, H., Feltovich, P., Glaser, R, Klopfer, D. & Wang, Y. (1988). Expertise in a complex skill: Diagnosing x-ray pictures. In M.T.H. Chi, R. Glaser & M.J. Farr (Eds.), *The Nature of Expertise* (pp. 311-342). Hillsdale, NJ: Erlbaum.

McKeithen, K.B., Reitman, J.S., Rueter, H.H. & Hirtle, S.C. (1981). Knowledge organization and skill differences in computer programmers. *Cognitive Psychology, 13,* 307-325.

Miller, G.A. (1956). The magical number seven, plus or minus two: Some limits on our capacity for processing information. *Psychological Review, 63,* 81-97.

Novick, L.R. (1988). Analogical transfer, problem similarity and expertise. *Journal of Experimental Psychology: Learning, Memory and Cognition, 14,* 510-520.

Patel, V.L. & Groen, G.J. (1991). The general and specific nature of medical expertise. In K.A. Ericsson & J. Smith (Eds.), *Toward a General Theory of Expertise* (pp. 93-125). Cambridge, England: Cambridge University Press.

Phelps, R.H. & Shanteau, J. (1978). Livestock judges: How much information can an expert use? *Organizational Behavior and Human Performance, 21,* 209-219.

Reyna, V.F. & Brainerd, C.J. (1991). Fuzzy-trace theory and children's acquisition of mathematical and scientific concepts. *Learning and Individual Differences, 3,* 27-60.

Reyna, V.F. & Ellis, S.C. (1994). Fuzzy-trace theory and framing effects in children's risky decision making. *Psychological Science, 5,* 275- 279.

Schmidt, H.G., Norman, G.R. & Boshuizen, H.P.A. (1990). A cognitive perspective on medical expertise: Theory and implications. *Academic Medicine, 65,* 611-621.

Schmidt, J.A., McLaughlin, J.P. & Leighton, P. (1989). Novice strategies for understanding paintings. *Applied Cognitive Psychology, 3,* 65-72.

Spilich, G.J., Vesonder, G.T., Chiesi, H.L. & Voss, J.F. (1979). Text-processing of domain-related information for individuals with high and low domain knowledge. *Journal of Verbal Learning and Verbal Behavior, 18,* 275-290.

Staszewski, J.J. (1988). Skilled memory and expert mental calculation. In M.T.H. Chi, R. Glaser & M.J. Farr (Eds.), *The Nature of Expertise* (pp. 71-128). Hillsdale, NJ: Erlbaum.

Sternberg, R.J. & Frensch, P.A. (1992). On being an expert: A cost-benefit analysis. In R.R. Hoffman (Ed.), *The Psychology of Expertise: Cognitive Research and Empirical AI* (pp. 191-203). New York: Springer-Verlag.

Voss, J.F., Green, T.R., Post, T.A. & Penner, B.C. (1983). Problem-solving skills in the social sciences. *The Psychology of Learning and Motivation: Advances in Research and Theory, 17,* 165-213.

White, B.Y. (1993). Intermediate causal models: A missing link for successful science education? In R. Glaser (Ed.), *Advances in Instructional Psychology,* Volume 4. Hillsdale, NJ: Erlbaum.

Zeitz, C.M. (1994). Expert-novice differences in memory, abstraction and reasoning in the domain of literature. *Cognition and Instruction, 12,* 277-312.

Zeitz, C.M. & Spoehr, K.T. (1989). Knowledge organization and the acquisition of procedural expertise. *Applied Cognitive Psychology, 3,* 313-336.

CHAPTER 3

Cognitive Models of Directional Inference in Expert Medical Reasoning

Vimla L. Patel & Marco F. Ramoni

Introduction

The purpose of this chapter is to give an account of the development of expertise in medical reasoning, and to compare the characterizations of expert reasoning which have emerged from our research with some of the models of expert reasoning provided by artificial intelligence (AI). It is important to begin by reminding ourselves that cognitive psychology and AI have their own paradigmatic approaches. However, there are ways in which cross-fertilization can take place. One is to develop a model that operates as both a psychological model and an AI system, a salient recent example being SOAR (Newell 1990). The second, which is far more common, is to make use of the ideas and techniques in one area to develop a theory in the other, resulting in a complementary evolution of parallel areas. The predominance of this latter approach stems from the fact that the demands made upon theories can be quite different in the two areas. The primary test of a psychological theory lies in its relationship to empirical data. Most areas of AI do not engage this constraint. On the other hand, AI models need to satisfy a requirement of precision of definition that tends to be difficult to achieve in psychological models except within highly delimited domains.

The differences between the areas of AI and psychology concerned with expert performance illustrate these issues (Hoffman 1992). Psychological research on the nature of expert-novice differences began in chess with the classic work of deGroot (1965) who, as well as Chase and Simon (1973), found clear differences in memory organization between experts and novices.

However, it is well known that programs capable of playing master chess do not yet analyze and generate their moves in a strictly human-like fashion. In particular, they do not make use of the kind of memory organization discovered by the psychological research (Ericsson and Smith 1991).

Much research on expert performance has been carried out in domains such as chess, physics and geometry, which have a prominent visuo-perceptual component. In physics and geometry, abstract representations can be expressed in terms of diagrams. Apart from areas such as radiology and dermatology, such a component has far less prominence in medicine. Physicians do not typically make use of diagrams when conducting their usual tasks.

The issue to be considered in this chapter is whether similar results to those found in perceptually-laden areas still holds in nonperceptual aspects of medicine. In particular, how close is the connection between enhanced recall, directionality of reasoning, and diagnostic accuracy? Our attempts to answer these questions forced us into a considerably more direct encounter with abductive reasoning. Two issues that seem important to AI in this regard are the following: what causes shifts in directionality and what screens out irrelevant processing?

This chapter will be structured as follows: After a preliminary review of the relevant background about the directionality of reasoning and the modeling of expert reasoning, we will summarize some models of reasoning that have emerged during the past decade in the field of AI. Then we describe the empirical investigations of expertise in medicine and their relationship to cognitive models. Finally, we propose some new directions for future research.

Background

In domains such as medicine, which make extensive use of explicitly defined verbal knowledge, much of the knowledge used in expert systems is somewhat similar in content to that used by humans. There are also important correspondences in the strategies that utilize this knowledge. However, the way this knowledge is organized in performance-oriented expert systems is normally different from that of the human. In particular, chunking of information, so important in human expertise, does not need to play a critical role (Patel and Groen 1991b). In this regard, it is important to distinguish between systems that are primarily oriented toward performing and achieving a solution from those oriented towards explanations and learning. Attempts to build the latter have encountered issues more closely resembling those encountered by psychologists (Patel and Groen 1991b).

One such set of issues is concerned with the role of directionality of reasoning in generating explanations. In early expert systems such as MYCIN

(Shortliffe 1976; Buchanan and Shortliffe 1984), expert knowledge was used to directly reach conclusions from the observed data. It is nowadays generally accepted within expert systems work that explanation requires a process of generation and testing of hypotheses in which inferences proceed in both forward and backward directions (Pearl 1988; Ramoni, Stefanelli, Magnani and Barosi 1992). Expert problem solvers tend to work forward from the given information to the unknown. This corresponds to the AI notion of forward chaining. Similarly, backward reasoning, where the problem solver works from a hypothesis regarding the unknown back to the given information, corresponds to backward chaining. The terms abduction and deduction are generally used to identify the inference patterns involved in the generation and in the testing of hypotheses, respectively. The implementation of abduction involves a number of important issues. One of these involves the nature of the inference patterns themselves. In most expert systems, rules have an inherent directionality: some of them lead from data to possible hypotheses and some others lead from possible hypotheses to observable findings (to test the hypotheses and discriminate among different solutions). Thus, reversing directionality involves using different rules. Pearl (1988) argues that far more efficient implementations are possible if the same rule can be used in both directions. However, such systems (i.e., those based on probabilistic reasoning) are prone to perturbation by irrelevant information. Their implementation also necessitates some kind of strategy for determining changes in directionality. This gives rise to two further questions. The first is what might cause such a shift in directionality. The second is how irrelevant information is ignored.

There is also a psychological tradition of research on directionality of reasoning. This began with the work of Simon and Simon (1978) and Larkin, McDermott, Simon and Simon (1980) who used protocol analysis techniques, developed by Newell and Simon (1972), to differentiate between the methods used by experts and novices in solving routine physics problems. A major theme from this research was the use of forward reasoning by experts. This pertains to the finding, primarily established in physical and mathematical problem solving. Superficially, it might appear that this is one instance in which AI theories and psychological theories dovetail. In fact, an important aspect of research in this area consisted of developing an expert system (OPS5) to account for the psychological data (Larkin, McDermott, Simon and Simon 1980). However, there are important differences, which is why we use the term "reasoning" rather than "chaining" when discussing these phenomena in a psychological sense.

First, the distinction between forward and backward *reasoning* is frequently defined in terms of goal-based (backward) versus knowledge-based (forward) heuristic search (e.g., Hunt 1989). This may be more general than the straightforward distinction between forward and backward *chaining*, since goal-based reasoning might be abductive and hence involve a mixed pattern of directionality.

Secondly, whereas forward reasoning by expert systems consists of straightforward chaining of rules, the forward reasoning of human experts invariably has "missing" steps in the inference process. People learn to circumvent long chains of reasoning and chunk or compile knowledge across intermediate states of inference (Newell 1990). This results in shorter, more direct inferences which are stored in long term memory and are directly available to be retrieved in the appropriate contexts. For example, if a physician has to reason about the effects of a pulmonary embolism on liver function, he or she may initially reason through a series of inferences which involve a representation of how certain vessels are blocked resulting in inadequate gas exchange, insufficient oxygenation of blood, and subsequently poor perfusion of tissues and organs, as well as incomplete elimination of carbon dioxide resulting in certain urinary findings indicative of liver dysfunction. Through experience this chain can be reduced to a cause-effect relation in which pulmonary embolism can result in liver dysfunction, given the goal of explaining certain urinary findings. This indicates that forward reasoning may be generated by a process considerably more complex than the simple chaining of rules.

Finally, there is an inherently close connection between the use of forward reasoning and the existence of a highly-evolved abstract representation of the problem (Larkin 1983). Thus inferences can be generated from these representations rather than directly from more concrete problem space distractions that tend to be used by expert systems. From this has evolved the notion that there is a close connection between experts' enhanced recall, of the type reported by Chase and Simon and the existence of forward reasoning, since both appear to reflect the use of highly evolved ways of encoding and organizing knowledge so that it involves the economical use of memory, especially working memory (Greeno and Simon 1988; Larkin 1983; Patel and Groen 1991a).

Human and Machine Cognition

Cognitive psychology and artificial intelligence share a common goal of providing systematic explanations of knowledge and reasoning. Hence, it is not surprising that both these fields address questions about knowledge and reasoning that traditionally belong to the discipline of epistemology. Behind most theories of human and machine cognition, an epistemological and ontological framework may be identified. Therefore, we will begin with some epistemological issues and illustrate how epistemological frameworks for computational models of expert reasoning "become" theories of cognition. In this analysis, we will focus on the medical diagnostic task and we will use it as an exemplar to describe the interplay between Cognitive Science and AI in the study of medical reasoning.

Epistemological Issues

Most theories of medical reasoning characterize the diagnostic task as a cyclical process of generating and testing possible explanations (hypotheses) for the abnormal state of the patient at hand (Elstein, Shulman and Sprafka 1978; Kassirer 1989; Joseph and Patel 1990; Ramoni et al. 1992). Commonly these theories described the process of generating and testing hypotheses in a way that was independent of the underlying structure of the domain knowledge, which could be organized as chains of causal relations among states, as prototypes of diseases, or as laws of behavior of the pathophysiological systems.

The only explicit assumption they made about the domain knowledge was its availability: All hypotheses needed to explain the current case had to be available when the diagnostic process starts, and the generation of hypotheses is a process of selection rather than a process of creation. This factor makes diagnostic reasoning different from the process of scientific discovery or creative thinking, in which all knowledge cannot be assumed always to be available.

These models of diagnostic reasoning shared an implicit ontological assumption of directionality. This assumption is consistent with the common image of medical knowledge: causal theories, nosological models, and prototypical definitions of diseases contain a directionality of thought from causes and diseases to observable signs and symptoms. Knowledge representation methods (based on logical, probabilistic or AI techniques) capture cause/effect or disease/symptom relationships in medical knowledge by means of asymmetric and transitive relations leading from causes and diseases to observable effects and symptoms.

In a broad sense, the task in diagnostic reasoning is to move backward along this chain of asymmetric and transitive relations in order to identify what is responsible for the observable abnormal effects in the patient. Many models of diagnostic reasoning break this process into two main phases (Joseph and Patel 1990):

> *Hypothesis generation:* On the basis of the available data (i.e., observable signs and symptoms), the diagnostician moves backward along the chain of asymmetric and transitive relations underlying the domain knowledge in order to identify a set of candidate hypotheses able to account for the situation at hand.

> *Hypothesis testing:* Each evoked hypothesis is evaluated on the basis of its expected consequences (i.e., those symptoms and signs that would be observable if the hypothesis were true). Hence, the hypothesis drives the process of gathering new information.

This is a basic model proposed by Duncker (1945). During the development of the problem, the solver's conception of the problem at any given time consists of the information he has about the problem, how he has evaluated this information, and how he has shaped his definition of what the problem is.

Within this generic definition, different models of diagnostic reasoning may be generated by specifying requirements or hypotheses (such as specificity, parsimony, adequacy) or the strategies to evoke and evaluate them. Moreover, one can take advantage of the structure of the domain knowledge to define specific diagnostic methods on the basis of the interaction between the reasoning strategy and the domain ontology (Bylander and Chandrasekaran 1988). In this respect, two major epistemological models of diagnostic reasoning have emerged during the past ten years: heuristic classification (Clancey 1985) and cover and differentiate (Eshelman 1988).

Heuristic classification has been introduced to capture the problem solving behavior involved in a broad class of tasks such as diagnosis, catalog selection, and skeletal planning. It originated in a retrospective analysis of the MYCIN knowledge based system, together with some psychological studies, and it was implemented in the NEOMYCIN system (Clancey 1987; Clancey and Letsinger 1984).

The ontology of heuristic classification is basically defined by two different sets of entities: data and solutions. Data and solutions are both organized into two hierarchies organized by the subsumption relation. When the subsumption relation is applied to data, it structures the data hierarchy, whereas when applied to solutions, it structures the solutions hierarchy. Moreover, a datum may be a qualitative or generic definition of another datum. Data and solutions are linked by an associative relation. This relation is intended to capture the compiled knowledge of an expert able to skip a long chain of inferences in just one heuristic step. In a medical diagnostic task, for instance, the associative relation may replace a long chain of causal relations.

The ontology of heuristic classification is defined by two parallel taxonomies, one for data and one for solutions, linked by a set of associative relations. In order for reasoning to occur on these two parallel classifications, Clancey defines an inference structure composed of three steps: abstraction, association, and refinement. Steps of abstraction and refinement "walk-through" source and target classifications, respectively, while association follows the associative relation across classifications.

The second major ontological system is the cover and differentiate model. This has been introduced to capture reasoning processes involved in some classes of diagnostic tasks, and has been also used to develop a knowledge acquisition tool in the field of troubleshooting diagnosis (Stefanelli and Ramoni 1992). The ontology of the cover and differentiate model may be represented as a network whose nodes are states and links are causal relations between states. In addition, there are entities called qualifiers. A qualifier may be linked to a state or to a causal relation to establish the likelihood of the state of the causal relation. Finally, there are two special kinds of states called initial cause (a state that is not caused by any other state) and symptom, respectively.

In this framework, the diagnostic process is regarded as an iterative process of proposing candidate solutions that will cover the symptoms, and evaluating them against new information. The cover and differentiate model relies on a causal ontology in which knowledge is represented as chains of states linked by a causal relation. Moreover, the cover and differentiate model relies on two basic assumptions: the exhaustivity assumption and the exclusivity assumption. The former states that "if a state can be explained, it has to be explained." This assumption implies only that an initial cause may be a solution, since it cannot be explained by any other state. The latter says that "all other things being equal, the minimum set hypothesis is preferred," thus introducing a strong variant of Occam's Razor.

Both heuristic classification and cover and differentiate can be subsumed under a more general inference structure, called the select and test model (Stefanelli and Ramoni 1992) given in figure 1. This model allows us to further specify the two-phase process at an epistemological level, without losing generality. In this framework, both the hypothesis generation and the hypothesis testing phases may be characterized in terms of four basic inference types, that is, fundamental components of reasoning (Peirce 1955): abstraction, abduction, deduction, and induction.

There is a general agreement in cognitive science research about the fact that humans work in problem solving space (Newell and Simon 1972; Koedinger and Anderson 1990). If we want to further characterize the hypotheses generation phase, we can therefore assume that the first step of this phase will be an abstraction operation performed on the data describing the problem at hand in order to select relevant features of the problem. Moreover, advances in AI (Clancey 1985) and cognitive science (Koedinger and Anderson 1990) pointed out a second property of abstracted features: they represent data in a qualitative way, ignoring some differences that may not be relevant for the solution of the problem. In geometry problem solving, for instance, one can safely ignore the difference between congruence and equivalence because both properties lead to the same results in almost all problems. In an abstraction process, data are therefore not only filtered according to their relevance for the problem solution, but they are also chunked in schemas representing an abstract description of the problem at hand. In the medical domain, for example, one can infer by abstraction that an adult male with hemoglobin concentration less than 14d/gl is an anemic patient.

Next, the hypotheses that could account for the current situation are related through a process of abduction, thus accomplishing the final part of the

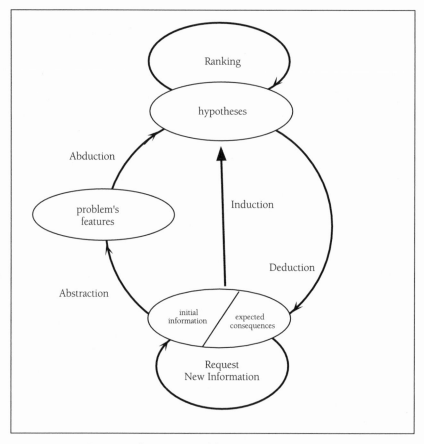

*Figure 1. The structure of the SELECT & TEST -MODEL
(from Stefanelli & Ramoni, 1992).*

generation phase. In the process of abduction, there is a "backward flow" of inferences across a chain of directed ontological relations which identify those initial conditions from which the current abstract representation of the problem comes. This provides tentative solutions to the problem at hand (hypotheses). For example, knowing that disease A will cause symptom B, abduction will try to identify the explanation for B, while deduction will forecast that a patient affected by disease A will manifest symptom B: both inferences are using the same ontological relation (cause) along two different directions.

Unfortunately, abduction can involve the fallacy of affirming the consequent. Due to logical fallibility, abduction tends to "postulate" these initial conditions, without necessarily proving them. Abduction is not collapsible on the inference to the best explanation (Peirce 1955), which seems to be the current intended interpretation of the term *abduction* within the AI community (Bylander, Allemang, Tanner and Josephson 1991; Poole 1989). Instead, it is conceived of as the inference to a possible explanation. The inference to the best explanation may be modeled by the entire cycle of generating and testing hypotheses. Abduction, as an inference type, has to be regarded as one of its building blocks.

It is easy to see that the solution to a problem may be sometimes provided by a composite hypothesis (Pople 1982), that is, a hypothesis that is the result of the interaction of more than one basic component. A clinical problem, for instance, may be the result of the interaction between two concurrent causes, and the solution to the diagnostic problem is to be composed by these two different hypotheses. Bylander *et al.* (1991) have argued that the process of finding the best set of hypotheses is logically intractable. This means that the size of the search space grows exponentially with the number of basic hypotheses available in the domain knowledge.

In the testing phase, hypotheses are incrementally tested according to their ability to account for the whole problem. Hence, deduction allows us to build up the possible world described by the consequences of each candidate hypothesis. A hypothesis is therefore correct if the world following from it is the same as the most similar world to the real one. This kind of reasoning is usually called prediction, and is regarded as the common way of evaluating diagnostic hypotheses (Kassirer 1989; Patel, Evans and Kaufman 1989).[1]

Once predictions have been derived from hypotheses, they have to be matched in order to choose the best one. Through a process of induction, one is able to synthesize singular statements into general concepts and laws, which can also be used to confirm or falsify (i.e., to evaluate) hypotheses. Through this process, a prediction generated from a hypothesis can be matched with one specific aspect of the patient problem. The major feature of induction is, therefore, the ability to falsify (i.e., rule out) those hypotheses whose expected consequences turn out to be not in agreement with the patient problem. This is because there is no way to logically confirm a hypothesis, but we can only disconfirm or refute it in presence of contrary evidence. This evaluation process closes the testing phase of the diagnostic cycle. Moreover, it determines which information is needed in order to discriminate among hypotheses and hence which information has to be collected.

Cognitive Issues

Within this epistemological framework, we can identify several different ways to characterize expert reasoning. The diagnostic task is believed to be intractable on logical grounds alone. This means that for a large enough number of hypotheses, the subject may not be able to deal with the combinatorial explosion of composite hypotheses. Hence, the major goal here is to constrain the number of selected hypotheses.

Expertise may be viewed either in terms of reasoning ability or in terms of additional (heuristic and compiled) knowledge. In the first view, expert performance may be defined as the result of superior abstraction ability. This ability allows the expert to select a few relevant features of the problem at hand, and to focus on a restricted set of hypotheses capable of explaining these abstracted features. As Greeno and Simon (1985) pointed out, experts' superior ability at chunking in terms of anticipated solution schemas, and their use of forward reasoning as the main pattern of inference, are intimately related. When the problem solver is able to summarize the features of the problem in an abstract schema, it can be covered by a small set of hypotheses. If there is just one hypothesis able to cover this schema, the solution is immediately found and no further cycles of reasoning (and hence no backward reasoning) are needed.

In the second view, expert performance is characterized by the presence of compiled knowledge (i.e., rules of thumb, shortcuts, and heuristics). Compiled knowledge refers to knowledge of causal expectations that people assemble directly from experience and partly by chunking results from previous problem-solving endeavors (Chandrasakeran 1991).

In psychological studies of problem solving, a primary method of data acquisition is the think-aloud task (Ericsson and Simon 1993). In these studies, subjects are instructed to think-aloud as they perform a particular task. In a typical problem-solving task, in which subjects are asked to "think aloud" as they make a medical diagnosis, the protocols generated tend to produce incomplete information regarding the nature of the knowledge being used. For example, in a routine case, experts tend to produce very sparse protocols which do not provide much of a basis for characterizing reasoning patterns. Kuipers and Kassirer (1984) suggest that expert knowledge is so compiled that it can be difficult for the expert to articulate intermediate steps. This is manifested in very short chains of inference by experienced problem solvers. A widely adopted solution has been to use various kinds of probing tasks to elicit a more detailed reasoning process. A probe that has been useful in our research is the *diagnostic explanation* task, in which the subject is asked to "explain the underlying pathophysiology" of the patient's condition (Patel and Groen 1986). This task was borrowed from Feltovich and Barrows (1984). We have found that physicians respond to this question by explaining the patient's symptoms in terms of a diagnosis.

A distinction is sometimes made in the literature between a clinical level of explanation and a pathophysiological level, with the latter involving basic pathology and physiology (e.g., Patil, Solovitz and Schwartz 1984). In general, the diagnostic goal of the physician is to explain a diagnosis by indicating its relationship to the clinical symptoms rather than giving a detailed exposition of the underlying mechanisms. The next section will show how this probe method has been used in our empirical investigations of forward reasoning.

Empirical Evidence

In our investigations of forward and backward reasoning, we embed the question about the underlying pathophysiology in the following overall paradigm: 1) Present a description of a case; 2) Obtain a free-recall of the case description; 3) Obtain a diagnostic explanation protocol; and finally 4) Ask for a diagnosis.

One of the motivations for using this paradigm is to establish some specific connections between comprehension and problem solving. There is a well established distinction in the psychological literature between the comprehension of a text and the comprehension of a situation underlying the text (e.g., van Dijk and Kintsch 1983). Free-recall tasks generate responses that sometimes reflect the one and sometimes the other, depending on the level of expertise of the subject. The theory of comprehension and its extension into problem solving proposed by Groen and Patel (1988) based on van Dijk and Kintsch (1983), divides the process of problem solving into two parts, one that involves developing a representation of a text and another that focuses on creating interactions between elements of this representation and a situation model based on prior knowledge of the domain.

It is important to note that in the diagnostic explanation task the diagnosis is requested *after* the diagnostic explanation. This is to give the subject the opportunity to provide a diagnosis during the explanation task. When this occurs, it seems reasonable to consider the possibility that the resulting protocol may reflect elements of the solution process. If the diagnosis is given first, then the subsequent protocol could be more a reflection of the diagnostic justification rather than the process of problem solving.

In this section, we will first describe the formal language we used to encode the protocols and how it can be used to characterize the directionality of reasoning. Greeno and Simon (1988) have suggested that there is an interaction between an expert's problem representation and the processes by which the problem is solved. Specifically, they claim that there is a close connection between superior recall phenomena by experts and a process commonly found in studies of expert problem-solving: reasoning in a forward fashion from the given data to a conclusion. In terms of their theory, the use of forward reasoning necessitates the existence of a small, manageable set of rules that can be accessed in a straight forward fashion without the need for extensive search. This involves the ability to recognize complex patterns of cues. Thus, there is an intimate connection between the ability to reason forward and superior pattern recognition (Greeno and Simon 1988). The problem in extending these notions to a verbally complex domain is that the notion of pattern recognition ceases to make sense. A phenomenon of perception must be extended to one of comprehension.

Propositional Representations

We have shown elsewhere (Patel and Frederiksen 1984; Patel, Groen and Frederiksen 1986) that techniques of propositional analysis yield evidence for both enhanced recall and forward reasoning in medicine; evidence which should be expected from studies in other domains. As it has been proposed by a number of authors (Kintsch 1974; Frederiksen 1975), verbal discourse can be decomposed into underlying units of meaning, usually termed propositions. The basic intuition behind the use of propositional representations is that they yield a precise method of empirically determining the verbal analogue to the perceptual notion of a pattern (Groen and Patel 1988). This implies the existence of a unit of analysis that can form the basis of chunking.

Intuitively, a proposition is an idea underlying the surface structure of a text. Following van Dijk and Kintsch (1983) and also Johnson-Laird (1983), it may be defined as a fact that is true in some possible world. The proposition's usefulness arises from the fact that a given piece of discourse may have many related ideas embedded within it. A propositional representation provides a means of representing these ideas, and the relationships among them, in an explicit fashion. Systems of propositional analysis (e.g., Kintsch 1974; Frederiksen 1975) have been developed that provide a uniform notation and classification for propositional representations.

In the field of AI, Sowa (1983) has evolved a similar system. What Sowa has done is to lay out sets of propositions using conceptual graphs. For the present purposes, the notational details of different propositional systems are relatively unimportant. What is critical is the underlying assumption that propositions preserve some of the meaning in mental representations of verbal information in episodic memory and, more generally, the notion that propositions form manageable units for knowledge representations.

Identifying Forward Reasoning

Our basic approach in analyzing data from a laboratory study begins by representing the propositional structure of a protocol as a semantic network. First, we distinguish between propositions that describe attribute information, which form the nodes of the network, and those that describe relational information, which form the links. Second, we distinguish between attributes that appear in the description of the clinical case, or in the subject's summary of the case, and those that do not. We will call the former *facts* and the latter *hypotheses*.

Our criteria for distinguishing between forward and backward reasoning were motivated by a resemblance between the causal and conditional relationships that predominated in the semantic networks arising from our data and the rule system of NEOMYCIN (Clancey and Letsinger 1984). This system incorporates a distinction between hypothesis-directed and data-directed rules that is roughly equivalent to the distinction between forward and backward reasoning. It therefore seemed reasonable to directly transform the semantic network into a set of production rules. A simple test for forward reasoning was to discover whether these rules would execute when implemented in a standard forward chaining production system interpreter. Backward reasoning could be defined, by default, as any rule that could not be executed.

This rule-based criterion has two potential disadvantages. The first is that it is somewhat noninformative where backward reasoning is concerned because backward reasoning is only defined in relation to forward reasoning. The second is that it contains a hidden theory. The production system interpreter provides a model of the reasoning process. Hence, it does not provide a "neutral" means of representing data. This had the effect of forcing us to treat the diagnostic explanation task as problem solving. While this conceptualization of the diagnostic explanation task is conceivable, it renders difficult the consideration of alternative possibilities.

An alternative criterion for determining the direction of reasoning can be formulated in terms of the semantic network representation, rather than the production rule representation. While difficult to define, the criterion is applied simply to small networks through visual inspection, without recourse to formal definitions. In order to justify this less formal approach, it is necessary to introduce some elementary concepts from graph theory (Sowa 1983). The terminology and the definitions are taken from Groen and Patel (1988).

In graph theory, a graph is defined as a nonempty set of nodes and a set of arcs leading from node N to a node N'. A graph is connected if there exists a path, directed or undirected, between any two nodes. In a directed path, every node has a source and a target connecting it to its immediate successor. If a graph is not connected then it breaks down into two or more separate graphs.

A semantic network is a directed graph formed by nodes and labeled connecting paths. Nodes may represent either clinical findings or hypotheses, whereas the paths represent directed connections between nodes. These networks provide a relatively precise means of characterizing the directionality of reasoning. Forward reasoning corresponds to an oriented path from data to hypothesis. Thus, forward-directed rules are identified whenever a physician attempts to generate a hypothesis from the findings in a case. Backward-directed rules correspond to an oriented path from a hypothesis to data. Pure forward reasoning refers to a network where all paths are oriented from data to hypothesis. Pure backward reasoning refers to a network where all paths are oriented from hypothesis to data.

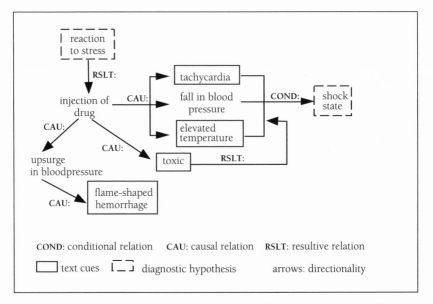

Figure 2. Semantic representation of explanation of a psychiatrist in a cardiology case (from Patel, Groen, & Arocha, 1990).

The use of these definitions is illustrated in figure 2. The figure gives the network representation of the diagnostic explanation by a psychiatrist for a cardiology problem described by Patel, Groen and Arocha (1990). The case is not within the subject's domain of specialization, and the diagnosis, *shock state*, is inaccurate. The underlying mechanism used by this subject to explain the signs and symptoms in the patient is the result of drug toxicity, due to antistress medication injected by the patient as a reaction to stress. This is an incorrect description of the patient's problem. This example is useful for illustrative purposes since it contains a mixture of forward and backward reasoning.

The diagram consists of nodes linked by arrows. The arrows have labels indicating the relationship between nodes. The two most important are CAU:, which means that the source node causes the target (e.g., *upsurge in blood pressure* causes *flame-shaped hemorrhage*), and COND:, which means that the source node is an indicator of the target (e.g., *tachycardia* indicates "shock state"). The arrows labeled CAU: represent causal relations, whereas those labeled COND: represent conditional relations. A difference between the two is in the strength of implication. Although we could define these terms formally, it is more important to note that subjects' attributions of causality or conditionality may deviate from appropriate usage in logic. The nodes containing facts from the problem text are enclosed in boxes.

The diagram also contains three "AND" nodes (conjunction), indicated by forks in the arrows. One of these is a target (*tachycardia, fall in blood pressure, and elevated temperature* indicate *shock state*). The remaining two nodes are sources (*injection of drug* causes *tachycardia, fall in blood pressure* and *elevated temperature*). If we compare the text and the semantic network, it is apparent that a network does not necessarily reflect the temporal sequence of concepts referred to in the text. For example, the same concept can be referred to repeatedly, but it is represented as inferences on a single node.

Using this graph, several different lines of reasoning can be illustrated, which can be rendered precise by introducing a few more concepts from graph theory. We define a cutpoint of a graph to be a node which, when removed together with all arrows leading to or from it, causes a graph to separate into disjoint components that are themselves graphs. Conversely, if two graphs have a common node, then their joining is the new graph formed by joining them at that node. This suggests that an algorithm for finding the components can be defined in terms of generating, at each cutpoint, two graphs whose joining is the original graph. What results from applying this algorithm is a hierarchy of components, some of which are uninteresting and some of which may actually distort the logic of the process we are attempting to represent. Because of this, we prohibit the application of the algorithm in the following two cases: (1) AND nodes, and (2) graphs that consist of a single path, without any branches. Carrying out this procedure results in the minimal components illustrated in figure 3. Although other components exist, they are all combinations of these minimal components. The directionality of these components is mixed.

The component where the inference is made by moving from data to hypothesis is coded as a forward-directed inference. In figure 3, *tachycardia, fall in blood pressure,* and *elevated temperature,* indicate the diagnosis of *shock state.* Conversely, a component where the inference is made in the direction from hypotheses to data is coded as backward-directed inference. An example here is *injection of drug* causes *flame-shaped hemorrhage.* Quantitative measures of directionality of reasoning can be obtained by coding inference as forward or backward. In a given protocol, one can determine the percentage of forward and backward reasoning inferences.

We develop a reference model for each case that represents a standard for a certain level of performance. The reference model represents an idealized knowledge representation that is constructed on the basis of domain expert judgement and pertinent medical texts (Patel and Groen 1986; Joseph and Patel 1990; Patel, Evans and Kaufman 1989). It serves as a benchmark for certain types of analysis which we perform on subjects' response protocols. The construction of a reference model is similar to a knowledge engineering task in the development of expert systems. The goal is not necessarily to develop a faithful cognitive representation of an expert, rather, it is to develop something like a normative or ideal model of the problem. It is an iterative

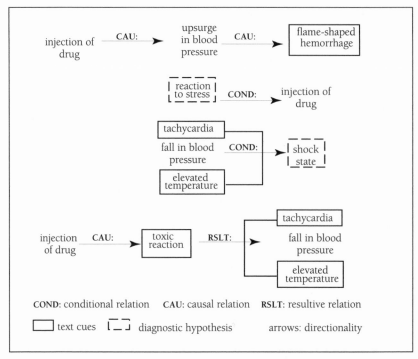

Figure 3. Components of semantic representation given in figure 2.
(from Patel, Groen, & Arocha, 1990)

process which begins with asking an expert (not participating in our studies) to explain the findings in a case. We can then consult other sources to verify and add to this information. We can also go back to the expert and probe for specific details. A more detailed account of the methods is given in Patel and Arocha (1995) and Groen and Patel (1988).

Empirical Results Concerning Directionality of Reasoning

The earliest results using this approach were obtained with a task involving the diagnosis of a case of acute bacterial endocarditis (Patel and Groen 1986). The subjects were seven specialists in cardiology. Four of these achieved an accurate diagnosis, whereas the remaining three achieved inaccurate or incomplete diagnoses. Using the production rule criterion described in the preceding section, it was shown that the diagnostic explanations of subjects making an accurate diagnosis consisted of pure forward reasoning. Two of the subjects with inaccurate diagnoses tended to make use of a mixture of forward and backward reasoning. The remaining subject used pure backward reasoning, beginning with a high level hypothesis and proceeding in a top-down fashion to the propositions embedded in the stimulus text or to the generation of irrelevant rules.

The results concerning forward reasoning led to a consideration of the conditions under which the pattern might be different. Patel, Groen and Arocha (1990) considered two factors. One was the relevance of expertise. The next experiment replicated the first, using psychiatrists and surgeons as subjects. All but one of these subjects made inaccurate diagnoses, and their explanations showed the same pattern of mixed directionality as was found in the subjects of the previous experiment.

The other factor was the structure of the clinical case. The next experiment utilized two cases, one more complex than the other, reflecting the domains of endocrinology and cardiology. The diagnostic explanations of subjects in cases both inside and outside their domain of specialization were investigated using a 1–2 page description of the patient problem. The subjects were endocrinologists and cardiologists. The subjects made accurate diagnoses of the case in their own specialty, but tended to yield inaccurate diagnoses of those outside their specialty. The representations of inaccurate diagnoses showed a mixture of forward and backward reasoning similar to that found for subjects with inaccurate diagnoses in the previous experiments. In the semantic network representation of the diagnostic explanation for accurate diagnoses, the line of reasoning leading to the diagnosis appeared as an unconnected component consisting of pure forward reasoning.

These cases contained complicating factors that were not directly related to the main diagnosis, and the subjects felt it necessary, after completing the diagnosis, to explain their causes. These appeared in the semantic network representation as disjointed components or loose ends, and frequently were related to backward reasoning.

An interesting result was found on the recall task, to evaluate the comprehension component of diagnostic reasoning; there were no differences in the recall of relevant and irrelevant propositions as a function of diagnostic accuracy in each of the two cases. The distinction between forward and backward reasoning is closely related to another distinction made in problem solving research between *strong methods*, which are highly constrained by the problem solving environment, and *weak methods*, which are only minimally constrained.

Forward reasoning is highly error prone in the absence of adequate domain knowledge, since there are no built-in checks on the legitimacy of the inferences that subjects make. In contrast, backward reasoning is slower and may make heavy demands on working memory, because one has to keep track of such things as goals and hypotheses. It is, therefore, most likely to be used when domain knowledge is inadequate. Backward reasoning is often taken as a "symptom" of a weak method. It is important to note that the term weak is being used in the technical sense of "weak constraints" as opposed to "strong constraints." This does not imply that it is a weak way of solving a problem. In fact, a weak method is preferable when relevant prior knowledge is lacking, as is likely to be the case with anyone but an expert.

In the paradigm used in the above experiments (Patel and Groen 1986; Patel, Groen and Arocha 1990), there is a certain ambiguity regarding the point in the procedure at which the diagnosis is actually made by the subject. An alternative approach is to present a patient problem in segments and obtain a diagnostic explanation after the subject has seen each segment of patient information (Feltovich, Johnson, Moller and Swanson 1984). Joseph and Patel (1990) used this procedure with a cross-domain comparison (cardiologists and endocrinologists working on both cardiology and endocrinology cases). Clearly, this would not be expected to yield pure forward reasoning, since subjects have far more opportunities to form inaccurate hypotheses on the basis of partial information. However, the results were actually consistent with the general pattern yielded in the two preceding experiments. Experts in their own domain reached tentative diagnoses by a forward reasoning process on the basis of the patient's history, which was presented in the initial segments of the case. Subsequent information, from the physical examination and laboratory tests, was used only to confirm the diagnosis. In contrast, experts outside their domain generated multiple hypotheses on the basis of the history, and added additional hypotheses as new information was provided. In addition, there were no significant differences between the groups in terms of selection of relevant and critical cues from the case.

In summary, there are two major findings: first, the presence or absence of forward reasoning does appear to be strongly related to diagnostic accuracy, and second, there is a lack of relationship between superior recall and diagnostic accuracy at high levels of expertise. All subjects with completely accurate diagnoses showed the use of pure forward reasoning in explaining evidence directly relevant to the main diagnosis, while none of the subjects with inaccurate diagnoses showed this phenomenon.

In cases with irrelevant cues, there were two explanation components. The main component consisted of an explanation of the disease which included the diagnosis. This was always generated by pure forward reasoning. The second essentially consisted of "tying up" the loose ends, which relate to information that was irrelevant to the main diagnosis. These did not necessarily consist of pure forward reasoning.

The most interesting question raised by these results is why inaccuracy is always associated with a transition from forward reasoning to backward reasoning. One plausible explanation is that such a transition is caused by feelings of uncertainty regarding one's conclusions. An explanation along these lines is consistent with the technique used by most expert systems for medical diagnosis, which is to attach a certainty factor to each decision that is made. On the other hand, it is possible to account for most of our data without invoking the notion of uncertainty. It can be assumed that rules that are present in an individual's knowledge will be fired by data and that a forward reasoning process will take place. However, if a diagnosis is inaccurate, then a number of rules will remain that are not linked to the main diagnosis. Facts in the text base that fire these rules essentially serve as loose ends. We have already discussed the results that indicate that even subjects with accurate answers/diagnoses appear to be aware of such unresolved components of what they remember about the clinical case, and frequently explain them by a process of backward reasoning.

It seems reasonable to assume that an expert may not be aware that his/her knowledge is leading to an inaccurate diagnosis, but is simply aware of the existence of the nonsalient cues that cannot be linked to the main diagnosis. In other words, the primary difference between accurate and inaccurate diagnosis may be the presence of loose ends. A diagnosis might be viewed as a theory about a clinical case. The loose ends are then essentially anomalies. Much as anomalies are highly correlated with an inaccurate theory, so loose ends are correlated with an inaccurate diagnosis. It should be noted that when faced with anomalies, scientists usually resort to the classical hypothetico-deductive method (e.g., Groen and Patel 1985), which is a form of backward reasoning. It should be also noted that scientific theories persist despite anomalies, hence inaccurate diagnoses may persist in an analogous fashion.

Development of Medical Expertise

Much of our discussion has focused on the nature of expertise. However, in an emerging area of medical informatics and cognition, the emphasis is more on the management of information rather than the generation of expert advice. Since issues involving the management of information arise more directly with the less than expert (subexpert) individuals, we briefly focus here on reasoning at this level.

Working definitions of expert, novice, and intermediate make sense primarily when taken in the context of a specific domain of expertise. An expert is somebody who has demonstrable mastery of the domain (the issue of "what is an expert?" is greatly elaborated elsewhere in this book). It should be noted that this often implies a criterion of mastery according to some kind of external standard. For example, the use of official ratings in the case of chess or board certifications in the case of medicine. However, such clear criteria are lacking in the case of novices and intermediates (Patel and Groen 1991b; Dreyfus and Dreyfus 1986; Hoffman, Shadbolt, Burton and Klein 1995).

A novice is a layperson or a beginner where a beginner is defined as an individual who has a prerequisite knowledge assumed by the domain. An intermediate is an individual in between novice and expert.

In a study that extended the Joseph and Patel research paradigm to include novice and intermediate subjects (see Braccio and Patel 1988), we adapted a method that was used to characterize the doctor-patient dialogue (Patel, Evans and Kaufman 1989). A new reference model that takes into account both novices and intermediates was developed. In order to characterize the performance of subjects, we built on an epistemological framework that identified appropriate units of knowledge together with a formal method of discourse analysis for coding interactions. Within this epistemological framework, clinical knowledge is hierarchically organized at increasing levels of abstraction from *observations* to *findings* to *facets* (diagnostic components) to *diagnosis* (Miller, Masarie and Myers 1988). *Observations* are units of information that are recognized as potentially relevant in the problem solving context. *Findings* are composed of sets of observations that are relevant in a diagnostic context. *Facets* are clusters of findings that are suggestive of diagnostic components. Specific combinations of facets lead to a diagnosis.

Facets can be considered as intermediate constructs leading to specific diagnosis through many possible permutations. Furthermore, specific diagnostic hypotheses are elicited via the use of retrieval structures which provide dynamic flexibility in their ability to partition the space of possible diagnoses. These structures provide access to information in long-term memory (Patel, Arocha and Kaufman 1994).

The verbal protocols that were collected with the presentation of partial patient information were transcribed and analyzed. Differences were observed between groups of subjects in terms of the types of inferences generated. Final year medical students generated inferences at the higher levels, focusing primarily on facets and diagnosis, showing a narrowing of the problem space. This is shown in figure 4. Second-year students focused on the facet and finding levels, with little ability to account for various intermediate constructs. This is given in figure 5. The first-year medical students functioned primarily at the local variable level of findings.

Systematic differences were also observed between groups of students in terms of problem-solving strategies used in developing problem representations. The strategies reflect the continuum from general "weak methods" to specific knowledge-based strategies. First-year students attempted to build a problem representation by aggregating local inferences (finding-level) to derive a partial account of the clinical problem. They used whatever knowledge they had available to them to explain fragments of the problem. Consequently, there was an accumulation of these isolated bits of information, without any integration.

Second year students had a great deal more knowledge available to them and tended to use more sophisticated strategies. They demonstrated an ability to generate facet-level hypotheses to account for some of the data. However, multiple hypotheses were generated without being evaluated, refined, or elaborated upon. At certain points they generated new, discrete hypotheses to account for each new piece of information. This achieved a degree of integra-

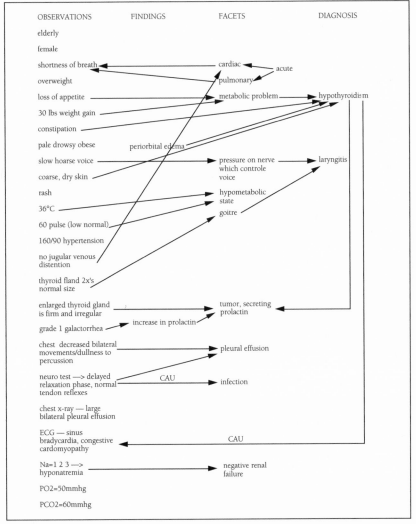

Figure 4. Schematic representation of a second-year medical student's problem solving in endocrinology.

tion in the problem space, but left the subject with multiple pathways to search, and difficulty invoking some kind of closure. The strategy was sometimes effective but highly inefficient in terms of time.

The major difference between final- and second-year students was the ability of the final-year students to effectively partition the problem-space and build on their intermediate-level or interim representations (viz., facets). They demonstrated that they had considerable knowledge of the appropriate clinical rules. But unlike the experts, they did not have sufficient knowledge

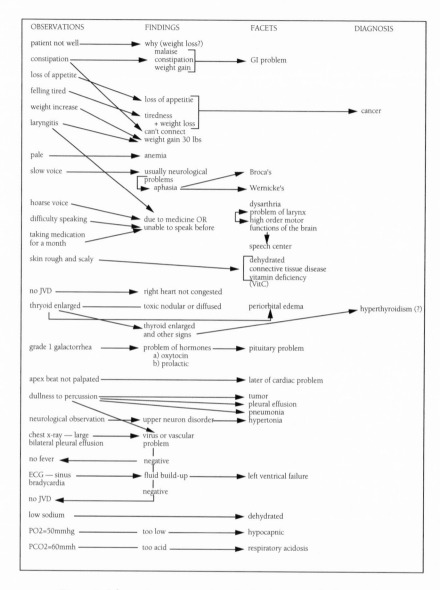

Figure 5. Schematic representation of a final-year medical student's problem solving in endocrinology.

to reason forward from information in the case to the diagnosis (Patel and Groen 1986). Consequently, they fell back on their intermediate-level hypotheses which they could evaluate, elaborate, and manipulate in various ways to organize the clinical information. These intermediate-level representations sometimes yielded insights towards finding solution state pathways (figure 4).

Intermediate-level or interim representations may also serve an organizational or chunking function, reducing the burden on working memory. First and second-year medical students tended to actually rehearse previously-acquired information, which we believe imposes considerable strain on available processing resources. This pattern was particularly evident in second-year students who recognized particular findings as relevant, but could not account for them (figure 5). They therefore needed to maintain these relevant findings in working memory until they could be accounted for or discarded as irrelevant. These results are also consistent with those of Arocha, Patel and Patel (1993).

In the next section, we present some final considerations about the interplay between medical cognition and expertise that we believe are critical for both cognitive psychology and AI research. We also present some of the new questions that our studies have explored.

Discussion

Given the close relationship between comprehension, problem solving, and explanation, to account for expert-intermediate-novice differences, our discussion will focus on the role of schemata, depth of expert reasoning, and the intermediate phenomenon.

The Role Of Schemata

Psychological theories postulate an intimate connection between the role of memory organization and the more procedural aspects of expertise. This is sometimes done through the introduction of the concept of a schema. This is a rather vague construct that has a long history in cognitive psychology (Rumelhart and Ortony 1977). Efforts to come to grips with the notion of schema have led some investigators (e.g., those in the situated cognition movement) to come to the conclusion that cognitive schemata are inherently nonrepresentable (Winograd and Flores 1986). Despite this, the concept of schema as an organizing unit of the effective memory organization typical of experts is important because it captures what is known in cognitive psychology about a basic reality of expertise.

What then, do such schemata consist of? A schema is assumed to be a structure that represents generic knowledge and is instantiated with specific new information in a given situation. Schemata, which are built up as a function of experience within a domain, guide a subject to key elements in a problem and serve to filter out irrelevant information. In a complex medical problem, there is an inordinate amount of potentially significant findings. An experienced physician can rapidly access appropriate schemata and delineate a problem into something manageable. The concept of schema is often used in cognitive psychology to explain phenomena of routine pattern recognition or prototypical patterns or something that is triggered by stimulus conditions. However, medical problem solving often necessitates more than a pattern recognition capability. We have to allow for composability of schemata in real time, not just in terms of fixed structures into which slots are filled.

Schemata can be viewed as a set of pointers from a problem encoding, residing in short term or working memory, to relevant knowledge in long term memory. Schemata also filter out the volume of information present in the space of a typical medical problem. The early work on expert-novice differences led to the postulation of an extremely close relationship between the phenomena of enhanced recall and forward reasoning, which would simplify the task of constructing a precise model (Chase and Simon 1973). However, our own research indicates that this is not the case. There appears to be a ceiling effect on the relationship between recall and expertise. In all our research using extremely well-qualified specialists as subjects, recall is quite independent of diagnostic accuracy. Moreover, the relationship of recall to expertise is also extremely subtle at pre-expert levels. In fact, the recall of clinical case material by intermediate subjects can actually be higher than that of either experts or novices (Patel and Groen 1991b). This is called the "intermediate effect" and is dealt with later in this chapter.

The characterization of the roles of schemata in the development of expertise becomes even more complicated if the directionality of reasoning is examined more closely. Koedinger and Anderson (1990) have recently obtained results in the domain of geometry that closely replicate our own. They also examined how closely the SOAR and ACT* models would account for their results. They found that while it was possible to make SOAR and ACT* perform as if there were a relationship between directionality and memory organization, there was no mechanism for the learning of such structures to take place. Once learned, these structures should provide the physician with the ability of effectively reasoning on the basis of an explicit knowledge of the structure and the laws of behavior provided by biomedical basic science. AI literature calls "deep systems" those systems able to reason on the basis of this explicit knowledge.

"Depth" of Expert Reasoning

In the AI literature, deep reasoning has often been equated with reasoning that involves a causal representation of the internal workings of a system. Using a causal representation is thought to add significant explanatory and predictive capabilities to the problem solver. This is an issue of some controversy in medical AI (Keravnou and Washbrook 1989). Reviewing the psychological research on expert-novice comparisons with special reference to the results from our own laboratory, there is very little evidence that experts always use "deep reasoning" as it has been defined in artificial intelligence literature.

Cognitive psychology contains little information that specifically corresponds to the sharp distinction between deep and shallow reasoning in AI. There are two issues that are directly related to our discussion: One is the research on areas such as explanation and causal reasoning that are directly relevant to the corresponding concerns in AI, and the other relates to the depth of representation, as indicated by the finding that experts categorize problems according to "deeper" domain principles, whereas novices organize problems according to their surface structure (Chi, Feltovich and Glaser 1981). Based on expert-novice studies in pediatric cardiology, Feltovich, Johnson, Moller and Swanson (1984) concluded that novices' knowledge of disease structure was "classically-centered," anchored in the most prototypical (usually the most common) instances of a disease category and lacking cross-referencing and connections between shared features of classes of diseases in memory. In contrast, experts' memory store of disease models was found to be extensively cross-referenced and with a rich network of connections among diseases that can present similar symptoms. We can assume that individuals, especially experts, are capable of reasoning at different levels of abstraction, that methods exist for switching between levels depending on task demands. The level of the representation is likely to be highly case-specific and domain-specific.

Our results indicate that experts, when asked to explain or justify a diagnosis, make little use of causal reasoning. Instead, they provide a minimal justification consisting of data-driven, forward inferences based on indicators rather than causes. This pattern changes only if the explanation is inadequate. In particular, any explanation that is inadequate has "loose ends" unconnected to the final diagnosis and tends to generate far more elaborate explanations which might be considered to satisfy some of the criteria of "depth" (Patel, Groen, Ramoni and Kaufman 1992). Such reasoning is sometimes causal in nature but, since it is not systematic, might better be characterized as reflecting a shift from data-driven to hypothesis-driven reasoning.

The importance of loose ends in diagnostic explanation indicates that people seem to use some kind of satisficing heuristic. This is based on a coherence criterion, where coherence is defined as the extent to which every finding is linked to a diagnostic hypothesis or, more technically, in terms of the connectedness of a semantic network representing a subject's protocol. The term satisficing refers to the use of a stop rule based on satisfaction with the pattern of one's reasoning (Simon 1989). The rule-out strategies of the expert guarantee early satisficing, and the pure forward reasoning characterizing accurate solutions of routine problems may reflect this satisficing. According to this view, the use of forward reasoning in generating incorrect diagnoses by novices may be due to a different kind of satisficing based on the lack of knowledge and the lack of sophisticated rule-out strategies. We can speculate that physicians may be guided by coherence constraints in determining the appropriate level of depth of reasoning to use.

While some of the differences between novices and experts are somewhat understood, insufficient attention has been paid to the intermediate level. The behavior of shallow expert systems bears some resemblance to that of novices who have been taught expert rules. However, the behavior of deep expert systems appears to resemble the performance of intermediates rather then experts (Patel, Groen, Ramoni and Kaufman 1992). Attempts to model the efficiency of expertise have tended to consist of transitions from shallowness to depth that appear to be somewhat unrealistic from a psychological point of view. What may be needed is a somewhat different approach that views the shallowness of the expert as more apparent than real and the study of the intermediate states of knowledge acquisition can be of some help in this process.

The Intermediate Effect

In much of the research characterizing the nature of expertise, the focal point is the "expert," and the novice is used as a basis of comparison. The theory of expertise really becomes a theory of the expert, in terms of the structure of knowledge and the various performance parameters.

It is also important to distinguish between intermediates and beginners, possibly on the basis of time devoted to learning the domain. If the category of subexperts is excluded, then a distinctive developmental phenomenon emerges, which has been termed the *intermediate effect*. This refers to the fact that, although it seems reasonable to assume that performance improves with training or time on task, there appear to be particular transitions, in which subjects can exhibit a certain drop in performance. This is an example of what is referred to as nonmonotonicity in the developmental literature (Strauss and Stavy 1982). What results most often is a learning curve or developmental pattern that is shaped like either a U or an inverted U. It should be noted that not all intermediate performance is nonmonotonic, and this phenomenon is more often associated with process-oriented variables, since the U-shaped phenomenon disappears when some global variables are used as criteria. The intermediate effect occurs with many tasks and at various levels of expertise (Patel and Groen 1991a). The tasks vary from comprehension of clinical cases and explanation of clinical problems, to problem solving, to generating laboratory data. Similar results were reported by Lesgold *et al.* (1988) in the domain of radiology.

One possible explanation of the phenomenon is detailed in Patel and

Groen (1991a) and Patel, Arocha and Kaufman (1994). It may be due to the
fact that intermediates have acquired an extensive body of knowledge, but
have not yet reorganized this knowledge in a functional manner to perform
various tasks. Thus, the knowledge has a sort of heterarchical or flat structure that necessitates considerable search and that also makes it more
difficult for intermediates to set up structures for rapid encoding and selective retrieval of information. Experts' knowledge is finely tuned to perform
various tasks, and they can readily screen out irrelevant information using
their hierarchically-organized schemata. The difference is reflected both in
the structural organization of knowledge and the extent to which it is proceduralized to perform different tasks. Both of these interrelated factors could
be responsible for this extraneous search and the accessing of irrelevant prior
knowledge. Schmidt and Boshuizen (1993) reported that the nonmonotonicity recall effects associated with intermediate level of experts disappear when
short exposure times (about 30 seconds) are used, demonstrating the emergence of the "intermediate effect" to be dependent on the amount of time
available for processing clinical information. The performance of experienced
physicians was relatively insensitive to manipulations of time in this study.
The results suggest that under time-restricted conditions, intermediates cannot engage in extraneous search. In other words, intermediates process too
much "garbage," whereas experts do not. Novices, on the other hand, do not
conduct irrelevant searches, simply because they lack a knowledge-base rich
enough to support such a search. While a novice's knowledge-base is likely
to be sparse and an experts' intricately interconnected, an intermediate may
have a lot of the pieces of knowledge in place, but lack the extensive connectedness of an expert. Until this knowledge becomes further consolidated,
the intermediate is more likely to engage in unnecessary and sometimes
counter-productive search.

Future Directions

While attempting to extend theoretical accounts of comprehension, directionality of reasoning, and the coordination of evidence and hypotheses as a
function of expertise, we have begun to rely on computational models that
have a certain generality. In particular, we have been working with Kintsch's
(1988) construction-integration computational theory (Arocha and Patel
1995; Patel, Arocha and Kaufman 1994) to investigate and model the learning process. The theory postulates that comprehension consists of two interrelated processes: the activation of concepts and the integration of those concepts into a situation model of the text. Although learning has been
traditionally conceived of as a cumulative process of knowledge and skill acquisition, research has provided evidence that learning is sometimes punctu-

ated by points of performance deterioration and increase in errors (Robertson and Glines 1985). In this regard, the study of the development of medical expertise has provided a picture of learning as a nonmonotonic process (Arocha, Patel and Patel 1993; Patel and Groen 1991b), which has been termed the *intermediate effect*. The intermediate effect may be due to the fact that at critical points in their learning, novices have acquired an extensive body of knowledge, but have not yet organized it in an efficient manner. Unlike experts, who are capable of imposing a hierarchical organization on their knowledge-bases (Patel, Arocha and Kaufman 1994), novices seem to generate many irrelevant concepts, which during clinical case comprehension and problem solving get activated. A hypothesis is that the "intermediate effect" occurs during those points at which large bodies of new knowledge from different sources is acquired (e.g., during a shift from classroom learning to "real world" learning).

In another research program, we are investigating the process of complex decision making with direct implications for the development of intelligent medical decision support. In one study (Kushniruk, Patel and Fleiszer 1995), physicians of three levels of expertise were presented with case descriptions of intensive care problems of systematically varied complexity. The physicians were asked to provide treatment decisions and the resultant think-aloud protocols were analyzed for differences in the reasoning and decision making of expert, novice and intermediate physicians. Based on the results of this analysis, which indicated deficiencies in the situational assessment abilities of the novices and intermediates, computer-based decision support is currently being designed to assist nonexpert physicians in the assessment of complex cases. In addition, the analysis indicated differences in the use of decision strategies by physicians of varied levels of expertise. Training and decision support is being designed to assist novices with these areas. In this line of work, it is argued that an understanding of the cognitive processes involved in decision making should provide an improved basis for the selection and design of appropriate forms of decision support and intelligent training systems.

There has been a great deal of research into the nature of expertise over the past twenty years. Most theories have tended to be local, focusing on specific phenomena, and have attempted to explain domain-specific empirical regularities. This has resulted in a pool of theoretical constructs that constitute a framework rather than a comprehensive theory of the nature of expertise. We recognize the same limitation in our research. The research reported in this chapter has emphasized cognitive and epistemological perspectives on expertise in medicine. In our psychological models, we have examined aspects of memory, knowledge structures, and reasoning strategies, largely in laboratory settings. Although these studies have been useful in developing theoretical models of expertise, reasoning, and more recently, learning, they have not yet been adequately tested in ecologically valid contexts.

Investigations in naturalistic settings are particularly critical for the development of ecologically valid learning theories and innovative instructional approaches. Recently, we have extended our work to a more naturalistic context (Leprohon and Patel 1995), in keeping with other works in the literature (e.g., Klein 1993). This transition from laboratory to the "real world" has necessitated an expanded theoretical framework and the development of methods to characterize the complex dynamics of real-world cognition and to determine how knowledge is applied in natural situations. This has included a shift in emphasis from studying the cognitive processes of the solitary individual to the investigation of the collective problem-solving processes involved in work groups (Patel and Kaufman 1996). It is apparent that much medical problem solving is a collective endeavor distributed among expert specialists, residents, medical students, nurses and other personnel such as laboratory technicians. Future research and related cognitive theories will need to take a broader range of factors into account. This point has been underlined by the recent challenge from situated theory (cf. Cognitive Science Special Issue: Situated Action 1993; Patel, Kaufman and Arocha 1995). It is our belief that theories of cognition could be enhanced by more serious consideration of the social context and the role of knowledge constructed in context. Patel, Arocha and Kaufman (1996) discuss some of these considerations in the context of acquisition of tacit knowledge and propose a mechanism by which such knowledge may be acquired through clinical practice.

Acknowledgments

We thank Robert Hoffman, Paul Feltovich and Kenneth Ford for their detailed constructive comments on the earlier draft of this paper. We acknowledge Michael Leccisi, José Arocha, David Kaufman and André Kushniruk for providing valuable suggestions at various stages of writing.

Note

Deduction as logical consequence is the most conservative form of prediction: If A is true in some world W, then all logical consequences of A will be true in W. Many studies have argued that the classical interpretation of deduction as logical consequence is too weak to capture the aim of prediction (Harman 1986; Poole 1989), and that different definitions, based on nonmonotonic logics or probability theory, for instance, are needed. The term deduction is here not committed to any representation formalism, but it is just used as a generic inference type.

References

Arocha, J.F. & Patel, V.L. (1995). Construction-integration theory and clinical reasoning. In C.A. Weaver III, S. Mannes & C.R. Fletcher (Eds.), *Discourse Comprehension:*

Essays in Honor of Walter Kintsch (pp. 359-381). Hillsdale, NJ: Erlbaum.

Arocha, J.F., Patel, V.L. & Patel, Y.C. (1993). Hypothesis generation and the coordination of theory and evidence in medical diagnostic reasoning. *Medical Decision Making,* 13, 198-211.

Braccio, A. & Patel, V.L. (1988). *On-line analysis of novice problem solving in medicine.* Paper presented at the annual meeting of the American Educational Research Association, New Orleans, LA.

Buchanan, B.G. & Shortliffe, E.H. (Eds.). (1984). *Rule-Based Expert Systems: The MYCIN Experiments of the Stanford Heuristic Programming Project.* Reading, MA: Addison-Wesley.

Bylander, T. & Chandrasekaran, B. (1988). Generic tasks for knowledge-based reasoning. *Knowledge-Based Systems, 1*, 65-77.

Bylander, T., Allemang, J., Tanner, R.C. & Josephson, J.R. (1991). The computational complexity of abduction. *Artificial Intelligence, 49*, 25-60.

Chandrasakeran, B. (1991). Functional representations and causal processes. In M. Yovits (Ed.), *Advances in Computers.* New York: Academic Press.

Chase, W.G. & Simon, H.A. (1973). Perception in chess. *Cognitive Psychology, 1,* 55-81.

Chi, M.T.H., Feltovich, P.J. & Glaser, R. (1981). Categorization and representation of physics problems by experts and novices. *Cognitive Science, 5,* 121-152.

Clancey, W.J. (1985). Heuristic classification. *Artificial Intelligence, 27,* 289-350.

Clancey, W.J. (Ed.). (1987). *Knowledge-Based Tutoring.* Cambridge, MA: MIT Press.

Clancey, W.J. & Letsinger, R. (1984). NEOMYCIN: Reconfiguring a rule-based expert system for application to teaching. In W.J. Clancey & E.H. Shortliffe (Eds.), *Readings in Medical Artificial Intelligence: The First Decade* (pp. 361-381). Reading, MA: Addison-Wesley.

Cognitive Science Special Issue: Situated Action (1993). *Cognitive Science, 17(1).*

deGroot, A.D. (1965). *Thought and Choice in Chess.* The Netherlands: Mouton, The Hague.

Dreyfus, H. & Dreyfus, S.E. (1986). *Mind Over Machine.* New York: Free Press.

Duncker, K. (1945). On problem-solving. *Psychology Monograph, 58* (270), 1-113.

Elstein, A.S., Shulman, L.S. & Sprafka, S.A. (1978). *Medical Problem Solving: An Analysis of Clinical Reasoning.* Cambridge, MA: Harvard University Press.

Ericsson, A. & Simon, H.A. (1993). *Protocol Analysis: Verbal Reports as Data.* Cambridge, MA: The MIT Press.

Ericsson, A. & Smith, J. (1991). Prospects and limits of the empirical study of expertise: An introduction. In A. Ericsson & J. Smith (Eds.), *Toward a General Theory of Expertise: Prospects and Limits* (pp. 1-38). New York: Cambridge University Press.

Eshelman, L. (1988). MOLE: A knowledge acquisition tool for Cover-and-Differentiate systems. In S. Marcus (Ed.), *Automating Knowledge Acquisition for Expert Systems,* (pp. 37-80). Boston, MA: Kluwer.

Feltovich, P.J. & Barrows, H.A. (1984). Issues of generality in medical problem solving. In H.G. deVolder & H.G. Schmidt (Eds.), *Tutorials in Problem Based Learning* (pp. 128-142). Assen, Holland: van Gorcum.

Feltovich, P.J., Johnson, P.E., Moller, J.H. & Swanson, D.B. (1984). LCS: The role and development of medical knowledge in diagnostic expertise. In W.J. Clancey & E.H.

Shortliffe (Eds.), *Readings in Medical Artificial Intelligence: The First Decade* (pp. 275-319). Reading, MA: Addison-Wesley.

Frederiksen, C.H. (1975). Representing logical and semantic structure of knowledge acquired from discourse. *Cognitive Psychology, 7,* 371-458.

Greeno, J.G. & Simon, H.A. (1988). Problem solving and reasoning. In R.C. Atkins, R.J. Herstein, G. Lindzey & R.D. Luce (Eds), *Steven's Handbook of Experimental Psychology.* New York: Wiley.

Groen, G.J. & Patel, V.L. (1985). Medical problem-solving: Some questionable assumptions. *Medical Education, 19,* 95-100.

Groen, G.J. & Patel, V.L. (1988). The relationship between comprehension and reasoning in medical expertise. In M.T.H. Chi, R. Glaser & M. Farr (Eds.), *The Nature of Expertise* (pp. 287-310). Hillsdale, NJ: Erlbaum.

Harman, G. (1986). *Change in View: Principles of Reasoning.* Cambridge, MA: MIT Press.

Hoffman, R.R. (Ed.). (1992). *The Psychology of Expertise: Cognitive Research and Empirical AI.* Hillsdale, NJ: Erlbaum.

Hoffman, R.R., Shadbolt, N.R., Burton, A.M. & Klein, G. (1995). Eliciting knowledge from experts: A methodological analysis. *Organizational Behavior and Human Decision Processes, 62(2),* 129-158.

Hunt, E. (1989). Cognitive science: Definition, status, and questions. *Annual Review of Psychology, 40,* 603-629.

Johnson-Laird, P.N. (1983). *Mental Models.* Cambridge, MA: Harvard University Press.

Joseph, G.-M. & Patel, V.L. (1990). Domain knowledge and hypothesis generation in diagnostic reasoning. *Journal of Medical Decision Making, 10,* 31-46.

Kassirer, J.P. (1989). Diagnostic reasoning. *Annals of Internal Medicine, 110,* 893-900.

Keravnou, E.T. & Washbrook, J. (1989). Deep and shallow models of medical expert systems. *Artificial Intelligence in Medicine, 1,* 11-28.

Kintsch, W. (1988). The role of knowledge in discourse comprehension: A construction-integration model. *Psychological Review, 95,* 163-182.

Kintsch, W. (Ed.). (1974). *The Representation of Meaning in Memory.* Hillsdale, NJ: Erlbaum.

Klein, G.A. (1993). A recognition-primed decision (RPD) model of rapid decision making. In G.A. Klein, J. Orasanu, R. Claderwood & C.E. Zsambok (Eds.), *Decision Making in Action: Models and Methods* (pp. 138-147). Norwood, NJ: Ablex.

Koedinger, K.R. & Anderson, J.R. (1990). Abstract planning and perceptual chunks: Elements of expertise in geometry. *Cognitive Science, 14,* 511-550.

Kuipers, B.J. & Kassirer, J.P. (1984). Causal reasoning in medicine: Analysis of a protocol. *Cognitive Science, 8,* 363-385.

Kushniruk, A.W., Patel, V.L. & Fleiszer, D. (1995). Complex decision making in providing surgical intensive care. In *Proceedings of the Seventeenth Annual Conference of the Cognitive Science Society* (pp. 287-292). Hillsdale, NJ: Erlbaum.

Larkin, J.H. (1983). Problem representation in physics. In D. Gentner & A.L. Stevens (Eds.), *Mental Models* (pp. 75-98). Hillsdale, NJ: Erlbaum.

Larkin, J.H., McDermott, J., Simon, D.P. & Simon, H.A. (1980). Expert and novice performance in solving physics problems. *Science, 208,* 1335-1342.

Leprohon, J. & Patel, V.L. (1995). Decision making strategies for telephone triage in emergency medical services. *Medical Decision Making, 15*(3), 240-253.

Lesgold, A.M., Rubinson, H., Feltovich, P.J., Glaser, R., Klopfer, D. & Wang, Y. (1988). Expertise in a complex skill: Diagnosing x-ray picture. In M.T.H. Chi, R. Glaser & M.J. Farr (Eds.), *The Nature of Expertise* (pp. 311-342). Hillsdale, NJ: Erlbaum.

Miller, R.A., Masarie, F.E. & Myers, J.D. (1988). Quick Medical Reference [Computer program, program version 10.22; knowledge-base version 06/15/88]. Department of Medicine, Section of Medical Informatics, University of Pittsburgh, Pittsburgh, PA.

Newell, A. (1990). *Unified Theories of Cognition.* Cambridge, MA: Harvard University Press.

Newell, A. & Simon, H.A. (1972). *Human Problem Solving.* Englewood Cliffs, NJ: Prentice Hall.

Patel, V.L. & Arocha, J.F. (1995). Cognitive models of clinical reasoning and conceptual representation. *Methods of Information in Medicine, 34*(1), 1-10.

Patel, V.L., Arocha, J.F. & Kaufman, D.R. (1994). Diagnostic Reasoning and Expertise. *Psychology of Learning and Motivation, 31,* 137-252.

Patel, V.L., Arocha, J.F. & Kaufman, D.R. (1996). Expertise and tacit knowledge in medicine. In R.J. Sternberg & J.A. Horvath (Eds.), *Tacit Knowledge in Professional Practise.* Hillsdale, NJ: Erlbaum.

Patel, V.L., Evans, D.A. & Kaufman, D.R. (1989). Cognitive framework for doctor-patient interaction. In D.A. Evans & V.L. Patel (Eds.), *Cognitive Science in Medicine: Biomedical Modeling* (pp. 253-308). Cambridge, MA: MIT Press.

Patel, V.L. & Frederiksen, C.H. (1984). Cognitive processes in comprehension and knowledge acquisition by medical students and physicians. In H.G. Schmidt & M.C. de Volder (Eds.), *Tutorials in Problem-Based Learning* (pp. 143-157). Assen, Holland: van Gorcum.

Patel, V.L. & Groen G.J. (1986). Knowledge-based solution strategies in medical reasoning. *Cognitive Science, 10,* 91-116.

Patel, V.L. & Groen, G.J. (1991a). The general and specific nature of medical expertise: A critical look. In A. Ericsson & J. Smith (Eds.), *Toward a General Theory of Expertise: Prospects and Limits* (pp. 93-125). New York: Cambridge University Press.

Patel, V.L. & Groen, G.J. (1991b). Developmental accounts of the transition from student to physician: Some problems and suggestions. *Medical Education, 25,* 527-535.

Patel, V.L., Groen, G.J. & Arocha, J.F. (1990). Medical expertise as a function of task difficulty. *Memory & Cognition, 18*(4), 394-406.

Patel, V.L., Groen, G.J. & Frederiksen, C.H. (1986). Differences between students and physicians in memory for clinical cases. *Medical Education, 20,* 3-9.

Patel, V.L., Groen, G.J., Ramoni, M.F. & Kaufman, D.R. (1992). Machine depth versus psychological depth: A lack of equivalence. In E. Keravnou (Ed.), *Deep Model for Medical Knowledge Engineering* (pp. 249-272). Amsterdam: Elsevier.

Patel, V.L. & Kaufman, D.R. (1996). The acquisition of medical expertise in complex dynamic environments. In A. Ericsson (Ed.), *The Road to Expert Performance: Empirical Evidence from the Arts & Sciences, Sports and Games* (pp. 127-165). Hillsdale, NJ: Erlbaum.

Patel, V.L., Kaufman, D.R. & Arocha, J.F. (1995). Steering through the murky waters of a scientific conflict: Situated and symbolic models of clinical cognition. *Artificial Intelligence in Medicine* 7, 413-438.

Patil, R.S., Szolovitz, P. & Schwartz, W. (1984). Causal understanding of patient illness in medical diagnosis. In W.J. Clancey & H.E. Shortliffe (Eds.), *Readings in Medical Artificial Intelligence* (pp. 339-360). Reading, MA: Addison-Wesley.

Pearl, J. (Ed.). (1988). *Probabilistic Reasoning in Intelligent Systems: Networks of Plausible Inference*. San Mateo: Morgan Kaufmann.

Peirce, C.S. (1955). Abduction and induction. In *Philosophical Writings of C.S. Peirce* (pp. 150-156). New York: Dover.

Poole, D. (1989). Explanation and prediction: an architecture for default and abductive reasoning. *Computational Intelligence, 5*, 97-110.

Pople, H. (1982). Heuristic methods of imposing structure on ill-structured problems: The structuring of medical diagnosis. In P. Szolovitz (Ed.), *Artificial Intelligence in Medicine* (pp. 119-190). Boulder, CO: Westview Press.

Ramoni, M., Stefanelli, M., Magnani, L. & Barosi, G. (1992). An epistemological framework for medical knowledge based system. *IEEE Transactions on Systems, Man, and Cybernetics, 22*, 1361-1375.

Robertson, R.J. & Glines, L.A. (1985). The phantom plateau returns. *Perceptual and Motor Skills, 61(1)*, 55-64.

Rumelhart, D.E. & Ortony, A. (1977). The representation of knowledge in memory. In R.C. Anderson, R.J. Spiro & W.E. Montague (Eds.), *Schooling and the Acquisition of Knowledge* (pp. 99-135). Hillsdale, NJ: Erlbaum.

Schmidt, H.G. & Boshuizen, H.P.A. (1993). On the origin of intermediate effects in clinical case recall. *Memory & Cognition, 21(3)*, 338-351.

Shortliffe, E.H. (1976). *Computer-Based Medical Consultations: MYCIN*. New York: Elsevier/North-Holland.

Simon, D.P. & Simon, H.A. (1978). Individual differences in solving physics problems. In R. Siegler (Ed.), *Children's Thinking: What Develops?* Hillsdale, NJ: Erlbaum.

Simon, H.A. (1989). The scientist as a problem solver. In D. Klahr & K. Kotovsky (Eds.), *Complex Information Processing: The Impact of Herbert A. Simon* (pp. 375-398). Hillsdale, NJ: Erlbaum.

Sowa, J.F. (1983). *Conceptual Structures. Information Processing in Man and Machine*. Reading, MA: Addison-Wesley.

Stefanelli, M. & Ramoni, M. (1992). Epistemological constraints on medical knowledge-based systems. In D.A. Evans & V.L. Patel (Eds.), *Advanced Models of Cognition for Medical Training and Practice,* NATO ASI Series F: *Computer and Systems Sciences* (Vol. 97, pp. 3-20). Heidelberg, Germany: Springer-Verlag.

Strauss, S. & Stavy, R. (Eds.). (1982). *U-shaped Behavioral Growth*. New York: Academic Press.

van Dijk, T.A. & Kintsch, W. (1983). *Strategies of Discourse Comprehension*. New York: Academic Press.

Winograd, T. & Flores, F. (Eds). (1986). *Understanding Computers and Cognition: A New Foundation for Design*. Norwood, NJ: Ablex.

CHAPTER 4

Experience and Expertise: The Role of Memory in Planning for Opportunities

Colleen M. Seifert, Andrea L. Patalano, Kristian J. Hammond, & Timothy M. Converse

Introduction

A commonsense notion about expertise is that experts differ from novices due to the number of experiences they have had within a particular domain. The experience acquired over time may form the basis of the complex knowledge organization that distinguishes experts from novices. But in addition to measures such as "years on the job," the quality of specific experiences may play a critical role in expertise. The content of these individual episodes may be preserved in memory and serve as a continuing resource for experts when faced with later problems. As such, they may serve as a context of experience with which to evaluate and refine the abstract knowledge comprising expertise.

In this chapter, we discuss an approach to expertise that emphasizes the role of specific past experiences in memory. We examine expertise in planning tasks, where decisions are made about which goals to pursue, which plans to select, and when to execute them. These decisions are likely to benefit from considering past experiences with similar cases. Our approach emphasizes the notion that "reasoning is remembering"—remembering successful plans so they can be repeated, remembering failed plans so they can be avoided, and remembering pending plans so they can be attempted later. Our main hypothesis is that expert planners are able to anticipate the circumstances related to satisfying goals, and therefore maximize their ability to respond to opportunities when they arise. We examine this opportunistic planning capability as a touchstone feature of human expertise at its best.

In the sections of this chapter, we briefly review the role of experience in expertise, and the central role of past experiences within our framework, case-based planning. Then, we present the problem of *opportunism*—taking advantage of unanticipated circumstances to satisfy one's goals—as a challenge for any model of expertise. After a discussion of competing models of opportunistic planning, we define our own model and identify its cognitive mechanisms. We then evaluate this model through two research methodologies: computational modeling and experiments with human participants. By combining evidence from these two approaches, we hope to develop a more complete theory of how opportunistic planning is accomplished. Our account of the role of memory for specific past experiences in identifying later opportunities provides evidence for the importance of the context of specific experiences in expertise.

The Need for Experience-Based Expertise

Most classical AI work on planning includes a separation of planning from execution. These theories (e.g., Sussman 1975) emphasize complete preplanning in order to guarantee that only a "correct" plan will ever be executed. They accomplish this by deriving a complete plan, projecting its effects on a model of the world, and determining that its outcome is successful. But complete planners, such as Sussman's STRIPS model (1975), also require assuming that the planner has complete and flawless knowledge of the world, that the world is stable and unchanging, and that the planner has all the time it needs to plan before any action is required. These assumptions may not hold in many situations; instead, we find our knowledge is incomplete, the world constantly changes, and unanticipated objects and events are perceived. As we begin to work with more realistic domain models, new issues arise that make complete preplanning less feasible (Hammond, Marks, and Converse 1985):

The Costly Information Issue: A planner cannot count on having complete information about a domain. Understanding the world "correctly," storing new information in a usable form, and deducing all potential outcomes of information can be expensive if not impossible operations.

The Planning Complexity Issue: If a planner searches for a correct and safe plan by projecting forward the effects of initial steps, the computational complexity can quickly become too time-consuming to be practical.

The Execution-Time Issue: A plan which seemed correct when it was constructed may turn out to fail during execution. To cope, a planner must have some facility for replanning, recovery, and repair.

The Multiple Goals Issue: As a planner interacts with the world, it is sometimes confronted with multiple, simultaneous goals, that interact in unexpected ways.

The Postponed Execution Issue: Because more goals can be created than can be pursued simultaneously, it is often the case that some goals will have to be postponed, and returned to when the time is right to achieve them.

We argue that many real-world domains have these characteristics (e.g., military exercises, stock purchasing, news programming), and require an expert to function with uncertain information about the world. However, one paradigm that explicitly attempts to address these problems is case-based reasoning (Bareiss 1989; Carbonell 1981; Hammond 1989; Kolodner, Simpson, and Sycara 1985; Schank 1982). The case-based approach to planning may be a tractable alternative to complete planners because, like human planners, it does not depend on having a complete solution in advance.

Case-Based Planning

Case-based planning (a specialization of case-based reasoning for planning tasks) proposes that the way to deal with the combinatorics of planning and projection is to let past experiences tell the planner when and where plans work and don't work. Rather than preplanning, a planner should reuse past successful plans. Rather than projecting the effects of actions into the future, a planner should recall what the outcomes were in the past. Rather than simulating a plan to identify problematic interactions, a planner should recall and then avoid those that have cropped up before.

The core notion of case-based planning is that expertise depends on the development of domain knowledge (a "case library" containing both memories of specific experiences and generalizations, abstractions, and rules based on those experiences). By experiencing failures and successes within a domain, the expert planner is prepared to deal with future failures and opportunities when they occur. Planning from past experiences is supported by some psychological evidence for making use of past experiences in planning for new goals (Byrne 1977).

In case-based planning, the case library is built up incrementally through experience. The framework (Hammond 1989) includes seven case-based processes:

1. An ANTICIPATOR that predicts execution problems on the basis of the failures that have been seen by the planner in the past.

2. A RETRIEVER that searches memory for a plan that satisfies current goals while avoiding any problems that the ANTICIPATOR has predicted.

3. A MODIFIER that alters the plan found by the RETRIEVER to achieve any other goals from the input that are not yet satisfied.

4. A PROJECTOR that uses past cases indexed by plans to predict outcomes.

5. A STORER that places new plans in memory, indexed by the goals that they satisfy and the problems that they avoid.

6. A REPAIRER that operates when a plan fails and attempts to explain and correct problems encountered.

7. An ASSIGNER that uses the causal explanation built during repair to determine the features which will predict this failure in the future. This knowledge is used to index the failure for later access by the ANTICIPATOR.

These seven modules define the case-based planning approach, and are presented in depth by Hammond (1989). Together, these modules act to anticipate and avoid execution problems before they occur, apply a variety of repairs to faulty plans that it creates, and store plans in memory so that they can be used again. The case-based approach includes the power of rule-based reasoning, since generalizations can be built from commonalities among cases. However, the case library is also preserved in memory, and can be accessed as a resource for future reasoning.

One example of a case-based planner is CHEF, which operates in the domain of Szechwan cooking (Hammond 1989). Its input is a set of goals for different tastes, textures, ingredients, and types of dishes, and its output is a single recipe that satisfies multiple goals. It finds a past plan that satisfies as many of the most important goals as possible, and then modifies that plan to satisfy additional goals as well. Before searching memory for a plan to modify, CHEF examines the goals and recalls any failures that have occurred in the interactions among plans. If a related failure is found in memory, CHEF adds a goal of avoiding the failure to its set of goals to satisfy, and this new goal is also used to search for a plan.

For example, suppose CHEF anticipates that stir frying chicken with snow peas can lead to soggy snow peas (because the chicken will sweat liquid into the pan). To avoid that problem, CHEF searches the case library for a stir fry plan involving vegetables getting soggy when cooked with meats. It finds a past plan for a beef and broccoli dish that solves this problem by cooking the vegetable and meat separately. The critical similarity between the current situation and the past plan is not the specific ingredients used, but the interaction of one plan (cooking meat) with another (cooking vegetables). CHEF's expertise in this example derives from knowing what similarities to attend to, and knowing what makes a past case especially relevant to a new problem.

As a result, CHEF, through its specific experiences, incrementally improves its ability to predict problems and create plans in response to its own failures. Its attempts at satisfying its own goals, successful or not, result in an improvement in its ability to do so in the future. Thus, the development of expertise in CHEF is dependent upon particular experiences and is bound to the context of previous cases. Experiences can also play a critical role in anticipating the success of possible plans. In the next section, we will examine the role of experiences in recognizing opportunities to satisfy goals.

Opportunistic Planning and Expertise

The CHEF system demonstrated the utility of learning from failures by anticipating and avoiding past failures. But expertise involves another important
role for experience: acquiring the ability to foresee and exploit future opportunities to satisfy one's goals. Taking advantage of improved circumstances to
solve problems displays the adaptive nature of expertise: Just as a system in a
changing world must contend with situations in which plans fail, it must also
deal with situations in which it succeeds in unanticipated ways.

In this section, we will look at the problem of anticipating and recognizing
planning opportunities. First, we discuss current models of opportunism,
and then present a new model, followed by a detailed example. The CHEF
planner (Hammond 1989) responds to failure by repairing its current plan
and by repairing the knowledge base (its expectations about the results of its
actions) which allowed it to create the plan. We now argue that execution-
time opportunities can be responded to in a similar way: the planner should
exploit the current opportunity and change its expectations to properly anticipate and exploit the future opportunity.

Models of Opportunistic Planning

Our approach builds on two views of opportunism in planning—that of
Hayes-Roth and Hayes-Roth (1979), and that of Birnbaum and Collins
(1984). Hayes-Roth and Hayes-Roth present the view that a planner should
be able to shift to a different planning strategy on the basis of perceived opportunities, even when those opportunities are unanticipated. Their model,
called "opportunistic planning," consists of a blackboard architecture (Lesser
et al. 1975) and planning specialists that capture planning information at
many different levels of abstraction. These specialists include domain-level
"errand plan" developers (e.g., specialists that know about routes, stores, or
conditions for specific plans) as well as more strategic operators (e.g., specialists that look for clusters of goals, and goals with similar conditions). The
planner can jump between strategies as different specialists "notice" that their
activation conditions are present. For example, in scheduling a set of errands, a specialist that groups errands by location can interrupt another specialist that orders them by priority. In this way, the planner can respond to
opportunities to visit nearby locations as they arise.

More recently, Birnbaum and Collins (1984) presented a theory of opportunism where goals are characterized as agents or "demons"—independent
processing entities—that have their own inferential power. In this approach,
a suspended goal continues to independently examine the ongoing input of
objects and events. If circumstances that allow for the satisfaction of the goal
arise, this demon mechanism recognizes them and inserts a plan into the

current action agenda. For example, consider an agent trying to obtain both food and water in the wild. Suppose the agent decides to suspend the goal to quench his thirst while pursuing the goal to satisfy his hunger. Then, while searching for food, the agent jumps over a stream, and is able to recognize that the stream contains water, and so affords an opportunity to satisfy the suspended goal (to obtain water).

Birnbaum and Collins (1984) argue that the agent is able to recognize the opportunity afforded by the stream because the suspended goal has the demon-based capability to examine the current situation and initiate inferences. This must be the case, they argue, because there can be no way to decide, at the time of suspending a goal, the exact conditions under which it should be reactivated. Birnbaum (1986) argues further that indexing suspended goals by descriptions of the conditions that both signal and allow their satisfaction is an unworkable approach. The problem is that the overall processing system will have to constantly compare the current state of the world to all of the goals waiting in a separate "memory of unsatisfied tasks." However, these arguments may address an overly constrained model of planning at the time of suspension. Instead of instituting a separate list of unsatisfied tasks in memory, a planner could integrate suspended goals into a single memory bank along with all other knowledge. Then, the normal processes that activate information in memory while processing the environment might sometimes also activate associated suspended goals.

Birnbaum and Collins (1984) also raised the problem of having no way to decide, at the time of suspending a goal, the exact conditions under which it should be reactivated. However, one may not need to anticipate the exact conditions for reactivation; instead, a more general category description may be adequate for recognizing types of opportunities. For example, the agent in the example may not have to anticipate coming across "a stream;" instead, simply noting that one should think about the suspended goal whenever one comes across "water" will specify a set of opportunities (a well, a water hole, a stream, a hollow stump) where it would be opportune to reconsider pursuing the thirst goal. Further, opportunism may be imperfect; that is, perhaps it is sufficient to anticipate some features related to opportunities, even at the cost of missing others. This compromise may be worthwhile in order to avoid the heavy computational costs of attempting to draw inferences from each new object to every suspended goal.

In the next section, we propose a model of opportunism that addresses these problems and can provide a better account of how people recognize opportunities during plan execution. We argue that the power of opportunism rests in the ability to reason at the time of goal suspension, before other activities are resumed. At that point, one can devote resources to drawing inferences about the features that indicate opportunities to satisfy the goal. Then, the elaborated inferences about features that signal opportunities can be stored in memory in association with the suspended goal. Later, when these features are perceived in the environment, the pending goal in memory can be automatically reactivated without any further inference required (Patalano, Seifert, and Hammond 1993; Hammond, Converse, Marks, and Seifert 1993). The successful recognition of opportunities will depend on the features chosen to index the suspended goal in memory. Identifying these features involves selecting a specific plan for satisfying the goal from among past plans in memory, abstracting necessary features for successfully executing the plan, and describing the features in a manner easily observed in the environment through normal understanding processes.

The Predictive Encoding Model of Opportunism

Our model of opportunism is based on the ability to anticipate the features in the world that indicate potential opportunities, and to use those features to index the pending goal in memory. At the time of initial encoding, one anticipates features related to circumstances where success would be possible, and then encodes the suspended goal into memory with those features. Then, while pursuing other activities, those same features may happen to be activated; if so, their activation automatically reactivates the suspended goal in memory just when the more favorable conditions have appeared in the world. We call this process predictive encoding, where the features that indicate the relevance of the plan are anticipated and used to index the plan in memory. This anticipation means that no separate or demon-based inference process has to operate; instead, the inference is prepared and stored in memory so that it is simply reactivated by the features perceived in the environment. The steps involved in the predictive encoding model are:

1. Goals that cannot be fit into a current ongoing plan are considered blocked and work on them is suspended.

2. Suspended goals are indexed (associated) in memory with features that are related to potential opportunities.

3. These memory structures are the same ones used to perceive events in the world as the planner executes other plans. No separate "list" of suspended goals is maintained.

4. Later, as elements of memory are activated by features in the world, the goals associated with them are also activated and then integrated into the current processing queue.

In this way, suspended goals are brought to the planner's attention when conditions change so that the goals can be satisfied. In the meantime, the planner can go on to pursue other goals without the need for further reasoning or inferencing regarding the suspended goal.

The success of this process will depend upon the quality of the indices selected for the initial encoding (Seifert, Hammond, Johnson, Converse, Mac-Dougal, and VanderStoep 1994; Johnson and Seifert 1992). We hypothesize that anticipating the circumstances in the world that are related to opportunities to satisfy the goal, and describing them in easily observable features, constitutes the expertise acquired with experience in a domain. Thus, the more one learns about the circumstances related to different types of opportunities, the better one will be able to predict the features and encode them in a way that maximizes successful recognition, and use of opportunities that arise.

For example, consider the goal of opening a locked door. Assume that all reasoning and activity towards accomplishing this goal is suspended while the planner pursues other, perhaps more important goals. Later, if a key is found, its association with locks may facilitate the retrieval of the goal from memory with no special preparation by the planner. But what if a credit card is found instead? Our model suggests that unless you consider the plan of "slipping the lock" at the time of the initial goal suspension, you will be unlikely to notice the credit card as an opportunity to pursue the suspended goal. By preparing such a memory association in advance, it is as if you were placing a "marker" to wait at the "right place" in memory. When these features are observed at a later point, the suspended goal in memory is then activated, and the planner is "reminded" of the goal awaiting pursuit. With careful predictive encoding, no special inference or reasoning process is needed in order to recognize the opportunity; instead, the normal processes occurring while simply recognizing objects in the current environment will automatically activate suspended goals waiting under appropriate indices in memory.

The advantage to this approach is that recognition of later opportunities is made effortless by formulating memory associations so that only normal, default inferencing about the world is required. The inference needed to connect a suspended goal with an opportunity for its satisfaction is prepared in advance, and indexed in memory in terms of readily observable features of the world. So, when initially encoding the "open door" goal, one might reason about plans like "slipping the lock," and determine the particular features of the needed tool; for example, "a thin, flat, yet stiff plane." Then, when one comes across the credit card, or any object fitting the description (such as a plastic knife), one may recognize an opportunity to open the door. Such "smart" indexing provides one solution to the problem of recognizing future opportunities: by anticipating—at the time of encoding—the circumstances that will comprise an opportunity, at least some opportunities will be easy to recognize. By contrast, the demon model of suspended goals predicts no advance preparation of indices; instead, each demon would actively work on-line to connect each perceived object to its triggering conditions. Rather than automatic activation, each demon would need to constantly reason about its potential relationship to each new object as they are perceived.

An Example of Opportunism in Planning

Consider the following example:

On April 14th, John realized that he needed tax forms in order to prepare his yearly income taxes. Because he was late for work, he had no time to do anything about it. He then goes on to pursue other goals throughout the day. Later, on his way out to lunch, John noticed that he was passing a First of America Bank branch, and recalled that he needed the tax forms. Since he had time, he stopped and picked up the forms and then continued on to lunch.

In this example, John decides to suspend a goal before deciding exactly how to satisfy it; in effect, he says, "I don't have all the resources (e.g., time) to pursue this goal right now." But later, John is able to recognize the conditions that lead to satisfying this goal. How could any processor accomplish this recognition? Our predictive encoding model specifies the following steps.

Suspending Goals

First, the planner suspends the blocked goals by associating them with the elements of memory that describe potential opportunities. In the example, John's goal to possess tax forms is blocked by lack of time. But before suspending the goal in memory, he does some planning about the goal. For novel or infrequent goals, this may involve identifying possible plans to try, resources needed, etc. After thinking for a bit, he recalls that he saw tax forms in the lobby of his bank last year, provided as a convenience for customers. Notice that "bank" may not be the first plan to come to mind for acquiring tax forms; certainly, other plans (like waiting until the forms arrive in the mail, calling the 800 number, or going to the post office) can be generated. But whichever plan he chooses, John is able to prepare for a later opportunity by reasoning out a potential plan and then linking the suspended goal to its preconditions; in the example, this involves "being at a bank."

Then, during the execution of other plans (like going to lunch), the planner naturally observes the effects of its own plans as well as any other events in its world. So later, while John is walking to a restaurant, he sees and recognizes a "First of America" sign as indicating a "bank." This concept in turn activates the prestored association with the suspended tax forms goal. He then recognizes the bank as an opportunity to look for tax forms, and can decide whether to interrupt his lunch to pursue the suspended goal. The key is that no inferencing or reasoning about the possible connection of "bank" to a suspended goal need be performed; instead, the inference is prestored, so that simply recognizing "bank" reactivated the inference made at the time of encoding. Thus, the planner's general recognition of a situation results in immediately activating any goals that have previously been associated with that situation.

What if John had not stopped to try to "predictively encode" the suspended goal? He could have simply realized he did not have time that morning, and then gone on to pursue other goals during the day. But without predictive encoding, would John have recognized the bank as an opportunity? To do so, John would have to examine every new feature of the world and reason about it in order to see if it is somehow related to the tax forms (Is this gas station going to lead to tax forms? What about that flower shop?); in addition, trying to connect everything observed to each of his pending goals would require many comparisons, and could consume much of his cognitive resources. However, by predictively encoding the pending goal, the inferences needed to connect "bank" to the tax forms has already been completed and "canned" into memory; now, all John needed to do was to notice a bank at any time and any place during his day.

Anticipating Opportunities

Predictive encoding requires the planner to anticipate a plan for the suspended goal and the necessary features for executing that plan. But how can a planner best anticipate the critical features of the world that will provide an opportunity for a plan? In general, opportunities to run plans can be derived from the conditions necessary to execute each of the steps of a plan. For example, in order to buy a newspaper, one has to have enough money, be at a store, the store has to have papers in stock, and so forth. So, with enough time, a planner could think through a plan step by step and collect the conditions that have to be true at each point in the plan. This process would require the examination of many conditions, and most may not be particularly helpful in detecting opportunities. For example, some conditions for obtaining tax forms—"have time" and "can carry the forms"—are not very distinctive as features that will allow one to recognize opportunities at the appropriate time. Features that indicate opportunities are more constrained than the conditions necessary for executing a plan; in fact, features indicating opportunities are further constrained by the need for ease of recognition, likelihood of occurrence, distinctiveness, and predictiveness. For example, "have time" is a necessary condition for finding tax forms, but if the suspended goal is associated in memory with time, the planner would be reminded of the goal far too often. While it is a needed condition, it does not isolate situations where acquiring tax forms specifically will be most likely to be successful.

Our solution involves a taxonomy of opportunity types to derive the conditions that will identify opportunities to satisfy goals. The following taxonomy is used to guide the planner's search through a plan to determine appropriate indices to be associated with the suspended goal in memory.

Does the plan require:

- a special resource? If so, index the goal in terms of the resource.
- a special tool? If so, index the goal in terms of the tool.

- a special location? If so, index the goal in terms of the location.
- a special agent or skill? If so, index the goal in terms of the agent or skill.
- a specific time? If so, index the goal in terms of the time constraint.

Using these tests, it is possible to associate the suspended goal in memory (to possess tax forms) with a location (BANK). Other conditions of the plan (such as "possess time") are checked before the plan is actually executed, but they are not used to index the suspended goal in memory. Anticipating the critical features that indicate an opportunity is the core of the predictive encoding process. Recognition of this prepared opportunity may then follow without any special effort, as described in the following section.

Recognizing Opportunities

The predictive encoding model also relies heavily on a model of memory where instances of concepts can be readily identified. For example, John can pick up tax forms at *any* bank, not just a particular one. It is necessary, then, to be able to recognize a wide variety of situations as instances of more general concepts. To accomplish this, we use a version of Martin's (1990) DMAP parser, a general purpose memory recognition system. DMAP uses a marker-passing algorithm in which two types of markers are used to activate and predict concepts (like plans and objects) in an ISA and PART-OF network. Activation markers are passed from primitive features up an abstraction hierarchy. When any part of a concept is activated, prediction markers are spread to its connected concepts, which themselves become active. Of course, this model will only be as good as the network of concepts upon which it operates; in human memory, this conceptual memory network is quite flexible and efficient (Smith and Medin 1981).

For opportunistic planning, we propose adding a new type of link to the memory structures in DMAP. This link associates suspended goals with conditions that represent opportunities to achieve them. Pointing from specific objects to goals, this SUSPEND link is traversed by any activation marker that is placed on the concept. Consequently, the activation of an object also activates any suspended goals associated with it. In the example, the suspended goal to get the tax forms is encoded into memory with the concept representing "you are at a bank." Then, as the world is perceived, a sequence of "parking lot," "building," and "First of America" sign is recognized. Because DMAP is passing activation markers up ISA links, the bank is recognized as a particular First of America branch, an instance of all First of America banks, and of a BANK. While the suspended goal is not directly associated with the concept "First of America," it is associated with BANK, and that causes the activation of the suspended goal to get the tax forms. Accomplishing the activation of the SUSPEND link is thus the same recognition process that occurs during the identification of any perceived object. The power of predictive encoding arises from prestoring the opportunity so that the suspended goal will be activated during normal perceptual processing.

Note that this process will result in sometimes failing to notice an opportunity for satisfying a goal. Some opportunities will be missed when they arise in a form that was not anticipated at the time of the goal suspension. Truly unique opportunities will be missed simply because this technique is aimed at recognition of previously experienced solutions. In addition, opportunities that could have been anticipated, but were not at the time of encoding, will also be missed. For example, if John also passes a library on his way to lunch, he may not recognize it as a potential place to pick up the tax forms. However, if, at the time of the blocked goal, John had anticipated the sources for tax forms, and remembered that libraries and post offices often provide them, he would then be more likely to notice an instance of one of these offices as a potential opportunity to satisfy his goal.

Of course, once a suspended goal is reactivated, it has to be evaluated for integration into the current execution agenda. In the example, the overall plan is changed to take the planner into the bank for a moment to pick up the forms before resuming the trip out to lunch. Successful retrieval and satisfaction of the pending goal serves to confirm and reinforce the predictions made at encoding time. The predictive encoding model as outlined here appears to account for some examples of opportunistic planning. In the next sections, we present some formal tests of the model, first through a computer simulation and then through empirical evidence from psychological experiments.

An Implementation of Opportunism

Our simulations with an implementation of an opportunistic planner were in the TRUCKER program (Hammond, Marks, and Converse 1989). Its domain is a UPS-like pickup and delivery task in which new orders are received during the course of a day. Its task is to schedule the orders and develop the routes for its trucks to follow through town. A dispatcher controls a fleet of trucks that roam a simulated city, picking up and dropping off parcels at designated addresses. Transport orders are "phoned in" by customers at various times during the simulated business day, and the planner must see to it that all deliveries are successfully completed by their deadlines.

TRUCKER's task involves receiving requests from customers, making decisions about which truck to assign a given request, deciding in what order given parcels should be picked up and dropped off, figuring out routes for the trucks to follow, and monitoring the execution of the plans it has constructed. A number of limited resources must be managed, including the trucks themselves, their gas and cargo space, and the planner's own planning time. TRUCKER starts off with very little information about the world that its trucks will be negotiating; all it has is the equivalent of a street map of its simulated world.

TRUCKER's central control structure is a queue-based executor, with planning and monitoring actions sharing space on the queue. The planner must also react to new goals as they arrive. The planner hands pickup and drop-off orders to trucks based on availability in the order they arrive, and integrates the new orders onto each truck's agenda. In the case where the truck is idle, no real integration is necessary, and the standard plan of traveling to the pickup point and then to the drop-off point is used; for example:

```
((GOTO (800 E-61-ST))
(PICKUP PARCEL.42 (850 E-61-ST))
(GOTO (6200 S-COTTAGE))
(DROPOFF PARCEL.42 (6230 S-COTTAGE)))
```

If no idle trucks are available, and if the planner decides the request cannot be merged onto any truck's current agenda, TRUCKER is forced to place the request on a queue of orders waiting for idle trucks. To suspend a goal, TRUCKER marks its representation of the goal's pickup and delivery points with an annotation that there is a goal related to those locations. Because the domain involves only one type of goal, TRUCKER doesn't need to do any more generalization in order to identify good opportunities to satisfy the suspended goals.

Then, as TRUCKER decides when to execute actions based on locations, landmarks, and addresses that it recognizes in the world, it must parse and interpret these objects as they appear in the environment. TRUCKER moves through its world, identifying the objects at its current location and responding with any actions it can now execute. For example, seeing "Woodlawn Street" enables it to execute a plan to turn south on Woodlawn. It also checks for any annotation of a goal with which the object might be associated. If found, the suspended goal is activated and integrated into the current schedule.

At this point the planner is invoked to construct a new route that will satisfy both goals. The fragment of program output in figure 1 illustrates the process of noticing the opportunity, the subsequent reassignment of a request from a different truck, and the construction of a new, combined agenda that includes the opportunity.

After having noticed the opportunity and suggesting the reassignment, TRUCKER uses planning techniques tailored to its domain to plan the new agenda (i.e., specifics about how to combine plans when scheduling trucks). Scheduling the initial pickup is trivial, in that a truck is already at the pickup location. The difficulty lies in scheduling the delivery. TRUCKER does so (though humans may not) by reviewing each location already scheduled and finding the section of the route that will be the least altered by the insertion of the delivery. This can be done even before the exact routes are selected by using the map.

8:17:12 AM *** Truck #1 starting new route at 800 block of E 61st Street. ***
*** Truck #1 has noticed opportunity to make pickup for REQUEST.49. ***
*** Request REQUEST.49 is assigned—Truck #1 inserting request in active agenda. ***
*** Noting combination opportunity in memory. ***
8:17:45 AM Planner Action:
                 (REASSIGN-BY-NOTICED-OPPORTUNITY REQUEST.49 #1)

—— Reassignment of REQUEST.49 means that truck #2 need not continue to destination.
PLANNER assigning REQUEST.49 to truck #1
Starting INTEGRATE-REQUEST REQUEST.49 #1 NOTICED-OPPORTUNITY
Current plan: ((GOTO (6200 S-COTTAGE) #Structure ROUTE 2)
                 (DROPOFF PARCEL.42 (6230 S-COTTAGE)))
Request-plan to integrate new plan with current plan:
                 ((GOTO (6100 S-COTTAGE))
                 (PICKUP PARCEL.50 (6150 S-COTTAGE))
                 (GOTO (900 E-63-ST))
                 (DROPOFF PARCEL.50 (925 E-63-ST)))
8:17:45 AM *** Truck #1 is stopping in 6100 block of S Cottage Grove. ***
Finishing INTEGRATE-REQUEST REQUEST.49 #1 NOTICED-OPPORTUNITY
Resulting combined plan:
                 ((GOTO (6100 S-COTTAGE))
                 (PICKUP PARCEL.50 (6150 S-COTTAGE))
                 (GOTO (6200 S-COTTAGE))
                 (DROPOFF PARCEL.42 (6230 S-COTTAGE))
                 (GOTO (900 E-63-ST))
                 (DROPOFF PARCEL.50 (925 E-63-ST)))
8:17:48 AM *** Truck #1 making pick-up at 6150 S-COTTAGE. ***

Figure 1.

This process for recognizing opportunities has several important features: The full planning mechanisms are invoked only when a suspended goal is activated, suggesting that it is an opportune time to incorporate it into the current agenda. In addition, the same memory for places and landmarks that is used to tell the trucks when to turn and where to stop is annotated with the suspended delivery goals that have not yet been satisfied. Finally, the overhead on this activation is trivial, in that all that TRUCKER has to do is look for a link to a goal on each of the objects it recognizes.

In TRUCKER, the experience of this successful use of opportunity is also saved in memory so that it may be exploited again. In TRUCKER's domain, where a major percentage of the orders are stable over time, certain conjuncts of orders will also tend to be stable and thus predictable. Thus, the plans for those conjuncts can be reused directly, saving both planning time (because the interactions no longer have to be reasoned about) and execution time (because an optimized version of the plan for the conjuncts is being applied). TRUCKER builds a library of routes and conjoined plans for groups of requests that have occurred together. This method of learning conjunctive plans confers three sorts of advantages to TRUCKER:

1. There is the benefit of having learned about profitable combinations of goals in the course of activity that had to be done anyway.

2. There is the benefit of having performed and saved the results of past planning for use in those situations where their utility has been demonstrated.

3. There is the benefit of reduced complexity of the remaining planning and scheduling problem because of the implicit policy decision to reuse combinations that have worked in the past.

However, there are two major limitations with TRUCKER as a testbed for the predictive encoding model. First, although opportunity recognition is crucial, there is really only one type of opportunity that can be exploited in this domain: the presence of a truck in a particular area. Second, although multiple trucks need to be tracked, and multiple orders need to be interleaved, there is not much in the way of interesting variations and interactions among plans in the delivery domain. A domain that is richer in the variety of plans that are executed and in the potential interactions among plans may provide more challenges. If the requirements for plan execution are less similar and more indirect, the need to anticipate opportunities in terms of more general indices will provide a more powerful test of the predictive encoding model.

The success of the TRUCKER program suggests that predictive encoding may be a functional approach to the problem of recognizing opportunities. However, is this approach the same as the one that human planners use? Ideally, we would like to examine the viability of the predictive encoding model as an account of the cognitive mechanisms operative in human experts. In the next section, we present several psychology experiments that address the psychological plausibility of the predictive encoding model. Specifically, the experiments examine the effects of preparing indices at the time of goal suspension on the later recognition of opportunities.

Empirical Evidence for Opportunism

A recent series of studies has addressed the specific predictions of predictive encoding in recognizing opportunities. These studies involved the domain of commonsense planning, where we could presume all of our college student participants are relatively expert. When participants are engaged in a multiple goal planning task, their ability to recognize opportunities to execute suspended goals provides a test of whether predictive encoding is a viable theory of opportunism.

The predictive encoding model previously presented provides several predictions about the recognition of opportunities:

1. that recognition is likely to occur based on features that could be anticipated from planning knowledge about the goal in general;
2. that features associated with opportunities at the time of suspension will be more likely to lead to retrieval of the pending goal;
3. that opportunities not anticipated may be missed;
4. that features requiring inferential links to connect to goals will be less likely to lead to recognition.

The predictive encoding hypothesis thus predicts specifically that opportunities to achieve goals will only be recognized at execution if they have been anticipated at the time of goal suspension.

These predictions from the predictive encoding model of opportunism distinguish it from demon-based models, and if verified, would support it in contrast to other models. Demon-based models, such as Birnbaum and Collins's (1984) "goals as agents" model, predict that all opportunities to achieve goals will be recognized regardless of encoding context. This prediction follows from the fact that the demons are free to make any inferences necessary at the time of exposure to the opportunity. Each goal "agent" can perform as much reasoning and inference as needed to attempt to connect its triggering conditions to the state of the world. Therefore, there is no cost to failing to prepare at encoding; instead, the agent can wait until it is exposed to the opportunity to form this connection. The contrasting predictions from these models are tested by (1) varying the degree to which plans to achieve pending goals are anticipated and (2) comparing whether or not recall cues that have been anticipated in the context of the earlier plans lead to more remindings than do unanticipated cues.

In order to examine these questions about opportunism, we need an experimental paradigm that will allow the creation of goals, exposure to various cues, and then measurement of retrieval of the original goals. This paradigm would allow the direct examination of the cue features leading to appropriate and inappropriate remindings of suspended goals. The method we developed involved a planning scenario including objects likely to be familiar to the college students who serve as our participants. The context of the task scenario for goal presentation was a college dormitory room. Each participant was asked to imagine that he or she must accomplish a number of goals in the dormitory room in a limited period of time. The scenario information provided was as follows:

Imagine that you are visiting your best friend, Chris, in her dormitory room. After chatting with one another for a while, you both hear a knock at the door.

A neighbor peeks her head in and summons Chris to attend a spur-of-the-moment hall meeting. Chris announces she'll be back soon and strolls down the hall to see what's up. In the first few minutes that you are alone in Chris's room, you realize that this is a perfect opportunity for you to do some snooping around. There are all kinds of things that you'd like to know about your friend Chris! And, if you are careful to leave no sign that you've tampered with anything, she'll never find you out.

Within this scenario, a series of goals were presented to the participants. These goal materials were designed with the physical setting in the dorm room in mind; consequently, they were constrained by the objects and activities likely to be possible in this setting. The set of goals presented included the following:

> You notice that Chris left her new college ring on her bureau. You try it on your finger and it gets stuck. Chris will kill you if she finds out that you were so careless with her new piece of jewelry. You need to get the ring off before Chris returns.

> You lean over Chris's bed. In the process, you manage to leave scuff marks high up on the white wall next to the bed. Though the marks are faint, they are in a very unusual and conspicuous location. You need to make the wall white again before Chris returns.

> When you open Chris's window to get some fresh air, a cold breeze blows her poster off the wall. You are not sure how the poster had previously been attached to the wall, but you do know that you need to reattach it before Chris returns.

Participants were told to read and make a mental note of each goal since they would need to retrieve the goals from memory at a later time. Thus, multiple goals were generated and remembered by the participants, and later retrieved during a cued recall task.

For the measurement of recall, a reminding paradigm was used based on prior studies of retrieving complex episodes from memory (Gentner and Landers 1985; Ratterman and Gentner 1987; Seifert, Abelson, and McKoon 1984). Descriptions of objects that might be found in this dormitory setting were presented to participants as later retrieval cues. The cued-recall task involved presenting a specific description of an object (e.g., "The only thing you find under the sink is a jar of Vaseline. If you could use the Vaseline in a plan to achieve any of your goals, record the plan(s) below"), and asking the participant to write down any prior goals that came to mind. The cue objects presented were assumed to present some salient or basic-level features during the process of comprehending the cue information. This feature information could potentially identify a particular goal previously encoded into memory, and thus retrieve a specific goal and its related information.

The set of cues was developed by identifying two different plans that could satisfy each of the ten goals. Each of these plans was then specified in terms of a specific object that would serve to execute the plan. For example, the goal of removing the stuck ring from the finger could be satisfied by lubricating the finger with Vaseline, or applying cold to the finger to shrink it using ice cubes. One of these two cues—"Vaseline" or "ice cubes"—was presented as a goal-related cue during the cued-recall test, and each was presented to half of the participants. In addition to these ten cues (one for each goal), each participant also saw the same five filler items that were not readily associated with any goal (e.g., comb, tea bags, shoe). As each cue was presented, participants were instructed to consider whether the object listed could be of any help with the goals presented earlier, and if so, to record the goal that "comes to mind." The dependent measure thus consisted of the remindings elicited by these fifteen cues.

The first experiment compared the memory task described above with a nonmemory task. In this No-Memory Control group (each of the groups in the study had over forty participants), all ten goals remained available throughout the session, so they did not need to recall the goals from memory. By comparing this group to a different Memory Control group, we could determine the effects of memory retrieval on the matching task. The reminding data were scored by counting a response as an instance of a reminding whenever it uniquely identified one of the earlier goals. The results showed that the No-Memory group generated 89% of the target goals in response to the object cues, illustrating that participants generally had little difficulty recognizing the intended uses of relevant objects. However, in the Memory Control group, participants generated about 75% of the relevant goals from the target cues. Though this number is less than the No-Memory group, this condition shows that participants were reliably able to recall many relevant goals from memory when cued by target objects.

Two other groups of participants were asked to perform some planning during the goal study phase in order to provide a comparison of goal retrieval when there was advance preparation of plans. In one planning group (the Given Plan condition), each goal was presented with a plan and a specific object for its execution; for example, for the "stuck ring" goal, the plan was "You think that if only you had some Vaseline, you might be able to grease your finger and slide the ring off." Participants in this group simply read the goal and plan information for each goal. In another planning group, the Guided Plan condition, participants were given a specific object with each goal, and were asked to generate the plan; for example, "You think that if only you had some Vaseline, you might be able to...". In this condition, the participants may work more actively to link the object with the goal to be achieved. In fact, all plans generated by participants during this phase were consistent with those intended by the experimenter (i.e., all plans matched those given in the Given Plan condition).

The mean percentage of target remindings generated in response to rehearsed versus unrehearsed cues was computed for each of the conditions. As expected, for both the Given Plan and Guided Plan conditions, a greater percentage of target goals were generated in response to rehearsed (89%) as compared with unrehearsed (71%) cues. A participant who, for example, associated Vaseline with the goal of removing a stuck ring and tape with the goal of re-hanging the fallen poster in the study phase of the experiment was more likely to be reminded of the stuck ring upon seeing "Vaseline" than to be reminded of the poster upon seeing "masking tape." This finding supports the hypothesis that associating a plan with a goal at the time of encoding facilitates opportunistic remindings.

Rehearsed cues not only led to a greater number of remindings than unrehearsed cues, they also led to a decrease in the mean number of unintended remindings generated for each cue. A greater mean number of unintended remindings was generated in response to each unrehearsed cue (32%) versus each rehearsed cue (20%) across Given and Guided Plan conditions, with an even higher rate of unintended remindings to the filler cues (44%). These differences suggest a task demand characteristic: that participants attempted to write a response to each cue, even if the response was not an appropriate one.

The study suggests that participants were more often reminded of goals when faced with anticipated cues because they had previously encoded each goal in terms of the cue. When processing the cue, the goal came to mind because it had previously been associated with the cue in memory. This predictive encoding effect is reminiscent of Tulving and Thomson's (1973) encoding specificity effect, where retrieval was shown to depend upon encoding. However, in our study, it was not simply *any* commonality between encoding and retrieval contexts that led to increased recall. Instead, the rehearsal of specific plan-related information, specified by the predictive encoding model, led to remindings from later cues. This finding contradicts a prediction from a demon-based model; if the inferences that connect an opportunity to a suspended goal are made at the time of exposure to the object, then differences in preparation should have little effect on recognition. But the results show that the specific associations formed at the time of suspension accounted for differences in recognizing opportunities.

It is possible that even less specific associations may serve to retrieve the pending goal at a later time; for example, recognition of opportunities that fit the same plan but are not instantiated in a particular specific object. Optimally, planning preparation could be more general and still produce appropriate remindings. In a second experiment, rather than rehearsing a specific plan and object, participants were either given or were asked to generate a general type of plan that would satisfy each goal. For example, in the Given Plan condition, the plan included only a type of plan: "You think that you might be able to lubricate your finger and slide the ring off." In Experiment 2, a "Guided" planning condition was not possible, since specific objects were to be avoided in the descriptions. Instead, a Generate Plan condition was added, wherein participants were asked to devise their own type of plan for each goal, without specifying a particular object that might be used to accomplish it. The instructions for plan generation made explicit the need to be general: "Keep in mind that we are not interested in what specific objects you would use to resolve each situation. Rather, we are interested in the kinds of approaches you would take. So, for example, you need not write plans like 'Use a sledgehammer to break down the door' since you could use any one of a number of objects to do so." In the Generate Plan condition, participants generated about two plans for each goal; for each participant, one of the plans generated was related to later reminding cues for around six of the ten goals.

The number of target remindings generated in response to rehearsed versus unrehearsed cues showed that, as expected, for the two conditions where advance planning occurred (the Given Plan and Generate Plan conditions), a greater percentage of target goals were recalled in response to rehearsed (82%) as compared with unrehearsed (65%) cues. Other measures, such as a free recall baseline at the end of the experiment, refute the possibility that participants were reminded of a greater percentage of goals associated with rehearsed cues simply because these goals were more available in memory. In fact, there were no differences in the groups or rehearsal conditions in overall free recall of the goals in memory.

A third experiment repeated the encoding of goals in association with potential plans to achieve them. In this study, all of the participants performed the Guided Planning task for all ten goals; for example, in studying the goal to remove the ring, they were given the object "Vaseline" and asked to generate a plan using that object to achieve the goal. But instead of seeing the identical object or a novel object as a recall cue, participants sometimes saw an object related to the specific plan they had studied. For example, in the cued reminding portion, participants who studied "Vaseline" saw either an unrehearsed cue ("ice cubes"), the rehearsed cue ("Vaseline"), or a different object that also fit the rehearsed plan ("butter"). (Note that all three cues are objects that can be used with some plan to satisfy the goal.) This manipulation will tell us whether the advantages of rehearsal are specific to the object studied, or whether participants spontaneously generated the more general plan category needed for the goal ("a kind of lubricant").

The results showed that all three types of cues resulted in more appropriate remindings than did unrelated cues. As expected, the cue actually rehearsed resulted in the most remindings (98%), while the unrehearsed related cue resulted in fewer (63%). However, the alternative version of the rehearsed cue ("butter") resulted in more remindings (76%) than the unrehearsed related cue, showing that rehearsal of a specific cue facilitated remindings from a more general version of that rehearsed cue. This finding suggests that predictive encoding does result in advantages to the planner in recognizing later opportunities: Not only is the rehearsed cue reliably tied to the suspended goal, but other unseen objects related to the rehearsed plan also result in more remindings than would occur without any rehearsal. So, attempting to encode the features related to potential opportunities benefits recognition not only of the specific case, but also more generally of items related to the rehearsed plan.

These results illustrate the advantages of preparing for later opportunities: when a participant had anticipated the type of plan for the goal, objects related to that plan were sufficient to enhance retrieval of the goal compared to unrehearsed objects. Associating a plan object with a goal *at the time of encoding* facilitated opportunistic remindings, but anticipating a type of plan more generally was also sufficient. Further, encoding specific rehearsed plans and objects resulted in remindings based on later objects that were only abstractly related to the plans studied. This finding raises questions about what level of generality is best for preparing features, because optimally, one would not want to be too general or too specific in preparing indices to goals in memory (and consequently be reminded too frequently or too infrequently to be of value). Further studies are pursuing this optimality issue through both experimental and modeling efforts.

In summary, these empirical studies support the predictive encoding hypothesis, in which planning needs are anticipated at the time of goal suspension, the goal is indexed with readily-observed features, and new experiences then retrieve the suspended goal from memory.

Conclusions

Opportunistic planning may represent a satisfying solution to the problem of how much to preplan efforts to achieve goals (as in complete planners) vs. waiting for the world to provide solutions to unsatisfied goals (as in situated approaches). The predictive encoding approach involves some preplanning to anticipate likely opportunities that may arise; however, it also involves reacting to the environment by allowing happenstance to activate pending goals. This predictive encoding solution is "intelligent" in that it takes advantage of both our ability to plan and our inability to predict the changes that might occur in the world we experience. Its consequence is that we may still miss opportunities that were potentially observable, while still maximizing the detection of opportunities that we know, from experience, are likely to occur.

Predictive encoding is important because it suggests that how people encode goal-related information is extremely important to their being able to recognize opportunities to achieve their goals. And recognizing opportunities is of great value when planning in a dynamic world. Given the continuous changes in circumstances as one moves through the environment, and the multiple-goal nature of most pursuits, it is not often possible to be aware of all of the features of the environment, let alone to stop and reason about the relevance of each to all pending goals. Predictive encoding allows a planner to retrieve goals from memory "on demand," while avoiding the need for heavy inferential processing of each new stimulus. Its functional utility for machine planners and its consistency with psychological evidence suggests predictive encoding is a viable account of a mechanism for opportunistic planning.

This work also suggests a mechanism for expertise to affect performance on other types of cognitive tasks. The ability to predict the circumstances leading to the solution of goals appears central to recognizing opportunities, but it may also affect success in generating potential diagnoses, avoiding errors, and in learning from experience. Perhaps this ability to project potential solutions helps the expert gain from experiences though comparing a strong "hypothesis" based on existing knowledge to the actual outcome of experience in the world. In this way, knowledge refinement and further learning may be driven by the active process of predicting potential paths to goal success. This suggests that specific experiences within a new domain may provide a critical training ground for the development of expertise, where experts can learn to anticipate and take advantage of opportunities to achieve their goals. And it is through ongoing experiences of attempting to satisfy goals in a dynamic world that opportunities for developing expertise can be encountered.

Acknowledgments

This work was supported by the Office of Naval Research under contracts N0014-88-K-0295 and N00014-91-J-1185 to the University of Chicago and contract N00014-91-J-1128 to the University of Michigan. Portions of this chapter have previously appeared in the *Journal of Machine Learning,* and some of the empirical results were first presented at the Cognitive Science Society meeting in 1994.

References

Bareiss, R. (1989). *Exemplar-Based Knowledge Acquisition.* San Diego: Academic Press.

Birnbaum, L.A. (1986). Integrated processing in planning. Ph.D. dissertation, Yale University, New Haven, CT.

Birnbaum, L.A & Collins, G.C. (1984). Opportunistic planning and Freudian slips. *Proceedings of the Sixth Cognitive Science Society,* Boulder, CO.

Byrne, R. (1977). Planning meals: Problem solving on a real data-base. *Cognition, 5,* 287-332.

Carbonell, J. (1981). A computational model of analogical problem solving. *Proceedings of the Seventh International Joint Conference on Artificial Intelligence.*

Gentner, D. & Landers, R. (1985). Analogical reminding: A good match is hard to find. *Proceedings of the International Conference on Cybernetics and Society* (pp. 607-

613), Tucson, AZ. New York: IEEE.

Hammond, K.J. (1989). *Case-Based Planning: Viewing Planning as a Memory Task*. San Diego: Academic Press.

Hammond, K.J., Marks, M. & Converse, T.M. (1989). Planning in an open world: A pluralistic approach. *Proceedings of the Eleventh Annual Cognitive Science Society*, Ann Arbor, Michigan.

Hammond, K.J., Converse, T.M., Marks, M. & Seifert, C.M. (1993). Opportunism and learning. *Machine Learning, 10* (3), 279-310.

Hayes-Roth, B. & Hayes-Roth, F. (1979). A cognitive model of planning. *Cognitive Science, 3*, 275-310.

Johnson, H.M. & Seifert, C.M. (1992). The role of predictive features in retrieving analogical cases. *Journal of Memory and Language, 31*, 648-667.

Kolodner, J., Simpson, R. & Sycara, K. (1985). A process model of case-based reasoning in problem-solving. *Proceedings of the Ninth International Joint Conference on Artificial Intelligence*, Los Angeles, CA.

Lesser, V.R., Fennell, R.D., Erman, L.D. & Reddy, D.R. (1975). Organization of the Hearsay-II speech understanding system. *IEEE Transactions on Acoustics, Speech and Signal Processing, ASSP-23*, 11-23.

Martin, C.E. (1990). *Direct memory access parsing*. Ph.D. dissertation, Yale University, New Haven, CT.

Patalano, A.L., Seifert, C.M. & Hammond, K.J. (1993). Predictive encoding: Planning for opportunities. *Proceedings of the Fifteenth Annual Cognitive Science Society Conference* (pp. 800-805), Boulder, CO.

Ratterman, M.J. & Gentner, D. (1987). Analogy and similarity: Determinants of accessibility and inferential soundness. *Proceedings of the Ninth Annual Meeting of the Cognitive Science Society* (pp. 23-24). Seattle, WA.

Schank, R. (1982). *Dynamic Memory: A Theory of Learning in Computers and People*. Cambridge: Cambridge University Press.

Seifert, C.M., Abelson, R.P. & McKoon, G. (1984). Being reminded of thematically similar episodes. *Proceedings of the Sixth Conference of the Cognitive Science Society* (pp. 310-314), Boulder, Colorado.

Seifert, C.M., Hammond, K.J., Johnson, H.M., Converse, T.M., MacDougal, T. & VanderStoep, S.W. (1994). Case-based learning: Predictive features in indexing. *Machine Learning, 16*, 37-56.

Smith, E.E. & Medin, D.L. (1981). *Categories and Concepts*. Cambridge, MA: Harvard Press.

Sussman, G. (1975). *A Computer Model of Skill Acquisition*, Vol. 1 of Artificial Intelligence Series. New York: American Elsevier.

Tulving, E. & Thomson, D. (1973). Encoding specificity and retrieval processes in episodic memory. *Psychological Review, 80*, 352-373.

CHAPTER 5

Issues of Expert Flexibility in Contexts Characterized by Complexity and Change

Paul J. Feltovich, Rand J. Spiro & Richard L. Coulson

Introduction

Extensive experience and the opportunity it provides for refining knowledge and for practicing skill have in the recent past been nearly definitive of expertise (e.g., Chase and Simon 1973), although criteria for the attribution of expertise have been expanded lately beyond personal experience (especially to include social and cultural factors: e.g., Agnew, Ford and Hayes; Stein, this volume). Despite the positive contribution experience makes to expertise (e.g., increases in speed and efficiency, heightened familiarity with many circumstances of a domain, the ability to identify relationships and pertinent past experiences—see, for example, Chi, Glaser and Farr 1988; Hoffman 1992), many of the changes to cognition that occur with extended practice are known to have rigidifying effects (as discussed in the next section). Under any circumstances, such inflexibility might be expected to have untoward repercussions, but these can only be exacerbated in a world characterized by complexity and rapid change. This is the kind of world in which we now find ourselves. Do individuals necessarily become more rigid in their thinking and acting at the same time they gain the experience that helps promote exceptional competence? Are there ways that flexibility can be engendered and rigidifying effects evaded? How are such developments affected by the orderliness and relative stability of the domain in which the expertise is achieved? These are some of the basic issues addressed in this chapter.

Some of the regularizing effects on cognition that can come with long-term

practice are discussed in the next section. Two examples of expert performance are presented in the third section, and these are used to characterize
two types of potential, desirable expert flexibility, one more fundamentally
adaptable than the other. In the fourth section, a tendency in thinking and
learning—the reductive bias—is discussed as a major potential impediment
(particularly in certain kinds of complex learning and practice environments)
both to sound understanding during learning and practice, and to the maintenance of adaptability. The discussion in the fifth section addresses ways
that flexibility might be maintained and enhanced as people gain experience
and skill. In the last section, we discuss why the topics of focus in this chapter are particularly germane in our current and coming world.

Rigidity and Extended Practice

It has been estimated that the development of outstanding understanding
and skill in any area of complex cognition, the kind of achievement to which
one might ascribe "expertise," requires at least ten years of diligent practice
(Hayes 1985). There are effects on cognition that come with such extended
practice that could lead to reduction in cognitive flexibility—to conditions of
relative rigidity in thinking and acting (while, as we have noted, effecting
other, more desirable gains, such as in efficiency and speed). Some of these
potentially rigidifying effects are discussed next.

Schematization/Routinization

Numerous constructs have been developed within cognitive science to describe abstractions from experiences that consolidate shared elements from
these experiences. Examples are frames (Minsky 1975), schemata (Rumelhart
and Ortony 1977), scripts (Shank and Abelson 1977), and prototypes (Rosch
and Mervis 1975). In particular, Minsky (1975, p. 212), described a frame as
"a data structure for representing a *stereotyped* situation, like being in a certain
kind of living room, or going to a child's birthday party" (emphasis ours).
Such mental structures enable carry-over of useful information from one situation to another, and they provide a kind of order for planning and for navigating in the world. But, because they are abstractions, they are reductive of
the reality from which they are abstracted, and they can be reductive of the reality to which they are applied. If this were not true, if they treated every experience as unique and in its full complexity, they would lose their value. The
reductiveness *is* part of the value. An undesirable result is that these mental
structures can cause people to see the world as *too* orderly and repeatable,
causing intrusion on a situation of expectations that are not actually there
(e.g., Bower, Black and Turner 1979; Spiro 1980), distorting memory in regu-

larizing, homogenizing ways (e.g., Bransford and Franks 1972; Bartlett 1934; Spiro 1980), or leading to an interpretation of a situation as something it is not (e.g., Feltovich, Johnson, Moller and Swanson 1984).

Functional Fixedness (and Other Fixations)

When one has thought about something or used it in a particular way for a long period of time, it can become difficult to think about that thing in novel ways or as being capable of supporting novel functions. This phenomenon was given the name functional fixedness by the psychologist Karl Duncker (1945). For example, in one of Duncker's experiments, subjects were given an assortment of objects that included a candle, a box of tacks, and a hammer. Their task was to mount the candle on a wall so that the candle could be burned safely. Few subjects thought of the best solution (given the materials available) that involved emptying the box containing the tacks and nailing it to the wall as a stand for the candle. The "container" of the tacks could not be thought of easily as something considerably different, a platform.

While functional fixedness refers classically to the constricted attribution of functionality, other types of fixation can contribute to inflexibility and, hence, to degradation of performance. All of these involve 'hanging on' to one interpretation, attribution, method, or point of view when more of these need to be considered (e.g., Cook and Woods 1994, pp. 274-277).

Automaticity/Proceduralization

Theories of skill development (e.g., Anderson 1992) typically posit a beginning of skill that is characterized by declarative (proposition-like) knowledge and ease of modification and adjustment. This is changed with extensive practice to a form of more proceduralized knowledge that is highly adapted to particular circumstances, that executes with relative ease, and, perhaps most importantly for current purposes, that is difficult to change. This is mirrored in theories of the development of cognitive automaticity in which cognition processes evolve from being consciously and deliberately controlled and controllable to becoming automatic and less amenable to regulation or modification. Significantly, for automaticity to be achieved in a cognitive activity the circumstances that elicit and drive that activity must remain stable over time (Shiffrin and Schneider 1977).

The Reductive Bias

This effect is somewhat different from the others that have been discussed, and it has not as yet been explicitly associated, as the others have, with the potential rigidifying effects of long term practice. However, our research suggests that it has great potential for reducing flexibility as individuals acquire experience. The reductive bias is a tendency for people to treat and interpret complex circumstances and topics as simpler than they really are, leading to misconception, as well as to error and to limitation in knowledge use due to inertness (e.g., Coulson, Feltovich and Spiro 1989; Feltovich, Spiro and Coulson 1989; Spiro, Feltovich, Coulson and Anderson 1989; see also Dember 1991). The reductive bias can be understood in relation to a number of dimensions, spanning a range from relative simplicity to complexity, by which concepts and phenomena can be characterized. Some examples of such dimensions are (after Feltovich, Spiro and Coulson 1993, pp. 193-194):

1. Discreteness/continuity. Do processes proceed in discernible steps, or are they unbreakable continua? Are attributes adequately describable by a small number of categories (e.g., dichotomous classifications like large/small), or is it necessary to recognize and utilize entire continuous dimensions (e.g., the full dimension of size) or large numbers of categorical distinctions?

2. Static/dynamic. Are the important aspects of a situation captured by a fixed "snapshot," or are the critical characteristics captured only by the *changes* from frame to frame? Are phenomena static and scalar or do they possess dynamic vectorial characteristics?

3. Sequentiality/simultaneity. Are processes occurring one at a time, or are multiple processes happening at the same time?

4. Mechanism/organism. Are effects traceable to simple and direct causal agents, or are they the product of more system-wide, organistic functions.[1] Can important and accurate understandings be gained by understanding just parts of the system, or must the entire system be understood for even the parts to be understood well?

5. Separability/interactiveness. Do processes occur independently or with only weak interaction, or is there strong interaction and interdependence?

6. Universality/conditionality. Do principles hold in much the same way (without the need for substantial modification) across different situations, or is there great context-sensitivity in their applicability?

7. Homogeneity/heterogeneity. Are components or explanatory schemes uniform (or similar) across a system—or are they diverse?

8. Regularity/irregularity. Is a domain characterized by a high degree of routinizability across cases, or do cases differ considerably from each other even when commonly called by the same name? Are there strong elements of symmetry and repeatable patterns in concepts and phenomena, or is there a prevalence of asymmetry and absence of consistent pattern?

9. Linearity/nonlinearity. Are functional relationships linear or nonlinear (i.e., are relationships between input and output variables proportional or nonproportional)? Can a single line of explanation convey a concept

or account for a phenomenon, or are multiple and overlapping lines of explanation required for adequate coverage?

10. Surface/deep: Are important elements for understanding and for guiding action delineated and apparent on the surface of a situation, or are they more covert, relational, abstracted?

11. Single/multiple: Do elements in a situation afford single (or just a few) interpretations, functional uses, categorizations, and so on, or do they afford many? Are multiple representations required (multiple schemas, analogies, case precedents, etc.)?

We have found that when what is to be understood is best described by the more complex, right-hand sides of these scales, it is instead frequently interpreted/treated by people as conforming to the simpler, left-hand sides. Thus, pervading the misconception, error, and inert knowledge we have found is a substrate of oversimplification. This simplificational tendency is widely present in education—on the part of the learner and in teaching and testing practices—and it is bolstered in many other ways, for example, sometimes by authorities and even by some inappropriate extensions of usually desirable practices of basic research (e.g., Coulson *et al.* 1989; Feltovich *et al.* 1989; Wimsatt 1980).

One can see that application of the reductive bias over the course of experience could have rigidifying effects like others we have discussed. For example, if principles are progressively taken to have more universal applicability than they actually do (universality/conditionality), flexible, condition-specific adjustments will not be made, nor will the need for such tailoring be recognized (e.g., Spiro, Coulson, Feltovich and Anderson 1988; Spiro, Vispoel, Schmitz, Samarapungavan and Boerger 1987). If concepts and phenomena are seen as compartmentalized (separability/interactiveness), external interacting sources contributing to the need for modification in (or even reinterpretation or reclassification of) that which is compartmentalized are again unlikely to be noticed or sought (Feltovich, Coulson, Spiro and Dawson-Saunders 1992). If only one point of view, attribution of function, or categorization (single/multiple) is routinely engaged when many are justifiable, this clearly has a constricting effect on cognition (e.g., Spiro *et al.* 1989). Despite these and other potential rigidifying effects associated with long-term practice, there is no doubt that experts at times perform with flexibility and adaptability. This is discussed next.

Evidence of Expert Flexibility

As we have discussed, there are a number of phenomena associated with long-term practice that could lead one to suspect that experts become less flexible. Indeed, there is evidence of some kinds of inflexibility in experts (e.g., Sternberg and Frensch 1992; Zeitz, this volume—but, see later discussions in this chapter). However, in some ways this is quite counterintuitive. In many areas of human performance, expertise is characterized by the ability to adapt quickly to changes in circumstances. Consider the major league baseball hitter. This individual can adapt nearly instantly to many different kinds of pitches, thrown from different angles, and at different speeds. It is the lesser hitters, those who do not make it to the highest leagues, who have always been characterized as "not being able to hit the curve ball," that is, not being able to adjust the swing appropriately to changing particular circumstances.

A prior study by Feltovich *et al.* (1984) was designed to address directly the flexibility of the expert. The research focused on reasoning within medical diagnosis and involved participants of widely different experience, ranging from new students in the area of medicine being studied (pediatric cardiology) to highly experienced and world renowned experts. These subjects diagnosed medical clinical cases which were chosen for use in the study because they had a special kind of structure, a "garden-path" structure. In particular, each case contained key information about the patient that would be discovered early by the diagnostician in working with the patient. These data would strongly suggest an incorrect diagnosis (a more classical, but incorrect, variant of the true disease—or a classical, but wrong, member of a category of diseases). Later data about the patient were inconsistent with the garden-path (wrong) disease, such that the flexible diagnostician would need to abandon this early formative diagnosis in favor of others, including the correct one.

Expert Flexibility of Type One: Extensive, Rich, Differentiated Schematization—Along with Precision in Expectations

The study showed that it was the *novices* who were rigid, in the sense of getting trapped on the garden path and not being able to adjust as they needed to (although, as we will see later, the experts exhibited another form of inflexibility). Experts were able to detect the need for a switch, and they usually also knew which disease items needed to be considered after abandoning the classical, garden path one. This ability to adjust flexibly was attributed in part to an expert memory of disease schemas that contained many different, finely discriminated variations on any one disease and many finely discriminated diseases within a disease class, or group.

Extensive, highly differentiated schematization was typified by an expert on one case who actively considered more than ten different subtle and not so subtle variations of the disease, Total Anomalous Pulmonary Venous Connection (TAPVC) en route to a successful diagnosis involving one of them. This extensiveness is reflected in his statement of a final diagnosis:

(Physician) My primary diagnosis is total anomalous pulmonary venous connection, without obstruction, and with a large atrial septal defect. The sites of total anomalous pulmonary venous connection which are consistent with this physiological picture are total anomalous pulmonary venous connection to the vertical vein, total anomalous pulmonary venous connection to the coronary sinus, total anomalous pulmonary venous connection directly to the right atrium, total anomalous pulmonary venous connection to the right superior vena cava, and total anomalous pulmonary venous connection to the azygus vein.... It is unlikely that this is total anomalous pulmonary venous connection below the diaphragm, either to the inferior vena cava, as seen in Scimitar Syndrome, uh, and extremely unlikely that it is total anomalous pulmonary venous connection to the, uh, portal venous system. Of the possible connections, the, uh, description of the anomalous vein in the right chest is most consistent with total anomalous pulmonary venous connection to the azygus vein.

(Experimenter) Do you wish to offer as many as two secondaries (diagnoses)?

(Physician) No.

Most novice subjects considered far fewer variations of the disease, and consideration of only one, the classical, text-book variant, was the most common.

Extensive differentiation of schemas in turn enabled the formation of precise clinical expectations for a particular patient and, hence, to abandonment of an hypothesis when these expectations were violated:

> The differentiation of disease knowledge aids the development of precision in the clinical expectations associated with any particular disease model. If possible distinctions among versions of a disease are not made, that is, if they are in a sense all seen as the same thing, then the associated variability in clinical manifestations among patients will be great. However, when an expert represents in memory, say, ten different versions of TAPVC, with each of these perhaps differentiated into more specific versions by severity and age of presentation in a child, then the clinical expectations associated with each of these "micro-models" can be highly specific. Precise clinical expectations, in turn, contribute to precise rules of evaluation of patient data (Feltovich et al. 1984, pp. 314).

Another striking example of expert flexibility based on extensive differentiation, from the same study, involved a case where the successful solution was highly influenced by the interpretation of a particular patient finding. If interpreted according to the "textbook," this finding (an electrocardiogram axis deviation) would lead, because of particular contextual features of the case, to the wrong diagnosis. Novices interpreted the finding according to the textbook directive and missed the case. Experts recognized that the textbook interpretation was not apt for the particular patient, adjusted the rule accordingly, and solved the case correctly (Feltovich et al. 1984, pp. 309-310).

A key point about this example of reasoning by experts, as well as the prior one involving TAPVC, is that even though the experts showed flexibility in the sense studied, their reasoning still appeared to involve working with schemas (i.e., they involved the retrieval from memory of prestored, abstracted packets of knowledge). The experts did not, for instance, appear to be piecing together a model of disease, on the fly, so to speak, using basic principles of pathophysiology (see also Patel and Ramoni, this volume). Hence, it might be proposed that one way that experts can have the advantages of schema-driven reasoning and still respond to the context sensitivity and to the great range of variability embodied in any real medical (or other kind of) case is to have a very large, well organized, and highly differentiated set of schemas that among them contains a particularized schema that is a fairly close match to any actual circumstance likely to be addressed.[2]

Expert Flexibility of Type Two: Basic Constructiveness

There have been demonstrations that experts retain a capacity to override schema-driven processing, to engage a deeper, more basic kind of reasoning from first principles *when they need to,* for instance, in particularly difficult cases (e.g., see Hoffman 1987; Patel and Ramoni, this volume; Patil, Szolovits and Schwartz 1984). The study by Feltovich and colleagues contained a case that has not until now been reported. The case involved Vena Caval to Left Atrial Connection, a condition in which the vena cava empties into the left atrium of the heart, instead of the right atrium as it normally does. This is a rare disease, and this case was used to test whether experts would engage more fundamental pathophysiological reasoning when confronted with an unusual medical condition. (Note that despite the unusualness of this case, we will argue later that situations requiring the type of basic, constructive reasoning that we will see is needed for the case are not all that uncommon, especially in modern society and work where increasingly events occur that have no clear precedents. That is, unusualness is becoming more the norm.)

The point that is pertinent for the present discussion is that almost all experts who worked on this case approached it in a standard schema-driven (albeit *rich* schema-driven) way, and they misdiagnosed the case. One expert was successful, and there appeared to be a key element to this success. This was a recognition (not elicited in the other experts) early on that something was strange about the case. The pertinent sections of verbal protocol from that case encounter are given below:

> (very first patient information) This is the case of a six year old Caucasian boy. His height is 45 inches and his weight is 45 pounds. The presenting problem is mild cyanosis discovered by a family physician during a pre-school exam.

> (physician) So, he's thought to be cyanotic at six years of age. That's really kind of unusual....

> (later) Right now, I just, I mean, I wonder if it is something unusual.... Blueness in the neonatal period can be an initial clue, but in older children it is usually a murmur.

> (still later—in response to the electrocardiogram from the case) I really kind of

expected the EKG to be normal. Notched atrial *p*-waves. I am wondering what the (heck?) is causing that. First of all, is there something that someone is over interpreting. But, if they are for real, it would mean that the left atrium is big. And that's unusual in that we didn't see it on the x-ray...and (also because I must then) try to think why we should have notched left atrial *p*-waves and blueness? You know, I guess the thing I'm thinking about is could this have been over-read and maybe something that they saw that was not really true. (But assuming it is true), it said normal axis, atrial *p*-waves, and questionable left ventricular enlargement. All that says to me is that the left atrium is big, and I am trying to see how I can fit that, use that information to come to some kind of diagnosis.

(NOTE, this appeared to be a critical incident in leading the physician to the correct diagnosis, along with some other diagnostic possibilities.)

As the physician states, cyanosis (or a degree of blueness), while not an unusual sign in the general field of pediatric cardiology, almost always is associated with congenital heart defects that are detected earlier in life—blue babies whose conditions are not detected and corrected early often do not live to be six years of age. Also, in the third episode above, the physician encountered a finding that would be so odd (given his current mental, diagnostic context) that he was first tempted to dismiss it as laboratory interpretation error.[3] But, then, choosing to take it as real, he was able to proceed to piece together an appropriate diagnosis. The appreciation of these oddities was a critical impetus for engaging a different style of reasoning that led to the successful conclusion.

Expertise Flexibility of Types One and Two and the Need to Detect Unusualness

One way to characterize expertise is that with long term experience the expert is one who has brought more and more of his or her world into the realm of the familiar. Even though much in this realm is context dependent, the expert has been able to see and codify (in schema-like structures) much of these relevant contexts and their effects (e.g., Chase and Simon 1973, Feltovich 1983). This enables a kind of rich knowledge-based flexibility—so long as the expert is functioning broadly within his or her usual domain and that domain is relatively stable. This was the kind of expert flexibility observed most often in the Feltovich *et al.* (1984) study.[4] However, there was some evidence for a second kind of even more flexible reasoning that was more fragmentary, basic, and constructive. This distinction between a normalized expertise and a more fundamental one has also been noted by Woods and colleagues in their studies of cognition in the workplace:

> Interestingly, practitioners are acutely aware of how deficient their rules of thumb may be and how certain situations may require abandoning the cognitively easy method in favor of more cognitively demanding "deep thinking" (Woods, Johannesen, Cook and Sarter 1994, p. 66).

However, for this more basic kind of reasoning to be engaged, it appears that there must be some tip-off to the expert that the current situation is outside the normal realm of inquiry. Otherwise, it is schema-driven processing as usual, even when this leads to bad outcomes. In this regard, Woods and colleagues go on to point out that failure to recognize when simplificational strategies are not adequate (in general) and when a situation is not within rountinized, normal practice and, hence, requires "deeper thinking" (in particular), are among the major contributors to workplace tragedies and mishaps (even when these involve highly experienced people).

Worlds One and Two and Their Implications for Expertise in Context: The Detrimental Role of the Reductive Bias

If we collect up all the items on the left-hand side of the dimensions of difficulty presented earlier, the picture painted by these can be seen a describing a kind of world. We will call this World One.[5] The epistemic stance associated with World One we refer to as the Reductive Worldview:

World One's *Reductive Worldview*
   discrete, static, sequential, mechanistic, separable, universal, homogeneous, regular, linear, surface, single

Stringing together the more complex right-hand descriptors yields a quite different kind of world. We call this one World Two and its associated epistemic stance the Complex Worldview:

World Two's *Complex Worldview*
   continuous, dynamic, simultaneous, organic, interactive, conditional, heterogeneous, irregular, nonlinear, deep, multiple

Our research suggests that World Two is much harder for people to understand than World One. When what is to be understood (e.g., a case, a concept, or a phenomenon) has features of World Two, there is a strong inclination instead to try to treat it as World One-like. In doing so, various reductive operations are engaged. We have referred to this general tendency as the reductive bias, and we have referred to individual operations of simplification as reductive biases (e.g., Feltovich et al. 1989; 1993).[6] Examples of the latter are the static bias, in which the dynamic phenomena are interpreted more statically; the step-wise bias, in which continuous processes are instead taken to occur in disjointed phases or steps; and the restricted perspective bias, in which too few of the legitimate different points of view, interpretations, or categorizations are considered.

The reductive bias can lead to misconception and error in domains that are complex in the sense that they are pervaded by such characteristics as dynamics, continuity, high interactivity, and ill-structuredness (i.e., domains that are characterized by the complex, right-hand sides of the dimensions of difficulty presented above). Biology, for example, is such a domain, and research on biological cognition has shown misconception (about difficult biological concepts) to be rather common, even at times among experts (e.g., Coulson *et al.* 1989; Feltovich *et al.* 1989, 1993; Feltovich, Coulson, Spiro and Adami 1994; Feltovich, Spiro and Coulson, in press; Patel, Kaufmann and Magder 1991; Myers, Feltovich, Coulson, Adami and Spiro 1990; Norman, Trott, Brooks and Smith 1994; Spiro *et al.* 1989).

The operation of the reductive bias can be rigidifying, if only because it can preclude engagement of a whole realm of thinking—a deep understanding of a realm of phenomena (those associated with World Two). The reductive bias forces thinking and understanding into highly constricted and limiting "slots." Based on our research, we can now recognize that a great deal of the novice (and even expert) performance in the Feltovich *et al.* (1984) study can be characterized as exhibiting various forms of the reductive bias. For example, some novices in the study treated disease as more static (an example of the static bias) than it really is, contributing to their rigidity when confronted with the real world variation of disease. Experts could comprehend any disease in a more fluid, dynamic, developmental way, with variation in disease depending on a formidable number of contextual factors including age of the patient, severity of the disease, fine structural distinctions in the disease, stage of progression of the disease, and many others. This understanding of disease as dynamic and variable undergirded the vast and rich schema base that the expert could bring to bear on a problem. Yet, this rich knowledge base was not sufficient at times, and a deeper kind of thinking appeared necessary.

We propose that, in addition to limiting understanding, the interpretation of the world in a reductive, World One-like way will also contribute to missing some cues to oddity/novelty that should suggest to an individual that a more basic, constructive, nonschema-based mode of mental operation is called for (see the earlier discussion in the previous section). Some examples: If a person sees a dynamic situation as more static, he or she may not see cues to unusualness that are based on *change*. If a person sees what are really highly interactive processes as being independent, he or she may not see cues to oddity that are based on the *interaction of components*. If a person sees what is in reality a continuous and integrated process instead as a sequence of relatively independent snapshots, he or she may miss cues based on incongruity with the integrated, emerging whole "story." (The expert physician's detection of incongruity of this kind was, we believe, a major reason for his picking up the cue to unusualness, cyanosis on a school physical, in the medical case that was reported on previously). If a person sees only the literal or superficial aspects of a situation, he or she may not notice cues to unusualness or difference that exist only at a more *abstract, "deeper" level* (cf. Chi, Feltovich and Glaser 1981), and so forth.

Thus far in this chapter we have discussed psychological mechanisms that suggest that with large amounts of practice, people can become rigid in various ways. However, we have also pointed to examples of experts who demonstrated flexibility, both of the structural kind (Expert Flexibility of Type One) associated with a large set of highly differentiated schemas (that results from extensive experience with a wide variety of instances/cases in a circumscribed domain), and, in one instance, a second kind of more fundamental, constructive flexibility (Expert Flexibility of Type Two).

Even though extended practice of some task can engage mechanisms leading to rigidity, practicing with lots of variations of the task is one way to inculcate a kind of flexibility, the structural kind. Under this argument, the baseball hitter we spoke of earlier has (deliberately) practiced hitting all the different variations of the pitched ball. Our physicians had practiced working with lots of different, even relatively odd, cases of heart disease, as subspecialty practitioners for many years in a major university-based and referral-based medical center. So, it appears that at least a kind of flexibility (which is limited—recall the erroneous performance of most of the experts on the second pediatric cardiology case, the one involving VCLAC) can be attained: 1) through practice, 2) on a wide sampling of cases, and 3) in a relatively constricted (and stable) domain of activity.

However, while wide sampling of cases within a domain is a necessary condition, it is probably not a sufficient condition for acquisition of this kind of flexibility (Type One). Some people could have the same opportunity, but end up thinking in an ossified manner. Or alternatively, by becoming progressively ossified, their performance might progressively deteriorate, leading to their loss of constituency—loss of their backing in various forms—leading to loss of opportunity to engage in rich experiences affording the opportunity to progress (Agnew *et al.*; Stein, this volume). In short, they might just not be able to succeed, and hence not be able to remain and practice, in the big leagues of baseball or in the world-class academic medical center.

Cognitive Flexibility Theory and the Expansive Possibility: Successfully Navigating World Two

If many people find it difficult to understand concepts and phenomena characterized by the descriptors of World Two, and if these failures of understanding can be a contributor to becoming rigid as experience is acquired, steps need to be taken to help people deal nonreductively with World Two (and the kinds of phenomena and structures characteristic of it). From our research over the last decade, we suspect that a major factor in determining whether experience will yield constriction or expansiveness is the degree of engagement of the reductive bias during opportunities for practice (Coulson, Feltovich and Spiro, in press). Hence, we propose that for individuals to retain flexibility as they gain experience and expertise, they must engage, in their ongoing practice and learning, measures that are antireductive and that consistently serve to open up knowledge and thought—this is in order to counteract forces tending to close these down. Such antireductive measures underlie educational approaches and tools we are building based on Cognitive Flexibility Theory (e.g., Spiro et al. 1987; Spiro et al. 1988; Spiro, Feltovich, Jacobson and Coulson 1991a,b; Spiro and Jehng 1990). We now address some of the ways tenets of Cognitive Flexibility Theory can be carried over to almost all learning and practice experiences.

First, learning for flexibility and for understanding in World Two involves adopting a personal epistemology, or worldview about knowledge and its application (as discussed earlier), that recognizes that what is to be learned can be messy, irregular, and exceptional. There is growing evidence that people vary in how they view their world and learning. For example, there is great variation in how regular and simple the world appears to them (Spiro, Feltovich and Coulson, in press). There is also variation in how difficult they believe learning to be (Schommer 1993). Quality of learning can be diminished when knowledge and learning are viewed in an oversimplified manner (e.g., Ainley 1993; Feltovich et al. 1989; Schommer 1993, 1995; Spiro et al. 1989). In addition, many processes associated with education and training reinforce simplistic views, for example, assessment and testing methods (e.g., Coulson et al. 1989; Fleming and Chambers 1983; Porter 1989). Devices and materials that are engaged in the learning process (e.g., certain kinds of hypertext) can themselves convey messages about the degree of orderliness and simplicity of knowledge and its use in the world, simply by the way they are structured and afford interaction with the learner (Mishra, Spiro and Feltovich, in press).

There is considerable pressure to oversimplify, but the learner/experiencer who would successfully remain flexible and gain the ability to become even more so needs to overcome this. At the heart of such an effort is the need to develop an underlying epistemic stance appropriate to World Two. In this regard, there is some emerging evidence that simply instructing learners about the various facets of complexity of knowledge and learning, as advocated by Cognitive Flexibility Theory, can contribute to better, more flexibly-usable learning of complex materials (e.g., Wang 1993). Of course, going beyond mere telling would be expected to have even greater facilitative effects.

An important characteristic of this epistemology for World Two is that it helps the individual maintain an open stance toward episodes of learning and experiencing. That is, rather than seeing knowledge as closed, the individual comes to expect variability, novelty, and interdependence in knowledge and its uses. He or she would look for connection, as well as for legitimate ways to compartmentalize; for change and patterns of change, as well as for what remains the same; for exceptions as well as rules; for context sensitivity (and its basic determinants), as well as more universal application of concepts and principles; for the *many* lessons provided by any rich learning experience, and not some canonical *one*; and so forth. The more some domain that is to be learned and navigated is characterized by the descriptors of World Two (as we argue many already are, and even more are bound to become), the more crucial such an expansive learning stance will be.

It will help the learner who would stay flexible (and expansive) to have and nurture a large "toolbox" of cognitive (and interpersonal) processes and methods to bring to bear in complex learning and understanding. This involves multiple ways of representing concepts and phenomena (Spiro *et al.* 1988, 1989); multiple languages and other formalisms; multiple connections among elements of knowledge; the ability to adopt multiple perspectives and frames of reference; and the ability to reason from multiple past cases and precedents (in addition to being able to apply multiple concepts and principles to cases in a context sensitive way). Also, the ability to utilize and collaborate with other people, yet another kind of multiplicity, becomes more important as the complexity of what is to be learned and understood increases (e.g., Feltovich, Spiro, Coulson and Feltovich, in press; Lesgold and Katz 1992).

This active inclination to see things many ways, to explain in many ways, to use in many ways, to connect in many ways, and so forth, can provide protection from the various forms of maladaptive rigidity discussed in the second section of this chapter. For example, Woods and colleagues (1994, pp. 76-77) propose multiple perspectives and modes of representation for helping people avoid fixation errors in the workplace.

Characteristics of World Two (e.g., simultaneity, irregularity, interactiveness, and conditionality) impose a complex relationship between abstracted knowledge (e.g., principles and rules) and the situations or cases where this knowledge needs to be applied (e.g., in problem solving). In other works, we have described this relationship as "ill-structure" (e.g., Spiro *et al.* 1988). In particular, many concepts, principles, or schemas (i.e., various kinds of abstracted knowledge), interacting in context-sensitive ways, are pertinent in any case of knowledge application. Furthermore, the collection of concepts etc. that is pertinent to a case may vary widely across cases all classified as being of the same type (e.g., different cases of hypertension in medicine—see Feltovich *et al.* 1992, for some detailed expositions of ill-structure in the field of medicine). Put another way, there are no intact, wide-scope abstractions that capture all of the goings-on of a case—no abstractions from which these particular happenings emerge as derivations. In addition, cases that may seem similar at some level of abstraction can be critically different in their particulars.

Because of these characteristics of ill-structuredness, Cognitive Flexibility Theory advocates a close coupling in learning and practice between abstractions, such as concepts and schemas, and their actual instantiations in real-world cases—reflecting their co-constituting nature (see Feltovich *et al.* 1992, for greater detail about this process of integrating abstractions and cases). The theory proposes that for a person to achieve and maintain cognitive flexibility, learning and experience should have two additional characteristics. First, any abstraction (e.g., concept or principle) must be explored in application across many diverse cases, to reveal the tailoring of the abstraction necessary to accommodate different particular situations. Second, actual cases (where numerous abstractions such as schemas or concepts are pertinent for any individual case) must be explored to gain a sense of how sets of concepts (and other abstractions) influence and modify each other in context. These kinds of exercises in learning and practicing have at least two intended ends. One is to undermine the perceived power of abstracted conceptual knowledge by revealing its context-sensitive limitations. Another is to inculcate a sense of this context-sensitivity itself and a sense of "how cases go" in a given domain, so that individuals learn how to piece together partial conceptual and case understandings to fit some particular new challenge. In this way, learning and practice guided by the tenets of Cognitive Flexibility Theory attempt to avoid another potential source of rigidity associated with increasing experience—that associated with an overreliance on intact, prepackaged schema-like knowledge structures that will not account for enough of the variability in the ill-structured domains of World Two.

Expert Flexibility and the New Workplace

The main issues that have been addressed in this chapter—the potential increase in inflexibility with the development of expertise, and how to engender flexibility despite this—are particularly timely. In part, this is because of changes that are now occurring in the way we work and live. The world of work is undergoing profound change, and these developments can be extended from the workplace to our societies in general, our "lifeplaces." The changes are dramatic enough that they have captured the attention of numerous study groups and analysts (e.g., Carnevale 1991; Davis and Botkin 1994; Hamal and Prahalad 1994; Handy 1990; Quinn 1992; Rifkin 1995; SCANS 1991; Tichy and Sherman 1994). There appears to be considerable commonality in the findings and predictions of these observers about current happenings and near-future directions. It is not necessary (or possible) to give a full account here (see Shalin, 1994, for an extensive discussion of the new workplace, as well as its implications for basic cognitive science research). Suffice it to say that World Two, as presented in this chapter, describes features of the new workplace (and general conditions of society) better than World One does.

The era of work and life from which we are now passing (and that has been in place since about the turn of twentieth century) aligned fairly well with the attributes of World One, for instance in the separability, sequentiality, uniformity, and linearity of processes (e.g., the assembly line and the pyramidic, hierarchical management structure) and in the relative uniformity of the products produced. It is also a world better suited to the regularization, schematization, relative constancy, and automaticity that can come with long term practice and experience. This world was one in which the route to expertise was relatively well served by accretion of a large knowledge base of differentiated and well organized schemas (Expert Flexibility of Type One).

It is clear that World Two describes better than World One the new kind of work and life that is already in place to some extent near the dawn of the 21st century and that is predicted to become even more pervasive. For example, the new workplace emphasizes such things as the need for dealing with deep understanding, the ubiquity of change and novelty, the simultaneous occurrence of processes, the interactiveness and interdependence of processes and people, the demand for customization/particularization in both products and procedures, nonhierarchical-nonlinear management structures, and the like. But these are precisely the kinds of things our research has shown that people, even experts, have difficulty understanding and managing—these are the kinds of processes and phenomena that are susceptible to the reductive bias. Such characteristics also militate against the usefulness and adequacy of fixed, pre-assembled cognitive structures (e.g., schemas) and routinized processes that can develop with practice—the same ones that are so helpful in dealing with World One. That is, the approach to development of expertise and to being able to navigate context-sensitivity that involves the creation of large numbers of differentiated schemas is also undermined to some extent; the new world is simply too fluid. In this new setting, the need for Expert Flexibility of Type Two is accentuated.

Not all of expertise should, or needs to, involve flexibility and change; elements of stability and continuity are also necessary. This is true of any system participating in life, from the genome to societies (e.g., Feltovich, Spiro, Coulson and Myers-Kelson 1995; Smith 1995; Waldrop 1992). Such systems need a degree of flexibility in order to respond to change and new challenges. However, there must also be stability, in order to take advantage of past experience and to retain assets that have proven themselves over time to be useful; we do not want to continuously jump-start our understanding of the world completely anew. Shalin et al. (this volume) describe nicely some of the benefits of relatively stable normal (and normative) "accepted methods," even in experts. These advantages include speed, support for communication of various sorts among work team members, the ability to track progress, and others. Those authors also note the importance of recognizing when the "usual" will not suffice. While both stability and flexibility are always necessary in a system, it is the balance between them for any current circumstance that is key. Part of our argument is that we are now in an era where this balance needs to swing more toward flexibility. As stated before, this is a time in which the "unusual" is becoming much more usual. Cognitive Flexibility Theory and educational approaches resulting from it have been responses to this perception of the need for greater flexibility (as well as to the related failures of learning that we have observed).

In conjunction with its requirement of greater flexibility, the nature of World Two and its relation to the new workplace raise a fundamental and intriguing question about the development of expertise in the future. In the past, a route to expertise involved practicing some relatively circumscribed task for many years. Likewise, most of the expertise that has been studied has involved endeavors where the fundamental "rules" do not change rapidly. For example, the basic rules of bridge and chess do not change at all, allowing accomplished adaptation to them over time. This is emphasized in the studies on bridge playing by Sternberg (1992; also Zeitz, this volume) noted earlier. Experts showed decrement in performance when the fundamental structure of the game was altered. What happens when there is no longer any stable "thing" to practice—when the fluidity of work does not have people doing any one kind of task for very long, when whole careers change every few years, and so forth? Proceduralization and automaticity require fairly stable environments for their development. It may be that such environments will not occur as frequently as they have in the past. A fundamental question is, can people practice *being flexible,* accruing benefits anything like those that in the past have been associated with practicing more delimited and predictable tasks?

Acknowledgments

Rachael Brady, Joan Feltovich, Ken Ford, Robert Hoffman, Tim Koschmann, Ann Myers, Valerie Shalin, and Paul Wohlmuth read drafts of this chapter and made many useful suggestions. Flaws that remain are, of course, our own. Preparation of this chapter was supported in part by a grant from the National Science Foundation (RED-9253157). Any opinions, findings, and conclusions or recommendations expressed in this material are those of the authors and do not necessarily reflect the views of the funding agency.

Notes

1. See Feltovich *et al.* 1989; Pepper 1942; White 1973, for more details about this distinction.

2. See O'Hara and Shadbolt (this volume) who discuss just this issue in relation to being able to find useful, extant problem solving models in libraries of such models that can be used "off the shelf" for designing expert systems.

3. Note in the EKG episode how the physician, although working alone here, is tied to parts of his broader context, in this instance the capability (expertise) of the original EKG reader. It was not uncommon for a physician participant to inquire about the identity of an x-ray or EKG reader and, depending on who that person was, accept, question, adjust, or even override that reader's report of findings. In a sense, a particular physician might be part of the constituency of some readers as experts, but not part of that constituency for other readers/interpreters (Agnew *et al.*, this volume). This episode, while coming from a study of expertise of the classical psychological variety, hints at some of the wider social and cultural ramifications of expertise explored in the present volume.

4. Although, in this study, this type of flexibility was seen only in experts, Arocha and Patel (1995) suggest that the foundations for this kind of flexibility can start to be laid down over the course of undergraduate medical education.

5. Our use of the terms "World One" and "World Two" is unrelated to the three "Worlds" proposed by Popper (1972).

6. What we call reductive biases are tendencies or inclinations in *conceptual* understanding and reasoning. Despite some similarity, these are different from biases that have been identified in the fields of judgement and decision making (see, e.g., Kahneman, Slovic and Tversky 1982; Elstein 1988, for discussions of the latter).

References

Ainley, M.D. (1993). Styles of engagement with learning: Multidimensional assessment of their relationship with strategy use and school achievement. *Journal of Educational Psychology, 85,* 395-405.

Anderson, J.R. (1982). Acquisition of cognitive skill. *Psychological Review, 18,* 396-406.

Arocha, J.F. & Patel, V.L. (1995). Novice diagnostic reasoning in medicine: Accounting for evidence. *Journal of the Learning Sciences, 4(4),* 355-384.

Bartlett, F.C. (1932). *Remembering.* Cambridge, UK: Cambridge University Press.

Bower, G.J., Black, J. & Turner, T. (1979). Scripts in memory for text. *Cognitive Psychology, 11,* 177-220.

Bransford, J.D. & Franks, J.J. (1972). The abstraction of linguistic ideas. *Cognitive Psychology, 2,* 331-350.

Carnevale, A.P. (1991). *America and the New Economy.* Alexandria, VA: American Society for Training & Development (in conjunction with the U.S. Dept. of Labor).

Chase, W.G. & Simon, H.A. (1973). Perception in chess. *Cognitive Psychology, 4,* 55-81.

Chi, M.T.H., Feltovich, P.J. & Glaser, R. (1981). Categorization and representation of physics problems by experts and novices. *Cognitive Science, 5,* 121-152.

Chi, M.T.H., Glaser, R. & Farr, M.J. (1988). *The Nature of Expertise.* Hillsdale, NJ: Lawrence Erlbaum.

Cook, R.I. & Woods, D.D. (1994). Operating at the sharp end: The complexity of human error. In M.S. Bogner (Ed.), *Human Error in Medicine.* Hillsdale, NJ: Lawrence Erlbaum.

Coulson, R.L., Feltovich P.J. & Spiro R.J. (1989). Foundations of a misunderstanding of the ultrastructural basis of myocardial failure: A reciprocation network of oversimplifications. *Journal of Medicine and Philosophy, 14,* 109-146.

Coulson, R.L., Feltovich, P.J. & Spiro, R.L. (in press). Cognitive flexibility in medicine: An application to the recognition and understanding of hypertension. *Advances in Health Sciences Education.*

Davis, S. & Botkin, J. (1994). *The Monster Under the Bed.* New York: Simon & Schuster.

Dember, W.N. (1991). Cognition, motivation, and emotion: Ideology revisited. In R.R. Hoffman & D. Palermo (Eds.), *Cognition and the Symbolic Processes* (pp. 153-162). Hillsdale, NJ: Lawrence Erlbaum.

Duncker, K. (1945). On problem solving. *Psychological Monographs, 58,* Whole No. 70.

Elstein, A.S. (1988). Cognitive processes in clinical inference and decision making. In D. Turk & P. Salovey (Eds.), *Reasoning, Inference, and Judgement in Clinical Psychology.* New York: Free Press/Macmillan.

Feltovich, P.J. (1983). Expertise: Reorganizing and refining knowledge for use. *Professions Education Researcher Notes* (A publication of the American Educational Research Assoc., Division I),4(3), 5-9.

Feltovich, P.J., Coulson, R.L., Spiro, R.J. & Adami, J.F. (1994). Conceptual understanding and stability, and knowledge shields for fending off conceptual change. Final Report, Cognitive Science Division, Office of Naval Research, Contract No. N00014-88-K-0077. [Also, Tech. Rep. #7, Dec. 1994, Conceptual Knowledge Research Project, SIU School of Medicine, Cognitive Science Division, Springfield, IL 62702.]

Feltovich, P.J., Coulson, R.L., Spiro, R.J. & Dawson-Saunders, B.K. (1992). Knowledge application and transfer for complex tasks in ill-structured domains: Implications for instruction and testing in biomedicine. In D. Evans & V.L. Patel (Eds.), *Advanced Models of Cognition for Medical Training and Practice* (pp. 212-244). Berlin: Springer-Verlag.

Feltovich, P.J., Johnson, P.E., Moller, J.H. & Swanson, D.B. (1984). LCS: The role and development of medical knowledge in diagnostic expertise. In W.J. Clancey & E.H. Shortliffe (Eds.), *Readings in Medical Artificial Intelligence: The First Decade* (pp. 275-319). Reading, MA: Addison Wesley.

Feltovich, P.J., Spiro, R.J. & Coulson, R.L. (1989). The nature of conceptual understanding in biomedicine: The deep structure of complex ideas and the development of misconceptions. In D.A. Evans & V.L. Patel (Eds.), *Cognitive Science in Medicine: Biomedical Modeling* (pp. 111-172). Cambridge, MA: MIT (Bradford) Press.

Feltovich, P.J., Spiro, R.J. & Coulson, R.L. (1993). Learning, teaching and testing for complex conceptual understanding. In N. Frederiksen & I. Bejar (Eds.), *Test Theory for a New Generation of Tests* (pp. 181-217). Hillsdale, NJ: Lawrence Erlbaum.

Feltovich, P.J., Spiro, R.J. & Coulson, R.L. (in press). A scheme for predicting difficulty of conceptual change: An example application to the concept of opposition to blood flow (cardiovascular impedance). In A. Pace (Ed.), *Beyond Prior Knowledge: Issues in Text Processing and Conceptual Change.* Norwood, NJ: Ablex.

Feltovich, P.J., Spiro, R.J., Coulson, R.L. & Feltovich, J. (in press). Collaboration within and among minds: Mastering complexity, individually and in groups. In T. Koschmann (Ed.), *CSCL: Theory and practice of an Emerging Paradigm.* Mahwah, NJ: Lawrence Erlbaum.

Feltovich, P.J., Spiro, R.J., Coulson, R.L. & Myers-Kelson, A. (1995). The reductive bias and the crisis of text (in the law). *Journal of Contemporary Legal Issues, 6,* 187-212.

Fleming, M. & Chambers, B. (1983). Teacher-made tests: Windows on the classroom. In W.F. Hathaway (Ed.), *New Directions in Testing and Measurement* (pp. 29-38). San Francisco: Jossey-Bass.

Hamel, G. & Prahalad, C.K. (1994). *Competing for the Future.* Boston, MA: Harvard Business School Press.

Handy, C. (1989). *The Age of Unreason.* Boston, MA: Harvard Business School Press.

Hayes, J.R. (1985). Three problems of teaching general skills. In J.W. Segal, S.F. Chipman & R. Glaser (Eds.), *Thinking and Learning Skills: Relating Instruction to Research* (Vol. 1, pp. 391-405). Hillsdale, NJ: Lawrence Erlbaum.

Hoffman, R.R. (1987, Summer). The problem of extracting the knowledge of experts from the perspective of experimental psychology. *AI Magazine, 8,* 53-64.

Hoffman, R.R. (1992). *The Psychology of Expertise: Cognitive Research and Empirical AI.* New York: Springer-Verlag.

Kahneman, D.L., Slovic, P. & Tversky, A. (Eds.). (1982). *Heuristics and Biases.* New York: Cambridge University Press.

Lesgold, A.M. & Katz, S. (1992). Models of cognition and educational technologies: Implications for medical training. In D. Evans & V.L. Patel (Eds.), *Advanced Models of Cognition for Medical Training and Practice* (pp. 256-264). Berlin: Springer-Verlag.

Minsky, M. (1975). A framework for representing knowledge. In P.H. Winston (Ed.), *The Psychology of Computer Vision* (pp. 211-277). New York: McGraw-Hill.

Mishra, P., Spiro, R.J. & Feltovich, P.J. (In press). Technology, representation, and cognition: The prefiguring of knowledge in Cognitive Flexibility Hypertexts. In H. van Oostendorp (Ed.), *Cognitive Aspects of Electronic Text Processing.* Norwood, NJ: Ablex.

Myers, A.C., Feltovich, P.J., Coulson, R.L., Adami, J.F. & Spiro, R.J. (1990). Reductive biases in the reasoning of medical students: An investigation in the domain of acid-base balance. In R.J. Heimstra, A.J.J.A. Scherbier & R.P. Zwierstra (Eds.), *Teaching and Assessing Clinical Competence.* Groningen, The Netherlands: BoekWerk.

Norman, G.R., Trott, A.D., Brooks, L.R. & Smith, E.K.M. (1994). Cognitive differences in clinical reasoning related to postgraduate training. *Teaching & Learning in Medicine, 6,* 114-120.

Patel, V.L., Kaufman, D.R. & Magder, S. (1991). Causal explanation of complex physiological concepts by medical students. *International Journal of Science Education, 13,* 171-185.

Patil, R.S., Szolovits, P. & Schwartz, W.B. (1984). Causal understanding of patient illness in medical diagnosis. In W.J. Clancey & E.H. Shortliffe (Eds.), *Readings in Medical Artificial Intelligence: The First Decade* (pp. 339-360). Reading, MA: Addison Wesley.

Pepper, S. (1942). *World Hypotheses.* Berkeley, CA: University of California Press.

Piore, M. & Sabel, C. (1984). *The Second Industrial Devide.* New York: Basic Books.

Popper, K.R. (1972). *Objective Knowledge: An Evolutionary Approach.* Oxford, UK: Clarendon Press.

Porter, A. (1989). A curriculum out of balance: The case of elementary school mathematics. *Educational Researcher, 18,* 9-15.

Quinn, J.B. (1992). *Intelligent Enterprise.* New York: Free Press.

Rifkin, J. (1995). *The End of Work.* New York: G.P. Putnam's Sons.

Rosch, E. & Mervis, C.B. (1975). Family resemblances: Studies in the internal structures of categories. *Cognitive Psychology, 7,* 573-605.

Rumelhart, D.E. & Ortony, A. (1977). The representation of knowledge in memory. In R.C. Anderson, R.J. Spiro & W.E. Montague (Eds.), *Schooling and the Acquisition of Knowledge* (pp. 99-135). Hillsdale, NJ: Lawrence Erlbaum.

SCANS. (1991). What work requires of schools: A SCANS report for America 2000. Washington, DC: U.S. Dept. of Labor, Secretary's Commission on Achieving Necessary Skills.

Schommer, M. (1993). Epistemological development and academic performance among secondary students. *Journal of Educational Psychology, 85,* 406-411.

Schommer, M. & Walker, K. (1995). Are epistemological beliefs similar across domains? *Journal. of Educational Psychology, 87,* 424-432.

Shalin, V.L. (1994). Human performance in the complex workplace: Implications for basic research in cognitive science. Report to NSF from workshop sponsored under Grant No. SBR-9216235, Sept. 11 & 12, 1992, Arlington, VA. [Working Paper No. 94-001, Dept. of Industrial Engineering, State University of New York at Buffalo.]

Shiffrin, R.M. & Schneider, W. (1977). Controlled and automatic information processing: Perceptual learning, automatic attending, and a general theory. *Psychological Review, 84,* 127-190.

Smith, J.W. (1995). The biological basis of attunement. *Journal of Contemporary Legal Issues, 6,* 361-371.

Spiro, R.J. (1980). Constructive processes in prose comprehension and recall. In R.J. Spiro, B.C. Bruce & W.F. Brewer (Eds.), *Theoretical Issues in Reading Comprehension* (pp. 245-278). Hillsdale, NJ: Lawrence Erlbaum.

Spiro, R.J., Coulson, R.L., Feltovich, P.J. & Anderson, D.K. (1988). Cognitive flexibility theory: Advanced knowledge acquisition in ill-structured domains. In *Proceedings of the 10th Annual Conference of the Cognitive Science Society* (pp. 375-383). Hillsdale, NJ: Lawrence Erlbaum. [Also appears in R.B. Ruddel, M.R. Ruddell & H. Singer, (Eds.). (1994). *Theoretical Models and Processes of Reading* (4th ed.). Newark, DE: International Reading Association.]

Spiro, R.J., Feltovich, P.J., Coulson, R.L. & Anderson, D.K. (1989). Multiple analogies for complex concepts: Antidotes for analogy-induced misconception in advanced knowledge acquisition. In S. Vosniadou & A. Ortony (Eds.), *Similarity and Analogical Reasoning* (pp. 498-531). Cambridge, MA: Cambridge University Press.

Spiro, R.J., Feltovich, P.J. & Coulson, R.L. (in press). Two epistemic worldviews: Prefigurative schemas and learning in complex domains. *Journal of Applied Cognitive Psychology.*

Spiro, R.J., Feltovich, P.J., Jacobson, M. & Coulson, R.L. (1991a). Cognitive flexibility, constructivism, and hypertext: Advanced knowledge acquisition in ill-structured domains. *Educational Technology, 31 (5),* 24-33. [Also appears in T.M. Duffy & D. H. Jonassen (Eds.). (1992). *Constructivism and the Technology of Instruction.* Hillsdale, NJ: Lawrence Erlbaum.]

Spiro, R.J., Feltovich, P.J., Jacobson, M. & Coulson, R.L. (1991b). Knowledge representation, content specification, and the development of skill in situation-specific knowledge assembly: Some constructivist issues as they relate to cognitive flexibility theory and hypertext. *Educational Technology, 31 (9),* 22-25. [Also appears in T.M. Duffy & D. H. Jonassen (Eds.). (1992). *Constructivism and the Technology of Instruction.* Hillsdale, NJ: Lawrence Erlbaum.]

Spiro, R.J. & Jehng, J.C. (1990). Random access instruction: Theory and technology for the nonlinear and multidimensional traversal of complex subject matter. In D. Nix & R.J. Spiro (Eds.), *Cognition, Education, and Multimedia* (pp. 163-205). Hillsdale, NJ: Lawrence Erlbaum.

Spiro, R.J., Vispoel, W., Schmitz, J., Samarapungavan, A. & Boerger, A. (1987). Knowledge acquisition for application: Cognitive flexibility and transfer in complex content domains. In B.C. Britton (Ed.), *Executive Control Processes* (pp. 177-199). Hillsdale, NJ: Lawrence Erlbaum.

Sternberg, R.J. & Frensch, P.A. (1992). On being an expert: A cost-benefit analysis. In R.R. Hoffman (Ed.), *The Psychology of Expertise: Cognitive Research and Empirical AI*. New York: Springer-Verlag.

Tichy, N.M. & Stratford, S.S. (1993). *Control Your Own Destiny or Somebody Else Will*. New York: HarperCollins.

Waldrop, M.M. (1992). *Complexity*. New York: Simon & Schuster.

Wang, S.R. (1993). The effects of cognitive styles and orientation procedures on learner performance in a complex computer-based learning environment. Unpublished doctoral dissertation, University of Colorado-Denver.

Watkins, K.E. & Marsick, V.J. (1993). *Sculpting the Learning Organization*. San Francisco: Jossey-Bass.

White, D.L. (1973). *Metahistory*. Baltimore, MD: Johns-Hopkins University Press.

Wimsatt, W.C. (1980). Reductionistic research strategies and their biases in the units of selection controversy. In T. Nickles (Ed.), *Scientific Discovery: Case Studies* (pp. 213-259). Dordrecht, Holland: D. Reidel.

Woods, D.D., Johannese, L.J., Cook, R.I. & Sarter, N.B. (1994). *Behind human error: Cognitive systems, computers, and hindsight*. Wright-Patterson Air Force Base, OH: CSE-RIAC.

Expertise in Context

CHAPTER 6

Cognitive Conceptions of Expertise

Robert J. Sternberg

Introduction

One does not have to read many Perry Mason novels to recognize Mason's expertise as a lawyer, nor does one have to read many Philip Marlowe mysteries to recognize Marlowe's expertise as a detective. Expertise has always held a certain fascination for us, as shown by the fact that so many novels, TV series, and other forms of dramatic production have been built around characters who are experts at what they do. In real life, true experts hold a similar fascination. Few laypeople would have doubted the expertise of Einstein as a physicist. Hence, they would not have doubted anything he said about physics, no matter how skeptical his fellow scientists may have been of particular claims that he made. At a lesser level, but still relevant, we depend on the expertise of lawyers, doctors, and other professionals when we seek their consultations, and at times put our lives in their hands.

What, exactly, is it that makes an "expert?" Psychologists have been studying expertise since the beginning of the century, although under a variety of different labels. For example, the studies of intelligence of Binet and Simon (1905) can be seen as studies of intellectual expertise, and many other studies in psychology equally could be viewed from the standpoint of the study of expert behavior. The study of expertise under its own name began in earnest about 20 years ago and continues through to the present day.

Curiously, very few of the studies of expertise take seriously the question of what is an expert. For the most part, investigators have defined expertise operationally, for example, by nominations of key people in professional disciplines, or by championships or games won in the case of studies of game playing. Such operational definitions are functionally useful, but do not come face to face with the question of just what constitutes an expert. That is the question I will address in this chapter.

I will briefly consider nine different views of expertise. The first three views are ones that have been generally held at one time or another, in the literature. These views include:

1. the general-process view, according to which experts are people who solve problems by different processes from those used by nonexperts, or who use the same processes more rapidly than do nonexperts;

2. the quantity-of-knowledge view, according to which experts simply know more than do nonexperts; and

3. the knowledge-organization view, according to which experts organize their knowledge more effectively than do nonexperts.

The next four views are based on the triarchic theory of intelligence (Sternberg 1985), but correspond to intuitions people have had as to what constitutes an expert. These conceptions include:

4) superior analytical ability in solving problems, which may be seen as the ability to use effectively the knowledge one has;

5) superior creative ability, which involves creating new knowledge on the basis of knowledge one already has;

6) superior automatization, according to which experts do things more adeptly and automatically than do nonexperts; and

7) superior practical ability, which involves "knowing the ropes" or knowing how to get ahead in one's field of endeavor.

The eighth view is based upon implicit theories, or people's conceptions of a construct. This eighth, labeling view holds that an expert is an expert by virtue of being labeled as such.

Finally, I will present a ninth, synthetic view, which combines elements of the others that will have been considered earlier. On this view, expertise is a prototype, and is rarely reached in its purely prototypical form. Rather, people have aspects of expertise, namely, the eight aspects that will have been considered in this chapter.

"Received" Views of Expertise

The General-Process View

The pioneering work of Newell, Shaw and Simon (1958) and Miller, Galanter and Pribram (1960) shifted much of the emphasis in experimental psychology from stimulus-response theories of behavior to cognitively-based theories. Instead of treating the mind as a black box that mediated between stimuli and responses to stimuli, psychologists started to treat the process of thought as being of interest and as being knowable in their own right. Cognitive psychologists studied the processes used to solve various kinds of problems, the strategies into which these processes were combined, and the latencies and error rates of these various processes. Implicitly, the notion of expertise was that an expert differed from a novice in variables such as these—in which processes and strategies were used, and in the speed and accuracy with which the processes were executed.

Consider, for example, a game such as chess. It seems obvious that an expert would have to think about chess in a way which was different from a novice. The expert could pick excellent moves after considering only a few possibilities, suggesting that his or her strategy was quite different from the novice, who would not recognize these excellent moves as being excellent. Perhaps the expert saw farther into the possible futures of the game, or considered more possible alternative moves, or simply had a clever method for selecting the better moves. Whatever the difference, the information-processing view provided welcome relief from the stimulus-response view, in that it actually considered what went on in the expert's head, rather than merely considering antecedents and consequences.

The view of expertise as based on superiority in general information processing was consistent with a view of intelligence that was developing at the time, namely, that more intelligent people are fundamentally superior information processors. A wide variety of studies was showing that more intelligent people could process information more rapidly than could less intelligent people (e.g., Hunt 1978; Jensen 1982; Sternberg 1977). Thus, intellectual expertise might consist of the ability to process information rapidly in a variety of tasks that anyone could do, given time, whereas specific forms of expertise might consist of the ability to process domain-specific information either faster or more accurately than could novices. The idea that there might be this conceptual link between general intelligence and the more specific abilities needed for domain-specific expertise was an attractive one, because it placed various kinds of cognitive expertise within a single rubric.

Knowledge-Based Views

The quantity-of-knowledge view. The study of expertise was revolutionized when first DeGroot (1965) and then Chase and Simon (1973) discovered that the difference between experts and novices in chess did not appear in their mental processing of information at all. Chase and Simon required both expert and novice chess players to remember configurations of chess pieces on chess boards that were exposed for brief periods of time. Perhaps the key difference between expert and novice chess players was in their ability to encode and then remember information, so that the experts would do much better on this task than would the novices. The experts did do better, but only when the chess pieces were arranged in a sensible configuration with regard to the game of chess. When the pieces were arranged in a random configuration that would never occur in a game of chess, the experts remembered no better than did the novices. These results were inconsistent with the view that the experts somehow processed information in general in a manner that was different than that of the novices. Rather, the results suggested that whatever the difference, it was specific to chess-board configurations. Chase and Simon suggested that the advantage of experts over novices was due to their having stored in memory tens of thousands of sensible configurations of chess pieces that potentially occur in games. They could recognize these configurations, and thereby encode them easily. To novices, on the other hand, the sense of a configuration looked no different from the nonsensical ones, and thus, they had no edge in remembering the sensible ones. They had no stored chess patterns to which to relate the given information. Other studies soon replicated the effect in other situations (e.g., Reitman 1976) and suggested that the difference between experts and novices in knowledge was not limited to chess.

At one level, the findings of Chase and Simon were very exciting. At another level, they were less so. The Chase and Simon findings failed the "grandmother test," by which a psychological finding gains interest if it is a finding that would not be obvious in advance to one's grandmother. The finding that experts know more than novices is not one of the great surprises of the century. It is hard to imagine how they would not know more. To the extent that the finding was exciting, however, it was not because experts knew more, but because the difference in knowledge seems to be causally related to their expertise.

From an educational point of view, these findings were perhaps disquieting. There has always been a strong conservative faction of educators and parents that has believed that the best education is the one that stuffs the most facts into children's heads. The modern emphasis on developing the thinking skills (Baron and Sternberg 1987) has no place in this conservative point of view. If anything, teaching for thinking can get in the way of teaching for knowledge, because it wastes time that might otherwise be used in stuffing in more facts. But it soon became apparent that although quantity of knowledge might be necessary for expertise, it almost certainly was not sufficient.

The organization-of-knowledge view. Studies of experts in physics by Chi, Glaser and Rees (1982), Larkin, McDermott and Simon (1980), and others suggested that, at least in the understanding of experts in physics, quantity of knowledge was not the most useful construct. Chi and her colleagues, for example, found that experts in physics sorted physics problems in a way that was different from the way that novices sorted the same problems. Experts tended to sort problems in terms of a deeper, more fundamental conceptual structure, whereas novices tended to sort them in terms of a more superficial surface structure. These results and others suggested that the difference between groups was not only in the amount of knowledge they had, but in how they organized that knowledge. Indeed, novices might not even be able to distinguish the deep structure from the surface structure, a sign of their inadequate understanding of the material in their field of interest. Many other studies reviewed in Chi, Glaser and Farr (1988), Hoffman (1992), and Sternberg and Frensch (1991) also suggest that organization of knowledge is at least as important as amount of knowledge in differentiating experts from novices in a variety of different disciplinary areas.

The organization-of-knowledge view is more interesting than the quantity-of-knowledge view, both conceptually and educationally. It suggests that there is more to expertise than just knowing more. One has to know how to organize what one knows. An expert could not simply memorize a book on a given topic or a series of encyclopedia entries, because the organization would not be one that he or she could exploit in order to do tasks effectively in the domain in which expertise is sought.

In order concretely to understand the difference between the two points of view, consider two people who study the French language. One of these hypothetical people memorizes an English-French-English dictionary as well as a book of French grammar. The other has spent fifteen years in France and has had to communicate with French people, but never has memorized any entries in a dictionary nor even read a book of grammar in more than a cursory way. Which individual is more likely expertly to communicate in French? Clearly the second. Although the first person may have an enormous quantity of information, the information is inert. She is unlikely to know when or how to use the information, and thus it is available, but inaccessible for use. The second person may actually have fewer items of information stored, but the information that is stored is encoded in a way that makes it readily accessible and usable. The result is that the second person is far more likely to be an expert communicator in French than is the first.

The difference between these two points of view is not limited to the learning of languages. Consider an aspect of mathematics such as algebra. Memorizing formulas and principles of algebra does not make an expert in algebra. The student who seeks to receive an A in the course by memorizing all the information he can get his hands on may well end up failing instead. A second student who memorizes nothing, but who understands how to use principles of algebra that he has acquired in the course of his problem solving, is much more likely to achieve expertise in algebra. Thus, the organization-of-knowledge viewpoint again seems to be the more useful one.

Clearly, in order to organize information well, one must first have information to organize. During the 1960s, a rash of new curricula appeared in the sciences and mathematics, devoted to teaching children to think in these disciplines. For the most part, these methods did not enjoy long-term success because they placed great emphasis on thinking concepts, but insufficient emphasis on children's learning the concepts in the first place. In order to think well, one first needs concepts with which to think.

The quantity-of-knowledge and especially the organization-of-knowledge points of view were attractive because they placed expertise within a framework that was becoming very popular within the study of cognitive development in general. According to this framework, preferred by Chi (1978), Siegler (1978), Keil (1989), and others, cognitive development centered largely around the acquisition and organization of information. On this view, Piaget (1972) was incorrect in his emphasis on general information processing. What distinguishes the more cognitively mature individual from the less cognitively mature one is the possession of a greater amount of knowledge and the superior organization of this knowledge. The work of these psychologists suggested that children's failure in a variety of tasks was not due actually to their inability to process information, but rather to their lack of knowledge needed for various tasks that they might seek to do. Thus, cognitive expertise became an advanced form of cognitive development within a specific domain. Just as one could develop cognitively at a general level and thus reach a level of higher maturity, so could one advance in a more specific domain, and achieve cognitive expertise in that domain.

Triarchic Conceptions of Expertise

The view of expertise presented here is based on a triarchic theory of human abilities (Sternberg 1985). Psychologists are sometimes satisfied with theories that astound laypeople either with their simplicity or with their complexity. For example, on the side of simplicity is Jensen's (1972) notion that the psychological basis of intelligence lie in a person's ability rapidly to solve choice-reaction-time tasks, in which one of two lights flashes, and the subject in turn must press one of two buttons. On the side of complexity are complicated production-system models such as those proposed by Klahr (1984). But there seem to be theories of intermediate complexity that are easier to grasp and that are more plausible, in some respects, than the theories at the extreme of either simplicity or complexity.

The knowledge-based views of expertise seem to be lacking in many of the aspects of expertise that fit into our everyday notions of what makes an expert. For example, Perry Mason was not an expert lawyer nor Philip Marlowe an expert detective simply because they knew a lot about lawyering or detecting, or even because they had organized the information they had acquired in an effective or streamlined way. Rather, it was their ability to analyze information—to extract from it clever inferences that would leave their readers in the dark—which distinguished these experts. The information that they used was available to any reader. What distinguished these experts from mere novices? Consider some possibilities.

Superior Analytical Ability

Drawing of inferences goes beyond quantity and organization of knowledge—it requires effective use of knowledge. Experts seem to be able to infer things from information that novices cannot infer. For example, the expert weather forecaster is able to infer what kinds of weather patterns are likely to follow from climatic trends, whereas a novice could have the same information and infer little or nothing from it about the future. The expert psychotherapist can take the results of psychological tests and interviews and infer the nature of a psychological disorder, whereas a novice would be more likely to make a wrong inference than a right one.

A true expert seems not only to have a great deal of knowledge, but also knows how to use the knowledge he or she has to analyze new information as it is acquired. On this point of view, organization of knowledge is only important to the extent that it permits a person to analyze information more effectively. It is not the organization per se that matters, but the utility of this organization in promoting analysis. An expert is not just a store house of facts, he or she is someone who knows how effectively to exploit the facts that are stored. On this view, cognitive psychologists might be faulted in their heavy use of memory paradigms, which seem to place the locus of expertise in memory. Cognitive psychologists have always felt comfortable studying memory, and perhaps it is therefore not surprising that the remembering of knowledge would become so key to their notion of expertise. We are reminded of how, if one gives a hammer to a carpenter, he is certain to find something to hammer. The hammer of cognitive psychologists in this case has been the study of the learning, organization, and recall of information. The expert witness in court, for example, would be of little use if he or she were able only to recite facts. The expert witness is expected to use his knowledge base to analyze the information presented to the court, and it is his superiority in performing this analysis that lends him his credibility as an expert.

Creative Ability

The view of expertise involving analytical ability may seem right as far as it goes, but it seems not to go far enough. Mason and Marlowe did not just analyze the information that they were given; they seem to have had creative insights that took information that other people saw in one way, but that they saw in another. Somehow, they were able to redefine the problems at hand, and thereby reach ingenious and insightful solutions that never occurred to others.

The processes of insight that they used correspond to what I have referred to as "selective encoding," "selective combination," and "selective comparison" (Davidson and Sternberg 1984; Sternberg 1985). A selective-encoding insight is one in which a person realizes the relevance of some information at the same time that she identifies other information as irrelevant. This filtering is critical in many kinds and perhaps all kinds of expertise. The expert lawyer needs to know which facts and which laws are critically relevant in the case at hand, and which may sound like they apply but do not. The expert doctor needs to know what symptoms are critical in leading to a diagnosis, and which of the many tests that she might perform are ones that will be helpful in making a diagnosis, given a certain set of symptoms. The expert detective needs to zero in on the critical clues to decide who is the guilty party. Many clues are irrelevant, and others may actually be misleading in the search for the guilty party. The expert mathematician seeking to do a proof needs to know which of the many postulates and theorems of mathematics are relevant to the proof, and which are not. Selective-encoding insights, thus, provide one basis for going beyond the information given.

Selective combination involves combining information in ways that may not be obvious to other people. Again, selective combination seems crucial in many forms of expertise. The lawyer needs to know how to combine the facts in order to yield a plausible case. The doctor needs to know how to combine the symptoms and the test results to lead to a diagnosis. A detective needs to know how to combine the facts to lead to a plausible scenario that might have led a certain person to commit a crime. The mathematician needs to know not only which postulates and theorems are relevant, but how to combine them in a logical order that makes for a mathematical proof. A person who identifies useful information but cannot combine it effectively cannot fully be an expert.

Finally, the expert needs selective comparison as well. Selective comparison involves applying all the information acquired in another context to a problem at hand. It is here that acquired knowledge becomes especially important, both with respect to quantity and organization. But again, it is not the knowledge per se that matters but the ability to exploit it effectively, to know when to apply it as well as when not to. A lawyer needs to know when past legal precedents are relevant and when they are red herrings. Similarly, a doctor needs to know when symptoms are genuinely similar to those of a past case and thereby suggest the same diagnosis, and when they are different enough only to seem to lead to the same diagnosis. Selective comparison may be viewed as a kind of analogy-forming, where an analogy is drawn between the present situation and some situation from the past. The idea that experts need to go beyond analysis to synthesis—to some kind of creative form of thought—fits well with other things we know. For example, in academic disciplines, the true experts in a field are not considered to be the ones who have taught courses on subject matter for many years and thus may have memorized what everyone else has done, but people who have made creative theoretical and empirical contributions to a given field. The most distinguished experts are usually the people who have advanced the field, not merely those who have learned where the field happens to be at a given time. The same would be true in other disciplines. In art, for example, the expert is not merely someone who can imitate the work of a famous artist, but someone who is well able to analyze the work of other artists, or who creates original art work of his own. In literature, one could be viewed as an expert either by virtue of superior criticism of literary work or by superior production of such work. But merely memorizing literary works and being able to retrieve them is not likely to be the basis for the recognition of a person as an expert. Thus, it appears that some kind of creative or synthetic contribution can be important, in addition to or instead of an analytical one.

Automatization

Experts seem not only to do more than can novices, they seem to do it more easily—more effortlessly. For example, an expert driver drives almost automatically, and makes driving look easy, as does an expert dancer with respect to dancing, or an expert violinist with respect to playing the violin. Performances that seem easy for this person are impossible for the novice, even when he or she expends great effort. Similarly, the expert speaker of French or any other language speaks automatically, whereas the novice speaks in a halting and insecure manner. Experts have automatized many of the aspects of performance that for novices required controlled processes (Shiffrin and Schneider 1977).

Automatization offers a further advantage to the expert. Presumably, humans have limited-capacity systems for processing information. It is widely agreed that controlled processing is resource-consuming, whereas automatic processing consumes few resources at all. By having much of their information processing automatized, experts free their cognitive resources for dealing with novel aspects of a situation. For example, a person who can hardly read German is in no position to make sophisticated inferences about a text written in German, whereas a person who has automatized the basic bottom-up comprehension skills of German will be in a better position to make these inferences. A person who is just learning to drive is more susceptible to accidents because he needs to spend many of his resources trying to manage the various aspects of driving a car, leaving him without the resources to cope with sudden perilous situations that may develop. An expert driver, on the other hand, has more resources available to devote to a sudden perilous situation. Thus, automaticity promotes or at least permits the use of higher levels of analysis and synthesis, and thus promotes expertise.

Practical Ability

A true expert does not operate in a social vacuum. In any field of endeavor, advancement requires a knowledge of how the field operates, and how successfully to navigate within it. A business executive, for example, might have excellent analytic and creative skills, but without practical savvy and understanding of how corporations really function, these analytic and synthetic abilities are likely to remain unused or useless. Even in the ivory-tower of academia, advancement to successively higher levels of expertise requires the knowledge of the ins and outs of publication, teaching, gaining tenure, obtaining grants, and the like. Similarly, no matter what the analytical or synthetic abilities of a Perry Mason, he could not have succeeded if he did not understand how courts and criminals work. The detective, similarly, does not operate in an abstract world, but rather has to have the practical savvy for knowing what leads can be pursued and what ones cannot be.

The general point here is that experts seem to have practical as well as analytic and synthetic abilities. They get to where they are not only on the basis of abstract abilities, but on the basis of their being able to apply these abstract abilities within the constraints of the field in which they work. Many a potentially brilliant writer or artist or scientist has probably never seen the limelight precisely because of a failure to understand how her field truly functions. Probably no one could argue that this kind of practical ability or common sense is sufficient for expertise, but for many kinds of expertise, it appears at least to be a necessary condition. Its necessity arises from our own necessity of operating within real, practical constraints rather than solely within ideal and hypothetical ones.

A Labeling Conception

When all is said and done, even cognitive psychologists who take a broader cognitive approach to the study of expertise probably will not fully understand the concept of expertise if they do not look at social factors as well. To some extent, expertise is a matter of labeling. From this point of view, a person is an expert because he or she is labeled as such.

People are designated as "expert witnesses," "expert chess players," or "expert photographers" because they meet certain organized criteria for designation as an expert. These criteria may differ from one field to another, and they may be loosely and even inconsistently applied from one case to another. But when we talk about expertise as it occurs in the real world, labeling is probably key. A doctor becomes an "expert" when he or she receives a certification to practice. We know that there is wide variation in the true expertise of various doctors, but once certified, they all have equal opportunities to be labeled as experts. We even consult them as experts, hoping that the ones we pick will be ones whose knowledge and ability to use that knowledge match their credentials. Their entitlement to the label of "doctor" identifies them as experts, and they are treated as such, almost without regard to their particular cognitive accomplishments. The same can be said for lawyers or Ph.D.s or people in any number of fields. Having received the credentials, they become "instant experts," regardless of their cognitive capabilities.

Some people may resist the notion that labeling has anything to do with expertise. It is important to distinguish exactly what it does have to do with, which is the way in which people use the concepts of expertise, more or less independently of any cognitive antecedents that we might create. One can dismiss such factors as "merely" social psychological. But the danger here, as is always true in cognitive psychology, is that in formulating theories of cognition, one will become detached from what happens in the real world, as opposed to what happens in some ideal world that cognitive psychologists might create in their laboratories. To an extent, expertise is a labeling phenomenon and this phenomenon needs to be taken into account as well as the cognitive ones.

Expertise as a Prototype

My own point of view in writing this chapter is not to promote one or another of these views as expertise, but rather to promote the view that expertise, like other constructs, is a prototype (Neisser 1976; Rosch 1973). It comprises all of the aspects described above, and probably others as well. Certainly, in specific domains, expertise may have aspects that do not apply in other domains. For example, the expert dancer needs a level of coordination and stamina that would not apply to the expert theoretical physicist. People are not really experts or nonexperts, but rather are experts in varying degrees. Their degree of expertise will depend on the extent to which they fulfill the criteria described above both singly and jointly. The more of each attribute they have, and the more of these attributes they have, the more likely they are to be "experts." Obviously, the labeling criterion is different in kind from the others, and may well depend on them to a certain degree. These criteria are by no means independent, nor are they even fully mutually exclusive. Rather, they represent correlated aspects of expertise. A multidimensional representation would thus have oblique rather than orthogonal axes.

The view of expertise as a prototype implies that within a given domain, people have a shared conception of what an expert is. The attributes of the prototype may differ somewhat from one domain to another. For example, the expert clinical psychologist might be viewed primarily as one who makes accurate diagnoses and then provides psychotherapy that maximizes the probability of a cure; in biology, the expert might be someone who does top-flight research on the nature of life; in theoretical physics, the expert might be someone who devises theories that compellingly account for large, important problems about the physical universe, and so on. A given field may have several alternative prototypes. For example, the expert academic psychologist might be viewed quite differently from the expert clinical psychologist: Research quality and productivity would be seen as far more important in the academic domain than in the clinical domain.

Prototypes of expertise can vary over time and space. For example, as the study of economics becomes more quantitative, knowledge and ability to use econometric techniques might increase in importance in the prototype of the economic expert. Moreover, the expert economist in a socialist country might be a rather different person from that in a capitalist country. Thus, prototypes are dynamic rather than static.

Although people may judge expertise against a prototype of what an expert is, we are fortunate that not everyone who is knowledgeable about and adept in a field conforms to any single prototype. As people with different kinds of qualifications emerge and show that they can be knowledgeable about and productive in a field, we find that we need to broaden our view of expertise in order to allow for the diversity of skills that can lead to outstanding performance.

Conclusion

Expertise is a multifaceted phenomenon. To a large extent, it is a cognitive phenomenon, but it is not exclusively a cognitive one. One needs to take into account as well the social conditions under which the label of expertise is granted. Expertise involves both general and specific processes, as well as knowledge and the ability to organize it.

Acknowledgment

Research for this article was supported under the Javits Act Program (grant No. R206R50001) as administered by the Office of Educational Research and Improvement, U.S. Department of Education. Grantees undertaking such projects are encouraged to express freely their professional judgment. This chapter, therefore, does not necessarily represent the positions or policies of the Government, and no official endorsement should be inferred.

References

Baron, J.B. & Sternberg, R.J. (Eds.). (1987). *Teaching Thinking Skills: Theory and Practice.* New York: Freeman.

Binet, A. & Simon, T. (1905). Méthodes nouvelles pour le diagnostic du niveau intellectuel des anormaux. *L'Année psychologique, 11,* 245–336.

Chase, W.G. & Simon, H.A. (1973). The mind's eye in chess. In W.G. Chase (Ed.), *Visual Information Processing* (pp. 215–281). New York: Academic Press.

Chi, M.T.H. (1978). Knowledge structure and memory development. In R.S. Siegler (Ed.), *Children's Thinking: What Develops?* (pp. 73–96). Hillsdale, NJ: Erlbaum.

Chi, M.T.H., Glaser, R. & Farr, M.J. (Eds.). (1988). *The Nature of Expertise.* Hillsdale, NJ: Erlbaum.

Chi, M.T.H., Glaser, R. & Rees, E. (1982). Expertise in problem solving. In R.J. Sternberg (Ed.), *Advances in the Psychology of Human Intelligence* (Vol. 1, pp. 7–75). Hillsdale, NJ: Erlbaum.

Davidson, J.E. & Sternberg, R.J. (1984). The role of insight in intellectual giftedness. *Gifted Child Quarterly, 28,* 58–64.

DeGroot, A.D. (1965). *Thought and Choice in Chess.* The Hague: Mouton.

Hoffman, R.R. (Ed.). (1992). *The Psychology of Expertise: Cognitive Research and Empirical AI.* New York: Springer-Verlag.

Hunt, E.B. (1978). Mechanics of verbal ability. *Psychological Review, 85,* 109–130.

Jensen, A.R. (1972). *Genetics and Education.* London: Methuen.

Jensen, A.R. (1982). The chronometry of intelligence. In R.J. Sternberg (Ed.), *Advances in the Psychology of Human Intelligence* (Vol. 1, pp. 255–310). Hillsdale, NJ: Erlbaum.

Keil, F.C. (1989). *Concepts, Kinds, and Cognitive Development.* Cambridge, MA: MIT Press.

Klahr, D. (1984). Transition processes in quantitative development. In R.J. Sternberg (Ed.), *Mechanisms of Cognitive Development.* San Francisco: Freeman.

Larkin, J., McDermott, J., Simon, D.P. & Simon, H.A. (1980). Expert and novice performance in solving physics problems. *Science, 208,* 1335–1342.

Miller, G., Galanter, E. & Pribram, K. (1960). *Plans and the Structure of Behavior.* New York: Holt.

Neisser, U. (1976). *Cognition and Reality: Principles and Implications of Cognitive Psychology.* San Francisco: Freeman.

Newell, A., Shaw, J.C. & Simon, H.A. (1958). Elements of a theory of human problem solving. *Psychological Review, 65,* 151–166.

Piaget, J. (1972). *The Psychology of Intelligence.* Totowa, NJ: Littlefield Adams.

Reitman, J.S. (1976). Skilled perception in Go: Deducing memory structures from interresponse times. *Cognitive Psychology, 8,* 336–356.

Rosch, E. (1973). On the internal structure of perceptual and semantic categories. In T.E. Moore (Ed.), *Cognitive Development and the Acquisition of Language* (pp. 112–144). New York: Academic Press.

Shiffrin, R.M. & Schneider, W. (1977). Controlled and automatic human information processing. II: Perceptual learning, automatic attending, and a general theory. *Psycho-*

logical Review, 84, 127–190.

Siegler, R.S. (1978). The origins of scientific reasoning. In R.S. Siegler (Ed.), *Children's Thinking: What Develops?* (pp. 109–149). Hillsdale, NJ: Erlbaum.

Sternberg, R.J. (1977). *Intelligence, Information Processing, and Analogical Reasoning: The Componential Analysis of Human Abilities.* Hillsdale, NJ: Erlbaum.

Sternberg, R.J. (1985). *Beyond IQ: A Triarchic Theory of Human Intelligence.* New York: Cambridge University Press.

Sternberg, R.J. & Frensch, P.A. (Eds.). (1991). *Complex Problem Solving: Principles and Mechanisms.* Hillsdale, NJ: Erlbaum.

Chapter 7

Metaphors for Expertise: How Knowledge Engineers Picture Human Expertise

Marianne LaFrance

Introduction

Human expertise has always had something of the exceptional and inimitable about it, or at least it had until the advent of artificial intelligence computer programs called expert systems. With the arrival of knowledge-based programs, human expertise has apparently become something that can be "tapped into" whenever needed. Press reports have likened expert systems to having "Experts in a box" or "Experience on a disc" (Laurie 1992). One recent business publication indicated that a particular expert system was like having an "Electronic partner" (Gallant 1991), while another system was like having "experts at your fingertips" (Touby, Romano, and Russel 1990). According to proponents of expert systems, human expertise, heretofore appreciated but seldom intentionally preserved, need no longer be intangible and inestimable. Expertise can be acquired and transferred to computer programs that have the ability to advise or the capacity to tutor, the power to create or the talent to enlighten (Michaelsen, Michie, and Boulanger 1985). In short, expert systems advance the possibility that human experience can be taken in and given back as packaged know-how.

It falls to knowledge engineers to figure out how to characterize human expertise so that it can be utilized in a computer system. But the process of discerning expert know-how has turned out be harder than anyone initially imagined. In fact, knowledge acquisition, as the process of eliciting and instantiating human expertise is called, is now an industry onto itself. There are books, manuals, journals, conferences, workshops and training programs devoted solely to the theory and practice of how to acquire human expertise and transfer it to a computer program (Scott, Clayton, and Gibson 1991; Westphal and Blanchard 1989). Part of the reason for all this activity stems from the fact that the elicitation of expertise has turned out to be considerably more complicated than having, as one expert system developer described, merely the time and the patience to ask an expert "why" 400 times in a row.

Much of what constitutes expert know-how is now recognized to be tacit and difficult to articulate (LaFrance 1990). One factor contributing to the very idea that expertise could be "transferred" from human to computer has been the adoption of particular metaphors by the builders of expert systems. Metaphors are used by people for a variety of reasons, not the least of which is the need to put into words something that escapes easy explication. According to Lakoff and Johnson (1980) metaphor is one of our most important tools for comprehending partially what cannot be comprehended totally. The core requirement for building a knowledge base for an expert system is that what the expert knows must be made excruciatingly explicit.

Chapter Overview

My thesis is that metaphors for the elicitation of expertise are central and salient in the expert systems community precisely because human expertise is deep and often esoteric. Although people believe that they know human expertise when they see it, it nonetheless escapes easy definition. Metaphors have been adopted to allow that which is nonverbal to be made verbal. In this chapter I describe some of the prevailing metaphors for the elicitation of expertise, a few of which may not be initially recognized as metaphors—being taken at face value as statements of what actually happens when people convey what they know to someone else. The chapter begins by defining briefly what a metaphor is, as well as presenting two dimensions on which any metaphor might be classified, namely metaphor strength and metaphor evolution. Next, four central metaphors are delineated. Expertise elicitation is likened respectively to excavation, capture, courtship, and creation. I draw on the existing literature in expert systems development to illustrate each of these metaphors. After portraying how knowledge engineers metaphorically conceive the elicitation of expertise, I next show how each of these metaphors propel the strategies that knowledge engineers use to conduct knowledge acquisition. Finally, I present some indications regarding how these metaphors may be subtly shaping what we conceive human expertise to be.

Theory of Metaphor

Although it might be argued that idioms abound in any field, the expert systems literature is a veritable treasury of metaphors. For example, developers of expert systems have described the acquisition of knowledge from an expert in a variety of striking ways. Feigenbaum (1980) referred to knowledge elicitation as a process of "extraction," Hayes-Roth (1984) compared the elicitation of expertise to "vacuum cleaning," Michealson, Michie, and Boulanger (1985) likened the process to a "skill transplant," and Davis (1985) described it as "the closest we can get to cloning." These metaphors are not only descriptive. I propose that they are also prescriptive in directing the development of techniques for knowledge acquisition.

Metaphors abound in AI not because computer scientists have poetry in their veins but because metaphors are eminently practical (Miller 1979).

> Explanations without metaphor would be difficult if not impossible, for in order to describe the unknown, we must resort to concepts that we know and understand, and that is the essence of metaphor—an unusual juxtaposition of the familiar and the unfamiliar (MacCormac 1985, p. 9).

Metaphors have been described as possessing two attributes (MacCormac 1985). The first has to do with *metaphor strength*, namely how effectively a metaphor expresses a similarity relationship between two objects that would otherwise be considered dissimilar and unrelated. The second concerns *metaphor evolution*, that is, the way in which a metaphor evolves from a poetic expression to a lexical assertion of truth and the conditions that support this evolution. I describe each of these attributes in more detail to support the argument that metaphor has played a significant role in knowledge acquisition.

Metaphor Strength

Metaphor strength deals with the degree of similarity between a known entity (the base system) and an unknown entity (the target system). The target system, in this case expertise to be transferred, is ill-defined or abstract, and the base system is familiar. For example, in characterizing expertise elicitation as extraction, "extraction" as the base system is relatively well-understood. The assertion of overlap does not, however, entail the mapping of whole entity to whole entity, but the partial mapping of some of the attributes of one entity to the other (Gentner 1982). Any entity has a number of referents, and hence a metaphor is a statement of analogy between specific paired referents (Ortony 1979). The proportion of analogous to nonanalogous referents determines the strength of the metaphor. It is important to keep in mind, however, that it is the nature of metaphors or analogies to have relatively few attributes within the base concept apply validly to a target concept (Indurkhya 1992). Nevertheless, stronger metaphors have a greater proportion of analogous referents.

The strongest metaphors are those that relate objects about which relatively much is known (the base system) to those which relatively little is known (the target system) because, at least at the outset, there is little awareness of areas of dissimilarity. As we will see, metaphors have played a significant part in the development of expert systems because little was actually known about how human expertise might be communicated to those having less expertise until work designed to do just that began. In general, as the nature of metaphorically related entities is studied and the dissimilarity of referents revealed, it is not at all uncommon for some metaphors to lose strength and appeal, often to be replaced by other metaphors.

Metaphor Evolution

Metaphors can also be described in terms of their evolution. Metaphors evolve in the sense that they tend to shift over time either toward greater "solidity," that is, toward becoming literal statements, or they can shift toward having fewer constructive referents and can weaken and fade from use. Thus, a poetic, suggestive metaphor, called a *diaphor* by Wheelwright (1962), can become a more descriptive metaphor, termed a *epiphor,* and maybe even change into a literal statement if there are a sufficient number of analogous referents. It can also shift in that direction purely by dint of repetition or surface appeal. But there is danger in such transformation.

Metaphors can be dangerous not only in bewitching us into thinking that what they suggest really does exist but also in leading us to believe that the attributes normally possessed by any of the referents in the metaphor are possessed by the others. "By forgetting that theories presuppose basic metaphors and thereby by taking theories literally, both scientists and theologians create myths." (MacCormac 1985, p. 17.)

Despite the fact that knowledge engineering is a technical enterprise, it has made very liberal use of metaphors; indeed some have achieved the status of myth. In what follows, I highlight four of these metaphors and show how each one has been incorporated into the language and the practice of knowledge engineering.

Metaphors for the Elicitation of Expertise

Knowledge engineering has accrued a large literature describing its theory and practice. This material, along with interviews I carried out with veteran knowledge engineers, constitutes the sources from which I draw four key metaphors. Although it is possible to discern more than four distinct metaphors as well as a number of hybrid metaphors in the expert systems literature, I will limit my discussion to these four, namely: *excavation, capture, courting,* and *creation.* They are presented in an order that roughly corresponds to their historical appearance (early ones first) and their prominence in the field. It should also be noted that the description of these four metaphors is not meant to suggest that proponents rigidly adhere to one and only one metaphor. Rather, my aim is to deliberately highlight the important features of prevailing views. This is done to accentuate what is unique to individual metaphors while at the same time drawing explicit contrasts with the others.

Expertise Elicitation as *Excavation*

One of the first and most enduring metaphors of how an expert's know-how is to be obtained involves the act of excavation or extraction. For example, a standard textbook on knowledge acquisition has a miner panning for gold on its cover (McGraw and Harbison-Briggs 1989). According to this metaphor, expertise is described as being *extracted* from an expert followed by transfer to a computer program. Since the essence of an expert system requires that the tacit performance know-how of an expert be made public and since experts are often hard-pressed to describe what they know, a second party was believed to be necessary to help get that knowledge out. That person became designated as a knowledge engineer (Feigenbaum 1977).

The idea that expertise can be extracted by an engineer became firmly entrenched in the literature with the publication of *Building Expert Systems* (Hayes-Roth, Waterman, and Lenat 1983). That volume, involving contributions by more than 40 AI scientists, presented the techniques and tools aimed at moving expert systems from ambition to reality.

The excavation metaphor gives voice to several aspects of knowledge elicitation. First, expertise is presented as a valuable resource. Several examples are as follows: "The importance of knowledge as a *resource* inspires people to build expert systems which could have distinct advantages over human experts" (Michie and Johnston 1985). "Expertise is a scarce *resource* whose refinement and reproduction creates wealth" (Hayes-Roth 1984, p. 5). "Individual computer scientists work with individual experts to explicate the expert's heuristics—to mine those *jewels of knowledge* out of their heads one by one (Feigenbaum and McCorduck 1984, p. 85).

The view of expertise as something that could be excavated also suggested that expertise could be "engineered." "Knowledge like a rare metal, lies dormant and impure.... Once *extracted,* an element of knowledge must undergo other transformations before it acquires commercial value" (Hayes-Roth 1984, p. 18). Hayes-Roth explicitly likened the four developmental stages of building an expert system—namely knowledge acquisition, system design, programming and refinement, respectively—to the four "knowledge processing tasks" of "mining," "molding," "assembling," and "refining."

A third attribute deriving from the excavation metaphor is subtle yet central to the comparison. That attribute makes expertise an "object." Knowledge can be excavated and bits can be removed. Note, for example, the following: "Knowledge acquisition techniques...enhance a knowledge engineer's ability to tap and extract at least portions of the expert's knowledge" (McGraw and Harbison-Briggs 1989, p. 8).

Knowledge engineering as *extraction* clearly highlights certain facets of how human expertise can be acquired for use in an expert system, even while hiding or imposing other questionable characteristics (Spiro, Feltovich, Coulson, and Anderson 1989). What is highlighted is the sighting of some pre-existing deposit, the digging out of this rare substance, and then the engineering of it by operators who have the skill to make it genuinely valuable.

The excavation metaphor is a familiar idea. In fact, Reddy noted that talking about ideas as though they were objects is a cultural metaphor. "The speaker puts ideas (objects) into words (containers) and sends them (along a conduit) to a hearer who takes the idea/objects out the word/containers" (1979, p. 10). In adopting this metaphor, knowledge engineers signed on to the idea which later came under serious scrutiny that expertise exists independently of the context of its development and use, that it is essentially incorruptible, and that it can be transferred intact to some other location (expert system).

But the excavation metaphor is a cultural metaphor in a narrower sense. Artificial intelligence has close ties with engineering science. So, excavation was a natural metaphor for those working in applied artificial intelligence. But excavation was also a useful, perhaps even a necessary, metaphor for the fledgling field of expert systems. By making expertise an object, it became possible to conceive of it as something that was solid and secure rather than transient and mercurial. Hence the business of getting a hold of it, while perhaps tricky, was nevertheless possible.

A close relative of the excavation metaphor for describing the elicitation of expertise is what in computing practice is referred to as a "memory dump." The ideal knowledge acquisition technique is seen as being one in which the expert dumps the contents of his or her knowledge base into the machine. In both extraction and dumping, the underlying view is of expertise as a substance, portions of which can be tapped into or hewn off by the knowledge engineer.

Expertise Elicitation as *Capture*

A second metaphor for the elicitation of expertise has to do with capturing it. According to this metaphor, expertise is something that needs to be seized. For example, an article characterized the process of knowledge acquisition as "the taming of an expert" (Brown 1989).

Expertise needs to be captured because once secured it can yield great benefits (Feigenbaum 1985). "The goal of the knowledge engineering process is to capture and incorporate a domain expert's fundamental domain knowledge" (McGraw and Harbison-Briggs 1989, p. 5).

Several attributes of expertise become apparent when it is seen as something to be captured. First, in capturing it, expertise will not disappear. Indeed one of the most compelling selling points of expert systems is that human expertise, which previously seemed highly perishable in the sense that human experts can leave, retire or even die, now could be made secure (Davis and Lenat 1982). "Expertise need not be lost when he retires; it could be *captured* in a computer system... (Scott, Clayton, and Gibson 1991, p. 6).

Secondly, capturing expertise means that it can be organized and consolidated. Where once conceived to be wild, unorganized and informal, expertise, under this view, can be catalogued. Indeed, instructions to would-be knowledge engineers are themselves very explicit on this point: "Successful information transfer requires...the knowledge engineer's capture of the information in a permanent record" (Scott, Clayton, and Gibson 1991, p. 383, 337). Natural existing expertise is at times disconcertingly vague and inconsistent. Captured in an expert system, it can be made to be systematic (Davis 1985).

Thirdly, if expertise can be captured in the knowledge base of an expert system, then it can be owned. An enthusiastic endorsement of this stance came with the publication of *The Fifth Generation* by Feigenbaum and McCorduck (1984). These authors predicted that knowledge, stored and manipulated by intelligent computers, would become a commodity like food or oil. They went on to write that this packaged knowledge would be:

A new form of power which will consist of facts, skills, codified experience, large amounts of easily obtained data, all accessible in fast, powerful ways to anybody who wants it—scholar, manager, policymaker, professional, or ordinary citizen. And it will be for sale. (1984, p. 55.)

A fourth referent included in the metaphor that expertise can be captured is that once captured, it can be put to use. Expertise can be pressed into service as a *"knowledge assistant"* (Davis 1982). In calling expert systems knowledge assistants, there was the added feature that experts might be persuaded of the value of relinquishing their expertise if they could be convinced that the system might be able to take over routine or time-consuming tasks (Waters and Nielsen 1988). An interesting variation of the notion of electronic knowledge assistant has been articulated by McCorduck: "This new version of the sorcerer's apprentice is called DENDRAL, and behaves as a chemist's assistant in interpreting the data from mass spectrography" (1979, p. 273).

Finally, the feature of expertise that becomes manifest when it is conceived as something requiring capture is the idea that experts might harbor reservations about being put to use for the building of an expert system. In other words, the conjecture was that some experts might resist the idea that their know-how would be collected from them and deposited elsewhere. Note the following: "Knowledge acquisition is sometimes considered a necessary burden carried out under protest so that one can get on with the study of cognitive processes in problem solving" (Stefik and Conway 1982, p. 4). Consequently, efforts were devised to wrest control of what experts know either through some enticement, such as suggesting that the resulting system will relieve them of the more repetitive or mundane aspects of their work, or through corporate power, which reminds them that their knowledge belongs in the final analysis to the organization that employs them.

Expertise Elicitation as *Courtship*

Some developers of expert systems have made reference to courting activities when describing how expertise can be transferred to an expert system. The following presents some examples of this metaphor: "High performance has to be *courted* with patience" (Buchanan 1982). "A famous rule of thumb about selecting your expert. The expert that the company doesn't want to give up is the *one that you want*" (Barr 1989).

A key feature suggested by the courting metaphor is experts are chosen. They may not necessarily be the most knowledgeable in an area but they are experts because others believe that they are (Agnew, Ford, and Hayes 1994). In other words, the expert is socially selected at a particular time and place. One implication of this selection notion is that the most desirable expert may not necessarily be the one that is most readily available. Using network analysis, Stein (1992, 1993), for example, found that the central information person in an organization—that is, the one others seek out for advice and information—was also the one who was relatively hard to get access to.

Another central attribute of the courting metaphor is that knowledge engineers need to establish a relationship with the expert in order for the know-how to be conveyed completely and without distortion. The expert will need to be entranced with the notion of expert systems because without his or her enthusiastic participation, the process of knowledge acquisition just won't work. Note the following description which emphasizes the participative nature of knowledge acquisition: "From a practical point of view, the knowledge acquisition task for developing knowledge-based systems may be viewed as a cooperative task between domain experts, knowledge engineers, and support systems" (Kinoshita 1989, p. 166).

With the courting metaphor, knowledge engineers acknowledge the fact that successful elicitation of expertise requires that the expert be fully involved in the process and keen about the opportunity to interact with the knowledge engineer (McGraw and Harbison-Briggs 1989). Anything short of this kind of participation will likely result in a partial or impoverished knowledge base.

The courting metaphor also indicates that the process of finding out what an expert knows is a more deliberate and skillful activity than that implied by either *excavation* or *capture*. The knowledge cannot not be blasted out by brute force nor can it be seized under duress but, rather, it must be acquired through subtle and collaborative efforts. With the courting analogy comes the recognition that the feelings the expert has for the knowledge engineer are not trivial.

Courting also implies that one needs to know something personally about the expert of interest. People who court others often do better if they have some information and insight about the person being courted. So too with attempting to secure the involvement of domain experts. It also helps if the person doing the courting has resources in order to do it well.

Expertise Elicitation as *Creation*

The final metaphor for expertise elicitation represents a significant departure from the preceding ones and is attracting considerable attention from the knowledge acquisition community. According to this metaphor, expertise is viewed not so much as something to be found but as something that is created by the knowledge engineer either during interaction with the expert, or is put together via inductive reasoning using various inputs provided by the expert. In short, the creation metaphor comes out of a more constructivist perspective to knowledge (Ford and Adams-Webber 1992).

The *creation* metaphor seems to have emerged for several reasons. As a number of theorists have pointed out, when information moves between people it is not so much gained, as it is qualitatively changed, made more or less meaningful (Axley 1984). In other words, knowledge emerges from the interactions that take place between expert and knowledge engineer. Moreover, what emerges from these interactions is not necessarily an exact replica of what experts know but is instead a present construction—a network of inferences that arise at the moment in response to the exchange between expert and knowledge engineer (LaFrance 1992).

Thus, knowledge acquisition is less a process of procuring the goods than it is an occasion for composing them. In their book, *Understanding Computers and Cognition,* Winograd and Flores (1986) hold that experts do not have, nor do they need, formal representations of their domains in order to act and hence "it is fruitless to search for a full formalization of the pre-understanding that underlies all thought and action" (p. 99). In other words, the elicitation of expertise taken as excavation, capture, or courting leads to the assumption that the knowledge needed for the knowledge base of an expert system already exists in the expert's head. According to the creation metaphor, knowledge acquisition does not obtain information; it generates invention:

> In developing such a system, there is an initial period of 'knowledge acquisition' during which professionals in the domain work together with 'knowledge engineers' to articulate the structure of the relevant concepts and rules. This is often described as a process of 'capturing' the knowledge that the experts already have and use. In fact, it is a creative design activity in which a systematic domain is created, covering

certain aspects of the professionals' work. (Winograd and Flores 1986, p. 99.)

According to the creation metaphor, the know-how that experts have does not pre-exist; it is manifest in the act of doing. It is what Schon calls "knowing-in-action": "Although we sometimes think before acting, it is also true that in much of the spontaneous behavior of skilled practice we reveal a kind of knowing which does not stem from a prior intellectual operation" (1983, p. 51).

In this view expertise is not an object: it can be prompted but it cannot be quarried. In knowledge acquisition, the expert answers questions, solves problems, explains solutions, and the like. These answers provide indications of what experts believe about what they do, but they are not themselves actual expertise that pre-existed the effort made to acquire it. The art of knowledge elicitation lies in devising situations and tasks that lead to behavior which in turn allows knowledge engineers to make good inferences about what constitutes know-how in this domain.

A specific metaphor that draws on the idea that transfer of expertise is a creative extrapolation has likened knowledge acquisition to crystallographic analysis, in which a beam of X-rays or electrons is shot at a crystal from a number of different angles (Young 1989). The resulting pattern of refraction and reflection, recorded on a photographic plate, is rich in information about the crystal structure, but it is not a copy of it.

Those working within the creation metaphor aim to "model" expertise, that is, they seek to contrive a representation of what know-how in a particular sphere might look like. What the expert says and does may be used as input but the input is reinterpreted and fashioned into a prototype. Note the distinction between conceiving of expertise elicitation as a process whereby existing knowledge is gotten hold of, versus elicitation conceived of as a process where expertise is contrived or modeled in one of a number of ways including induction or extrapolation. "There is currently a major paradigm split in knowledge acquisition research and practice between techniques for the transfer of existing knowledge from human experts and those for the creation of new expertise through empirical induction or 'machine learning'" (Gaines and Boose 1988, p. 12).

In machine induction, for example, the human expert provides important information such as examples from a particular domain as well as attributes by which the cases can be described. But then a program takes over and induces rules that link these features and then applies these induced rules to new examples. In short, the knowledge engineer and/or an induction mechanism goes beyond the information provided by the expert.

A comparison of the four prevailing metaphors is given in Table 1. As Table 1 shows, each metaphor tends to highlight certain features while simultaneously hiding others.

	Features or assumptions about expertise that are highlighted or made salient	Features or assumptions about expertise that are denied or de-emphasized
EXCAVATION	Expertise is a thing	Expertise is dynamic and context-dependent
CAPTURE	Expertise is often tacit, ineffable, hidden	Much expertise is public and verbalizable
COURTSHIP	Expertise is highly personal and idiosyncratic	Expertise is often equivalent across experts and transferable
CREATION	Expertise emerges in the process of eliciting it	In some domains, there exist a priori criteria for recognizing expertise

Table 1.
Comparison of major metaphors in terms of their conceptions of "expertise"

Assessing Metaphors for Expertise Elicitation

Each metaphor describing the elicitation of expertise highlights some features, ignores others, and sometimes even misleads recipients as to what goes on in the process (Spiro, Feltovich, Coulson, and Anderson 1989). Nonetheless, the four metaphors of excavation, capture, courtship, and creation can be appraised along two dimensions described previously, namely the dimensions of metaphor strength and metaphor evolution.

Assessing the Metaphors on Metaphor Strength

A metaphor can achieve strength in two ways. First, it can become strong because there are many overlapping attributes with the phenomenon being modeled. Second, a metaphor can be strong if it is repeated enough. On both counts, the *excavation* metaphor appears stronger than capture, courting, or creation.

As to overlap among attributes, those who adopt the excavation metaphor see expertise as something that can be mined, molded, and refined. It is clearly valuable and scarce; its tacit quality gives it the quality of being buried and embedded and not easily brought to the surface. Moreover, it seems to require a special kind of engineer to know how to handle it; and it achieves its maximum value after it has been processed. And underlying all these attributes is the idea that human expertise exists as a thing. Expertise viewed as extractable is not intangible or context specific. It can be grasped and transported; it does not loose anything in the process; indeed it becomes even more valuable. The idiosyncratic and incalculable qualities typically ascribed to human expertise become a thing of the past. Thus, the considerable overlap among entity attributes makes expertise elicitation as excavation a strong metaphor in the culture of knowledge engineering.

The *capture* metaphor also shows considerable metaphor strength. It possesses a number of attributes in common with excavation, but it stresses other features. For something to require capture means that it might resist being ensnared. When work on expert systems began to proliferate, it became clear that knowledge elicitation was not always welcomed by the expert (Hoffman 1987). Experts were occasionally unwilling or averse to being exploited in this fashion.

Knowledge engineers often assume that they will face a "difficult expert" and they are on the lookout for ways to bring this person into line (LaFrance 1991). The capture metaphor possesses considerable strength as a metaphor precisely because it expresses knowledge engineers' uneasy accord with the social side of knowledge elicitation. A significant proportion of knowledge engineers find the extended contact with experts required by the demands of knowledge acquisition to be unnerving and hopefully soon, unnecessary, if automated knowledge acquisition becomes a reality (LaFrance 1991).

Capture also calls attention to the idea that expertise must be managed, not just engineered. The capture metaphor, while used to make the point that expertise can be marketed and sold, also conveys the point that it is not just there for the taking but tends to be guarded and controlled. So the capture metaphor also shows a number of areas of overlap among attributes of the target and base systems.

The *courtship* metaphor for expertise elicitation appears to possess less strength perhaps because courtship itself seems at first pass to possess fewer relevant features than either excavation or capture. Nevertheless, *courtship* accentuates some attributes ignored by the prior two metaphors and appears to be gaining strength. For one thing, courtship conveys a social dimension, a dimension not discernible in the idea of excavation and underestimated in the notion of capture. The social aspects are subtle yet significant. For example, courtship strongly suggests the need to find the right person. Likewise, expert system developers describe the difficulty of finding the right expert, that is, someone who is not only knowledgeable about the domain but someone who is also known and trustworthy (Stein 1992). Courtship also connotes some aspects of the need to convince or persuade and hence implicates the importance of social skills for knowledge engineers. Experts often need to be attracted to and committed to the process or else the knowledge acquisition may botch the very thing it is designed to secure. Finally courtship implicates the need for commitment (Winograd and Flores 1989).

Finally, the *creation* metaphor is also gaining popularity. While AI researchers are drawn to the idea that expertise might be generated via induction, the idea that expertise is an invention generated by the knowledge acquisition process itself is a controversial idea (Clancey 1987). If Winograd and Flores (1986) are correct that knowledge emerges in the communication between expert and knowledge engineer, then system builders are paradoxically both more and less dependent on the expert. They are more dependent because the expert's specific experience is essential to define the problem and evaluate the solutions; less dependent because what gets put in the knowledge base is actually the knowledge engineer's inference about what the expert knows. Time will tell whether expertise elicitation as *creation* develops as a strong metaphor within AI. Outside AI, it appears to be picking up steam (Resnick, Levine, and Teasley 1991).

Assessing the Metaphors on Metaphor Evolution

Each of the four metaphors evolved somewhat separately over the last two decades, but each has also changed as the result of coming up against alternative metaphors. *Excavation* was present almost from the beginning. It provided for the possibility that expertise could be acquired and that fairly crude methods would get at it. *Capture* emerged with the insight that human expertise might resist acquisition and that it may need to be appropriated. *Courtship* suggested the need for solicitation and collaboration. *Creation* represents somewhat of a departure. If expertise is constructed rather than found, and if expertise elicitation represents just one stage in the ongoing creation of meaning, then knowledge engineering is an entirely different sort of activity than conceived when extraction was the prevailing metaphor.

The next section presents the elicitation strategies that have originated from conceiving of the elicitation of expertise as being like excavation, capture, courtship, and creation.

Elicitation Strategies

At an applied level, the four major metaphors have suggested different strategies for knowledge elicitation. Table 2 summarizes what each strategy concentrates on and what each tends to overlook.

Regarded as *excavation*, methods were devised for "getting the knowledge *out* of the expert and *into* the system" (Olson and Rueter 1987, p. 22). Sophistication was not required; what was imperative was digging to the point where you found what you were looking for. The key thing was to find the right expert and then to keep at that person until one had extracted whatever was there. Although knowledge acquisition has now been described more as a "chisel than a bulldozer" (McGraw and Harbison-Briggs 1989, p. 9), extraction nevertheless implies that expertise elicitation can be a laborious and even a rather crude process.

	Features or assumptions about expertise that are highlighted or made salient	Features or assumptions about expertise that are denied or de-emphasized
EXCAVATION	Elicitation is straightforward although labor-intensive	Elicitors need not worry about personalities or context
CAPTURE	Elicitors need to take charge and lay claim to the relevant body of knowledge	Expertise is subtle and experts are sometimes willing to oblige
COURTSHIP	Elicitation depends critically on relationship building and collaboration with the expert	Sometimes expertise is obtainable by teams of knowledge engineers
CREATION	Care needs to be taken, so that inaccurate or specious knowledge is not modeled	The same expertise can come from several sources and different methods

Table 2. Comparison of major metaphors in terms of their conceptions of "expertise elicitation"

For those who think of expertise elicitation as *capture,* the knowledge acquisition process is described as one in which the knowledge engineer needs to be in control of the expert. Note the following: "Knowledge engineers must give up as much control as is necessary for the expert's comfort. At the same time, they must *retain sufficient control* to ensure that they acquire the necessary information" (Scott, Clayton, and Gibson 1991, p. 434).

The *capture* metaphor led to emphasis being placed on learning how to deal with problematic experts. The focus shifted from getting the know-how out of the expert to getting the expert to be cooperative and compliant. For example, there are personality traits to look for in an expert [e.g., patience, ability to communicate, and honesty (McGraw and Harbison-Briggs 1989); cooperativeness, affability, and commitment (Prerau 1987)], and strategies for how to manage unruly experts [e.g., solutions for how to deal with those experts who provide incorrect information or explanations that wander aimlessly (Brown 1989; Walters and Nielsen 1988)].

Regarded as *courtship,* the knowledge acquisition strategy requires first securing consensus as to who is the best expert and then creating a climate in which the selected expert wants to be engaged. Thus, knowledge acquisition is from first to last an interpersonal encounter and the knowledge engineer is a person needs to possess high-quality social skills. With the *creation* metaphor, successful knowledge acquisition depends much more heavily on the knowledge engineer's talent and training for inference and invention.

Conclusions

Expertise elicitation for the purpose of building knowledge-based systems can be a complex and dynamic enterprise. It is no wonder that a number of metaphors have emerged to characterize features that are at various times salient and problematic. While no single metaphor can lay claim to the entire "truth" of expertise elicitation, researchers and programmers alike might profit by attending to what is both made visible and rendered hidden by the choice to adopt one metaphor over another.

All four major metaphors, namely, excavation, capture, courtship and creation, share the idea that expertise is valuable. For the first two metaphors especially, expertise is regarded as too valuable to be left in the hands of experts for there it is frequently unavailable, or worse, it could disappear altogether. The first two also imply that expertise is an object and that it can exist independently of the context in which it is enacted or elicited. While the metaphors of excavation and capture do not exclude the notion that each expert has a unique perspective, nevertheless the implication is that expertise is more or less equivalent in any given domain and wherever found, can be transported and transferred without variation or change in meaning. In contrast, the more recent metaphors of courtship and creation metaphors give voice to the more contextual and transactional qualities of expertise elicitation.

Metaphors help the system builder deal with the complicated task of explicating know-how, but the predominant metaphors of expertise elicitation show signs of having moved from being suggestive descriptions to being taken as literal statements of reality. In taking metaphors literally, myths rather than truth may come to prevail (MacCormac 1985; Spiro, et al. 1989). In addition, literalness implies that blame for the knowledge acquisition bottleneck lies solely on the human expert. That is, experts store their knowledge in ways that make it extremely difficult for them to access it. Often, most experts implicitly know where to go for what they need. It is the knowledge engineer who has trouble gaining access to this automatic process. With the exception of the creation metaphor, there is little recognition of the fact that the difficulty in expertise elicitation may be a problem as much of knowledge representation as it is of acquisition. In other words, the fault may lie in the limitations currently available for representing the complexity and range of expertise in even very bounded domains.

The problem of acquiring knowledge from an expert has rekindled questions as to how one person can come to understand what someone else (of considerably more experience) already knows. Metaphors provide both insight into and precautions about this human cognitive activity. Knowledge engineers would do well occasionally to reflect on how they talk and think about what they do, especially when encountering obstacles in eliciting expertise. Having adopted a particular metaphorical perspective, they may inadvertently close off other solution options which become visible when one ponders another metaphor. And because expertise elicitation is important both theoretically as well as practically to those who build expert systems, the channels should always be kept open for new metaphors.

Acknowledgments

This research was supported by grant number BNS-8721882 from the National Science Foundation.

References

Agnew, N.M., Ford, K.M. & Hayes, P.J. (1994). Expertise in context: Personally constructed, socially selected, and reality-relevant. *International Journal of Expert Systems, 7,* 65-88.

Axley, S.R. (1984). Managerial and organizational communication in terms of the conduit metaphor. *Academy of Management Review, 9,* 428-437.

Brown, B. (1989). The taming of an expert: An anecdotal report. *SIGART Newsletter, 108,* 133-135.

Buchanan, B.G. (1982). New research on expert systems. In J.E. Hayes, D. Michie, & Y.H. Pao (Eds.), *Machine Intelligence 10.* New York: Wiley.

Clancey, W.J. (1987). Book review of Winograd's and Flores' "Understanding Computers and Cognition: A new foundation for design". *Artificial Intelligence, 31,* 233-251.

Davis, R. (1985). Problem solutions with expert systems: Approach, tools available, how to begin. From Texas Instruments Satellite Symposium: *Knowledge-based Systems and Their Applications.* Dallas, Texas.

Davis, R. & Lenat, D.B. (1982). *Knowledge-based systems in artificial intelligence.* New York: McGraw Hill.

Feigenbaum, E.A. (1977). The art of artificial intelligence: Themes and case studies of knowledge engineering. *Proceedings of the Fifth International Joint Conference on Artificial Intelligence.*

Feigenbaum, E.A. (1980). *Knowledge engineering: The applied side of artificial intelligence.* Stanford, CA: Stanford University Heuristic Programming Project.

Feigenbaum, E.A. & McCorduck, P. (1984). *The Fifth Generation.* London: Pan Books.

Ford, K.M. & Adams-Webber, J.R. (1992). Knowledge acquisition and constructivist epistemology. In R.R. Hoffman (Ed.), *The Psychology of Expertise: Cognitive Research and Empirical AI* (pp. 121-136). New York: Springer-Verlag.

Gaines, B.R. & Boose, J.H. (Eds.). (1988). *Knowledge acquisition for knowledge based systems.* London: Academic Press.

Gallant, M. (1991). An electronic partner at the negotiation table. *Canadian Business Review, 18*(3), 42.

Gentner, D. (1982). Are scientific analogies metaphors?. In D.S. Miall (Ed.), *Metaphor: Problems and Perspectives.* Harvester Press.

Hayes-Roth, F. (1984). The knowledge-based expert system: A tutorial. *IEEE Computer, 17,* 11-28.

Hayes-Roth, F., Waterman, D.A. & Lenat, D.B. (Eds.). (1983). *Building Expert Systems.* Reading, MA: Addison-Wesley.

Hoffman, R.R. (Ed.). (1992). *The Psychology of Expertise: Cognitive Research and Empirical AI.* New York: Springer-Verlag.

Indurkhya, B. (1992). *Metaphor and Cognition: An Interactionist Approach.* Dortrecht/Boston: Kluwer Academic.

Johnson, G. (1986). *Machinery of the Mind.* Redmond, WA: Microsoft Press.

Kinoshita, T. (1989). A knowledge acquisition model with applications for requirements specification and definition. *SIGART Newsletter, 108,* 166-168.

LaFrance, M. (1990). The special structure of expertise. In K.L. McGraw & C.R. Westphal (Eds.), *Readings in Knowledge Acquisition: Current practices and trends.* New York: Ellis Horwood.

LaFrance, M. (1991). What are experts for? *AI & Society: The International Journal of Human and Machine Intelligence,* 161-170.

LaFrance, M. (1992). Questioning knowledge acquisition. In A. Graesser, E. Peacock, & T. Lauer (Eds.), *Questions and Information Systems.* Hillsdale, NJ: Lawrence Erlbaum.

Lakoff, G. & Johnson, M. (1980). *Metaphors We Live By.* Chicago: University of Chicago Press.

Laurie, S. (1992). Experience on a disc. *The Banker, 142(795),* 56.

McCorduck, P. (1979). *Machines Who Think: A Personal Inquiry into the History and Prospects of Artificial Intelligence.* New York: Freeman.

MacCormac, E.R. (1985). *A Cognitive Theory of Metaphor.* Cambridge, MA: MIT Press.

McGraw, K.L. & Harbison-Briggs, K. (1989). *Knowledge Acquisition: Principles and Guidelines.* Englewood Cliffs, NJ: Prentice Hall.

Michaelsen, R.H., Michie, D. & Boulanger, A. (1985). The technology of expert systems. *Byte,* April, 303-312.

Michie, D. & Johnston, R. (1985). *The creative computer.* London: Pelican.

Miller, G. (1979). Images and models, similes and metaphors. In A. Ortony (Ed.), *Metaphor and Thought* (pp. 202-253). New York: Cambridge University Press.

Olson, J.R. & Rueter, H.H. (1987). Extracting expertise from experts: Methods for knowledge acquisition. *Expert Systems, 4.*

Ortony, A. (1979). Beyond literal similarity. *Psychological Review, 86,* 161-180.

Prerau, D.S. (1987). Knowledge acquisition in the development of a large expert system. *AI Magazine, 8,* (Summer), 215-223.

Reddy, M. (1979). The conduit metaphor. In A. Ortony (Ed.), *Metaphor and Thought.* New York: Cambridge University Press.

Resnick, L., Levine, J. & Teasley, S. (1991). *Socially Shared Knowledge.* Washington, DC: American Psychological Association.

Schon, D.A. (1983). *The Reflective Practitioner: How Professionals Think in Action.* New York: Basic Books.

Scott, A.C., Clayton, J.E. & Gibson, E.L. (1991). *A Practical Guide to Knowledge Acquisition.* Reading, MA: Addison Wesley.

Spiro, R., Feltovich, P.J., Coulson, R.L. & Anderson, D.K. (1989). In S. Vosniadon & A. Ortony (Eds.), *Similarity and Analogical Reasoning*. Cambridge: Cambridge University Press.

Stefik, M. & Conway, L. (1982). Toward the principled engineering of knowledge. *The AI Magazine*. Summer.

Stein, E.W. (1992). A method to identify candidates for knowledge acquisition. *Journal of Management Information Systems, 9*, 161-178.

Stein, E.W. (1993, May). Validating attributed knowledge and expertise. Paper presented at *The Third International Workshop on Human & Machine Cognition, Special Topic: Expertise in Context*. Seaside, Florida.

Touby, L., Romano, C. & Russel, A.M. (1990). The thinking machines: How to have experts at your fingertips. *Working Woman, 15(11)*, 87.

Waterman, D.A. (1986). *A Guide to Expert Systems*. Reading, MA: Addison-Wesley.

Waters, J.R. & Nielsen, N.R. (1988). *Crafting Knowledge-Based Systems: Expert Systems Made Easy/Realistic*. New York: Wiley.

Westphal, C.R. & Blanchard, D.R. (1989). A compendium of knowledge acquisition references. *SIGART Newsletter, 108*, 33-57.

Wheelwright, P.E. (1962). *Metaphor and Reality*. Bloomington, IA: Indiana University Press.

Winograd, T. & Flores, F. (1989). *Understanding Computers and Cognition: A New Foundation for Design*. New York: McGraw Hill.

Young, R.M. (1989). Human interface aspects of expert systems. In L.A. Murray & J.R.E. Richardson (Eds.), *Intelligent Systems in a Human Context*. Oxford: Oxford University Press.

CHAPTER 8

A Look At Expertise From A Social Perspective

Eric W. Stein

Introduction

Human beings live in multiple social contexts that guide and shape their behavior and ideas. The purpose of this chapter is to review works that consider human expertise in context. My desire is to broaden our notion of expertise to include social considerations. The chapter is structured as follows. Following the introduction, I examine emerging views and theories of expertise in context. Next, I discuss empirical methods for measuring expertise in the social context. Finally, I close with a summary and some final reflections.

Views of Expertise in Context

Research on human expertise may be divided into several streams. Most modern research focuses on the individual attributes of experts (e.g., skills, cognitive structures). For recent research in this area, the reader is referred to other chapters in this volume as well as prior works in the field.[1] However, in the past few years, there has been growing interest in expertise from a social perspective, a view that complements study of expertise from a cognitive psychological perspective.

Emergence of Works on Expertise in Context

Research on expertise in context comes to us from organization theory (Stein 1992, 1995), constructivism, evolutionary epistemology, and the philosophy of science (Agnew, Ford, and Hayes 1994), communication theory (Harvey 1992), and marketing (Ohanian 1990). Table 1 provides a summary of the

Social Referent	Theoretical/Empirical Approach	Representative Thinkers	Reference Disciplines
Constituents	Constituencies select experts based on goodness of fit between their knowledge and the criteria of the constituents.	Agnew et al. (1994)	Philosophy of Science & Psychology
Organizational members	Experts provide members of the social network with core knowledge about business activities. May be measured using social network analysis	Stein (1992, 1995)	Organization Theory
Consumers	Consumers perceive people as being an expert in one or more areas. May be measured using multi-dimensional survey instruments.	Ohanian (1990)	Marketing
Information receivers	Expertise viewed as system of exchange between sender (expert) and receiver (non-expert). System may be modeled via signal detection theory.	Harvey (1992)	Communication Theory

Table 1. Streams of research on expertise from a social perspective.

major areas of research in expertise from a social perspective.

In essence, each view considers the expert in relation to a referent social group such as a social network, an organization, a constituency, or a market. As indicated in figure 1, experts interact with members of the social context locally and globally. For example, experts may interact with the members of their organizations or may serve constituencies at large. In each case, the perceptions of the members of the social referent play a significant role in designating who has expertise, as well as codetermining the quality of that expertise.

This line of thinking opens up several research possibilities. The social perspective differs from the view that expertise resides merely in the expert. Instead, the construct of expertise is seen as jointly determined by individual skills and knowledge, and the needs, perceptions, and activities of the members of the social system with whom the expert interacts. Put another way, we might say that expertise resides in the *expert-in-context*. Following a discussion of different views of expertise, I discuss ways to measure it.

Expertise from a Constituency Perspective

One conceptualization is that of the expert as serving a constituency (Agnew, *et al.* 1994, see also Agnew & Ford this volume). This conception is grounded in evolutionary epistemology, constructivism, and the philosophy of science.

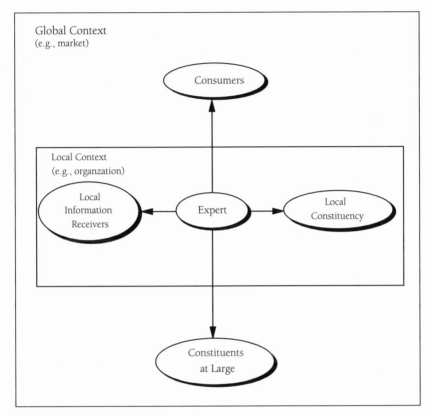

Figure 1: The Expert in context.

Agnew *et al.* propose that constituencies select their experts based on the perceived usefulness of their knowledge. They argue that some are chosen to play the role of expert based on the goodness of fit between their characteristics and the various selectors employed by the constituency in question. Each constituency may apply different criteria in the evaluation and selection of their experts. For instance, Agnew *et al.* observe that scientific communities usually subject their experts to more rigorous evaluation criteria than is found in some other communities. Thus, the expertise that emerges from different constituencies may be of varying degrees of quality or levels.

Agnew *et al.* define Level 1 experts as those who offer personal constructions that have meaning for their constituencies, although these constructions may not be "reality relevant." In other words, a Level 1 expert provides functional, yet possibly fallible, advice for his or her constituency. This expertise may be grounded in an empirical base of personal "cases," but is not knowledge derived from controlled experimentation, which allows for the identification of variables and their causal relationships. Experts in this first category include "snake-oil" salesmen, politicians, and used car sales people. However, even doctors, lawyers, stock brokers and other professionals may fall into this category for the following reasons. All constituencies have a "most trusted" method of validation to satisfy the condition of reality relevance. Scientific method properly practiced is Agnew *et al.*'s most trusted method of validation. Agnew *et al.* only award Level 2 status to experts whose knowledge claims have been subjected to the rigors of empirical scientific testing, their most trusted selector for reality relevance. Very few experts fall into this category because most constituencies do not apply the principles of rigorous scientific testing in their evaluations.

This conception of expertise is useful because it explains the emergence of different types of expertise. It accounts for witch doctors among native peoples, who, prior to the introduction of formal science, provided the best available knowledge to their constituents. Yet even in modern life, communities choose some of their experts for various reasons and under different systems of evaluation. Churchman (1971) observed that members of a "Lockean" community of inquirers construct their knowledge based on intersubjective agreement among the members.

> Thus the design of a Lockean (inquiring system) requires the design of a community of inquiring systems in which virtually all "agree" that an input is simple or not simple, and if any disagreement ever occurs, the disagreement can be removed by re-presenting the stimulus to each of the members of the community of inquiring systems, and eventually so large a majority will agree that the voice of dissent is lost. Evidence that such a design can be accomplished seems to follow from the common experience of sensory agreement among human observers with a common language and psychological attitude (p. 105).

High levels of observer agreement occur in many professional and scientific contexts. For example, if Dr. Smith is perceived as solving "most" of the hard medical cases in the community, then his expertise may stand undisputed for some time, even if there is statistical evidence to the contrary. Scientific communities may also fall prey to this limitation, as Kuhn (1970) has observed. Agnew *et al.* therefore expose the soft underbelly of the notion of individual expertise and offer an alternative in their constituency view of expertise.

Although Agnew *et al.* position science as their most trusted selector of expertise, there are other rigorous, yet nonscientific, forms of expert evaluation. For instance, organizations employ checks and balances to discriminate between experts and nonexperts (see next section), and industries employ strict licensing procedures to select and gauge the quality of their experts. Various requirements such as milestone-based learning outcomes (e.g., the Ph.D., RN, JD, etc.), as well as on-going training and quality classifications (e.g., professional engineer classification) also serve to ensure expert quality. These other evaluations are critically important because the knowledge of relatively few experts is subjected to scientific testing. The degree to which these criteria approximate the rigor of scientific testing is worthy of further study. Such work may suggest an alternative expert classification scheme based on a continuum rather than a set of discrete categories or levels.

Expertise from an Organizational Perspective

Many experts serve members of their organizations or "networks" (Stein 1992, 1995). A social network is an interdependent social group of which the expert is part. Experts act as sources of knowledge for the network by responding to requests from the members. An argument can be made that members of an organization (i.e., the constituency) select experts whose knowledge results in positive personal and organizational outcomes over time. While this expertise does not qualify as Level 2 according to the framework put forth by Agnew *et al.* (1994), expertise in organizational contexts can none the less be subjected to rigorous selection.

There are two observations that support this contention. First, organizations, especially business organizations (e.g., Federal Express, IBM), are highly interdependent. Serial interdependence, where the outputs of one process become the inputs to the next process, provides the most effective check on input quality. For example, if the marketing department's sales forecast is used by manufacturing to gauge production runs, then the data must be of high quality or manufacturing will come to reject marketing's figures. Furthermore, business organizations hold their members and the business units to outcome measures such as profit/loss, market share, return on investment (ROI), and so on. If one member of the marketing department is better at providing forecasts than others, then, over time, manufacturing should request information from this person in order to maintain manufacturing's bottom line. Based on these observations, I proposed (Stein 1992, 1995) that the rate that information is retrieved from certain employees is indicative of expertise in one or more areas. This variable was operationalized using the techniques of social network analysis and is discussed in the Measurement section of this chapter.

Expertise from a Market Perspective

Another way to conceive expertise is from a market perspective, which illustrates how experts can serve constituencies at large. Expertise can be regarded as a transaction between an expert (who is viewed as a service provider) and a consumer. This conceptualization has been used by marketers to examine the variables that affect advertising effectiveness, where the perceived quality and credibility of an expert spokesperson can sometimes translate into market share changes equaling tens and hundreds of millions of dollars.

In the words of Ohanian (1990):

> The selection of an appropriate spokesperson for a product or a service is an important, yet difficult, decision. Is an effective and credible spokesperson someone who is attractive, trustworthy, or an expert.... Marketing and advertising practitioners share the belief that a communicator's character has a significant effect on the persuasiveness of the message. (p. 39)

One of the benefits of modeling expertise this way is that the techniques of attitude measurement are highly developed in the field of advertising, and these techniques may be utilized to examine expertise in context. One of these techniques is discussed in the Measurement section of this chapter.

Expertise from a Communication Theory Perspective

It is possible to look at expertise through the lens of classic communication theory (Shannon and Weaver 1964). Together, an expert (the sender) and a nonexpert (the receiver) form a communication system. An expert renders an opinion and this opinion is "sent" to a nonexpert who receives it in order to choose an appropriate course of action (Harvey 1992). Examples of this situation abound in everyday life: weather experts "send" forecasts to farmers who must decide how best to protect their crops; experts testify to jurors who must decide the fate of defendants. This characterization in terms of senders and receivers is consistent with the view that communication patterns in organizations are indicative of where expertise resides. Harvey (1992) argues that rendering an opinion to a receiver is in principle no different from deciding whether a particular stimulus was present to an observer, which may be modeled using signal detection theory.

Using the framework of signal detection theory, Harvey distinguishes between the accuracy of an expert and his or her performance. *Accuracy* is defined strictly as a function of the expert's knowledge and skills. *Performance* on the other hand takes into account the receiver's characteristics and biases. Harvey suggests that the performance of an expert can be modeled as a joint probability of the latter's characteristics and the receiver's goals and evaluation criteria. Thus, the level analysis becomes the expert in context rather than the expert alone. This characterization is consistent with Agnew et al.'s (1994) assumption that the designation of "expert" arises from the attributions of the constituency, as well as the individual characteristics of the expert. According to Harvey's framework, an expert can be accurate but not necessarily show high levels of performance. For example, if a constituency embraces the advice offered by an expert, his or her performance will be positively regarded; if the advice offered by the expert is out of sync with the constituency's needs, then performance will be negatively regarded. Harvey's work thus operationalizes the coupling between experts and members of the social referent.

Measuring Expertise in Context

Having reviewed four different ways to theoretically describe *expertise-in-context*, we turn to an examination of the techniques available to measure it.

Measuring Expertise Using a Multi-Dimensional Scale

One way to measure expertise in context is to measure the attitudes of an expert's constituency using a multi-dimensional scale. This method is applicable for rank-ordering the perceived status of a few well-known experts.

Ohanian (1990) demonstrated a way to measure the expertness and trustworthiness of celebrity endorsers based on consumer attitudes using a multi-dimensional psychometric scale. The instrument was utilized in the following way. First, the celebrities were chosen by 40 students who were asked to list all the celebrities who came to mind. The most frequently mentioned gender pair was John McEnroe and Madonna, and they were then used in the study with other celebrity pairs. Next, items for the source credibility scale were selected. Several (52) students were asked to evaluate lists of words that pertained to the constructs of expertise, trust, and attractiveness. Items with 75% or more agreement were assigned to that construct. These words were then used to construct a semantic differential scale to evaluate source credibility. A semantic differential scale "seeks to measure the meaning of an object to an individual...on a series of 7-point, bipolar rating scales. Any concept, whether a political issue, a person, an institution, or a work of art can be rated" (Miller 1991, p. 183). Examples of such bipolar scales include fair-unfair, good-bad, novice-expert, trustworthy-untrustworthy, etc. Factor analysis resulted in the identification of 11 word items associated with expertise. The final model found the construct of expertise to be described by five key adjectives: (1) "expert," (2) "experienced," (3) "knowledgeable," (4) "qualified," and (5) "skilled." Construct reliability was reported at .885 and above. Once the scale was validated, several hundred students were asked to evaluate the McEnroe-Madonna pair in terms of source credibility.

What is the significance of this work? Ohanian demonstrates that expertise can be measured as a construct having multiple dimensions. Second, this work offered a validated instrument that may be used to assess expertise in contexts at large; that is, to measure the expertise of a small number of well-known experts. Researchers may find this instrument useful in the measurement of expertise in other contexts. However, if the experts are not well-known or in the context of large organizations, then an alternative method such as social network analysis may be used.

Measuring Expertise Using Network Analysis

One way to systematically tap the knowledge of "who knows what" in organizational contexts is to apply social network analysis. The earliest expression of a social network was the sociogram (Moreno 1934), which is a diagram of the relationships between members of a social system. Relations between individuals may be represented as directed graphs or matrices (Hage and Harary 1983). For example, if A seeks knowledge from B, then that relation can be represented on a digraph by drawing an arrow from A to B. The same information can be represented as a "1" in a matrix of senders and receivers. An entire organization can be represented in this format. The quality of an exchange also may be measured such as its importance, accuracy, and timeliness.

Once the data are collected, they may be analyzed at the system, group, and individual levels. The interested reader is referred to Alba (1982), Burt (1983), Hage (1983), Knoke (1982), and Lincoln (1982) for complete coverage of these topics. Individual network measures convey the degree to which a member of the network is valued by other members of the network for one or more interactions or relationships. For example, if we ask each person in an n-person network: "To what degree do you *trust* each of the following people listed below?," each member would receive $n-1$ scores along the dimension of trust. One can determine who is most trusted by the other members by rank ordering the scores. In the parlance of network analysis, high-scoring members are considered "central" to the network. Almost any attribute can be measured with network centrality scores, including communication centrality, information retrieval centrality, cooperation centrality, trust centrality, etc.

Network surveys are designed according to several specifications. First, the researcher must select the relations to be profiled (e.g., information retrieval, trust). Second, the researcher must scale each interaction as a binary choice (e.g., as 0 or 1), a nominal choice (e.g., high, medium, or low), or on an interval scale (e.g., 1–10). For studies involving information retrieval, the researcher must select the type of knowledge under consideration. Questions are then constructed to measure the strength of the interactions. For example, if we want to know who is an expert on hazardous waste regulations, we would ask: "From whom do you retrieve information about hazardous waste regulations?" All members of the organization are listed under each question. In my experience, network surveys can be completed in 3–5 minutes by pen and paper or 1–3 minutes by telephone, and the data are easily tabulated in a spreadsheet. Electronic mail can also be used to distribute and collect network data. A department of 30–40 people can be surveyed in less than a day while a hundred people can be surveyed in as little as a few days.

Network data may be tabulated and analyzed using spreadsheets or specialized programs (for information on specialized programs, see Borgatti, Everett, and Freeman 1992; Burt 1987). The convention is to set up a matrix of respondents and sources of knowledge. Each respondent (N_i) is assigned an identification number (ID). These identification numbers may be listed across the top row of a spreadsheet. In the left-hand column, the names of the potential information resources (R_i) are listed. Frequency-scaled scores may be obtained by calculating the row sums or means. The row scores, which indicate retrieval centrality, are then ordered from the highest to the lowest. Members with the highest retrieval scores are central sources for the organization.

This method was first used in the context of identifying candidates to participate in knowledge acquisition for use in the development of expert systems (Stein 1992). Human experts and sources of documented knowledge that supported problem-solving were identified in a small library services organization. Expertise was measured by determining retrieval centrality for each member and then ranking the results. The higher the centrality score, the greater the defined level of expertise. The network survey consisted of questions such as: "From whom do you retrieve information about administrative procedures?" followed by a list of names of the members of the network. Each respondent was asked to indicate on a scale how often he or she retrieved particular information from other members of the organization. Expertise in five broad areas of knowledge was identified: Service Support, Public Services, Administrative Procedures, Historical Information, and Rules and Norms. The categories were chosen because they represented the core of the organization's knowledge base according to prior interviews with senior management. The response rate on the survey was 100% (21 out of 21). Retrieval centrality scores were normalized by the maximum retrieval score for each category of knowledge. Normalized scores were then rank-ordered by total scores across all categories of knowledge. Members of the organization with scores greater than one standard deviation above the mean for one or more types of knowledge were designated experts for that category.

These results were validated several ways. First, the scores were compared to a chi-square distribution. It was assumed that if people were indifferent to the quality of the source, then each person would receive approximately the same retrieval score. A chi-square test was performed comparing the observed scores to the number of responses expected from a uniform distribution (i.e., the mean retrieval score). The chi-square values indicated that the observed retrieval scores for people were significantly different ($p < .001$) from what would have occurred under an assumption of uniformity. This result supported the contention that source quality was a factor in the selection of experts.

The results of the study were also cross-checked by conducting interviews, before and after data collection, with key personnel in the organization (larger organizations would require the application of independent measures of expertise in addition to the interviews). Finally, the method was applied to a second field site to verify that it could be administered in an efficient manner.

In sum, network analysis was found to be a useful means of identifying experts in organizational contexts. Given the relative success of the method, another study was initiated to measure expertise in context.

Measuring Expertise in an Organizational Context

One important research question concerning expertise is: "What are the differences between experts and nonexperts in organizational settings?" This question was addressed in a recent study (Stein 1995). The members of two organizations (a biotechnology firm and an educational institution) were partitioned into groups of experts and nonexperts to examine their differences in terms of demographic, organizational, and social-psychological variables. Organizational variables included job level and the number of employees reporting to each person. Social-psychological variables included cooperativeness, accessibility, trust, and leadership. It was hypothesized that experts would display different levels of these variables than nonexperts. A two-way Analysis of Variance was conducted to detect differences in mean scores for experts and nonexperts for the variables indicated at the 95% confidence level.

Data for the study were collected at two organizations located in the greater Philadelphia area. The first site was a small biotechnology start-up firm known by the pseudonym BIOTEC. The second site was a division of an established eastern educational institution, which was identified as EDSYS. Experts were identified using the techniques of network analysis described above. Those who scored $z > 2$ on at least one of the categories of core knowledge for the organization were designated experts.

This procedure yielded seven experts and 24 nonexperts at BIOTEC and 15 experts and 38 nonexperts at EDSYS. The results of the expert identification were validated through interviews with key informants at both sites, which was considered adequate because the sites were small (for larger sites, I recommend that experts be evaluated using independent instruments; e.g., performance evaluations, in-depth interviews; tests of domain knowledge; etc.). Once experts were identified, data were collected for each of the study variables. Experience (age, industry, and organizational experience) was measured using clearly worded questions such as "How old are you?"; "How long have you worked in this organization?". Education was measured using a scale similar to the one developed by Hollingshead and Redlich (1958). Job level within the organization was determined by analyzing formal reporting data and organizational charts at both sites. Cooperation, accessibility, trust, and leadership were measured using network analysis; that is, respondents were asked to indicate the degree (on a 5-point Likert scale) that they trusted others, considered them cooperative or accessible, and showed leadership.

The results of the study were as follows. In terms of education, the evidence was unequivocal: experts had significantly higher levels of formal education than nonexperts. This result was consistent with an earlier work by Abdolmohammadi and Shanteau (1992). Experience was defined here in terms of life experience (e.g., age), industry experience, and organizational experience. The study found no difference between experts and nonexperts in terms of age or industry experience. This study did not find a significant difference between experts and nonexperts in terms of organizational experience. However, the analysis revealed an interaction effect, which showed that organizational experience was greater for experts at one organization, while less at the other.

This study found experts to have significantly higher job levels and numbers of people reporting to them than nonexperts. There was almost no difference between experts and nonexperts in terms of cooperation as measured. Another interesting finding was that experts were trusted more than nonexperts. Finally, support was found for the hypothesis that experts show higher levels of leadership than nonexperts. This result is not entirely surprising since knowledge, experience, intelligence, confidence, and communication effectiveness can be the basis for leadership in organizations (Griffin 1993).

Final Thoughts

I have tried to demonstrate that expertise can be usefully thought of as a function of social context as well as individual skills, knowledge, and experience. One of the results of this work is that the expert and his or her social referent can be viewed as a coupled system. Beginning with Agnew et al. (1994), the expert is linked to a constituency, which has a role in his or her selection. Harvey (1992) showed how the attitudes of the members of the social referent could determine the success of an expert, even though he or she was individually accurate. Ohanian (1990) examined the relationships between experts and consumers in a market context. I have argued (Stein 1992, 1995) that experts serve members of the social network in organizational contexts, and that members' information-seeking behaviors and attitudes are reflective of who had expertise. In this chapter, I have also outlined ways to measure expertise in context. A multi-dimensional scale like the one described by Ohanian (1990) may be used to measure the expertise of a few experts known to constituents at large. In organizational contexts, the efficacy of using network analysis to identify experts and their characteristics was demonstrated.

This work has implications for both theory and practice. The notion of *expertise in context* adds new scope to research in this area. Expertise will continue, of course, to be studied from a cognitive psychological view. On the other hand, study of the social context may offer further insights into the nature of expertise not yet accessed by cognitive psychological methods. New research questions can be framed and investigated from a social-psychological perspective using communication theory, social network analysis, and a constituency view of expertise. For example, we might consider whether experts are trusted more than other people (i.e., if someone is an expert, is he or she then trusted more by others?). Do people who are simply trusted become experts? These questions and many others can be explored perhaps more easily if we consider the expert in context.

For those embarking on research on expertise in organizational contexts, network analysis may be used to identify expert subjects (as I have defined them) instead of using the ad hoc methods frequently employed. For instance, when Shanteau (1987, 1992) identified experts for study in two recent works he did so by peer review:

> My suggestion is to let those in a domain define the experts. In every field, there are those who are considered by their peers to be best at what they do. In some domains this is reflected by official recognition or job titles. In others, it comes from consensual acclamation. In my research, experts are operationally defined as those who have been recognized within their professional as having the necessary skills and abilities to perform at the highest level. (1992, p. 255)

Now at least researchers have a systematic means to identify subjects.

A practical application of this work is in the field of knowledge engineering and the building of expert systems. Waterman (1986) suggested that experts be identified on the basis of the opinions of the members of the organization. Toward that end, network analysis provides an operational method to identify experts for use in knowledge acquisition. I encourage others to test the assumption that information retrieval rates are indicative of expertise (see Stein 1992) by comparing these data to performance measures and the results of psychological tests.

It is beneficial for expertise to be considered in context. Viewing expertise from a contextual view provides a way to explain aspects of expertise that do not fit neatly into cognitive psychological models. An expert is more than the sum of his or her cognitive abilities and skills—he or she is also codefined by context.

Acknowledgments

Preparation of this article was supported by Penn State (Great Valley campus, Malvern, PA), which provided funds that enabled the author to travel to international conferences to present and refine these ideas. The author thanks the editors of this volume for their helpful guidance and feedback.

Note

Discussions in the field of cognitive psychology regarding the differences between experts and novices can be found in Dreyfus and Dreyfus (1986); Chi, Feltovich, and Glaser (1981); Chi, Glaser, and Farr (1988); Larkin, McDermott, Simon, and Simon (1980); Anderson (1985); Benner (1984); and the role of mental models in problem solving Gentner and Stevens (1983). A discussion of levels of competence is found in Sternberg (1992). Those interested in empirical applications are directed to Hoffman (1992). Some work on expert systems and human task performance can be found in Prerau (1987) and in Keller (1987).

References

Abdolmohammadi, M.J., & Shanteau, J. (1992). Personal attributes of expert auditors. *Organizational Behavior and Human Decision Processes, 53*, 158-172.

Agnew, N.M., Ford, K.M., & Hayes, P.J. (1994). Expertise in context: personally constructed, socially selected, and reality relevant? *International Journal of Expert Systems: Research and Applications, 7(1)*, 65-88.

Alba, R.D. (1982). Taking stock of network analysis. *Research in the Sociology of Organizations, 1*, 39-74.

Anderson, J.R. (1985). *Cognitive Psychology and its Implications.* New York: Freeman.

Benner, P. (1984). *From Novice to Expert: Excellence and Power in Clinical Nursing Practice.* San Francisco, CA: Addison Wesley.

Borgatti, S., Everett, M.G., & Freeman, L. (1992). *UCINET IV manual.* Columbia, SC: Analytic Technologies.

Burt, R. (1987). *Structure: Version 3.2* (Tech. Report No. TR2). Center for the Social Sciences at Columbia University.

Burt, R.S. & Minor, M.J. (1983). *Applied Network Analysis: A Methodological Introduction.* Beverly Hills, CA: Sage.

Chi, M.T.H., Feltovich, P.J., & Glaser, R. (1981). Categorization and representation of physics problems by experts and novices. *Cognitive Science, 5*, 121-152.

Chi, M.T.H., Glaser, R., & Farr, M.J. (Eds.). (1988). *The Nature of Expertise.* Hillsdale, NJ: Erlbaum.

Churchman, C.W. (1971). *The Design of Inquiring Systems.* New York: Basic Books.

Dreyfus, H. & Dreyfus, S. (1986). *Mind Over Machine.* New York: The Free Press.

Gentner, D. & Stevens, A.S. (Eds.). (1983). *Mental Models.* Hillsdale, NJ: Erlbaum.

Griffin, R.W. (1993). *Management.* Boston: Houghton Mifflin.

Hage, P. & Harary, F. (1983). *Structural Models in Anthropology.* New York: Cambridge University Press.

Harvey, L.O. (1992). The critical operating characteristic and the evaluation of expert judgement. *Organizational Behavior and Human Decision Processes, 53*, 229-251.

Hoffman, R.R. (Ed.). (1992). *The Psychology of Expertise: Cognitive Research and Empirical AI.* New York: Springer-Verlag.

Hollingshead, A.B. & Redlich, F.C. (1958). *Social Class and Mental Illness: A Community Study.* New York: John Wiley.

Keller, R. (1987). *Expert Systems Technology.* Englewood Cliffs, NJ: Yourdon Press (Prentice Hall).

Knoke, D. & Kuklinski, J.H. (1982). *Network Analysis.* Beverly Hills, CA: Sage.

Kuhn, T. (1970). *The Structure of Scientific Revolutions.* Chicago: University of Chicago Press.

Larkin, J., McDermott, J., Simon, D.P., & Simon, H. (1980). Expert and novice performance in solving physics problems. *Science, 208(20),* 1335-1342.

Lincoln, J.R. (1982). Intra-(and inter-) organizational networks. In *Research in the Sociology of Organizations* (pp. 1-38). Greenwich, CT: JAI Press.

Miller, D.C. (1991). *Handbook of Research Design and Social Measurement* (5th. Ed.). Newbury Park, CA: Sage.

Moreno, J.L. (1934). *Who Shall Survive?* Washington, D.C.: Nervous and Mental Disease Publishing.

Ohanian, R. (1990). Construction and validation of a scale to measure celebrity endorsers' perceived expertise, trustworthiness, and attractiveness. *Journal of Advertising, 19(3),* 39-52.

Prerau, D.S. (1987). Knowledge acquisition in the development of a large expert system. *AI Magazine, 8(2),* (Summer), 43-51.

Shannon, C. & Weaver, W. (1964). *The Mathematical Theory of Communication.* Urbana, IL: University of Illinois Press.

Shanteau, J. (1987). Psychological characteristics of expert decision makers. In J.L. Mumpower, O. Renn, L.D. Phillips, & V.R.R. Uppuluri (Eds.), *Expert Judgement and Expert Systems.* Berlin: Springer-Verlag.

Shanteau, J. (1992). Competence in experts: the role of task characteristics. *Organizational Behavior and Human Decision Processes, 53,* 252-266.

Stein, E.W. (1992). A method to identify candidates for knowledge acquisition. *Journal of Management Information Systems, 9,* (Fall), 161-178.

Stein, E.W. (1995). Social and individual characteristics of human experts. *International Journal of Expert Systems: Research and Applications, 8(2),* 121-143.

Sternberg, R.J. & Frensch, P.A. (1992). On being an expert: A cost-benefit analysis. In R. Hoffman (Ed.), *The Psychology of Expertise: Cognitive Research and Empirical AI.* New York: Springer-Verlag.

Waterman, D.A. (1986). *A Guide to Expert Systems.* Reading, MA: Addison-Wesley.

CHAPTER 9

Expertise in Dynamic, Physical Task Domains

Valerie L. Shalin, Norman D. Geddes, Dennis Bertram, Michael A. Szczepkowski, & David DuBois

Introduction

Laboratory studies of expertise have usually focused on the individual expert's selection and sequencing of problem solving inferences and the relationship between these inferences and the expert's initial understanding of a problem description (Chi, Feltovich, and Glaser 1981; Patel and Groen 1986). The results of such studies emphasize the regularities of expert behavior across tasks. However, a criticism of laboratory studies is that such tasksenvironments are lacking broader context and missing many of the features and constraints that ordinarily influence human behavior in real-world tasks (Lave 1988). The results of research motivated by this criticism emphasize the idiosyncrasies of behavior across situations.

In this chapter we first contrast the two approaches to the study of human behavior and examine the accounts of expertise they provide. Then we review our own observational studies of expertise conducted in three different complex, risk-laden, physical task environments: aviation, internal medicine, and on-foot land navigation. The remainder of the chapter presents verbal protocols obtained from these task domains and lays out some of their implications for an account of expertise that merges theoretical emphases from both laboratory and real-world studies of expertise.

In keeping with the accounts of expertise provided by laboratory studies, the protocols are used to suggest that abstract, accepted methods constrain the activities of practitioners and render the activities of practitioners predictable. Thus, social convention motivates the adoption of accepted methods in order to control risk in complex physical task domains. This perspective on expertise provides a normative basis for judging behavior as correct or incorrect, and a necessary foundation for the development of intelligent aids to support the observed regularities. However, in keeping with studies of behavior in real-world task contexts, the protocols are also used to suggest that an expert's ability to execute accepted methods depends critically on perceptual experience and temporal awareness obtained through engagement with the physical world—supported by aspects of expert cognition that are often overlooked in the domains and task formulations submitted to laboratory study.

Theoretical and Methodological Paradigms for the Study of Human Behavior

Two apparently contrasting paradigms seem to have guided recent studies of expertise: 1) Laboratory studies and 2) Observational studies in a social and operational context. These paradigms and the task settings they employ have yielded different characterizations of expertise, with different perspectives on the predictability of human behavior and the viability of artificially intelligent aids.

Laboratory Studies of the Individual

In many laboratory studies of the individual, an experimenter prepares written problem descriptions (sometimes with a diagrammatic representation of a problem setting) and a problem-solving goal. The individual attempts to solve the problem in the laboratory, often while thinking aloud (Larkin 1983; Patel and Groen 1986; Patel, Groen, and Arocha 1990; Soloway and Erlich 1984). Alternatively, the individual may engage in tasks related to problem solving. For example, the individual sorts a set of problems into categories corresponding to a solution approach or common conceptual underpinnings (Chi et al. 1981). These studies have revealed striking differences between the manner in which experts and novices interpret problems and search for solutions.

Studies conducted within this paradigm have emphasized the predictability and regularity of behavior and generally conclude that expert behavior derives from the mental manipulation of symbol structures that denote features in the environment, motor behaviors or other symbols (Vera and Simon 1993). Accordingly, experts are said to solve problems by matching problem statements in the external environment to features of pre-stored, "generic" problem types. Once experts identify a match to a problem type, they select and apply one of a number of potentially relevant problem-solving operations (Newell 1973). This characterization of expertise suggests that the creation of intelligent aids is a matter of duplicating the expert's representation of problem types and associated problem-solving operations.

Limitations of this paradigm for the study of expertise arise from the use of preformulated problems in written and diagrammatic form. One limitation is the risk of assuming (rather than observing) a decomposition of the domain. For example, laboratory studies of medical expertise may artificially partition the diagnosis process away from treatment selection (Patel and Groen 1986). An alternative decomposition of the domain could be considered, in which treatment options interact with the diagnostic process (Shalin and Bertram, in press). A second limitation of using preformulated problems is the potential for ignoring the process whereby problems are discovered in actual situations (Clancey 1993). The assumption behind the paradigm is that the form of the preformulated problem is similar to the results from a straightforward process of matching the task environment to stored symbolic knowledge. The content of the symbol structures and the mental operations they support are thought to be more interesting and informative about the nature of expertise. Yet, attempts both to simulate the process of matching new tasks to stored knowledge (Hammond 1989) and to define the precise scope of proposed mental symbols (Dreyfus 1981) suggest that the matching of real task environments with mental representations can be highly problematic.

Observational Studies of the Individual in a Social and Physical Context

An alternative to the study of individuals in the laboratory involves interviews, observation, diaries, and simulation experiments with individuals performing real tasks in typical task environments including other individuals (Hutchins 1990, 1993; Lave 1988; Scribner 1984; Suchman 1987).

Studies conducted within this paradigm highlight the responsiveness of human behavior to properties of ordinary task environments. Reminiscent of ecological psychology (Gibson 1979) and task analysis in human factors psychology, researchers working within this paradigm often do not seek explanations of human behavior based on abstract, transferable, symbolic representations of knowledge. For example, Suchman's (1987) study of behaviors in the operation of a copying machine suggests that abstract representations of knowledge are inherently underspecified and cannot in principle determine the specific properties of an observed action in the face of an unpredictable, ever-changing environment. Rather, properties of "situations" (e.g., the laboratory-experiment situation, the presence of paper and pencil, institutional settings such as the supermarket) guide human behavior as the task unfolds.

In contrast to the laboratory paradigm, the observational paradigm corresponds to a different philosophical perspective on human behavior. In emphasizing the context sensitivity of behavior, the paradigm discourages the comparison of behavior against normative expectations, which presumably can be operative only in the tightly controlled, delimited task environment of the experiment. In arguing that expert behavior cannot be predicted by *a priori* abstractions, the theory associated with the observational paradigm often casts a veil of pessimism on the utility of artificially intelligent systems using predetermined symbolic representations of knowledge (e.g., Winograd and Flores 1986). However, when the observational paradigm invests the environment with total control over behavior, the resulting explanations of behavior may omit regularities that are better understood with respect to mental processes, particularly in the context of dynamic task domains. For example, Von Wright's work demonstrates that tracking performance improves when subjects have the opportunity to develop expectations for future movements (von Wright 1957 cited in Welford 1968, p. 297). These expectations arise from practice with the tracking route. In the absence of such practice, subjects cannot anticipate future requirements while they execute current movements. Performance suffers in these cases because there is insufficient time to process and react to unfamiliar circumstances, thus demonstrating the inadequacy of current engagement as a sole influence on performance in dynamic task environments.

Observational Studies of Expertise in Dynamic Task Domains

Rather than regarding the two paradigms as merely competing accounts of human cognition, the paradigms may be especially informative about the properties of the task environments in which the research is conducted (Clancey 1992; Simon 1969). Lave (1988) suggests that the abstract accounts of problem-solving knowledge depend on the study of scholastic task domains that inflate the value of normative behavior (e.g., mathematics). On the other hand, contextually rich, observational studies tend to focus on task domains in which there are few consequences for idiosyncratic, unpredictable behavior, such as meal preparation, grocery shopping, retail sales, or the operation of a copy machine. These are domains in which most actions are very low risk, provisions for timely communication between participants exist, and corrective actions are often possible.

However, normative behavior need not be exclusively associated with scholastic task domains. Our own observational and experimental research in contextually rich environments addresses performance in what Woods (1988) calls "complex, dynamic, and physical domains": commercial aviation, on-foot land navigation and internal medicine. These domains have some interesting properties. They encompass indefinitely large systems and integrate multiple individuals with unique expertise that shapes their understanding of the work (Hutchins 1990). The tasks severely limit the amount of time a problem solver can take to enumerate, deliberate and execute possible responses (Klein, Calderwood, and MacGregor 1989). Expert responses impact the physical world, although representations of the world (such as a map) may be used. The effects of physical action are not always immediate or even apparent to the actor (Norman 1991; Woods, in press), although errors in these domains may result in the loss of life. Experts are personally accountable for their actions and may be asked to justify their actions to external authorities, under the threat of losing their professional livelihood. The distinctive properties of these domains encourage regularities in behavior that serve to control risk and render individual behavior predictable. Although the domains are indeed complex, ill-structured and unpredictable in their lowest level of detail, human behavior in these domains is predictable at some level of abstraction, as an adaptation of pre-existing knowledge (Feltovich, Coulson, Spiro and Dawson-Saunders 1992; Zeitz, this volume).

In the following subsections, we describe the goals and data collection methods for three studies of expertise in such domains, originally conducted to address specific applications concerns, such as testing or aiding. In each case, the subjects were aware of the applied purpose of our studies, but none of the theoretical issues described in later sections were discussed with them in advance of data collection.

On-foot Land Navigation

On-foot land navigation tasks include the planning and execution of a route for troop movement across unimproved terrain. The applications purpose of the study we conducted was to develop a methodology for creating paper-and-pencil job knowledge tests to substitute for time- and labor-intensive performance tests.

We collected 30 hours of videotape from experienced, two-person navigation teams, selected from the training staff at two different Marine Bases. Two experimenters participated in a variety of land navigation activities, serving as prompters to a think-aloud task, and in some respects, as novice subjects to be instructed. We also collected 10 additional hours of video or audiotape of novice land navigation during actual training sessions. The job knowledge test that resulted from our analysis of these data showed improved correlations with hands-on performance measures, compared to existing land navigation tests and to other job-knowledge correlations found in previous research (DuBois and Shalin 1995).

Commercial Aviation

Commercial aviation tasks include take-off, climb, level flight, descent, and landing of a passenger-carrying aircraft. The purpose of our study was to examine the potential pilot performance consequences of automated, intelligent information management.

Bloomfield, Shalin, and Corwin (1991) audiotaped 8 hours of four different training pilots in repeated take-off, level-flight, and descent scenarios in a 6-degree of freedom motion-based flight simulator. One of the experimenters served as a novice first officer. The experimental methodology included thinking aloud tasks, conversations with the first officer, and limiting pilot access to the flight instruments. Analyses of these data contributed to the design of displays specialized for different tasks, validated in a second study using different combinations of these displays and tasks in a desk-top simulation environment. This study demonstrated enhanced performance with displays matched to the tasks for which they were designed (Shalin, Geddes, and Mikesell 1992; Shalin, Geddes, Mikesell, and Ramamurthy 1993a,b).

Medical Intensive Care

Internal medicine tasks in the intensive care unit include admitting a patient, collecting patient information, discussing patient cases with consultants, issuing treatment orders and instructions, and performing procedures. The purpose of our study was to develop a method for a task analysis that characterized physician workload at varying levels of expertise, supported by a reliable non-intrusive measure of workload.

We videotaped 60 hours of interns, residents and attending physicians conducting their normal activities in two different inner-city teaching hospitals. We also videotaped an attending physician while he commented on another videotape of rounds in which he participated. The analysis of these data yielded a positive correlation between measures of physician workload and engagement in written and oral communication (Szczepkowski, Shalin, Bertram, Drury, Aquilina, and TenBrock 1994).

In the next section, we rely on the verbal data from all three of these studies to illustrate three properties of expertise in these domains: 1) the expert's use of accepted methods, 2) an awareness of elapsed and required time as they impact discretionary decision making, and 3) the importance of perceptual skill.

The Use of Accepted Methods

In these three domains, feedback from ongoing experience may arrive too late to serve as a guide for compensating action. For example, pilots do not lower the flaps of their aircraft during takeoff, after sensing a lack of lift. Pilots lower the flaps of their aircraft *before takeoff*, in anticipation of well-described consequences of the failure to do so. Therefore, rather than empha-

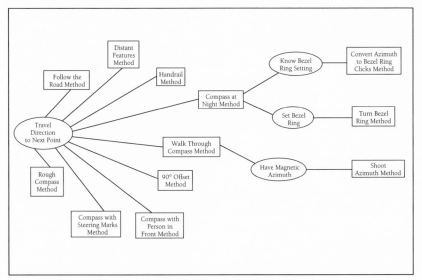

Figure 1. Alternative methods for travelling in an intended direction.

sizing the responsiveness of human behavior to immediate experience, we emphasize the influence of knowledge on the execution of actions in these domains, in the form of pre-determined, accepted methods.

We often describe these methods as plans within a plan-goal graph, described by Sewell and Geddes (1990). An example plan-goal graph is illustrated in figure 1, with plans indicated by boxes and goals by ovals. Plans consist of different methods and tools to achieve the same goal. We utilize the term *methods* here, in keeping with Livingston (1987), to distinguish our weak notion of plans from the stronger, traditional AI notion of plans (Sacerdoti 1977). Moreover, real-world problems seldom depend on the solution of a single isolated goal. Accordingly, we do not suggest that humans perform a set of completely pre-specified operational steps, independent of their interactions with the environment or the current set of active goals. Rather, the expert selects from among frameworks for action based on world conditions, current goals and previous experience (see also Hoffman 1987; Klein 1993; Newell 1973; Seifert, Patalano, Hammond and Converse, this volume). Then the expert adapts the selected set for the specific conditions and goals, and monitors the execution of these adapted methods based on expected results. The dominance of accepted methods provides a basis for predicting and evaluating individual behavior across a range of task settings. We now turn to evidence for accepted methods and a rationale for their utility.

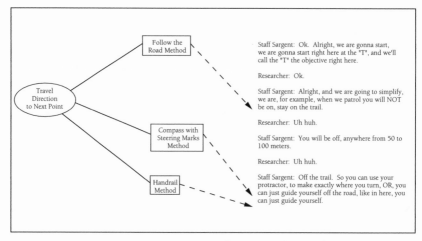

Figure 2. An expert's appeal to accepted methods.

Evidence for Accepted Methods

Though it appears to us that experts nearly always respect accepted methods in the domains considered here, the methods are not likely to be mentioned during ordinary verbal exchange between experts. As part of their shared knowledge, the necessity of these methods is often assumed in their conversations (Clark and Schaefer 1987). To support the role of accepted methods in determining performance, we present three kinds of evidence: 1) the expert's post hoc appeal to an accepted method, 2) the evaluation of another individual's actions against an accepted method, and 3) discussions between individuals about alternative methods.

The excerpt in figure 2 from our study of land navigation exemplifies an expert's appeal to accepted methods in planning a route. The example indicates three alternative accepted methods for traveling in an intended direction. Each method has slightly different side-effects making it more or less appropriate for different circumstances. The "Follow the Road Method" offers accuracy, but possible visibility to an enemy. The "Compass with Steering Marks Method" involves preparation to plot a course on a map. The "Handrail Method" involves knowledge about the direction in which the road is headed but requires knowledge about the suitability of the existing terrain as a source of cover.

Figure 3 provides an attending physician's commentary while viewing a videotape of morning rounds. In his commentary, he discusses the rationale for choosing between two pre-defined methods, this time for emergency diagnosis and treatment. The protocol enumerates two valid treatment ap-

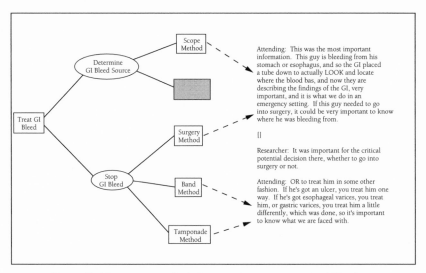

Figure 3. Alternative methods for treating gastrointestinal bleeding.

proaches to gastrointestinal bleeding. The point of this illustration is not whether other options actually exist, but that practice proceeds *as if* only a pre-enumerated set of options exists. This convention allows for the explicit evaluation of another individual's treatment selection and execution as correct or incorrect against normative expectations, as in the following excerpt, in which the attending physician evaluates a resident.

> *Attending:* And that is very important. His blood gas is very abnormal, and he should have been put on a ventilator. And so this resident, a very good resident made a *decision* not to put him on a ventilator, and now we are discussing why he made the decision NOT to put him on the ventilator. Clearly, any other asthmatic should have been on a ventilator. A young otherwise healthy guy should not have had a carbon dioxide as elevated as his was.

> *Researcher:* He was lucky.

> *Attending:* It was a good decision.

The above examples are post-hoc commentary, potentially epiphenomenal to observed performance, informed by the positive outcome of the reasoning and encouraged by interaction with the experimenter (Ericcson and Simon 1993; Suchman 1987). Though still dissociated from the execution of action, the following excerpt illustrates an evaluative process within the work group itself, and not at all motivated by experimenter interaction. A lab value provided by the intern is met with joking and laughter. The intern repeats the attending's instruction, as if to confirm that she was following instructions.

Attending: How is [next patient] doing? Did we get the, she is on heparin now?

Intern: Yes, PTT was over 100 last night.

Resident: Ok, good, super therapy [laughter].

Attending: Good [laughter] that's all right.

Intern: You *said* anticoagulant.

Resident: Let no stone go unturned, better too much than not enough. Let no blood go unthinned.

The resulting value was actually too high. Perhaps the joking and laughter are covering for an overly aggressive (and hence somewhat incorrect) treatment. The example shows that evaluation of work according to accepted, instructed methods is an ongoing, natural occurrence in a realistic workplace setting. However, unlike the classroom, the example illustrates that the outcome matters, which is part of the rationale for accepted methods.

Rationale for Accepted Methods

In the kinds of domains we study, the adoption of accepted methods reduces risk to the outcome in several respects, illustrated by the discussion of route planning presented in the following protocol.

Researcher: Are we going to have any checkpoints in the middle?

Sergeant: Yes.

Researcher: Why?

Sergeant: In case anybody gets lost, that way they know where to go to, or in case we get hit by enemy fire, we've got a reference to call for fire, or if we need resupply, we can say, hey, we are at checkpoint three, we need water or ammo, or we need a corpsman.

Researcher: Ok.

Staff Sergeant: We need the checkpoints so we'll have a reference, I know, ok for example here, we'll get to the creek, so I'll say, all right, we are already, approximately around in here somewhere, so just to know....

Researcher: Uh huh.

Staff Sergeant: Then, uh, also, like you said, you would stop me here and you say "we're lost." Well, that won't happen to me because, I always do what I call, what we already know, is called an escape route.

Researcher: Yes.

Staff Sergeant: So that means you could turn me around 360, blindfold me, and I'll open my eyes up, and break out my compass, follow this azimuth, follow 270, ok and it will take me to the road.

The example illustrates three advantages of accepted methods for reducing risk. First, they establish expectations at certain points in executing the route, so that deviations can be recognized and corrected early, when the ease of recovery is greatest. Second, accepted methods are associated with anticipated but unintended consequences (in this case, getting lost), and they drive the planning of a compensating escape route. Third, they facilitate the coordination of multiple team members in case of an emergency (Orasanu 1990; Orasanu and Fischer 1992).

Our conclusions regarding the predominance of accepted methods are based on our participation in these studies as outside observers. Though we view expert actions as predetermined and deliberative, we follow Headland, Pike and Harris (1990) in distinguishing our experiences from those of practitioners. But for the purposes of the present work, practitioners do not need to experience their work as deliberative. The key requirement for the development of intelligent aids to support human behavior in apparently complex environments is a foundation of expectations for expert behavior. The broader purpose of developing a theory of expertise requires an explanation for the apparent predictability of behavior across different individuals and variable task settings, part of which likely lies in the training and experience of the individual.

Temporal and Perceptual Bases of Accepted Methods

The cases discussed above support the conceptualization of expert knowledge in terms of standard generic methods acquired by the agent in advance of the need for their use, and executed in anticipation of future conditions. This characterization converges with those obtained from the analysis of standard laboratory studies of expertise. However, we note two important refinements to this conclusion. First, the preponderance of accepted methods is a function of the task domain, as well as both cognitive and social influences on behavior. Social influences include, for example, the presence of multiple individuals and the consequences of failure. Second, and discussed next, temporal awareness and perceptual experience are extremely important components of expert knowledge, and must be present to render accepted methods functional.

Temporal Awareness

Expert performance in dynamic task domains attempts to direct physical processes towards prespecified goals. Due to time constraints, dynamic tasks also usually involve interweaving the multiple methods in use for different simultaneous goals. These task properties suggest that the expert has a sense of how much temporal leeway the current problem setting provides, how much time is required for executing alternative methods in the current task setting and how a particular method might be adjusted to meet the available time.

A key concept here, drawn from the human factors literature is the *stable situation.* In this situation, the expert feels in control and with sufficient time to react to changes. The following two excerpts from aviation illustrate the notion of a stable situation, and in addition, the expert's discretion in timing the execution of the methods.

Pilot: So we have 10 miles to go 1,000 feet. So I'm just doing the mental arithmetic, do I need to increase my speed, do I need to put slats out to slow it down any?

First Officer: 11 for 10.

Researcher: You have lost your DME; there we go.

Pilot: So everything is fine the way it is. On some of these the rates of descent are so much that you start having to put your speed brakes or your slats to slow you down.

Researcher: Uh huh.

Pilot: To meet the profile itself. Ok, we have the altitude, throttles are going forward to maintain the 250, we can select 9,000 feet now and arm it. Just staying a little bit ahead of the airplane.

Pilot: Ok, I've got it. We're kind of caught up, and that was kind of a whiz-bang get down. I would hate to have to do that in actual weather. It would be a little bit quick.

The importance of temporal awareness is perhaps obvious in aviation, given its reliance on the control of aircraft position that changes over time. However, we see a similar role for temporal awareness in intensive care medicine.

Attending: If I am happy that the patient is stable and I understand enough about him, made our teaching pitch, now even though there is a lot more we can do about that patient, we move on…we went in there, found out the guy was awake and alert, he was a little tremulous, *he wasn't withdrawing badly, he was stable, he was able to give us some information,* I was happy to say that he was stable, and we left. So basically, when I went in there, I did very few things, but I wanted to make sure that he was stable enough that we didn't have to *do* anything right away.

Appreciation of the potential for rapid deterioration encourages advance planning, which in turn allows for the utilization of expert consultation that would otherwise not be available during an unstable situation, as described to the researcher this way:

Attending: …so the next step, if he continued to bleed, would be to put a special tube in that has a big gastric balloon, and an esophageal balloon and it actually *poof* tamponades, like putting your finger in a duct. And so they were thinking about that. That's pretty aggressive therapy, because it [unintelligible]. So *he had already anticipated the next step, if he was not gonna do well, he was already set to think about having that put in.*

Researcher: Why did he tell you that?

Attending: That's important. That's an important piece of information, I wanted to know what his thought process was, so he was telling me what his next step would be if he continued to bleed. *He* had made the anticipatory feeling about what the game plan was gonna be *if* something changed. So, he was on a pitressin drip, he was on, getting blood, he was on the nitroglycerin, the next *step* would have been, and ask questions about how effective that would be....

Attending: So they probably talked to consultants the night before and came up with together, with, *if something happens to him, this is what you need to do.* So they not only probably have thought about it, they've talked to their consultants last night and that the consensus was....

Researcher: This, this multiple people....

Attending: You see, there's people that *aren't* here that....

Researcher: Have impact.

Attending: have major impact on...probably the GI who came in at 8:00 at night and didn't finish til 10:00 probably said, I'm not gonna come back and re-endoscope him. Call the surgeons, and consider, reconsider putting a Blakemore tube down him.

To know that one is in a stable situation and in control requires a sense of the time it takes for a situation to deteriorate, and the time requirements of alternative responses. In other words, temporal awareness requires knowledge to interpret the current situation and select and refine alternative methods. For example, in land navigation, novices typically underestimate the time requirements of a planned route. Temporal properties of situations and treatment methods form the basis of explicit instruction for inexperienced medical residents, as illustrated by the following three protocols.

Intern: What's the point of putting in a trach at this point?

Attending: Well, the question is, you know, with the life support system that she is on, *how long is she likely to survive?*

Intern: Right, that's what I mean.

Attending: She very well could survive for a number of weeks.

Resident: For a while.

Intern: Oh, I see.

Attending: Anytime you see a pneumonia that flares like this [motions with his hand like a blooming flower—with sound effects] it is almost always either pseudomonas or kleb. And you have to act on it right away, because those individuals can develop necrotizing pneumonia, and—and basically die in 48 hours.

Attending: Well you did the right thing. You know, I think the ideal way to treat a trans [unintelligible] effusion is with diuretics. *But* if you have somebody who is in respiratory failure, you don't screw around, you tap 'em, and that way you can immediately relieve their restrictive lung disease.

Knowledge for managing temporally constrained dynamic tasks is largely overlooked in cognitive theories of expertise. While research on musical cognition does address the importance of temporal knowledge (Sloboda 1991), this work suggests relationships between loudness, timing and emotional impact with unclear bearing on the functions and processing of temporal content of interest here. Research in artificial intelligence has addressed the representation of temporal information (Allen 1983), but only rarely the use of temporal reasoning in expert human problem solving (cf. Allen and Schubert 1991). Research on naturalistic decision making provides one of the rare bodies of literature concerned with the role of temporal constraints on the decision making process (Klein, Orasanu, Calderwood, and Zsambok 1993).

Human factors research recognizes the performance degradation that results from the failure to manage dynamic processes in keeping with their temporal constraints (Hollnagel 1991; Sanderson 1989). Prabhu, Sharit, and Drury (1992) suggest that adequate information about current and projected situations will improve performance. Our complementary concern here is with the experience and knowledge that must be present to render such information useful. In keeping with the above examples, we suggest that expert knowledge includes the temporal requirements of alternative accepted methods in the present situation (e.g., diuretics or tapping) relative to the possible time course of the dynamic process they address (e.g., restrictive lung disease). Knowledge for determining temporal requirements includes knowledge for determining when to initiate an accepted method and must also include knowledge for selecting a method to initiate given the available time.

Perceptual Processes

Expert knowledge of accepted methods includes knowledge about their conditions of applicability. Certainly, early laboratory studies of expertise suggested that experts have a well-developed ability to identify relevant patterns in a task environment (Chase and Simon 1973; see also Zeitz, this volume). Many of the ensuing studies focused on what we call relation-based recognition, involving relations among "things" where the material content of the "things" is largely irrelevant (Biederman and Shiffrar 1987; Palmer 1977; Winston 1975).

Relation-based recognition appears in land navigation, in which patterns of objects on the map are associated with patterns of the objects in the terrain, as illustrated below.

Staff Sergeant: We just left the Harbaugh, left the Harbaugh Road, and we moved upstream. The stream runs uh, southeast up to the junction of the stream. *At approximately this point, I can see the, the y of the stream,* the junction. And one y is running uh, one part of the stream is running like, southwest, the other one's running southeast. We know—it should be in front of us—*the place where the junction is—in front of—we should see some high ground, north of us,* which is the place that I'm looking at—we should see north of us—north of us is high ground. I use terrain association, which is what we are doing, the stream moves to our leftside; follow the stream and it bends around to approximately 200 meters.

The novice eventually develops relation-based recognition in land navigation to acquire a sensitivity to the relevant properties of both the map and the environment and to the quality of match required for a map to be in proper registration with the environment. The novices in the protocol below failed to attend to the north-south direction of the stream.

Researcher: So you thought you were at a different fork?

Private (trainee): We thought we were here, where it bends around.

Researcher: Uh huh.

Private (trainee): And that was our box in the middle, that little dot right there. But actually we are back here.

Researcher: Yeah.

Private: So we could have another, about 800 meters to go from that, 500 meters. We'll follow that creek all the way up, go south.

Researcher: So, do you see now that it was the wrong fork?

Private: Yeah.

Researcher: How do you know?

Private: How do we know?

Researcher: Yeah.

Private: Because that creek right here breaks off and runs west to east; it's supposed to run north to south; we are supposed to be going north to south, so it must be another creek.

Relation-based recognition is a type of perceptual process that lends itself to symbolic representation, and for that matter, linguistic representation as well. With a relation-based perspective on perceptual processes, the use of case descriptions to study medical reasoning, for example, seems quite legitimate (Boshuizen and Schmidt 1992; Patel and Groen 1986; Patel, *et al.* 1990). However, our research in natural task settings indicates a role for other perceptually based processes performed by experts: 1) functional analysis, 2) perception of continuously valued physical dimensions, and 3) the monitoring of events or processes over time that are not amenable to precise verbal description.

The protocol below illustrates what we call functional analysis, in which the meaning and the material of the perceptual inputs are far more important than in relation-based recognition. By functional analysis, we refer to the functions afforded by the environment (Gibson 1979), but driven by professional training and experience. The following excerpt was selected from a route planning session prior to route execution, in which the expert discusses terrain properties using perceptually-based knowledge, similar to the examples of terrain analysis provided by Hoffman and Pike (in press).

Researcher: So everyone on a recon fire team would be, would get lots of map reading experience?

Staff Sergeant: Yes.

Sergeant: They'd have to be familiar with the map and how to read the terrain itself. As far as the (density) of roads, is this stream fordable or not by vehicles, or do they have to have special equipment to ford it, or you know, how fast is the current running, what's the bottom of the stream like, stuff like that there. The roads, is it you know, is it accessible for heavy traffic vehicles or just light vehicles, um, if you shell it, how much damage would be done to the road? Would it just make potholes, or would it you know totally make the road useless. Along with the vegetation and stuff like that, even the trails, the deer trails out there, we use those a lot, because you know, its an animal trail. Could the enemy use those as a route to us?

Here, the kinds of material involved are crucial for a seemingly infinite set of potential inferences, based on combining common sense with instructed knowledge.

Other perceptually-based tasks require an evaluation of continuously valued physical dimensions. For example, Lesgold noted the deficient ability of resident radiologists to discriminate the degrees of tissue density on an x-ray (Lesgold, *et al.* 1988). The two case descriptions discussed below were obtained prior to morning rounds and illustrates that internal medicine involves a recognition of properties such as the redness of palms (palmar erythema) and the firmness of an abdomen, in addition to the relational knowledge discussed previously. Just as the philosophers have insisted (e.g., Harnad 1990), knowing the name for a phenomenon is not the same as having experienced it.

Resident: Did she have any AV nicking?

Intern: No, her discs were sharp, no hemorrhages, *I was really excited, I thought I'd see my first papilledema.*

Attending: Chest was clear?

Intern: Chest was clear, heart....

Attending: Neuro exam.

Intern: Oh, she did have a grade 2 over 6 systolic murmur at the apex....

Attending: See any fresh tracks?

Intern: No. I don't think she shoots up now.

Attending: Well, I know she says she doesn't, but....

Intern: Well, we didn't see any, and we didn't see any petechia, or any problems with the skin.

Intern: Review of systems was only significant for a rash, which she has had for years, on her scalp, which is pruritic, and was at one point in some hospital treated with a shampoo and went away. *But, we don't know what it is, the daughter insisted that it was not infectious,* but we all thought it was some bug and everybody started itching.

Resident: I didn't see that, where was that?

Intern: Oh, you'll see it, just take a look at her scalp. *We're all going, what does scabies look like? What do fleas?* Was it [unintelligible]? And the surgery residents are going like this [motions with her hands scratching her head]. Physical exam, she was tachycardic at 120, afebrile, blood pressure 148 over 80, she was pale and lethargic, not very comfortable. Her heart was tachycardic, but no murmurs. Her abdomen, she had generous hepatomegaly, *her liver was palpable at 3 cm below the costal margin, even an intern like myself could feel it.* She had positive bowel sounds, her abdomen was firm, her rectal—she had rectal prolapse, with heme-positive stool. Her skin, as I said she had multiple excoriations on her scalp, on her left hip, on her legs, she had some spider angiomas on her lower extremities. *Dr. X said she has palmar erythma, but I compared her to my palms, and I wasn't convinced.*

The intern's reference to her own palms indicates both her curiosity and her doubt. She truly does not know what red palms look like, and she realizes that this is an important judgment.

A third perceptual process involved in expertise in these domains incorporates a perceptual parsing of events over time. Even aviation, with its technical base of quantitative sensors and information displays, involves perceptual experience of events over time, illustrated in the following protocol.

Pilot: …Looks like we've got a power split. Now my [unintelligible] just off to the right. First there was the feeling of the airplane kind of lurching, which is kind of unusual, and I just heard a circuit breaker pop. We've got the master caution light. I'm guessing that it feels like maybe the left engine. Take a look at the Number 1 N2 and see what it's reading.

As illustrated by the protocol below, the practice of medicine also requires perceptual experience in monitoring events indicative of patient condition.

Attending: Any sternocleido mastoid retractions? Did it look like his respiratory rate was high? Low? In between?

Intern: His respiratory rate was about 95, but no additional muscles were used for breathing.

Attending: Was he tachycardic?

Intern: Yeah, it was 120…uh [looks through chart]…uh 120.

Attending: And so generally, *how did he look to you when you saw him, just by looking at him? Did he look comfortable, did he look stressed, tired, fatigued?*

Intern: Uh.

Attending: Or did it look like he was, comfortable?

Intern: Certainly he was not looking comfortable. I would say that he was looking in mild stress. But he was not looking like he was having respiratory fatigue of his muscles. His movements, breathing movements were quite active, and I didn't get the impression that he has respiratory fatigue and would get into respiratory failure at that point....

Attending: Well, you know, he's got that upper airway noise and that bothers me. And he *is* in significant respiratory difficulties. *Ah, you've got to very carefully look at these people. They are not going to have rapid shallow breathing all the time.* He's very muscular, he's got a very deep breath, but a very low rate for his mean ventilation time can fool you.

Resident: Would you have intubated just on the basis of the gas?

Attending: No, I think you've got to make a decision where he doesn't look tired. He looks tired in there, and then you start talking to him, and he can talk.

Resident: When he first came, he couldn't finish a sentence.

Attending: Ok.

Resident: He would go on, stop for a while, and then continue the sentence. Now he can carry on a conversation without any problem. So he is doing better, clinically.

The above examples illustrate a number of roles for perceptual content in expert performance. A relation-based, verbally-oriented conceptualization of perceptual content justifies experimental settings that substitute words for experience, in effort to study "higher" mental processes But words may not function in the same manner as perceptual experience in the direction of attention (Neisser 1976), the activation of prior experience (Brooks, Norman, and Allen 1991; Klein 1987), their compatibility with parallel processing (Treisman and Sato 1990) and the apprehension of events as they unfold over time in significant, meaningful patterns. A premature characterization of expertise without taking these functions into account potentially creates an inappropriate prioritization of research questions, and misdirects remedial technology and instructional efforts.

Summary and Conclusions

The two major paradigms in the study of expertise have tend to confound a particular theoretical perspective with the specific task domains and task environments in which the supporting empirical work occurs. Though observational studies of practice often emphasize human responsiveness to specific details of the task environment, our observations are consistent with Klein (1993), and suggest the complementary role of accepted methods as the basis of task performance in high-risk, dynamic physical task domains. Though laboratory studies of expertise, in turn, typically reveal the consistencies in expert performance across different problems, our observations suggest that the laboratory setting has omitted many of the temporal and perceptual phenomena that invoke abstract knowledge and direct its refinement for the current task.

The use of "accepted methods" by experts reconciles the conclusions from apparently disparate perspectives on expertise. This use is generally compatible with the conclusions of traditional laboratory studies of expertise and the regularity they emphasize, but with several notable refinements. First, we emphasize the social (rather than cognitive) rationale for the dominance of accepted methods in practice, which is critical for coordinated team performance and the effective use of expertise distributed across individuals. Hence the requirements of the domain—particularly the social significance of error—should moderate the preponderance of accepted methods. As Feltovich, *et al.* (1992) notes (in chapter 10), some domains require flexible skills. And our use of the term "accepted methods" does not imply an expert's strict compliance with an apparently fully specified sequences of action. Indeed, the slavish execution of fully specified procedures is often characteristic of the novice. Instead, we conclude that accepted methods are prepared frameworks for action and coordination that are specialized to the opportunities provided by specific situations (Feltovich, *et al.* 1992; Hayes-Roth and Hayes-Roth 1979; Lesgold 1989).

In keeping with the conclusions of observational studies of expertise, accepted methods are not functional without an ability to interact with a changing physical environment. The selection among alternative accepted methods requires an appreciation for the possible and likely time courses of events, and consideration of the temporal requirements for executing alternative methods. The descriptions of behavior presented here suggest that expertise is anchored in perceptual sensitivity to auditory, kinesthetic, tactile and visual experience, even while numerical, pictorial, and verbal representations are also in use. Perceptual sensitivity extends beyond a relation-based conceptualization, to include functional analysis, the perception of continuously valued physical dimensions and the monitoring of events and processes over time. We hope that our observations of perceptual processes in practice lend support to those researchers whose experimental efforts address the processes of perception in expert reasoning (e.g., Klein and Hoffman 1993), and that our findings as a whole encourage other researchers to incorporate a richer task environment including dynamic processes in their experimental work.

Because accepted methods with well-defined conditions of applicability appear to dominate performance in these domains, we are optimistic about the viability of artificial aids for certain functions ordinarily thought to be intelligent. For example, alternative courses of action might be suggested to the expert. Or, guided by an analysis of the content of alternative accepted methods, appropriate displays might be configured automatically to reduce display clutter and relieve the expert of display management and data acquisition tasks. Such uses harken to the earliest days of cognitive science, when ambitions for machine competence were more moderated. The critical current research issue for the use of artificially intelligent aids is to understand the fuzzy boundaries between the applicability and nonapplicability of accepted methods and ensure the apprehension of information that identifies nonroutine cases.

Acknowledgments

This research was partially supported by NASA Langley Research Center, under grant NASA-NAG11342; the Manpower, Personnel and Training Program, Office of Naval Research, under contract N00014-91-C-0224; and the Mark Diamond Research Fund at SUNY Buffalo. The authors gratefully acknowledge helpful feedback from the editors of this volume, comments from the Center for Cognitive Science at SUNY Buffalo obtained during a colloquium presentation of this material, and later interactions with Center members Don Pollack and Len Talmy. The views discussed in this chapter represent the authors and not their employers or funding agencies.

References

Allen, J.F. (1983). Maintaining knowledge about temporal intervals. *Communications of the ACM, 26(11),* 832-843.

Allen, J.F. & Schubert, L.K. (1991). *The TRAINS Project* (TRAINS Technical Note No. 91-1). Rochester, NY: University of Rochester, Department of Computer Science.

Biederman, I. & Shiffrar, M.M. (1987). Sexing day-old chicks: A case study and expert systems analysis of a difficult perceptual-learning task. *Journal of Experimental Psychology: Learning, Memory and Cognition, 13,* 640-645.

Bloomfield, J.R., Shalin, V.L. & Corwin, B. (1991). Knowledge sensitive task manipulation: Acquiring knowledge from pilots flying a motion-based flight simulator. In *Proceedings of the 6th International Symposium on Aviation Psychology* (pp. 1068-1073). Columbus, OH: Ohio State University.

Boshuizen, H.P.A. & Schmidt, H. (1992). On the role of biomedical knowledge in clinical reasoning by experts, intermediates and novices. *Cognitive Science, 16,* 153-184.

Brooks, L.R., Norman, G.R. & Allen, S.W. (1991). Role of specific similarity in a medical diagnostic task. *Journal of Experimental Psychology: General, 120(3),* 278-287.

Chase, W.G. & Simon, H.A. (1973). Perception in chess. *Cognitive Psychology, 4,* 55-81.

Chi, M.T.H., Feltovich, P.J. & Glaser, R. (1981). Categorization and representation of physics problems by experts and novices. *Cognitive Science, 5,* 121-152.

Clancey, W.J. (1993). Situated action: A neuropsychological interpretation response to Vera and Simon. *Cognitive Science, 17,* 87-116.

Clancey, W.J. (1992). Model construction operators. *Artificial Intelligence, 53,* 1-115.

Clark, H.H. & Schaefer, E.F. (1987). Concealing one's meaning from overhearers. *Journal of Memory & Language, 26,* 209-225.

DuBois, D. & Shalin, V.L. (1995). Job knowledge test design: Cognitive contributions to content oriented methods. In P. Nichols, S. Chipman & R. Brennan (Eds.), *Alterna-*

tive Diagnostic Assessment (pp. 189-220). Hillsdale, NJ: Lawrence Erlbaum.

Dreyfus, H.L. (1981). From micro-worlds to knowledge representation: AI at an impasse. In J. Haugeland (Ed.), *Mind Design* (pp. 161-204). Cambridge, MA: Bradford Books.

Ericcson, K.A. & Simon, H.A. (1993). *Protocol Analysis: Verbal Reports as Data* (rev. ed.). Cambridge, MA: MIT Press.

Feltovich, P.J., Coulson, R.L., Spiro, R.J. & Dawson-Saunders, B.K. (1992). Knowledge application and transfer for complex tasks in ill-structured domains: Implications for instruction and testing in biomedicine. In D. Evans & V. Patel (Eds.), *Advanced Models of Cognition for Medical Training and Practice* (pp. 213-244). Berlin: Springer-Verlag.

Gibson, J.J. (1979). *The Ecological Approach to Visual Perception*. Boston: Houghton-Mifflin.

Hammond, K.J. (1989). *Case-based Planning*. Boston: Academic Press.

Harnad, S. (1990). The symbol grounding problem. *Physica D, 42,* 335-346.

Hayes-Roth, B. & Hayes-Roth, F. (1979). A cognitive model of planning. *Cognitive Science, 2,* 257-310.

Headland, T.N., Pike, K.L. & Harris, M. (Eds.). (1990). *Emics and Etics: The Insider/Outsider Debate*. Newbury Park: Sage Publications.

Hoffman, R.R. (1987, Summer). The problem of extracting the knowledge of experts from the perspective of experimental psychology. *The AI Magazine, 8,* 53-64.

Hoffman, R.R. & Pike, R.J. (1995). On the specification of the information available for the perception and description of the natural terrain. To appear in P.A. Hancock, J. Flach, J.K. Caird & K.J. Vicente (Eds.), *Local Applications of the Ecological Approach to Human-Machine Systems* (285-323). Hillsdale, NJ: Lawrence Erlbaum.

Hollnagel, E. (1991). The phenotype of erroneous actions: Implications for HCI design. In G.R.S. Weir & J.L. Alty (Eds.), *Human Computer Interaction and Complex Systems* (pp. 73-121). London: Academic Press.

Hutchins, E.F. (1993). Learning to navigate. In S. Chaiklin & J. Lave (Eds.), *Understanding Practice* (pp. 35-63). Cambridge: Cambridge University Press.

Hutchins, E.F. (1990). The technology of team navigation. In J. Galegher, R. Kraut & C. Egido (Eds.), *Intellectual Teamwork: Social and Technological Foundations of Cooperative Work* (pp. 191-220). Hillsdale, NJ: Lawrence Erlbaum.

Klein, G.A. (1993). A recognition primed (RPD) model of rapid decision making. In G.A. Klein, J. Orasanu, R. Calderwood & C.E. Zsambok (Eds.), *Decision Making in Context* (pp. 138-147). Norwood, NJ: Ablex.

Klein, G.A. (1987). Analytical versus recognitional approaches to design decision making. In W.B. Rouse & K.R. Boff (Eds.), *System Design: Behavioral Perspectives on Designers, Tools and Organizations* (pp. 175-186). New York: North Holland.

Klein, G.A. & Hoffman, R.R. (1993). Seeing the invisible: Perceptual-cognitive aspects of expertise. In M. Rabinowitz (Ed.), *Cognitive Science Foundations of Instruction* (pp. 203-226). Hillsdale, NJ: Lawrence Erlbaum.

Klein, G.A., Orasanu, J., Calderwood, R. & Zsambok, C.E. (Eds.). (1993). *Decision Making in Context*. Norwood, NJ: Ablex.

Klein, G.A., Calderwood, R. & MacGregor, D. (1989). Critical decision method for eliciting knowledge. *IEEE Transactions on Systems, Man, and Cybernetics, 19(3),* 462-472.

Larkin, J.H. (1983). The role of problem representation in physics. In D. Gentner & A.L. Stevens (Eds.), *Mental Models* (pp. 75-100). Hillsdale, NJ: Lawrence Erlbaum.

Lave, J. (1988). *Cognition in Practice.* Cambridge, England: Cambridge University Press.

Lesgold, A. (1989). Context-specific requirements for models of expertise. In D.A. Evans & V.L. Patel (Eds.), *Advanced Models of Cognition for Medical Training and Practice* (pp. 373-400). Berlin: Springer-Verlag.

Lesgold, A., Rubinson, H., Feltovich, P., Glaser, R., Klopfer, D. & Wang, Y. (1988). Expertise in a complex skill: Diagnosing x-ray pictures. In M.T.H. Chi, R. Glaser & M.J. Farr (Eds.), *The Nature of Expertise* (pp. 311-342). Hillsdale, NJ: Lawrence Erlbaum.

Livingston, E. (1987). *Making Sense of Ethnomethodology.* London: Routledge & Kegan Paul.

Newell, A. (1973). Artificial intelligence and the concept of mind. In R.C. Schank & K.M. Colby (Eds.), *Computer Models of Language and Thought* (pp. 2-60). San Francisco: W.H. Freeman.

Neisser, U. (1976). *Cognition and Reality.* New York: W.H. Freeman.

Norman, D.A. (1991). Cognitive artifacts. In J. Carroll (Ed.), *Designing Interaction* (pp. 17-38). Cambridge: Cambridge University Press.

Orasanu, J.M. (1990). *Shared mental models and crew decision making* (CSL Report No. 46). Princeton, NJ: Princeton University, Cognitive Science Laboratory.

Orasanu, J.M. & Fischer, U. (1992). Team cognition in the cockpit: Linguistic control of shared problem solving. In *Proceedings of the 14th Annual Meeting of the Cognitive Science Society* (pp. 189-194). Hillsdale, NJ: Lawrence Erlbaum.

Palmer, S.E. (1977). Hierarchical structure in perceptual representation. *Cognitive Psychology, 9,* 441-474.

Patel, V.L. & Groen, G.J. (1986). Knowledge-based solution strategies in medical reasoning. *Cognitive Science, 10,* 91-116.

Patel, V.L., Groen, G.J. & Arocha, J.F. (1990). Medical expertise as a function of task difficulty. *Memory and Cognition, 18,* 394-406.

Prabhu, P., Sharit, J. & Drury, C. (1992). Classification of temporal errors in CIM systems: Development of a framework for deriving human-centered information requirements. *International Journal of Computer Integrated Manufacturing, 5(2),* 68-80.

Sacerdoti, E. (1977). *A Structure of Plans and Behavior.* New York: Elsevier.

Sanderson, P.M. (1989). The human planning and scheduling role in advanced manufacturing systems: An emerging human factors domain. *Human Factors, 31(6),* 635-66.

Scribner, S. (1984). Studying working intelligence. In B. Rogoff & J. Lave (Eds.), *Everyday Cognition: Its Development in Social Context* (pp. 9-40). Cambridge, MA: Harvard University Press.

Seifert, C., Patalano, A., Hammond, K. & Converse, T. (this volume). Experience and expertise: Preparing for opportunities. In P.J. Feltovich, K.M. Ford, & R.R. Hoffman (Eds.), *Expertise in Context.* Menlo Park, CA: AAAI/MIT Press.

Sewell, D.R. & Geddes, N.D. (1990). A plan- and goal-based method for computer-human system design. *Human Computer Interaction: INTERACT 90* (pp. 283-288). New York: North Holland.

Shalin, V.L. & Bertram, D.A. (1996). Functions of expertise in a medical intensive care unit. *Journal of Experimental and Theoretical Artificial Intelligence: Special Issue on the Psychology of Human and Artificial Expertise,* 8, 3/4, 209-227. R. Campell & R. Mathews (Eds.).

Shalin, V.L., Geddes, N.D. & Mikesell, B.G. (1992). *Information management for the commercial aviation flight deck.* Presented at the Poster Session of the 36th Annual Meeting of the Human Factors Society, Atlanta, GA.

Shalin, V.L., Geddes, N.D., Mikesell, B.G. & Ramamurthy, M. (1993a). Evidence for plan-based performance and implications for information management on the commercial aviation flight deck. In *Proceedings of the 4th International Conference on Human Machine Interaction and Artificial Intelligence in Aeronautics and Space* (pp. 1-17). Toulouse, France: European Institute of Cognitive Sciences and Engineering.

Shalin, V.L., Geddes, N.D., Mikesell, B.G. & Ramamurthy, M. (1993b). Performance effects of plan-based information displays in commercial aviation. In *Proceedings of the 7th International Symposium on Aviation Psychology* (pp. 138-143). Columbus, OH: Ohio State University.

Simon, H.A. (1969). *The Sciences of the Artificial.* Cambridge, MA: MIT Press.

Sloboda, J.A. (1991). Musical expertise. In K.A. Ericsson & J. Smith (Eds.), *Toward a General Theory of Expertise* (pp. 153-171). Cambridge: Cambridge University Press.

Soloway, E. & Erlich, K. (1984). Empirical investigations of programming knowledge. *IEEE Transactions on Software Engineering, 10*(5), 595-609.

Suchman, L.A. (1987). *Plans and Situated Actions.* Cambridge, England: Cambridge University Press.

Szczepkowski, M.A., Shalin, V.L., Bertram, D.A., Drury, C.G., Aquilina, A. & Ten-Brock, E. (1994). Observable measures of physician mental workload in the medical intensive care unit. In *Proceedings of the 12th Triennial Congress of the International Ergonomics Association* (Vol. 6, pp. 229-231). Ontario, Canada: Human Factors Association of Canada.

Treisman, A. & Sato, S. (1990). Conjunction search revisited. *Journal of Experimental Psychology: Human Perception and Performance, 16,* 459-478.

Vera, A.H. & Simon, H.A. (1993). Situated action: A symbolic interpretation. *Cognitive Science, 17,* 7-48.

Welford, A.T. (1968). *Fundamentals of Skill.* London: Metheuen.

Winograd, T. & Flores, F. (1986). *Understanding Computers and Cognition.* Norwood, NJ: Ablex.

Winston, P.H. (Ed.). (1975). Learning structural descriptions from examples. *The Psychology of Computer Vision* (pp. 157-209). New York: McGraw-Hill.

Woods, D. D. (1988). Coping with complexity: The psychology of human behaviour in complex systems. In L.P. Goodstein, H.B. Andersen & S.E. Olson (Eds.), *Tasks, Errors and Mental Models* (pp. 128-148). London: Taylor & Francis.

Woods, D.D. (in press). Towards a theoretical base for representation design in the computer medium: Ecological perception and aiding human cognition. In J. Flach, P. Hancock, J. Caird & K. Vicente (Eds.), *Global Perspectives on the Ecology of Human-Machine Systems.* Hillsdale, NJ: Lawrence Erlbaum.

Zeitz, C. (this volume). Some concrete advantages of abstraction: How experts' representations facilitate reasoning. In P.J. Feltovich, K.M. Ford & R.R. Hoffman (Eds.), *Expertise in Context.* Menlo Park, CA: AAAI/MIT Press.

CHAPTER 10

Expertise In Context: Personally Constructed, Socially Selected and Reality-Relevant?

Neil M. Agnew, Kenneth M. Ford & Patrick J. Hayes

Introduction

What do snake oil salesmen, TV evangelists, chicken sexers, small motor mechanics, geologists, radiologists, and computer scientists all have in common? They all meet the minimum criterion of expertise, namely they all have a constituency that perceives them to be experts. But surely there is more to it than that. What other criteria or guidelines should we add to help us scale, or at least order, expertise? How might we rank order the knowledge possessed by the above experts? Discussions with various colleagues suggest that the snake oil salesman and the TV evangelist occupy the bottom rung; next come chicken sexers, then small motor mechanics, then a tie between geologist and radiologists, with computer scientists at the top of the heap. But of course those polled involved a majority of computer scientists. Not surprisingly, when asked about the matter, geologists and radiologists each placed themselves above computer scientists, while using the same ordering for the lowest and middle rungs.

The following themes emerged when our colleagues were asked to justify their ranking:

- The snake oil salesmen and TV evangelists were ranked lowest because it seemed that there was no "real" basis for their presumed expertise and they were perceived as experts only by naïve, relatively uneducated constituencies. However, one observer noted that some TV evangelists were expert at reading "human nature," if financial success is used as one "objective" criterion.

- The chicken sexer demonstrates ability to read subtle biological nature, but only in a narrow sense. Furthermore, selected apprentices can acquire the skill in a relatively short time.

- The small motor mechanic demonstrates the ability to read "mechanical nature" and deals with a wider and more complex range of problems than does the chicken sexer, and it takes a longer apprenticeship to acquire this skill.

- Petroleum geologists and radiologists both required a long period of formal and theoretical training. Nevertheless, they have only a limited ability to deal with areas of high uncertainty in their respective fields. When they are correct in their predictions, they produce significant payoffs in terms of profits or life extension. But when they are wrong, their mistakes incur very high costs. Determining whether they are right or wrong frequently takes years and involves multiple criteria.

- Computer scientists require a long period of formal theoretical and technical training. Furthermore, their training is anchored in the fundamental sciences of physics and mathematics, and the applications of their knowledge are employed by those in almost every other scholarly or applied discipline. However, the geologists and radiologists tended to see the computer scientists as knowledgeable about artificial, not "real" or natural worlds.

These classifications and justifications, though casually made, reflect some of the themes we will carry through this chapter, including the following:

- The minimum criterion of expertise is to have at least one reasonably large group of people—a constituency or niche—who consider that you are an expert; in this sense, expertise is socially selected. Note that we are making a distinction here between being an expert and having knowledge. "Expert" is a *role* that some are selected to play on the basis of all sorts of criteria, epistemic and otherwise.

- Different constituencies apply a variety of quasi-stable criteria in selecting their experts. So while those designated as experts may share some common characteristics (e.g., high confidence), there are also many niche-specific characteristics and performance criteria.

- Experts competing for the same constituency (e.g., computer scientists competing for grants and journal space) while sharing a common core, differ in the constellation of skills, knowledge, and personality that they bring to a given competition. Such individual differences indicate not only that expertise is a social attribution, but also that it arises from and utilizes personally constructed knowledge.

- Finally, among the different quasi-stable selective criteria that various constituencies apply in choosing their experts, some selectors are more "reality-relevant" than others. For example, certain constituencies, such as the scientific and engineering communities, have evolved some relatively robust cross-cultural criteria in selecting their experts.

Thus, we think of experts less in terms of their possessing some particular rare cognitive competency, or a greater quantity of 'true' knowledge than their colleagues, than as having been selected by a constituency willing to attribute expertise to them. Snake oil salesman *are* experts on this view.[1] Expertise is not synonymous with knowledge. Expertise, unlike knowledge, does not reside in the individual, but rather emerges from a dynamic interaction between the individual and his physical/cultural domain. Whether or not an individual is selected to serve in an expert role for a constituency is often independent of the absolute accuracy of their knowledge. Experts are not necessarily the most knowledgeable among us.

A radiologist with whom one of us works trusts that patients he categorizes as having heart disease will generate feedback (e.g., they die or require surgery) that fit his anticipation. To the extent he perceives a fit, we have an instance of personally constructed knowledge. To the extent that a constituency selects and nourishes his constructions, our radiologist's knowledge/behavior becomes socially selected, and he is permitted to serve in the role of expert. In fact, our radiologist's continuing expert status is as much a function of his capacity to construct and maintain confidence, both his own and that of his constituency, as it is a function of his particular beliefs about heart disease. His capacity to construct personally robust beliefs is a necessary, but not sufficient, condition of expert status. Given this capacity for confidence, he is in the running with other competitors to be socially selected. Those selected to serve as experts have constructed personally and socially functional anticipations—beliefs that fit the personal and social constraints of the time and the context.

In short, we here propose that "selection theory" (Campbell 1977) provides a useful model for considering the production and maintenance of expertise. Selection theory is based on the notion that a variation-selection-and-retention process is fundamental to all inductive achievements, to all increases in knowledge, and to all increases in fit of system to environment. In such processes there are three essentials: 1) mechanisms for introducing variation; 2) selection processes; and 3) mechanisms for preserving and/or propagating the selected variations. Note that, in general, the generation mechanism (1) and the preservation mechanism (3) are inherently at odds, and one must be traded off against the other (Campbell 1977, p. 421). From this perspective, potential experts can be seen as trial-and-error cognitive/technical gambits or variations, some of whom are chosen by selection processes operating in their environments or contexts. Once selected, these newly minted experts become selectors themselves since they function to preserve and propagate their own expertise, while either constraining or fostering the emergence and selection of other potential experts.

Guided by selection theory, we will commence at a general level of analysis examining the historical and social aspects of expertise and then from within a constructivist framework move to an individual psychological/cognitive level of analysis. Selection theory emphasizes the constraints rather than the variations that influence human behavior. In contrast, constructivist epistemologies are largely concerned with the variations and, in particular, the processes of individual construing. The perspective described here provides an integrated view of expertise as personally constructed and socially selected. Further, we address the issue of justifying our confidence, or lack thereof, in the knowledge claims made by our experts. In brief, we assume that historical and social contexts, human nature, and reality's hidden-hand editing function represent quasi-stable selectors and preservers, thus placing constraints on which knowledge trials are selected to play the role of expert and which remain for the time being undernourished or rejected.

Expertise: Socially Selected and Historically Situated

Today's experts become tomorrow's endangered species. Expertise remains at the mercy of its context. Historical context constrains expertise, and nested within that larger temporal framework, cultural and disciplinary constraints select the fittingest. We say "the fittingest" not the "fittest," thus indicating that in studying expertise we must focus as much upon the selectors (the context) as upon the selected (the experts). As in the evolutionary analogy, the degree of fit is not assumed to be perfect. Potential competitors continue to challenge for dominance, and the selective criteria change, thus affording opportunities for competing beliefs and their champions.

As a result of such winnowing, expert knowledge is functional but fallible. It is functional in that it has been selected from among legions of competitors to (more or less) fit quasi-stable sociophysical niches. It is fallible on at least two count. First, no perfect fits are assumed in the natural selection analogy where niches are multi-dimensional, quasi-stable systems—so fit becomes a matter of degree. Second, changes in selectors can lead to a growing degree of obsolescence in any previously selected expert knowledge. Evidence for this general thesis can be found in several disciplines, including the history, philosophy, and sociology of science.

The History and Philosophy of Science

We face a puzzle posed by history in general and the history of science (e.g., Kuhn 1970) in particular. The puzzle is this: how can one have high confidence in modern expertise when history shows that knowledge is often highly fragile, that it is at the mercy of shifts in historical context, and that yesterday's experts are today's museum pieces. While we acknowledge that beliefs are strongly shaped to fit historical contexts, we do not believe it is necessary to accept the implied extreme relativism or nihilism proposed by some investigators (e.g., Collins 1981a,b).

Like the history of science, the modern philosophy of science (e.g., Lakatos 1968; Meehl 1990; Popper 1974; Quine 1969) challenges the confidence we have placed in our traditional methods (epistemologies) of generating knowledge. Many of humankind's most trusted methods rely on induction—which survives at the mercy of a biased selection of positive instances and the rejection or rationalization of negative instances. Even when applied without bias, inductive strategies remain at the mercy of the future. Our inductively produced beliefs are threatened both by paradigm shifts—changes in the quasi-stable cultural or discipline-specific selectors—and by yet-to-surface salient negative instances. Furthermore, the logic of confirmation leaves many explicit competing hypotheses (cognitive trials) and legions of implicit or unthought-of hypotheses still in the running. Fallible though it may be, however, induction is a functional and affordable strategy for most decision makers (Agnew and Brown 1989b). Alternative epistemological mechanisms have been generated—but not widely selected. The robustness and success of induction, in spite of its apparent logical flaws, is itself a phenomenon which requires explanation.

In seeking to reduce errors associated with induction, Karl Popper proposed a "logic of falsification." He recommended that we revise our selectors and that science focus its energy on seeking and displaying negative instances relating to an hypothesis rather than on seeking and displaying (selecting) positive instances. But the costs of such a strategy are enormous, involving a drastic reduction in the type of problems scientists can seriously engage, and as Popper acknowledged, it is only a logical solution. In theory, one negative instance would disprove the hypothesis of a meticulously specified theory. However, the history of science suggests that this falsification logic is a paper tiger (at least descriptively), and that negative instances typically lead not to the rejection of a prized theory, but rather to the rejection of the negative instance, or at best, to cosmetic retrofits of auxiliary or disposable subhypotheses (e.g., Lakatos 1968; Meehl 1990; Minsky 1983). The connection between theory and instance is often long and complex and has many safety valves which allow consistency to be restored. Much of the arcane craft of experimental design is devoted to attempting to close as many of these as possible to increase the logical pressure of experimental data on some sufficiently fragile part of a theory.

As noted by Bickard (1993, personal communication), Popper was well aware of the practical limits of the "logic" of falsification. He merely wished to establish the logical "asymmetry" between confirming and falsifying instances. It is simply true that accepting a falsifying instance logically requires rejecting the theory, whereas accepting a positive instance does not logically force acceptance of the theory. In practice, whether an instance is accepted or rejected is more than a matter of logic; it is one of research design, error variance, experimenter preference, disciplinary pressures, etc. In this sense, the popular and relatively stable selectors of science, its epistemology, deliver knowledge and expertise that is context dependent and historically fragile.

How then are we to maintain confidence in modern knowledge and expertise, given the limitations of our knowledge-making and expertise-selecting methods as portrayed by the history and philosophy of science? While accepting the epistemological constructivism such arguments support, we reject ontological nihilism. Specifically, we allay our ontological angst by relying on a variation of selection theory; that is, we see some selectors (e.g., certain scientific selectors) as relatively cross-cultural, and as selecting for "fit" to larger space/time frames than those selectors serving more local contexts. Further, while individual scientists typically do not practice the logic of falsification on their own hypotheses, they happily attempt to practice it on competing hypotheses, thus affording the evolution of a modest logic of falsification at some level, over the long haul.

The sociology of science provides further evidence for the context dependency of knowledge and expertise and, in particular, support for the notion that expertise is selected to fit the quasi-stable constraints of respective disciplines or professions.

The Sociology of Science

Sociologists of science (e.g., Knorr-Cetina 1987; Knorr-Cetina and Mulkay 1983) and social psychologists (e.g., Campbell 1987b; Gergen 1981) have engaged the historical and philosophical issues noted above. Sociologists are bringing to bear on science their general models of social determinism. Not only can we see historical context effects (e.g., the trend for science to replace religion in occupying the how-to-deal-with-unobservables niche), but we see also how larger social systems place constraints on the beliefs and practices of subsystems (e.g., senate reviews of scientific priorities, projects, and spending). Furthermore, we see how scientific disciplines establish and exercise further constraints (i.e., selectors) through various rites of passage, thus determining who is selected in and who selected out, which hypotheses and methods are tolerated and nourished, and which are deprived of editorial or grant support.

Like anthropologists studying primitive tribes, some sociologists (e.g., Knorr-Cetina and Mulkay 1983; Latour 1987) have moved into scientific laboratories where they peer over the shoulders of scientists in the process of creating expert knowledge. Not surprisingly, the sociologists report that knowledge is brought to life by social bargaining, that "facts" are constructed through negotiations over what meter readings (or other proxies representing the phenomenon under investigation) to keep and which to discard. As a consequence, other hopefuls attempting to replicate the study now have clear (expert) guidelines as to which meter readings they should select in and which to select out.[2]

We should not be surprised that sociologists can compile (induce) many positive instances of social determinism. That is their job and basic premise—they select and display positive instances supporting their hypotheses. Sociologists are not alone...all disciplines conduct the same epistemological practice...as noted by Simon (1983) *no conclusions without premises!* Thus, at the local level, we see evidence for "professional" constraints acting like homogenization and extrusion processes where the product is the expertise of the specialty. While we agree that expertise is socially selected, with contexts serving as variance reduction valves, we do not believe that this is the whole story.

Our natural selection model suggests that mechanisms have evolved not only to reduce variance and maintain social cohesion but also to give competing variations or hypotheses a chance. Over the long haul, for example, the courts and science represent institutionalized opportunities for both variation and the winnowing of beliefs. Furthermore, deviant "meter readings" arising from carefully crafted experiments by theoretical opponents are not so readily negotiated away. While backing the status quo remains the best bet, it is not the only one, and periodically it is rejected. Eventually, some marginal sociologist of science will weather an academic storm and start gathering and displaying instances in which the pressures of social determinism were overcome by a deviant "experiential reality" constructed by socially mutant scientists who provide "seed" concepts or technologies around which the young Turks and disaffected crystallize, sometimes with startling rapidity.

In contrast to the historical and social levels of analyses sketched above, most research on expertise has traditionally focused on the individual (e.g., studies of the memory of chess players). This useful line of research is sustained by the assumption that expert knowledge or expertise is best understood in terms of cognitive competence. At first glance, this assumption may seem in conflict with our notion of expert as a role that some are selected to play as a result of a social attribution. It may, however, be helpful to make a process/product distinction here. Expertise, along with painting, poetry and physics, can be seen as a product of the interplay between cognitive and cultural/social processes. The processes involved in the development and deployment of expertise can be gainfully conceptualized and studied from both an intra- and inter-individual basis. In the next section, we shift from the macro to the micro level of description and examine expertise as personally constructed.

Expertise: Personally Constructed

While expertise operates within (is selected to fit) the constraints of histori-cal, cultural, and professional/scientific contexts or niches, such selective forces are not perfectly efficient, and therefore, individual differences be-tween experts in the same discipline still remain to be accounted for. Sociolo-gists would account for some (most?) of this variance in terms of subcultural influences within the larger culture. Some cognitive psychologists might credit such variations in expertise to differences in cognitive competence. We accept both these accounts and see the variations arising as a result of indi-vidual differences interacting with subcultural and cultural variables. Inher-ent individual differences in cognitive capacity, energy level, aggressiveness, etc., are selected and nourished by some physical/cultural niches.

The selective forces at work in disparate areas of expertise or specialization differ. For example, one would expect areas of scientific expertise (selected to play a societal devil's advocate role and so conditionally sheltered from certain cultural constraints), to attract proportionally more stubborn young Turks and provide them with relatively more degrees of freedom than afforded new en-trants into more culturally accountable specialities (e.g., medicine and account-ing). Although certain institutions (e.g., university-based science) offer increased freedom, significant constraints (selectors) still operate. In mature scientific dis-ciplines, highly concentrated training and testing practices will lead to "selecting in" those who buy the current orthodoxy and thus become practitioners of "normal science" in a Kuhnian sense and at the same time "selecting out" the deviants. Still, between these two poles—between the establishment experts and unprogrammable deviants—remains a residue of functional marginals, or conceptual/technical mutants, to seed future developments.

Marginals can be successful in the sense of having obtained and main-tained group membership in spite of thinking and practicing in some con-ceptual or technical ways on the fringe of the central core of current ortho-doxy. Some are conservative marginals who still practice various past orthodoxies, while others will be radical marginals who revise and extend current beliefs and practices, ideological sports, if you will. In natural selec-tion terms, we have modest ideological mutants or variations, most of whom will fade away. Nevertheless, a few will not only survive but thrive in a nour-ishing but untapped portion of the niche or even provide a bridge into an evolving niche—in both cases becoming an expert's expert. But how are we to explain ideological mutants or variants?

Pragmatic Constructivism

Pragmatic constructivism provides one way of conceptualizing expertise as a product of individual-cultural interactions. Personal construct theory as formulated by Kelly (1955) and summarized by Adams-Webber (1987), provides for high variability in individual constructions of experience; our natural selection model requires this variability, but we have not yet accounted for it. Reality does not reveal itself to us directly, and any given event is open to a variety of alternative interpretations. This fact does not imply, however, that all interpretations are equally good. On the contrary, different ways of construing the same event can be evaluated by comparing them systematically in terms of their relative predictive utility or viability. It is likely that some interpretations of an event will prove more useful than others. Thus, although we deny the traditionally posited iconic relation between knowledge and ontological reality, we have substituted for it a different but no less specific relation—pragmatic viability. It is within this framework that we see expertise as socially selected and personally constructed.

Not Anything Goes

The radical constructivists and others operating within the skeptical tradition claim that since we have no direct access to "reality"—our beliefs are shadows—science, like religion, politics, and literature, merely reflects the myth-making tendencies of the human tribe, with one myth being no more reality-based than another. Collins (1981a, p. 3) expresses the antiepistemic (and perhaps also antiscientific) stance found among many radical constructivists, relativists, and sociologists of science when he says: "the natural world has a small or nonexistent role in the construction of scientific knowledge." Collins has noted that the behavior of real scientists typically does not follow the abstract ideal of disinterested pursuit of truth. There is a widely accepted vision of science disinterestedly uncovering truth, the kind of thing that inspires marble statues at the portals of older university buildings; but as Collins correctly emphasizes, this isn't what really goes on.[3] In any case, it doesn't stand up to logical criticism, since the best that science could ever have is a theory, and a theory can be no more than a collection of guesses written in some conceptual framework which itself must be provided by society. So, a certain naïve story is wrong, and absolute truth is unattainable. But Collins draws the startling and extreme conclusion that "reality" is merely a construction of a social game.

In contrast, Kelly stresses the salience of our idiosyncratic constructions and the futility of worrying about our lack of direct access to the world-as-it-is.

> The fact that my only approach to reality is through offering some responsible construction of it does not discourage me from postulating that it is there. The open question for man is not whether reality exists or not but what he can make of it. If he does make something of it, he can stop worrying about whether it exists or not. If he doesn't make something of it, he might better worry about whether he exists or not (Kelly, 1969, p. 25).

As Kelly emphasizes here, the constructivist view does not have to lead to any kind of ultimate skepticism or rejection of the possibility of truth. That someone's view of a tree is something idiosyncratic constructed in his mind and that the very concept of "tree" has arisen from social intercourse and takes its authority ultimately perhaps from faith in arborists—all of this does not entail that the tree is not real or that it is inaccessible to discussion. Arborists, cognitive theorists, and semanticists, of course, all construct their views of the world, and none have privileged access to it other than by utilizing more or less successful constructions. But a constructivist's analysis of the tree-perception process might be no less successful at tree-construction than anyone else's and indeed might borrow from the same authority as any other discussion of trees, so if we acknowledge that some kind of world is really there—and we surely had better at least do that—then to give a constructivist account of the relationship between perceiver and perceived does not force us all into ontological skepticism.

Ironically, the only thing that distinguishes the work of descriptive sociologists or ethnomethodologists from novel-writing is precisely their comparatively careful attention to data, thereby accepting the hidden hand of the real world as an editor of one's ideas. This acceptance is a defining characteristic of our optimistic pragmatic constructivism. As noted above, they (e.g., Collins) sometimes claim that the world-as-it-is plays little or no part in the beliefs of scientists; but what can be the basis for *their* beliefs other than empirical observation of the natural world, which, of course, includes the scientists they study? Are sociologists somehow issued special glasses that allow them to see more clearly than other scientists?

While we acknowledge the skeptic's ontological angst, we explicitly reject the nihilist view that "anything goes." Alternatively, we concur with Quine's (1969) gently limiting interpretation that "almost anything goes." We do so not only as an article of faith but also as a means of understanding some of the profound impacts of science...impacts which deliver cross-cultural bewilderment—like atom bombs—and wonder—like penicillin. Although beliefs may be representational shadows, they are *about* the real world, which in the long (and sometimes not so long) run serves as a hidden-hand editor of both beliefs and believers. Thus, we contend that "reality," writ small or large, provides some constraints on what is believed and practiced.

We see "physical nature" and "human nature" as multi-dimensional quasi-stable selectors providing a hidden-hand editing function that shapes many of our beliefs. In brief, we claim that some knowledge and expertise are more than disposable cultural myths or highly personal empirical or symbolic fabrications (Agnew & Brown, 1989a). Anyone who has carried out experiments (or for that matter written computer programs) has not only experienced social context pressures but also felt the non-negotiable force of the constraints imposed by the ontic world. Ontological reality manifests itself to us (sometimes quite emphatically) when we bump into some of the constraints that it imposes on our activities...and on our beliefs. Some of the shadows on the wall of Plato's cave kick back.

In our view, reality plays a more or less direct role of editor for the beliefs of both individuals and societies. For example, in the case of visual perception, reality seems to play a very precise role in that some of our retinal cells are sensitive to just a few photons. On the other hand, our beliefs about politics seem only tangentially influenced by the world-as-it-is. Even if all our current beliefs are of unknown validity in terms of their degree of correspondence with an independent reality underlying events, they may still prove useful for anticipating new possibilities as we persevere in our efforts to improve the range of convenience of our constructions and to explore still unknown potentials of human experience (Ford & Adams-Webber, 1992).

Returning to our evolutionary analogy, these personal and societal hypotheses can be seen as trial-and-error gambits that can be highly functional in certain socio-physical niches. Relatively primitive creatures, such as insects, make little or no use of anticipatory hypotheses—they rely on their perceptual feelers to warn them just before something bad happens. In contrast, highly evolved risk-averse creatures such as humans avail themselves of what Dennett (1996) calls "temporally distal" anticipations. It has been proposed (Campbell, 1987a) that our trial hypotheses are evolved mechanisms for distance perception, higher order evolutions than the eye, or the random trial-and-error explorations of the insect's feeler, or the cilia of primitive water organisms. Thus, our hypotheses can die in our stead, enabling us to hypothesize another way, another day.

From a selection theory perspective, our anticipations reflect our ontological assumptions. In this sense, we construct our own "realities" through trial-and-error gambits, some of which in turn are selected to fit quasi-stable constraints: individual such as comfort and hunger, cultural such as esteem and wealth, and cross-cultural such as death and gravity.

Ontological Pitons

Stephen Hawking (1988) opens his book with the story of a little old lady who confronted Bertrand Russell at the end of his lecture on orbiting planets, telling him that "What you have told us is rubbish. The world is really a flat plate supported on the back of a giant tortoise." Russell reportedly gave a superior smile before asking what the turtle was standing on. "You're very clever, young man, very clever," replied the old lady, "but it's turtles all the way down."[4]

Likewise, for an individual knower (whether man or machine), it's "beliefs (i.e., constructions) all the way down." Thinkers cannot think of anything except through a process of active (but not always conscious) construction involving the building and manipulation of representations, and all representations must embody a perspective and make suppositions. One might hope that an analysis of the process of perception or of the relationship between believer and believed might reveal the ways in which our thoughts are anchored in reality—perhaps psychology or semantics will show where the turtle stands. But all thinking, including this entire story of the world, our beliefs and perceptions, and the relationships between them, is as much a construction as any other of our thoughts. One who believes that any *constructed* conceptual framework cannot be firmly enough attached to the world-as-it-is cannot obtain a firmer grip on that elusive ontic world through this kind of metalevel discussion, phrased as it is in a framework which has no better claim to direct authority. No amount of thinking about meanings can ever reach Cartesian bedrock; indeed, it *is* turtles all the way down.

As a consequence, there doesn't seem to be any certain knowledge on which to stop and stand—at least no place that adequately answers the skeptics, that doesn't generate logical paradoxes, that doesn't involve the scandal of induction, and, as underlined by Simon (1983), that doesn't rely on unproven assumptions. Once we reject naïve realism—the comfortable notion that "reality" somehow etches veridical pictures or messages on "the wax plates of our minds"—we encounter a formidable puzzle. How can our conviction that there is a reliable fit between at least some of our beliefs and their referents be justified? How can we release the comfortable brass ring of naïve realism and yet keep from sliding into a logically coherent but pragmatically unworkable and philosophically unsavory relativist stew as depicted in figure 1? Where should we drive our ontological pītons? The skeptics and radical constructivists propose that there is no principled way of anchoring our beliefs, and so anything goes; there are no ways of deciding whose knowledge claims to trust: tinker, tailor, soldier, sailor, Indian chief, politician...the Bible or the *Scientific American*.

However, in spite of this apparent dilemma, everyone does locate trusted stopping places. In Kelly's terms, these core constructs, trusted turtles, sustain a repertoire of functional if fallible anticipations. In most cases, core constructs remain implicit. Only when people encounter pervasive and salient negative feedback do they become aware of the fallibility of heretofore trusted turtles, and the world trembles—we experience cognitive earthquakes. Personally constructed expertise requires robust and sustaining core constructs. In this sense, expertise is based on a kind of cognitive bigotry, on logically indefensible but stubbornly held assumptions which support anticipations with a functional range of personal and constituency relevance.

They do not, indeed, provide the kind of ultimate certainty that seems to motivate so much philosophical handwringing, but we do not draw tragic conclusions from this apparent failure. A confident skeptic (to the extent there can be such a thing) is one who is certain that his beliefs are uncertain;

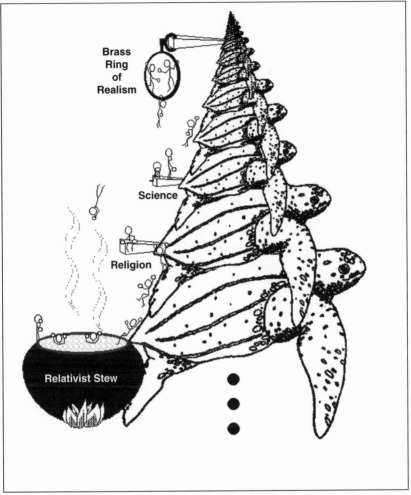

Figure 1. Although it's turtles all the way down, we all find trusted stopping places.

while a naïve realist is one who is certain they *are* certain (equivalent to intellectual foot-stamping)—a fight between the confused and the redundant. Such absolute certainty is a chimera, according to a constructivist view of thought and perception, which could never possibly be obtained. A phenomenological analysis of "direct" perception suggests some of the difficulties. Try to imagine seeing, and *knowing* that what one saw was true, as a result of having some kind of *direct* access to the world. How would one know that one had this knowledge? It is difficult to imagine in what such certainty could consist, other than extreme confidence in oneself. And of course such bigoted self-confidence is a common phenomenon in human affairs already.

Nonetheless, among the most trusted cortico/cultural constructions are representations of REALITY writ large. When in need of an ontological piton, we all look first to those personal constructions of reality selected by constraints in our personal experience, our perceptual constructions of the everyday world. Even the most radical constructivist ducks the flying brick.

When confidence in our personal constructions is low or uncertain, people turn to experts (and expert institutions) as a source of trusted belief. In particular, knowledge able to "pass" the tests of our preferred "courts of knowledge"—whether these courts be tribal lore, religious doctrines, or the pronouncements of modern science—is accorded high status and constitutes a likely candidate for the role of piton or most trusted belief. The production and selection by both individuals and society of knowledge treated as objective—knowledge that we are able to project confidently and viably beyond our own sphere of experience into that of others—plays an important role in the stabilization of individual beliefs. Individuals construct, maintain, and revise their own trusted beliefs through continuous interaction with the trusted beliefs of their subcultures, which, in turn, reflect to some degree the trusted beliefs of the wider culture.

We find two of society's most evolved institutions, religion and science, sometimes competing to provide the most trusted representations of the unobservable past and the future (e.g., big bang vs. Genesis). These religious and scientific experts produce models of possible worlds for their respective constituencies. These very different models are supported by selected and trusted proxy representations of relevant worlds. Of course the models in each case are well protected by robust damage control mechanisms to help avoid or discount counter examples. Evolved trusted selectors provide long-term functional beliefs of high social and individual salience.

The Scientific Context

We take the position that some of our knowledge is more than social, that to some degree, it reflects the hidden-hand editing of selectors that cross cultures and time. In this sense, the larger culture has selected the evolving scientific tribe to serve as an institutionalized devil's advocate and generator of more trusted beliefs to replace current arbitrary place holders (temporary experts).

Although based on logically indefensible assumptions and arbitrary closures, science remains one of our most trusted generators of knowledge and expertise. Here we are suggesting that certain of the conceptual and methodological aspects of science have evolved and have been selected by the larger culture as damage control mechanisms. Such mechanisms help protect the culture from total reliance on beliefs that are short-term functional but long-term dysfunctional.

In its search for reliable constructions, science has evolved and institution-alized mechanisms for evaluating the durability of knowledge constructions. Such winnowing mechanisms as empirical replication, logical consistency, mathematical representation, and institutionalized critical forums underlie the "courts" of science. Society endows science with the resources to identify higher order invariants or proxies than those produced by knowledge claimants who are driven by short-term goals. Nevertheless, these critical representations do not provide infallible winnowing because the shape of the future may not be represented in past samples and because hidden con-founding variables may invalidate previously trusted findings. But, at least, some products of science appear relatively independent of highly local selec-tors and seem to reflect long-term stabilities in cross-cultural selectors.

Part of the conventional definition of scientific method emphasizes publi-cation, review, and reproducibility of results. This elegant story, the sociolo-gists have observed, fits the actual behavior of individual members of the sci-ence tribe only rather loosely. We are not assuming that most individual scientists actually try to falsify their theories by devising tests that permit re-ality to edit their beliefs, but that SCIENCE writ large does a functional (but always fallible) job at falsification. This process occurs through peer review and by the fact that the scientific culture has institutionalized the defeating of another scientist's published opinions as a recognized form of success. Whole careers can be made by utilizing the logic of falsification on ideas which oth-ers have been careless enough to assert, but there are strong social pressures on most academic scientists to regularly assert *something*. Perhaps no single scientist operates according to the ideal rules, as sociologists delight in telling us, but the approximate global effect is to produce knowledge which the hid-den editor has had an opportunity to grip as firmly as it can be made to.

Our Expert in a Scientific Context

What do we find if we place our expert radiologist in a scientific context? In figure 2 (after Agnew & Brown 1989a), we present an example of what we mean by feedforward and feedback proxies in a scientific sense. Feedforward proxies are typically hypotheses concerning predicted relationships between variables, and feedback proxies are typically relevant sample data generated in a controlled context. The basic assumption is that in order to claim that a relationship exists between an X and a Y variable, we must have access to systematic data *in all four cells* of the simplified 2 X 2 matrix. For example, let X-cutoff define the dividing line between patients diagnosed as having heart disease and those designated as normal. That is, all patients who "score" equal to or above Xc by whatever criteria our radiologist relies upon are diagnosed as having heart disease. All those scoring below Xc are desig-nated as normal. So our expert has sorted his population of patients into two

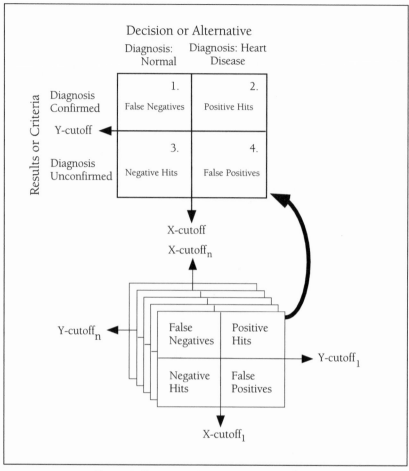

Figure 2. Do experts "construct" positive hits?

groups, one that he hypothesizes belong in Cell 2 (heart disease), and the other group occupying Cell 3 (normal). In this sense, the physician's salient representational space includes only two of the four cells, so there is not enough information available to test the hypothesis. Furthermore, his Cell 2 and 3 designations are questionable since our "expert" lacks *systematic* follow-up data (Y-cutoff proxies) on both his "normals" (to determine if they are "negative hits") and his "heart disease" designations (to determine if they are "positive hits"). His main efforts go to displaying and generating diagnostic clues for his supposed Cell 2 designations—to *constructing* positive hits. In this sense, his goal is to build an island of consistency (Minsky 1985) supporting his belief that 'if *X* then *Y*.'

Notice expertise not only involves making decisions valued by constituents but also involves another vital factor, namely damage control. Experts must be able to maintain their confidence and that of their constituents in the face of nonsystematic but periodic negative feedback. They must be able, with finesse, to successfully "manage" evidence concerning casually discovered False Negatives (e.g., a patient the expert has diagnosed as normal has a heart attack while leaving the office); or casually discovered False Positives (e.g., a patient diagnosed as having serious disease shows no evidence of heart disease on the available Y criteria—catheteratization, exploratory surgery, etc.). But, of course, maintaining confidence in his Xc diagnostic hypothesis remains less challenging under the above impoverished database and casual feedback than it would be if standardized Y-cutoff criteria had been systematically applied to both his normals and heart disease designations and if he were forced to confront such data collected and displayed in all four cells. In brief, many "experts" have not demonstrated expertise in a scientific context as defined by the logic and data requirements of rational empiricism and as represented in the four-cell model.

Our radiologist neither seeks nor receives systematic data on the fate of his designated normals (Cell 3 feedback). Furthermore, he is in a position to ignore or rationalize Cell 4 patients, those he designated as heart diseased yet for whom the surgeon produces no supporting feedback from catheterization. In most professional contexts, the Y-cutoff is frequently fuzzy and under the control of the expert (and/or the profession) so it can be manipulated—wittingly or otherwise—thus enabling the expert to harvest positive instances and ignore or discount negative ones. For example, if the catheterization feedback is negative, our radiologist can shift to, and select from among, any one of Yn criteria—fuzzy or otherwise—that support his prophecy. Finally, the probability of his patients falling into Cell 4 is very low. These patients have been well winnowed before they get to him: They have been designated as having heart problems first by themselves, then by their general practitioner, and perhaps then by a referring specialist. They have been multiply designated as Cell 2 occupants before they see our expert. Thus, his major contribution does not concern the ones he designates as Cell 2 (heart diseased) but rather those he designates as Cell 3 (normal). And, of course, it is those patients about whom he receives little or no feedback.

Other professionals, hostile or indifferent to his hypotheses, may focus their attention on collecting and displaying negative evidence (i.e., Cell 1 and Cell 4 data). But in many instances of professional expertise, such testing is not feasible because the X-cutoff and Y-cutoff criteria are subjective or are themselves the focus of debate. For example, the radiologist's X-cutoff criteria involve subjective patterns he perceives in computer-generated images (e.g., blue fingers, ballerina foot, etc.). At this stage, we do not know the degree of their relationship to reliable, arms-length Y-cutoffs. Furthermore, the currently trusted Y-cutoff criteria are costly and involve risk (e.g., catheterization and surgery) and so cannot be applied to "normals" merely to accommodate our desire to test our expert in a scientific context. Other less costly and intrusive criteria could be employed as proxies (e.g., mortality rates, EEG's, stress tests, etc.), but it should be noted that the matter of selecting a specific alternative criterion must be negotiated and institutionalized. In the meantime, the various medical constituencies (which include all of us) require someone to sort patients into normal and diseased categories regardless of the logical or empirical flaws in the process.

We have suggested that in the typical professional domain (e.g., sorting patients in and out of diagnostic categories in medicine or sorting potential students in and out of graduate programs in universities), knowledge claims are not based on rational-empirical tests of the type outlined above. Critical information is often lacking in Cells 1 and 3. In other words, the Yc accuracy criteria are not applied to patients designated normal or to rejected graduate students. Furthermore, a large number of positive hits can be accounted for by prior screening (patients already designated as highly suspected of heart disease, graduate students pre-selected by having earned good grades in undergraduate work). Thus, in either case, a coin-toss decision rule may do as well as a sorting by experts. Finally, those improbable patients/grad students who fall into Cell 4 can usually be explained away by the experts and their constituencies, who rely on professionally evolved damage control heuristics.

Two Levels of Expertise

All experts have been selected by their constituency. But some knowledge claims have survived the harsher test of being fitted against the real world more firmly than merely by mass opinion, no matter how loud the chorus of a constituency might be. We will call this *reality-relevant* or Level 2 expertise, a stage beyond the first level of *socially selected* knowledge. In using this term, we do not (of course) mean to claim that Level 2 expertise has achieved absolute status as truth, which is probably unattainable in this world, as Popper has convincingly argued. Rather, we grant the accolade of reality-relevance to knowledge claims which continue to pass the tightest empirical tests that our culture can devise. At present the most demanding filter on opinion seems to be the kind of aggressive attempts at falsification represented by the four-cell model.

Interestingly, only rarely does society subject those it has selected to play the role of expert to the kind of careful scrutiny required for elevation to Level 2 status in our model. Many "experts" have not had their expertise subjected to the logic and data requirements of rational empiricism as represented in the four-cell model. Level 1 expertise is personally constructed and socially selected—but not necessarily reality-relevant. As may be expected, Level 1 experts include those who are subsequently labeled as con artists, quacks, delusional, sincere but misguided, etc. However, most Level 1 experts are not obvious frauds but may in fact be found among the professionals—doctors, lawyers, accountants, coaches, teachers, technicians, etc. In addition to passing the confidence-generation test, these experts must sometimes pass extensive domain entry hurdles and keep passing domain-specific performance tests. Nevertheless, while serving useful and sometimes crucial roles in society, the empirical status of their professional beliefs remains undecided—their expertise may actually be reality-relevant, but until it is subjected to our highest courts of knowledge, we relegate it to Level 1.

We observe that many visible experts operating in nontrivial domains are Level 1 experts, who in turn select compatible colleagues, and that such serial selections can account for the appearance of high consensually validated expertise. For those unfamiliar with the medical domain, look in your own domain for comparable examples. For instance, university faculty are selected as promising academics; then a certain proportion are further selected for promotion and tenure. They are generally perceived to be experts by the general public and by students, but not necessarily by all or even most of their colleagues. Gradually they stream apart, some gravitating to administrative roles, others to teaching, others to research. Among the latter are those who become successful grant generators and publishers—thus meeting the selection criteria of other subgroups. Among such successful experts will be those with radically different, if not opposed, views concerning the target domain. Who are the *real* experts among these socially selected and short-term functional knowledge claimants?

As a filter on Level 2 expertise we can do no better than to rely on our most highly evolved models for finding reality-relevant knowledge, namely those developed by our culture's devil's advocate—science. We have presented one such model, the four-cell model (see figure 2), to illustrate how Level 1 experts might be distinguished from Level 2 experts. But we should also emphasize that our test for reality-relevance is that the knowledge claims have been subjected to the most trusted empirical selectors available, and that this trustworthiness is ultimately to be decided by empirical success. If a better way is ever found to test ideas against the world, then we will regard knowledge which passes *that* test as reality-relevant. So this entire notion is ultimately defined empirically: quite appropriately, we submit. No better ultimate test of correctness of theories can be found than that they succeed, and we are here suggesting that this very same criterion be applied at the higher level of testing the tests.

The Radiologist, the Snake Oil Salesman, and the Chicken Sexer Revisited

Consider an expert radiologist to whom other physicians refer their patients. He must, like all experts, be socially selected, perceived to be an expert by a constituency. He must, like all experts, have evolved through trial-and-error gambits, a set of trusted beliefs which provide him with firm decision aids in dealing with salient anomalies for his constituency, and of course, he must have been selected to be an expert's expert from among competitors. But what, if anything, sets this radiologist apart from the snake oil salesman and the chicken sexer?

On all these points, the snake oil salesman, along with the TV evangelist, the chicken sexer, the physicist and the radiologist, can be classified as an expert. But we presume that while the snake oil salesman produces trusted representations for his constituency, they are less likely to be selected by scientific selectors than are the representations of the chicken sexer or the radiologist. In fact, the chicken sexer would readily pass our simple 2 X 2 test for knowledge claims; that is, arms-length Yc criteria could be readily established which would support his sorting of male and female chicks with very few false negatives or false positives.

Assuming a random process operating within our target space/time domain and given perfect perception, one would anticipate, in the "long run," chance distributions of outcomes resulting from the ministrations/predictions of both the snake oil and radiological experts. But this expectation assumes a specific replicable decision or sorting process on the X axis and an objective, reliable method of assigning treatment/prediction outcomes. The snake oil salesman has it easy—everyone is sorted into the diseased category, and he promises that his treatments will move them all, regardless of the disease ("good for whatever ails ya"), into the positive treatment result cell.

Under a few plausible assumptions: 1) that most ailments are self-limiting (the Doc keeps you busy while nature effects a cure); 2) that the Y category is multidimensional so that the degree of membership in treatment outcome set is fuzzy; and 3) that a placebo effect works on at least some of the treatment dimensions, the snake oil salesman will end up with an impressive distribution of clients in the "successful" treatment cell (positives). If we stop there, as classical clinical trials do, then we suspect that the radiologist and the snake oil man will both accumulate a significant number of testimonials.

We should not be seen as denigrating experts for not validating their expertise against *our* most trusted test for reality relevance. We are merely observing that in many of the most important and nontrivial domains, knowledge claims are not (and frequently cannot be) subjected to scientific scrutiny of the sort represented by the four-cell model. In all cultures and societies, the role of an expert is to reduce uncertainty and serve as a source of trusted representations when other sources fail—to be a sort of human piton. That is, they readily make functional decisions that their constituencies value and find difficult to make for themselves. Specifically, constituents believe that experts (whether TV evangelists or radiologists) can help them manage salient uncertainty. To a large extent, the foundation of this expertise is "blind" confidence, the experts' own confidence and that of their constituents in them. In fact, some experts come and go like fads, as their capricious constituents desert them for the newest champion—a case of the confident blind leading the uncertain blind. Thus, while the scientific context remains our most trusted ideal, the required controls and restrictions place severe limitations on the kind of questions that can be addressed. Hence for many significant questions, whether asked by stockbrokers or bushmen, we all rely heavily on unverified (and often unverifiable) expert opinion.

Consider the expert potter described in Evans-Pritchard's famous study of the Azande as related by Clifford Geertz (1983). When discussing the case of a pot that had inexplicably cracked in the making, the expert exclaimed that it must be witchcraft. Evans-Pritchard suggested that this explanation was nonsense and that pots just sometimes break. But, replied the expert potter, he had selected the clay carefully and removed all the pebbles and dirt, and he had abstained from sexual intercourse the night before. Thus he had considered all the obvious (at least in Zande culture) causes of failure in pottery—and yet the pot still cracked. Witchcraft seemed the only explanation.

This account provides a clear instance of an expert offering functional but totally culturally situated (Level 1) expertise. It was functional in that for the Azande (if not for Evans-Pritchard) the expert's diagnosis of witchcraft reduced uncertainty about the cause of the pot's breaking, served as a damage-control mechanism for the expert, and defended the coherence of their cultural knowledge base.

A characteristic of Level 2 expertise is that one can be relatively more confident about its success when it is used outside the time and place of its origin. In contrast, much Level 1 expertise is only locally functional and does not travel well either in terms of social selection or otherwise. The Azande potter's views would not serve him well outside his culture, either as a source of social expertise or as an empirical predictor of success. But if the potter were to fall sick with yellow fever he could, indeed, be cured by the application of antibiotics. Western medicine is closer to Level 2 than theories of the supernatural, even though it probably has a considerably smaller constituency. This is not to claim that Level 2 expertise will automatically be recognized as such outside its cultural context—*that* would be quite a different matter, essentially orthogonal to pragmatic success.

Discussion

Many in the early knowledge engineering community construed knowledge acquisition as a sort of cognitive mining operation in which the goal was to extract "…those jewels of knowledge out of their heads [experts] one by one" (Feigenbaum and McCorduck 1983; p. 2). This vision held out the hope of merging all these nuggets into a superhuman expert, perhaps resulting in an artificial genius in the near future (Lenat and Feigenbaum 1991). But many difficulties were encountered, and the term "knowledge acquisition bottle-neck" was coined as knowledge engineers searched, often in vain, for these rational-empirical underpinnings of expertise. It was discovered, for example, that the stories experts tell when queried about the basis of their expertise typically cannot account for their behavior. This fact was generally attributed to an inability of experts to access and report the knowledge they had buried away deep in their subconscious. It seemed that to find the gold we must only dig a little deeper. Hence knowledge acquisition researchers focused on developing tools aimed at avoiding the expert's cognitive defenses.

Next, many in the knowledge acquisition community began to adopt a more constructivist perspective (Boose 1985; Ford and Adams-Webber 1992; Ford, Petry, Adams-Webber and Chang 1991; Ford, Stahl, Adams-Webber, Cañas, Novak and Jones 1991; Gaines 1987; Gaines, Shaw and Woodward 1993; Shaw and Woodward 1990). This led away from the notion of veridical pictures or maps of reality stored in the heads of experts and toward thinking of expertise as functional but fallible *constructions*. Rather than as a process of extraction or elicitation, knowledge acquisition became widely seen as a collaborative modeling activity involving the knowledge engineer and domain expert—a process of knowledge construction. The focus was now on the dialogue between expert and knowledge engineer; however, it was still concerned largely with the individual expert and his idiosyncratic construal of the world.

Although their philosophical assumptions differed dramatically, both the "miners" and the "modelers" regarded the system under study to be the individual expert, and neither gave substantial consideration to the surrounding social/physical/cultural context in which expertise is embedded. Likewise, research on expertise in cognitive psychology focused rather narrowly on issues of individual cognitive competence. This focus is now being criticized by several authors (Clancey 1993; Ford, Bradshaw, Adams-Webber and Agnew 1993; Sternberg 1994; Sternberg and Frensch 1992) and more emphasis is being correctly placed on the context-dependent and socially situated nature of expertise. But some have concluded rather over-zealously that the very idea of individual knowledge is somehow mistaken or inappropriate and that all of AI and cognitive psychology must be thrown out and re-thought from a more radical perspective. Some old, very simple visions are naïve and misleading. We need to throw out that bathwater. But it is a mistake to throw away everything—water, baby, and even the bath.

The distinction we have emphasized between personal knowledge and the "expert role" permits us to acknowledge the under-appreciated socially and culturally mediated nature of expertise while still maintaining a crucial role for the individual construer and his constructions. Likewise, it leads to neither relativism nor nihilism. Various constituencies select their experts on the basis of all sorts of criteria—rational and otherwise. But some selectors (e.g., certain scientific ones) are relatively cross-cultural and select for fit to larger space/time frames than those selectors serving more local contexts.

Since expertise is most fundamentally a matter of social attribution rather than cognitive competence or special knowledge, we would expect it to be at the mercy of shifting selection criteria and therefore often have a relatively temporary and local domain of application. The survival of expertise, like the survival of a species, is at the mercy of its fit to context. Expertise may be short lived and also narrowly travelled; that is, most experts operate in relatively small and somewhat unique niches. Obsolescence arises when the constituency or their selectors evolve beyond the expert's ability to accommodate change. This fact applies as equally to human experts as to machine expert systems. Lack of portability should not be seen as a symptom of some inherent weakness or inadequacy of mechanical thinking or of computer representation. It is implicit in the very notion of expertise itself. Any expert system, human or otherwise, is context-bound and will typically not be directly transportable to a new constituency that relies on different selectors than the original constituency.

Early obsolescence and lack of portability are as much problems for human experts as for the artificial reasoners we construct. We will only begin to make systems more portable by understanding more thoroughly the ways in which experts are attached to the social constituencies which give them authority. We can, of course, build relatively weak expert systems using only consensual knowledge, but then they will not be very "expert" and will more resemble an automated encyclopedia than an expert. Given that we are interested in building *expert* systems, knowledge engineers should try to model expertise in a way that is (more) sensitive to the interactions between the expert and the context that shapes and sustains his expertise, that is, the selectors. In particular, knowledge engineers ought to look for what constitutes a functional solution not only in terms of formal domain content but also in terms of knowledge that can help explain the expert's selection by the constituency network. Although we expect, in general, that systems constructed on the basis of Level 2 expertise will be more resistant to obsolescence than systems relying on other less "reality" relevant forms of expertise, such is not *always* the case. Thus, when considering the feasibility of a particular project, the knowledge engineer must gauge the stability, across both time and cultures, of the selectors (whether political or otherwise) for the expertise upon which the envisioned system is to rely. We recognize that this task is not an easy or precise one, but it is nonetheless important. Sociometry and structural analysis are examples of ways to describe the structure of social networks and may be useful in mapping the range and concentration of the constituents of given experts. Several researchers are engaged in empirical studies of the sort suggested here (Stein 1996).

In contrast to some in the situated cognition movement, we do not doubt that experts actually possess knowledge, and in contrast to the radical social constructivists, we do not deny that the natural world has an important role in the construction of knowledge. Collins and others of heightened social awareness have provided a valuable critical response to a kind of naïve certainty, an unwarranted overconfidence in one's ideas or methods. It can rinse away a certain kind of conceptual grime which sometimes clouds our thinking. But we must not overreact and throw away everything. Such absolute rejections reflect thinking which is just as rigid and dogmatic as the simplistic naïvete they purport to overcome. Reality has always been, and will always continue to be, complex and elusive, but it is there. We can only represent reality, using terms which are socially embedded, but we *do* have representations of it. We may never describe it accurately (and in any case could never be certain that we had), but we can indeed be always reaching toward it.

Acknowledgments

We express our appreciation to Jack Adams-Webber, Jeff Bradshaw, Alberto Cañas, John Coffey, Paul Feltovich, Robert Hoffman, Kathy Howell, Stephen Soldz, and Jeff Yerkes for their contributions and support.

Notes

1. Of course, snake oil salesman might have several constituencies, one of which may be largely filled with Federal investigators who recognize their skills at hoodwinking their other constituencies.

2. The recent history of the cold fusion debate provides a condensed time capsule account of the issue.

3. Einstein understood this quite clearly, saying of the individual scientist that he "will never be able to compare his picture with the real mechanism (reality) and he cannot even imagine the possibility or the meaning of such a comparison" (Einstein and Infeld 1966, p. 30).

4. Robert Hoffman (1993, personal communication) informs us that it was not Russell but William James who generated this story.

References

Adams-Webber, J.R. (1987). Personal construct theory. In R. Corsini (Ed.), *Concise Encyclopedia of Psychology* (pp. 824-825). New York: Wiley Interscience.

Agnew, N.M. & Brown, J.L. (1989a). Foundations for a theory of knowing: I. Construing reality. *Canadian Psychology, 30,* 152-167.

Agnew, N.M. & Brown, J.L. (1989b). Foundations for a theory of knowing: II. Fallible but functional knowledge. *Canadian Psychology, 30,* 168-183.

Boose, J.H. (1985). A knowledge acquisition program for expert systems based on

Personal Construct Psychology. *International Journal of Man-Machine Studies, 23,* 495-525.

Campbell, D.T. (1977). Descriptive epistemology: Psychological, sociological, and evolutionary. *William James Lectures.* Harvard University.

Campbell, D.T. (1987a). Neurological embodiments of belief and the gaps in the fit of phenomena to noumena. In A. Shimony & D. Nails (Eds.), *Naturalistic Epistemology,* (pp. 165-192). Boston: D. Redidel.

Campbell, D.T. (1987b). Selection theory and the sociology of scientific validity. In W. Callebaut & R. Pinxten (Eds.), *Evolutionary Epistemology: A Multiparadigm Program* (pp. 130-158). Boston: D. Reidel.

Clancey, W.J. (1993). The knowledge level reinterpreted: Modeling socio-technical systems. *International Journal of Intelligent Systems, 8(1),* 33-49. [Reprinted in K.M. Ford & J.M. Bradshaw (Eds.), (1993). *Knowledge Acquisition as Modeling.* New York: Wiley.]

Collins, H.M. (1981a). Stages in the empirical programme of relativism. *Social Studies of Science, 11,* 3-10.

Collins, H.M. (1981b). Son of seven sexes: The social destruction of a physical phenomenon. *Social Studies of Science, 11,* 33-62.

Dennett, D.C. (1996). Producing future by telling stories. In K.M. Ford & Z. Pylyshyn (Eds.), The *Robot's Dilemma Revisited: The Frame Problem in Artificial Intelligence* (pp. 1-7). Norwood, NJ: Ablex.

Einstein, A. & Infeld, L. (1966). *The Evolution of Physics.* New York: Simon and Schuster.

Feigenbaum, E.A. & McCorduck, P. (1983). *The Fifth Generation.* New York: Addison-Wesley.

Ford, K.M. & Adams-Webber, J.R. (1992). Knowledge acquisition and constructivist epistemology. In R.R. Hoffman (Ed.), *The Psychology of Expertise: Cognitive Research and Empirical AI* (pp. 121-136). New York: Springer-Verlag.

Ford, K.M., Bradshaw, J.M., Adams-Webber, J.R., & Agnew, N.M. (1993). Knowledge acquisition as a constructive modeling activity. *International Journal of Intelligent Systems, 8(1),* 9-32. [Reprinted in K.M. Ford & J.M. Bradshaw (Eds.), (1993). *Knowledge Acquisition as Modeling.* New York: Wiley.]

Ford, K.M., Petry, F.E., Adams-Webber, J.R., & Chang, P.J. (1991). An approach to knowledge acquisition based on the structure of personal construct systems. *IEEE Transactions on Knowledge and Data Engineering, 3,* 78-88.

Ford, K.M., Stahl, H., Adams-Webber, J.R., Cañas, A.J., Novak, J., & Jones, J.C. (1991). ICONKAT: An integrated constructivist knowledge acquisition tool. *Knowledge Acquisition, 3,* 215-236.

Gaines, B.R. (1987). An overview of knowledge acquisition and transfer. *International Journal of Man-Machine Studies, 26(4),* 453-472.

Gaines, B.R., Shaw, M.L.G., & Woodward, J.B. (1993). Modeling as a framework for knowledge acquisition methodologies and tools. *International Journal of Intelligent Systems, 8(2),* 155-168. [Reprinted in K.M. Ford & J.M. Bradshaw (Eds.), (1993). *Knowledge Acquisition as Modeling.* New York: Wiley.]

Geertz, C. (1983). *Local Knowledge: Further Essays in Interpretive Anthropology.* New York: Basic Books.

Gergen, K.J. (1981). The meager voice of empiricist confirmation. *Personality and Social Psychology Bulletin, 2,* 373-337.

Hawking, S.W. (1988). *A Brief History of Time: From the Big Bang to Black Holes.* New York: Bantam Book.

Howard, I.P. (1974). Proposals for the study of Anomalous Perceptual Schemata. *Perception, 3,* 497-513.

Kelly, G.A. (1955). *The Psychology of Personal Constructs.* New York: Norton.

Kelly, G.A. (1969). A mathematical approach to psychology. In B.A. Maher (Ed.), *Clinical Psychology and Personality: The Selected Papers of George Kelly* (pp. 7-45). New York: Wiley.

Knorr-Cetina, K.D. (1987). Evolutionary epistemology and the sociology of science. In W. Callebaut & R. Pinxten (Eds.), *Evolutionary Epistemology: A Multiparadigm program* (pp. 179-201). Dordrecht, Holland: D. Reidel.

Knorr-Cetina, K.D. & Mulkay, M. (1983). *Science Observed.* Beverly Hills, CA: Sage Publications.

Kuhn, T. (1970). *The Structure of Scientific Revolutions.* University of Chicago Press.

Lakatos, I. 1968. *The Problem of Inductive Logic.* North Holland, Amsterdam.

Latour, B. (1987). *Science in Action: How to Follow Scientists and Engineers through Society.* Cambridge, MA: Harvard University Press.

Lenat, D.B. & Feigenbaum, E.A. (1991). On the thresholds of knowledge. *Artificial Intelligence, 47,* 185-250.

Meehl, P.E. (1990). Appraising and amending theories: The strategy of Lakatosian Defence and two principles that warrent it. *Psychological Inquiry, 1,* 108-141.

Minksy, M. (1983). Jokes and the logic of the cognitive unconscious. In R. Groner, M. Groner, & W.F. Bischof (Eds.), *Methods of Heuristics* (pp. 171-193). London: Lawrence Erlbaum.

Minksy, M. (1985). *The Society of Mind.* New York: Simon & Schuster.

Popper, K.R. (1974). Autobiography of Karl Popper. In P. Schilpp (Ed.), *The Philosophy of Karl Popper, Book 1,* (pp. 2-181). LaSalle, IL: Open Court.

Quine, W.V. (1969). *Ontological Relativity and Other Essays.* New York: Columbia University Press.

Simon, H. A. (1983). *Reason in Human Affairs.* Stanford, Stanford University Press.

Shaw, M.L.G. & Woodward, J.B. (1990). Modeling expert knowledge. *Knowledge Acquisition, 2(3),* 179-206.

Stein, E. (1996). A look at expertise from a social perspective. In P.J. Feltovich, K.M. Ford & R.R. Hoffman (Eds.), *Expertise in Context* (pp. 181-194). Menlo Park, CA: AAAI/MIT Press.

Sternberg, R.J. (1994). Cognitive conceptions of expertise. *International Journal of Expert Systems, 7(1),* 1-12.

Sternberg, R.J. & Frensch, P.A. (1992). On being an expert: A cost-benefit analysis. In R.R. Hoffman (Ed.), *The Psychology of Expertise: Cognitive Research and Empirical AI* (pp. 191-203). New York: Springer-Verlag.

Socially Situated Expertise

CHAPTER 11

The Conceptual Nature of Knowledge, Situations, and Activity

William J. Clancey

Background: The Audience and the Problem

Research papers are ultimately personal statements, locating the author's developing thought along a path from what is now seen as naive toward what is viewed as a hopeful redirection. From 1974 to 1987, I was part of a community of AI researchers who devised computer programs that could diagnose diseases, engage in case-method discourse for teaching, and model students' problem solving strategies (Buchanan and Shortliffe 1984). Following the rubric of "knowledge-based systems," we believed not only that knowledge could be represented in rules ("If there is evidence of bacterial meningitis and the patient is an alcoholic, then therapy should cover for diplococcus organisms"), but also that a body of such rules would be functionally equivalent to what an expert physician can do. We knew that the physician knew more, but we assumed that his or her knowledge simply consisted of *more rules.*

The assumption that human knowledge consists exclusively of words organized into networks of rules and pattern descriptions ("frames") guided the creation of hundreds of computer programs, described in dozens of books such as *Building Expert Systems* (Hayes-Roth et al. 1983), *Intelligent Tutoring Systems* (Sleeman and Brown 1982), and *The Logical Foundations of Artificial Intelligence* (Genesereth and Nilsson 1987). Certainly, these researchers realized that processes of physical coordination and perception involved in motor skills couldn't easily be replicated by pattern and rule descriptions. But such aspects of cognition were viewed as "peripheral" or "implementation" concerns. According to this view, intelligence is *mental,* and the content of thought consists of networks of words, coordinated by an "architecture" for matching, search, and rule application. These representations, describing the world and how to behave, serve as the machine's knowledge, just as they are the basis for human reasoning and judgment. According to this "symbolic approach" to building an artificial intelligence, descriptive models not only *represent* human knowledge, they correspond in a maplike way to *structures stored* in human memory. By this view, a descriptive model is an explanation of human behavior because *the model is the person's knowledge*—stored inside, it directly controls what the person sees and does.

The distinction between representations (knowledge) and implementation (biology or silicon), called the "functionalist" hypothesis (Edelman 1992), claims that although AI engineers might learn more about biological processes of relevance to understanding the nature of knowledge, they ultimately will be able to develop a machine with human capability that is not biological or organic. This strategy has considerable support, but unfortunately, the thrust has been to *ignore the differences* between human knowledge and computer programs and instead to tout existing programs as "intelligent." Emphasizing the similarities between people and computer models, rather than the differences, is an ironic strategy for AI researchers to adopt, given that one of the central accomplishments of AI has been the formalization of *means-ends analysis* as a problem-solving method: Progress in solving a problem can be made by describing the difference between the current state and a goal state and then making a move that attempts to bridge that gap.

Given the focus on symbolic inference, cognitive studies have appropriately focused on aspects of intelligence that rely on descriptive models, such as in mathematics, science, engineering, and medicine—the professional areas of human expertise. Focusing on professional expertise has supported the idea that "knowledge equals stored models" and hence has produced a dichotomy between physical and intellectual skills. That is, the distinction between physical skills and "knowledge" is based on an assumption, which was instilled in many professionals in school, that "real knowledge" consists of scientific facts and theories. By this view, intelligence is concerned only with articulated belief and reasoned hypothesis.

But understanding the nature of cognition requires considering more than the complex problem solving and learning of human experts and their tutees. Other subareas of psychology seek to understand more general aspects of cognition, such as the relation of primates to humans, neurological dysfunction, and the evolution of language. Each of these requires some consideration of how the brain works, and each provides some enlightening insights for robot builders.[1] In this respect, the means-ends approach I promote is a continuation of the original aim of cybernetics: to compare the mechanisms of biological and artificial systems.

By holding current computer programs up against the background of this other psychological research, cognitive scientists can articulate differences between human knowledge and the best cognitive models. Although questions about the relation of language, thought, and learning are very old, computational models provide an opportunity to test theories in a new way—by building a mechanism out of descriptions of the world and how to behave and seeing how well it performs. Gardner (1985; p. 385) says this is precisely the opportunity afforded by the computational modeling approach: "Only through scrupulous adherence to computational thinking could scientists discover the ways in which humans actually *differ* from the serial digital computer—the von Neumann computer, the model that dominated the thinking of the first generation of cognitive scientists." Gardner concludes from such comparisons that cognitive scientists should substantially broaden their view of mental processes. This chapter is in the same spirit, stepping out from what AI programs do to inquire how such models of cognition relate to human knowledge and activity. I frame strategies for bridging the gap, as well as appropriately using the technology developed to date.

An exposition of the differences between people and computers necessarily requires examples of what computers cannot yet do. Such descriptions are to some extent poetic—a style of analysis promoted by Oliver Sacks in books such as *The Man Who Mistook His Wife for a Hat*—because they cannot yet be programmed. This analysis irks some AI researchers and has been characterized as "asking the tail of philosophy to wave the dog of cognitive science" (Vera and Simon 1993). Through an interesting form of circularity, descriptive models of scientific discovery shape how some researchers view the advancement of their science: If aspects of cognition cannot be modeled satisfactorily as networks of words, then work on these areas of cognition is "vague," and comparative analysis is "nonoperational speculation." Here lies perhaps the ultimate difficulty in bridging different points of view: The scientific study of human knowledge only partially resembles the operation of machine learning programs. In people, nonverbal conceptualization can organize the search for new ideas. Being aware of and articulating this difference is pivotal in relating people and programs.

To understand people better, a broader view of conceptualizing is required, one which embraces the nonverbal, often called "tacit," aspects of knowledge ("Concepts are More than Networks of Words" subsection and "Relating Knowledge, Activity, and Situations" subsection). "Situated action" can then be understood as a psychological theory. To illustrate how knowledge, situations and activity are dynamically related to descriptions, I present the example of how the Seaside community developed from a central plan ("Constructing a Community" section). This example reveals how descriptions such as blueprints, rules of thumb, and policies are used in practice—they are not knowledge itself, but *means* of guiding activities and resolving disputes. In this analysis, I will distinguish between *concepts* (what people know), *descriptions* (representations people create and interpret to guide their work), and *social activity* (how work and points of view are coordinated). On this basis, I articulate the difference between information-processing *tasks*, as described in cognitive models of expertise (Chi *et al.* 1988), and *activities*, which are *conceptualizations* for choreographing how and where tasks are carried out ("Activities Versus Tasks" section). The confusion between tasks and activities is rooted in the identification of descriptions with concepts, and accounts for the difficulty in understanding that *situations are conceptual constructs*, not places or problem descriptions ("What Is Conceptualizing..." section). Finally, from this perspective, having reconstellated knowledge, context, and representational artifacts, I consider specific suggestions for using tools such as expert systems and computer programs in general ("Activity-Based Tool Design" section).

Concepts Are More than Networks of Words

In this chapter, I explain the idea of situated cognition (e.g., see Gardner 1985; Lakoff 1987; Sacks 1987; Bruner 1990; Edelman 1992), which I take as a broad approach for re-relating human knowledge and AI programs. In contrast to the dominant view of AI in the past decades, the theory of situated cognition claims that knowledge is not a *set of descriptions*, such as a collection of facts and rules. AI researchers and cognitive scientists model knowledge by descriptions in cognitive models and expert systems. But the map is not the territory (Korzybski 1941): Human conceptualization has properties relating to learning and flexibility that make human knowledge different from procedures and semantic networks in a computer program. Situated cognition research explores the idea that conceptual knowledge, as a capacity to coordinate and sequence behavior, is inherently formed as part of and within physical performances.

The force of this claim is that a machine constructed from networks of words alone, which works in the manner of the production rule architecture described by Newell (1991), cannot learn or perform with the flexibility of a human (Dreyfus and Dreyfus 1986). The hypothesis is that a theory of knowledge that equates meaning and concepts with networks of words fundamentally fails to distinguish between *conceptualization* (a form of physical coordination), *experience* (such as imagining a design), and *cultural artifacts* (such as documents and expert systems). Such distinctions are made by Dewey (1902), most obviously in his critique of Bertrand Russell's "devotion to discourse" (Dewey 1939). Today Dewey's view is associated with the "contextualism" of ecological psychology (Barker 1968; Turvey and Shaw 1995) and the sociology of knowledge (Berger and Luckman 1966). Earlier in the century it was called "functionalism" (Harrison 1977), meaning "activity-oriented,"[2] in the philosophy of James (1890), Dewey, and Mead (1934), and carried further into a theory of language as a tool by the social psychology of Bartlett (1932) and Vygotsky (Wertsch 1991).

In contrast, the AI literature, exemplified by a collection (vanLehn 1991) that presents the work of many distinguished researchers, equates the following terms:

"knowledge"

"knowledge representations"

"representations"

"mental models"

"knowledge base"

"concepts"

For example, the following recently appeared in the *AI Magazine*: "The situationalists are attacking the very *idea* of knowledge representation—the notion that cognitive agents think about their environments, in large part, by manipulating internal representations of the worlds they inhabit" (Hayes *et al.* 1994, p. 17). Here the idea of "knowledge representation" is equated with the idea that "knowledge is representational." By this view, a representation of knowledge is not just a description in a model, *a scientist's representation of a subject's knowledge*, but literally something manipulated internally in the subject's brain. The computational view hypothesizes that the scientist's model and the subject's knowledge are equivalent in both notation (knowledge representation language) and architecture (the knowledge base interpreter and the relation of sensation and models to motor processes). Zenon Pylyshyn stated this hypothesis explicitly in his commentary presented at an AI symposium in 1988:

> The choice of both notation and architecture are central empirical issues in cognitive science, and for reasons that go right to the heart of the computational view of mind. It's true that in the physical sciences, theoretical notation is not an empirical issue. But in cognitive science our choice of notation is critical precisely because the theories claim that representations are written in the mind in the postulated notation: that at least some of the knowledge is explicitly represented and encoded in the notation proposed by the theory. The architecture is likewise important because the claim is that these are literally the operations that are applied to the representations.... In cognitive science, theories claim that the mind works the way the model does, complete with notation and architecture. What is sometimes not appreciated is that computational models are models of what literally goes on in the mind (Pylyshyn 1991, p. 219).

Sometimes human knowledge and descriptions in a model are equated quite deliberately, as in Zenon Pylyshyn's frank statement; other claims about concepts, mental models, and knowledge bases become so ingrained that scientists do not reflect upon them. George Lakoff (1987) provides perhaps the best historical review of the paradigm:

> A collection of symbols placed in correspondence with an objectively structured world is viewed as a representation of reality.... Thought is the mechani-

cal manipulation of abstract symbols. The mind is an abstract machine, manipulating symbols essentially in the way a computer does, that is, by algorithmic computation. Symbols that correspond to the external world are internal representations of an external reality....

Though such views are by no means shared by all cognitive scientists, they are nevertheless widespread, and in fact so common that many of them are often assumed to be true without question or comment. Many, perhaps even most, contemporary discussions of the mind as a computing machine take such views for granted (pp. xii-xiii).

Since the late 1980s, with the airing of alternative points of view, some AI researchers have argued that claims by situated cognition adherents about the descriptive modeling approach were all straw men, or that only expert systems were based on the idea that human memory consisted of a storehouse of descriptions. Certainly, the idea that "knowledge equals representation of knowledge" is clear in the expert systems literature:

Traditionally the transmission of knowledge from human expert to trainee has required education and internship years long. Extracting knowledge from human and putting it in computable forms can greatly reduce the costs of knowledge reproduction and exploitation (Hayes-Roth et al. 1983, p. 5).

Knowledge engineers in the decade starting about 1975 viewed expert systems as just a straightforward application of Newell and Simon's physical symbol system hypothesis:

A consequence of the prominence of the physical symbol system hypothesis is the recent emergence of the representation of knowledge as one of the most central enterprises of the field. Almost every AI project of recent vintage—from natural language understanding to visual perception to planning to expert systems—has employed an explicit symbolic representation of the information in its domain of concern. General languages for representing arbitrary knowledge are becoming a focus in this preoccupation with using symbols for facts and metainformation for a given domain.... One of the working hypotheses in this field is that knowledge is representational; that is, "knowing" consists in large part of representing symbolically facts about the world. This lends support to Newell's physical symbol system hypothesis... (pp. 45-46).

Notice how the claims go beyond saying that "knowledge is representational" to argue that knowledge is "explicit" and "symbolic," which in expert systems means that knowledge is represented as rules or other associational patterns in words. The symbols are not just arbitrary patterns, they are *meaningful encodings*:

It is sufficient to think of symbols as strings of characters and of symbol structures as a type of data structure.... The following are examples of symbols: Apple, Transistor-13, Running, Five, 3.14159. And the following are examples of symbol structures: (On Block1 Block2) (Plus 5 X) (Same-as (Father-of Pete) (Father-of (Brother-of Pete)))" (Hayes-Roth et al. 1983, p. 61).

Although it is true that this point of view, equating knowledge with word networks, remained controversial among philosophers, it was the dominant means of modeling cognition throughout the 1980s. Some researchers, stopping to reflect on the assumptions of the field, were surprised to see how far the theories had gone:

> More interesting, and perhaps more serious, is the confusion between purposive and mechanistic language that characterizes much of the writing in cognitive science. As if it were the most natural thing in the world, purposive terminology has been imported into an information-processing framework: subgoals are stored in short-term memory; unconscious expectations are processed in parallel; opinions are represented propositionally; the mind contains schemata... (Miller *et al.* 1984, p. 6).

Perhaps nowhere are the assumptions more clear and the difficulties more severe than in models of language (Winograd and Flores 1986). Bresnan even reminds her colleagues that they all operate within the paradigm of the identity hypothesis, that knowledge consists of stored descriptions, and, by assumption, this is not the source of theoretical deficiencies:

> The cognitive psychologists, computer scientists, and linguists who have questioned the psychological reality of grammars have not doubted that a speaker's knowledge of language is mentally represented in the form of stored knowledge structures of some kind. All theories of mental representation of language presuppose this. What has been doubted is that these internal knowledge structures are adequately characterized by transformational theory... (Bresnan 1984, p. 106).

Although Hayes, Ford, and Agnew in particular have tried to associate the view that knowledge representations are knowledge exclusively with expert systems research, it is easy to find examples in the cognitive psychology literature, as the quote from Bresnan attests. For example, Rosenbloom recently described how Soar's architecture "supports knowledge": "Productions provide for the explicit storage of knowledge. The knowledge is stored in the actions of productions, while the conditions act as access paths to the knowledge." (Rosenbloom *et al.* 1991, p. 81) Again, by this view knowledge is something that can be stored. Soar's productions *are* knowledge.

But Hayes *et al.* are correct that one can find more balanced treatments. Michalski provides the following appraisal of machine learning:

> An intelligent system must be able to form concepts, that is classes of entities united by some principle. Such a principle might be a common use or goal, the same role in a structure forming a theory about something, or just similar perceptual characteristics....

> In research on concept learning, the term "concept" is usually viewed in a narrower sense...namely, as an equivalence class of entities, such that it can be *comprehensibly described* by no more than a small set of statements. This description must be sufficient for distinguishing this concept from other concepts (Michalski 1992, p. 248, emphasis added).

When knowledge is equated with descriptions comprehensible to human readers, a mental model is equated with the data structure manipulations of a computer program, and all representing in the mind is reduced to a vocabulary of symbols composed into texts. Consequently, when situated cognition researchers deny that mental representing is a process of manipulating text networks (e.g., Brooks 1991; Suchman 1987), some AI researchers interpret this as claiming that there are "no internal representations" *at all* (Hayes *et al.* 1994) or "no concepts in the mind" (Sandberg and Wielinga 1991; Clancey 1992b). Actually, the claim is that human concepts cannot be *equated* with descriptions, such as semantic networks. Put another way, manipulating symbolic expressions according to mathematical transformation rules and conceptualizing are different kinds of processes.

"Knowledge," as a technical term, is better viewed as an analytic abstraction. Like energy, knowledge is not a substance that can be in hand (Newell 1982). Sometimes it is useful to view knowledge metaphorically as being a thing; describing it and measuring it as a "body of knowledge." For example, a teacher planning a course or writing a textbook adopts this point of view; few people argue that such forms of teaching should be abolished. But more broadly construed, human knowledge is dynamically forming as adaptations of past coordinations (Edelman 1992). Therefore we cannot inventory what someone knows, in the sense that we can list the textual contents (facts, rules, and procedures) of a descriptive cognitive model or expert system.

AI researchers are often perplexed by these claims. One colleague wrote to me:

> There is something of great value that humans store in libraries—usually called knowledge—that helps us to interact successfully with our environment (not to mention entertaining us). There is something (knowledge seems like a good word for it) that is useful to various degrees across people, cultures, and time. It sounds like you are denying this.

Identifying knowledge with books in a library is identifying human memory with texts, diagrams, and other descriptions. This is indeed the folk psychology view. But just as we found that the brain is not a telephone switchboard, situated cognition claims that progress in understanding the brain is inhibited by continuing to identify knowledge with *artifacts* that knowledgeable people create, such as textbooks and expert systems. AI needs a better metaphor if it is to replicate what the brain accomplishes. In the next subsection, I introduce the epistemological implications of situated cognition. The suggested metaphor is not knowledge as a substance, but as a dynamically-developed coordination process.

Relating Knowledge, Activity, and Situations

From a psychologist's perspective, the theory of situated action (Mills 1940; Suchman 1987) claims that knowledge is *dynamically constructed* as we conceive of what is happening to us, speak, and move (Thelen and Smith 1994). Most importantly, social scientists emphasize that a person's *conception of activity* is with respect to social norms, and this is how we coordinate our experience and action. Action is thereby *situated in a person's role* as a member of a community. The common idea in the literature of AI that "situated" means "in a physical setting" or merely "interactive" (Vera and Simon 1993) distorts the psychological nature of the theory and the social nature of activity.

An activity is not merely a movement or action, but a complex choreography of identity, sense of place, and participation, which *conceptually regulates* our behavior. Such conceptual constraints enable value judgments about how we use our time, how we dress and talk, the tools that we prefer, what we build, and our interpretations of our community's goals and policies. That is, our conception of what we are doing, and hence the *context* of our actions, is always social, even though we may be alone. Professional expertise is therefore "contextualized" in the sense that it reflects knowledge about a community's activities of inventing, valuing, and interpreting theories, designs, and policies (Nonaka 1991; Collins, this volume). This conceptualization of context has been likened to the water in which a fish swims (Wynn 1991); it is tacit, pervasive, and necessary.

The construction of the planned town of Seaside, Florida illustrates how a community's knowledge enables it to coordinate *scientific facts* about the world (such as hurricane and tide data), *designs* (such as architectural plans), and *policies* (social and legal constraints on behavior). Schön (1987, p. 14) claims that "professionalism"—"the replacement of artistry by systematic, preferably scientific knowledge"—ignores the distinction between science, design, and policy. Expertise is defined by professionalism as if it were scientific knowledge alone, in terms of what can be studied experimentally, written down, and taught in schools. Correspondingly, the nature of knowledge is narrowed to "truths about the world," and facts for solving problems are viewed in terms of mathematical or naturally-occurring objects and properties. Professionalism thus equates *the work of creating designs* and *interpreting policies*, in which we construct a social reality of value judgments, artifacts and activities, with *the work of science*. Consequently, the "social construction of knowledge" (Berger and Luckman 1966) is equated with the development of theories about *nature*, when its force should instead be directed at understanding the social origin and resolution of problems in *everyday work*. As a result of this confusion, claims about knowledge construction in design and policy interpretation are viewed as forms of "relativism" and hence "antiscientific."

Identifying the application of theory *in* practice with the development of theory itself (science) has led to some unfortunate exchanges in print. For example, when Lave says "The fashioning of normative models of thinking from particular, 'scientific' culturally valued, named bodies of knowledge is a cultural act" (1988, p. 172), she is referring to how cognitive researchers and schools apply mathematical theory to evaluate everyday judgments, such as using algebra to appraise grocery shoppers' knowledge in making price comparisons. Shoppers may measure as mathematically incompetent in tests, but on the store floor be fully capable of making the qualitative judgments that fit their needs (by comparing packages proportionally, for example). Thus, human problem solving is seen primarily through the glasses of formal theories—a normative model of "how practice should be" is fashioned from the world view of science. This is essentially how professionalism characterizes expertise in general. But Hayes *et al.* read this as *an attack on science*: "RadNanny claims that ... science merely reflects the mythmaking tendencies of the human tribe, with one myth being no more reality-based than another." (p. 23)

The two points of view are at cross purposes: Lave criticizes the application of scientific norms of measurement and calculation to understanding human behavior; Hayes *et al.* criticize the application of cultural studies to understanding science. Reconciling these points of view involves allowing that some human knowledge is judgmental, nonverbal, and contextually valued, that is, not reducible in principle to scientific facts or theories.[3] Attempts to replace or equate all knowledge with descriptions leaves out the perceptual-conceptual coordination that makes describing and interpreting plans possible, as the Seaside example illustrates.

Constructing a Community

Seaside is a planned community, a beach front tract of about 80 acres located in the Florida panhandle. Practice, pattern descriptions, and theory all play a part in the ongoing development of the town. A brochure describes how the town was originally designed:

> Careful study of small towns in the south and in Florida in particular provided the planning team with a set of planning and building standards that had withstood the test of time. Street widths, distances between structures, sidewalks, street trees and lighting, building forms and material in these towns were documented and distilled into a code which made explicit the unwritten rules which for generations had guided the making of building and towns in the region. In reviving this neglected tradition, buildings would be produced which were well-adapted to the local climate and which worked together to form coherent streets and squares and a community with a strong sense of place. (From a Seaside brochure.)

Against the backdrop of freshly-painted pastel homes of varying sizes, one finds BMWs and Weber grills, the stuff of the late twentieth century. Amid this oddly familiar and Disneyesque superorganization, one finds adaptations for the place and time (Dunlop 1989):

> Though it is a strong plan armed with an equally strong companion code, it is

not so rigid that it can't be modified. Along the way, Leon Krier [builder of a prominent home in Seaside] looked at the plan and suggested adding the pedestrian paths that now form a second network through the town. Homeowners chose to pave the streets in red brick; they originally were of crushed shell, more pleasing to the eye but less so to bare feet.

Given the scale and ownership by individuals, the results were not entirely intended or controlled by the organizing committee:

> Duany [one of the architects hired to produce the town plan] notes that in the plan were certain inadvertent "errors of alignment and misinterpretations," which today he views as fortuitous. "We've found that it added vitality. Now we're less concerned about perfection. Urbanism thrives on a certain amount of irregularity."

The regularity can be jarring, but not all the patterns were dictated by the plan:

> Concoctions have become more elaborate, even excessive, as if a dozen or more Victorian ship captains had landed there at once. "The code," says Duany, "does not actually generate cute Victorian houses. That just happens to be the taste of America today." The code does call for a variety of housing types, ranging from the Charleston side-yard house to the antebellum manse, and mandates what goes where....

Certainly the deliberate patterning makes Seaside a curiosity, but what makes it of artistic interest is the unexpected juxtaposition: "That is not to say that Seaside has become a neatly patterned patchwork quilt. It still retains small elements of surprise and serendipity."

The Seaside example primarily illustrates how prescriptive theories are reinterpreted in a changing context. Rules for "how to build a Victorian house" are adapted to the Florida climate in a planned community. This goes beyond claiming that plans must be modified in action. One view is that plans must be modified because the world is messy, so our ideals can't be realized—as if the forces of darkness work against our rational desires. The rubric, "reducing theory to practice" suggests not merely an application or change in form, but a *loss* of some kind.

But in practice, standardized methods and procedures are as much *a problem* as a resource. The plan calls for certain kinds of wind or rain protection, but the available wood is not the oak of the Carolinas, only weaker pine. Certainly, we turn to the plans to know what to do, but as often we are turning elsewhere to decide what to do about the plans. Design rules and policies create problems; they are the origin not only of guidance and control, but of discoordination and conflict. Generally, rules only strictly fit human behavior when we view a community over a short time period, ahistorically.

Furthermore, the Southern towns we see today, on which Seaside is patterned, weren't generated by single coherent plans, dictating all homeowners' choices—just as Seaside today isn't rotely generated from the code. So the pattern descriptions and code are abstractions, lying between past practice and what Seaside will become, neither a description of the past in detail, nor literally what will be built.

Variations are produced by errors in the plan (e.g., irregularities in how the code is applied to produce the more detailed plans of blocks and streets), misinterpretations, and serendipitous juxtapositions. Neighboring builders on the street make independent decisions whose effect in combination is often harmonious. The pattern of six honeymoon cottages on the beach is intentional; the preponderance of sea captain Victorians is a reflection of taste; and some of the irregularity reflects personal wealth and different preferences for using a home. Patterns we perceive in physical juxtapositions are emergent effects that we as observers experience, describe, and explain. Without some freedom—choices not dictated by the central control of the code—the effect would seem artificial precisely because it was too regular, and hence predictable. Openness to negotiation will vary; some restrictions (e.g., number of floors and building materials) are relatively constrained.

Understanding the nature of expertise requires understanding the negotiation process in the context of the emerging practice—not as an appeal to literal meanings and codes, but a dynamic reexamination of what's been built so far. What patterns are developing? How do the patterns relate to previous interpretations and developing understanding of what we are trying to accomplish? That is, expertise is as much the participation within a community of other designers, an *inductive* process of constructing new perspectives, as a deductive process of applying previously codified rules and theoretical explanations. In the next section, I consider in more detail how human knowledge in using plans is different from descriptive models of deliberation and learning. Human action is not, as the descriptive modeling view suggests, an artful combination of *either* following plans *or* situated action; rather, attentively following a plan involves *reconceiving* what it means during activity itself, and *that* is situated action.

The Future-Orientation of Prescriptive Models

The interplay by which practice (what people do) and theory (descriptions of behavior and the world) shape each other is *dialectic*. What people do and produce is not dictated by the theory. The value of a theory, by this view, is not simply in how it corresponds to past practice, but in how well it serves to guide future practice.

A simple view of science is that scientists formulate experiences and observations about the world in scientific models. The models are valued because they describe the observed patterns and predict future phenomena in detail. Furthermore, models are valued when they have engineering value; they enable us to build buildings that withstand a hurricane and tell us how far back

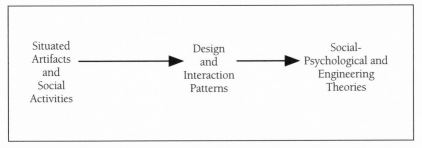

Figure 1. Relation of the experienced world, pattern descriptions, and theories.

and high off the sand to build the houses of Seaside. In this respect, the models of Seaside homes are intended to accurately describe the past, but exist for their value in predicting a harmonious effect in the new community.

Christopher Alexander (1977) conceived of architectural design in just this way (summarized by figure 1). On the one hand, we have artifacts and activities in the world. We perceive the world and sense similarities, in our everyday process of making sense and acting in our world (Schön 1979). In our practice as designers (architects, city planners, robot builders), we represent our experiences of similarity descriptively, using classifications, grammars, and rules to represent patterns. Examples include a botanical classification, a bug library in a student modeling program, and Alexander's "pattern language" of hundreds of design configurations found in homes and communities that people find satisfying. Next, as scientists we seek to understand why these patterns exist, so we can control or create them deliberately or predict what will happen next. We create causal stories about how the patterns developed, indicating how properties of objects influence each other over time. As engineers, we then use our theories to build and manipulate things in the world.

In this way, models of architecture (and social practice in general) have predictive and explanatory value: Proceeding deductively (from the right side of figure 1), theories predict that certain patterns won't occur. Or perhaps, the incidences of a type will be rare. For example, the theories behind Alexander's architectural pattern language suggest that given a choice people will put their bedrooms on the east side of a house, and not in the basement.

This view of how patterns are discovered and explained fits Dewey's (1902 1939) argument that representations are tools for inquiry. Dewey emphasized that such representations may be external (charts, diagrams, written policies) or internal imaginations (visualizations, silent speaking). The notion of representational accuracy is future-directed, in predicting success in making something. In traditional science, this "making" is experimental, in a laboratory. In business, procedures predict organizational success in efficiency and

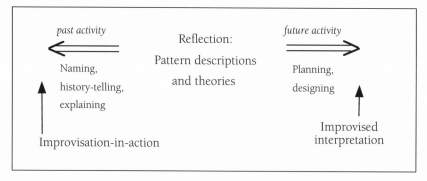

Figure 2. Descriptions lie between performances.

competitive effectiveness. The purpose of description is forward-looking, an orientation of control and/or change. The purpose of theorizing isn't accurate description of the past, per se, but to be knowledgeable of and in the future.[4]

Representational artifacts play a curious role in changing human behavior: On the one hand, the reflective process of observing, describing, and explaining promotes change by enabling invention of alternative designs. But these ways of seeing, talking, and organizing can become conservative forces, tending to rigidify practice. Understanding social change, particularly how to promote change in professions and business is a fundamental problem that is trivialized by the view that human behavior is driven by descriptions of fact and theory alone (or equivalently, that emotions and social relations are an unfortunate complication).

To understand change, we need to understand stability. This entails understanding the nature of interpretation by which theories are comprehended and used to guide activity. Agreement isn't reached by just sharing facts, but by sharing ways of coordinating different interests—a choreography, not a canon. Coherence and regularity are phenomena of a community of practice—a group of people with a shared language, tools, and ways of working together (Wenger 1990). Theories (codes, plans, rules) are developed and interpreted within the ongoing development of values, orientations, and habits of the group.

Relating figure 1 to the Seaside example, Southerners didn't literally apply a "code for building a Southern town" in their past activity. Instead, the descriptions created today are abstractions and idealized reorderings that tell a rationalized story about how building occurs. In contrast, the past activity itself was, to paraphrase Schön, "improvisation-in-action." This is depicted in figure 2. Rules neither strictly describe the past nor control the future. Creating and interpreting (standards, exceptions, repairs) occur within activity. Vocabularies and rules fit human behavior only when viewed in narrow contexts, ahistorically. Similarly, now that people have a representation in hand, a plan for Seaside, they won't rotely apply it in the future. Within practical limits, they *improvise interpretations* that suit their activity as it develops, for example, changing the paths to suit barefoot walks to the beach.

Describing the world and describing behavior occur in reflection, as actions that will at some level be automatic or immediate. Some interpretations of situated action miss this point, viewing action as *either* improvised *or* planned:

> The shooting-the-rapids example illustrates one important way in which experts make use of plans. The plan normally consists of an approximate path through rapids, as broad as feasible, taking advantage of the main currents and avoiding the obvious obstacles.... The most important property of such a plan is that it minimizes the number of occasions when an emergency calling for situated action will arise (Vera and Simon 1993, p. 41).

But situated action is not reverting to something more primitive or out of control. Rather, a dynamic adaptation is always generalizing our perceptions, our conceptions, and coordinations as we act. This reconceptualization occurs moment by moment and is a necessary part of abandoning a plan and looking more carefully to recategorize the situation: Rafting down a river, I might be reflecting on the rapids that just narrowly overturned my boat, telling myself that the water is higher than I expected, realizing that the deep holes have shifted from last season's run. I decide that I will have to portage around the next bend. A descriptive account abstracts my behavior and sees only smooth, "deliberate" execution or highly-reactive adjustments. Situated cognition claims that we are *always automatically adjusting* even as we follow a plan. That is, the relation is *both-and:* We are always recategorizing circumstances, even as we appear to proceed in lock-step with our predescribed actions. The claim is that descriptive cognitive models do not work this way, but the brain does. Descriptive models of "opportunistic planning" suppose a mixture of bottom-up and top-down processing, but this is again manipulating descriptions within a given ontology—a fixed language of objects, attributes, and events by which a model is indexed and matched against situation descriptions. In the brain, recoordination is dynamic, involving a mixture of perceptual recategorization and reconceptualization, sometimes on many levels at once (Varela 1995; Edelman 1992).

This example should make clear that situated action is not action without internal representations (leading to the claims that the baby has been thrown out with the bathwater)—indeed, the claim is starkly different! The claim is about the nature of the *representing process*. Our internal representing is *coupled* such that perception, movement, and conceptualization are changing with respect to each other moment-by-moment in a way that descriptive "perceive-deliberate-act" models do not capture. But identifying knowledge with text and all knowledgeable behavior with deliberation, a descriptive modeling theorist finds a dynamic model to be incomprehensible, a violation of the traditional engineering approach:

> Apparently one cannot talk about the brakes of a car without mentioning the engine, the steering wheel, the tires, the ignition system and the seat belts in one breadth. The need for "wholeness" denies the possibility of characterizing and explaining the mechanisms that govern components (Vera and Simon 1993, p. 124).

Indeed, the point is that the brain is not like a car in its linear, causal coupling of fixed entities, but operates by a kind of mechanism engineers have yet to replicate in an artificial device (Freeman 1991). Structures in the brain form during action itself (Merzenich *et al.* 1983), like a car whose engine's parts and causal linkages change under the load of a steeper hill or colder wind. Such mechanisms are "situated" because the repertoire of actions becomes organized by what is perceived.

The rapids example is obviously on a different time scale than building a town. But the relation between conceptualization and planful descriptions I have characterized occurs throughout human life. In general, human conceptualization is far more flexible than the stored knowledge representations of a cognitive model suggest. Just as the river forces adjustments at nearly every moment, building the town involves flexibility and negotiation that expert system models of reasoning do not capture. Individual decisions and behaviors are in general shaped by an *a priori* mixture of personal and social descriptions, plans, and codes. The pace of surprise in the town is different from running rapids, but local adaptations are occurring when new buildings are proposed and blueprints are interpreted during construction. Knowledge base characterizations of expertise, even with respect to these relatively static diagrams, are impoverished precisely because they attempt to equate practice—what experts actually do in real settings over time—to a code, the rules and scripts of the knowledge base. A more appropriate understanding of the relation views knowledge base representations—insofar as they are part of the discourse of the expert or expressed in text books, policies, etc.—as something the expert refers to in his or her own practice, as a guide, a resource, something that must be interpreted.

Human activity, whether one is rafting down a river or managing a construction site, is broadly pre-conceived and usually pre-described in plans and schedules (even the rafting company uses computer reservations). But the details are always improvised (even when you are pretending to be a robot). At some level, all "actions" happen in a coordinated way without a preceding description of how they will appear. The grainsize of prior description depends on the time available, prior experience, and your intentions (which are also variably pre-described depending on circumstances).

This analysis raises questions about packaging theories and policies in a computer system and delivering it to some community as an expert system or instructional tool. Knowledge engineers could build an expert system that embodied the Seaside plan, but would such a tool address the practice of collaboration? Would it relate to the participants' problems in negotiating the points of view of different expertise? The "capture and disseminate" view of "reproducing knowledge" (cf. Hayes-Roth, cited in the "Concepts are More than Networks of Words" subsection) does produce useful tools. But situated cognition suggests knowledge engineering hasn't considered the conceptual problems people have in reconciling different world views, which is what forces reconceptualization in conversations between the carpenter, the home owner, the town council, the county inspector, etc. That is, the original expert system approach ignores the fact that *there are many experts* and they would benefit from tools for working together. Ironically, our view in 1975 of "many experts" when building Mycin was that *physicians* might disagree about how to build the knowledge base, not that there were different professional *roles* to reconcile. Problems are "ill-structured" not just because there are many constraints and too much information, but also because *different participants are playing different roles and claiming different sets of "facts."*

To understand how situated cognition suggests new ways of using expert system technology in tools for collaborative work, we need to explore further what people are conceptualizing, which produces these different views of the world, and why these conceptualizations cannot be replaced by a program constructed exclusively from descriptions. In the next section, I contrast *how people conceive of activities* with the task analysis of knowledge engineering, which equates intentions with goals, context with data, and problems with symbolic puzzles.

Activities Versus Tasks

To understand the idea that *knowledge* is inherently social (as well as inherently neural), we must first understand that human *action* is inherently social.[5] The difficulty is understanding that "action" is meant in the broad sense of an "activity." The activity of being a construction site coordinator comprises many individual "tasks," such as "test hypothesis" or "combine conjunctive goals," as found in expert systems and cognitive models. In this section I will explicate how a person's conception of his or her activity is socially *oriented* and *shaped*. On this basis I will then describe the relation of activities to tasks and goals in expert systems, reformulate the meaning of "the social construction of knowledge," explain what constitutes and "problem," and then discuss the social nature of work.

The Conception of Activity

Our everyday way of talking about social activity places primacy on the individual and marks "social" as being a matter of choice or a *kind* of activity. For example, we socialize at a party; we engage in "social chat" before settling down to work; we may decide to join others for a drink after work in order to "be social." In common parlance, social activities are things that people do together: parties, meetings, tours. We may "opt out" of a social activity, and go our own way. By the cognitive "individualist" point of view, social activities par excellence are special occasions, such as weddings.

Social activities in our everyday experience may also be things we do reluctantly, such as attending a meeting. In business settings, meetings appear to take time away from "the real work," which is individually-directed. Work is having your nose to the grindstone; social activity is having fun talking to people about nonserious things.

In each of these examples, activity is viewed as being social or not: Individual activity is when I am alone, social activity is when I am interacting with other people. This is essentially the biological, either-or view of "activity"—a state of alertness, of being awake doing something. But the social scientist, in describing human *activities as social,* is not referring to kinds of activities per se. Rather what we do, the tools and materials we use, and how we conceive of what we are doing, are *culturally* constructed. Even though an individual may be alone, as in reading a book, there is always some larger social activity in which he or she is engaged. Indeed, as we will see, descriptive accounts provide an inadequate view of subjectivity and, hence, the attitude of "individualism," because they do not emphasize the inherently social aspect of identity.

For example, suppose that I am in a hotel room, reading a journal article. The cognitive perspective puts on blinders and defines my task as comprehending text. From the social perspective, I am *on a business trip,* and I have thirty minutes before I must go by car to work with my colleagues at Nynex down the road. The information processing perspective sees only the symbols on the page and my reasoning about the author's argument. The social scientist asks, "Why are you sitting in that chair in a hotel room? Why aren't you at home?" That is, to the social scientist my activity is not merely reading—I am also on a business trip, working for IRL at Nynex in White Plains, NY.

We are always engaged in social activity, which is to say that our activity, as human beings, is always shaped, constrained, and given meaning by our *ongoing* interactions within a business, family, and community. Sitting in my hotel room, I am still nevertheless on a business trip. This ongoing activity shapes how I spend my time, how I dress, and what I think about.

Why has the social nature of all activity been so misunderstood in common parlance and cognitive science? Social activity is probably viewed in a commonsense way as being *opposed to* work because of the tension we feel when *we are engaged in an activity* and because of the time or place are obligated (by our commitments) to adopt another persona. In our culture, we engage in multiple, contrasting activities every day, which split our attention and loyalty. We leave the family in the morning in order to "go to work." We end our pleasantries at the start of the meeting in order to "get down to business." We end a discussion with a colleague in our office in order to "do something meaningful." Ending one form of engagement, we experience a tension and conflict in the change of theme, which is marked conventionally as a shift from "socializing" to "working." Both activities are social constructions, but the limiting of our options leads us to view the more narrowly-defined style as being "work" and the freedom we have left behind as "being social."

Although a social scientist may cringe to have it put this way, a cognitive scientist might begin by thinking of activities as being forms of *subjugation,* or more neutrally, *constraint.* Human activities are always constrained by cultural norms. During a movie in a theater, I cannot yell out to a friend across the room whether he would get me some popcorn. I cannot in general talk very loudly to the person next to me. If my back hurts, I cannot stand by my seat (and block the view). Sitting in a hotel room on a business trip, I cannot decide to take a bath or go for a walk if I am expected to be over at Nynex in 10 minutes.

The standard examples of activities suggest a form of passivity: being on a tour in a museum, attending a religious service, listening quietly to a lecture. The trick in understanding activities is realizing that such *following* or *adherence to a norm* is inherent in all activities. Day by day, you make choices, identifying with a group of people and participating in social practices that limit (and hence give meaning to) your behavior.

Again, the individualist will object: But what about *after work,* when I am sitting at home alone in my easy chair, reading *Atlas Shrugged?* I'm in control of my time, I do what I want to do. And what about on the weekend, when I am gardening or taking a walk by myself. Surely these are not social!

But how we conceive of free time, the very notion of "after work," "weekend" and "gardening" are socially constructed. Again, "constructed" here means that what people tend to do occurs within a historically-developed and defined set of alternatives, that the tools and materials they use develop within a culture of manufacture and methods for use, and that how they *conceive* of this time is with respect to cultural norms.[6] Weekends in Bali are not the same as weekends in Detroit. Our very understanding of "time alone" is codetermined with respect to our understanding of "being at work," "being on a business trip," and "being at a party." Although we are not literally confined in the same way we might be while sitting at a contract negotiation meeting, on the weekend we are nevertheless engaging and acting within an understanding of the realm of possible actions that our culture makes available. Sitting at home on Sunday morning reading the NY Times over coffee is a culturally-constructed event. The meaning of any activity depends on its context, which includes how we conceptually contrast one range of activities with another.

Of course, someone can "opt out" and go live in the Na Pali Headlands of Kauai out in the jungle. But if you have left Detroit and your desk job, you are now engaged in the activity of "opting out." You are "going back to nature," "seeking a simple life." Although free to romp around naked, you cannot escape the historical social reality that defines your activity in terms of making one choice and not another, of participating or not. The meaning of your activity of being in Kauai will be codetermined by your understanding of the activity of working in Detroit. Sitting in a chair in a lecture hall, we may be bored by a lecture and dream about the beaches of Kauai. But even then, we are still in the activity of "attending a lecture," though our activity might be best described as "not paying attention to the lecture."[7]

An activity is therefore not just something we do, but a *manner* of interacting. Viewing activities as a *form of engagement* emphasizes that the conception of activity constitutes a means of coordinating action, a manner of being engaged with other people and things in the environment, what we call a *choreography.* Every human actor is in some state of participation within a society, a business, a community. My activity within the Institute for Research on Learning is "working at home," an acceptable form of engagement, a way of participating in IRL's business. Within Portola Valley, where I am working, I am not participating in the activities of the schools or the town council. Like most people I am in the activity of "going about my own business." Like most of my neighbors, I don't know the names of the people who live around me; we are all in the activity of "minding our own business." Even *not* talking to my neighbor is a kind of choreography.

The idea of activity has been appropriately characterized in cognitive science as an *intentional state,* a mode of being. The social perspective emphasizes time, rhythm, and place (Hall 1976): An activity is a *participation framework,* an encompassing fabric of ways of interacting that shapes what people do. Activities tend to have beginnings and ends; activities have the form "While I am doing this, I will only do these things and not others." While I am working at home, I will stay in my office and write; I will not call my spouse and chat, I will not read my electronic mail, I will not make phone calls, I will not stop in mid-morning and go out for a walk (but I will swim at noon).

People understand *interruptions, "being on task,"* and *satisfaction* with respect to activities. For example, contrast your experience when interrupted by different people when you are reading: a stranger in a train, a colleague in your office, your spouse when you're reading the paper in the morning. Your conceptual coordination of the interruption is shaped not just by your inter-

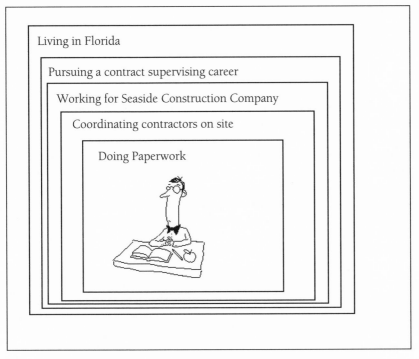

Figure 3. Ongoing activities of a Seaside contractor, "working alone."

est in what you are reading (and why you are reading it) but by the activity in which you are engaged. Activities provide the background for *constructing situations;* they make locations into events. Different activities allow me to walk casually down the middle of the street on the afternoon of Palo Alto's Centennial Saturday, but run for my life when crossing on any other day.

With these considerations in mind, I return to the descriptive view of goals and knowledge, specifically as formulated in expert systems. How is the conception of activity related to what a knowledge engineer represents? What other kinds of tools would be useful?

The Relation of Activities to Tasks and Goals in Expert Systems

Activities are broadly intentional, but not confined by the kinds of goals that define an expert system's operation. People conceive of goals and articulate them *within* activities. From the descriptive modeling perspective, the encompassing and composed nature of activities is often missed because the modeler starts by choosing *one activity* to model and the point of view of one role fulfilling one predefined goal within this activity. With such a design approach, human action appears to be a relation between defined goals, data, and decisions. For example, in modeling medical diagnosis (Buchanan and Shortliffe 1984), we chose the physician's activity of examining a patient. We even viewed this narrowly, focusing on the interview of the patient, diagnosis, and treatment recommendation, ignoring the physical exam. But the physician is also in the activity of "working at the outpatient clinic." We ignored the context of patients coming and going, nurses collecting the vital signs, nurses administering immunizations, parents asking questions about siblings or a spouse at home, etc. In designing medical expert systems like Mycin, we chose one activity and left out the life of the clinician. We ignored union meetings, discussions in the hallways about a lost chart, phone calls to specialists to get dosage recommendations, requests for the hospital to fax an x-ray, moonlighting in the Emergency Room. Indeed, when we viewed medical diagnosis as a *task* to be modeled, we ignored most of the *activity* of a health maintenance organization! Consequently, we developed a tool that neither fit into the physician's schedule, nor solved the everyday problems he encountered.

This is not to say that Mycin, if it had been placed in the clinic, would not have been useful. Rather, the thrust of this shift in perspective, broadening our point of view from goals to activities, partially explains *why Mycin was never used at all,* and second, reveals *opportunities for using the technology that we never considered.* Indeed, the design of Mycin reveals how our conception of activity shapes the design process. We viewed physicians as the center, knowledge as stored, knowledge acquisition as transfer, and the knowledge base as a body of universal truths (conditional on universal situation descriptions). Rather than developing tools for facilitating conversations, this *rationalist approach works to eliminate conversations* and replace human reasoning by automatic deductive programs (Winograd and Flores 1986). In a similar analysis, Lincoln, *et al.* (1993) suggest that medical practitioners need notational devices with spreadsheet-like operations that help manage the interactions of tentative inferences within volatile, uncertain situations. But if the expert performances of a physician are explained only in terms of knowledge stored in the head, tools for developing models interactively in a team are not considered.

To provide another example, figure 3 represents the activities of a contractor who is sitting alone in his trailer on the Seaside site. The contractor has many identities: on his job that morning, he might be thinking about struggling with a county building code form which needs to be filed. In this activity, he is coordinating the contractors on the site, perhaps reconciling the work of the plumbers and electricians at a particular home. He wears the badge of the "Seaside Construction Co.," to which his decisions must also be accountable. But at the same time, he holds certain principles about how to be a supervisor, which he seeks to bring to his company to change their practices, and has a conception of how to advance his career by doing well in this company. Of course, we can include this worker's conception of how living in Florida influences his decisions about pursuing this career in the Florida Panhandle, rather than Miami, etc.

Although these activities are described as nested levels, other relatively disjoint identities and participation frameworks will not fit strictly into such a hierarchical ordering. For example, the worker is a sports fan, attends a certain church, supports a political party, volunteers for community service, etc. Any of these may or may not be relevant conceptions having a bearing on day-to-day contracting work. The important point is that this person has all of these identities and will experience a conflict if an activity suggests a way of coordinating his views, talk, and actions that is different from how he might behave in another context, which he perceives is also a relevant conception of what he is currently doing. For example, if the county requests an action that he believes is not in accord with the union's principles, he will have a problem. One source of creativity lies in juggling multiple identities and carrying ideas from one community to another.

To recapitulate: All human action—deliberation, goal defining, theory application, information description, policy interpretation, planning—occurs within activities. Conception of activities is usually implicit, serving as the *background* against which problems arise and judgment is based. In Winograd and Flores' (1986) analysis this background is the origin of our sense of trouble in a situation, which they called "breakdown." Breakdown is not just a difficulty in interpreting text, a failure for a description to apply to a new situation (as Winograd and Flores emphasized), but more generally is *any conceptual discoordination* between perspectives within and between people, suggesting different ways of characterizing facts and evaluating judgments.

In contrast with this view of situated action, the idea of "rational action," also called "cognitivism," suggests that goals and prescriptive rules *control* actions. By this view, tasks are isolated things to do and context is just the given world of data to operate upon. That is, behavior is "conditional" on the facts. The contrary, "situated," view is that defining goals, claiming what constitutes the facts, and following plans and policies all occur within nested activities. In this sense, all action is *situated* in the actors' conceptions of what they are *supposed to be* doing, that is, norms, values, and roles—their identities. Articulation of goals, facts, and methods—that is, creation of descriptions and interpretations of representational artifacts—arises within this *conceptual* frame.[8]

Activities are *the grounding of intentionality*—"what I am doing now" is defined with respect to my activities. Hence, my intention is not just to finish reading a journal article or to write a report, but "to make a contribution to the research project," "to convince the client that I should continue to belong to this project," "to convey what IRL means by participatory design." Viewed narrowly, cognitive goals are *information* oriented—developing models and choosing actions. The goals of activities involve—conceptually and physically—reaffirming and developing forms of engagement, membership, and identity (Wenger 1990; Lave and Wenger 1991); they are *participation* oriented.

What I take to be information and see in a situation depends on my conception of my activity. When I walk into the medical clinic with the conception of a medical anthropologist, I see notes on paper and hear conversations that constitute data by how they are arranged in space and time. When I walk into the medical clinic as a cognitive scientist, I listen to the physician's information requests and hear the names of symptoms and diseases. To understand the process by which people segment the world into objects and events, we need to understand that *perceiving is situated in activities.*

In these respects, activities are the context for all that we do. But by reducing activities to descriptions of goals, data, and actions in the descriptive approach (as in the "Concepts are More than Networks of Words subsection"), knowledge engineering and cognitive modeling unwittingly reduced *conceptions* of context to descriptions. This research misunderstood the functional character of conceptions to *coordinate* what we perceive, our judgments, and how we interact.

Given the relation between knowledge and activities, we can better understand how knowledge is socially constructed.

Social Construction of Knowledge

An individual's capacity to engage in an activity may be characterized as *knowledge*. Thus, "knowledge is socially constructed" means first, that *knowledge develops and has value within activity,* and second, *activities are socially constructed.* Descriptive modelers often interpreted the phrase "social construction of knowledge" in terms of their assumption that knowledge consists of statements about beliefs and theories. But activities are the primary construction: Ways of interacting and viewing the world, ways of structuring time and space, pre-date human language and descriptive theories. We can see this today in chimpanzees and other animals who conceive of social relations, build and maintain homesites, and distinguish between activities such as food gathering and play—all without a descriptive language for modeling what they are doing.[9] Within a discourse, an activity mediated by language (Wertsch 1991), statements about beliefs and theories provide a way of changing activities (Mills 1940; Schön 1979; cf. figure 2). Again, situated action does not deny the role or importance of plans, but emphasizes that planning occurs within an *already conceptually-coordinated* activity.

To understand what "social construction of knowledge" means, you must first understand that *activities,* the choreographies of human action, *develop within ongoing activities.* Our capacity to plan what we will do, to design new methods and tools, and to formalize what we know, develops within and depends upon our pre-existing activities. For example, when caregivers at a health maintenance organization join to form a new outpatient clinic, they are already engaged in activities such as "being a technical clinical assistant at the County Hospital," "being a physician escaping from private practice," and "representing the union advocating greater responsibility for nurses." These pre-existing conceptions of interacting and these identities provided the context within which a new clinic was formed.

Knowledge, then, develops *within activities.* The knowledge required to accomplish goals, such as caring for a patient, is determined, in large part, by the scientific and health care establishment to which the clinicians belong. The members of the local clinic help define what constitutes competence by their choices of whom they want to work with and how they talk about each other's work.

The idea that knowledge is a possession of an individual person is as limited as the idea that culture is going to the opera.[10] Culture is pervasive; we are participating in a culture and shaping it by everything we do (Hall 1976). Knowledge is pervasive in all our capabilities to *participate* in our society; it is not merely beliefs and theories *describing* what we do.

The difficulty in understanding how knowledge is socially constructed partly stems from social scientists' lack of success in articulating the conceptual nature of knowledge. For descriptive modelers, social construction of knowledge is by default understood to mean the social construction of written facts about nature and equated with relativism (e.g., see Slezak 1989; Lakoff 1987). The practice of science is cultural (Gregory 1988), but the effect is not so much on what someone sees when looking in a microscope and even less on how numbers are tallied to formulate an equation. Rather, social construction operates on and through concepts, activities, designs, and policies. Expertise is not just about scientific facts and laws, but about value-laden artifacts and conventions and how to coordinate them.

For example, the physics researchers at Stanford University's Linear Accelerator Center (SLAC) are constrained in their work by government funding, the politics of promoting international science competitively against other states such as Texas, the terrain that limits building around a major fault zone, etc. The "science" we see at SLAC in the next decades will not be a purely experimental effort, but will reflect the savvy of the Director in securing funding and building huge new devices within the context of engineering and political constraints. Again, the activities of the scientists at SLAC cannot be understood solely in terms of the scientific horizon of physics, but are framed by being a member of SLAC, being a Californian competing for federal dollars, and being an American scientist rushing in time to beat the efforts at Cern in Switzerland. Choices of what to explore next in the realm of physics are generated and evaluated in this context.

Similarly, the medical profession is not just deductive application of physiological science. Drug dosages, diets, exercise programs, etc. must all be designed with respect to the practices of people, which constrain time, memory, and will to carry through procedures (Feltovich et al. 1992).

The social construction of knowledge includes the construction of written theories and facts about the world. But, as these examples illustrate, the force is not on what scientists find out about nature, but which facts are relevant and what designs are valued within the constraints of engineering and social affairs. In these choices, we are always involved in *constructing communities of practice:* SLAC, a school district, a seaside town, a subdiscipline of AI. Knowledge in this realm, particularly the professional knowledge called "expertise," concerns how to make interpretations of policy ("judgments") that generate successful, harmonious designs.

According to Schön (1987), the difficulty of formulating design knowledge lies in a combination of the rapidly-changing character of activities and the difficulty of codifying rules about "the ill-defined melange of topographical, financial, economic, environmental, and political factors" (p. 4). This is summed up by Kyle: "We know how to teach people how to build ships but not how to figure out what ships to build" (quoted by Schön 1987, p. 11). In effect, it is difficult to formulate *a priori* what kinds of problems will arise and on what basis they should be resolved. The next section elaborates this distinction between problems in practice and the formal problem solving of "professionalism" studied in cognitive science of the 1970s and 80s.

Problematic Situations, Not Puzzles

The scientific view of problem solving is that one starts with certain data, a goal, and certain theories about how goals and facts are related. But in practice the problem is often which *kinds* of facts are relevant and how to justify action within a matrix of conflicting regulations and competing judgments. Following Dewey, Schön emphasizes that a problem must be *constructed* to fit the methods and theories of a practice:

> When a practitioner sets a problem, he chooses and names the things he will notice. In his road-building situation, the civil engineer may see drainage, soil stability, and ease of maintenance; he may not see the differential effects of the road on the economies of the towns that lie along its route. Through complementary acts of naming and framing, the practitioner selects things for attention and organizes them, guided by an appreciation of the situation that gives it coherence and sets a direction for action. So problem setting is an ontological process—in Nelson Goodman's (1978) memorable word, a form of worldmaking. (Schön 1987, p. 4)

Casting a situation in some language defines a "space" for reasoning about alternative designs, diagnoses, and plans. Schön calls this process "problem framing." In contrast with the classical AI view of problem solving (Newell and Simon 1972), Schön argues that framing a problem is not a matter of searching and filtering through given facts, per se, but of *creating* information (cf. von Foerster's 1970 critique of information processing theories of memory). The descriptive view maintains, for the most part, that the world is encountered as objects with properties. The situated cognition view is that we segment the world perceptually, within the rubrics of our activities. In our interpretative process of qualifying and weighing experiences, we participate in such a way that our process of seeing and naming has created a world, the conceptual space in which we coordinate our thought and action. "Creating information" means that our *interpretations* claim which facts are meaningful to the problem at hand; by this we define the problem (reifying our conceptions into what Newell and Simon call a "problem space" description).

Schön goes on to describe how differences in opinion are not reducible to arguments about facts. Instead, different conceptualizations lead professionals with different backgrounds to perceive and name *different sets of facts* as being relevant. These differences derive from conceptualization of activities—not more names and facts—that underlie each professional's attending, valuing, and sense-making:

> Depending on our disciplinary backgrounds, organizational roles, past histories, interests, and political/economic perspectives, we frame problematic situations in different ways. A nutritionist, for example may convert a vague worry about malnourishment among children in developing countries into the problem of selecting an optimal diet. But agronomists may frame the problem in terms of food production; epidemiologist may frame it in terms of diseases that increase the need for nutrients or prevent their absorption; demographers tend to see it in terms of a rate of population growth that has outstripped agricultural activity; engineers, in terms of inadequate food storage and distribution; economists, in terms of insufficient purchasing power or the inequitable distribution of land or wealth. In the field of malnourishment, professional identities and political/economic perspectives determine how people see a problematic situation, and debates about malnourishment revolve around the construction of a problem to be solved. Debates involve conflicting frames, not easily resolvable—if resolvable at all—by appeal to data. Those who hold conflicting frames pay attention to different facts and make different sense of the facts they notice. It is not by technical problem solving that we convert problematic situations to well-formed problems; rather, it is through naming and framing that technical problem solving becomes possible (Schön 1987, p. 4-5).

In terms of the "practice <-> pattern <-> theory" framework (figure 1), Schön is characterizing how a practitioner comes to perceive a difference, articulate a pattern, and frame a problem in technical terms. In contrast, the process of structuring the world, of perceiving and naming order, has been characterized in AI research, not so much as a conceptual capability of people, but as inherent in types of situations. The laboratory perspective of giving problems to a subject suggested that there were two kinds of problems: *well-structured problems,* which could be mapped directly into a known problem-solving language and procedure, and *ill-structured problems,* which were experienced as confusing in some way, requiring restatement and often more information before they could be resolved. Observing that this classification was relative to the subject's knowledge, Simon (1973) concluded that all problems are potentially ill-structured and there is nothing fundamentally different between playing chess and designing a ship—both can be described by categorizing states and operators in the General Problem Solver. Design problems and their solutions are thereby reduced to puzzles and mathematical operations.

Situated cognition argues that problem solving is a particular kind of activity occurring within other ongoing activities, which are the context that produces the troublesome situation and provides the framing values and goals for justifying our action. By this process, judgments are made objective—our justifications relate to the principles, methods, and practices of the communities to which we belong (Berger and Luckman 1966).

In contrast, cryptarithmetic, theorem proving, chess, and other "problems" studied by Newell and Simon (1972) are merely puzzles existing in a mathematical world of well-defined rules of play. Carrying over these ideas to medical expert systems in the early 1970s, knowledge engineers viewed medical practice as the rote application of facts and causal relations between organisms and therapies. In viewing every patient encounter as a "problem," designers of consultation systems never understood either the conceptual nature of *trouble* as a discoordination, or how it was resolved in everyday situations.

In reducing medical knowledge to descriptive, scientific models of disease, knowledge engineers, as well as cognitive psychologists adopting the expertise perspective (Chi *et al.* 1988) lumped together written scientific facts, conceptions, experience with therapeutic designs (regimens). For the most part, this viewpoint ignored the political factors underlying the distribution of decision-making between the medical subspecialties and between nurses and physicians. For example, it is common to find in a module of caregivers three MDs, one physician's assistant, and four nurses of different varieties. Whose professional knowledge is coded in Mycin? From this perspective, Mycin models the knowledge of an infectious-disease specialist in a large, tertiary care hospital. That is, Mycin doesn't contain "medical knowledge," per se, but was intended to *model one role in a certain activity.* This role and activity were rarely reflected on or deliberately pursued in the design because the content of the knowledge base was viewed as "medical knowledge," *universal truths* about medicine. "Case-based reasoning" and "roles" are well-known ideas in AI research, but experience from the past and the choreography of roles tend to be reduced to *more descriptions,* which get thrown into the pot of scientific facts and rules.

The flattening of knowledge into facts about the world can be seen clearly in how the term "frame" was used in anthropology to refer specifically to activities (Frake 1977), while in AI's knowledge representation research it meant any "unit" of knowledge, from a description of a political context to a description of a chair. By this "atomization" of knowledge into uniform pieces, the nesting of concepts and communities by which the world is segmented, facts are interpreted as relevant, and designs are invented, is represented as a hierarchy of graphs (called "contexts"). In this view, every surrounding "frame" becomes a "context," and the distinctions among scientific data, practical design constraints, and interpersonal choreography are lost. Any claim of "openness to interpretation" and "creating of information" suggested arbitrariness and scientific relativism, so the difference between nature and culture became muddled. "Cultural knowledge" becomes just more facts in long-term memory (Lave 1988, p. 89).

To summarize, human knowledge comprises much more than written scientific facts and theories. Problems arise not in selecting facts, but in conceptualizing how we should view the activity we are currently engaged within: What *differences* (Bateson 1972)—kinds of facts—make a difference? What perspective (economic, physical, political, medical) should be adopted? How are conflicting judgments to be reconciled in the practice of our conversations, design procedures, and regulating policies? Who should be invited to participate in this discourse and what rights should they be accorded? How will we reach a decision? On what time frame? How will we answer to the competing viewpoints, which suggest that our designs are unproven, that they have failed in the past, that they are too costly? Expertise consists of the ability to make value judgments for framing problems, which in turn establishes a reified "problem space," in which the technical methods of science and engineering may proceed (Schön 1987).

Knowledge, context, and trouble are conceptual. Through the thought process of conceptualization—which is still poorly understood—we articulate problem descriptions, facts, and rules for guiding our action. Dewey called this process of thinking, describing, and manipulating descriptions "inquiry." He argued in 1939 that Bertrand Russell's rationalist view (which became the foundation of descriptive modeling) fundamentally confused the origin and role of statements ("propositions") in problem solving:

> The exclusive devotion of Mr. Russell to discourse is manifested in his assumption that *propositions* are the subject-matter of inquiry, a view assumed so unconsciously that it is taken for granted that Peirce and I likewise assume it. But according to our view—and according to any thoroughgoing empiricist—*things and events* are the material and objects of inquiry, and propositions are *means* in

inquiry, so that as conclusions of a given inquiry they become means of carrying on further inquiries. Like other means they are modified and improved in the course of use. (p. 573)

Thus, Dewey saw statements as being out in the world of our conscious experience, lying between performances (figure 2). Once we understand that conceptual coordinations in different modalities—including for example rhythm, imagery, accent, and gestures—are not equivalent to *descriptions* of the world and our behavior, we can better understand the activity of describing and comprehending in recoordinating our activity. But if we equate conceptualizations and descriptions, we will have little idea *how problems arise* and what resources we draw upon for generating and improving our descriptions of the situation, how we will decide, and what we will do.

As we have seen, the view of knowledge as true descriptions does not adequately explain what is problematic when professionals from different disciplines attempt to work together. Correspondingly, by the descriptive view, an individual is just a repository and applier of knowledge. By the social view, the individual's contribution is more dynamic and unique. The relationship of the individual to the group is different than is suggested by the "cognitive tasks" view of work.

"Social Activity" Versus Individual Work

The reduction of problem solving to rote rule manipulation and parsing of text has distorted not only our view of expertise and context, but our understanding of how work actually gets done. Having decomposed knowledge in terms of technical calculi, knowledge engineers and cognitive modelers are left with a residue of "value judgments," which appear as immature forms of real (scientific) knowledge, and a residue of "social relations," which appear as messy, but necessary considerations for getting information and communicating decisions. The resulting dichotomization makes the core of knowledge individual cognition and the remainder "social factors." The core is "hard science" and the periphery (so-constrained) is "soft."

The dichotomization of individual and society is reflected in the Cold War drama between the forces of democracy and communism. The theory of situated action suggests that our identity as supporters of individual rights may have inhibited our scientific understanding that knowledge and work are inherently social (Hall 1976). It is perhaps not a coincidence that Soviet psychologists were deeply affected by the relation between the state and the individual and sought to understand how the influences interpenetrated. For example, Lev Vygotsky emphasized that an individual's understanding develops within the pre-existing social fabric of activities—the conceptual segmentation and ordering of time, place, and events, which develops into and is manifest in habits, norms, means of labor, and roles. What is "socially shared" is not just language, tools, and expressed beliefs, but conceptual ways of choreographing action, by which descriptions and artifacts develop and are given meaning.

As individuals we participate in the process of constructing what will be the norm, how performance will be evaluated, what ideas will be valued, and what tools will be used. The experience of being in an activity is not usually that of subjugation, as I first introduced the notion, but what people usually call "being constructive." Norms of the group allow redirecting its path: Activities may include means of communication and negotiation by which individual ideas and preferences are heard and incorporated. Conflicts are foremost differing conceptions of activities in which *individuals* believe themselves to be engaged. If the permissible styles permit a trade-off, a complainer may compromise; the activities of the group, or what constitutes a norm or acceptable variation, will change.

When work is identified with technical knowledge, interpersonal capability and knowledge about other people and their abilities are viewed as nonessential or simply nice add-ons for getting the job done. In this way, the view that knowledge is objective and technical obscures that knowledge is *about what people do during their lives.* Rather than being about things and properties, knowledge is first and foremost about how to belong, how to interact, what to do productively with your time. That is, knowledge is inherently *personal,* as Polanyi (1958) put it, because it has a tacit dimension and develops within cultural commitments. Again, the conception of activities provides a way of understanding subjectivity without relegating it to "uncertain belief" (opinion) or "misconception" (theoretical error). In this respect, the theory of the social construction of knowledge, because it emphasizes values, roles, and interpersonal choreography, provides a better accounting for the nature of individual knowledge than cognitivism. How ironic that raising the banner of "the social" appears to deny the importance of the individual!

To bring this back to "knowledge-level" descriptions appearing in cognitive models (Newell 1982), knowledge is therefore not just about a social *world,* but about *activities* and the *social-political-physical reality* in which activities occur. Knowledge is not just about tasks, but about forms of *participation*—the who, what, where, and why of behavior. Reality for a human being is not just the facts of nature, but an *identity* as a person. The social construction point of view tries to show that identity is not just a collection of technical procedures and scientific beliefs, as for example in a student model of a teaching program. A knowledge-level description would, in its entirety, not merely characterize the information-processing (or model-building) behavior of a person, but the timing, the locations, the roles, and the identities of that person's life (Wenger 1990). For example, in the everyday workplace, knowledge about what other people know is essential for assigning jobs, getting assistance, and developing teams. This social-psychological viewpoint does not replace "goal" or "task" by

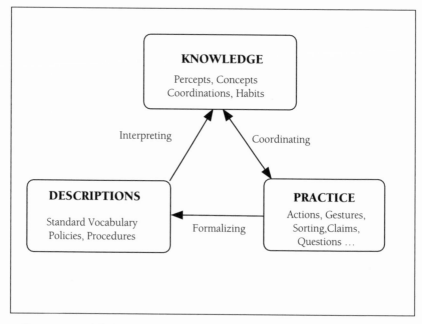

Figure 4. Simplified view distinguishing between conceptualization (knowledge), action in the world (practice), and text, diagrams, and computer programs (descriptions, commonly called "representations").

"activity," but places behavior in a broader analytic context.

In this section, I presented a theoretical perspective contrasting knowledge about activities and task descriptions. I will conclude by considering briefly two areas in which this perspective can be applied—in pursuing the goals of AI to replicate human intelligence ("What Is Conceptualizing if Not Manipulating Stored Descriptions?" section) and in applying knowledge engineering to produce useful tools ("Activity-Based Tool Design" section).

What Is Conceptualizing if Not Manipulating Stored Descriptions?

The foundational assumption that "representations" in the brain and "representations" on paper can be treated isomorphically (Vera and Simon 1993), although useful in some pedagogical respects, has limited value as a productive simplification for cognitive science. Dewey argued this point with Russell 55 years ago, so why hasn't the idea taken hold? Bartlett (1932) posed the same question, and concluded:

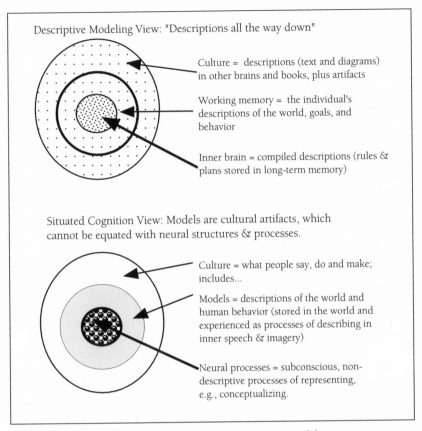

Figure 5. *Philosophical positions relating models to the individual brain and culture.*

It is because the force of the rejection of associationism depends mainly upon the adoption of a functional point of view; but the attitude of analytic description is just as important within its own sphere....

In various senses, therefore, associationism is likely to remain, though its outlook is foreign to the demands of modern psychological science. It tells us something about the characteristics of associated details, when they are associated, but it explains nothing whatever of the activity of the conditions by which they are brought together (p. 308).

Bartlett contrasts the functional point of view, an understanding of social and biological conditions, with *description of patterns of behavior* (e.g., associations expressed as rules or semantic networks). Again, AI seeks not only to provide useful explanations of behavior, but to replicate the associational capability of the brain. Modern psychological science has been slow to develop a mechanism other than stored descriptions of associations. However, through the work of Hebb (1949) and his followers in connectionism a different kind of architecture, not based on networks of words, has been explored. In this section I will briefly survey some considerations in developing a machine with human capabilities of speech and understanding, as framed by the situated cognition perspective.

Figure 4 summarizes how situated cognition relates human knowledge, practice, and representational artifacts. Broadly speaking, the box labeled "knowledge" corresponds to conceptualizing and other representing processes in the brain. Cognitive scientists describe these dynamic capabilities and processes in terms of static perceptual categories, named concepts and properties, habitual procedures, etc. The box labeled "practice" corresponds to human behavior, including conversations, ways of talking, turn-taking, posturing, gesturing, etc., studied by subfields of discourse analysis, interaction analysis, etc. The box labeled "descriptions" corresponds to documents of all kinds, standardized database record structures (vocabularies), dictionaries, knowledge bases of expert systems, cognitive models, corporate policies, etc. Although all speech could be placed in this box, it is useful to separate written and other codified representations that can be stored, transferred to other people, and later viewed and interpreted. This separation is useful because documents, as artifacts, play a special role historically in the development of a community, which speech (even memorized narratives) does not have (Donald 1991).

In terms of the Seaside example, the contractor's *knowledge* includes his conception of his activities; his *practice* includes how he spends his time, his manner of speaking to other workers, how he organizes mail and requests in his office, etc.; his *descriptions* include letters he writes, forms he fills out, regulations he posts on the company bulletin board, etc. By this view, conceptual coordinating occurs in all actions, including the formalizing and interpreting of descriptions. Conceptualizing is a dynamic process of reconstructing "global maps" relating perceptions, other conceptualizations, and motor actions (Edelman 1992). Conceptualizing is inherently *multimodal* (even when verbal organizers are dominating), *adaptive* (Vygotsky: "Every thought is a generalization"), and *constitutes an interactive perceptual-motor feedback system.* Conceptualizing is itself a behavior in animals capable of imagery and inner speech. ("Hearing" a tune in one's head is also an example of conceptualizing.) "Concepts," as formalized in descriptive cognitive models, are *names for conceptualizations* of objects, events, and relations, which may or may not be articulated in the discourse of a practice.

What physical recoordinating occurs as we speak and comprehend text? When cognitive modelers identify concepts with text networks, this scientific question does not arise—physical coordinating is viewed as an *effect* of comprehending text, not its basis. Examining the extremes of human experience, studies of creativity and dysfunction have discovered that conceptualization concerns much more than relating words; our knowledge includes conceptualization of scenes, rhythm, sequential ordering, identities, and values (e.g., see Gardner 1985; Sacks 1987; and Rosenfield 1992).

Figure 4 is also intended to represent that knowledge and practice are codetermined: What we are doing is conceived as we are doing it. The effects are of course serial, as any conversation reveals. But the effects are also dialectic, in the sense that what we perceive and what we conceive, although separable categorizations in the brain, are postulated to codetermine each other. This is a kind of parallelism and interactivity different from modular architectures based on simultaneous, but independent formation. Chaos models probably come closest to characterizing how areas of the brain, functioning together, but generalized and "modularly" substitutable, can co-organize each other (Freeman 1991).

Figure 5 illustrates the distinction between the descriptive and situated perspectives in another way. By the view that knowledge consists of text networks, called "representations," representations are viewed as a single kind of thing, called "symbol structures," located in the world, in working memory, and in long-term memory (e.g., see Simon 1973; Vera and Simon 1993). By the situated cognition view, a distinction is made between models on paper or in computer programs, imagined experiences, and conceptual processes. Human knowledge and culture can be described, *but are not reducible* to a body of descriptions. Put another way, we cannot understand how descriptions are created and given meaning unless we make a distinction between representations that are consciously manipulated and other forms of representing. That is, we cannot understand the nature of language if we call all forms of representing, inside and out, "symbol processing" (Lakoff 1987; Edelman 1992).

In the information-processing view (Newell and Simon 1972; vanLehn 1991), there is a sharp line between the individual and the environment, such that the relation is of input-output—taking in data and putting out what has been created inside. Neural processes are viewed as being similar in kind to conscious reasoning, involving storage, matching, assembly of descriptions (Vera and Simon 1993).

In the situated cognition view, the functional distinction between conscious and subconscious is emphasized, and the line between culture and individual experience is less distinct. Individual experience is coupled through the conceptualization of activity to what other people say and do. Neural processes are not viewed as analogous to writing text, matching descriptions, or deducing the implications of rules. By this view, perception operates without a preconceived *description* of what is interesting in the world to perceive (Schön 1979).

Figure 5 suggests that people are not information processors in the man-

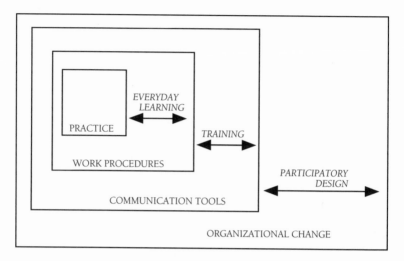

Figure 6. Aspects of organizational learning: Coordinating everyday practice, procedures, tools, and organizational change.

ner of expert systems. There are at least two ways of approaching this argument: Looking inwards to consider the nature of memory and perception, and looking outwards to consider the nature of social action. Both arguments relate to the idea of interpretation and meaning. Some philosophers and linguists argue that meaning cannot be equated with stored descriptions. Social scientists argue that descriptions must be creatively interpreted in practice. Both arguments claim that "creative interpretation" (however it may work) cannot be deduced from other descriptions alone. That is, the social and philosophical arguments of situated cognition ultimately make claims about the architecture of intelligence, and this is not the architecture of expert systems or most cognitive models. What are the implications of this shift in perspective for the design and use of tools in practice?

Activity-Based Tool Design

The Seaside example reveals how narrowly the task analysis of knowledge engineering views the knowledge, context, and problems of workers. When we view the construction manager in isolation, we describe his tasks as scheduling workers, planning construction, allocating space on site, and repairing equipment. Within these tasks, we describe the manager as modeling, gathering information, and explaining decisions. The expertise of being a construction manager is well-defined by such a framing of tasks, allowing us to describe problem spaces and rules that express his work in terms of solving a puzzle.

In developing a tool for Seaside, knowledge engineers might have first thought to *deliver* a knowledge base that embodied the "Seaside Community Town Plan" and tools for *enforcing* that plan in the various decisions of the builders and homeowners. We now see the problem differently: Who interprets plans with whom, how can the plan be questioned and modified? How can we help people deal with difficult cases?

First, different personnel are engaged in different activities, suggesting that different tools might be needed. Indeed, it is perhaps more fruitful to view people who are collaborating as creating problems for each other (often inadvertently) and creating information (descriptions and evaluations of past designs, interpretations of policy) to help solve problems. The *work* of collaboration is partially caused by the need to coordinate different activities occurring in one place with shared resources.

The idea of collaboration as "reading from the same score" or "singing with one voice" is misleading; people are following *many scripts* because they are expected to fulfill different roles. In a medical clinic, for example, seven workers might be following five scripts based on their professional jobs which will have names like MD, PA, LVN, TCA, and RN. Software designers need to customize tools in terms of activities and not only tasks.

Kukla *et al.* (1992) describe how an activity-based analysis of conversations reveals what people need to see about other people's work, when they need to see it, and where. On this basis, Kukla created collaborative tools for process control in a Monsanto chemical plant. The key design idea is to facilitate conversations by studying what people want to show each other when they are discussing different issues ranging from routine quality control and scheduling to troubleshooting. The study focused on unexpected problems that arise and that could not be easily automated; hence the tool provides assistance in situations of high risk and high cost. The program provides a means of accessing and comparing historical data from different viewpoints, video of current conditions, and instrument readouts. A surprising aspect of Kukla's designs is that there is not "one collaboration tool" per se, but *different components and interface designs* for different roles in conversations about different topics.

Second, although some problems are common, tool design can go beyond automating what is routine to provide tools for helping people with nonroutine situations. Studies of problem framing (Schön 1979) indicate different phases that the puzzle view of cognition has poorly characterized:

- Framing, giving a name to a situation.
- Recounting the history of what you observed and did.
- Telling related stories from experience.

- Ordering events, claiming temporal relationships.
- Tentatively configuring a causal explanation of underlying processes.
- Reconceptualizing the meaning of observations, theories, and policies.

Lincoln *et al.* (1993) have described how the conception of a "computerized patient record" fails to relate to the representational work of clinicians who need a notational structure for describing the story of the patient, the patient's disease, and encounters with the patient. Similarly, Zuboff (1988) applied situated cognition ideas to suggest how computers can be used to "informate" and not just automate the workplace. These investigators claim that providing access to historical information is the first problem. How strange that we proposed to give physicians Mycin in 1977, when the medical community didn't even have databases!

Third, the idea that *learning is a process of conceiving an activity,* and activities are inherently social, puts emphasis on improving learning by addressing issues of membership, participation in a community, and identity. Participatory design of computer tools follows this approach (Greenbaum and Kyng 1991). Participatory design deliberately brings together tool designers, workers, and researchers in a multidisciplinary collaboration (i.e., a choreographed conflict). Through scenarios, role-playing, and other ways of projecting design implications, the design of the computer tools is oriented to the practice of the users.[11]

Figure 6 puts these ideas together to show how learning can be conceived as recoordinating occurring on different time scales:

- *everyday practice* (relating conception of practice to procedures and regulations),
- *training* (relating conception of procedures and regulations to workplace tools), and
- *participatory design* (relating workplace tools to the redesign process).

In contrast, a theory of knowledge based on descriptions would view behavior as constrained by designs and plans: procedures coordinate practice; tools coordinate the application of procedures; the design process coordinates the invention of tools. Both views are useful: One imposes order by design, the other explains how order actually develops and is sustained.

To summarize, an activity-based perspective suggests how to design computer tools to promote learning: Facilitate conversations and hence participation, allowing multiple perspectives to be viewed and compared. Focus especially on how problematic situations arise and are resolved.

Conclusions

In this chapter, I considered the conceptual relation of knowledge, situations, and activities. I emphasized that knowledge is more than written scientific facts and theories. Professional expertise in particular is framed by a person's conceptualization of multiple, ongoing activities, which are essentially identities, comprising intentions, norms, and choreographies. These conceptions are an important source of conflicts, judgments, and values in human action. Expertise consists of generally useful concepts for coordinating activities, especially ways of framing problematic situations so that technical, descriptive methods can be applied in a routine manner (Schön 1987).

By equating knowledge with scientific theory, designs, and policies, the "symbolic approach" of AI equated knowledge with text networks such as classifications, grammars, dictionaries, and causal networks, and other forms of scientific representations such as equations and diagrams. This view serves us well for describing some of the patterns of human reasoning. But machines based on this "architecture of intelligence" inadequately replicate the human ability to coordinate conceptions of meaning, physical skills, intention, visual scenes, timing, and attitude (Sacks 1987).

By equating knowledge, situations, and activities with descriptions, the descriptive approach reduced "context" in problem solving models to goals and data. Consequently, the conceptual nature of context was oversimplified and its *content,* the aspect of identity in making judgments and choreographing action, was often ignored.

Ironically, by treating social conception as merely context (and context as just more data), the individual nature of cognition was glossed by descriptive modeling—personal differences were viewed as matters of opinion, different knowledge (stored in the head), or just differing awareness of the facts. Knowledge was viewed as universal because it consists mainly of scientific theories. Knowledge representation research consequently focused narrowly on topics such as "qualitative models of physics." Indeed, the lingering worry that "individual differences" were not yet accounted for in descriptive models of learning reflects not understanding and relating *kinds of conceptualizing* and hence forms of representing other than describing (Gardner 1985). Even studies of diagrams reduce pictures to words (Larkin and Simon 1987).

With so many ideas equated or conflated in the descriptive modeling approach—knowledge, science, descriptions, and context—the rail against "decontextualized knowledge" (Brown et al. 1988) was interpreted as an attack on "abstract description" (Sandberg and Wielinga 1991) and even an attack on science itself (Slezak 1989). Instead, the force of the criticism was not upon the formalization of descriptive models, but upon their adequacy in directing everyday human affairs. Descriptive modeling has made solid contributions to scientific and engineering modeling (Clancey 1992a). But building expert systems and intelligent tutoring systems on these principles alone produces tools that don't address the dilemmas of everyday design in arguments about which facts are relevant and how to interpret policies (Greenbaum and

Kyng 1991; Kukla *et al.* 1993; Sachs 1995). That is, the epistemology of expert systems is inadequate for understanding or enhancing collaboration.

The descriptive view of knowledge suggested that knowledge engineers should just codify theories and plans in tools and deliver them to workers. More recent efforts go beyond packaging expertise, to help people converse about designs and policy in unanticipated situations. These new tools use the same representational and automated modeling techniques originally developed for expert systems. But the design process starts with a better understanding of interpersonal aspects of interpreting, questioning, and modifying theories and rules—and this perspective is applied to the software design process itself. On this basis, we focus not just on delivery of preordained plans, but on construction of new conceptions, helping reconcile inherent conflicts in resources, timing, and values that arise as people with different expertise work together.

Acknowledgments

This research has been supported in part by Nynex Science and Technology, Inc., a major health maintenance organization in southern California, and a gift from the Xerox Foundation. I would like to thank my colleagues at IRL and our partners for sharing their insights: Gitti Jordan, Charlotte Linde, Judith Gregory from IRL, Jean Gilbert at Kaiser-Permanente, and at Nynex, Pat Sachs, Dave Torok, Maarten Sierhuis, and David Moore. But especially I have benefited from my friends in AI, who have encouraged me to keep trying to make sense of social theories: John McDermott, Luc Steels (Brussels), Rolf Pfeifer (Zurich), Kurt vanLehn, and the editors of this volume.

Notes

1. See especially the articles and commentary in *Behavioral and Brain Sciences,* for example, Donald (1993).

2. "Functionalism" is a theory about the evolutionary, developmental, instrumental content of knowledge, not to be confused with the "functionalist" hypothesis that a physical symbol system in a computer is "functionally equivalent" to the operation of the human brain.

3. Lave places "scientific" in quotes to highlight that using mathematical theory to model certain cultural phenomena is itself a cultural activity. She wishes to distinguish scientific *theories* from the *application of theories* in studying human behavior. This application is often equated with science itself, hence the scare quotes: Cognitive "science" is partly about the design of schools; cognitive research embodies certain cultural assumptions about what should be learned in schools (by virtue of what school subjects are studied) and how to assess the adequacy of teaching (in applying rational models of optimality to evaluate practical choices). Using science to direct everyday affairs is a cultural value, not part of science itself.

4. Minsky's initial idea of "frames" considered them as schemas for directing future action. But such descriptions, as in the cognitive models that were based on this idea,

were assumed to be mostly subconsciously manipulated. The situated cognition view is that descriptions and mental models are consciously generated and interpreted. By hypothesis, other forms of internal representing in the brain (e.g., the signal processing of primary vision) are different in kind—they are perceptual-conceptual "couplings" not inferences (e.g., see Edelman, 1992; Freeman, 1991; Thelen and Smith, 1994; Clancey, in press). Put another way, when descriptive models involve interpreting what rules and frames mean, they are modeling conscious human behavior. When they suppose that such descriptions are just "symbols" mechanically related, they are modeling subconscious neural processes. Situated cognition claims that these two forms of interpretation have dramatically different capabilities for reorienting behavior. As Bartlett emphasized, conscious story telling and interpretation provide a means of "turning around on our own schemata." Recently Polk and Newell (1995) have modeled how text manipulation in reading occurs consciously as a behavior; this begins to distinguish between texts, descriptive models, and neural processes.

5. I am trying to convey a "both-and" point view: Both social and neural. But "inherently" has different implications. Knowledge is inherently social in *content* and inherently "neural" in *form*. This doesn't mean that we won't be able to reproduce the functions of neurons by silicon or some other substrate. I am simply emphasizing that 1) there is of course an internal aspect, and 2) we need to reproduce the dynamic characteristics of neurons relative to categorization and coordination. One could say "inherently psychological," but this wouldn't convey that it is *how the neural mechanism works* that we need to understand and replicate if we are to create a machine capable of situated action.

6. Again, saying that tools are cultural does not mean that they are not physical. I am trying to convey how a "both-and" causal process operates: Tools are both culturally conceived and physical at the same time. The either-or perspective suggests that we can "understand" a phenomenon from a single point of view at a time. This is true for the operation and use of mechanical devices; refer again to Vera and Simon's characterization of a car. The linear perspective prefers to say "*partly* cultural" and "*totally* physical." This attempt to divide up the causal influences is adequate for some purposes. But understanding historical change requires understanding how cultural, biological, and physical interactions interpenetrate. Gould's (1987) critique of linear views of evolution is based on the same notion of dialectic causality. The dialectic view claims that *understanding the interactions between physical and social constraints* is essential for understanding what has evolved. This is perhaps most clear in the evolution of language (Donald 1991).

7. This example comes from Frake (1977).

8. In this respect, the focus of the sociology of knowledge and social psychology on conceptual interactions and constructions is more inclusive than ecological psychology, which emphasizes perceptual interactions in physical niches (Turvey and Shaw 1995).

9. By a descriptive language, I mean a language like natural language or many AI knowledge representation and planning languages, with syntactically-distinguished subjects, actions, objects, and modal qualifiers, enabling historical, prescriptive, or explanatory statements to be made about objects in the world, their properties, and events. As AI research has demonstrated, such distinctions are necessary in order to *model* the world and behavior (Edelman 1992).

10. Again, knowledge as a functional capacity is historically-personal (subjective), and knowledge as a coordination process is neurological. The problem with the "possession" metaphor is not that it denies the social character, but too quickly slips into

viewing knowledge as a static thing and the cultural aspect as just a coloring or flavoring of objective truths. For example, it is common in AI to define knowledge as "true belief." By this view, culture is what we do on Saturday evenings or explains why some cooking pots are made from iron and others from clay.

11. For further examples and discussion, see the special issue of the *Communications of the ACM*, "Representations of Work," Volume 38, Number 9, September, 1995.

References

Alexander, C. (1977). *A Pattern Language*. New York: Oxford University Press.

Barker, R.G. (1968). *Ecological Psychology: Concepts and Methods for Studying the Environment of Human Behavior*. Stanford, CA: Stanford University Press.

Bartlett, F.C. (1932/1977). *Remembering—A Study in Experimental and Social Psychology*. Cambridge: Cambridge University Press. Reprint.

Bateson, G. (1972). *Steps to an Ecology of Mind*. New York: Ballentine Books.

Berger P.L & Luckmann, T. (1966). *The Social Construction of Reality: A Treatise in the Sociology of Knowledge*. Garden City, NY: Anchor Books.

Brooks, R.A. (1991). Intelligence without reason. In *Proceedings of the 12th International Conference on Artificial Intelligence* (pp. 569-595). San Mateo, CA: Morgan-Kaufmann.

Brown, J.S., Collins, A. & Duguid, P. (1988). *Situated cognition and the culture of learning*. Institute for Research on Learning, Technical Report No. 88-0008. Palo Alto, CA. [Shorter version appears in *Educational Researcher, 18(1)*, 32-42, February, 1989.]

Bruner, J. (1990). *Acts of Meaning*. Cambridge, MA: Harvard University Press.

Buchanan, B.G. & Shortliffe, E.H. (Eds.). (1984). *Rule Based Expert Systems: The MYCIN Experiments of the Stanford Heuristic Programming Project*. Reading, MA: Addison-Wesley.

Chi, M.T.H., Glaser, R. & Farr, M.J. (Eds.). (1988). *The Nature of Expertise*. Hillsdale, NJ: Lawrence Erlbaum.

Clancey, W.J. (1992a). Model construction operators. *Artificial Intelligence, 53(1)*, 1-124.

Clancey, W.J. (1992b). Representations of knowing: In defense of cognitive apprenticeship. *Journal of Artificial Intelligence in Education, 3(2)*, 139-168.

Clancey, W.J. (1993). Situated action: A neuropsychological interpretation (Response to Vera and Simon). *Cognitive Science, 17(1)*, 87-116.

Clancey, W.J. (In Press). *Situated Cognition: On Human Knowledge and Computer Representations*. New York: Cambridge University Press.

Collingwood, R.G. (1938). *The Principles of Art*. London: Oxford University Press.

Dewey, J. (1939). Experience, knowledge, and value: A rejoinder. In P.A. Schilpp (Ed.), *The Philosophy of John Dewey* (pp. 515-608). Evanston, IL: Northwestern University.

Dewey, J. (1902/1981). *The Child and the Curriculum*. Chicago: University of Chicago Press. [Reprinted in J.J. McDermott (Ed.), *The Philosophy of John Dewey* (pp. 511-523). Chicago: University of Chicago Press.]

Donald, M. (1991). *Origins of the Modern Mind: Three Stages in the Evolution of Culture and Cognition.* Cambridge, MA: Harvard University Press.

Donald, M. (1993). Multiple book reviews of *Origins of the Modern Mind. Behavioral and Brain Sciences, 16(4),* 737-791.

Dreyfus, H.L & Dreyfus, S.E. (1986). *Mind Over Machine.* New York: The Free Press.

Dunlop, B. (1989). Coming of age. *Architectural Record* (July), 96-103.

Edelman, G.M. (1992). *Bright Air, Brilliant Fire: On the Matter of the Mind.* New York: Basic Books.

Effken, J.A. & Shaw, R.E. (1992). Ecological perspectives on the new artificial intelligence. *Ecological Psychology, 4(4),* 247-70.

Feltovich, P.J., Coulson, R.L., Spiro, R.J. & Dawson-Saunders, B.K. (1992). Knowledge application and transfer for complex tasks in ill-structured domains: Implications for instruction and testing in biomedicine. In D. Evans & V. Patel (Eds.), *Advanced Models of Cognition for Medical Training and Practice* (pp. 213-244). Berlin: Springer-Verlag.

Fodor, J.A. (1975). *The Language of Thought.* Cambridge, MA: Harvard University Press.

Fodor, J.A. (1981). *Representations: Philosophical Essays on the Foundations of Cognitive Science.* Cambridge, MA: The MIT Press.

Frake, C.O. (1977). Plying frames can be dangerous: Some reflections on methodology in cognitive anthropology. *The Quarterly Newsletter of the Institute for Comparative Human Development, 1(3),* 1-7. [Also in C.O. Frake, (Ed.), *Language and Cultural Description* (pp. 45-60). Stanford, CA: Stanford University Press, 1980.]

Freeman, W. J. (1991). The Physiology of Perception. *Scientific American* (February), 78-85.

Gardner, H. (1985). *The Mind's New Science: A History of the Cognitive Revolution.* New York: Basic Books.

Genesereth, M.R. & Nilsson, N.J. (1987). *The Logical Foundations of Artificial Intelligence.* Los Altos, CA: Morgan Kaufmann.

Gould, S.J. (1987). *An Urchin in the Storm: Essays about Books and Ideas.* New York: W.W. Norton.

Greenbaum J. & Kyng, M. (1991). *Design at Work: Cooperative design of computer systems.* Hillsdale, NJ: Lawrence Erlbaum.

Gregory, B. (1988). *Inventing Reality: Physics as Language.* New York: John Wiley.

Hall, E.T. (1976). *Beyond Culture.* New York: Doubleday.

Harrison, R. (1977). Functionalism. In B.B. Wolman (Ed.), *International Encyclopedia of Psychiatry, Psychology, Psychoanalysis, and Neurology,* Vol. 5 (pp. 144-6). New York: Aesculapius.

Hayes, P.J., Ford, K.M. & Agnew, N. (1994). On babies and bathwater: A cautionary tale. *AI Magazine, 15(4),* 14-26, Winter.

Hayes-Roth, F., Waterman, D.A. & Lenat, D.B. (1983). *Building Expert Systems.* Reading, MA: Addison-Wesley.

Hebb, D.O. (1949/1961). *The Organization of Behavior, a Neuropsychological Theory.* New York: Wiley.

Korzybski, A. (1941). *Science and Sanity.* New York: Science Press.

Kukla, C.D., Clemens, E.A., Morse, R.S. & Cash, D. (1992). Designing effective systems: A tool approach. In P.S. Adler & T.A. Winograd (Eds.), *Usability: Turning Technologies into Tools* (pp. 41-65). New York: Oxford University Press.

Lakoff, G. (1987). *Women, Fire, and Dangerous Things: What Categories Reveal about the Mind.* Chicago: University of Chicago Press.

Larkin, J.H. & Simon, H.A. (1987). Why a diagram is (sometimes) worth ten thousand words. *Cognitive Science, 11(1),* 65-100.

Lave, J. (1988). *Cognition in Practice.* Cambridge: Cambridge University Press.

Lave, J. & Wenger, E. (1991). *Situated Learning: Legitimate Peripheral Participation.* Cambridge: Cambridge University Press.

Lincoln, T.L., Essin, D.J. & Ware, W.H. (1993). The Electronic Medical Record: A challenge for computer science to develop clinically and socially relevant computer systems to coordinate information for patient care and analysis. *The Information Society, 9,* 157-88.

Mead, G.H. (1934). *Mind, Self, and Society.* Chicago: University of Chicago Press.

Merzenich, M.M., Kaas, J.H., Wall, J., Nelson, R.J., Sur, M. & Felleman, D. (1983). Topographic reorganization of somatosensory cortical areas 3b and 1 in adult monkeys following restricted deafferentation. *Neuroscience, 8(1),* 33-55.

Michalski, R.S. (1992). Concept learning. In S.C. Shapiro (Ed.), *Encyclopedia of Artificial Intelligence,* Vol. 1 (pp. 249-259). New York: John Wiley.

Mills, C.W. (1940). Situated actions and vocabularies of motive. *American Sociological Review, 5,* 904-913.

Nonaka, I. (1991). The knowledge-creating company. *Harvard Business Review* (Nov.-Dec.), 96-104.

Newell, A. (1982). The knowledge level. *Artificial Intelligence, 18(1),* 87-127, January.

Newell, A. (1990). *Unified Theories of Cognition.* Cambridge, MA: Harvard University Press.

Newell, A. & Simon, H.A. (1972). *Human Problem Solving.* Englewood Cliff, NJ: Prentice-Hall.

Polk, T.A. & Newell, A. (1995). Deduction as verbal reasoning. *Psychological Review, 102(3),* 533-566.

Polanyi, M. (1958/1964). *Personal Knowledge: Towards a Post-Critical Philosophy.* New York: Harper and Row.

Pylyshyn, Z. (1991). Cognitive architecture in theories of cognition. In K. vanLehn (Ed.), *Architectures for Intelligence: The Twenty-Second Carnegie Symposium on Cognition* (pp. 189-223). Hillsdale: Lawrence Erlbaum.

Rosenbloom, P.S., Newell, A. & Laird, J.E. (1991). Toward the knowledge level in Soar: The role of the architecture in the use of knowledge. In K. vanLehn (Ed.), *Architectures for Intelligence: The Twenty-Second Carnegie Symposium on Cognition* (pp. 75-112). Hillsdale: Lawrence Erlbaum.

Rosenfield, I. (1992). *The Strange, Familiar, and Forgotten.* New York: Vintage Books.

Sachs, P. (1995). Transforming work: Collaboration, learning, and design. *Communications of the ACM, 38(9),* 36-44, September. Special issue on "Representations of Work."

Sacks, O. (1987). *The Man Who Mistook His Wife for a Hat.* New York: Harper & Row.

Sandberg, J.A.C. & Wielinga, B.J. (1991). How situated is cognition? In *Proceedings of* the 12th International Conference on Artificial Intelligence (pp. 341-346). San Mateo, CA: Morgan-Kaufmann.

Schön, D.A. (1979). Generative metaphor: A perspective on problem-setting in social policy. In A. Ortony (Ed.), Metaphor and Thought (pp. 254-283). Cambridge: Cambridge University Press.

Schön, D.A. (1987). Educating the Reflective Practitioner. San Francisco: Jossey-Bass.

Scribner, S. & Sachs, P. (1991). Knowledge acquisition at work. IEEE Brief, No. 2, Dec. New York: Institute on Education and the Economy, Teachers College, Columbia University.

Simon, H.A. (1973). Ill-structured problems. Artificial Intelligence, 4, 181-201.

Sleeman, D. & Brown, J.S. (1982). Intelligent Tutoring Systems. London: Academic Press.

Slezak, P. (1989). Scientific discovery by computer as empirical refutation of the Strong Programme. Social Studies of Science, Vol. 19, (pp. 563-600). London: Sage.

Suchman, L.A. (1987). Plans and Situated Actions: The Problem of Human-Machine Communication. Cambridge: Cambridge Press.

Thelen, E. & Smith, L.B. (1994). A Dynamic Systems Approach to the Development of Cognition and Action. Cambridge, MA: Bradford Books.

Turvey, M.T. & Shaw, R.E. (1995). Toward an Ecological Physics and a Physical Psychology. In R.L. Solso & D.W. Massaro (Eds.), The Science of the Mind: 2001 and Beyond (pp. 144-169). New York: Oxford University Press.

vanLehn, K. (1991). Architectures for Intelligence: The Twenty-Second Carnegie Symposium on Cognition. Hillsdale: Lawrence Erlbaum.

Varela, F.J. (1995). The re-enchantment of the concrete. In L Steels, & R. Brooks, (Eds.), The "Artificial Life" Route to "Artificial Intelligence": Building Situated Embodied Agents (pp. 11-22). Hillsdale, NJ: Lawrence Erlbaum.

Vera, A.H. & Simon, H.A. (1993). Situated action: A symbolic interpretation. Cognitive Science, 17(1), 7-48.

Von Foerster, H. (1970). Thoughts and notes on cognition. In P.L. Garvin (Ed.), Cognition: A Multiple View (pp. 25-48). New York: Spartan Books.

Wenger, E. (1990). Toward a theory of cultural transparency: Elements of a social discourse of the visible and the invisible. Ph.D. Dissertation in Information and Computer Science, University of California, Irvine.

Wertsch, J.V. (1991). Voices of the Mind: A Sociocultural Approach to Mediated Action. Cambridge, MA: Harvard University Press.

Winograd, T. & Flores, F. (1986). Understanding Computers and Cognition: A New Foundation for Design. Norwood, NJ: Ablex.

Wynn, E. (1991). Taking Practice Seriously. In J. Greenbaum & M. Kyng (Eds.), Design at Work: Cooperative Design of Computer Systems (pp. 45-64). Hillsdale, NJ: Lawrence Erlbaum.

Zuboff, S. (1988). In the Age of the Smart Machine: The Future of Work and Power. New York: Basic Books.

CHAPTER 12

Rat-Tale: Sociology's Contribution to Understanding Human and Machine Cognition

H. M. Collins

The Sociological Questions

At the conference that formed the inspiration for this volume, Pat Hayes asked, rather mischievously, what sociology had to contribute to the study of artificial intelligence. I will take this question seriously.

Different sociologists have different views about what sociology is, and even among those who agree that sociology has a bearing on artificial intelligence, there is a range of ideas about just how it should be applied (Collins 1994). Some of these approaches have already had a substantial impact on AI research (Suchman 1987). These differences should not come as a surprise; it would be equally difficult to represent the relations of psychology as a whole or philosophy as a whole to the question of artificial intelligence. The answer I give represents, then, one view of sociology's contribution. Having been scrupulously fair for nearly two paragraphs, let me add that this is not just "a personal view," or a "perspective among others;" I think it is the right view. I start by trying to explain this sociological viewpoint.

Sociology's Fundamental Units of Explanation

One might characterize and order the sciences by what they take as their fundamental units of explanation; those things that explain but which do not require further explanation. Physics is the exception because it tries to explain everything. Chemistry, on the other hand, *doesn't* try to explain protons, neutrons, and electrons. Biochemistry just accepts atoms, and perhaps molecules; biology accepts the elements of cells; while general medicine takes muscles, bones, and organs as their fundamental units. Continuing up the scale, the fundamental units of enquiry of psychology and social psychology are individual minds and their interactions with other minds. Right at the top, sociology's fundamental units are *collectivities;* groups of people who are the location of certain types of knowledge and sets of activities. People are collections of quarks for physicists, protons, neutrons, and electrons for chemists, atoms for biochemists, cells for biologists, organ systems for doctors, minds for psychologists, but for sociologists they are collections of collectivities. People are the "symptoms" of the social collectivities of which they are a part.

One of the things that can make sociology difficult is that its fundamental units of explanation can be hard to see or even imagine. Of the other sciences listed above, only physics resembles it in this respect. The entities of all the other sciences are relatively easy to imagine or to see. One can picture simplified versions of atoms, molecules and cells, and one can see organs and interacting individuals, but to imagine a collectivity is almost as hard as imagining a "superstring" or an "*n*-dimensional space." This can be frustrating because the surface phenomena pertaining to collectivities, human beings, are so easy to see. To the sociologist, individuals are tantalizing indications of a deeper reality. They relate to collectivities as, say, colors relate to quantum transitions in the atom (except that collectivities are bigger than their symptoms whereas quantum transitions are smaller) or, better, as the conversation of an individual English speaker relates to a dialect of native English as it is collectively spoken.

Let us give an indication of what is involved in taking collectivities seriously. Societies differ: in British society in the 1990s I can go to the cinema, drive to work, play darts, supervise a student, take out a mortgage, test for the existence of a natural phenomenon by reference to its consistent behavior in repeated experiments, and so on. If I were a member of Zande society (before it was invaded by Westerners), I could do none of these. The Azande believe that disasters befall people because of the influence of witches. To test whether someone is a witch they consult the "poison oracle." They prepare a special poison called "benge" and feed it to a chicken. If the chicken dies, the accused is a witch, but if it lives, the accused is not a witch. They check the oracle's reliability by poisoning a second chicken with the same benge. This time if the chicken lives the person is a witch, but if it dies he or she is not a witch. If I were an Azande I could accuse someone of being a witch, prepare benge, consult the poison oracle, check its veracity by reference to its varied behavior in repeated tests, and so forth; in current British society I could do none of these. (That is to say, I might go through all the motions of accusation, chicken poisoning, and so forth, but it would not result in anyone being counted as a witch within British society).

The reason I could do some things in one society and not in the other has little to do with what is legal and illegal. It has little to do with the psychology of the individuals in the two societies. It does not even have to do with what the respective members of the two societies have been trained to do, because if I transferred myself to Zande society tomorrow I would not be able to take out a mortgage in that society in spite of my knowledge of mortgages, nor would an Azande transported here be able to designate witches. The problem is that the two societies have different social and conceptual structures. It just does not make sense to do the things in one society that do make sense in the other. The (antediluvian) Azande do not have the concept of a mortgage, and we do not have the concept of the poison oracle. Taking out mortgages and oracular divination, like team games, are things one can only do in combination with others who understand the point of what one is trying to do. Something must follow from the actions, such as the purchase of a house or the ostracizing of the witch; otherwise one might as well be speaking a "private language." We are correct, then, to talk of differences in social and *conceptual* structure.

And yet it is a little more subtle even than this because in many ways the social and the conceptual are the same thing. Perhaps the easiest way to see this is to go back to the example of natural language. A language is both a conceptual structure and a form of social activity. The content and shape of a language is determined by its historical legacy and what people do when they speak, read, and write. Yet people do not learn how to speak just by thinking about it, or even by internalizing a set of rules. Neither my son nor I know why in current teenage argot the old word "cheeky"—meaning insolent—has been adapted to refer to a person who turns in an irritatingly sharp sporting performance, nor do we know why that usage will last for a few months at most. The meaning will be found in no dictionaries and the only way to get the nuance is to practice the use of the term within my son's social circle. The word is alive in that temporally and spatially local collectivity and, almost certainly, it will soon die. (Having read the above passage, my son informs me that I've got the word wrong—which rather reinforces the point.) The point is that the word "cheeky" does not exist in some kind of conceptual "space" in my son's head, because its subtle and continually changing meaning comes out of the flux of speech activity that takes place in my son's social circle. He does not quite know what it means, firstly because he can not tell me, and secondly because it does not stand still for long enough. No individual nor subset of individuals is in control of where it is going; its fate is in the hands of the collectivity. To "know" the word is to "live" the word.

A more well-worked and concrete example of the relationship between the way we think and the way we act is found in the idea of germs (Winch 1958,

p. 121 ff). The swabbing, washing, scrubbing, draping, and rubber-gloving that precedes a modern surgical intervention is well known. One could not understand this seemingly interminable procedure if one did not also understand the idea of germs. Why do surgeons pull on their rubber gloves in that curiously difficult fashion? Knowing about germs, one can see that they are trying to avoid touching the possibly nonsterile inside of the glove with the sterile outside. One can make sense of the activity—and see how one might blend one's own actions into the activity—only because one can understand the idea of germs. Likewise, if one wants to watch a major operation from within an operating theatre one has to understand the idea of germs to know where to stand and what not to touch. Correspondingly, one would not be able to maintain the idea of germs if surgeons regularly operated with bare hands and dirty waistcoats or even if they felt they could move about freely during the operation.

Just as the meaning of "cheeky" is made and maintained by what is uttered in my son's social circle, the meaning of germ is made and maintained by what surgeons do in operating theatres. All this scrubbing and draping "makes" the world of surgeons full of germs; each scrub affirms the existence of germs rather than eliminates them. The way surgeons act in the operating theatre is part and parcel of our world of germs, just as the way we speak comprises our language. The scrubbing and draping and the concept of germs are facets of the same surgical "form of life."

The term "form of life" is taken from the later philosophy of Wittgenstein (1953; Winch 1958; Collins and Pinch 1982). Any philosophy that deals with the structure of ideas is pretty well indistinguishable from sociology just as, deep down, sociology is philosophical; understanding how concepts work involves understanding how people act in their lives. The meaning of concepts is not to be found by looking at dictionaries but by looking at what people say and do, just as making sense of what people say and do involves understanding them.

This difficult idea—the mutual constitution of the social and conceptual—precipitates questions we will call "the sociological questions" (though they are equally philosophical). They are: Can elements of our conceptual life be given to entities, such as computers, that do not share our social life? If they can, is this range of elements constrained? If yes, where are the boundaries and how is the trick accomplished? The answer to Pat Hayes's query about sociology's contribution, or potential contribution, to artificial intelligence is to be found in the answers to the sociological questions set out above.

The plan of the rest of this chapter is as follows. I will first try to explain in greater detail what is meant by saying that knowledge is the property of social collectivies. I will try to make the point convincing by discussing science and arithmetic. In picking these cases I am adopting the strategy of "the hard case." I am not sure if the strategy of the hard case has a scholarly pedigree in the philosophy of science but it was introduced in the social study of science to justify the early concentration on physics and mathematics rather than targets such as economics or sociology where the influence of social factors was so much easier to find. If physics and mathematics could be shown to have a social foundation, so the argument went, then it would be obvious that the same would hold true of, say, biology and the social sciences. Investigating the much easier social sciences first would carry none of the same implications for the natural sciences.

The next two sections will be devoted to science and arithmetic, and they will pose a difficult question. How does a pocket calculator fit into society given that we have established that even arithmetic is the kind of activity that needs an understanding of social context if it is to work properly? In the fourth section I will show how the question might be answered by introducing first the idea of "repair and attribution." Repair and attribution are what humans do, usually without noticing, when they compensate for the deficiencies of the computers in their midst. Then I will introduce the theory of "mimeomorphic actions." These are a special class of actions that can be performed without our needing to understand the context in which they are set.

In the fifth section I will describe briefly how the new theory can be put to work. The final section sets out a new version of the Turing Test—the Editing Test—which could be used to try out the sociological analysis.

Science and Society

It is not easy to put substantial flesh onto the skeleton of the sociological framework because some areas of life look so completely conceptual that is hard to believe that a social element enters anywhere. For example, the truths of science and mathematics have long been thought of as independent of social life. There are, however, different sciences for different societies (Kuhn 1962). For two decades sociologists have been studying social/conceptual differences within science and the way that these develop and are then maintained (Collins 1975; MacKenzie 1981; Collins and Pinch 1982; Pinch 1986). One way of explaining matters in respect of the experimental sciences is to think in terms of the "experimenters' regress," a problem to do with knowing what the outcome of an experiment means (Collins 1985).

The experimenter's regress happens because to know whether "x" exists, whether "x" be gravity waves, the constancy of the speed of light, or the indivisibility of the charge on the electron, one needs to build a good "x-detector," but to know whether you have built a good x-detector you have to see whether it does what it is supposed to do, but to know what it is supposed to do you have to know whether or not it ought to detect x when it is working properly, but to know whether it ought to detect x when it is working properly you need to know whether x exists, but to know whether x exists you need to build a good x-detector, and so forth.

The experimenters' regress arises because experiments are hard and they usually do not work first time if they work at all. To learn to carry out a new and difficult experiment is a matter of transferring a set of skills that can sometimes be learned only through social intercourse with those who already possess them. This was how it was when the "Transversely Excited Atmospheric Pressure Carbon Dioxide Laser" (TEA-laser) was developed (Collins 1974, 1985). In the normal way, repeating experiments, hard though it is, presents no *conceptual* problems because we know roughly what the result of an experiment should look like—there is social consensus about this—and we carry on until we get the experiment right. For example, in the case of TEA-laser building, experimenters who could not make their devices work either sought more knowledge or gave up; they did not conclude that working lasers could not exist.

In frontier science, the proper outcomes of experiments are in dispute. In these areas the skill-laden nature of experimentation becomes more obvious to everyone. Typically scientists whose findings are disputed claim that their rivals did not do the experiments with sufficient skill and that is why they cannot find the phenomenon. The rivals will claim that there is no phenomenon and the original experiments were inadequate. There is no way to settle such a dispute with further experiments alone for each further experiment is subject to the same uncertainty about the adequacy of the procedure. The usual surrogate indicator—the experiment produces a result in the right range—is not available because there is no agreement about what is the right range. Thus the "purely scientific" dispute can go on for ever. The disagreement is usually settled for all practical purposes when one side can no longer get published.

This pattern was followed in the case of the dispute over the detection of cosmic gravitational radiation (Collins 1975, 1985; Collins and Pinch 1993). Related processes have been found in many other scientific controversies such as the dispute over magnetic monopoles (Pickering 1981), over free quarks (Pickering 1983), over the chemical transfer of memory (Travis 1981), over phenomena related to parapsychology (Collins and Pinch 1982; Collins 1985), over the flux of solar neutrinos (Pinch 1986), over the nature of the vacuum (Shapin and Schaffer 1987), over the experimental confirmation of the special and general theories of relativity (Collins and Pinch 1993) and so forth.

Disputes such as these are settled, as I have said, not when scientists change their minds, but when one side loses its voice in the scientific community. This closure of debate entails agreement by the larger part of the scientific community about which phenomena are genuine and, coextensively, what counts as a skillfully-executed experiment. New ideas about what things are real and the acceptance of new sets of experimental practices are two sides of the same coin. What count as results, then, are specific to social collectivities of scientists. The discovery of a new natural phenomenon is, at the same time, learning a new way to act within the scientific community; it's like learning the special meaning of the word "cheeky" sufficiently thoroughly to pass as "cool" in my son's social group.

In sum, scientific conclusions are reached in science by scientists agreeing to agree and acting as though they agree. To think of it another way, one might say that the inexpressibility of what has become known as "tacit knowledge" comes about because skill is a mixture of situated mental and physical accomplishments that one can only learn by being a member of the local group (Polanyi 1958; Collins 1974, 1985).

It is not surprising that one can find collectivities with heterodox views about which natural phenomena exist. The community of scientists who believe in the existence of paranormal phenomena are one such collectivity, and at the time of writing, the community that believes in "cold fusion" is another; both are flourishing, continuing actively with their experiments and finding what seems to them to be positive results.

Science and Computers

The experimenter's regress and the social nature of scientific research have a clear consequence for computers as we know them. One would not expect isolated computers to be able to "discover" scientific laws, since discovery is a matter of embedding within a community rather than a matter of a lonely dialogue with nature. It has been claimed that computers can discover (Langley et al. 1987), but these claims must be misguided if the ideas put forward here are correct. Closer examination of so-called "discovery programs" reveals that they are fed with data already filtered and cleaned by reference to the theory that the larger part of the scientific society currently counts as correct (Collins 1990). Given this, the ability to calculate a formula immanent in some numbers and an algorithm does not bear on the question of the nature of scientific knowledge with all its disputes about what is to count as data and what as "noise" and error.[2]

Now consider the consequences of these ideas for, say, expert systems. One ought no longer expect to be able to transfer much of the knowledge of experts from their heads to machines because the knowledge is not just "in the head"; expert knowledge is also a matter of belonging to and interacting in a community. One might characterize the course of development of expert systems as going from ambitious but failed attempts to replace humans to less ambitious but more successful efforts to build programs that can advise humans. This is what has happened with medical diagnostic systems which began with the much-hyped MYCIN[3] and have now turned into help systems (Lipscombe 1989). The train of development is easy to understand given the way of looking at the world being proposed here: an expert system can "know" a lot more information than a human expert, it can even "know" a lot more tricks of the trade (heuristics, or rules of thumb) than a human, therefore it can be a good helpmate, but it cannot blend that knowledge into the social flux nor have the knowledge pertaining to the social flux without being a participant within it; expertise depends on this and has to be supplied by the operator. In other places I have tried to work out the details of the consequences of these ideas for expert systems (Collins, Green, and Draper 1985; Collins 1990).

I now return to the main argument, working it through with a still "harder case."

Arithmetic

Mathematics and arithmetic represent a harder case than experimentally based science because, appearing to be a matter of pure individual thought rather than skill, they seem still less likely to depend on collective activity. But, just as what counts as a successful experiment depends on social agreement, what counts as "proof" in mathematics is a matter of people agreeing to agree that something has been "proved" and that the content of the world of mathematical entities should be seen this way rather than that. Currently we are witnessing the mathematical community's coming to terms with computer-based proofs.

I am unable to provide details of historical case studies that would point to the social agreements upon which what we call "the logic of arithmetic" are based, but the work is being done. We can, however, say a little about arithmetic that usefully illustrates the general point.

Arithmetic cannot be put to use without approximation. How many significant figures count when some variable is measured experimentally or calculated? How close do theoretically calculated and experimentally measured values have to be to count as being "in agreement"? (Kuhn, 1961, explains the point wonderfully well.) Knowing how to approximate comes with experience—experience of the whole world of things as we know, live, and interact with them. Measure your height. You will find that the proper way to report the measurement varies from place to place and time to time. Your height is one thing as far as you are concerned, another as far as a police description is concerned, another again as far as a tailor is concerned, another again for the designer of a space suit, and another again for a scientist researching the consequence of horizontal sleep for the decompression of the spine.

Or consider the sum "7/11*11." The answer for most purposes is "7," but there are purposes for which it is "6.99999 recurring." The mathematician will say "6.99999 recurring is 7." The mathematician is talking about mathematical conventions; 7 and 6.9999…are far from identical as far as the designer of computer rounding algorithms is concerned. The designer's problem is to make 6.9999…appear as 7 under a range of circumstances. Schoolteachers, in trying to explain the relationships between fractions and decimals, and in trying to explain the conventions of arithmetic, rely on the long tail that you get when you use arithmetical algorithms for certain sums. So, even knowing what counts as the right outcome of the sum 7/11*11 requires socially acquired context-sensitivity.

This simple example can be developed to show the complexity of our interactions with something as simple as a pocket calculator (Collins 1990). There is an interesting problem regarding the calculator: How does an unsocialized thing do arithmetic when arithmetic is something that requires social skills when humans do it? If there is a problem with pocket calculators that we can solve, then we have dealt with a hard case. That is, we can say that if we can understand the social element in something as apparently unsocial as a pocket calculator, we will be in a better position to understand the cases of more obviously social devices such as those that interact through natural language. Let us try to explain pocket calculators.

Understanding Computers:
'RAT' and the Theory of Mimeomorphic Actions

The explanation I offer of how an unsocialized entity, such as a calculator or other computer, can appear to do tasks that require the abilities of a member of society, has firstly to do with "Repair, Attribution and all That" which I will refer to as RAT. What we do with RAT, as I will explain below, is what makes it possible for us to use computers for some of the more complex tasks that humans usually fulfill. RAT is what we do when we fit computers into the social context. A full blown, fully socialized, artificial intelligence would have to do as much RAT as we normally do. As I will explain, I believe no significant progress in this direction has been made.

RAT

We have to understand that the success of calculators and other machines has a lot to do with how much we do when we encounter them. For example, when I pick up a cheap pocket calculator and do the sum "7/11*11" I get the answer 6.9999996, but I do not immediately write an angry letter to the manufacturers telling them that they have sold me a dud calculator. I look at the result and I "see" 7. Seeing 7 where there is only 6.9999996 is part of the work I do in making the interaction between me and the calculator look like ordinary arithmetic. If I analyze the process more carefully, I will find that I do a lot of work at the input stage as well as at the output stage (Collins 1990, ch. 5).

This work is of the same sort that I do when I hear the strange accents and intonations of a voice-generating chip giving me a telephone number, or telling me that "a door is a jar" (a phrase frequently evinced by a car I once rented). I can turn mangled vocalizations into English words because I can provide enough context for what such a device is "trying to say" to make sense of it. On the input side, voice-operated computers require me to speak in a special way if they are to work at all accurately. This is because they *cannot* do the same sort of intepretative, contextualizing work on humans' varying vocalizations that we can do on theirs. The special way of speaking that I have to adopt in order to be "understood" by a computer is equivalent to my being ready to insert my arithmetical sum into the calculator through a keyboard that offers me a limited choice of options in the way I express the sum.

What I am doing when I see 6.9999996 as 7 and hear the voice chip as saying ordinary words is known as "repair." I am repairing the deficiencies of the computer. Insofar as I do such repair work without noticing it, I can easily think of the calculator (voice chip) as doing arithmetic (speaking). This is rather like the process of anthropomorphisation. I might attribute human characteristics to my dog, to my car, and to my calculator. This is what I do when I say that my calculator is "better at arithmetic than I am." Thus the first thing we need to understand if we are know how computers interact with humans is repair and attribution (see also Garfinkel 1967).

Hiding the RAT

What one might call "hiding the RAT" is the most general principle of computer interface design. The interface is designed so that the user is unaware of how much RAT he or she is putting into the interaction. The way to do this is to have the computer need only the kind of RAT that we are accustomed to using in our everyday lives. In other words, make the interface require only ubiquitous skills. This is usually called making interfaces "user-friendly." It is less a matter of making the interface do skillful things and more a matter of making it natural and easy for us to use skills we already have.

The examples given in the previous section are like this. Any precalculator era arithmetician was already accustomed to approximating. Logarithm tables and slide-rules require more approximating skills than calculators. That is why the calculator's mistakes are so easy to repair, and why it is so easy to attribute arithmetician's skills to it. Ubiquitous skills are "transparent"; one does not notice that one has them. The repair of broken speech patterns is another ubiquitous skill; we have to do it all the time in normal conversation. One of the things that designers are doing as programs become more user-friendly is, then, to make their programs touch our culture in places where the skills of repair are already in place (Collins 1990).

One design mistake is to think that a computer that thoroughly hides the RAT does not need RAT at all. This kind of mistake led, for example, to the overblown claims for the power of expert systems such as automated medical diagnosticians like MYCIN. It happens when the designer does not understand how much work and skill humans put into their day-to-day interactions with each other and with machines. If one does not notice how skill-laden ordinary social life is, one may think that a system with which people can interact easily is a social creature. But it is not a social creature unless the pattern of skill use is roughly symmetrical between all parties. Once again, the asymmetry is easily seen in systems that involve speech, but careful analysis will show its presence in nearly all computer-human interactions, including human-calculator interaction. (For a hilarious account of what I would call "unbalanced RAT" in automated photocopiers see Suchman, 1987.) Only in special cases (to be discussed below) is symmetry achievable with current or immediately foreseeable machines.

Balancing the RAT

Balancing the RAT is one of the ultimate aims of artificial intelligence research. It means building devices that are as good at repair and attribution as we are, so that the burden of RAT can be shared equally between all parties as it is in normal human interactions. In most current computer-human interactions nearly all the repairing is done by the humans.

This is not to say that computers and other machines cannot do various bits of pseudo-repair such as spell-checking and so forth. Close analysis shows, however, that this type of checking is substantially different in process and effect to that done by humans. For example, my spell checker will correct the misspelling in antidisestablishmentareanism, a mistake that many humans would miss, but not in world processor, which nearly every human would spot. What is more, nearly every human would also see that both antidisestablishmentareanism and world processor are correctly spelled in the context of this passage!

To return to balancing the burden of repair, part of the answer to the sociological questions is that no ordinary balanced-RAT interchange can be managed unless, one way or another, we put social knowledge into computers. At the moment we have no idea how to do this.

Killing the RAT

There is another way of dealing with RAT, however. This is to eliminate the need for it. Machines can take the role of ordinary, socialized, human beings without being members of society under some circumstances. The circumstances are that ordinary humans beings want to do things that could be done without the skills, ways of conceptualizing the world, and ways of acting and speaking that are normally mastered with socialization. I believe there is a class of actions that can be managed without RAT if we so wish. These I call "mimeomorphic actions" (Collins 1990; Collins and Kusch 1995); they are to be understood by contrasting them with our more ordinary actions—"polimorphic actions." I now explain these terms along with some other concepts that are emerging as the theory of mimeomorphic actions is developed.

Polimorphic Actions and Mimeomorphic Actions

The simplest way to understand polimorphic actions is to note that the same *action* can be carried out by an indefinite number of different behaviors. Here the term behavior is being used to refer to bodily movements—for example, as they would be described by an observer—in contrast with actions that, for our purposes, are identified by intentions. In this terminology we might say that a certain behavior "corresponds to" or "instantiates" an action. We might also say that an observer could *not* identify a particular action through observing the behavior associated with it. To give an example of a polimorphic action, paying money can be done by passing metal or paper tokens, writing a check, proffering a plastic card and signing a slip, and so forth, and each of these can be done in open-ended variety of ways. At the same time, the same piece of behavior may be the instantiation of many different actions. For example, signing one's name might be the act of paying money, or it might be agreeing to a divorce, the final flourish of a suicide note, or a specimen signature for the bank.

Most of the time most of our actions are polimorphic actions of this type or closely related types, all characterized by the fact that they involve socially appropriate responses to contexts that vary open-endedly, or meaningfully varied responses to fixed contexts, or combinations of both (Collins and Kusch 1995). Our ability to operate smoothly and concertedly in these kinds of contexts is a puzzling feature of ordinary social life. This is the ability we learn as we become socialized.

I call these actions polimorphic because the prefix "poly" means many and these actions must be executed in many different ways. "Poli" is a pun on "poly." It refers to the fact that the way the action is carried out is related to societal context; it is related, that is, to the *polis*.

Polimorphic actions are "rule-bound" in the sense that it is clear when they are being done the wrong way. For example, there are wrong ways of doing something even so ill-defined as going for a walk. One way to do it wrong in many societies is to brush against others on the sidewalk. Though polimorphic actions are rule-bound, it is not possible to provide a recipe for doing them the right way that could be followed by someone who did not already understand the society in which they are embedded—there are too many context-dependent ways of doing them right.

The starting point for understanding mimeomorphic actions is to see them as actions where, by contrast with polimorphic actions, we attempt to maintain a one-to-one mapping between our actions and observable behaviors; in other words, to instantiate the same act, we perform the same behavior. I call these actions mimeomorphic because one may think of them as actions where the actor is trying to *reproduce* the behavior which comprises the execution of the action rather than to vary it.[4] Mimeomorphic actions are also rule-bound, but here there is a chance of providing a description of correct execution as well as listing the wrong ways to do things.

Matters soon become complicated (Collins and Kusch 1995). We want to talk about repeating the execution of actions in the "same" way, but since there are always parameters within which every behavior is different from those that preceded it (e.g., the time of day is different, the Sun might be shining on one occasion and not on another), and since the level of accuracy of the space-time description of any movement can be increased almost indefinitely, there can always be said to be variation of behavior whatever the intentions of the actor. Whether we see variation depends on frame of reference. Thus, by "the same behavior" we have to mean "the same behavior *within* those parameters that mark the outer edges of the actor's indifference." *Sameness and indifference are logically related ideas.* Mimeomorphic actions are marked by either our preference for them to be carried out in the same way each time or our readiness for them to be carried out with a range of differences to which we are indifferent.

Another complication is that mimeomorphic actions may sometimes consist of actions carried out by behaviors that vary systematically and predictably in response to a prespecified and exhaustive set of contexts; instead of reproducing just one pattern of behaviors, one might reproduce one of a set of prespecified patterns. For example, on production lines run under the "scientific management" ideas developed by F.W. Taylor (e.g., Rose 1988), workers are instructed on exactly how to move their limbs and bodies to be maximally efficient. But a worker may well be given instruction in two or more sets of movements which correspond to the two or more tasks he or she is expected to do as the line moves along. An action where a choice between sets of prespecified behaviors is required is referred to in the theory of morphicity as a "disjunctive mimeomorphic action" (Collins and Kusch 1995). There are further subtypes within these categories.

Note also that the characteristic feature of (simple) mimeomorphic actions is that we may *try* to execute them with the same spatio-temporal behavior; we can fail to execute our intentions. Like all intentional actions, what we intend is not necessarily what we accomplish. Given these qualifications, we can see that mimeomorphic actions include, for example, work on Taylorist production lines as described above, the ideal golf swing (since about 1930), high-board competition diving, simple arithmetical operations, and so forth.

It is important to note that in the case of most actions, the way we carry them out—polimorphically or mimeomorphically—varies with historical setting. There are a few actions the meanings of which are bound up with their being either mimeomorphic or polimorphic; in contemporary society an example of the first type of action is marching, while an example of the second type is writing love letters. The "morphicity" of these actions cannot change without changing the action itself: one cannot be said to be marching unless one is trying to repeat the length of step; one cannot normally be said to writing love letters if one writes one identical letter after another. Many actions, however, change morphicity during the course of their history. Furthermore, many actions can be executed in either way depending on intention and desired outcome. For example, while I nearly always execute my golf swing mimeomorphically, I might decide to clown about, trying to amuse my partners rather than execute a proper shot. In that case I would still be swinging the club, and I might even meet with greater success in terms of the effect on the ball, but I would not be engaged in a mimeomorphic action. As we will see, because the morphicity of actions can change, computers can mimic actions more easily at some times than others.

Every action, it should be noted, is an element of a higher-order action. A set of embedded actions that an individual executes in order to complete a higher-level action is described as an "action path" while a set of actions executed partly by others in order to complete a higher-level action is an "action cascade." Many higher-level actions are polimorphic actions but contain elements which are mimeomorphic actions lower down their action paths or action cascades.

We can now return to computers and try to work out the different ways in which they can fit into society.

RAT, Mimeomorphic Actions, and
Human and Machine Cognition

To execute a polimorphic action successfully requires sensitivity to social context. To reproduce the effect of a mimeomorphic action, however, it is necessary only to reproduce the behavior that is always associated with that action (or a behavior that lies within the envelope of indifference). As far as an observer is concerned, or for that matter, the other party to an interaction, such behavior is indistinguishable from the action itself. This is not the case where polimorphic actions are concerned because there is no behavior that maps into the actions one-to-one (nor any set of behaviors that map into an envelope of indifference). It is because the reproduction of behavior does not *normally* reproduce actions that artificial intelligence is so hard to attain. If, however, we decompose actions so that the mimeomorphic elements are evident, we can see those places where computers can slip into the context of social life *without* needing the services of humans who continually repair and attribute. Thus, if we decompose the work of arithmeticians carefully enough we will understand just what it is that a pocket calculator (or slide rule), does by itself, and just what it does not.

The research program that follows from the above analysis is the reexamination of many of our actions in terms of their morphicity. Where mimeomorphic actions are embedded within action paths and action cascades that are otherwise made up of polimorphic actions, computers can accomplish some parts of our actions for us. It is we who must continue to take responsibility for the rest of the polimorphic actions in the paths and cascades. Note how this differs from previous approaches.[5] We no longer analyze the competence of computers by thinking in terms of whole domains of knowledge such as arithmetic (Dreyfus 1992), we now analyze elements of actions within domains (Collins 1996). Under this analysis, the boundary of computerization is as flexible and shifting as our idea of how best to carry on our lives within domains. Let me now return to the sociological questions with which we began.

The Editing Test

I began by explaining a sociological perspective: human cognition happens within forms of life or social contexts. I have gone on to explain the point of the resulting "sociological questions" in more detail and to sketch a way of approaching the answers. Can our conceptual life *appear* to become the property of entities, such as computers, that do not share our social life? Yes!—so long as we are prepared to engage in all the repair and attribution that makes computers seem to do what we do. Are there elements of our conceptual life that can become the property of entities, such as computers without needing repair and attribution? The answer is again yes. Is this range of elements constrained? The answer, once more, is yes—the elements involve mimeomorphic actions.

How, then, can computers fit into social life? The answer shifts depending on the ingenuity of designers, the amount of work that the user is prepared to do in order to make up for the deficiencies of the computer, and the way we do things (in a mimeomorphic manner or not) in our ordinary life at any particular time and place. There is, however, an absolute boundary for any unsocialized machine; no unsocialized machine can do repair, attribution and all that—the work that makes the unsocialized fit into social context. This means that in circumstances where computers need to do this work, current and immediately foreseeable devices will fail; what I have called "balancing the RAT" is impossible.

Design of the Editing Test

It is quite easy to test this claim with an appropriately designed but simplified version of the Turing Test which I call the Editing Test (Collins 1996). The test requires a determined judge, an intelligent and literate control who shares the broad cultural background of the judge, and the machine with which the control is to be compared. The judge provides both "Control" and "Machine" with copies of a few typed paragraphs (in a clear, machine-readable font), of somewhat misspelled and otherwise mucked-about English, which neither Control nor Machine has seen before. It is important that the paragraphs are previously unseen for it is easy to devise a program to transliterate an example once it has been thought through.

Once presented, Control and Machine have, say, an hour to transliterate the passages into normal English. Machine will have the text presented to its scanner and its output will be a second text. Control will type his/her transliteration into a word processor to be printed out by the same printer as is used by Machine. The judge will then be given the printed texts and will have to work out which has been transliterated by Control and which by Machine. Here is a specimen of the sort of paragraph the judge might present:

Mary: The next thing I want you to do is spell a word that means a religious ceremony.

John: You mean rite. Do you want me to spell it out loud?

Mary: No, I want you to write it.

John: I'm tired. All you ever want me to do is write, write, write.

Mary: That's unfair, I just want you to write, write, write.

John: OK, I'll write, write.

Mary: Write.

The point of this simplified test is that the hard thing for a machine to do in a Turing Test is to demonstrate the skill of repairing typed English conversation—the interactional stuff is mostly icing on the cake. The test is designed to draw on all the culture-bound common-sense needed to navigate the domain of error correction in printed English learned by being embedded in society. This is the only kind of skill that can be tested through the medium of the typed word but it is quite sufficient, if the test is carefully designed, to enable us to tell the socialized from the unsocialized; it is enough to tell whether we have balanced the RAT.[6] It seems to me that if a machine could pass a carefully designed version of this little test all the significant problems of artificial intelligence would have been solved because we would have learned how to embed a computer in society—all that would remain would be research and development.

Conclusion

Finally, to sum up the argument: How do we manage the trick of making unsocialized computers do things that require socialization among humans? By humans making up for computer deficiencies—RAT; by making the process invisible—hiding the RAT; and, since balancing the RAT is impossible, by killing the RAT. Killing the RAT is accomplished only in the special case where actions are mimeomorphic, and only in that case can current computers mimic the actions of socialized human beings. Expert system designers have probably discovered most of this through trial and error; I hope to have systematized some of this experience and revealed why machines designed to embed mimeomorphic rather than polimorphic actions are the way forward where usefulness is important.

Acknowledgments

I am grateful to Georgina Rooke for helpful comments on an earlier draft of this chapter. The editors, too, did heroic work in helping me revise, resulting in a much improved draft; in particular, at the cost of a large number of self-citations, there is now at least a small chance of cross disciplinary communication. Work on this chapter was supported partly by grant R000234581 from the UK Economic and Social Research Council.

Notes

1. For the first use of this argument of which I am aware of see Collins (1981).

2. For an extended but not always well-focussed debate on the matter, see *Social Studies of Science*, Vol. 19 (1989) pp. 563-695, and Vol. 21 (1991) pp. 143-56. The second reference contains an illuminating contribution from Herbert Simon followed by a revealing discussion.

3. "In evaluations of MYCIN's skills at diagnosis and therapy, MYCIN was judged to perform at the level of human specialists in infectious diseases and above (sometimes far above) the level of other nonspecialist physicians." (Feigenbaum and McCorduck 1984, p. 65.)

4. In earlier work (e.g., Collins 1990) the two kinds of actions have been referred to as "regular actions" (polimorphic) and "behavior-specific actions" (mimeomorphic).

5. I am mainly concerned with contrasting this approach with notions based on domains of knowledge, but note also that in contrast to theories such as Minsky's (1987) *Society of Mind*, the socially embedded feature of polimorphic actions is *not reduced* by analysis into mimeomorphic specific elements. Higher-level polimorphic actions can be executed only by properly socially embedded actors. Entities which simply reproduced the behaviors corresponding to the lowest level of an action tree would not be able to match the choice of behaviors to social context.

6. It is worth noting for the combinatorily-inclined that a look-up table *exhaustively* listing all corrected passages of about the above length—300 characters—including those for which the most appropriate response would be "I can't correct that," would

contain 10^{600} entries, compared to the, roughly, 10^{125} particles in the universe. The number of potentially correctible passages would be very much smaller of course but, I would guess, would still be beyond the bounds of brute strength methods. Note also that the correct response—of which there may be more than one—may vary from place to place and time to time as our linguistic culture changes.

References

Bloor, D. (1983). Wittgenstein: *A Social Theory of Knowledge*. London: Macmillan.

Collins, H.M. (1974). The TEA set: Tacit knowledge and scientific networks. *Science Studies, 4,* 165-86.

Collins, H.M. (1975). The seven sexes: A study in the sociology of a phenomenon, or the replication of experiments in physics. *Sociology, 9,* 205-24.

Collins, H.M. (1981). Stages in the empirical programme of relativism. *Social Studies of Science, 11,* 3-10.

Collins, H.M. (1985). *Changing Order: Replication and Induction in Scientific Practice* [2nd ed., 1992]. Chicago: University of Chicago Press.

Collins, H.M. (1990). *Artificial Experts: Social Knowledge and Intelligent Machines*. Cambridge, MA: MIT Press.

Collins, H.M. (1993). The structure of knowledge. *Social Research, 60,* 95-116.

Collins, H.M. (1994). Sociology and artificial intelligence. In S. Jasanoff, G.E. Markle, J.C. Petersen, & T. Pinch (Eds.), *Handbook of Science and Technology Studies* (pp. 286-381). Beverley Hills: Sage.

Collins, H.M. (1996). Embedded or embodied: Hubert Dreyfus's "What Computers Still Can't Do". *Artificial Intelligence, XX.*

Collins, H.M., Green, R.H., & Draper, R.C. (1985). Where's the expertise: Expert systems as a medium of knowledge transfer. In M.J. Merry (Ed.), *Expert Systems 85* (pp. 323-334). Cambridge: Cambridge University Press.

Collins, H.M. & Kusch, M. (1995). Two kinds of actions: A phenomenological study. *Philosophy and Phenomenological Research, 55,* 799-819.

Collins, H.M. & Pinch, T.J. (1982). *Frames of Meaning: The Social Construction of Extraordinary Science*. London: Routledge and Kegan Paul.

Collins, H.M. & Pinch, T.J. (1993). *The Golem: What Everyone Needs to Know About Science*. Cambridge & New York: Cambridge University Press. [Canto paperback ed., 1994.]

Dreyfus, H. (1992). *What Computers Still Can't Do*. Cambridge, MA: MIT Press.

Feigenbaum, E.A. & McCorduck, P. (1984). *The Fifth Generation: Artificial Intelligence and Japan's Computer Challenge to the World*. London: Michael Joseph.

Garfinkel, H. (1967). *Studies in Ethnomethodology*. New Jersey: Prentice-Hall.

Kuhn, T.S. (1961). The function of measurement in modern physical science. *ISIS, 52,* 162-76.

Kuhn, T.S. (1962). *The Structure of Scientific Revolutions*. Chicago: University of Chicago Press.

Langley, P., Simon, H.A., Bradshaw, G.L., & Zytkow, J.M. (1987). *Scientific Discovery: Computational Explorations of the Creative Process*. Cambridge, MA: MIT Press.

Lipscombe, B. (1989). Expert systems and computer-controlled decision making in medicine. *AI and Society,* 3, 184-97.

Mackenzie, D. (1981). *Statistics in Britain 1865-1930.* Edinburgh: Edinburgh University Press.

Minsky, M. (1987). *The Society of Mind.* London: Heinemann.

Pickering, A. (1981). Constraints on controversy: The case of the magnetic monopole. *Social Studies of Science, 11,* 63-93.

Pickering, A. (1984). *Constructing Quarks: A Sociological History of Particle Physics.* Edinburgh: Edinburgh University Press.

Pinch, T.J. (1986). *Confronting Nature: The Sociology of Solar-Neutrino Detection.* Dordrecht: Reidel.

Polanyi, M. (1958). *Personal Knowledge.* London: Routledge and Kegan Paul.

Rose, M.J. (1988). *Industrial Behavior: Research and Control.* Harmondsworth: Penguin Books.

Shapin, S. & Schaffer, S. (1987). *Leviathan and the Air Pump: Hobbes, Boyle and the Experimental Life.* Princeton: Princeton University Press.

Suchman, L.A. (1987). *Plans and Situated Action: The Problem of Human-Machine Interaction.* Cambridge: Cambridge University Press.

Travis, G.D.L. (1981). Replicating replication? Aspects of the social construction of learning in planarian worms. *Social Studies of Science, 11,* 11-32.

Vallacher, R.R. & Wegner, D.M. (1985). *A Theory of Action Identification.* Hillsdale, NJ: Lawrence Erlbaum.

Winch, P.G. (1958). *The Idea of a Social Science.* London: Routledge and Kegan Paul.

Wittgenstein, L. (1953). *Philosophical Investigations.* Oxford: Blackwell.

Expert Systems in Context

CHAPTER 13

Model-Based Expert Systems and the Explanation of Expertise

Nigel Shadbolt & Kieron O'Hara

Introduction

In this chapter, we will discuss the relevance of expert system technology to the study of expertise. Expert systems are common in industrial contexts, and often deal with relatively mundane problems. It is our contention that, despite their engineering image, expert systems can provide valuable insights into the expertise that they attempt to replicate. To support this claim, we shall sketch a particular class of expert systems, and show how that class of systems can provide psychological insight.

Expert systems are computer systems that attempt to store large amounts of data (or *knowledge*) of a particular domain, organized in such a way as to enable them to solve problems and make inferences in that domain. As such, an expert system can be divided into two separate components: the *knowledge base*, which contains the pieces of knowledge that the system uses, organized and represented in a *knowledge representation language;* and the *inference engine*, which is the part of the program which manipulates the pieces of knowledge in order to produce new pieces of knowledge. We shall not be concerned here with the details of the inference engine; our claim is that the development of the knowledge base of a particular system can shed light on the expertise the system is to model.

We begin with a historical discussion of expert systems: how they began, how they are developed, and what problems needed to be solved along the way. Fuller discussions of the history of expert systems can be found in Jackson (1990, pp. 35-56) and Shadbolt (1989). We then emphasize the use of *models* in the development of expert systems, and attempt to show how regarding expert system development as a modelling activity can solve a number of pervasive difficulties. Finally, we end with a brief discussion of the value of such systems for understanding the psychology of expertise.

A Brief History of Expert Systems

Many would regard MYCIN (Shortliffe, Axline, Buchanan, Merigan and Cohen 1973; Shortliffe 1976), which assisted doctors in the selection of an appropriate course of treatment for patients with bacteremia, meningitis and cystitis, as the first and original expert system. Others would argue in favour of DENDRAL (Buchanan and Feigenbaum 1978), whose function was to infer the molecular structure of unknown compounds from mass spectral and nuclear magnetic response data. Another contender is MIT's MACSYMA system (Genesereth 1979). This system (originally designed by Carl Engleman, William Martin and Joel Moses on the basis of their MATHLAB 68 system) used mathematical expertise to recognise a user's problem and then selected appropriate methods and techniques of mathematical analysis; it is still in widespread commercial use by engineers and scientists.

Whichever one is accorded the title, what these early systems had in common was that they incorporated substantial amounts of knowledge. Research on other large expert systems continued through the late 1970s across a range of application domains. These are now regarded as landmarks in the development of expert systems.

CASNET (Szolovits and Parker 1978; Weiss, Kulikowski, Amarel and Safir 1978) was a large medical expert system that diagnosed and proposed treatments for disease states related to glaucoma. One of the distinctive features of CASNET was that knowledge was represented in a semantic network that attempted to provide a causal-association model of symptoms, disease processes and treatments.

The PROSPECTOR system (Gaschnig 1982) helped in the interpretation of geological data and attempted to assess the likelihood of finding various types of mineral deposits. Its knowledge representation was rule and network based. It used certainty factors and probability propagation methods to encode the idea of confidence in evidence and certainty in conclusions.

XCON/R1 (McDermott 1980) configured DEC VAX computer systems. It decided upon the components needed to produce an operational system given a customer's order. It was a constraint driven system—it had knowledge about what components could go together, what the constraints at the installation site were, etc. It used this knowledge, expressed in a rule-based format, to reason forward from the constraint data to a configuration that satisfied the constraints. This commercial system is still in use and is considered one of the most successful in the history of expert systems.

These systems had large knowledge bases, ran on large computers, and consumed man years of research and development. It is also interesting to note that they employed a wide range of techniques to represent knowledge and reason with it. In some of the earliest systems we see mixed representation methods; rules, nets and frames. However, it is also salutary to note that four out of the six named systems only reached what is termed the *prototype* stage. Clearly this was not yet a completely mature and exploitable technology.

A new direction in the evolution of expert systems was provided by the work on EMYCIN (van Melle 1979; van Melle, Shortliffe and Buchanan 1984). The acronym, which stands for *essential* MYCIN, indicates the skeletal nature of the system, which was that part of MYCIN that dealt with inference and explanation (i.e., MYCIN stripped of its domain knowledge). This abstraction away from the problem domain left a "clean" kernel system. The system was restricted to representing and reasoning with knowledge in a particular way. However, it provided an uncomplicated tool with which to build applications. In particular, it could be used to build diagnostic and classification systems. The age of the expert system *shell* had dawned.

Once the paradigm for such shells became apparent, they proliferated. Early shells tended to be primarily rule-based. They also began to migrate from costly hardware to PCs, and from LISP to a variety of other programming languages. The simplicity of a kernel rule-based shell made this process straightforward.

A great deal of interest was shown in this first generation of shells. As awareness increased and money poured in, more and more companies and academic sites became active in the area (Szolovits 1987; Feigenbaum and McCorduck 1984, appendices B and C). As momentum gathered and expectations rose, perhaps it is not surprising that a sense of what the technology could realistically achieve was not always retained (Feigenbaum and McCorduck 1984, pp. 83-126).

Nevertheless, this interest, together with the emergence of an expert system shell technology, led to real progress. Many of the first generation applications were diagnostic in nature—one particular generic class of expert systems. But there is in fact a range of types of problem-solving we could imagine expert systems performing. A number of classifications have been proposed; the one in Table 1 derives from Waterman (1986). This is a rather coarse characterization, and if we take just the category of diagnosis it can be further analysed into subtypes; heuristic diagnosis, systematic diagnosis through causal tracing, systematic diagnosis through localization, etc.

Each of these different types was proposed to have a different underlying problem-solving structure. As researchers recognised the breadth of problem-solving types, they began to develop characteristic descriptions or models of them (e.g., Clancey 1985; Chandrasekaran 1983; Stefik, Aikins, Balzer, Benoit, Birnbaum, Hayes-Roth and Sacerdoti 1983). Thus one could imagine a shell containing not only a mechanism for reasoning with rules and frames

Type	Description
Diagnosis	Inferring system malfunctions from observables
Interpretation	Inferring situation descriptions from sensor data
Prediction	Inferring likely consequences of given situations
Design	Configuring objects under constraints
Planning	Designing and sequencing actions
Monitoring	Comparing observations to plan vulnerabilities
Debugging	Prescribing remedies to malfunctions
Repair	Executing a plan to administer a prescribed remedy
Instruction	Teaching of any knowledge level component
Control	Governing overall systems behaviour

Table 1. Generic problem-solving categories (after Waterman, 1986).

but one that would apply a particular problem-solving method. We now go on to show how the emergence of such problem-solving models can be used to facilitate knowledge acquisition and expert system development.

Using Models to Develop Expert Systems

The idea of using models in expert system development is relatively recent (Breuker and Wielinga 1989), and there are several competing approaches. However, there does seem to be some convergence around a general form (e.g., Motta, Rajan, Domingue and Eisenstadt 1991), and we shall try to give a more or less neutral characterization of the field.

Conceptual Models and Design Models

The key concept that is used to govern the use of models in the development of expert systems is that of model refinement. Every stage in the development process involves a relatively straightforward step of transformation from one model to the next. The process can be seen in figure 1.

The initial stage of expert system development according to this rough methodology is the creation of a user requirements document. Basically, the aim of this is to set out the job the expert system will have to do, which users it will be aimed at, how quickly it will have to work, what hardware it will run on, and so forth. The user requirements may be negotiable over the course of the development project—often requirements turn out to be contradictory, or technologically infeasible—but the main aim is that they set out the context, as well as specifying the goal, of development.

The second stage is the production of a conceptual model (we will see an

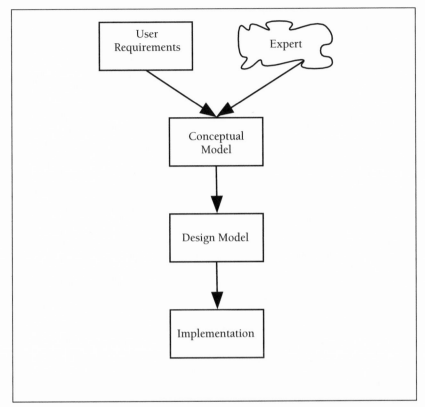

Figure 1. Expert system development as model refinement.

example of such a model in the next subsection). This is generally produced by one or more experts with a knowledge engineer, on the basis of the user requirements. The aim of the conceptual model is to specify the expertise required to solve the problems which the system will have to solve. There are differing views about what factors should influence the conceptual model; for instance, the KADS methodology (Wielinga, Schreiber and Breuker 1992) insists that a conceptual model be created with an eye to the implementation of the target system, while the VITAL methodology (Shadbolt, Motta and Rouge 1993) recommends that a conceptual model be drawn up without such constraints. It is not clear that the difference between these two views is very great. On the one hand, since the target system has not yet been built, its final form is to some extent still a matter for conjecture, while on the other, the computational context of the system development will always act as a constraint to modelling. What is clear is that the conceptual model will be created constructively between the expert and the knowledge engineer. It is therefore the conceptual model which has most claims on being an account of the expertise.

The next stage of the development process is the transformation or refinement of the conceptual model into a design model. The conceptual model is a model of the required expertise; the function of the design model is to specify a representation scheme of the conceptual model on the implementation platform specified in the user requirements. In other words, where the conceptual model specifies what needs to be computed, the design model will specify *how* (in the particular computational context) it will be computed. Ideally, there will be few changes between the conceptual model and the design model; nevertheless, in many contexts, substantial changes have to be made. However, the transformation from conceptual model to design model should, where possible, be *structure preserving;* there should be a relatively straightforward translation from the high level structures in the conceptual model to the high level structures in the design model. We shall see the reasons for this when we discuss the positive aspects of model-based development in the next section.

Since the design model has been drawn up with an eye on implementation, the implementation process itself, therefore, should also be relatively straightforward. Again, changes to the design model may be required, for example, to allow various optimizations and computational short cuts. But the general structure should be preserved in this transformation. Note that if the transformations from conceptual model to design model, and from design model to implementation, are both structure preserving, the implementation will be isomorphic at some level of abstraction to the conceptual model, despite the fact that the conceptual model was not necessarily developed with implementation in mind.

The distinction between conceptual model/design model/implementation can be seen as different ways of answering the question of what the system is actually going to do. For example, if we take a system designed to perform some classification task, the conceptual model will specify *what* the system will do (e.g., by finding the most specific match between an object and various class distinctions). The design model will specify *how* that is to be done (e.g., establish-and-refine—a specific computational technique for matching). The implementation will be the *computational realization* of this strategy (e.g., using left-right matching of nested lists).

This is a very general view of expert system development as model refinement; most individual methodologies make different suggestions as to which models are useful, and which can be ignored. There is, however, a consensus around this general structure.

Having seen how models can be used in expert system development, we should now look at an example of such a model.

Epistemological Typing Within Models: the Domain Layer, the Inference Layer and the Task Layer

There is a variation among various different accounts of what such models will look like, although work has been done to suggest that, despite structural differences, the differences in content are not great (Karbach, Linster and Voss 1990). We will take as an exemplar a KADS-style model, the form of which seems to be becoming a European standard. We will also restrict our attention to conceptual models, although what we say should apply to design models too since the model refinement process should be structure preserving.

The key notion in such models is that of *epistemological typing*. The knowledge that each model contains is relevant either to particular inferences about the domain, or to the drawing of such inferences, or to the organization of such inferences to perform tasks. On the basis of this tripartite distinction, a model can be built in three "layers."

The first layer is the *domain layer*. In this layer goes all the knowledge or data about the domain. So, for example, if our domain was a medical domain, then such knowledge might involve the particular concepts that the system is likely to use, such as "body-temperature," "abstracted-body-temperature," "wheezing," "finger-clubbing," "blood-pressure," "pneumonia," "streptococcal-pneumonia," etc., together with the values that these concepts can take (e.g., "body-temperature" might take an integer value, while "abstracted-body-temperature" might take a value from the set {very-low, low, normal, high, fever}, and such concepts as "wheezing" and "finger-clubbing" might be Boolean in form). Also there may be knowledge contained in implications between concepts, such as "(all x) (all y) body-temperature(x,y) and greater-than$(y,40)$ => abstracted-body-temperature$(x,$fever)." This is the sort of knowledge contained in the domain layer.

The second layer is the *inference layer;* this layer contains the ways in which the knowledge in the domain layer can be manipulated to perform inferences. The insight is that the same piece of knowledge (or better, the same sentence) can play different roles in different problem-solving situations. For example, the claim that "x has pneumonia" might, in different circumstances, be an observational input to the diagnostic process, or a hypothesis to be tested about x's health, or a diagnosis of x's illness, and so on. These different roles can be arrayed in an inference structure.

One well-known inference structure which can serve as an example is *heuristic classification* (Clancey 1985), shown in figure 2. In this diagram the boxes represent the *roles* that knowledge can play in problem-solving, while the ovals represent the *inferences* that are performed.

The process of heuristic classification consists of the following inferences. The input to the classification is a set of observables; in our medical example, these might be items of knowledge such as "body-temperature(x,41)" or "finger-clubbing(x,yes)." This input is then abstracted into usable form by the diagnostician. The abstraction knowledge is the domain knowledge that will enable this abstraction to take place (an example of such knowledge then might be "(all x) (all y) body-temperature(x,y) and greater-than(y,40) => abstracted-body-temperature(x,fever)"). The result of such abstraction will be a set of findings (such as "fever(x,yes)," the statement that x has a fever, which we are able to deduce from his high body temperature). At this point, the diagnostician is then able to match the findings heuristically against some general abstract solutions.

In a medical example, the collection of findings, or symptoms, could be matched against the likely symptoms of, say, a pneumonia sufferer; the information enabling the diagnostician to do this would be referenced under the match inference step. Then the final classification or diagnosis is produced by a refinement of the general solution down to a specific one (e.g., from pneumonia to streptococcal pneumonia).

In this way, the inference structure suggests a way of classifying or diagnosing. Note that there are alternative inference structures for classification. For example, the heuristic matching could be replaced by a systematic series of tests, which could be more exact, while also being more expensive in time and effort. Another method would attempt classification by looking at underlying causal factors as opposed to this symptom-based approach.

The third epistemological type required is a way of combining inferences to achieve specific goals. This knowledge is collected in the *task layer,* a control structure fitted over the inference structure. The inference structure both groups inferences together and links these inferences to the underlying domain knowledge. However, what is needed at the task layer is a set of pointers indicating how to navigate through the inference structure.

Consider our example of heuristic classification (figure 2). This is a relatively simple, linear inference structure. Even so, there are various ways of moving through it. The diagnostician can take the observables as input and diagnose the solution as output—this is the "default" use of the structure that we described above. However, the structure could be navigated in reverse; given a solution, the knowledge contained in the roles and inference steps of the diagram could be used to move round to the observables (working "backwards" through the inferences). This would be an appropriate course of action in the event that the task to be solved was that of stating what symptoms the patient could expect as a result of his contracting some disease. A third possibility would be to take the observables and the solution as input, and work towards the findings. This would be appropriate if a tentative diagnosis had been made, which the diagnostician wished to test; she could then confirm that the observables, such as the patient's temperature, blood pressure, etc., were consistent with the tentative diagnosis.

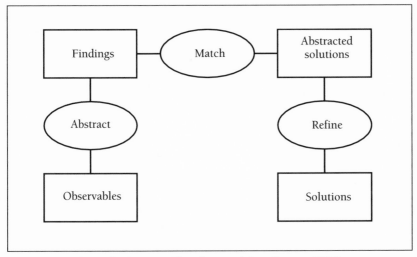

Figure 2. Heuristic Classification (after Clancey, 1985).

We have sketched a way of developing expert systems: model the expertise required to perform the task at hand, then transform that model into a system design, and finally implement that design. There are a number of variations on that theme, from various researchers in the field, but as a general characterization of model-based expert system development methodologies, it is adequate for our purposes.

There is one more innovation we should discuss. Since expert system developments are often large projects involving a large number of staff, it is logical that insights from software engineering, the science of managing large software projects, should be employed if and where possible. One such principle is that of *reuse;* time, effort and space can be saved if items can be reused. This leads to the notion of a *library,* in which various modules are stored and indexed, ready to be transplanted.

Model Libraries

In model-based expert system development, as we have seen, the early phases of any project will be heavily involved with modelling, and it is here that the software engineering principles can be put to use. It may well be just as difficult to model an expert as it is to build an expert system without guidance from a model. Even if the development process is easier with a model, the modelling process may place an extra overhead on development.

However, as Chandrasekaran (1983) and Clancey (1985), among others, have argued, certain problem-solving structures or methods can be seen to

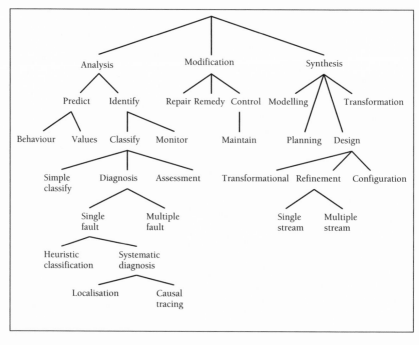

*Figure 3. The taxonomic hierarchy of KADS-I interpretation models
(after Breuker et al., 1987).*

be common across domains. For example, a medical diagnostician, a petroleum geologist and possibly even the much-maligned chicken sexer might all be seen as performing acts of heuristic classification (figure 2). This idea led to much work to discover particularly ubiquitous problem-solving structures; perhaps the most comprehensive is Joost Breuker *et al.*'s monumental set of models written for the KADS project (1987), which isolated the hierarchy of structures shown in figure 3.

Each of these problem-solving types was described at a certain level of abstraction, of course. Clearly no general problem-solving type could apply to all domains in full, simply because the essential domain layer knowledge would have to be omitted from any domain-independent model. But it was quickly seen to be possible to draw up *skeletal* models that partially specified what inferences were pertinent in a number of domains. The description of each type could be done in great detail (e.g., diagnosis in Benjamins 1993).

For example, consider the heuristic classification inference structure we have already seen (figure 2). In the context of an actual conceptual model, that inference structure is a part of a model—the inference layer of a model, with specified relations to the domain layer and the task layer. However, we can also see it in isolation from particular domains and tasks, and see it as a skeletal model. It specifies a class of models—to apply it to a new domain, the inference steps and roles need to be filled with new domain knowledge, and to use it to perform a new task a new task layer (i.e., control structure) needs to be written to navigate through it.

Such skeletal models can be collected, and placed in a library. Then, assuming the library is well-organized, a knowledge engineer can begin the modelling process by selecting the model from the library that most nearly describes the expert's problem-solving. When he goes on to acquire the domain knowledge, that process, driven by the model, should thereby be facilitated. In this way, model libraries can be an important aid to knowledge engineering; each model, in effect, is an equivalence class of domain-specific models.

Having presented a model of expertise and illustrated its use in expert system development, we now need to address the question of why such a model should be employed.

Reasons for Wanting Model-based Development Methodologies

There are a number of reasons why a model-based expert system development methodology might be preferred to a rival, with respect to both the efficiency of the system development process, and the verification of the target system. In this section, we shall briefly canvas some of these considerations; however, we should begin by showing what advantages and disadvantages alternative types of methodology can have.

Alternatives to Model-Based Methodologies

There are only two well-articulated alternatives to model-based system development. The first group of methodologies is based around the notion of *rapid prototyping* (Buchanan, Barstow, Bechtel, Bennett, Clancey, Kulikowski, Mitchell and Waterman 1983; Waterman 1986). On the basis of a few discussions with the expert, the knowledge engineer will build a small running prototype of the target system. This can then be tested by the expert. It will, of course, turn out to be faulty in some respects, and the expert will locate these faults. On the basis of her report, the knowledge engineer can then program another prototype, incorporating the expert's comments; the expert will then test this system, and so on.

Rapid prototyping does have a number of advantages. In the first place, the expert does get a sense of how her expertise will be presented. It is important for the expert to critique the knowledge engineer's interpretation and representation of her expertise, and this can be difficult if she only has a mathematical or logical description at which to look; rapid prototyping can obviously avoid this latter pitfall.

Secondly, rapid prototyping can be useful when there is a hierarchical organization of experts. It is often the case that the time of the experts high up in the organization is too expensive and precious for them to give full attention to an expert system development project. Rapid prototyping allows a system to be built quickly with the minimum of fuss. After the main expert has given his or her input at the early stage, the experts lower down can then attend to the fine tuning of the system in later iterations of the methodology. Or, alternatively, those lower down the hierarchy can supply the basic information and structure, while the main expert adds his or her special contribution in fine detail. Further, the process of rapid prototyping is simple to execute and understand.

Hence there are good reasons to use a rapid prototyping methodology. However, there are also a number of disadvantages. For example, if a system is built around a prototype, the possibility may arise of redundant code remaining in the system. There may be difficulties in maintenance, since the need to develop prototype systems quickly can lead to a preponderance of "hacks" as opposed to well-motivated code. Most importantly, rapid prototyping provides little guidance for the knowledge engineer; it tells him to build a series of systems, but not how.

The other alternative to using a model-based development methodology is to use a "deep model," a highly detailed and accurate model of the underlying causal relationships between the various concepts relevant to the domain. The idea is that the surface, context-relative knowledge which constitutes the operational expertise would be derived by the system from "first principles," rather than merely used or articulated (Keravnou and Washbrook 1989).

The deep model paradigm may represent a future for expert system development, but at present it is not poised to take over from standard or "shallow" model-based development. Pragmatically, the loss in efficiency in representing knowledge of the domain at a deep level is too great for such systems to be practicable in the short to medium term.

What is more important is that such systems, by explicitly not representing the context-dependent, functional but fallible abstractions on which expertise often relies (Agnew, Ford and Hayes 1994), fail to represent expert knowledge. Such a "deep" expert system would actually be a model of the domain, rather than of the expertise, and hence the psychological results in which we are interested would not necessarily be forthcoming.

Expert System Development as Model Refinement

Model-based development methodologies score over their rivals by having a clear methodological story about expert system development from establishment of user requirements down to implementation. At each stage, the transformations—from requirements to conceptual model, from conceptual model to design model, and from design model to code—are relatively well-understood. Once the knowledge engineer knows (from the user requirements) what the system is supposed to do, what task it is supposed to perform and with whom it is supposed to interact, he can then construct with the expert a model of her expertise that would be sufficient to support the intended capabilities of the system. Transformation of the conceptual model to a design model, and transformation of that to a functioning system, should be relatively straightforward. Hence the problem of building the system specified in the user requirements is broken down into a series of smaller, better-understood, steps.

Knowledge Acquisition

Another advantage of model-based methodologies is that knowledge acquisition (KA) can be facilitated. A dangerous temptation is to see the "expertise" as some sort of mechanism causally underlying the performance of the expert, which just has to be retrieved and encoded to get the system going (e.g., Feigenbaum and McCorduck 1984, seem to have succumbed to this temptation). However, as the above discussion (and many other chapters in this volume) indicates, expertise itself is often as constructed as the expert's performance; it cannot legitimately be seen as some more or less complex collection of "nuggets" to be "mined" out of the expert's head. Rather, the expert and the knowledge engineer together have to construct a view of the expertise.

This exercise is more problematic than one might hope, and KA can be both time-consuming and labour intensive. All types of expert system development methodology have to crawl through this process, and model-based methodologies do not offer any panaceas. However, the advantage that model-based methodologies do have is that they make a clear separation between the expertise required to do the task and the knowledge required for the system to run successfully. The knowledge engineer finds himself with a model of the expertise without worrying too much at that stage about how this expertise is to be deployed.

Added to which, the models built by knowledge engineers can act as useful structural principles for KA. For instance, if a knowledge engineer has decided that the inference structure of the expertise is, say, heuristic classification (figure 2), then, since that structure indexes the domain knowledge for him in its roles (boxes) and inference steps (ovals), it actually tells him what to look for: observables, findings, abstraction rules connecting observables and findings, a hierarchical structure of more or less abstract solutions or diagnoses, matching rules connecting findings and abstract solutions, and refinement rules for navigating through the solution hierarchy. Anything else will not be relevant. Clearly this will not solve all KA problems, but it does mean at least that some strategic decisions in KA (i.e., what to look for, and how) will be made, thereby speeding up the development process.

Explanation

It is vital that expert systems be able to explain their output to their users; if they do not, then they may not be used (cf. Davis 1987, pp. 19-20). To dramatize this, if a medical expert system recommends that the patient's leg be amputated, it is crucial to distinguish between the system's functioning correctly and the system's producing garbage courtesy of a bug in the code. Hence the system needs to produce a verifiable rationalization of its output. Chandrasekaran, Tanner and Josephson (1989) discuss the historical evolution of this idea, and its implementation. The key word is "rationalization." What is essential in the general case is that the user comes to understand, at a relatively deep level, how the system's recommendation came to be made. In this, of course, expert systems are no different from experts.[1]

What follows from this is that the system cannot take its own structure for granted. For example, the developers of the pioneering system MYCIN had the good idea of enabling the system to give a rule trace of its activity (Davis 1982). This had the effect of explaining the output in terms of the rule-based knowledge that was stored in the knowledge base, together with the goals driving the inferences.

This is a perfectly legitimate type of explanation in a number of circumstances. However, for many classes of user, the presentation of the knowledge solely in terms of the (very fine-grained) rules in the knowledge base would be too cryptic and detailed, and therefore unconfirmable—the explanation would fail to convince its intended audience. The explanation would be better couched at a conceptual level, and this would only be possible if the system had access to a representation of its high-level problem-solving strategies. In other words, the expert system's explanation of its output should be similar to the expert's own explanation/justification of her behaviour. This is a major insight behind NEOMYCIN's explanation strategy (Clancey 1983).

In this respect, model-based expert systems have a natural advantage. The implementation shares many aspects of its structure with the conceptual model, thanks to the structure-preserving nature of the model refinement steps. Hence the high-level strategies that the system uses are likely to be reflected in the conceptual model. But the conceptual model is merely a model of expertise—it is largely based on the expert's own account of her behaviour. Therefore it is relatively easy in many cases to connect actions of the system with the original expertise, by following the transformation from conceptual model through design model to implementation.

Efficiency

Another advantage of model-based systems is that their development affords potential long-term gains in efficiency. In many ways, these gains are traded off against the gains in efficiency made possible by other types of methodology such as rapid prototyping, although the life-cycle models of most model-based development methodologies include a prototyping dimension, and so can capitalize on some of the advantages of rapid prototyping. A model-based system will never be up and running very quickly, as a rapid prototype must be. But since each aspect of implementation has an ancestor in the conceptual model, it is easier to avoid redundancies in the code (assuming no redundancy in the model!) (e.g., Dillon and Tan 1993, p. 16).

Furthermore, as we have already noted, the model's inference structure can be used to index the domain knowledge, thereby aiding knowledge acquisition. This argument can be carried further, since the knowledge base of the target system itself can also be indexed by the inference structure. To each role and inference step in the structure would correspond a partition in the knowledge base. Hence, when inference is performed by the system, the finding of relevant rules or data required for continuing the inference is facilitated by the principled organization of the rules and data in those partitions. Fensel and Straatman (1996) and O'Hara and Shadbolt (1996) debate the various ways in which different model-based methodologies can aid efficiency.

As an example, figure 4 shows how backward chaining could be speeded up by exploitation of indexing in accordance with inference structure. At the foot of the figure we have a simple fragment of an inference structure, which gives a single inference step (match) and its context (findings and abstract solutions). Related to the items in this inference structure are three partitions of the system's knowledge base, each containing relevant pieces of knowledge. At the top of the figure we are shown a simple control structure for backward chaining (i.e., reasoning in reverse from a hypothesis to be proved). The knowledge base might be potentially very large; for instance, imagine the complete model containing, say, ten similar fragments, each based around an inference step. In that case, then, the inference structure-based partitioning of the knowledge base might well cut down the search time by an order of magnitude.

Verification, Validation and Maintenance

Before an expert system can be released either commercially or in sensitive environments, it is essential that it is verified (it is proven to conform to the specification) and validated (the specification is shown to meet the user re-

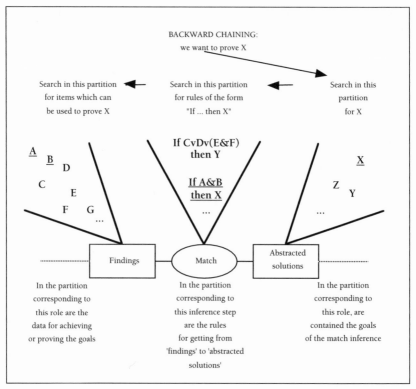

Figure 4. Using the inference structure of the conceptual model to partition (index) the knowledge base.

quirements). Bugs must be located and eradicated. This can be difficult, because there may well be bugs in the way that the knowledge has been represented, not just in the code. The separation of model development into a conceptual modelling phase, a design phase and an implementation phase can be an advantage for verification and validation. This is achieved by making a clear conceptual distinction between the representation of knowledge or expertise, the design of the system, and the building of the system on the basis of the design. Hence errors in knowledge representation, faulty design, and buggy code can each be isolated and treated independently of each other (Tansley and Hayball 1993).

As a simple example, consider the room allocation system described in Motta, O'Hara and Shadbolt (1994). This system was intended to allocate people to offices under a series of constraints, and to find an optimal solution without backtracking. The original conceptual model was only 80% correct with respect to the test data, since certain orderings of the data resulted in an incomplete allocation. On occasion, the system was left with two people who were debarred from sharing an office by some mutual incompatibility, and only one office. The division of the effort into conceptual modelling, design and implementation enabled the problem to be identified as a modelling problem. The code itself faithfully implemented the design, and the design mapped onto the model. The fault had to be in the original conceptualization of the domain, and it was discovered that an implicit constraint had been overlooked. Once the conceptual model had been corrected, the changes rippled through the various other stages (i.e., the parts of the design or code that were connected to the faulty part of the model were rewritten) and the bug was excised (Motta *et al.* 1994, pp. 339-340). The model-based methodology doesn't make finding a bug trivial, but it helps to know that its source was conceptual.

Further, this point is equally applicable when the completed and operational system is maintained. The three-way distinction helps service engineers understand the operation of large expert systems in the same way as with debugging (e.g., Tansley and Hayball 1993, p. 18).

Archiving and Reuse

Finally, since the building of the system is a separate phase of development from the modelling phase, it follows that a more general conceptual model can be used to build more than one system. For example, one could imagine a system to diagnose disease in environments where an expert could not be assumed to be available, a second system to aid an expert diagnostician, and a third system to train novice diagnosticians all being built from the same conceptual model of an expert diagnostician. The expertise itself can be held in a model relatively independently of the uses to which the model might be put. Furthermore, no matter how many systems are built, the conceptual model will remain as an archival record of the expertise that an organization holds.

Hence a system developer would only need to acquire the task-specific knowledge for his system from scratch. For the rest, the system could interact with systems containing shared knowledge bases, facilitating the building of larger and cheaper systems. To this end, standardization of knowledge representation languages, interfaces, and the like, is being pursued by the Knowledge-Sharing Initiative (Neches, Fikes, Finin, Gruber, Patil, Senator and Swartout 1991).

Conceptual Models as Explanations

We have argued that model-based methodologies can be useful for expert system development. We don't claim that they solve every problem. Indeed they sometimes create extra problems, such as the extra time required to produce a model that is saved in rapid prototyping. But the main point is that there is a central class of problems associated with expert system development that model-based methodologies can ameliorate, and as a result of that, increasingly many systems are being developed—in real-world contexts—in a model-based way.

Our claim is that the conceptual models—the models of expertise—built as part of the development process can be useful to psychologists by *explaining* the expertise modelled. However, this claim is often misunderstood, and it is important to get its content clear. In this final section, we will first discuss which notion of explanation we are relying upon, and then discuss how that notion applies to the conceptual models of expert systems. A defence of this position is given at length in O'Hara (1994).

Functional Analysis as Explanation

It is important to realize that there are various types of explanation, not all of which are appropriate in particular circumstances. As a result of the large influence of Hempel's deductive-nomological model of explanation (1965), in which an explanation is said to involve the logical deduction of the explanandum from a set of initial conditions and covering laws, many have assumed that explanation is an act of deduction. Others have tried to assimilate all explanation to an account of the causal antecedents of the event to be explained (Lewis 1986).

Both these types of explanation are valid in many areas. However, contrary to some of the stronger claims, they do not exhaust the possibilities. In particular, explanations do not take place in a vacuum; they are accounts of events or processes that are produced for purposes and for audiences. Any attempt to insist rigidly that all explanations fit these patterns is likely to fall foul of this pragmatic constraint (Achinstein 1983).

One type of explanation that is not one of these types is the functional analysis of dispositions (Cummins 1975). This type of explanation applies to a dispositional regularity, which is particularly resistant to explanations of the deductive and the causal types. Because such regularities are dispositional, they will not necessarily be universal. If an object is disposed to d, it cannot be assumed that it will always d. For example, a gun may be disposed to fire a shell over 1 kilometer, but it may fall short once in a while. Because such regularities are not universal, that makes them very difficult to subsume under covering laws according to the deductive-nomological model. And the individual manifestations of a disposition may have many varying and unrepeatable causes, which will make a lawlike causal account impossible (Jackson and Pettit 1990).

The analytical strategy deals with the difficulty by taking the complex dispositional process d, and analysing it into a series of other dispositional processes $d1,\ldots, dn,$ such that (a) each of the di are less complex and better understood, and (b) the $di,$ when carried out in a suitably programmed or connected way, will be equivalent to the performance of $d.$ In other words, the process to be explained is broken down into a set of individual steps, each of which is better understood. Cummins (1983) shows how such an analytical strategy has a long and distinguished tradition in cognitive psychology.

Our claim is that a conceptual model of some expertise is a functional analysis of that expertise as defined by Cummins (1975). In this case, the expertise itself is the complex disposition. It is dispositional, not deterministic; the expert will not always give the same response to the same input, and will not always exercise her expertise successfully. The disposition, unanalysed, is difficult to understand for the outsider. The purpose of the conceptual model is to break down the complex inference into a series of smaller and better-understood steps.

The domain layer of the model shows how domain-based inferences are made. The inference layer shows how inference types are put together to make larger inference structures. For example, in heuristic classification, a complex classification inference is analysed into a series of three inferences, an abstraction, a heuristic match, and a refinement of a coarse classification. Each of the three minor inference steps is relatively transparent, as opposed to the coarse-grained classification from observables to solution. The task layer shows how a practitioner marshalls such inferences to solve particular tasks (i.e., it analyses high level tasks in terms of particular inferences). All these three layers contribute towards an analysis of the expertise.

We can also see how such an account of expertise is perfectly designed for its audience. Conceptual models are aimed primarily at knowledge engineers who have to design and build a functioning system that will reproduce the expert's performance. The beauty of this type of explanation is that the expertise itself is opaque; there is no simple, easily capturable function to take the system from input to output. However, when the conceptual model has broken the expertise down into a number of individual steps, those individual steps are likely to be easier to reproduce. The task and inference layers of the model should tell the knowledge engineer how to combine those individual steps to recreate the expertise.

The conceptual model is not all that the knowledge engineer needs to know; the design phase of development will impose further considerations of efficiency, etc. But it has explained the expertise in terms of simpler steps. Given that a conceptual model is explanatory in this way, our final task is to examine the effect of the context of the model on the evaluation of its explanatoriness.

Explanation and Context

It is important to note that the extent to which a conceptual model is explanatory of expertise is limited by the scope of the expert system as set out in the user requirements. In particular, the requirements, by setting out strict limits to the ambit of the system, restrict the explanatory value of the models produced during development to the context of use of the system.

This contextualized understanding of the expertise manifests itself in a number of ways.

- The explanation provided by the conceptual model takes a certain set of primitive inferences and domain objects. These inferences and objects are chosen, ideally, because they can be a basis for computational development, and they are irreducible. The point of functional analysis explanations is that the complex top level disposition is analysed into more basic dispositions. Hence the conceptual model will only be explanatory for someone for whom the primitives of the explanation are not themselves in need of explanation.

- The target system will be intended to solve a range of tasks in a range of contexts. Hence the conceptual model cannot be expected always to explain the expertise as it operates in different tasks or in different contexts (although it may provide such an explanation).

- The target system's operation will make assumptions about the world which need not always hold. Certain types of data will not be usable by the system. This is the problem of brittleness; a human expert can adapt relatively easily to new circumstances, whereas an expert system will often be unable to cope. Hence the explanatory value of the conceptual model will vary with the type of data that the expertise is expected to operate on.

- The human expertise will be integrated into a whole set of cognitive abilities and functions in the expert (e.g., the expert will be able to make jokes using her expertise). The conceptual model, by contrast, explains the expertise in isolation from the expert's other abilities.

It can therefore be seen that the conceptual model does not provide a context-free explanation of the expertise, either in the sense of an explanation that is explanatory in all contexts, or in the sense of an explanation of the operation of the expertise in all contexts. Context is limited by the scope of the expert system, in terms of both the context of use of the system and the context of operation of the expertise.

Indeed, this brittleness of the explanation is an essential aspect of it. The performance limitations of an expert system must be clear to users; a system which operates flexibly across contexts may seduce its users into using it outside its intended context of operation. Generally speaking, it is better that performance degrades dramatically, to restrict use of the system to areas in which its performance is guaranteed to be reliable.

Hence a conceptual model will not provide the whole explanatory story about expertise. But then, it is not clear that any type of explanation could achieve that. Different audiences require different generalizations, different primitives, and different assumptions from their explanations. A conceptual model will provide adequate explanation to anyone who requires a functional decomposition of the operation of the expertise over well-defined data sets for well-defined tasks. There are many other aspects to the psychological study of expertise, but, we feel, such a decomposition is an important step in the understanding of the operation of expertise.

Acknowledgments

This chapter has grown out of two papers ("Conceptual Models, Competence Models and Psychological Explanation" by Kieron O'Hara, and "Interpreting Generic Task Structures" by Kieron O'Hara and Nigel Shadbolt) presented at the Third International Workshop on Human and Machine Cognition, Seaside, Florida, May 13-15, 1993. We would like to thank the participants at the workshop whose contributions have aided the development of the paper. Particular thanks are due to Robert Hoffman and Martin Davies.

Note

Interestingly, this point may well bear heavily on the notion of an expert's *constituency* (Agnew, Ford and Hayes 1994). Society does provide a number of relatively neutral contexts in which experts may well have to justify themselves (e.g., courts of law). Some theorists have argued that it is essential in a democratic society that expertise is justifiable in such a forum (e.g., Feyerabend 1978). Agnew *et al.*'s informal ranking of experts from snake oil salesmen up (down?) to computer scientists does seem to reflect the extent to which such experts could justify their own output in such neutral contexts.

References

Achinstein, P. (1983). *The Nature of Explanation*. Oxford: Oxford University Press.

Agnew, N.M., Ford, K.M. & Hayes, P.J. (1994). Expertise in context: personally constructed, socially selected and reality-relevant? *International Journal of Expert Systems, 7*, 65-88.

Benjamins, R. (1993). *Problem solving methods for diagnosis*. Ph.D. thesis. Amsterdam: University of Amsterdam.

Breuker, J. & Wielinga, B. (1989). Models of expertise in knowledge acquisition. In A. Guida and T. Tasso (Eds.), *Topics in Expert System Design* (pp. 265-296). Amsterdam: Elsevier.

Breuker, J., Wielinga, B.J., van Someren, M., de Hoog, R., Schreiber, G., de Greef, P., Bredeweg, B., Wielmaker, J., Billault, J.-P., Davoodi, M. & Hayward, S. (1987) *Model driven knowledge acquisition: interpretation models* (KADS project deliverable AI). Amsterdam: Dept. of Social Science Informatics, University of Amsterdam.

Buchanan, B.G., Barstow, D., Bechtel, R., Bennett, J., Clancey, W., Kulikowski, C., Mitchell, T. & Waterman, D.A. (1983). Constructing an expert system. In F. Hayes-

Roth, D.A. Waterman & D.B. Lenat (Eds.), *Building Expert Systems* (pp. 127-168). Reading, MA: Addison Wesley.

Buchanan, B.G. & Feigenbaum, E.A. (1978). DENDRAL and Meta-DENDRAL: their applications dimension. *Artificial Intelligence, 11,* 5-24.

Chandrasekaran, B. (1983). Towards a taxonomy of problem solving types. *AI Magazine, 4(1),* 9-17.

Chandrasekaran, B., Tanner, M.C. & Josephson, J.R. (1989). Explaining control strategies in problem solving. *IEEE Expert, 4,* 9-24.

Clancey, W.J. (1983). The epistemology of a rule-based expert system—a framework for explanation. *Artificial Intelligence, 20,* 215-251.

Clancey, W.J. (1985). Heuristic classification. *Artificial Intelligence, 27,* 289-350.

Cummins, R. (1975). Functional analysis. *Journal of Philosophy, 72,* 741-764.

Cummins, R. (1983). *The Nature of Psychological Explanation.* Cambridge, MA: MIT Press.

Davis, R. (1982). Teiresias: applications of meta-level knowledge. In R. Davis & D.B. Lenat (Eds.), *Knowledge-Based Systems in Artificial Intelligence* (pp. 227-490). New York: McGraw-Hill.

Davis, R. (1987). Knowledge-based systems: the view in 1986. In: W.E.L. Grimson & R.S. Patil (Eds.), *AI in the 1980s and Beyond* (pp. 13-41). Cambridge, MA: MIT Press.

Dillon, T. & Tan, P.H. (1993). *Object-Oriented Conceptual Modelling.* Sydney: Prentice-Hall.

Feigenbaum, E.A. & McCorduck, P. (1984). *The Fifth Generation* (rev. ed.). Reading, MA: Addison Wesley.

Fensel, D. & Straatman, R. (1996). Problem-solving methods: making assumptions for efficiency reasons. In N. Shadbolt, K. O'Hara & G. Schreiber (Eds.), *Advances in Knowledge Acquisition* (pp. 17-32). Berlin: Springer-Verlag.

Feyerabend, P.K. (1978). *Science in a Free Society.* London: New Left Books.

Gaschnig, J. (1982). PROSPECTOR: an expert system for mineral exploration. In D. Michie (Ed.), *Introductory Readings in Expert Systems* (pp. 47-64). New York: Gordon & Breach.

Genesereth, M.R. (1979). The role of plans in automated consultation. In *Proceedings of IJCAI-79* (pp. 311-319). San Mateo, CA: Morgan Kaufman.

Hempel, C.G. (1965). *Aspects of Scientific Explanation.* New York: Free Press.

Jackson, F. & Pettit, P. (1990). Program explanation: a general perspective. *Analysis, 50,* 107-117.

Jackson, P. (1990). *Introduction to Expert Systems* (2nd ed.). Reading, MA: Addison-Wesley.

Karbach, W., Linster, M. & Voss, A. (1990). Model-based approaches: One label—one idea? In B. Wielinga, J. Boose, B. Gaines, G. Schreiber & M. van Someren (Eds.), *Current Trends in Knowledge Acquisition* (pp. 173-189). Amsterdam: IOS Press.

Keravnou, E.T. & Washbrook, J. (1989). What is a deep expert system? An analysis of the architectural requirements of second-generation expert systems. *The Knowledge Engineering Review, 4,* 205-233.

Lewis, D. (1986). Causal explanation. In D.-H. Ruben (Ed.), *Explanation* (pp. 182-206). Oxford: Oxford University Press.

McDermott, J. (1980). *R1: A rule-based configurer of computer systems* (Research rep. CMU-CS-80-119). Dept. of Computer Science, Carnegie-Mellon University, Pittsburgh, PA.

Motta, E., O'Hara, K. & Shadbolt, N. (1994). Grounding GDMs: a structured case study. *International Journal of Human-Computer Studies, 40,* 315-347.

Motta, E., Rajan, T., Domingue, J. & Eisenstadt, M. (1991). Methodological foundations of KEATS, the knowledge engineers' assistant. *Knowledge Acquisition, 3,* 21-47.

Neches, R., Fikes, R., Finin, T., Gruber, T., Patil, R., Senator, T. & Swartout, W.R. (1991). Enabling technology for knowledge sharing. *AI Magazine, 5(3),* 36-56.

O'Hara, K. (1994). *Mind as machine: can computational processes be regarded as explanatory of mental processes?* D.Phil. thesis. Oxford: Worcester College, Oxford.

O'Hara, K. & Shadbolt, N. (1996). The thin end of the wedge: efficiency and the generalised directive model methodology. In N. Shadbolt, K. O'Hara & G. Schreiber (Eds.), *Advances in Knowledge Acquisition* (pp. 33-47). Berlin: Springer-Verlag.

Shadbolt, N. (Ed.). (1989). Expert systems—a natural history. In *Research and Development in Expert Systems VI* (pp. 1-11). Cambridge: Cambridge University Press.

Shadbolt, N., Motta, E. & Rouge, A. (1993). Constructing knowledge based systems. *IEEE Software, 10(6),* 34-38.

Shortliffe, E.H. (1976). *Computer-Based Medical Consultations: MYCIN.* New York: Elsevier.

Shortliffe, E.H., Axline, S.G., Buchanan, B.G., Merigan, T.C. & Cohen, S.N. (1973). An artificial intelligence program to advise physicians regarding antimicrobial therapy. *Computers and Biomedical Research, 6,* 544-560.

Stefik, M., Aikins, J., Balzer, R., Benoit, J., Birnbaum, L., Hayes-Roth, F. & Sacerdoti, E. (1983). The architecture of expert systems. In F. Hayes-Roth, D.A. Waterman & D.B. Lenat (Eds.), *Building Expert Systems* (pp. 59-86). Reading, MA: Addison Wesley.

Szolovits, P. (1987). Expert systems tools and techniques: past, present and future. In W.E.L. Grimson & R.S. Patil (Eds.), *AI in the 1980s and Beyond* (pp. 43-74). Cambridge, MA: MIT Press.

Szolovits, P. & Parker, S.G. (1978). Categorical and probabilistic reasoning in medical diagnosis. *Artificial Intelligence, 11,* 115-144.

Tansley, D.S.W. & Hayball, C.C. (1993). *Knowledge-Based Systems Analysis and Design: A KADS Developer's Handbook.* New York: Prentice-Hall.

Van Melle, W. (1979). A domain-independent production-rule system for consultation programs. In *Proceedings of IJCAI-79* (pp. 923-925). San Mateo, CA: Morgan Kaufman.

Van Melle, W., Shortliffe, E.H. & Buchanan, B.G. (1984). EMYCIN: A knowledge engineer's tool for constructing rule-based expert systems. In B. Buchanan & E. Shortliffe (Eds.), *Rule-Based Expert Systems* (pp. 302-328). New York: Addison-Wesley.

Waterman, D.A. (1986). *A Guide to Expert Systems.* Reading, MA: Addison Wesley.

Weiss, S.M., Kulikowski, C.A., Amarel, S. & Safir, A. (1978). A model-based method for computer-aided medical decision-making. *Artificial Intelligence, 11,* 145-172.

Wielinga, B.J., Schreiber, A.T. & Breuker, J.A. (1992). KADS: A modelling approach to knowledge engineering. *Knowledge Acquisition, 4,* 5-53.

CHAPTER 14

A Study of Solution Quality in Human Expert and Knowledge-Based System Reasoning

Caroline Clarke Hayes

Introduction

It is difficult to find useful metrics for evaluating knowledge-based systems (KBS's). Furthermore, there may be several relevant ways in which to evaluate a system. This chapter presents a study in which a method is developed for evaluating the experience level of a KBS, and the quality of the solutions it produces relative to those produced by humans with various levels of experience. Additionally, the method allows one to put an upper and lower bound on the estimated experience level of the KBS.

The objective of this work is to provide a measure that allows one to answer the question, "How expert is my expert system?" Just as grade school children are given achievement tests to assist in determining at what grade-level they are performing, one can consider this method to be a type of achievement test for knowledge-based systems. Most literature on KBS evaluation deals with validation, verification, and testing (VVT) (Nazareth and Kennedy 1993) in which the primary concern is with the correctness of a knowledge-based system and other properties such as circularity, inconsistency, and redundancy in the databases and rulebases. Other KBS evaluations address properties such as modifiability, ease of use, and cost (Lane 1986; Liebowitz 1986). Although correct solutions and consistency of knowledge-bases are important, these properties alone may not be sufficient to make a system useful; solution quality and the range of problems the system can solve are also crucial in determining a system's overall competence. The work reported here addresses the problem of measuring system competence as a function of solution quality.

This method is an advancement over more approximate metrics used in earlier work (Hayes 1990) in which the experience level of a KBS was also estimated by comparing the quality of the solutions it produced to those of human experts. This method allowed the experience level of the KBS to be approximated by determining that its performance was higher than one particular expert but lower than another particular expert. However, without knowing whether these particular experts were skilled or unskilled relative to their peers, it was hard to say how accurate the experience estimate for the system was. The method presented in this chapter produces a precise experience interval for the KBS which bounds the experience estimate. It does so by constructing a function to describe the relationship between experience and solution quality for a group of subjects. Since solution quality is often hard to quantify by automated methods, this method utilizes human experts' abilities to judge solution quality.

Overview of the Chapter

The method is demonstrated on a particular KBS system, Machinist, which is designed to automatically generate manufacturing plans when given a description of a metal part and the material from which it is to be made. In addition to information on the skill level of the KBS, this study also yields some insights concerning the differences between inexperienced and experienced human machinists and the changes they undergo in development. Human machinists are highly skilled individuals. Machinists report that it may require as much as 8 to 10 years of intensive practice to achieve master level status. This is consistent with developments of skill in other complex tasks such as musical composition and painting (Hayes 1985).

The Domain of Machining

Machining is the art of shaping metal with a variety of tools. The task addressed in this work involves shaping metal parts on a computer numeric controlled (CNC) machining center. A machining center is a machine tool that can perform a variety of different types of machining operations such as drilling, milling, or reaming. CNC machine tools use computer programming to control the motion of the tool and workpiece. In contrast, older style manually controlled machine tools, developed before World War II (and still commonly in use today), control the motion of the cutting tool through a set of manually operated levers that either raise or lower the tool, move the workpiece forward and backward, or from side to side. CNC control allows more complicated and precise motions of the tool and workpiece than does the older manual-style control.

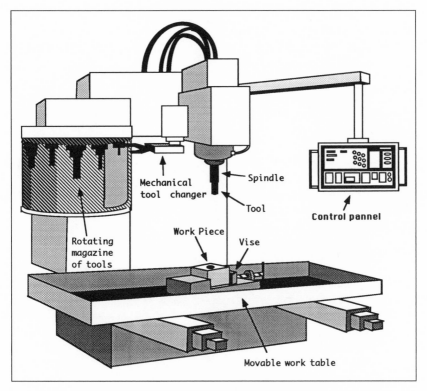

Figure 1. A three-axis vertical machining center.

Figure 1 shows a CNC machining center. The spindle holds and drives the tool. On the left-hand side is a rotating magazine holding a variety of types and sizes of tools. There is a mechanical tool changer which can automatically take tools from the magazine and load them in the spindle. The machinist can run the machine tool either by typing commands into the control panel on the right-hand side or by down-loading a program from another computer. The workpiece is shown clamped in a vise, which is mounted on a movable work table.

Figure 2 shows an example of a product that can be created on the machining center. This part starts out as a solid rectangular block of metal, and a series of machining steps is used to cut away various volumes from the part. Each volume that is removed by one process (or a tightly related set of several processes) is called a feature. The part depicted in Figure 2 has eight features: four holes, a pocket, two angles, and a slot. Features represent subgoals in the machining task.

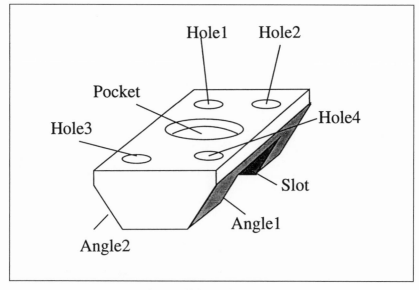

Figure 2. A part that could be made on the machining center.

Architecture of the Machinist System

Figure 3 shows a simplified version of the architecture of the Machinist system, which automatically generates machining plans (Hayes 1990; Hayes and Wright 1989). This architecture is modeled after the behavior of expert machinists. Some of the special properties of this problem solver are that it uses a search strategy called LCOS (Least Commitment to Operator Selection) (Hayes 1996). In this strategy, several alternative operators are enumerated for each of the goals in the problem. Once all goals have been explored, then selections of operations to satisfy specific goals are made. This can be contrasted to a depth first search (DFS) operator selection strategy in which operators are selected based on information local to the particular goal being examined. Commitments to particular operator selections are changed through backtracking only if a globally consistent solution cannot be found. The DFS strategy will generate the first feasible solution found, which is not necessarily a highly efficient solution. The advantage of the LCOS approach is that it allows operator selections to be made which utilize global problem information. The LCOS strategy is important in problem solving situations where overall solution efficiency is important. Another property of interest in the Machinist architecture is that operator descriptions and instantiations are formulated by a process of successive refinement, reminiscent of the process used by MOLGEN (Stefik 1980) but more flexible. However, operators in Machinist are constructed from descriptions of the effectors that create actions.

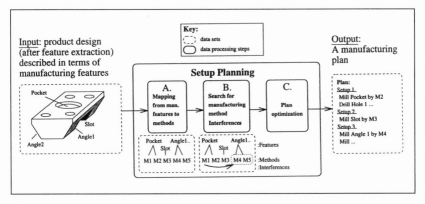

Figure 3. A simplified diagram of the Machinist System's architecture.

Input. The input to the system is a description of a product as a rectangular block with an x, y and z dimension, and a list of features which much be cut away from the block in order to make the part. East feature's description specifies its feature-type (hole, pocket, slot, etc.), location, and orientation.

Output. The output is a plan consisting of an ordered list of setups. A setup represents a major plan step. Each setup specifies one clamping operation and one or more cutting operations. Each time the clamps are changed it is considered to be a new setup. Human machinists often use the number of setups in the plan as an estimate of the cost. Figure 4 shows an example of a setup: a rectangular part is shown clamped in a vise. Several blocks of metal, called parallels, may be inserted underneath the part (like the phone book under a small child at the dinner table) to lift the part up to the right height in the vise. As depicted, the part in figure 4 does not yet have shapes cut into it.

The Machinist system's task (and the machinist's task) is to select, sequence, and organize manufacturing operations into setups to create a step-by-step plan that is capable of producing a specified part with a given set of tools. Such a manufacturing plan is often called a setup plan, and the task of creating it is called setup planning. Creating a setup plan requires a great deal of expertise. Solutions produced must be feasible, reliable, and efficient. Machinists must accurately select appropriate manufacturing steps for each situation, detect interactions between steps, and understand how to optimize solutions. This process requires numerous skills that are acquired through years of experience.

There are three major challenges in setup planning. The first challenge (represented by box A in figure 3) is to determine what manufacturing methods can create each of the features. One or more methods must be consid-

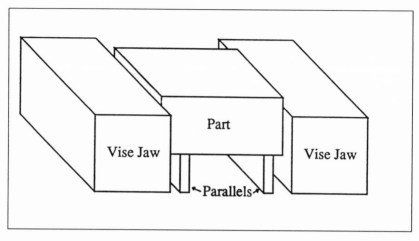

Figure 4. A setup using the vise and two parallels.

ered for each feature in order to make plan optimizations possible later.

The second challenge (represented by box B in figure 3) is to make a plan that avoids interference between plan steps (i.e., setups). Sometimes performing one step will make it difficult or impossible to perform other steps later in the plan. For example, figure 5 shows a clamping interference between the angles and the holes. The vise jaws will slip if they clamp on the angles located on the left and right sides of the part, making it difficult to drill the holes. However, this interference can be avoided by intelligently ordering the methods so that the holes are cut first, and then the angles. The difficulty is in identifying the interferences and ordering the steps to avoid them.

The third challenge (represented by box C in figure 3) is to create a plan that is of high quality (produces highly accurate products), yet is efficient (few steps, and low-cost). Some operations can share work among them. For example, two manufacturing operations, such as drilling Hole1 and Hole2, may share work between them if the operations are executed one right after the other. If the holes have the same diameter then the same drill can be used to drill both of them. The work of one tool change can be saved if Hole1 and Hole2 are performed in sequence. Likewise, since both holes are on the same side of the part they can both use the same clamping arrangement. The work of setting up the clamps for the second hole can also be saved. Searching for work-sharing opportunities by carefully selecting and sequencing operations can result in large cost savings in the plan.

The Machinist architecture provides the mechanisms to meet these challenges and produce feasible manufacturing plans. However, it was not clear initially what the level of quality of those plans was. The machinists infor-

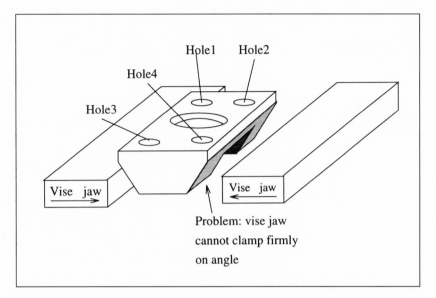

Figure 5. An interaction between features.

mally commented that they were pretty good, but how good was pretty good? Were the plans as good as those produced by experts or were they only as good as those produced by apprentices? It was important to know the answer if Machinist is to be used as a tool to aid machinists in planning. The level of quality of the plans determines how it can be used.

Background for the Present Project

The present study arose from the desire to measure the quality and experience level of Machinist. Initially, a prototype of the Machinist system was implemented to test the basic problem-solving approach and system architecture. However, before pushing ahead with a major effort to improve the system, the basic soundness of the approach had to be evaluated. In other words, if the best solutions produced by the system were of low quality, then it might be best to revamp the basic approach. However, if the plans produced proved to be of high quality, development of the current approach could be continued.

The task of measuring solution quality proved difficult for a number of reasons. The initial approach applied to the Machinist program utilized a scoring method which provided a numeric estimate of solution quality. In devising this scoring method, it was deemed desirable to utilize the same component factors utilized by human experts. Some of the major criteria included solution feasibility, cost, and reliability. A function consisting of a weighted sum of these factors was composed. This approach proved to be inadequate, in that the quality and feasibility ratings produced by this function did not agree well with experts' assessments. Furthermore, after revising the function several times, it became apparent that an accurate function would be very difficult to construct because accurate computation of the component factors (feasibility, cost and reliability) presented a formidable challenge. For example, with sufficient effort and cost data, solution cost can be fairly accurately estimated (within 10% of the true value) (Hetem 1994). However, solution reliability is not as easy to predict. To predict reliability for a wide range of part shapes, cuts, tooling, and fixturing arrangements, a large quantity of unavailable empirical data are required.

Eventually, the author started to question why it was necessary to devise a function to assess quality when there are already a number of apparently robust quality estimating devices available in any machine shop, that is, human experts. Thus, the initial approach of building an automated quality function was abandoned (for the time being) and human experts were utilized to assess quality. However, this approach raised a range of new questions. How closely would two or more experts agree? Would two different experts assign vastly different quality ratings to the same problem solution? How would such a difference affect quality measurements?

Method

The approach used in this work to use expert judgment in assessing the KBS's solution quality is as follows. A range of subjects at different experience levels are asked to produce manufacturing plans for several problems. The KBS is also made to produce solutions for the same problems. The plans for each problem are then rank ordered by two or more expert judges. Two or more judges are used in order to smooth out individual biases that particular judges may have. The best solutions are put at the top of the pile and the worst at the bottom. The worst solution is assigned a score of 1 and the best is assigned the highest score. Next, the average rank received by each subject is computed. If each plan produced by a subject is considered to be like each competition that a gymnast enters, then the average rank is like the gymnast's average performance over several competitions, where all scores from all judges in each competition are averaged.

These average rank data are used to produce a "skill function" that plots the experience of the subject against the average quality ranking of their solutions. This function shows for any given experience level, the quality of solutions one would expect that person to produce on average. Additionally, confidence bands constructed around this function show the expected range of variation in subjects at a given experience level. Thus, the plot looks similar to a plot of the age of children against their weight. There is a distinct relation between age and weight, but at any particular age, particular individuals will fall within a range.

To estimate the achievement level of a KBS in terms of the quality of the solutions it produces, the KBS;s average quality ranking is plugged into the equation for the skill functions, and an estimate of the KBS's experience level is produced. Thus, one can make statements such as "my KBS produces solutions equivalent in quality to those produced by humans having eight years of experience." The confidence bands can be used similarly to bound the estimate.

One might ask why not simply use the average quality ranking directly as an assessment of the skill-level of a person or KBS? The reason is that quality rankings are relative rather than absolute measures of quality. Subject A might have a higher quality ranking than subject B, but it does not really tell us how skilled or unskilled A and B are. It is necessary to map these relative comparisons onto some scale (such as experience level) to give them meaning.

Subjects

Two types of subjects were used in this study: problem solvers, who created solutions for each of the tasks, and judges, who judged the quality of each of the problem solvers' solutions.

Judges. Two expert judges were used to judge the quality of the problem solver's solutions. The judges had 15 and 18 years of experience respectively, starting from the beginning of their apprenticeships. The judges were experienced in CNC machining on a three-axis machine tool. Since the judges stated that they felt that background and training strongly influence the way in which quality judgments are made, each judge was also asked to describe his background.

The first judge had his training in a shop that produced small batches of very large parts. A typical part in this type of shop is very hard to manipulate because of its weight. Such parts require a large amount of careful machining time. If they are manufactured out of tolerance, they must be scraped or re-machined. This judge stated that reliability and accuracy of operations were the most important criteria in judging solution quality. Given the choice between having a more concise plan versus a more accurate plan, he claimed he would choose the more accurate plan rather than risk having to remake and re-manipulate the part.

The second judge received his training in a large batch production shop. In this shop, parts were mass-produced. Small amounts of wasted time on each individual part added up to a large amount of wasted time over the course of the whole batch run. This judge stated that to him, plan length was

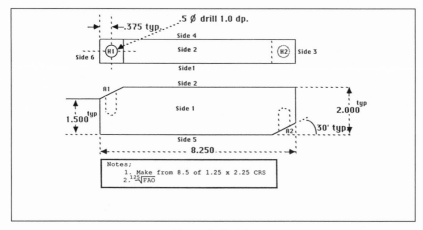

Figure 6. Part 1.

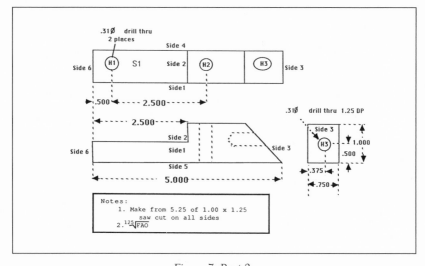

Figure 7. Part 2.

the most critical aspect of solution quality, and if he were forced to make a choice, he would prefer to sacrifice some accuracy in order to achieve a concise, low-cost plan.

Problem Solvers. Seven problem solvers were used in this study. The problem solvers came from a variety of machine shops and backgrounds, but all had three-axis CNC machining experience. These problem solvers had experience levels ranging from 2 to 10 years. Their individual experience levers were: 2, 2, 5, 5, 7, 8, and 10 years of experience. The first four years of a ma-

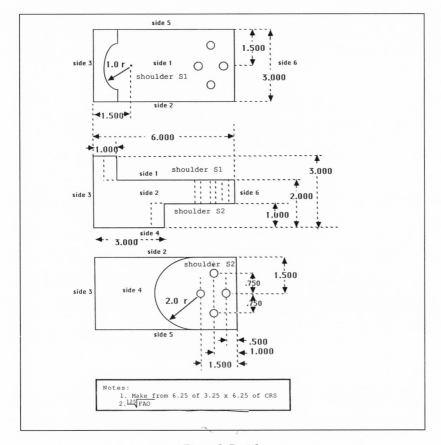

Figure 8. Part 3.

chinist's professional life are typically spent in an apprenticeship. Sometimes they spend a few years prior to apprenticeship as machine tool operators, thus they may graduate from the apprentice program after having anywhere from 4 to 8 years of total experience. Problem solvers with only two years of experience were considered novices. By 5 years of experience they are considered to be at a competent but intermediate level. Problem solvers having 7 and 8 years of experience were considered by the judges to be quite promising, but were clearly viewed as still being at an advanced intermediate stage of skill. The subject having 10 years of experience was described as an expert by the judges prior to the experiment.

Also used in this study were two versions of the KBS, Machinist: an early version, "frozen" 2 1/2 years after the start of system development, and a later version, frozen 5 1/2 years after the start of development. They were counted as the eighth and ninth "problem solvers." The early version will be labeled problem solver M1 and the later version, problem solver M2. These two programs were also used to generate manufacturing plans.

Tasks

Each problem solver (including the two versions of the KBS) was instructed to create a manufacturing plan for each of three parts shown in figures 6, 7 and 8. For each problem, the box at the bottom of each diagram contains a description of dimensions and surface properties of the stock material from which the part would be made (the initial state). None of these tasks had been used in the development of the KBS, and the KBS had not been tested previously on any of these problems. The human subjects had also not seen these problems before.

Problem solvers were told that the parts would be made on a CNC vertical machining center and that they could use standard tools and clamps that would be available in most shops. The level of detail of the plan should include all the machining and clamping operations, but it should not include programming statements, or speeds and feeds for the tool.

Procedure

The problem solvers (both human and computer) were given each of the three problems in succession (figures 6, 7 and 8). They were asked to create manufacturing plans for each of these parts. Human problem solvers were given a blueprint of the parts, and KBS's were given electronic descriptions. "Think aloud" protocols were also taken as problem solvers worked out solutions. Problem solvers were allowed to develop and modify the manufacturing plan as much as they wanted until they stated that they were done. At that point, they were shown the next problem, but they could not go back to the previous problem.

When all solutions from all problem solvers had been collected, all solutions (that is, plans) were written up in a uniform format and handwriting. The plans were sorted into three groups containing nine plans each. Each solution group contained all the solutions to one problem.

Next, each of the expert judges was asked to rank the plans in each group from best to worst. The best plan was given a score of 9 and the worst was given a score of 1. As they rated the plans, the judges made comments about the feasibility of the plans, or pointed out mistakes and suggested possible improvements. Some sample plans created by the problem solvers are shown in figures 12 and 13. These plans have been annotated in the right hand margins with both judges' comments.

Initially, the author considered asking the judges to assign quality scores (instead of ranks) indicating the absolute quality of each plan (as Olympic

Problem Solver	Years of Experience	P1	P2	P3	P1	P2	P3	Average Solution Quality Rank
S1	2	2	2	8	1	1	1	2.50
S2	2	1	1	5	2	5	5	3.17
S3	5	5	3	7	4	4	4	4.50
S4	5	3	-	4	7	-	2	4.0
S5	7	4	5	6	3	3	3	4.5
S6	8	8	8	1	8	8	7	6.67
S7	10	-	7	9	-	6	-	7.33
M1	*	6	6	3	5	2	6	4.67
M2	*	7	4	2	6	7	8	5.67

Table 1. Solution Quality

judges do). However, this approach was rejected on the grounds that machinists do not have a standard or agreed upon method for assigning quality measures to plans. Correlating the scores assigned by two judges would be difficult; on a scale from one to nine an enthusiastic judge might give many nines while a conservative judge may never give more than a seven at best. Thus, it was decided that the machinists should rank order the plans.

Results

The initial intent of the study was to examine solution quality. However, the data collected contained information on a number of other solution properties. Tables 1, 2, and 3 show the data collected on solution properties: quality, feasibility, and length for the solutions created by the various problem solvers. The length data were obtained simply by counting the number of steps (i.e., setups) in each solution. The feasibility data were obtained from the judges comments which they wrote on the plans as they ranked them. The feasibility data were an unexpected outcome of the study. Although the judges were asked only to provide quality ranking, they often provided additional information in the form of comments which they wrote on the solutions concerning errors, possible improvements, and feasibility. Table 3 summarizes their comments on feasibility.

The goal of the analysis of these data was to examine several properties of the solution (quality, length, feasibility) and to see if any were strongly correlated with experience. If so, that solution property could be used to estimate

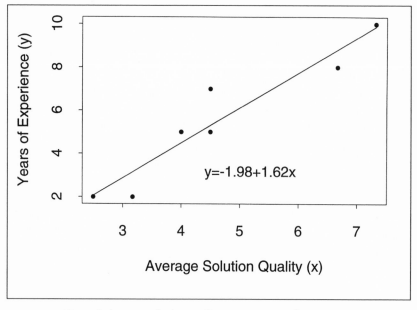

Figure 9 Average solution quality versus years of experience.

a knowledge-based system's experience level.

It is also of interest to note that machinists report that the properties of plan efficiency (estimated by length) and feasibility are important components of solution quality. Another, second goal was to see if these reports were borne out in the data. More specifically, machinists report that a short, efficient solution is favored over a long one, provided that the short solution does not sacrifice accuracy. However, feasibility is by far the most important factor in determining quality.

Solution Quality

Table 1 shows the quality rankings assigned by the two judges to each of the problem solutions. Problem solvers and their experience levels (in years) are listed on the left-hand side. S1 through S7 are the human problem solvers. M1 and M2 are respectively the early and later versions of the Machinist program. Judges (Judge1, Judge2) and problems (P1, P2, P3) are listed across the top. Since M1 and M2 are programs, years of experience are not a relevant quantity, and this value is filled in by a star (*).

The missing data points (indicated by a dash (−) in Table 1) resulted from the fact that the experimenter's time with each problem solver was often very limited since their service was being donated by the manufacturing company

Problem Solver:	Years of experience	Judge 1 p1	Judge 1 p2	Judge 1 p3	Judge 2 p1	Judge 2 p2	Judge 2 p3	% feasible plans
S1	2	0	0	1	0	0	0	0.17
S2	2	0	0	1	0	-	1	0.40
S3	5	1	1	1	0	-	-	0.75
S4	5	0	-	1	1	-	-	0.67
S5	7	1	1	1	0	1	-	0.80
S6	8	1	1	1	1	1	1	1.00
S7	10	-	1	1	-	-	-	1.00
M1	*	1	1	1	1	1	1	1.00
M2	*	1	1	1	0	-	1	0.80

Table 2. Solution Feasibility

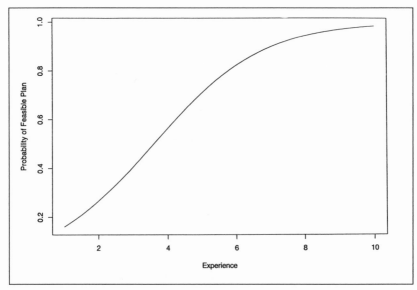

Figure 10. Probability of producing a feasible solution versus years of experience.

Problem Solver:	Years of Experience:	Problem P1	Problem P2	Problem P3
S1	2	5	4	4
S2	2	6	7	5
S3	5	4	5	4
S4	5	9	8	7
S5	7	5	6	5
S6	8	6	5	5
S7	10	-	4	2
M1	*	4	7	7
M2	*	4	4	5

Table 3. Solution Length

or facility where he or she worked. In two cases, the available time was less than the time required for the subject to complete all three problems, so the last problem was left only partially complete. This happened for both subject S4 and S7. S4 did not complete problem P2, and S7 did not complete problem P1. Additionally, Judge2 failed to provide a ranking for S7 on problem P3, but he provided no explanation as to why.

The Spearman rank correlation coefficient was computed for each of the three problems to see how closely the judges tended to agree with each other. The following coefficients were found: problem 1, $r = 0.74$; problem 2, $r = 0.42$; problem 3, $r = -0.71$. A factorial analysis was also performed on the data. Experience was found to be statistically significant, but judge and part were not.

A linear regression was used to generate a function to describe the relationship between quality and experience for the data in Table 1. The following equation was found.

(1) $y = -1.98 + 1.62x$

The result is shown in figure 9. Experience is plotted on the y axis and average solution quality ranking on the x axis. The solid line shows the experience-quality function found for the data. The curved bands flanking the diagonal line represent a 95% confidence interval around the function.

Several types of curves were fit to the data, including logarithmic and several polynomials. However, a simple linear regression fit the data quite well.

Solution Feasibility

Solution feasibility is shown in Table 2. A "1" means feasible, "0," infeasible. The dashes in Table 2 indicate either that there was no solution generated by the subject for a particular problem (true for subject S4, problem P2; and subject S7, problem P1) or that the judge made no comment on the solution's feasibility.

A logistic regression was used to fit a curve to these data. The relationship was found to be statistically significant. Figure 10 shows the result. This graph shows the probability of producing a feasible solution against the experience level of the problem solver. A logistic regression was selected instead of a linear regression because a logistic regression can produce a function where y is bounded by 0 and 1, while a linear regression can not. Since it is known that the y value of the function which fits these data is bounded by 0 and 1, a logistic regression makes more sense; for a given experience level, one can never produce fewer than 0 feasible plans or more than 100% feasible plans.

Solution Length

Table 3 shows the number of setups in each plan. These data were obtained simply by counting the number of setups in each plan. Note that there is a value for plan length for S4's solution to problem P2 in Table 2 (despite the missing quality ranking for this same subject and problem in Table 1). The reason for this discrepancy is that S4's solution to problem P2 was obtained by the experimenter on a return trip to the subject's place of employment several months after the solution rankings had been obtained. Therefore, there is a plan and a plan length for this problem, but no ranking.

An analysis of variance (ANOVA) showed that experience was statistically significant, although not strongly so. The relationship between individual problem and plan length was not statistically significant.

The average plan length for each subject was plotted against experience. However, no simple linear, logarithmic or exponential function was found that produced a good fit to the data, so this graph is not shown.

Discussion

Of the three solution properties examined, quality, feasibility, and length, it appeared that solution quality was the most suitable property to use in estimating experience. The skill function, shown in figure 9, is used to estimate experience level of the Machinist system.

Agreement Between Judges

The Spearman rank correlations indicate that the judges agreed strongly on problem 1, agreed weakly on problem 2, and disagreed on problem 3. However, it is not clear whether the low correlations on problem 2 are due to a difference in evaluation criteria, or to the fact that many of the plans were almost equal in quality. The latter reason is most likely since the judges repeatedly commented that many of the plans were almost equal in quality. On problem 2, Judge2 identified a group of 5 plans which he believed to be almost equal in quality. In an earlier study, a correlation of $r = 0.92$ was found between the same two judges for a different set of plans (Hayes 1987).

Solution Quality, Feasibility, Length

For solution quality, there was a statistically significant relationship between experience and solution quality, and a simple function relating the two. The same was found for the relationship between experience and solution feasibility. The function obtained by a logistic regression relating experience and solution feasibility showed that between 2 and 6 years of experience, the increase in machinists' ability to produce feasible plans is fairly linear. Beyond 6 years, this increase appears to slow.

There was a weak but statistically statistically significant relationship found between experience and plan length, but no simple function that related the two could be found. This supports the judges' assertions that solution efficiency (length) plays a role in determining quality, but that feasibility plays a stronger role.

One might expect to find that the greater the experience of the problem solver, the shorter and more efficient the solutions. However, this did not appear to be the case. In fact, some of the inexperienced machinists produced very short plans, intermediate machinists produced the longest plans, and experienced machinists produced plans of intermediate length. The reason that the inexperienced machinists produced such short plans is because essential steps had been omitted. The plans were usually not feasible. The reason the experienced machinists did not make particularly short plans appears to be that they may have reached some sort of a limit. The length of the plan was probably not the shortest possible, but it was the shortest possible without a large increase in planning effort and plan cost. Additionally, length is only one of many factors, such as cost and accuracy, that they aim to optimize. Expert machinists report that the structure of the plan is far more important in determining quality than the exact number of steps.

Assessing the Expert System's Experience Level

The goal of the first part of the analysis was to find some solution property that was strongly correlated with experience so that this solution property could be used to estimate a KBS's experience level. In particular, the goal was to estimate the experience level of the Machinist system.

Since both solution quality and solution feasibility appeared to have strong relationships to experience, either could probably be used to estimate the experience level of the Machinist system. In this study, it was decided that solution quality would be used for this purpose. The author's reasoning was that since solution quality was the original focus of the experiment, and solution feasibility data were an unexpected positive by-product which was unevenly reported, the data on solution quality was likely to be more accurate.

Table 1 shows that the average solution quality rating received by the early version of the Machinist system (M1) was 4.67. The average solution quality rating received by the later version of the Machinist system (M2) was 5.67. In order to compute an estimate of the Machinist system's experience level, these quality values were substituted into equation (1), which is the function found earlier relating experience and solution quality. The estimated experience level of the early version of the Machinist system was found to be 5.6 years. The estimated experience level of the later version of the Machinist system was found to be 7.2 years.

However, since it is possible that a range of different experts might produce a solution of the same quality, there are really a range of experience levels one must consider for a given quality value. An experience interval for the KBS was constructed by using the confidence bands around equation (1) (shown in figure 9). An experience interval is a 95% confidence interval bounding the experience estimate. It was found that the later version of the Machinist system produced plans equivalent in quality to those produced by humans between 6.3 to 8.4 years of experience.

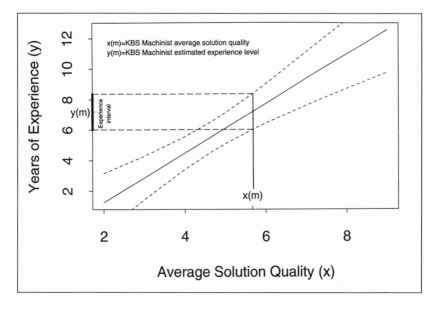

Figure 11. The experience interval of the later version of the Machinist program, M2.

The experience estimate for the later version of the system is graphically shown in figure 11. In this figure, the horizontal line represents the KBS's average quality ranking, while the vertical lines and the gray region between them shows the estimated experience range.

These estimates were used to measure the program's performance on a yardstick of human experience. The results showed that the system has a high skill level and is capable of achieving a high level of competence, supporting the hypothesis is that the Machinist system's problem-solving approach is a reasonable one.

Summary and Conclusions

The method presented here for measuring the experience level of a knowledge-based system (KBS) has several benefits. First of all, it allows assessments to be made of a KBS's skill level without necessarily requiring the expert system to be complete, or broad in problem coverage. Such measures can be useful for testing the validity of an approach before spending additional effort to make the system more complete and robust.

Second, the method appears to be fairly robust since it produced a reasonably small experience interval despite the fact that many of the solutions used to construct the experience-quality function were very close in quality, and

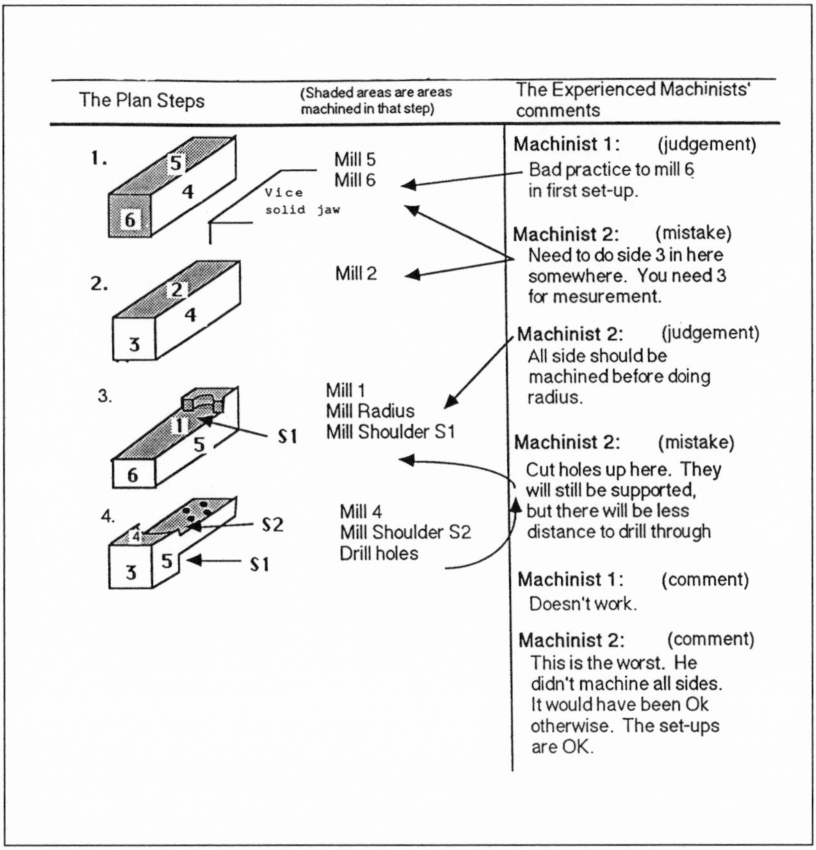

The Plan Steps	(Shaded areas are areas machined in that step)	The Experienced Machinists' comments

Figure 12. A plan for part III produced by a machinist with 2 years experience.

the experts did not always agree on the ranking assigned to a given solution.

Third, it can provide a way to compare two or more KBS's. It is often difficult to benchmark two expert systems against each other even when the systems operate on the same domain. Two separate tests can be made, one on each KBS using problems suited to its domain. When the tests are complete the experience levels of the two systems can be compared.

In addition to providing a way to measure the experience level of a KBS, this study also provides some insights into differences between novice and expert machinists. At the start of this study, the author expected one difference to be that novices would require more time to solve problems, and that they would sometimes be frustrated by being unable to figure out how to start on some problems. However, for the sample of parts examined, all machinists took roughly the same amount of time to produce solutions (be-

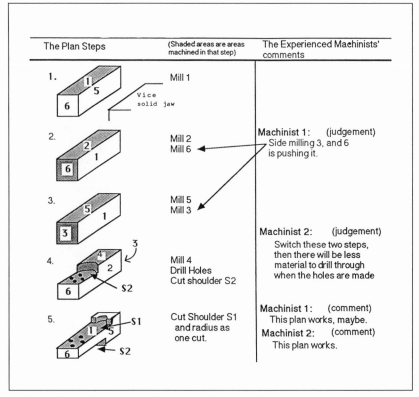

Figure 13. A plan for part III produced by a machinist with 5 years experience.

tween 10 and 30 minutes, depending on the complexity of the problem), and none of the machinists complained of not being able to start or solve problems. Novices and experts would both generate solutions fairly rapidly and would express satisfaction with their solutions at the end. One of the main differences seemed to be that the novices' solutions were often infeasible, although they were completely unaware of this fact. They would construct a solution, carefully double check it, and declare the solution satisfactory without ever noticing that the solution was completely unsound.

One possible explanation for this behavior is that there is a difference in the knowledge possessed by novice and expert machinists about their own problem solving processes and limitations. In other studies by the author on experienced machinists, it was found that they appear to have significant knowledge about their own knowledge boundaries. This knowledge helps experienced machinists avoid the pitfalls that apprentices fall into of generating solutions which they believe to be correct, but which fail (sometimes in dangerous ways) when they are executed. Experienced machinists report that they are rarely surprised by plan failures. Plan failures still occur in the plans of experienced machinists but they can usually predict where these failures are likely to occur, and proceed with great caution at those steps. The second and third year machinists appeared to lack this type of knowledge completely.

The practical consequence of the novices' inability to detect dangerous errors in their plans which may result in catastrophic equipment damage or worse, serious bodily injury, is that new apprentices are rarely allowed to plan out and execute a job until it has been checked over by a more experienced machinist. They must be carefully supervised until they acquire the ability to recognize when they are out of their realm of experience.

This chapter has described the development of a general method for estimating the experience level of a KBS, and has demonstrated this method to estimate the experience level of the Machinist program, a KBS that automatically creates manufacturing plans. In order to find a way of estimating experience, several solution properties were examined to see if any were strongly correlated with experience including solution quality, feasibility, and length.

Solution quality was selected as the property to be used in estimating the experience level of the KBS. A function relating quality and experience was constructed. This function was used to estimate the experience level of the KBS, given the average quality ranking of the solutions it generated. The Machinist program was estimated to have an experience level between 6 and 8 years. The advantages of this method are that it allows knowledge-based systems to be assessed on a yardstick of human performance, and it allows 2 or more knowledge-based systems to be compared, even if those systems operate in different domains.

Acknowledgments

A special thanks to all the machinists who provided data or served as judges for this study including Jim Dillinger, Dan McKeel, Dave Belotti, Jack Rude, Steve Rosenberg, Bill Knight, Dare Hire, and Mike Westjohn. Another thanks to Bill Burtle for his data collection, to Michael I. Parzen for his advice on logistic regressions and other statistical matters, to J.R. Hayes for his Spearman rank correlation advice, and to Michael Dorneich for his statistical and numerical analysis advice and editorial comments.

References

Anderson, J.R. (1993). Development of expertise. In B.G. Buchanan *et al.* (Eds.), *Readings in Knowledge Acquisition* (pp. 61-77). San Mateo, CA: Morgan Kaufman.

Charness, N. (1976). Memory for chess positions: Resistance to interference. *Journal of Experimental Psychology: Human Learning and Memory*, 641-653.

Chi, M., Glasser, R. & Farr, M.J. (Eds.) (1988). *The Nature of Expertise*. Hillsdale, NJ: Lawrence Erlbaum.

Hayes, C.C. (1990). *Machining Planning: A Model of an Expert Level Planning Process*. Ph.D. Thesis. Pittsburgh, PA: Carnegie Mellon University.

Hayes, C.C. (1987). Observing machinists' planning methods: Using goal interactions to guide search. *The Ninth Annual Conference of the Cognitive Science Society* (pp. 952-958). Seattle, WA.

Hayes, C.C. (1996). P3: A process planner for manufacturability analysis. *IEEE Transactions on Robotics and Automation, special issue on Assembly and Task Planning, 12(2)*.

Hayes, C.C. & Wright, P.K. (1989). Automated process planning: Using feature interaction to guide search. *Journal of Manufacturing Systems, 8(1)*, 1-16.

Hayes, J.R. (1985). Three problems in teaching general skills. In C.F. Chipman, J.W. Segal & R. Glaser (Eds.), *Thinking and Learning Skills, Volume 2: Research and Open Questions*. Hillsdale, NJ: Lawrence Erlbaum.

Hetem, V. (1994). *Cost Estimation*. Ph.D. Thesis. Urbana-Champaign, IL: University of Illinois.

Lancaster, J.S. & Kolodner, J.L. (1987). Problem solving in a natural task as a function of experience. *The Ninth Annual Conference of the Cognitive Science Society* (pp. 727-736). Seattle, WA.

Lane, N.E. (1986). Global issues in evaluation of expert systems. *Proceedings of the 1986 IEEE International Conference on Systems, Man and Cybernetics* (pp. 121-125).

Liebowitz, J. (1986). Useful approach for evaluating expert systems. *Expert Systems, 3(2)*, 86-96.

Nazareth, D.L. & Kennedy, M.H. (1993). Knowledge-based system verification, validation and testing. *International Journal of Expert Systems, 6(2)*, 143-162.

Stefik, M.J. (1980). *Planning with Constraints*. Ph.D. Thesis. Stanford, CA: Stanford University.

CHAPTER 15

Abduction and Abstraction in Diagnosis: A Schema-based Account

Carl R. Stern & George F. Luger

Introduction

The activity of constructing explanations is strongly goal-dependent. This dependency has recently been emphasized in the "content theory of explanation" proposed by Leake (1992). Leake observes that the information that a good explanation must provide is closely tied to the reasons for constructing the explanation. Leake fleshes out his analysis with a taxonomy of general explanatory goals and an analysis of the requirements imposed by each type of goal.

Our study of expert performance in the area of semiconductor component failure analysis supports Leake's account of goal-dependency. We find that the patterns of diagnostic explanation produced by failure analysts are closely correlated with the need to support different kinds of remedial practices (i.e., different ways of addressing the reliability concerns raised by component failures). Explanations of component failures exhibit a distinct range of forms corresponding to the different causal dimensions addressed by remediation, for example, the component design, the component manufacturing process, the surrounding circuit design, and the stresses (electrical, mechanical, thermal) originating from an external environment. We have frequently observed that failure analysts working in different settings (e.g., for a component manufacturer vs. a circuit assembly manufacturer) tend to emphasize different causal dimensions.

Despite the fact that component failures typically result from an interaction of factors, diagnostic explanations usually focus on only one causal dimension, treating the others as incidental. The diagnostician's selection of a diagnostic hypothesis provides a context for interpreting evidence, for selectively emphasizing or ignoring certain kinds of data, and for constructing causal theories about the sequence of events resulting in the failure. Within the framework of this general hypothesis, the diagnostician's application of causal knowledge is controlled by the goal of producing a detailed causal explanation of a certain form.

Our model of diagnosis is based on the observation and analysis of expert performance in the area of semiconductor component failure analysis. We have worked with five failure analysts over nearly half a decade in the process of constructing a failure analysis expert system.[1] The weakness of our original rule-based expert system in capturing the diagnostic problem solving behavior of human experts motivated the development of a second architecture. In this architecture, explanation patterns are encoded in *schemas*. A schema specifies a general pattern of causation as a causal sequence in which each step of the sequence is characterized by causal processes of a certain type. Using this schema representation, we have developed a schema-based abduction algorithm that implements an important modification of the usual abductive chaining algorithm (Levesque 1989). In schema-based abduction, search for causal processes to explain unexplained conditions is restricted to the class of causal processes specified by the schema at the current step.

We now present some observations regarding the patterns of investigation and hypothesis formation followed by human experts in semiconductor component failure analysis; this is followed by a general discussion of certain related cognitive issues. In the next two sections we give a specification of our architecture for diagnosis. We then present an extended example of failure analysis using this architecture.

Expertise in Context: Component Level Failure Analysis

Semiconductor component failure analysis offers an important example of expertise in context (Luger and Stern 1992). The failure analyst is presented with an initial set of signs, for example, the abnormal behavior of a diode after *burn in*,[2] and is required to organize an investigation based on an interpretation of those signs. The analyst begins the analysis by gathering information about the history and vulnerabilities of the device as well as the particular circumstances of the current failure. The initial visual and electrical examinations are conducted against the background of this information. Based on the initial examination, the analyst adopts a prioritized list of hypotheses—the failure mechanisms which could account for the abnormal device behavior. Data gathering then proceeds, focused by the active hypothesis set.

As new information is acquired, some hypotheses are dropped while others are modified. In the light of hypothesis revision, observations that once were considered relevant are pushed aside, and new observations become critical. Eventually the investigation stabilizes on a sufficiently well-established hypothesis and the focus changes. The goal becomes one of establishing certain details in the causal scenario which are relevant to the task of fixing the problem or preventing it in the future. The final outcome of this process, if it is successful, is an explanation of the device malfunction suitably focused and precise enough to support corrective action.

An essential element of the investigative process is the use of hypotheses to organize search. The problem solver hypothesizes conditions which are not directly in evidence, conditions which might account for the device's anomalous behavior. Initially these conditions may be specified in a very general or abstract way. Evidence gathering is then directed towards confirming or disconfirming these hypotheses as well as elaborating the hypotheses in more detail.

Although the initial stage of the investigation involves a parallel investigation of competing hypotheses, each hypothesis can be seen to define a particular investigative context. These contexts are distinguished by the scope of relevant data, the set of patterns used for reasoning about the evidence, and the set of methods appropriate for correcting the problem. For example, environmentally-induced failures are investigated and remediated differently from manufacturing defects, which are in turn handled differently from failures resulting from wearout mechanisms. It is therefore important to constrain the type of failure mechanism involved as soon as possible in order to narrow the scope of the investigation.

Semiconductor failure analysis involves the initial adoption of candidate hypotheses, that is, conditions not in evidence, to explain the failure. This pattern of reasoning was characterized by the philosopher Peirce as a peculiar form called *abduction,* to be distinguished from the more familiar *deduction* and *induction* (Peirce 1958). It has been studied recently by workers in the AI research community (e.g., Levesque 1989; Charniak and Shimony 1990; Pearl 1987), as well as in the cognitive science community (e.g., Feltovich *et al.* 1984; Kuipers and Kassirer 1984).

Our study of semiconductor failure analysis has led us to examine abductive problem solving more closely. In an effort to understand better the inner logic of diagnostic investigations, we have analyzed the structure of abductive hypotheses in semiconductor failure analysis and examined the way in which these hypotheses organize investigations.

The abductive hypotheses used in semiconductor failure analysis are called *failure mechanisms.* Failure mechanism represent abstract patterns of causation, codifying the accumulated experience of experts both in understanding and responding to recurring patterns of failures over time. During initial hypothesis formation, failure mechanisms are treated as simple associations between sets of symptoms and types of causes. However, as the investigation of individual hypotheses progress, *deeper* knowledge from the domain of semi-conductor physics is brought to bear. To understand the *logic* underlying the application of this deeper domain knowledge, we believe it is necessary to view failure mechanisms as complex structures representing key elements of the causal chains which produce failures. Viewed in this way, these abstract causal patterns help us to understand the specific sequence of data gathering steps and interpretive reasoning by which human problem solvers pursue the investigation of hypotheses.

We call the representation of these recurring patterns of causation *schemas* because of their role in organizing and interpreting the diagnostician's experience. A schema is defined as a cognitive structure which guides the application of concepts, in this case causal laws, to experience. Schema-based pattern recognition involves the interpreter's use of schemas to actively construct perceptual or conceptual patterns which fit the data. This notion is distinguished from simple pattern matching, where the interpreter selects one of a predefined set of stored patterns based on criteria such as identity or closeness to the data. The term schema is thus used in a sense similar to that first proposed by Kant (1781/1964) and later developed by Bartlett (1932), Newell and Simon (1972), and Piaget (1970).

Causal Associations and the Heuristics of Diagnosis

In the area of semiconductor failure analysis, as in many other diagnostic domains, knowledge of first principles is insufficient for proficiency in diagnosis. In addition to a knowledge of semiconductor physics, engineers require an extensive period of training and experience before they become competent failure analysts. One reason for this is that there can be a large gulf between observed symptoms on the one hand and the laws of semiconductor physics on the other. Computationally speaking, the search for explanations from first principles involves too large a search space.

The gulf between first principles and observed symptoms is mediated by the recognition of recurring causal patterns or scenarios. The diagnostician searches for indications of these causal patterns in the preliminary data. The semiconductor component failure analyst learns to recognize and reason about a set of potential *failure mechanisms*. These represent the commonly occurring patterns of causation to which experts attribute component failures. For transistors and diodes, the experts we interviewed recognize between 40 and 60 different failure mechanisms.

Failure analysts associate failure *mechanisms* with failure *modes*. A failure mode is a general class of behavior under which a set of observable symptoms has been subsumed. For transistors, failure modes include: short, open, resistive, reverse bias leakage, low gain, intermittent, etc. Examples of associations

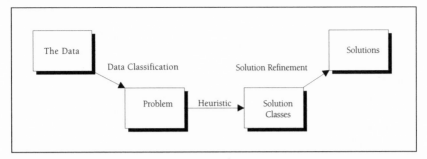

Figure 1. Clancey's heuristic classification architecture. The essential steps are data classification, heuristic matching, and solution refinement.

between mechanisms and modes are: contamination causes reverse bias leakage; particles cause intermittent shorts; faulty die attach causes high series resistance; electrical overstress causes opens; faulty wire bonds cause opens.

It is a mistake to construe such associations as deterministic relations between cause and effect. Contamination does not always produce leakage; particles do not always produce shorts. It would be more appropriate to view these as rough statistical correlations between types of effects and types of causes, that is, between failure modes and failure mechanisms. The rules in our expert system estimate the likelihood of failure mechanisms based on the failure mode along with contextual factors such as device structure and history. The important point, however, is that failure modes denote general types of failures and failure mechanisms denote general patterns of causation. To attempt to redefine these associations in a way that renders them more deterministically causal would undermine their heuristic function in the formation of hypotheses. It is precisely the generality of these associations that allows them to provide a useful decomposition of the global solution space during the early stages of inquiry.

This pattern of problem solving follows closely that described by Clancey (1985) in his analysis of *heuristic classification* architectures. Clancey discovered that a large class of expert systems employ a similar method of problem solving. This architecture is illustrated in Figure 1. The method is based on identifying a finite set of problem classes and solution classes. Problem data are first analyzed and identified with a problem class. Then a method of heuristic classification or matching is used to map the problem class into a solution class. Clancey used the term *heuristic classification,* as opposed to *simple classification,* to describe the process of associating elements from distinct classification hierarchies. Finally, a solution refinement method is used to generate and validate a concrete solution from the solution class. Clancey recognized that this order of steps was not necessarily sequential; the stages of the problem classification, heuristic matching, and solution refinement are often interleaved. He did, however, propose this as a knowledge level specification of the logical structure of problem solving in an important class of expert systems.

Our experience indicates that semiconductor component failure analysts use symptom classification and heuristic matching in generating an hypothesis set. What remains to be described is how these hypotheses are investigated and elaborated into viable causal explanations. This corresponds to the solution refinement stage described by Clancey. We believe we have discovered an interesting and important characterization of solution refinement with respect to semiconductor failure analysis. We have observed that causal hypotheses function as schemas for the construction of causal explanations from the domain laws and the facts of the case.

Failure Mechanisms and Explanation Schemas

When expert failure analysts are asked to explain their actions and reasoning, much of their discussion is phrased in terms of the failure mechanisms whose presence they are trying to establish or eliminate. Experts, however, do not usually articulate the content and structure of these failure mechanisms unless asked. Nonetheless, this content and structure is part of the understanding implicit in their practice, and it is useful to ask them to articulate it. When they are pushed, what experts often describe is a set of stereotyped failure scenarios. These are patterns of causation consisting of events or device states connected by transitions, where the transitions are law-governed processes or mechanisms.

It is important for the knowledge engineer to determine the structure corresponding to each failure mechanism in order to understand why particular test procedures or measurements are performed and how test results are interpreted. Simply put, a failure mechanism represents a story pattern explaining why a failure occurred. A story conforming to this pattern has events or states of a specific type linked by processes or mechanisms of a certain type. The failure analyst attempts to match events in the current situation to those in the story. Once those events are known he or she can then verify that the processes or mechanisms linking events or states conform to the constraints imposed by the causal first principles of the domain. (We have created a set of schema graphs corresponding to the causal mechanisms which experts use in transistor failure analysis, and describe several of them later in this chapter.)

Situated Versus Context Free Knowledge

The scientific laws used in diagnosis, for example, the laws of semiconductor physics, represent a context free form of knowledge. The generality of these laws can be seen from the fact that the same laws can be applied to a wide variety of different situations or circumstances. The heuristic associations between failure mechanisms and failure modes represent the other extreme. These correlations vary both in content and strength depending on a variety of circumstances, including device structure, failure history, and failure analysis goals. The process of identifying failure mechanisms is thus *semiotic* in the sense that it involves interpreting signs within a pragmatic context.

In forming an hypothesis regarding the cause of leakage,[3] for example, an expert will take into account whether a transistor is NPN or PNP[4] because contamination induced inversion[5] is much more strongly correlated with leakage in PNP transistors. He may also take into account whether the manufacturer has had a history of problems with contamination, and whether other devices from the same lot show signs of contamination. Similarly, experts take into account at what stage in its life cycle a device failed, because, for example, wearout mechanisms such as metal migration and whisker formation become more likely when a device has seen extended testing or use.

We also found that analysts with different goals and resources generally produce explanations with a different focus and structure. For example, failure analyses conducted by engineers at a manufacturing facility employed a larger set of causal mechanisms relating to process control in manufacturing than commercial failure analyses conducted on behalf of end users. Moreover, even when the same manufacturing defects were described, the explanation of defects in the manufacturer's failure analysis reports were focused on the details required to determine necessary changes in the manufacturing process, whereas the customer's failure analysis reports were focused on the details required to *detect* those defects in the lot acceptance process.

It is useful to contrast the schema-based approach to diagnosis with that of model-based diagnosis (Davis and Hamscher 1992). Both methods use reasoning based on first principles to identify and refine causal explanations. Both methods need to employ knowledge of device structure in order to apply causal knowledge. However, in model-based reasoning, the device structure is formalized in advance into a context free description. As Davis and Hamscher acknowledge, the construction of useful and appropriate models is, to a great extent, a black art. A model is necessarily an abstraction: it captures only certain aspects of device structure, while omitting others. The trick in creating a model is to choose a suitable abstraction, one that does not abstract out any elements of device structure required to account for a malfunction in some future situation.

In our approach the device structure is formalized in the context of an hypothesis regarding the type of causality responsible for a failure. This means that only those aspects of device structure are examined that are relevant to the hypothesized failure mechanism. Thus the hypothesis provides a context, determining what aspects of structure need to be formalized.

A Computational Architecture for Schema-Based Diagnosis

The architecture we propose uses schemas to investigate causal mechanisms and construct explanations. Explanation schemas represent an organized body of knowledge related to a causal pattern. Each schema describes a causal mechanism which is capable of producing a determinate range of effects. The mechanism is characterized by a set of events or states and their causal connections. This defines the attributes that must be specified in order to instantiate the causal mechanism vis-à-vis the current situation. The schema is also associated with a body of "compiled knowledge" used by human problem solvers to test for the presence of the mechanism and to propose corrective action. Finally the schema *graph* gives a concise description of the pattern of causal connections between events or states, serving as a template for constructing explanations from the causal domain theory and the facts of the case.

Schema-based diagnosis involves five steps: 1) generation of an hypothesis set, 2) hypothesis pruning, 3) hypothesis instantiation, 4) explanation construction and validation, and 5) explanation repair. In the following subsections we describe each of these steps.

Generation of an Hypothesis Set

We use a heuristic classification approach to identify a set of candidate mechanisms that will account for the observed fault/malfunction. Initial observations regarding the symptom or malfunction must be elaborated by further observations or measurements. Additional evidence gathering in conjunction with data abstraction is used to locate the malfunction within a classification hierarchy of problem types. Problem types are then matched against solution types, that is, causal mechanisms which can produce the observed problems. Each mechanism corresponds to an abstract pattern of causation. A mechanism is composite in the sense that it comprises a causal chain, distinguished by the constituent event types and causal processes. The identification of a mechanism activates a schema for reasoning about that type of mechanism.

Hypothesis Pruning

The hypothesis set, represented by the set of activated schemas, is tested and pruned. As mentioned above, each schema is associated with a set of tests or observations designed to confirm or disconfirm the presence of that mechanism. Some tests provide specific support for individual mechanisms while others provide general criteria for discriminating between classes of causal mechanisms. General tests discriminate between classes by producing additional data which some mechanisms can "explain" and others cannot. The test procedures are collectively assembled and correlated in order to select the least cost test for pruning the hypothesis set. Testing and planning steps are alternated until the number of hypotheses on the "discriminant" cannot be further reduced. The remaining mechanisms are ranked in order of likelihood.

Hypothesis Instantiation

The most likely remaining hypothesis is selected for expansion. The corresponding schema graph is applied to the current situation. Nodes in the schema graph, representing the events in the causal scenario, are correlated with observed or hypothesized events in the current situation. Facts or data from the current situation are used to determine event attributes and properties in the schema graph. Attributes or properties required by the schema but currently unknown may trigger further testing or observation.

Explanation Construction and Validation

The schema graph is used as a template to construct an explanation from the causal domain theory and the known facts of the case. The causal links in the uninstantiated schema graph represent causal relations at a very general and abstract level. Consider, for example, one of the simplest schema graphs, that for an electrical overstress[6] induced open. This is illustrated in Figure 2. In this schema graph, two key causal links are "excessive current causes temperature elevation" and "excessive temperature causes melting."

Once the nodes of the graph are bound to a specific set of events, these causal links need to be reconstructed from the causal domain theory at a more concrete and detailed level. The application of the causal domain theory starts from the observed symptoms or malfunction (the bottom of the schema graph) and proceeds upwards from effect to cause through the instantiated nodes of the graph. This procedure propagates constraints, inferring characteristics of the cause from those of the effect. This procedure can serve to confirm or disconfirm the explanation.

In the current example, if we are using electrical overstress to explain a melted bond wire, we can determine from the composition of the bond wire material the minimum temperature required to melt it. We thus specify "excessive temperature" with an exact number. We can then infer from the thickness and resistance of the bond wire material an exact range of current over time which would be required to cause the melting. If, for example, the device could not have seen that level of current, then an inconsistency is detected which disconfirms the hypothesis of simple electrical overstress.

Explanation Repair

The detection of an inconsistency between the inferred and actual properties of an object in the schema graph constitutes a potential disconfirmation of

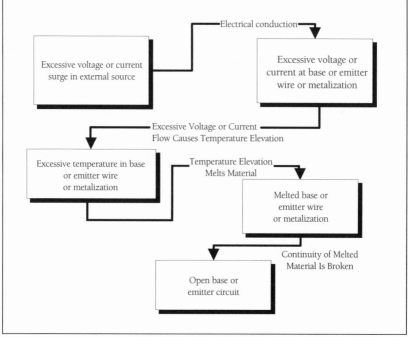

*Figure 2. A linear schema graph for electrical-overstress-induced-open
Excessive voltage or current causes localized temperature elevation,
resulting in melted wire or metallization.*

the explanation. At this point, two courses of action are possible. Either the current hypothesis is discarded or we attempt to repair it. If the hypothesis is discarded, the procedure returns to step 3 and begins to instantiate the next hypothesis on the hypothesis list.

If, on the other hand, no other hypotheses remain, or no other hypothesis has a similar weight of evidence supporting it, we may choose to repair the current explanation. In the melted bond wire example, we may conjecture that the bond wire was pinched or otherwise thinned at the location where it melted, thus reducing the amount of current required to melt it. To accomplish such an explanation repair, we need to locate the source of the inconsistent constraint, the causal link where it originated, and modify one of the conditions on which the constraint depended.

The problem of explanation repair is one of the most difficult faced by our method. We explore two general approaches to the problem: 1) to encode the repair strategies employed by human experts in the area and 2) to use abductive reasoning to reconstruct from scratch the schema subgraph where the inconsistency was detected.

Schema-Based Abduction

At the heart of the procedure described above is a process of reasoning which we call *schema-based abduction*. This refers to the method by which the causal links specified by the schema graph are reconstructed from the causal domain theory in the context of a set of situation-specific bindings. We next characterize this mode of reasoning more precisely, relating it to the conventional notion of abduction.

Abduction, as it is ordinarily understood by the logic community in AI, is a mode of inference which generates candidate explanations for an otherwise unexplained set of observations O. Abductive inference allows us to *assume* facts not directly in evidence. More formally, an hypothesis H is a minimal abductive explanation for observation set O if:

i O is not entailed by the current background knowledge K

ii $H \cup K$ entails O

iii No proper subset of H has property ii

iv H is consistent with K

Abductive reasoners have been implemented that generate the complete set of minimal abductive explanations using a relatively straightforward backchaining approach. They rely on the "inference rule":

abduce$(B, \alpha \rightarrow B) = \alpha$

where α is a conjunction of literals. Backchaining proceeds by taking each $a_i \in \alpha$, $a_i \notin K$, as a new abductive subgoal. Such algorithms work best over sets of propositional Horn clauses. Typically these systems take as input a set A of abducible propositions, that is, propositions which the abductive reasoner is allowed to include in the hypothesis H. Even for a propositional Horn clause language, however, this task has been shown to be NP-hard.

The schema-based abduction which we employ represents a highly constrained form of abductive reasoning. In schema-based abduction the objects related as cause and effect are already given in abstract form in the schema graph. Abductive reasoning consists not in inferring causes from effects but in inferring *properties* of the cause from the *properties* of the effect. More precisely, for any given link in the schema graph, the set A of abducibles is restricted to properties of the objects or events playing the role of cause in that particular link. The effect of abduction is thus a kind of constraint propagation, where instance bindings representing known properties in the effect are used to create new instance bindings in the cause. Backchaining search in schema-based abduction is thus considerably simplified. Its flow is determined by the preset pattern of links in the schema graph.

There are many cases where backward constraint propagation requires a method other than simple abductive inference. Consider the case discussed earlier in which electrical overstress is the hypothesis used to explain a melt-ed bond wire. We can infer from the composition of the bond wire and its thickness the temperature required to melt it. From this we can infer a mini-mum range of current over time required to produce that temperature. The propagation of constraints in this case requires an equation solving and equality substitution capability. We thus identify the term *schema-based abduction* with a broadened notion of abduction that includes methods for backward constraint propagation such as equation solving and equality sub-stitution.

Schema-Based Diagnosis: An Extended Example

We next analyze a typical situation from the semiconductor failure analysis domain in terms of schema-based problem solving. A bipolar transistor is brought in with a complaint of "low gain." A series of standard electrical measurements confirms low gain at low current (low gain in low current hFE) as well as discovering a second abnormal electrical characteristic: high collector base[7] leakage (high ICBO).

The first phase of reasoning, corresponding to the data abstraction phase in heuristic classification, involves the firing of a classification rule. High ICBO and low hFE together are classified as a collector base leakage problem:

result(ICBO, high) $\wedge$ result(hFE_lo, low gain) $\Rightarrow$ problem(C-B, leakage)

This reduction can be readily reconstructed from the domain theory. The ex-planation is that collector base leakage reduces gain by lowering the effective base drive. Note that reasoning so far relies solely on representations of inter-nal device structure and function. This type of reasoning is well handled by the model-based paradigm.

In the next phase of reasoning, we seek the cause of high collector base leakage. Heuristic classification rules identify three types of causal mecha-nisms which can explain collector base leakage:

problem(C-B, leakage) $\Rightarrow$ hypothesis(electrical overstress)

problem(C-B, leakage) $\Rightarrow$ hypothesis(contamination)

problem(C-B, leakage) $\Rightarrow$ hypothesis(mask misalignment/overetch)

These rules all fire, causing the activation of three schemas. The data struc-ture for a typical schema is described in Figure 3.

Each of the schemas is located within a schema hierarchy, reflecting the hi-erarchical structure of causal abstractions used to organize the search for ex-planations. An example of a schema hierarchy for *bridging faults* is given in Figure 4.

We use the available evidence to activate the most specific hypotheses pos-

Name	electrical overstress induced leakage
Attribute	type of overstress (voltage/current)
	location of overstress (emitter/base)
	intensity (pulse/power)
	source type
Indications	test equipment or application clustering
	linear junction characteristic
	leakage is stable over temperature
Test Procedures	delid: visual examination; look for orange peel or burn
	delid: SEM; look for pitting or tunneling
	delid: deprocessing: look for channels, damage to Si crystalline structure
Micro-theory	overstress induced leakage
Schema Graph	EOS-Leakage
Subschemas	ESD induced leakage
	oscillation overstress induced leakage
	pulse power overstress induced leakage

Figure 3. The data structure used for electrical-overstress-induced-leakage. The schema includes not only needed values but also "compiled knowledge" relating to indications and testing.

sible, that is, the deepest hypothesis in the schema hierarchy. Suppose, for example, that our transistor is a PNP device. In the schema hierarchy for bridging faults, we first activated the *contamination* schema among others. Using additional evidence, we then specialize the hypothesis of *contamination.* The most common form of contamination is Na^+. Na^+ contamination in PNP transistors typically produces *inversion,* resulting in a characteristic signature of high ICBO leakage. Because our transistor is PNP and because of the presence of ICBO leakage, we thus specialize the hypothesis of contamination using the following rule:

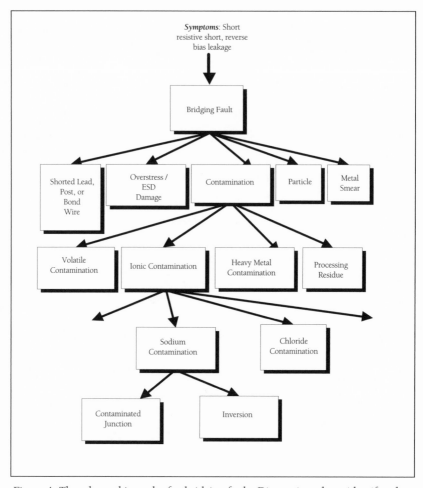

Figure 4. The schema hierarchy for bridging faults Diagnosis seeks to identify a hypothesis as deep in the hierarchy as possible.

hypothesis(contamination) ∧ device(polarity, PNP) ∧ problem(C-B, leakage) ∧ NOT(problem(E-B, leakage)) ⟹ hypothesis(inversion)

Similarly, we might fire a rule activating ESD[8] as a subhypothesis of electrical overstress based on the fact that the degradation is localized and that small signal devices are particularly sensitive to ESD damage:

hypothesis(overstress) ∧ problem(C-B, leakage) ∧ NOT(problem(E-B, leakage)) ∧ device(power, small signal) ⟹ hypothesis(ESD)

After the hypothesis set is generated, the *hypothesis pruning* stage begins.

Each schema provides a standard set of procedures for gathering evidence related to that particular causal mechanism. Electrical overstress, for example, is investigated by gathering details about the device's history and its possible exposure to an overstress or ESD environment. Similarly, mask misalignment is generally a wafer level problem; it can thus be investigated by determining if other chips from the same wafer are similarly degraded.

The internal verification procedures for overstress and mask misalignment/over-etch both involve cutting off the package lid and examining the internal structure of the device. Since these procedures are potentially destructive of evidence, we put them off as long as possible. The internal verification procedure for contamination, on the other hand, is usually nondestructive. This procedure depends on the temperature sensitivity of contamination. Since many contaminants are dispersed by elevated temperatures, the device is baked and then electrically retested to see if its electrical characteristics have improved. Let us suppose that they have. This fact then increases the probability of contamination, without completely eliminating the other hypotheses.

Up until now we have pruned and ordered the hypothesis list using nondestructive procedures. A nondestructive approach was necessary in order to allow for the possibility of backtracking. Beyond this point we engage in procedures which involve irreversible changes to the device and thus potential destruction of evidence. From this point on, we organize testing based on a careful consideration of potential gains versus potential costs, including destruction of evidence. To focus evidence gathering and precisely define the goals of each procedure, we continue the investigation in the context of constructing a detailed explanation based on the most likely hypothesis.

Explanation construction proceeds by instantiating the schema graph for the hypothesized mechanism. We illustrate again the notion of a schema graph by presenting the schema graph for *Inversion Induced Leakage* in Figure 5.

In constructing an explanation, the instantiated schema graph is traversed backwards or abductively, reconstructing the causal links using the causal domain theory. This serves two main purposes: to test the viability of the explanation by determining consistency with known facts, and to serve as a source of potential tests by fleshing out required conditions or assumptions. Returning to our example, the hypothesis of *inversion* is elaborated by proceeding backwards from the node *High ICBO* (at the lower right hand corner of the *Inversion Schema* graph). According to the graph, high ICBO is caused by an exposed junction along the edge of the chip. To reconstruct this causal link from the domain theory, we must make use of the fact that the chip surface along the edge is rough because of the way the chip is split off or sawed from the wafer. It is this roughness, the absence of a regular crystalline structure, that produces low level leakage when there is an exposed junction. Reconstructing this causal link from the domain theory thus fleshes out a hid-

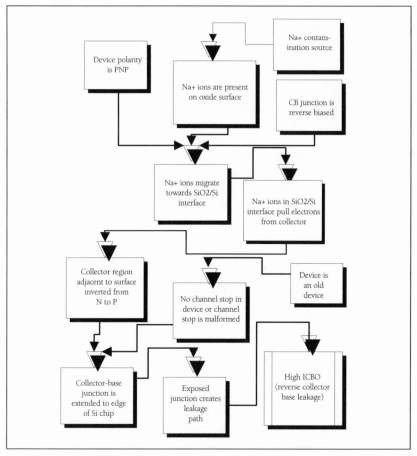

Figure 5. The schema graph for inversion-induced-leakage. Sodium ions produce an inverted region, extending junction out to the edge of the chip. Leakage occurs at the chip's edge.

den assumption, an assumption which might be violated if, for instance, a new method for separating chips from the wafer were invented.

Let us suppose that we have abductively regressed to the condition *Collector-base junction extended to edge of chip* (lower left-hand corner of the schema graph). The two conditions required to produce this result are 1) the collector base region is inverted and 2) no channel stop is present to prevent the extension of the inverted region to the chip's edge. Inversion has been such a common cause of PNP transistor problems that modern PNP transistors are almost always built with a channel stop to prevent the inverted region from reaching the edge of the chip. The presence of a properly functioning channel stop in the transistor would thus be inconsistent with an explanation based on inversion. The reconstruction of this causal link thus requires that we establish either 1) the absence of a channel stop or 2) a defect in the channel stop.

Suppose we determine, after a low power internal visual examination, that a channel stop is present. This determination then focuses the examination of the die on the search for a defect in the channel stop. The discovery of such a defect would significantly increase the force of evidence behind an inversion-based explanation. It would also specialize the explanation, adding an important twist: the cause of the leakage problem is Na+ contamination in conjunction with a faulty channel stop. The process of explanation construction thus results in an explanation richer in detail and more useful than the abstract explanatory hypothesis from which we started.

Conclusion

We propose an architecture for integrating heuristic problem solving and causal reasoning. This approach uses heuristic matching at a high level of abstraction to frame initial hypotheses. These are then refined to form fully articulated explanations. The schema-based architecture we propose involves a dynamic process of interrogation, explanation generation, and hypothesis evaluation. This in effect supports search through alternative interpretation spaces constrained by the fit of hypotheses to data.

In addition, the schema-based architecture provides a means for modeling the practical dimension of explanation construction. We have observed in our work with human failure analysts that the structure and focus of explanations generally reflect the practical need to support specific remedial practices. The use of a schema-based architecture to control explanation construction allows us to model this practical dimension, generating explanations which are consistent with the evidence and the applicable laws of semiconductor physics but which at the same time embody a structure developed over time to support certain types of corrective action.

Notes

1. This expert system, called DSFAX, was developed for Sandia National Laboratories from 1988 to 1994.

2. *Burn in* is a test procedure in which a device is powered up over an extended period of time under carefully controlled conditions in order to identify potential defects.

3. Leakage denotes the existence of a small channel current path between device locations or across a junction which is reverse biased.

4. NPN and PNP stand for the two possible polarity structures of bipolar transistors.

5. Inversion is a phenomenon in which positively charged ions attract negative ions from an adjacent P region, effectively creating a thin N region across which a leakage current can flow.

6. Electrical overstress is an excessive current or voltage applied to the device.

7. The two junctions of a bipolar transistor are the collector base (CB) and emitter base (EB).

8. ESD, or ElectroStatic Discharge, is a short duration high voltage current resulting from a static buildup, usually from a human source.

References

Bartlett, F. (1932). *Remembering*. London: Cambridge University Press.

Charniak, E. & Shimony, S. (1990). Probabilistic semantics for cost based abduction. *Proceedings of the Eighth National Conference on Artificial Intelligence* (pp. 106-111). Menlo Park, CA: AAAI/MIT Press.

Clancey, W.E. (1985). Heuristic classification. *Artificial Intelligence, 27,* 289-350.

Davis, R. & Hamscher, W. (1988). Model based reasoning: Troubleshooting. In W. Hamscher, L. Console, & J. deKleer (Eds.), (1992), *Readings in Model Based Diagnosis.* San Mateo, CA: Morgan Kaufman.

Doyle, J. (1983). Methodological simplicity in expert system construction: The case of judgments and reasoned assumptions. In I. Shafer & J. Pearl (Eds.), (1990), *Uncertain Reasoning* (pp. 689-693). San Mateo, CA: Morgan Kaufman.

Eco, U. (1976). *A Theory of Semiotics.* Bloomington: Indiana University Press.

Feltovich, P.J., Johnson, P.E., Moller, J.H., & Swanson, D.B. (1984). LCS: The role and development of medical knowledge in diagnostic expertise. In W.J. Clancey & E.H. Shortliffe (Eds.), *Readings in Artificial Intelligence in Medicine: The First Decade.* Reading, MA: Addison Wesley.

Gallanti, M., Roncato, M., Stefanini, A., & Tornielli, G. (1989). A diagnostic algorithm based on models at different levels of abstraction. *Proceeding of the Eleventh International Joint Conference on Artificial Intelligence* (pp. 1350-1355). San Mateo, CA: Morgan Kaufman.

Kant, I. (1781/1964). *Critique of Pure Reason.* N.K. Smith (Trans.). New York: St. Martin's Press.

Kass, A., Leake, D., & Owens, C. (1986). SWALE: A program that explains. In *Explanation Patterns: Understanding Mechanically and Creatively* (pp. 232-254). Hillsdale, NJ: Lawrence Erlbaum.

Kuipers, B. & Kassirer, J. (1984). Causal reasoning in medicine: analysis of a protocol. *Cognitive Science, 8,* 363-385.

Leake, D. (1992). *Evaluating Explanations: A Content Theory.* Hillsdale, NJ: Lawrence Erlbaum.

Levesque, H.J. (1989). A knowledge level account of abduction. *Proceeding of the Eleventh International Joint Conference on Artificial Intelligence* (pp. 1061-1067). San Mateo, CA: Morgan Kaufman.

Luger, G.F. & Stern, C. (1992). Expert Systems and the abductive circle. In R. Jorna & B. von Heusden (Eds.), *Cognition and Semiotics.* Berlin: Walter de Gruyter.

Newell, A. & Simon, H. (1972). *Human Problem Solving*. Englewood Cliffs, NJ: Prentice Hall.

Ng, H.T. & Mooney, R.J. (1990). On the role of coherence in abductive explanation. *Proceedings of the Eighth National Conference on Artificial Intelligence* (pp. 337-342). Menlo Park, CA: AAAI/MIT Press.

Patil, R. (1981). Causal representation of patient illness for electrolyte and acid-base diagnosis. In *MIT/LCS/TR-267*. Cambridge: MIT Press.

Pearl, J. (1987). On evidential reasoning in a hierarchy of hypotheses. *Artificial Intelligence, 28,* (1986) 9-15. [Reprinted in I. Shafer & J. Pearl (Eds.), (1990), *Uncertain Reasoning* (pp. 449-451). San Mateo, CA: Morgan Kaufman.]

Peirce, C.S. (1958). *Collected Papers: 1931-1958*. Cambridge MA: Harvard University Press.

Peng, Y. & Reggia, J.A. (1990). *Abductive Inference Methods for Diagnostic Problem-Solving*. Berlin: Springer Verlag.

Piaget, J. (1970). *Structuralism*. New York: Basic Books.

Poole, D. (1989). Normality and faults in logic-based diagnosis. *Proceeding of the Eleventh International Joint Conference on Artificial Intelligence* (pp. 1304-1310). San Mateo, CA: Morgan Kaufman.

Reggia, J., Nau, D.S., & Wang, P.Y. (1983). Diagnostic expert systems based on a set covering model. *International Journal of Man-Machine Studies, 19(5),* 437-460.

Selman, B. & Levesque, H.J. (1990). Abductive and default reasoning: A computational core. *Proceedings of the Eighth National Conference on Artificial Intelligence* (pp. 343-348). Menlo Park, CA: AAAI/MIT Press.

Torasso, P. & Console, L. (1989). *Diagnostic Problem Solving: Combining Heuristic, Approximate, and Causal Reasoning*. London: North Oxford Academic.

Chapter 16

Integrating Skill and Knowledge in Expert Agents

Henry Hexmoor & Stuart C. Shapiro

Introduction

An empirical characteristic of the development of expertise is the transformation of deliberative, "conscious" activity to more automatic forms. In this chapter, we will discuss knowledge organization and representation for skills, and the integration of skills with knowledge. We will illustrate our concepts by discussing a few implemented agents in hardware and software. An underlying theme for our formal representations is *embodiment* of knowledge. "We define *embodiment* as the notion that the *representation and extension of concepts* is in part determined by the *physiology* (the bodily functions) of an agent, and in part by the *interaction* of the agent with its environment" (Hexmoor, Lammens and Shapiro 1993, p. 326). With this prior definition, all computer representations are embodiments of their hardware and how they are used in interaction with other agents. We intend our definition to apply to agents that physically manipulate the environment and themselves have physically moving parts. Furthermore, we use our definition as a prescription for developing representations instead of a description of all possible representations. We have developed an autonomous agent architecture that incorporates action and perception which are embodied in terms of the moving parts and the dynamics of the moving parts when the agent interacts with the world.

It seems clear that book knowledge differs from practical knowledge. For example, an automobile driver uses a combination of his book knowledge of driving rules and tips as well as practical knowledge in his actual driving. In this chapter, we will not focus on this distinction. Instead, we are concerned with the balance of using knowledge and skill over time as two components of expertise. Henceforth, skills in this chapter refer to motor skills. For us, skills are that part of expertise that is acquired through practice. Furthermore, once a skill is acquired it is largely inaccessible to explanation, without reflection and reasoning.

This inaccessibility leaves an unclear breakdown of expertise into book knowledge and practical knowledge. By focusing on the distinction between knowledge and skills, one can see that the expertise of a medical specialist lies mostly in his knowledge about his area of specialization, while the expertise of a surgeon includes his skills in surgical procedures. The expertise of an athlete is mostly his skills. Skills are often hard to put into words. Athletic coaches often speak in strange jargon that does not refer to body parts. Examples from bowling are over-turn, "applying too much spin to the ball and not enough finger lift"; loafing, "not lifting or turning the ball properly with the result that the ball lags and lacks action"; and yanking the shot, "hanging onto the ball too long and pulling it to across the body" (Taylor 1991). But what are skills and how does an agent possess them? Why is it sometimes hard to verbalize skills? Can skill knowledge be represented by a production system or a declarative representation? Anderson's (1983) Act* assumes the answer is yes to the last question. Instead of empirical tests and psychological investigation, we build computer models that seem to mimic the internal mechanisms of an expert in acquiring skill and knowledge (i.e., expertise). We hope that our computational models and synthetic agents will provide an alternative mechanism for exploring issues about knowledge and skill which is somewhat independent of ethnomethodology and biological organisms.

Traditionally, expert systems addressed the knowledge component of expertise. These systems were often designed with an impoverished ontology of percepts and actions (e.g., IF symptoms A and B are present THEN prescribe medication C). We posit that the knowledge used in expertise is necessarily embodied in the expert and ought to be represented in terms of the agent's physiology and the interaction of the agent with its environment. We don't use embodiment as merely meaning that the agent has a body. Knowledge resides in various parts of the expert agent (e.g., cerebellum versus cerebral cortex), and is used in different cognitive processes.

Once a skill is acquired, it changes with experience. However, natural language plays an important role for skills that are primarily acquired through communication. We hypothesize that the human brain's natural language comprehension mechanism translates representations to embodied representations which are more natural for representing skills. We believe that many current implemented natural language comprehension systems ignore the role of body-centered understanding. With this hypothesis we believe we need to model multi-level representations within an agent. This chapter focuses on embodied representations of knowledge that are "natural" for the agent, and leaves the natural language abstractions which make communication easier as a separate problem.

We believe that in order to understand expertise, it is important to understand the ability to use, coordinate, and learn the knowledge involved in different cognitive processes that exist in different parts of the expert agent's body. In our investigations, we are examining the mechanisms for acquiring knowledge and skill, the migration of knowledge in the agent, and the nature of expertise, by designing and implementing an agent architecture. In this chapter, we describe our architecture and give an ontology of concepts in our approach. We also describe a representational formalism for encoding skills. We then describe "agents" that have been developed using our architecture. We demonstrate several of our concepts about expertise concretely using our implemented agents. This will be followed by a discussion of knowledge migration in our architecture and implemented agents as examples. We will conclude this chapter by pointing out how agents use and gain knowledge and skills with our architecture.

Architecture

To model an expert, we have developed an architecture called grounded layered architecture with integrated reasoning, GLAIR (Hexmoor, Lammens and Shapiro 1992), schematically presented in figure 1.

The figure shows three distinct levels: knowledge, perceptuo-motor, and sensory-actuator. These levels provide a framework for modeling distinct types of behavior generation. The Knowledge Level (KL) is considered to contain the agent's "conscious" beliefs and plans. The KL is the only level in GLAIR accessible to natural language use and generation. This accessibility to natural language sets the KL apart from the other levels. We use the SNePS Knowledge Representation and Reasoning system (Shapiro and Rapaport 1992; Shapiro and Group 1992) to represent the knowledge at the KL. Knowledge representation and reasoning systems such as SNePS are general purpose tools to explicitly and symbolically encode the contents and processes of a cognitive agent's "mind." These systems have formal properties that help in the analysis of what is represented.

The other two levels, Perceptuo-Motor Level (PML) and Sensori-Actuator Level (SAL), are considered to contain "unconscious" processes. The PML is used to model skills. The SAL models the actuator hardware and all unchanging and least complex agent-centered processing of actuator input and output. For detailed discussions of GLAIR and comparisons with competing architectures see (Hexmoor et al. 1992).

We have adopted an ontology of terms used in various parts of GLAIR which primarily reflects our choice of levels for modeling various parts of an autonomous agent. In the next section, we describe our terms.

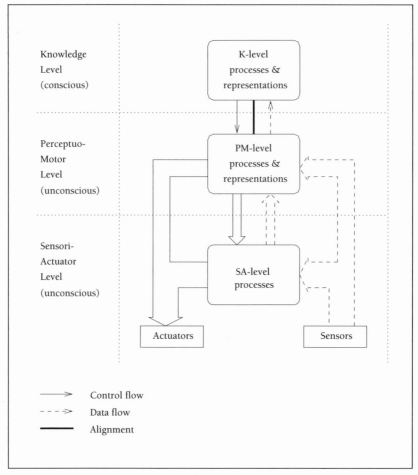

Figure 1. Schematic representation of the GLAIR architecture. Width of control and data paths suggests the amount of information passing through (bandwidth). Sensors include both world-sensors and propio-sensors.

An Ontology

The entities modeled at the KL are *plans, goals, actions, acts, intentions,* and *beliefs.* These terms are described elsewhere (e.g., Kumar and Shapiro 1991), and in this chapter the reader can think of them as having their common sense meanings. The entities modeled at the PML are *sensations, actuators, commands, behaviors,* and *tendencies.* We use *sensations* as atomic terms used in describing perception. *Actuators* are the effecting parts of the agent (e.g., muscles or motors). We assume that actuators can be commanded independently.[1] A *command* is an instantaneous atomic control signal for an actuator.

In the case of continuously changing actuator parameters, a command is a control signal for the rate of change of the values for the actuator. By a *behavior* we mean a cluster of possibly simultaneous commands, at most one for each actuator.[2] A *tendency* is a measure of an agent's preference when there are alternative commands. This preference is computed and maintained based on the agent's prior experiences.

In order to transfer information between levels, either all terms in the levels have a one-to-one correspondence, or some terms do not correspond to anything in the other levels. For example, a sequence of commands at the PML may map into a single primitive act (see Kumar and Shapiro 1991) at the KL. For another example, intentions do not map to anything at the PML because intentions at the KL refer to a decision to execute that action. At the PML there is no need to consider decisions about actions.

When there is a one-to-one correspondence, there is a correspondence between terms in the Knowledge Representation and Reasoning (KRR) system on one hand and perceived objects, properties, events, and motor capabilities on the other hand. We call this correspondence *alignment*.

Obviously, beyond what the ontology dictates, there is no domain-independent way of deciding what goes into each level. We consider the locus of knowledge and skills to be dynamically changing between levels. *Perceptual reduction* and *action elaboration* are two salient features that guide location of knowledge and skills. Perceptual reduction is the grouping of perceptual data into perceptual concepts at higher levels. Action elaboration is the expansion of motor actions into finer actuator controls at lower levels.

In addition to the changing locus of knowledge and skill, the locus of control also changes. We will discuss exact mappings between levels in the context of projects and domains later in this chapter.

In the following subsection we describe Perceptuo-Motor Automata (PMA) as our representational tool in the PML. PMA can be considered to be a specialized production system as much as Soar (Laird 1987) is a specialized production system. Our tool is specialized for modeling situated actions in intelligent agency. Many features, like concurrency of behavior activation, distinguish it from similar systems.

Perceptuo-Motor Automata

In order to generate commands for actuators, we have developed a representation mechanism and a modeling tool for representing and generating behaviors (metaphorically at the "unconscious" level) of an autonomous agent (Hexmoor 1992). PMA is a tool used in modeling the PML behavioral components of a GLAIR-agent. Behavioral modules that PMA (as a tool) models are also called PMA. Therefore, we might refer to a PMA for *chewing* behavior and a PMA for *walking*. Our use of the term will be clear from the context.

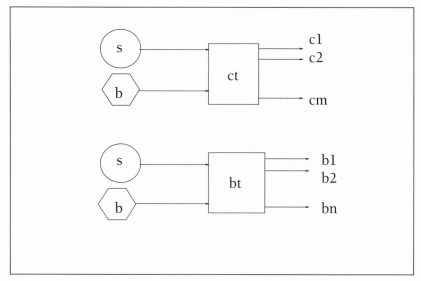

Figure 2. A command transition is shown on the left that maps a Situation, s1, and Behavior, b1, to a Command, c1. A Behavior transition is shown in the right that maps a pair of Situations, s2, and Behavior, b2, to a Behavior, b3.

PMA as a system is designed to constantly produce signals/impulses for the actuators. We consider these signals/impulses to be instantaneous controls that determine actuator activation levels. For example, for a mobile robot, signals would be activation levels of motors and each signal/impulse would be a fraction of a second in duration. In the context of a GLAIR-agent, PMA models rapid and automatic behaviors of the agent.

We assume that agent's have a finite number of actuators. An actuator is an effecting part of the agent that can be independently commanded. A behavior is a set of commands, one for each actuator. Multiple behaviors can be active at the same time. Therefore, an actuator can be commanded simultaneously by multiple behaviors. In PMA as part of a GLAIR-agent, all commands for an actuator issued by different behaviors are passed directly to the SAL.

The set of behavioral modules that PMA models in a domain is formally represented by <Sensations, Commands, Command Transition, Behaviors, Behavior Transition, Rewards>. For example, a Sensation for a mobile robot that walks in building hallways can be its *distance to the wall*. In Air Battle Simulation (ABS) (Hexmoor *et al.* 1993), *relative distances from the enemy in X, Y, and Z axes* are Sensations. We assume that all possible situations for a PMA can be specified by a combination of one or more Sensations. We call a pattern of Sensations that is used for input to a PMA a Situation. In ABS, instantiations of <*distanceX, distanceY, distanceZ, orientation*> are Situations (e.g.,

<close-front, close-right, close-above, parallel> is a Situation). In summary, PMA input is a Situation, an *n*-tuple of Sensations. Commands are a set of primitive activations that can be sent to actuators. Command Transitions (CT) are transformation functions that produce commands for execution for inputs of situation or situation/behavior pairs. This is shown in figure 2. CTs are functions since the output of a CT is a set of one or more Commands. The simplest CTs are mappings of Sensations to Commands (Sensations ↦ Command). CTs can be disabled by inhibiting them. Inhibition is useful when the agent needs to override "unconscious" behaviors generated by PMA with "conscious" behaviors generated by the KL.

CTs use Behaviors and previous Commands in producing output. When the latest sensations along with the current Behavior match a command transition, that command transition activates a command which is then executed. Our implementation of PMA is object-oriented and written in Common Lisp and C. Our descriptions of PMA operation therefore consider CTs as objects that can process their input and activate output nodes. CTs may take into account an estimated accumulated reward for Commands. We call the latter "tendencies." Tendencies are computed using reinforcement based learning techniques (Sutton 1988). Below is a list of Command Transition types.

- Sensations ↦ Command
- Previous command X Sensations ↦ Command
- Behavior X Sensations ↦ Command
- Tendency X Sensations ↦ Command
- Previous-command X Behavior X Sensations ↦ Command
- Tendency X Behavior X Sensations ↦ Command
- Previous-command X Behavior X Tendency X Sensations ↦ Command

Behaviors partition a PMA into smaller PMAs, each a set of command transitions. Behavior Transitions (BT) are transformations that update the Behavior in effect. When the agent decides on a different course of action at the KL, that effects a change in Behavior at the PML, a BT is used to guide the change of behavior. Alternatively, a BT can be used at PML without a "conscious" decision. BT is Behavior1 X Sensations ↦ Behavior2 where Behavior1 and Behavior2 are Behaviors.

Rewards are used for learning. Rewards are static "goodness values" associated with situations. Estimated accumulated rewards are estimations of accumulations of rewards over time used in delayed credit assignment. These are determined prior to PMA execution and remain unchanged throughout.

Behaviors, Behavior Transitions, and Rewards in a PMA can be empty. The simplest class of PMA is that in which all three of these elements are empty. Below is the pattern of combinations of tuples, each defining a class of PMA. For example, *<Sensation, Commands, Command Transitions, NIL, NIL, NIL>*

models a PMA consisting of sensation/command pairs. It does not include PMAs partitioned into behaviors or rewards in CTs. Therefore it allows the possibility of nondeterminism (i.e., one situation can be mapped into several commands). The following is the pattern for all possibilities for CT types.

[Previous command **X**] [Behavior **X**] [Tendency **X**] Sensations ↦ command set

The capacity to produce asynchronous and concurrent behaviors and concurrent Commands for actuators allows the modeling of certain interactions with the agents in the world. What is interesting is: (a) the serendipity of behavior combinations unbeknownst to the agent (i.e., emergent behaviors), and (b) the way the agent makes use of the successful interactions in the world by various kinds of learning processes: PMA is used as the agent's lowest level mechanism to learn from the positive interactions in the world.

In the following section, we describe examples of agents we are developing that illustrate the principles of the GLAIR architecture. Each agent is designed to exemplify different features of our architecture.

GLAIR Agents

We have developed several agents among which are a player of a video-game Air Battle Simulation (ABS) named Gabby, for GLAIR Air Battler, and an autonomous mobile robot named Gerry (the "G" stands for GLAIR and the two "r"s stand for "roving robot"). Gerry and Gabby differ in their mapping of terms between the KL and the PML. This difference reflects their different modes of interaction with the world. We conjecture that Gabby is more "mindful" of its actions and monitors its actions. We need to further analyze the mapping of terms between the KL and the PML to understand the modes of interactions.

All agents display a variety of integrated behaviors. We distinguish between deliberative, reactive, and reflexive behaviors. These behaviors are mostly exhibited by the KL, the PML, and the SAL respectively. As we move down from the KL to the PML and the SAL, computational and representational power is traded for better response time and simpler control. The agent learns from and automates its interactions with the environment.

Gabby and Air Battle Simulation

Figure 3 schematically presents the structure of the GLAIR agent that plays the ABS video-game. We will refer to this agent as Gabby. Before it starts learning, Gabby does not have a PMA and therefore uses "conscious" level reasoning (i.e., SNePS rules; Kumar and Shapiro 1991), to decide what move to make. Once transitions are learned and cached in a PMA, Gabby uses the PMA for deciding its next move whenever possible. By adding learning strategies, a PMA is developed that caches moves decided at the KL for future

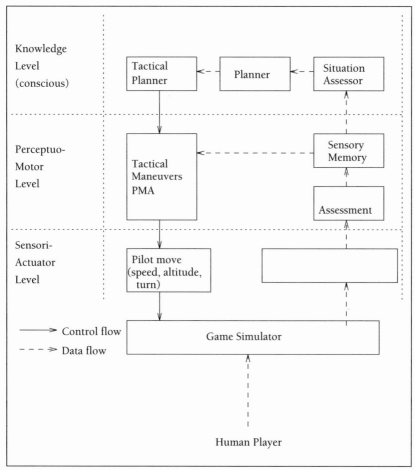

*Figure 3. Schematic representation of the Air Battle Simulation
playing GLAIR agent, Gabby.*

use. Here again, learning is used to mark PMA moves that proved unwise
and to reinforce moves that turn out to be successful. Gabby demonstrates
real time behaviors and the interlevel alignment mechanism.

The ABS video game runs on SparcStations and simulates World War I-
style air plane dog-fights between Gabby and a human player. The game display consists of a main window giving a horizontal view, a side window giving a vertical view, and two "damage reports." This is shown in figure 4. The
control panel window is shown in figure 5. The human player's plane is always considered to be in the center of the two shaded areas. The horizontal
two-dimensional position and orientation of Gabby's plane are displayed by

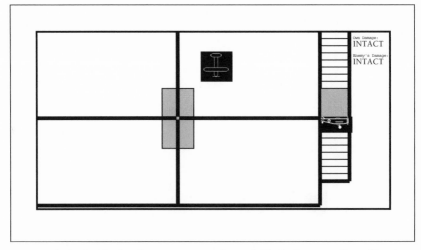

Figure 4. Air Battle Simulation game windows. Gabby's plane is indicated by the drawing of a plane in the upper right quadrant of the main window and by the drawing of a plane in the side window. This figure shows Gabby fleeing, flying parallel to and at a higher altitude than the human. The shaded regions denote shooting range. If Gabby's plane appears in both shaded regions, whichever plane is facing the other (possibly both) will fire.

the drawing of a plane in the main window, and its height relative to the human's plane is indicated by the drawing of a plane in the side window. The condition of the human's plane is indicated by the report labeled "Own Damage," and the condition of Gabby's plane by the report labeled "Enemy's Damage." When the two planes are close in all three dimensions, as indicated by Gabby's plane being shown in the two shaded areas, whichever plane is facing the other one automatically fires: That is, neither Gabby nor the human makes a separate decision about when to fire.

The human player uses the control panel to choose a move, which comprises a combination of changing altitude, speed, and direction. When the human player presses the GO button, Gabby also selects a move. The game simulator then considers the two moves to determine the outcome, and updates the screen and the accumulated damage to the two planes, thus simulating simultaneous moves. The game ends when one or both of the two players' planes are destroyed.

Gerry

Gerry began as an Omnibot 2000 toy robot (Amherst Systems, Inc.). Gerry is a 2.5 feet tall mobile robot with two independently driven wheels, an in-

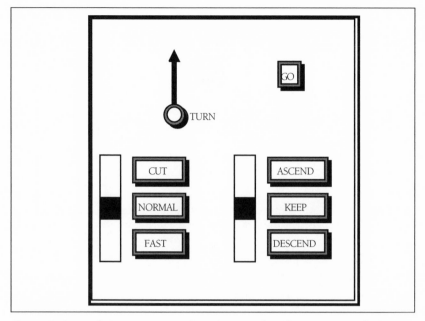

Figure 5. Air Battle Instrument Panel window. To select/change a move, the human player pushes one of the buttons in each column and adjusts the TURN dial by repeatedly clicking on it. CUT, NORMAL, and FAST are used for speed selection.

frared transmitter, four infrared sensors, a front and rear bumper, and four corner whiskers controlled by a 6.270 board developed at MIT for use in their 6.270 class. These boards have a 6811 microprocessor with multitasking capabilities. Gerry has four primitive abilities: going straight, turning right, turning left, and stopping. When a whisker or a bumper senses contact with an external object, Gerry performs a reflex. There are reflexes corresponding to each whisker and bumper Reflexes are implemented in Gerry's SAL. At the PML of Gerry, behaviors are implemented using PMA.

Currently, Gerry has PMAs and some basic knowledge at the KL for searching for another robot, Garry. Garry is one foot tall, has two independently driven wheels, an infrared transmitter, two infrared sensors, and three front bumper/whiskers controlled by a 6.270 board. When a whisker or a bumper senses contact with an external object, Garry performs a reflex. Garry is a Lego robot.

Figure 6 shows that Gerry's KL knowledge consists of three separate components of knowledge for spotting Garry, catching up with Garry, and grabbing Garry. At the KL, Gerry doesn't know that these are parts of a task for getting Garry. Perceptual reduction is implemented by having concepts at the KL correspond to patterns of stimulus at the PML. For example, "no-garry" at

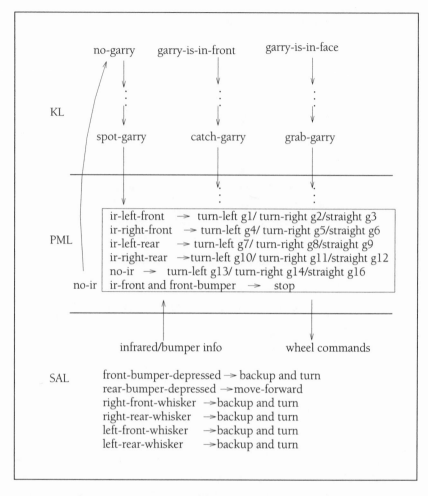

Figure 6. Schematic representation of the Gerry's GLAIR components. The box in the PML shows a PMA for spotting Gerry. There are others for catching up with Garry and grabbing Garry. Variable gi next to each action in the PMA box represents goodness of action in the context of a corresponding situation.

the KL corresponds to the pattern of no infrared being sensed at the PML. At the KL, no concepts for specific infrared signals as in percetuo-motor level exist. Each action in the knowledge level is expanded into a PMA in the perceptuo-motor level. This is an implementation of action elaboration in which actions at the PML are finer compared to the KL actions. As shown in Figure 6, action elaboration is implemented by mapping an action in the KL to a PMA. For example, "spot-garry" is shown to map to a PMA in the PML, which is shown in the solid box. Transitions in the PMA map infrared situations to commands. With Gerry, each situation in the PMA is mapped to all commands. What determines applicability of a command, in a given situation, is its goodness level shown by *gi* in figure 6.

At the SAL, Gerry has six reflexes for avoiding obstacles. Figure 6 shows mnemonic forms of these reflexes. The actual implementation of actuator commands is given in terms of wheel commands.

Concurrent behaviors at the PML are allowed, as are concurrent reflexes. Behaviors and reflexes produce wheel commands. All wheel commands are given a priority level when they are generated. The PML wheel commands have lower priority than the ones for reflexes. One exception is that behaviors have higher priority than reflexes if a reflex needs to be suppressed. For example, to catch Garry, Gerry needs to have its front bumper touch Garry and sense high levels of infrared radiation with its front sensors. Normally, touching an object with the front bumper triggers a reflex to backup and turn. However, we want to suppress this reflex. There is a module at the SAL for arbitration and combination of all wheel commands. This module examines flags for suppression and, if reflexes are not suppressed, it sums the effect of reflex-generated wheel commands and passes it to the wheels. If no reflex is active, it sums all behavior-generated wheel commands and passes the result to the wheels. If reflex suppression is turned on, it ignores reflexes and attends to the behavior generated commands.

We have programmed PMAs and the knowledge at the KL so Gerry will look for Garry and will stop when it finds Garry. At the PML, Gerry is to resolve nondeterminacy using reinforcement based learning. Gerry's actions can be controlled either completely by the KL or by the PML.

In the following section we describe learning in a GLAIR level that is based on the contents and influence of a neighboring level. We call this type of learning knowledge migration. We will use Gerry and Gabby to illustrate this learning strategy.

Knowledge Migration

An important feature of GLAIR is that it allows knowledge to migrate from one level to another and in doing so change the representation in order to be consistent with the representation used at the new level. The underlying assumption here is that parts of an agent's knowledge about its world have "natural" loci either as deliberative knowledge, as reactions, or as reflexes. As the agent interacts with the world, the knowledge may be gained at some level and later find its "natural" locus at a different level and migrate there. In the following subsection, we will describe learning in the PML from the KL.

"Conscious" to "Unconscious" Migration

"What to do next" is a the ability to choose an action to perform, given the current situation (Hexmoor and Nute 1992). Our migration of knowledge from the "conscious" to "unconscious" is limited to "what to do next." As in *automaticity,* migration of knowledge about actions from the KL to the PML makes the agent's reactions in the environment faster and less deliberate.

> In novel situations or in situations requiring moment-to-moment decisions, controlled processing may be adopted and used to perform accurately, though slowly. Then as the situations become familiar, always requiring the same sequence of processing operations, automatic processing will develop, attention demands will be eased, other controlled operations can be carried out in parallel with the automatic processing, and performance will improve (Shiffrin 1977, p. 161).

Knowledge compilation (Anderson 1983) is a twofold procedure of *proceduralization* to convert declarative knowledge into productions and *composition* to combine several productions into one. Our knowledge migration is similar to Anderson's knowledge compilation in that the migration process produces PMA transitions which are a kind of production rules. However, unlike Anderson's knowledge compilation, our transitions in the PMA are maintained separately from the initial knowledge.

We describe two implementations of knowledge migration. In both, migration transforms representations of knowledge into PMA transitions.

In the process of knowledge migration, Gabby drops all the intermediate reasoning and only retains the stimuli/response pair in the PML. Furthermore, Gabby adds what it learns in each novel situation to the existing structure of the PML. By enriching existing structures in PML and extracting/reformatting knowledge existing at the KL we feel we have modeled a form of *chunking* (Miller 1956).

At the PML, commands have a one to one correspondence with KL actions, and behaviors have a one-to-one correspondence with KL goals. Consider C and B in the PML to be unique counterparts of A and G respectively in the KL and S to be the current situation. If $S \textbf{ X } B \mapsto C$ is not already a CT in the PML, it is made one. B is the behavior in effect and remains so until a new goal is selected at the "conscious" level. If a new G (corresponding to new behavior B' in the PML) is transmitted to the PML, the behavior in effect is updated to B'. If $S \textbf{ X } B \mapsto B'$ is not a BT, it is made one.

Example of Migration in the Agents. We started Gabby with an empty PMA. Whenever an appropriate PMA CT existed, it was used. Otherwise, the KL handled command generation, and a new PMA was created. As the game was played, we observed that the agent became more reactive since the PMA was used more often to generate behaviors instead of the KL.

Figure 7 shows a small, typical sample of PMA transitions Gabby learned while playing ABS. Many other transitions were learned. Only four CTs and

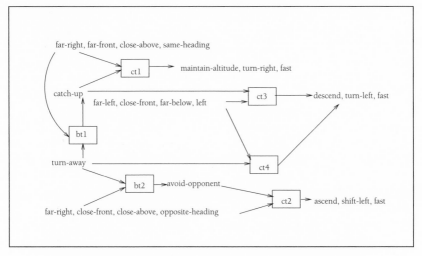

Figure 7. Sample of Learned Command and Behavior Transitions.

two BTs are shown in the figure. We narrowly consider knowledge of "what to do next" (Hexmoor and Nute 1992; i.e., given the current situation what action should be performed) to illustrate automaticity. In GLAIR, migration of knowledge about actions from the knowledge level to the PM-level can be thought of as a form of automaticity.

When Gabby in the knowledge level determines an action, it submits a pair of an action A and a goal G to the PML. At the PM-level, commands are one to one associated with K-level actions, and behaviors are one to one associated with K-level goals. Let's consider command C and behavior B to be the unique counterparts of action A and goal G respectively, and situation S to be the current situation. If $S \mathbf{X} B \mapsto C$ is not a CT, it is made one. B is the behavior in effect and unless a new goal is selected at the conscious level, it remains to be the behavior in effect. If a new G (corresponding to new behavior B' in the PM level) is transmitted to the PM-level, the behavior in effect is updated to be B'. If $S \mathbf{X} B \mapsto B'$ is not a BT, it is made one.

In figure 7, if the behavior is turn-away and the situation of the opponent is far-right, far-front, close-above, and same-heading, according to *bt1* the effective behavior will change to catch-up. With catch-up as effective behavior, if the situation persists, according to *ct1,* the command will be to maintain-altitude, turn-right, and fast. On the other hand, if the effective behavior is turn-away and the situation of the opponent is far-right, close-front, close-above, opposite-heading, according to *bt2,* the effective behavior will be avoid-opponent. If this situation persists and the effective behavior is avoid-opponent, according to *ct2,* ascend, shift-right and fast is the command to execute. $ct3$ and $ct4$ are two other command transitions that are learned and the transitions are self-evident from the figure.

Instead of learning through repetition as it occurs with automaticity, mappings for every novel situation in PMA were stored in the PML (i.e., one trial learning). After the first game ended, Gabby began succeeding games with partially learned PMAs and continued learning. The game involved highly recurring patterns of interaction. Interactions in situations perceived as near range and in pursuit were far more common than other patterns of interaction. Because patterns of interaction were repeated, novel situations became rare, and the rate of learning was inversely proportional to time.

We now turn to Gerry. In this agent, when the KL determines an action, it submits that action to the PML, where actions have a one to one correspondence with behaviors. The PML commands have no direct counterparts in the KL. In Gerry, we assume that at the PML there are a finite number of actuators and corresponding commands. When the KL decides on action A, say *approach an object,* at the PML, a number of command transitions are constructed, one for each actuator command. Unlike Gabby, in which a command transition is built for each stimulus/response pair at the KL, in Gerry for each KL stimulus/response pair a set of command transitions is constructed.

In the following subsection, we discuss learning at the KL as a result of migration from the PML.

"Unconscious" to "Conscious" Migration

When a recurring pattern of interaction between an agent and its environment is detected at the "unconscious" level and this interaction is consistently beneficial for the agent in the sense that it always puts the agent in a more "desirable" state, a concept can be constructed at the "conscious" level to represent this pattern. We consider this type of migration from the PM-level to the KL a form of *skill acquisition* or *habit formation*.

To illustrate, a pattern of interaction at the PML consists of a sequence of commands, C (e.g., c_1; c_2; ...; c_n) and the situations, S (e.g., s_1; s_2; ...; s_n) for which these commands were generated. All commands in the sequence were generated while behavior B was in effect. B may or may not have a goal counterpart, G, at the KL. If it has, a new act, A, is created to stand for C, and the triple $<s_1, G, A>$ is migrated to the KL. At the KL, the knowledge that s_1 is the precondition of C is constructed. In case there is no corresponding goal in the KL, a primitive act and the situation s_1 that triggered the sequence of commands, C (i.e., the precondition for c_1:) is migrated. The situation, s_1, will play the role of a precondition for the act.[3] From this triple, knowledge constructs are created to reflect the fact that s_1 is the precondition of C. Also learned is the planning knowledge that every time G needs to be achieved, A should be performed.

Skill Refinement

Our premise for skill refinement is that we have an agent who has some basic skills but for certain situations can't choose the best alternative because the consequences of the actions are unknown and there are inadequate biases from experience. In skill refinement, we are concerned with "unconscious" choices of action. Often what is migrated from the KL to the PML introduces nondeterminacy (i.e., for certain situations, more than one action is applicable). In this subsection, we will look at how an agent can improve its skills by improving its choice of action.

The rules of Gabby's PMA are situation/command pairs where a situation is paired with multiple commands. The object of learning is to learn which command, when performed in a given situation yields, the better result (i.e., results in a situation that is more "desirable").

Some situations in ABS are more desirable for Gabby than others (e.g., being right behind the enemy and in shooting range). To each situation, S, we assign a reward value, $R(S)$, between -1 and 1. As Gabby makes a move, it finds itself in a new situation. This new situation is not known to Gabby beforehand since the situation also depends on the other pilot's move. Since the new situation is not uniquely determined by Gabby's move, the game is not Markovian. The reinforcement-based learning we describe in this section has been proven to be effective only in Markovian environments.[4] Although we have successfully applied reinforcement learning in the non-Markovian domain of ABS, we cannot prove convergence of reinforcement learning in ABS.

In all of our modeling, we used Q-learning (Watkins 1989), which is a particular variety of reinforcement-based learning. In Q-learning, Utility($S(t)$, $C(t)$) is the evaluation of the appropriateness of command C in situation S when C is executed at time t in response to S at t. $R(S(t+1))$ is the "reward" received by being in state $S(t+1)$. For the agent, rewards are determined as the game is played and can not be determined beforehand. This is called the immediate reward. The following equality is maintained and propagated as each command is executed: At the start of the game, all Utility(S, C) in PMA are set to 1.

$$\text{Utility}(S(t), C(t)) = R(S(t+1))$$
$$+ \gamma \, [\lambda \, \text{Utility}(S(t+1), C(t+1))$$
$$+ (1-\lambda) \max_{C(t+1)} \text{Utility}(S(t+1), C(t+1))]$$

The parameter γ determines how important it is to be in the state that Gabby ends up in after his move. In reinforcement based learning, this is known as the discount factor. Parameter λ is known as the recency/learning factor.

Example of Skill Refinement in the Agents.   To test our implementation of reinforcement-based learning we tested Gabby in some playing situations. We developed a programmed opponent (a pseudo-human player) for Gabby

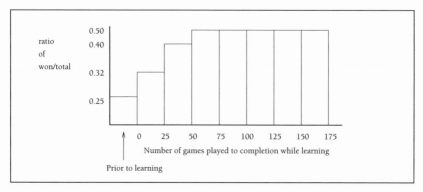

Figure 8. Learning rate using reinforcement based Q learning

that plays according to a fixed strategy written to simulate a strategy that a human player might use. We had the two programs play 25 games without learning. Gabby won about 30% of these games. We then turned on Gabby's reinforcement based learning, had the programs play an additional 175 games, and recorded the number of winning games for each set of 25. Gabby won 32% of the first learning set, 40% of the second set, 50% of the third set, and remained at that level thereafter. Gabby learned to be just as good as its opponent in winning the game. Once one of the planes gets behind the other, it is very hard to shake off the enemy. Gabby learned to be just as good as its enemy in finishing the enemy once in pursuit and attack. From our analysis of starting the game positions, it was equally probable for either plane to be in a position of pursuit and attack. When one plane had the opportunity to be in pursuit, losing by the pursuant became highly likely since both pilots are equally competent. Given its opponent's strategies, we conjecture that Gabby learned as much as possible. If we now were to improve the strategies of the pseudo-human player, we believe Gabby would improve again to match the level of competence of its opponent.

We assume that Gabby does not "know" about the long-term consequences of its actions. At the PML, we want to preserve reactivity and therefore, don't want the agent to learn long-term consequences of its actions. We also do not want to rely completely on learning "unconsciously" through reinforcement. The agent must, therefore, observe interactions with the world in order to learn sequences of actions that are in no way guaranteed to be successful but that are commonplace for the agent and have been used frequently with a high degree of success. In the following subsection, we briefly discuss learning from routine activities in the world.

"Routines" as Emergent Skills or Habits

"Routines are patterns of interaction between an agent and its world" (Agre

1987, p. 269). At times, these routines coincide with a *skill* or a *habit*. Our definition of a routine is "a course of action that is habitually (or by choice) adhered to." For simplicity, we can consider a routine as any frequently repeated sequence of actions. The adherence to a sequence of actions is a "desire" to follow one action after another without regard to applicability of actions. Since by routine we imply a tendency to follow a sequence of actions "blindly," at first glance this definition might seem to run counter to the situatedness view of activity (e.g., Clancey 1996) we have opted for in the PML. In contrast to traditional views, situated activity and situated cognition promote shallow internal models of the world.

Situated activity replaces "thinking ahead" with experiences of interactions with the world using the world as its own best model. In our situated approach, we want actions based on current situations, not based on reasoning about consequences of actions. With a routine, we want actions performed in sequence based merely on succession from previous actions. Such a course of action is squarely in the spirit of situated theory.

Not all routines are noticed by the agent. An agent may engage in a routine and not be "aware" of it. We call routines that the agent becomes "aware" of *emergent routines.* We use the term emergent to mean unpredictable and necessarily arising from interaction between the agent and its world. For instance, when an agent observes a substantially improved situation over a finite number of actions, the agent may recognize a successful routine. We associate all conscious routines with concepts available for the agent's reasoning. Some routines that reach the KL may be treated as a single action.

We see two ways emergent routines might be learned. We discussed one way of learning emergent routines in the section on migration of knowledge from the "unconscious" to the "conscious." A second technique is for the agent to "unconsciously" monitor the primitive actions at the KL that start off PMAs. When there is sufficient repetition in the sequence of KL actions, the sequence of actions is learned as a new complex action made up of the primitive actions.

At the PML, routines are like programs that compete to gain control. Like a skill or habit, once a routine gains control, it will usually run to completion without interruption. However, if a routine is interrupted by a process in another part of the agent's architecture, something out of the ordinary (unexpected) must have happened in the world. This is reminiscent of classical planning problems and recovery from failures (Georgeff 1987). However, we believe that with the emergence of situated cognition and the fact that reactive systems make no predictions about the results of actions, the concept of routine failure will be avoided.

Related Work

Our architecture and approach has been an attempt at bridging the gap between modeling deliberation (i.e., knowledge driven activity) and reactivity (i.e., skill driven activity). Our three layered architecture facilitates mediation between deliberation and reactivity. There are similar layered architectures with specific mediating layers (e.g., Bonasso et al. 1992; Gat 1992). A system for the role of mediation is the Reactive Action Packages (RAPS) of Jim Firby (1992). RAPS takes a set of high-level tasks generated by a planner and recursively decomposes them into a set of reactive skills that can be run on the robot. RAPS then activates and deactivates these sets of skills in order to accomplish tasks. RAPS is also responsible for monitoring the execution of the skills to see if they are moving the robot towards the goal. If the task is not being achieved, RAPS can choose another method for achieving the same task or take other corrective action.

Our agents learn within a layer and migrate expertise in between layers. A similar learning scheme is described in Bonasso and Kortenkamp (1994). Learning in the highest level improves cognitive skills. Learning in the middle layer improves the coherence between the other levels. Learning in the lowest level improves the agent's reflexive actions. In our architecture, and Bonasso's, knowledge that is migrated from the highest level to lower levels makes a task that is highly cognitive in the beginning (i.e., cognitive expertise), reactive and skilled in the future. In our architecture we go one step further and allow for repeated patterns of interactions (i.e., motor skills) at the low level to be redefined using cognitive concepts at a later time.

Summary and Conclusion

Our approach to the study of expertise is to build agents that use and acquire knowledge and skill. Our architecture for intelligent agency distinguishes between "conscious" and "unconscious" processes. Our approach involves the embodiment of actions in that it addresses migration of knowledge and the acquisition of new skills that emerge from repetition.

We used our architecture in modeling agents in several domains. One of these domains is a video-game in which a computer agent flies a WWI-style airplane. As the game progresses, this agent learns to maneuver the airplane more "unconsciously" and improves its decision making ability. This improvement shows a style of building skills from the agent's own knowledge and its interactions in the world. Our capturing skills are rather novel, especially among advocates of symbolic AI.

We have developed some preliminary techniques for learning routines from an agent's interactions with the world. By learning routines, an agent can become more automatic in its interaction in the world, and with certain routines, it can enrich its "conscious" knowledge about actions.

Acknowledgment

This work was supported in part by Equipment Grant No. EDUD-US-932022 from SUN Microsystems Computer Corporation. We are grateful to Johan Lammens and William Rapaport for their comments on the issues discussed in this chapter. The first author thanks Jeff Shrager of Xerox PARC for useful comments. We are grateful to editors Ken Ford, Paul Feltovich, and Robert Hoffman for many comments that improved our chapter.

Notes

1. This is a highly simplistic model of perception and action. For a more detailed theory of perception and action, see Kelso (1985).

2. Our distinction between acts and behaviors and the levels we choose to place them in GLAIR are consistent with "Acts, as I use the term, are what humans do when they intend to do something, whereas behavior is unintended" (Collins 1990, p. 30). As does Collins, we see intentionality to be the distinguishing characteristic of acts and behaviors.

3. We will either have all the commands as acts at the KL or just invent a new act for the sequence of commands, but the commands themselves will not exist at the KL.

4. The Markovian assumption for an agent is that the effect of an agent's actions only depends on its current state.

References

Agre, P.E. & Chapman, D. (1987). Pengi: An implementation of a theory of activity. In *Proceedings of American Association for Artificial Intelligence* (pp. 268-272). Seattle, WA: AAAI Press.

Anderson, J. (1983). *The Architecture of Cognition*. Cambridge: Harvard University Press.

Bonasso, R.P., Antonisse, H.J. & Slack, M.G. (1992). A reactive robot system for find and fetch tasks in an outdoor environment. In *Proceedings of the Tenth National Conference on Artificial Intelligence* (pp. 801-808). Menlo Park, CA: AAAI Press.

Bonasso, R.P. & Kortenkamp, D. (1994). An intelligent agent architecture in which to pursue robot learning. In *Working Notes: MCL COLT 1994 Robot Learning Workshop*.

Clancey, W.J. (1996). The conceptual nature of knowledge, situations, and activity. In P.J. Feltovich, K.M. Ford & R.R. Hoffman (Eds.), *Expertise in Context* (pp. 247-291). Menlo Park, CA: AAAI/MIT Press.

Collins, H. (1990). *Artificial Experts: Social Knowledge and Intelligent Machines*. Cambridge, MA: The MIT Press.

Firby, R.J. (1992). Building symbolic primitives with continuous control routines. In *Proceedings of the International Conference on AI Planning Systems*.

Gat, E. (1992). Integrating planning and reacting in a heterogeneous asynchronous architecture for controlling real-world mobile robots. In *Proceedings Tenth National Conference on Artificial Intelligence* (pp. 809-815). Menlo Park, CA: AAAI Press.

Georgeff, M.P. (1987). Planning. In *Annual Reviews of Computer Science,* Vol. 2, (pp. 359-400). Palo Alto, CA: Annual Reviews.

Hexmoor, H., Caicedo, G., Bidwell, F. & Shapiro, S. (1993). Air battle simulation: An agent with conscious and unconscious layers (TR93-14). In *University of Buffalo Graduate Conference in Computer Science-93*. Dept. of Computer Science, SUNY at Buffalo, NY.

Hexmoor, H., Lammens, J. & Shapiro, S. (1992). *An autonomous agent architecture for integrating perception and acting with grounded, embodied symbolic reasoning* (Tech. Rep. CS-92-21). Dept. of Computer Science, SUNY at Buffalo, NY.

Hexmoor, H., Lammens, J. & Shapiro, S.C. (1993). Embodiment in GLAIR: A grounded layered architecture with integrated reasoning. In D.D. Dankel (Ed.), *Proceedings of the Sixth Florida Artificial Intelligence Research Symposium* (pp. 325-329). [Also available as CS Dept. TR93-10. SUNY at Buffalo, NY.]

Hexmoor, H. & Nute, D. (1992). *Methods for deciding what to do next and learning* (Tech. Rep. AI-1992-01). AI Programs, University of Georgia, Athens, GA. [Also available as CS Department TR-92-23. SUNY at Buffalo, NY.]

Kelso, J.A.S. (Ed.). (1985). *Human Motor Behavior.* Hillsdale, NJ: Erlbaum.

Laird, J.E., Newell, A. & Rosenbloom, P.S. (1987). Soar: An architecture for general intelligence. *Artificial Intelligence Journal, 33,* 1-64.

Kumar, D. & Shapiro, S.C. (1991). Modeling a rational cognitive agent in SNePS. In P. Barahona, L.M. Pereira & A. Porto (Eds.), *EPIA 91: 5th Portugese Conference on Artificial Intelligence, Lecture Notes in Artificial Intelligence,* 541 (pp. 120-134). Heidelberg: Springer-Verlag.

Miller G. (1956). The magical number seven, plus or minus two: Some limits on our capacity for processing information. *Psychological Review, 63-2,* 81-97.

Shapiro, S.C. & Group, T.S.I. (1992). *SNePS-2 User's Manual.* Dept. of Computer Science, SUNY at Buffalo, NY.

Shapiro, S.C. & Rapaport, W.J. (1992). The SNePS family. *Computers & Mathematics with Applications, 23(2-5),* 243-275.

Shiffrin, R.M. & Schneider, W. (1977). Controlled and automatic human information processing: II. perceptual learning, automatic attending, and a general theory. *Psychological Review, 84-2,* 127-190.

Sutton, R. (1988). Learning to predict by the methods of temporal differences. *Machine Learning, 3,* 3-44.

Taylor, D. (1991). *Bowling Strikes.* Chicago: Contemporary Books.

Watkins, C. (1989). *Learning from delayed rewards.* Ph.D. thesis, King's College, Cambridge, UK.

CHAPTER 17

Toward Automated Expert Reasoning and Expert-Novice Communication

Michael Miller & Donald Perlis

Introduction

The formal study of inference has undergone an explosion over the past 15 years with the introduction of nonmonotonic (default) reasoning (e.g., Reiter 1980; McDermott and Doyle 1980; McCarthy 1980). Here we consider some ramifications of default reasoning that may be applicable to automated expertise. It is now well recognized that a great deal of practical knowledge about any domain is in the form of defaults. This fact suggests the possibility of characterizing expertise in terms of defaults and default use. We will do so toward the end of the chapter after developing some prerequisite machinery. One ingredient in our characterization is the capacity to explicitly deny defaults; this concept has received little attention in the literature and seems to require some new technical devices.

We first discuss defaults and their pervasiveness in reasoning, both for experts and novices. Then we consider special defaults, which we call *range* defaults, and argue that they are needed in expert reasoning, and that novices learn in part by substituting range defaults for simple defaults.

Default Reasoning

The commonsense world is far too complex for reasoners, human or otherwise, to be aware of all information that may be germane to a situation at any given time. Therefore, very often a conclusion one draws is not necessarily true; additional information might have "defeated" the conclusion and even prevented the inference in the first place. When I learn that Tweety is a bird, it is reasonable for me to conclude that Tweety can fly, since birds *typically* fly; but the conclusion may be false nevertheless. An endless supply of counterexamples can be constructed: Tweety may have had her wings clipped or may have become a victim of an oil-spill or may be a penguin; all good reasons for her not to be a flyer. Moreover, had I known the additional information that Tweety was a penguin, I would not have concluded that she could fly in the first place. Very many cases of practical reasoning are of this sort. Yet this form of reasoning lies outside the framework of traditional monotonic logic in which more information leads to more (not fewer) conclusions (Minsky 1975).

Researchers have addressed this issue by developing formalisms for default (or nonmonotonic) reasoning, in which something inferred from one set of information may fail to be inferred from that set augmented with additional information. Three well-known such formalisms are Reiter's (1980) default logic (DL), McDermott and Doyle's (1980) nonmonotonic logic (NML), and McCarthy's (1980) circumscription. Each of these offers a formal treatment of a reasoner coming to a reasonable yet defeasible conclusion, based on whatever knowledge is available plus some default rule(s). Just what is a reasonable conclusion, how it is reached, and what the default rules are vary from formalism to formalism.

In looking more closely at the Tweety example, we can see two elements at work. The first is a default principle (which we will usually refer to simply as a *default*) about typical features of birds, such as "birds typically fly," and the second is a means to employ that knowledge to draw a conclusion about particular birds (e.g., Tweety). Research in default reasoning has dealt with these two elements in varying ways. It is our contention in this chapter that for some purposes, such as representing novice-expert differences, it is important to separate these two aspects sharply. As a matter of notation, we will write $Bird(x) \rightarrow_{typ} Fly(x)$ for the default "birds typically fly"; more generally we write $\Psi \rightarrow_{typ} \Phi$ for "Ψ's typically are Φ's" (or "Ψ's typically have property Φ"). This notation is intended to be neutral among all the standard default formalisms: in DL, $\rightarrow_{typ}$ would be expressed as an inference rule; in NML it would involve a consistency predicate; and in circumscription it would involve an abnormality predicate.

Expertise

Cognitive scientists have intensively studied expertise in many settings. Not surprisingly, it is novice-expert differences that motivate many of these studies. Mayer (1992), among others, describes several knowledge-based distinctions between experts and novices including the following: 1) novices tend to store their knowledge in small fragmented units, while experts store theirs in larger interconnected functional units and 2) experts tend to know and use "deep" knowledge while novices use more superficial knowledge.

Experts have substantial knowledge about their domain of expertise, yet there is some indication that their judgments can be based on surprisingly little information (see Ebbesen and Konechi 1975; and Einhorn 1974). For instance, some studies indicate that in medical diagnosis, experts form a few, well-focused hypotheses early in the process (even before adequate data is presented), and use that to guide what data they seek; in contrast novices follow more of a broad searching strategy, don't have well-formulated hypotheses early on, and obtain much more information (much of which is not of value) (Kassirer and Gorry 1978).[1]

Feltovich, Johnson, Moller and Swanson (1984) suggest several postulates regarding different characteristics of novice and expert knowledge bases (in the domain of medicine). Included is that the novice's knowledge base is sparse—it lacks the cross-referencing and clustering structure of the expert's dense knowledge base. Also, the novice's knowledge is more imprecise than the expert's. This fact is, in part, due to the expert's "fine-tuning" of her knowledge to different contexts through clinical experience. These differences result in novice expectations being "either overly general, allowing clinical findings that should not occur, or overly specific, not allowing the legitimate range." Rau (1993) provides a computational treatment of breadth and salience of knowledge that appears to be related to the appropriate range of application of knowledge in making judgments.

Both experts and novices draw conclusions based on their knowledge. They may differ in their knowledge; for example, an ornithologist will likely believe the default that cardinals are either red (males) or russet (females)—with rare exceptions being white (albinos)—while a casual observer (i.e., a novice) may mistakenly believe simply that cardinals are typically red, a narrower range of possibilities than that used by the expert.[2]

Experts and novices may also differ in how they draw conclusions from their knowledge. This knowledge/conclusion-drawing distinction can be misleading, though. The inference procedures by which one draws conclusions can be partly encoded as declarative knowledge, such as in typicality statements. This fact will become important as our discussion proceeds.

An Example

For much of this chapter we rely on motivation from a seemingly simple dialog between Tommy, a young boy or even a (novice) robot, and Sue an (expert) ornithologist responsible for teaching Tommy about birds. Sue, but not Tommy, knows that female cardinals are russet and males are red. Sue takes Tommy to the zoo and the following conversation ensues:

Tommy: "Look, someone's feeding all those birds!"

Sue: "Do you know what kind of birds they are?"

Tommy: "No."

Sue: "They're cardinals."

Tommy: "But they're not red. I thought cardinals were supposed to be bright red."

Sue: "I used to think that also. Quite a few are red, but many others are russet, like these."

Tommy: "Are all cardinals red or russet?"

Sue: "Almost; a very few are white albinos. I wonder why only russet ones are here."

Sue (to the zookeeper): "Why are there only female cardinals here?"

Zookeeper: "We put the males in another cage for an experiment."

From the dialog we can presume that in the past Tommy has picked up a "bad," though not uncommon, default: that cardinals typically are red. Sue, the expert, teaches him otherwise. Among other things, this requires that she express to Tommy the denial of a default (e.g., roughly, "it is not the case that cardinals typically are red"). She gets the point across by saying *"Quite a few are red, but many others are russet, like these."*

Denying a default requires explicit recognition of that default as a mistake to avoid. Although empirical studies have not addressed this, this recognition, we suggest, is more abundant in an expert's repertoire and less so in a novice's.

We turn to the topic of default denial and formal representation next. We do so within the larger picture of range defaults. Ranges explicitly depend upon denials, as we shall see, and are somewhat commonplace, thereby providing a further motivational context for denials.

Range Defaults and Default Denials

In the dialog there is evidence that Sue holds a special kind of default called a *range default* about the color of cardinals. Specifically, she believes that cardinals typically are red *or* russet (the range of the default), though there are exceptions—the albinos—and she denies that cardinals are typically red. Moreover she would, given the opportunity, also deny that cardinals typically are russet: there are proportionately too many red and too many russet cardinals for these latter defaults to be sensible. Here's another example: People typically are male or female. Note that this too is a default, not a universal fact. There are rare hermaphroditic or neuter persons who are neither (singularly) male nor (singularly) female; and perhaps gender-changes can be similarly construed. There are too many male and *too* many female people to exclude either maleness or femaleness as typical. Both of the defaults "people typically are male" and "people typically are female" are too restrictive and hence inappropriate.

More formally, a range default is an accepted default of the form "P's are typically Q" where Q is a disjunction (i.e., $Q = \Phi_1 \vee \Phi_2 \vee ... \Phi_n$, or $Q = V_{i=1...n} \Phi_i$) and for every shorter disjunction S formed from the (disjunctive) components of Q, the (sub) default "P's are typically S" is denied. Thus a range default has two parts: an affirmed disjunctive default (e.g., "cardinals typically are red *or* russet") and various default denials (e.g., "it is not the case that cardinals typically are red" and "it is not the case that cardinals typically are russet"). The example dialog presented earlier suggests that some of the detailed, fine-tuned, substantial quantity knowledge that experts have may take the form of range defaults, as opposed to simple, nondisjunctive defaults. In a sense we all become less "novice" and more "expert" about everyday matters concerning people, relationships, gender, etc. as we grow up. The fine-tuning of our defaults, at times accomplished by refining a simple default into a range default, is part of this process.

Why bother with default denials at all? Knowing that a particular bird is a cardinal and that typically cardinals are red or russet, the latter being the affirmative disjunctive part of a range default, should lead one to conclude that the bird is red or russet, unless one knows to the contrary. A reasoner need not go on to deny the individual defaults "typically cardinals are red" and "typically cardinals are russet" in reaching that conclusion. Why do range defaults, and specifically the default denial component, deserve special mention? There are two reasons: 1) their representation presents a challenge (see Miller and Perlis, in preparation), and 2) they can play a role in reasoning that is not accomplished with "ordinary" defaults alone. There are cases in commonsense reasoning where it is important not only to reach the correct default conclusion, but also to have meta-knowledge about one's own defaults which itself can be reasoned with and about.

In the example dialog Sue notices that the collection of birds in the zoo is unusual: they are all russet and hence female. But the plain disjunctive default, namely that cardinals typically are red or russet, does not itself prompt this conclusion. Sue does have excellent reason to think the collection is an oddity though, because she has the additional information that it is *not* the case that cardinals typically are russet. She uses this fact in forming the observation that an *unusual* collection of cardinals has gathered at the zoo, and hence to wonder: Why have only female cardinals gathered? A novice or layperson, on the other hand, without Sue's knowledge, might have no reason to inquire further.

The sort of knowledge that an expert may have regarding cardinals is precisely what a range default about cardinal color expresses, and this knowledge can be crucial to reasoning, as has been illustrated. Given such pragmatic ramifications of range defaults for commonsense reasoning, it is of interest to examine their formal representation and theoretical aspects. We turn to these issues now.

The Problem of Denying Defaults

The representation and use of range defaults clearly hinges on the representation and use of two components. First, a plain disjunctive default principle which affirms the range of the default, and second, (a collection of) denied defaults—default principles explicitly believed to be false. Taken together, these denials assert that the disjunctive range of the affirmed component cannot be restricted any further.

Formally, let I be any nonempty, finite set of (at least two) indices used to specify the disjuncts in a range and let $V_{i \in I} \Phi_i$ be the range of a default about Ψ. Then the first component of the range default, namely the plain disjunctive default principle, is represented (using our neutral $\rightarrow_{typ}$ notation) by:

(1) $\Psi \rightarrow_{typ} V_{i \in I} \Phi_i$

Rule (1) specifies a range but it's accuracy depends on there being no proper subset J of I which is itself the range of a default about Ψ. That is, for every nonempty proper subset J of I, when the potential default principle

$\Psi \rightarrow_{typ} V_{i \in J} \Phi_i$

is denied, giving

(2) $\neg (\Psi \rightarrow_{typ} V_{i \in J} \Phi_i)$

then Rules (1) and (2) together formalize a range default.

To cast this in terms of our cardinal-color example, let $I = \{1,2\}$, $\Phi_1 =$ Red and $\Phi_2 =$ Russet. Then the disjunctive component (corresponding to Rule 1) of the cardinal-color range default reduces to

$Cardinal(x) \rightarrow_{typ} Red(x) \vee Russet(x)$

and the denial component (corresponding to Rule 3) contains both

$\neg (Cardinal(x) \rightarrow_{typ} Red(x))$ and $\neg (Cardinal(x) \rightarrow_{typ} Russet(x))$.

Notice that the generic form (1) is doing double-duty. On the one hand, it encodes a typicality statement about the population of Ψ-things (i.e., a statement asserting a "population trend"), and on the other it encodes a means of drawing a conclusion about a specific Ψ-thing.[3] But then (2) is puzzling: Which is being denied, the typicality statement or the inference procedure? If we take denial literally and use classical negation—as indicated in (2)—then a problem surfaces immediately in DL where defaults are written as inference rules, since there is no recognized formal notion of the negation of a rule of inference. In NML and circumscription, negating a default results in a *counterexample* axiom, which simply records that the default can lead to an error in at least one case and is *not* an assertion that the default itself is a bad one that should not be used. (We analyze these issues in detail in Miller and Perlis, in preparation.)

In short, default denial seems to create difficulties for standard formalisms. We will utilize the approach discussed in (Miller and Perlis, in preparation)

which appears to handle all of the problems simultaneously and uniformly across all the standard formalisms. We next summarize this approach briefly and then apply it to our sample expert-novice dialog in the next subsection.

Formally Separating the Two Default Features

In the traditional formalisms (e.g., DL, NML, and circumscription) defaults are formally represented in combined form containing a conflation between a general typicality (or trend) about a population on the one hand, and a sanctioning of inferred conclusions about a particular member of the population on the other hand. The negation of such a representation (when possible at all) then mixes together both the unsoundness of the inferences and the denial of the population-trend, even if (as in the case of range defaults) only the latter is wanted.

The key, then, is to view a default as having two complementary features. One is the typicality statement *Typ* giving default information as a trend about the commonsense world. The other is the inferential mechanism *Inf* by means of which *Typ* is used to produce default conclusions. *What is needed for default denial is negating Typ, not Inf.* But when *Inf* and *Typ* are combined in a single representation, then negating *Typ* without negating *Inf* is problematic.

Our approach is as follows: we treat standard default mechanisms as largely playing the role of *Inf* and adjoin a separate typicality statement to play the role of *Typ*. Should we want to deny the trend itself, we assert ¬*Typ*, the negation of the typicality statement. This can be achieved quite easily in each of DL, NML, and circumscription.

As an example consider DL where the default $\Psi \to_{\text{typ}} \Phi$ is rendered as the inference rule

$$(3) \qquad \frac{\Psi : \Phi}{\Phi}$$

Rule (3) can roughly be interpreted as meaning "If Ψ is believed, and if Φ is consistent with all that is believed, then Φ is inferred (believed). This standard DL rule mechanism is what we use to fill the role of *Inf*, but not as it stands. We must pull out the population trend specifics, thereby neutralizing a theory's rule(s). This is accomplished by first replacing each of a theory's existing default rules by an axiom of the form

(4)   *Typically* (Ψ, Φ)

which has the intuitive meaning that typically Ψ's are Φ's: a statement about a population trend and not itself an inference procedure. Each of these axioms plays the role of *Typ*. Next we adjoin a *single* new neutralized inference rule:

$$(5) \qquad \frac{Px \ \& \ \text{Typically}(P,Q) : Qx}{Qx}$$

to fill the role of *Inf*. Here P and Q are second-order variables which can be bound to first-order expressions such as Ψ and Φ in the expression *Typically*(Ψ, Φ). Given an individual a, Rule (5) says this: If it is believed that $\Psi(a)$ and it is believed that *Typically*(Ψ, Φ), then $\Phi(a)$ is concluded when $\Phi(a)$ is consistent. If, on the other hand, for a particular Ψ_0 and Φ_0, $\Psi_0(a)$ is believed and *Typically*(Ψ_0, Φ_0) is not, then (5) does not produce $\Phi_0(a)$. Thus it is the presence or absence of statements like (4) which controls the use of (5), and the two together produce the effect of (3) by binding P to Ψ and Q to Φ. For a particular Ψ_0 and Φ_0, we can explicitly deny population trend typicalities by asserting

(6) $\neg$ *Typically*(Ψ_0, Φ_0)

This is a default denial asserting that it is *not* the case that typically Ψ_0's are Φ_0's.

Once typicality statements are separated from the inferential mechanism, range defaults can be specified. The cardinal-color range default is formally expressed as the conjunction of the following three statements:

Typically(*Cardinal, Red* $\vee$ *Russet*)

$\neg$ *Typically*(*Cardinal, Red*)

$\neg$ *Typically*(*Cardinal, Russet*)

To return momentarily to the issue of expertise, the analysis above lends itself to the idea that a single general-purpose default-use mechanism, as in Rule (5), may suffice for experts and novices alike. We do not suggest that *all* reasoning mechanisms are necessarily shared by experts and novices; rather we speculate that a specialized default mechanism may be. We do suggest, however, that default reasoning differences between experts and novices may hinge on differences in knowledge of the form (4) as well as denials (6); we pursue these ideas in the next section.

Sue and Tommy Revisited—Pieces of a Formal Treatment

Once the representation issue is settled range defaults perform as desired. We illustrate this by casting fragments of the knowledge evident in our sample dialog into a more formal setting.

The dialog suggests that Sue holds a range default about cardinal color, that she also holds simple defaults concerning female cardinal color (that females are russet) and male cardinal color (that males are red), and a firm (nondefault) belief about all possible cardinal colors (that cardinals are either red, russet or white). Sue indicates that she has additional knowledge regarding birds as well. For one, that cardinals are birds. For another, that birds typically fly. Tommy shares these last two beliefs, but not the others, at least initially. Instead either he believes the firm statement that all cardinals are red or the simple default that typically cardinals are red. Exactly which, is irrelevant for our purposes, so we'll suppose it to be the default. At the start of the conversation then, Tommy's and Sue's knowledge bases (KB) include the following:

Fragment of Tommy's Starting KB	Fragment of Sue's Starting KB
$Typically(Cardinal, Red)$	$Typically(Cardinal, Red \lor Russet)$
$(\forall x)\, Cardinal(x) \to Bird(x)$	$\neg\, Typically(Cardinal, Red)$
$Typically(Bird, Fly)$	$\neg\, Typically(Cardinal, Russet)$
	$(\forall x)\, Cardinal(x) \to Bird(x)$
	$Typically(Bird, Fly)$
	$Typically(Cardinal\ \&\ Female, Russet)$
	$Typically(Cardinal\ \&\ Male, Red)$
	$(\forall x)\, Cardinal(x) \to Red(x) \lor Russet(x) \lor White(x)$

From the above knowledge bases, the following initial conclusions are readily drawn (say, in DL) about an individual cardinal b_0, given the additional fact $Cardinal(b_0)$. (Starred (*) conclusions are default inferences, produced using Rule 5.)

Tommy's Initial Conclusions	Sue's Initial Conclusions
$*Red(b_0)$	$*Red(b_0) \lor Russet(b_0)$
$Bird(b_0)$	$Bird(b_0)$
$*Fly(b_0)$	$*Fly(b_0)$
	$Red(b_0) \lor Russet(b_0) \lor White(b_0)$

From the still further information $Male(b_0)$, Sue would conclude $Red(b_0)$; and from $Female(b_0)$ she would conclude $Russet(b_0)$. Tommy could conclude nothing further if given either $Male(b_0)$ or $Female(b_0)$.

At the end of the dialog, after Sue's instruction, Tommy's knowledge base still contains a single default about cardinal color, but now it is a range default, as represented by the first three statements of Tommy's new knowledge base:

Fragment of Tommy's New KB

$Typically(Cardinal, Red \lor Russet)$
$\neg\, Typically(Cardinal, Red)$
$\neg\, Typically(Cardinal, Russet)$
$(\forall x)\, Cardinal(x) \to Bird(x)$
$Typically(Bird, Fly)$

Tommy still lacks some of Sue's knowledge about cardinal color, namely $Typically(Cardinal\ \&\ Female, Russet)$ and $Typically(Cardinal\ \&\ Male, Red)$, but his previously held (bad) default is now gone. From $Cardinal(b_0)$ Tommy now can conclude $Red(b_0) \lor Russet(b_0)$.

A Tentative Formal Characterization of Expertise

We can use our analysis and sample dialog to motivate a characterization of expertise in terms of a default-reasoning framework. Of course the scenario depicted in the dialog, and our formal treatment of it, cannot justify strong or overly general claims about human experts and novices. At best it is suggestive, and may lead to both studies of human subjects and to algorithms for automated expertise and for novice learning.

Recall that Sue (the expert) enters the scenario with more defaults than Tommy, including a range default about cardinal color which better matches the facts about the world than Tommy's cardinal-color simple default. Her defaults are presumably well-grounded in breadth, that is, many observations (not only her own, but also of others who have taught her) have led her to believe them. She also has beliefs comprised of default denials; knows about exceptions to her (range) defaults (e.g., albino cardinals); she knows that the collection of female cardinals is unusual or abnormal; and she knows when she does not know enough to explain the unusual collection of cardinals.

We thus offer the following hypotheses about expertise:

- *Experts hold a substantial number of defaults (compared to a novice) in the domain of expertise.* Sue holds more, but related, defaults than does Tommy, even after she has given him some instruction. After the instruction Tommy still remains unaware of some related defaults, for instance, that female cardinals typically are russet, and males typically are red.

- *Expert's defaults are well grounded in breadth.* Many observations and much instruction leads the expert to believe defaults in the area of expertise. (See Rau 1993 for a discussion of a computational approach to breadth of knowledge.)

- *Novices' defaults tend to be overly specific or overly general.* Tommy's original default concerning cardinal color, that "cardinals typically are red" (indicated in the dialog when he says "I thought cardinals were supposed to be bright red.") is too narrow. Sue provides a more accurate range (red or russet) for his default by informing him that "Quite a few are red but many others are russet...." (See Feltovich et al. 1984 for a discussion of this and related issues.)

- *Experts hold a substantial supply of default denials, each indicating a common mistake to be avoided.* Sue's statement "Quite a few are red but many others are russet..." indicates that she also holds the default denial that "it is not the case that cardinals typically are red" as well as the default denial that "it is not the case that cardinals typically are russet."

- *Experts have the ability to deal with individual exceptions to defaults.* Sue knows that some exceptional cardinals are white, indicated when she says that "a very few are white albinos."

- *Experts know when collections of things are abnormal, based on combined defaults and default denials.* Sue wonders why only russet cardinals have gathered at the zoo ("I wonder why only russet ones are here")—an abnormal situation given her default (that "cardinals typically are red or russet") together with her default denial ("it is not the case that cardinals typically are russet").

- *Experts know when they don't know; that is, they know when it's time to ask for help.* Sue does so when she asks, "Why are there only female cardinals here?"

Conclusion

In this chapter we have considered expertise from the point of view of default (nonmonotonic) reasoning, and have suggested a number of connections. In particular, we noted the importance of the ability to deny a default principle, and illustrated a formal mechanism for representing such denials in the context of a dialog between an expert and a novice. While we do not claim that defaults (and denials) are all there is to expertise, we do think that this connection is a fruitful dimension along which to explore expert reasoning, including novice-expert shifts.

We did not give a formal treatment of the entire Tommy-Sue dialog. That would have involved many additional technical mechanisms which are beyond the scope of this chapter, and indeed beyond the state of the art in automated reasoning. Among other things, appropriate means would be needed for reasoning about groups, including statistical and set-theoretic aspects, in ways compatible with default reasoning; also time, change-of-mind, advice-taking, and learning would enter importantly. All of these factors, and more, would have to be combined into a single robust system to achieve a satisfactory automated reasoner like Tommy (or Sue). While there is much progress on these various themes, integrating them has not to our knowledge even been attempted. Such an integration is a major goal of our on-going work.

Acknowledgments

This research was supported in part by NSF grant IRI9311988 and by ARO grant DAAH0494G0238.

Notes

1. While one might suppose that the expert knows which relevant pieces of information to pick out and which pieces to ignore, there is some evidence indicating that this is not always the case. Experts are sometimes influenced by irrelevant information and as a result their decisions may turn out to be incorrect or unreliable (Shanteau 1984). Moreover, experts are at times unable to provide convincing accounts of how they make their judgments (see Clancey 1993). These issues are, however, controversial. For other views see (Ericsson and Smith 1991) and (Glaser and Chi 1988).

2. We conjecture that such "default ranges"—which will be addressed in what follows—are important aspects of the phenomenon studied in (Feltovich *et al.* 1984) and (Rau 1993).

3. The reader may wish to view the neutral $\rightarrow_{typ}$ notation in terms of a particular formalism, say DL, to see the dual functions served by Rule (1). In DL, $\Psi \rightarrow_{typ} \Phi$ is represented by the default inference rule $\Psi : \Phi / \Phi$. This rule encodes a population trend, that Ψ's are typically Φ's, and also the mechanism by which to draw an inference about an instance of the population. (We discuss this below and in further detail in Miller and Perlis, in preparation.)

References

Clancey, W.J. (1993). *The situated cognition perspective on knowledge and context.* Presented at the Third International Workshop on Human and Machine Cognition, Seaside, Florida.

Ebbesen, E. & Konechi, V. (1975). Decision making and information integration in the courts: The setting of bail. *Journal of Personality and Social Psychology, 32,* 805–821.

Einhorn, H. (1974). Expert judgment: Some necessary conditions and an example. *Journal of Applied Psychology, 59,* 562–571.

Ericsson, K.A. & Smith, J. (Eds.). (1991). *Toward a General Theory of Expertise.* New York: Cambridge University Press

Feltovich, P., Johnson, P., Moller, J., & Swanson, D. (1984). LCS: The role and development of medical knowledge in diagnostic expertise. In W.J. Clancey & E. Shortliffe (Eds.), *Readings in Medical Artificial Intelligence: The First Decade* (pp. 275–319). Reading, MA: Addison-Wesley.

Glaser, R. & Chi, M.T.H. (Eds.). (1988). *The Nature of Expertise.* Hillsdale, NJ: Lawrence Erlbaum.

Kassirer, J. & Gorry, G.A. (1978). Clinical problem solving: A behavioral analysis. *Annals of Internal Medicine, 89,* 245-255.

Mayer, R.E. (1992). *Thinking, Problem Solving, and Cognition* (2nd ed.). New York: W.H. Freeman.

McCarthy, J. (1980). Circumscription: A form of nonmonotonic reasoning. *Artificial Intelligence, 13 (1,2),* 27-39.

McDermott, D. & Doyle, J. (1980). Nonmonotonic logic I. *Artificial Intelligence, 13 (1,2),* 41-72.

Miller, M. & Perlis, D. (In preparation). *Defaults Denied.*

Minsky, M. (1975). A framework for representing knowledge. In P. Winston (Ed.), *The Psychology of Computer Vision.* New York: McGraw-Hill.

Rau, L.F. (1993). *A Computational Approach to Meta-knowledge: Calculating Breadth and Salience.* GE AI Laboratory Tech. Rep. 93CRD094. Aspects of this material were presented at the Third International Workshop on Human and Machine Cognition, Seaside, FL, 1993.

Reiter, R. (1980). A logic for default reasoning. *Artificial Intelligence, 13(1,2),* 81–132.

Shanteau, J. (1984). Some unasked questions about the psychology of expert decision makers. In *Proceedings of the 1984 IEEE Conference on Systems, Man, and Cybernetics* (pp. 408–412). New York: IEEE.

CHAPTER 18

The Turing Effect: The Nature of Trust in Expert System Advice

F. Javier Lerch, Michael J. Prietula & Carol T. Kulik

Introduction

Information systems (computers, telecommunications, video systems, etc.) are fundamentally changing the nature of work in all forms and in all sectors of society (Adler 1989; Davidow and Malone 1992; Haeckel and Nolan 1993). An aspect of that change involves the realization that knowledge is a fundamental asset that must be characterized, represented, distributed, and used within an organizational or societal context (Keen 1991; Quinn 1992). A primary mechanism for delivery and use of knowledge is via information systems. Thus, a major research concern has been to understand and predict how discretionary users (e.g., managers and professionals) decide to make use of available computer-based tools (Davis, Bagozzi and Warshaw 1989; DeSanctis 1983; Robey 1979). Obviously, organizations do not accrue any gain from their investments in information systems if these systems are not utilized. Several researchers and practitioners have proposed methods for assessing and increasing the likelihood of system use (Alavi 1984; Alavi and Henderson 1981; Anderson and Reitman-Olson 1985; Gould and Lewis 1985). The purpose of this chapter is to investigate a particular aspect of systems use—trust.

In this chapter, we introduce and explore what we call the *Turing Effect*. The foundation for our work thus stems from an idea proposed over forty years ago. Turing (1950) proposed the imitation game as a fair test for answering the question, "Can machines think?"[1] The imitation game, as posed by Turing, essentially asks whether a (human) judge can distinguish between a human and a computer (i.e., machine) imitating a human (with the interaction occurring through a typed medium, thus masking the source). Success in imitation was deemed as correctly "fooling" the human ninety percent of the time in a five-minute, typical conversation.

In our adaptation of the Turing test, we take a slightly different focus. Rather than have our human participants (judges) try to *guess* if a communication source is a human or computer, we *tell* our participants who (or what) is the source. The nature of the communication is not a conversation, but advice presented to the participant from the communication source. The purpose of our game is to examine how participants *trust* the advice given to them if it is characterized as a human or a computer.

Specifically, we present a series of simple financial problems (via a computer program simulating electronic mail) to our participants, along with proposed "advice" (solution) for each problem from a particular type of source described by introductory materials. Our experimental method compares how advice characterized as coming from a computer is trusted vis-a-vis the *identical* advice characterized as coming from human sources. The main manipulation ascribes the same advice to three different sources: an expert system, a human expert and a human novice. Therefore, it compares how the same advice generates different trust judgments when the attributed source of the advice is manipulated.

We define the Turing Effect, in general, as the differential impact on trust judgments resulting from attributing advice to a computer. In this chapter we demonstrate this effect and begin to explicate the psychological mechanism underlying this phenomenon.

Background in Social Psychology

Social psychologists have argued that trust (in general) is partially the result of an attribution process (Reeder and Brewer 1979; Rempel, Holmes and Zanna 1985). An *attribution* is an inference about why an event occurred in term's of a person's dispositions, personality, or beliefs. The goal of an attribution process is the attempt to understand the causes behind others'—and our own—behaviors (Kelley 1967). There are some indications in social psychology literature that interactions with computers can indeed trigger attribution processes. For example, in a study of self-supplied (computer-generated) versus supervisor-supplied performance feedback, Earley (1988) found that computer-generated data regarding performance were perceived as more trustworthy than supervisor-supplied feedback. In addition, some studies have noted that trust in a computer may have an impact on behavior. For example, Woods, Roth and Bennett (1987) found that when technicians do not trust a decision aid, they may either reject its advice or attempt to manipulate the output of the decision aid toward their own preconceived solutions.

Empirical work has yet to explicitly study trust in computer advice by measuring and comparing levels of trust in humans and computers engaged in similar tasks, or by investigating how trust in computer advice influences intentions or behaviors. However, research on trust and source credibility in general suggests that source characteristics do have an impact on attributional activity and that trust may have an impact on subsequent behavior. How this research applies to the Turing Effect is explained next.

Interpersonal Trust and Source Credibility

Interpersonal trust has been defined by Rotter (1980) as "a generalized expectancy held by an individual that the word, promise, oral or written statement of another individual or group can be relied on" (p. 2). Scanzoni (1979) states that interpersonal trust sometimes requires a willingness to place oneself in a position of risk. These and other characterizations of interpersonal trust are broad enough to encompass the concept of trust in computers.

Trust studies have sometimes emphasized the component of trust that is related to the ability to forecast desired or gratifying behavior (Deutsch 1973; Scanzoni 1979). Other researchers highlight the dispositional attributions present in trusting relationships by which individuals are regarded as reliable (Reeder and Brewer 1979). The former component reflects the influence of the predictability of an individual's actions on specific tasks, while the latter component focuses on whether individuals, rather than their actions in a specific situation, are *reliable*. Both of these components are regarded as relevant when considering the nature of interactions with computer systems or individuals. Therefore, we selected a model (Rempel *et al.* 1985) that incorporates these components.

Predictability, Dependability and Faith

Rempel *et al.* (1985) identified three distinct and coherent dimensions of trust: predictability, dependability and faith. According to this model, the most specific and concrete component of trust is based upon the predictability of the individual's actions. A judgment of predictability can be made whenever one observes consistent behavior over time in a stable environment. With this component of trust it is not necessary to "interpret" the individual's behavior or to make dispositional attributions toward the person. Instead, the stable pattern of behavior allows the individual's behavior to be predicted reliably as long as there are no disruptions from the environment (i.e., out of an individual's control). This component of trust can be measured by the extent to which one *agrees* with the specific behaviors of an individual.

A second component of trust is dependability, which reflects the common understanding of trust. This component is based largely on instances in which environmental factors are thought to be an insufficient explanation for the individual's behavior. In dependability, the individual's behavior is attributed to internal, dispositional characteristics of the person. Thus, a judgment of dependability goes beyond a prediction based on recurring, observable specific behaviors and involves attributions to personal characteristics that account for those behaviors. This component is usually measured (as in this research) by the extent to which one has confidence in a person or a computer system.

In addition to the research on interpersonal trust, the literature on persuasive communication has consistently identified source credibility as a central factor for predicting the impact of a message (Birnbaum and Stegner 1979; Hovland and Weiss 1951; Sternthal, Dholakia and Leavitt 1978). The pattern of results indicates that the greater the perceived credibility of a source of communication, the greater the effectiveness or persuasiveness of the message. Source credibility has been an important variable in applied research fields such as the design of advertising messages and the elicitation of information from witnesses. For example, Devine and Ostrom (1985) found that in the pre-deliberation task of jurors, the credibility of even one witness can substantially impact jurors' verdicts. In marketing, research factors such as communicator physical attractiveness have been found to have a considerable influence on persuasiveness because of the attributions of credibility they may evoke (Baker and Churchill 1977; Chaiken 1979; Dion and Stein 1978; Mills and Aronson 1965; Patzer 1983). The extent to which the perceiver accepts or rejects the position advocated in the communication is considered to be an outcome of the inferences made by the perceiver about the characteristics of the communicator (Eagly and Chaiken 1975). Therefore, source credibility should be closely linked to dependability because source credibility affects opinions on a given position by influencing the recipient's attributional activity.

Credibility of a source has historically been defined to include expertise and experience (Hovland, Janis and Kelley 1953). Brock (1965) reported that respondents' behavioral change following communications was related to the amount of experience the source had with the topic of the communication. Greater experience with specific participant increased the likelihood of the respondent following the directions of the communication. McGinnies and Ward (1974) found that sources of communication identified as "expert" produced more changes in attitude in the desired direction than sources lacking expertness. In more recent studies, credibility of the source has been manipulated via experience with the problem (Bannister 1986) or levels of expertise (Birnbaum and Mellers 1983). A similar manipulation is used in this research in order to influence inferences on the trustworthiness of the advice received from different ascribed sources. The next step is to relate the concept of advice to the context of a computer advisor.

Expert Systems and Explanations

An intriguing but little-researched belief about expert systems is that it is essential to provide a capability for explaining results offered by an expert system in order to increase user acceptance (Buchanan and Shortliffe 1984;

Chandrasekaran, Tanner and Josephson 1988; Ellis 1989; Langlotz and Short-liffe 1989; Wick and Slagle 1989). Swartout (1983) rationalized this relationship between the existence of explanation capabilities in expert systems and increased user acceptance as "Trust in a system is developed not only by the quality of its results, but also by a clear description of how they were derived. This can be especially true when *first* working with an expert system (p. 292).

Thus, in our imitation game we include explanations about the advice in order to compare trust levels among human and computer sources at the early stages of interaction with the system. Finally, Muir (1987) has made an additional recommendation for calibrating users' trust in decision aids, based on the theoretical work by Rempel *et al.* (1985) on interpersonal trust. Muir suggested that one should provide explicit data on a decision aid's output in terms of its competence in order to improve the perception of trustworthiness.

The Present Research

In our imitation game, the advice from all sources is the same, the explanations for the advice are the same, and the competence of the advice is rated identically for all sources by a fictitious independent judge. Therefore, if a Turing Effect is found with our imitation game, it can be traced to the attributional activity generated by the different qualifications of the source—the source pedigree.

The first experiment examined how three different source pedigrees (a human expert, a human novice, and an expert system) affected agreement ratings (predictability), confidence ratings (dependability), and performance attributions. The second experiment explored the nature of the attributions made about a human expert and an expert system, in order to explain the differential trust judgments found in the first experiment. The third experiment examined how three alternative explanation modes (no explanation, rule explanation and prose explanation) given by an expert system affected agreement ratings (predictability) and confidence ratings (dependability). Finally, experiment four explored how to increase trust in expert systems by manipulating user attributions.

Experiment 1: The Effects of Source Pedigree

The first experiment was designed to examine the effects of source pedigree on trust judgments through the analysis of the effects of source pedigree on agreement, confidence and performance attribution ratings. The main manipulation consisted of three source pedigrees: an expert system, a human expert and a human novice.

Method

Participants. The participants were ninety-two undergraduate students in introductory organizational behavior and marketing courses at Carnegie Mellon University who volunteered in partial fulfillment of a course requirement.

Materials and Apparatus. The stimuli for the experiment consisted of ten financial management decision problems cast as two-alternative choices, such as a decision between leasing or purchasing, or a decision between public versus private financing. Each problem was presented in a brief paragraph. The presentation of the experimental instructions and decision problems, as well as data collection, were conducted on an individual basis using personal computers.

Design and Procedure. Source pedigree was a between-subjects factor with each participant randomly assigned to one of three treatment groups: expert system, human expert and human novice. Source pedigree was manipulated through a brief paragraph (the source description) that participants read at the beginning of the experiment. The three paragraphs describing the sources of advice are shown in Table 1.

Before the trials began, participants were given a written questionnaire assessing their computer background. Participants reported that their knowledge of computer technology was between "Considerably Adequate" and "Borderline" (scale 1-5, M = 2.56, sd = 0.82) and their knowledge of artificial intelligence and expert systems between "Borderline" and "Considerably Inadequate" (scale 1-5, M = 3.34, sd = 0.62) making them relatively naive users of the technology. However, they rated the importance of computer technology and artificial intelligence between "Very Important" and "Important" (scale 1-4, M = 1.28, sd = 0.47; M = 1.51, sd = 0.64 respectively) for business decision making in the next twenty years.

Each participant then received verbal instructions explaining the task, and then proceeded to interact with the personal computer. After reading the source description from the computer screen, participants proceeded to the ten financial problems. For each problem, the participant was presented with a description of the decision to be made and a solution (i.e., the advice) proposed by the source. For example, a participant assigned to the human novice group was presented with problem solutions attributed to the human novice. After reading the source's proposed advice, participants rated the extent to which they agreed with the advice (assessing predictability) by responding to a displayed six-point agreement scale. We selected a six-point scale in order to force the participants to commit themselves either to agree or disagree with the advice, instead of remaining neutral. The computer then provided feedback, in the form of a memo from a fictional supervisor (Mr. Watson), regarding the appropriateness of the advice. An example of a problem, advice, agreement scale, and feedback memo sequence is shown in

---

Expert System—MIDAS

MIDAS is an artificial intelligence program that was constructed as a joint effort between Carnegie Mellon's Computer Science Department and the Graduate School of Industrial Administration. MIDAS has a large amount of knowledge about general business principles. It has been reviewed by experts from two major firms in the Pittsburgh area and revised accordingly.

Human Expert

William O'Neil received his undergraduate business degree in May of 1975. He was a very good student and worked four years as a financial analyst in a large bank. He then joined a major consulting firm and has worked there for nine years as one of their top financial consultants. In fact, he has just been promoted to "partner" in the firm.

Human Novice

William O'Neil received his undergraduate business degree in May of 1987. He was a very good student and started working for a major bank in July of the same year as a financial analyst.

Table 1. Descriptions provided to participants for different sources of advice.

Table 2. This sequence of events (problem, advice, agreement, feedback) was repeated for each of the ten problems and is shown in Table 3. The ordering of the problems was the same for all participants.

Though agreement ratings were obtained after each problem (necessarily), the assessment of confidence involved judgments about the source. Accordingly, we grouped the problems into sets, and assessed confidence after each set as follows. The ten problems were divided into three sets comprising four, two and four problems each (though the participants were unaware of any such grouping). The problems in the first set (P1–4) were simple, and the advice given was described as correct and appropriate in the feedback from Mr. Watson. The problems in the second set (P5 and 6) were described ambiguously and with little information. The advice suggested for P5 was *incorrect* and the feedback memo from Mr. Watson correctly identified the impropriety. However, the advice supplied for P6 was correct and so noted in the feedback memo. The problems in the last set (P7–10) were more complicated than those in the first set, but all of the presented advice was correct and therefore the feedback was positive. In summary, the advice received on all problems was correct except for one—P5.

Confidence in the source of advice (assessing dependability) was measured on a four-point scale. The wording of the scale alternatives was selected in order for the intervals between phrases to be as nearly equal as possible (see Scale 11, Meister 1985, p. 388), increasing the reliability of interpreting changes in confidence ratings. Since confidence is related to the source of advice (and not to specific problems), it was requested only on *four* occasions: before the presentation of the first problem and after the completion of each of the three problem sets (i.e., after P4, P6, and P10).

Following the confidence ratings (except after the first rating, which was given prior to the presentation of the problems), four performance attribution ratings (ability, task difficulty, effort and luck) were collected using the same scale used for assessing confidence ratings. The presentation order of the attribution ratings was the same for all problems and for all participants. The set of four performance attributions used was adopted from a general framework for eliciting causal explanations regarding success and failure of events (Frieze 1976; Weiner 1986; Weiner, Frieze, Kukla, Reed, Rest and Rosenbaum 1971). In this framework, two types of causal locus of control (internal, external) are crossed with two types of causal stability across time (stable, unstable). The resulting table identifies four types of causal attributions for observed behavior as shown in figure 1.

In summary, the dependent variables for Experiment 1 were ratings of agreement (with the advice given for each problem), confidence (in the source of the advice) and four performance attributions (indicating primary causes for performance). Agreement (ten observations) and confidence (four observations) were measured using single rating scales. Performance attributions were measured three times after each problem set (twelve attribution measurements in total per participant).

Hypotheses

Since predictability judgments induce little effort in making attributions about the source of advice and are facilitated by the presence of data on source's competence on prior situations (Muir 1985), we did not expect significant differences in agreement ratings in the *advice* among the source pedigrees (H1). Agreement with the advice should be a function of the specific problem characteristics and of the adequacy of the source's advice and explanation within the problem domain. In other words, agreement with the advice should be related to the predictability of the source's behavior *on the specific decision problem*. Since the advice, the explanation for the advice, and the problem situation are the same across sources, agreement with specific advice should be equivalent, regardless of source pedigree.

On the other hand, significant differences in confidence ratings in the *source* of the advice should be observed across source pedigrees (H2a). In particular, higher confidence ratings should be obtained for the human expert than for the human novice (H2b). This follows directly from the work

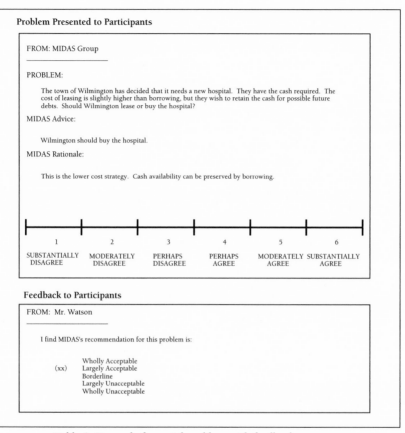

Problem Presented to Participants

FROM: MIDAS Group

PROBLEM:

The town of Wilmington has decided that it needs a new hospital. They have the cash required. The cost of leasing is slightly higher than borrowing, but they wish to retain the cash for possible future debts. Should Wilmington lease or buy the hospital?

MIDAS Advice:

Wilmington should buy the hospital.

MIDAS Rationale:

This is the lower cost strategy. Cash availability can be preserved by borrowing.

1	2	3	4	5	6
SUBSTANTIALLY DISAGREE	MODERATELY DISAGREE	PERHAPS DISAGREE	PERHAPS AGREE	MODERATELY AGREE	SUBSTANTIALLY AGREE

Feedback to Participants

FROM: Mr. Watson

I find MIDAS's recommendation for this problem is:

               Wholly Acceptable
(xx)   Largely Acceptable
               Borderline
               Largely Unacceptable
               Wholly Unacceptable

Table 2. Example financial problem with feedback response.

Step	Trial Event
1	Assessment of Confidence Rating in Source
2	Presentations of P1–4: Advice, Agreement, Feedback for each problem
3	Assessment of Confidence Rating in Source
4	Assessment of Performance Attribute Ratings
5	Presentations of P5 and 6: Advice, Agreement, Feedback for each problem (Incorrect Advice for P5)
6	Assessment of Confidence Rating in Source
7	Assessment of Performance Attribute Ratings
8	Presentations of P7–10: Advice, Agreement, Feedback for each problem
9	Assessment of Confidence Rating in Source
10	Assessment of Performance Attribute Ratings

Table 3. Sequence of trial events for participants in Experiment 1.

		Locus of Control	
		Internal	External
Stability	Stable	Ability	Task Difficulty
	Unstable	Effort	Luck

Figure 1. Performance attributions framework for causal factors.

on source credibility discussed earlier—experts should be perceived as fundamentally different (and better) than novices. Confidence ratings require an assessment of the source's dependability that goes beyond specific observed performance. Source pedigree should be an essential component of the evoked processes underlying the confidence rating. We did not make formal a priori predictions for confidence in the expert system in comparison to the human sources because confidence in the expert system should depend on the specific description of the expert system, and on the extent of the participants' knowledge about expert systems in general.

Relatedly, differences should be found in the perceived importance of the causal factors affecting the specific problem performance of different sources of advice. As performance attributions to source ability should vary directly with the *confidence* held in the source, performance attributions for "internal factors" (ability and effort) should dominate over "external factors" (task difficulty and luck) in explaining the performance of different sources of advice (H3a, for ability). Therefore, there should be higher ability attributions for the human expert than for the human novice (H3b). However, no differences should occur among the sources in the perceived importance of external factors—task difficulty and luck (H3c and 3d). We did not make specific predictions on effort attributions given the difficulty of hypothesizing how effort attributions are interpreted when interacting with computers, and the uncertainty of how attributions are made by novices toward experts, so the results on this are exploratory.

Summarizing, the hypotheses for Experiment 1 were:

H1. There will be no differences in agreement ratings among the source pedigrees.

H2a. There will be directional differences in confidence ratings among the source pedigrees.

H2b. Confidence ratings for the human expert will be higher than those for the human novice.

H3a. There will be directional differences in ability attribution ratings among the source pedigrees.

H3b. Ability attribution ratings for the human expert will be higher than those for the human novice.

H3c. There will be no differences in task difficulty attribution ratings among the source pedigrees.

H3d. There will be no differences in luck attribution ratings among the source pedigrees.

Results

Agreement with the Advice. To test H1, a multivariate analysis was performed in order to avoid overestimating differences in the between-subject factor in a repeated measures experiment (Cole and Grizzle 1966; LaTour and Miniard 1983). A Hotelling-Lawley Trace statistic was used for the within-factors associated F-tests. No statistically significant overall Source Pedigree effect was detected between participants, and no statistically significant Source Pedigree by Trial (i.e., Problem) interaction was detected within participants. As expected, source of advice was not a statistically significant factor for agreement ratings, supporting H1.

However, the participants did pay attention to the advice presented to them (a manipulation check on the task stimuli), as a statistically significant Problem effect was detected within participants ($T_o^2 = 2.01$, p < .001). When presented with incorrect advice in P5, participants lowered their agreement levels accordingly—agreement ratings for P5 were significantly lower than those for all the previous four problems (Scheffé, p<.01). Agreement ratings decreased even further in the sixth problem even though the advice was correct (Scheffé, p<.01).

Confidence in Source of Advice. A similar analysis was performed to test H2a and 2b. There was a statistically significant overall effect of Source Pedigree (F(2,89) = 12.42, p < .001) supporting H2a. No significant differences were found for mean confidence ratings between the expert system ($\underline{M}$ = 2.53, $\underline{sd}$ = 0.63) and the novice ($\underline{M}$ = 2.60, $\underline{sd}$ = 0.61). However, confidence levels for the human expert ($\underline{M}$ = 2.96, $\underline{sd}$ = 0.56) were significantly higher than those for the human novice (Newman-Keuls, p<.01), supporting H2b. Figure 2 shows the confidence ratings for the three Source Pedigree conditions across trials.

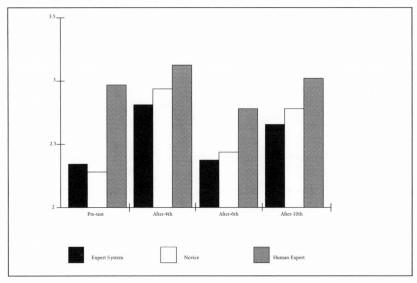

Figure 2. Confidence ratings for Experiment 1.

There was a significant Trial effect ($T_o^2 = 0.720$, p < .001), but not a Trial by Source Pedigree interaction within participants, indicating the stability of the Source ratings relative to variations induced by responses to Trial events. Recall that confidence ratings in the Source Pedigree were taken four times: before the task problems were given, after the completion of the first problem set (four problems, all advice was correct), after the completion of second problem set (two problems, one containing incorrect advice), after the completion of third problem set (four problems, all advice was correct). In all three Source Pedigree conditions, confidence ratings increased significantly between the pre-task assessment and after the first problem set (Scheffé, p<.01). Confidence ratings after the first problem set were significantly higher than all three other confidence assessments (Scheffé, p<.01). Confidence assessed after the second problem set eroded to pre-task levels (Scheffé, p<.05). Confidence assessed after the third problem set increased again, but did not return to the high level obtained after the first problem set (Scheffé, p<.01).

Performance Attributions. Analyses were conducted on the four causal factors comprising the performance attributions for confidence. No statistically significant differences were found among the Source Pedigree conditions for attributional ratings of ability, task difficulty, and luck. Similarly, no statistically significant effects were found for Trial on ratings of ability, task difficulty, and luck. As there was neither an overall Source Pedigree effect, nor a statistically significant rating of experts over novices on ability, H3a and 3b were not supported. No statistically significant differences were found among groups

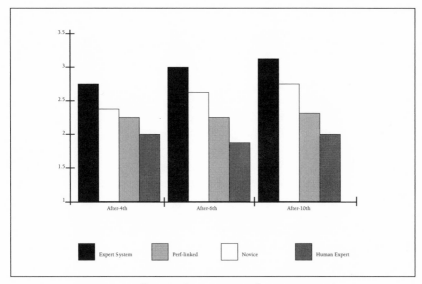

Figure 3. Effort attribution ratings for Experiment 1.

for the two external factors, task difficulty and luck, supporting H3c and 3d.

There was, however, a statistically significant overall effect of Source Pedigree on ratings of effort ($F(2, 89) = 15.7$, $p < .001$) as well as a statistically significant overall effect of Trial on effort ($T_o^2 = 0.150$, $F(2,88) = 6.63$, $p < .01$). There was no Source Pedigree by Trial interaction, indicating the relative stability of effort attribution ratings across fluctuations related to Trials.

Figure 3 shows the results for effort attributions. Participants in the expert system condition rated effort to be significantly *less* important ($M = 1.96$, $sd = 0.52$) in determining performance than participants in the other two conditions (novice $M = 2.59$, $sd = 0.72$; expert $M = 2.91$, $sd = 0.64$; Newman-Keuls, $p<.01$). Furthermore, participants in the human expert condition gave significantly *higher* ratings to the role of effort than the participants did in the human novice condition (Newman-Keuls, $p<.01$).

Discussion

Confidence in Source and Agreement with Advice. As expected, the source pedigree had a statistically significant effect on confidence ratings but not on agreement ratings. The specific descriptions for three sources of advice generated similar confidence levels for the expert system and the novice, but significantly higher confidence levels for the human expert. These results are the first indication that confidence ratings are generated by an *attributional* process (regarding the source) while agreement ratings are based on the source's *behavior* in specific situations (i.e., in each problem).

Performance Attributions. As expected, no statistically significant differences were found among the three source pedigrees for the two external factors: task difficulty and luck. Participants perceived these external factors as equally influential in determining the performance of the human expert, human novice, and expert system. However, we had expected participants to attribute greater *ability* to the performance of those sources in which they had higher confidence. Instead, no statistically significant differences were found across the three source pedigrees in ratings of ability.

The difference in performance attributions was found in how participants responded among the Source Pedigree conditions when considering the other internal factor, effort. Participants judged human expert performance as more attributable to effort than that of a human novice. This is somewhat surprising since novices could be expected to have to exert a higher level of effort than experts (or at least the same level of effort) when generating the same advice in order to compensate for less knowledge and/or experience. Yet, this also may be the reflection of the participants' naive perspective of an aspect of expert versus novice differences. Participants also attributed increased effort to the novice and human expert as the difficulty of the problems increased.

What is also interesting is that the participants in the expert systems condition rated effort the lowest among the three sources in determining performance. From this finding, we might speculate that these participants saw effort as an internal attribution that can only be applied to describe *human* performance. While human performance is perceived to be influenced by changes in human effort, these participants may believe that effort is irrelevant or strange for predicting the performance of a computer.

To pursue the findings regarding ability and effort, in Experiment 2 (below) we collected open-ended descriptions of ability and effort attributions to investigate how participants distinguish between these two internal attributions. We also wanted to examine how participants interpret these two attributions in both the human expert and computer context, as the characterizations of "expert" and "expert system" are, at least on the surface, somewhat similar in function, if not in form.

Experiment 2: Ability and Effort Attributions

The purpose of Experiment 2 was to investigate how participants interpret the role of *ability* and *effort* in performance. This issue was important because in Experiment 1, no significant differences were found for *ability* attributions between the expert system and the human expert. We suspected that effort attributions may include some of the dimensions commonly ascribed to ability, such as knowledge or experience. Furthermore, there was a significant difference for effort attributions between the two human sources even though there was no explicit mention of effort either in the description of these two sources or in the stimuli for each problem. An understanding of how participants interpret effort attributions may indicate those characteristics of the source of advice that are considered important in making confidence ratings.

Method

Participants. The participants were forty-four undergraduate students in introductory organizational behavior and marketing courses at Carnegie Mellon University who volunteered in partial fulfillment of a course requirement. None of them participated in Experiment 1.

Materials and Apparatus. The stimuli and approach for Experiment 2 consisted of the same ten financial management decision problems and computer apparatus described in Experiment 1.

Design and Procedure. The procedure of Experiment 2 paralleled that of Experiment 1 except for three changes. First, attributional ratings were not collected after confidence ratings. Second, each student was randomly assigned to one of two source pedigree groups: the expert system and the human expert. Third, at the end of the experimental session, each participant was asked to provide overall ability and effort attribution ratings of the performance of the source of advice, and to justify their ratings by providing a written explanation. Although independent rating measures like the ones used in Experiment 1 (i.e., ability, task difficulty, effort, and luck) have been shown to be reliable and valid for assessing causal attributions, Elig and Frieze (1979) recommend open-ended measures for assessing causal attributions in novel situations in order to assess the degree to which common people distinguish among the four measures.

Results

Participants were classified into two groups for each of the causal factors (ability and effort) based on their ratings of the importance of the casual factor in determining the quality of the source's advice. Participants who rated the factor as "Very Important" or "Important" were classified into the Important group, and participants who rated the factor as "Not important" or "Very Unimportant" were classified into the Unimportant group.

Participants' explanations for their ratings were sorted into sets based on the content of the explanations. One of the experimenters read all the explanations and established a categorization scheme. A second independent judge then sorted the explanations into sets using the classification scheme developed by the experimenter. The second judge disagreed with the classification made by the experimenter on only three occasions (out of eighty six explanations). When this occurred, the participant's explanations were excluded from further analysis (two participants in the human expert condition and one participant in the expert system condition were excluded). The results of this classification process are shown in Table 4, which shows the percentage of answers for each group falling into a particular explanation category.

A large percentage of ability explanations were classified as "other" by the two judges in both conditions within the Important group, where most of these explanations simply repeated the question (e.g., "ability is important in order to perform well"). Beyond that, the most frequent categories said to underlay expert ability were: experience, knowledge, and education. By far, the dominant explanation for expert systems ability was knowledge. An example of an explanation making reference to experience for the human expert was: "He obviously based his judgments on past experiences with such problems—his ability to deal with them was obvious." Similar explanations were given for the human expert when making reference to knowledge while explaining why performance was a function of ability. The last category for the human expert was "education." Not surprisingly, none of the expert system explanations fit into the education category. An example of knowledge attributed to the expert system was: "Its performance was based on its general knowledge of financing."

More substantial differences were found for effort attributions. When a participant considered effort as important for the human expert, the most likely reason reported was the human expert "tried hard" (50%). For example, one participant stated: "O'Neil obviously tried hard, especially in the last problems." The second most likely response was "experience" (38%). Another participant provided a good example of explaining effort in terms of experience: "Important if we think of his advice as being the result of many years of hard work in his field." In this participant's explanation, effort is not defined as the current effort exerted to solve the problems (trying hard) but as the past effort exerted during the long period of acquiring expertise.

Discussion

In Experiment 1, participants did not distinguish between the performance of expert systems and the performance of human experts in terms of ability, but did make a distinction in terms of effort (i.e., relevant for human experts, not relevant for expert systems). Experiment 2 provided insight into how participants viewed expert systems and human experts differently. In particular, although these participants viewed the impact of ability the same for human experts and expert systems, they viewed what constituted (i.e., ex-

Ability

	Human Expert	Expert System
Important group		
No. of answers	24 (100%)	16 (100%)
Percentage of answers making reference to:		
Knowledge	24 %	56 %
Experience	28 %	6 %
Education	12 %	0 %
Other	36 %	38%
Unimportant group		
No. of answers	1 (100%)	0
Percentage of answers making reference to:		
Need only of basic knowledge		100 %

Effort

	Human Expert	Expert System
Important group		
No. of answers	15 (100%)	0
Percentage of answers making reference to:		
Tried hard	50 %	
Experience	38 %	
Other	12 %	
Unimportant group		
No. of answers	10 (100%)	16 (100%)
Percentage of answers making reference to:		
Not able to...		
measure effort	40 %	69 %
Only knowledge...		
and ability needed	30 %	6 %
No need for effort...		
(easy problems)	20 %	19 %
Other	10 %	6 %

Table 4. Results of attribution explanation analysis.

plained) ability differently. Human expert ability was explained in terms of knowledge, experience and education, while the ability of expert systems was explained in terms of knowledge alone.

Experiment 2 also provided some insight into how effort was interpreted and why effort attributions differed. For human experts, effort was interpreted as the combination of trying hard and having experience. For expert systems, effort was essentially meaningless—expert systems can not "exert" effort.

In Experiment 1, effort attribution ratings were not only different between the expert system and the two human source pedigree conditions, but also between the human expert and the novice: effort was perceived as playing more of a role in the performance of human experts than human novices. We may draw some inferences regarding this latter difference from the results of Experiment 2. One explanation for the differences in effort attributions made to human experts and novices may be that participants consider the effort of acquiring knowledge through many years of hard work as part of an *overall* effort attribution, and that this component of effort is missing for the human novice. In other words, effort attributions are used as surrogates for experience and knowledge and, consequently they reflect differences between humans with different levels of expertise. Thus, it is possible that attributions about expertise based on the differences in experience (as presented in the description of the source pedigrees) may account for the difference in confidence ratings between the human expert and the other two conditions. Confidence may be based on the perceived historical "effort" put in by the human expert for the acquisition of expertise.

Given that participants perceived expert systems differently from human experts in terms of the fundamental attributions underlying performance, and that effort attributions were essentially "undefined" for expert systems, Experiment 3 examined another possible source of variation on how participants viewed the advice of expert systems.

Experiment 3: Expert System Explanation Modes

Since designers of expert systems often have often claimed that explanation capabilities may have a considerable impact on aspects of use, Experiment 3 was designed to specifically examine the effect of explanation mode on *trust*. The manipulation consisted of varying the form of the explanation (how, and if, it was presented to the participant), but keeping the substance (i.e., advice) constant.

Method

Participants. The participants were sixty-seven undergraduate students in introductory organizational behavior and marketing courses at Carnegie Mellon University who volunteered in partial fulfillment of a course requirement. None of them participated in the first two experiments.

Materials and Apparatus. The stimuli for the experiment consisted of the same ten financial management decision problems and computing apparatus described in Experiment 1.

Expert System — No Explanations

MIDAS Advice:
    Wilmington should buy the hospital

Expert System — Prose Explanations

MIDAS Advice:
    Wilmington should buy the hospital

MIDAS Rationale:
    This is the lower cost strategy. Cash availability can be preserved by borrowing.

Expert System — Rule Explanations

MIDAS Advice:
    Wilmington should buy the hospital

MIDAS Rules:
    IF Cash_Level = ACCEPTABLE and
        Cost (LEASE) > Cost (BORROW) and
        Cash_Goal = RETAIN CASH AVAILABILITY
    THEN
        Funding_Strategy = PURCHASE

Table 5. Examples of explanation modes.

Design and Procedure. Experiment 3 followed the same procedure as Experiment 1, except that the mode of explanations generated by the expert system was the between-subjects factor. Each participant was randomly assigned to one of three treatment groups: expert system with no explanations (No-Explanation), expert system with explanations in the form of English sentences as in Experiment 1 (Prose-Explanation), and expert system with explanations in the form of "if-then" production rules (Rule-Explanation). Explanation mode was manipulated by omitting the explanations in the first condition and by changing the prose explanations to "if-then" production rules in the third condition. Table 5 presents an example of each of the three treatment stimuli.

Hypotheses

Explanation mode should have an impact on agreement ratings (H4a). Specifically, agreement ratings for the No-Explanation condition should be lower than for either the Rule-Explanation or Prose-Explanation conditions (H4b). This is because the user of an expert system, when provided explanations, should be able to follow the reasoning behind the advice given in a specific situation. On the other hand, there should be no significant differences in confidence among the three expert systems explanation conditions (H5), since confidence ratings require an assessment of the source's dependability that goes beyond observed behavior in a specific situation. Based on the results of Experiment 2, explanations should not change the value of this assessment since explanations are related to situation-specific behaviors (giving advice for each specific problem). If explanation mode does not have an impact on confidence, then the attributional process should be similar for all three expert systems conditions. Therefore, there should be no significant differences in the four attribution ratings for the three expert systems (H6).

In summary, our hypotheses for Experiment 3 are the following:

H4a. Agreement ratings will differ according to explanation modes.

H4b. Agreement ratings for the No-Explanation condition will be lower than the Rule-Explanation and the Prose-Explanation conditions.

H5. Confidence ratings will not differ according to explanation modes.

H6. All four attribution ratings will not differ according to explanation mode.

Results

Agreement with Advice. Explanation mode had a significant effect on agreement ratings ($F(2,64) = 6.23$, $p < .01$), supporting H4a. No statistically significant differences were found between the Rule-Explanation ($\underline{M} = 4.62$, $\underline{sd} = 1.26$) and Prose-Explanation conditions ($\underline{M} = 4.47$, $\underline{sd} = 1.19$). Agreement levels with the No-Explanation condition ($\underline{M} = 4.15$, $\underline{sd} = 1.02$) were significantly lower than those for the other two conditions (Newman-Keuls, p<.01), supporting H4b.

There was a statistically significant Trial effect within-subjects for the mean agreement ratings for the three explanation mode conditions ($T_o^2 = 2.90$, $p < .001$), but no Trial by Participant interaction. In all three conditions, agreement ratings declined for P5 (the problem with the wrong advice supplied) and are significantly lower than those for all the previous four problems (Scheffé, p<.01). Paralleling the results of Experiment 1, agreement ratings declined even further for P6, even though the advice was correct (Scheffé, p<.05).

Confidence in Source of Advice. Explanation mode did not affect confidence ratings, supporting H5. There was an overall Trial effect ($T_o^2 = 1.01$, $p < .001$), but no Trial by Explanation Mode interaction. The pattern across the four trials paralleled the results found in Experiment 1. Participants reported the highest confidence levels immediately after the first problem set (Scheffé, p<.01); there was a statistically significant decrease in confidence levels reported after the second problem set (Scheffé, p<.01) that approached the levels found in the pretest assessment; there was a statistically significant increase in reported confidence levels after the fourth problem set (Scheffé, p<.01) that did not achieve the levels reported after the first problem set.

Performance Attributions. Supporting H6, explanation mode did not have a statistically significant effect for the four attribution ratings: Ability, Task Difficulty, Effort, and Luck.

Discussion

As expected, explanation mode had a significant effect on agreement ratings, but neither on confidence nor on attribution ratings. Both types of explanation increased the agreement with the advice but failed to boost confidence in the expert system. These results supplement the findings of Experiment 1, where manipulations of source pedigree had an impact on confidence and effort attributions ratings, but failed to modify agreement ratings.

The findings of Experiments 1 through 3 strongly suggest that confidence is the result of an *attributional* process (regarding the source) while agreement is based on the evaluation of specific *behavior* with the evidence from each specific situation and of past behavior in similar situations. Accordingly, participants reported being more confident in human experts' judgment and less confident in the judgments of human novices or expert systems. The performance of human experts was explained by these participants in terms of effort in expertise acquisition, a factor these participants believed an expert system cannot possess.

These results raise an important question: Is it possible to *increase* confidence levels (and hence, trust) in the expert system by linking its description to the description of a human expert? This was the focus of Experiment 4.

Experiment 4: Linking Expert Systems and Experts

Prior to Experiment 4, a pilot study was conducted to assess the dominant features participants perceived in the original descriptions of the human expert and expert system (see Table 1 for the original descriptions). Sixteen participants from the same population group received the same stimuli as in Experiment 1 (eight participants with expert system advice, eight with human expert advice). A surprise recall task at the end asked the participants to write down the background information about the description of their source of advice (the expert system and the human expert respectively).

An analysis of the recall data revealed that two of the three features used in the original description of the expert system (see Table 1) met an arbitrary recall criterion (a feature recalled correctly by at least half of the partici-

---

First Revised Description: Knowledge-Linked

MIDAS is an artificial intelligence program that was constructed as a joint effort between Carnegie Mellon's Computer Science Department and the Graduate School of Industrial Administration. MIDAS has a large amount of knowledge about general business principles. **The source of this knowledge is William O'Neil.*** William O'Neil received his undergraduate degree in May of 1975. After working for four years as a financial analyst, he joined a major consulting firm and has worked there for nine years as one of their top financial consultants. In fact, he has just been promoted to "partner" in the firm.

Second Revised Description: Performance-Linked

MIDAS is an artificial intelligence program that was constructed as a joint effort between Carnegie Mellon's Computer Science Department and the Graduate School of Industrial Administration. MIDAS has a large amount of knowledge about general business principles. **The advice produced by MIDAS when solving financial problems is consistently better than the advice given by an experienced financial analyst (William O'Neil).*** William O'Neil received his undergraduate degree in May of 1975. After working for four years as a financial analyst, he joined a major consulting firm and has worked there for nine years as one of their top financial consultants. In fact, he has just been promoted to "partner" in the firm.

* **Boldface** indicates the sentence added.

Table 6. Revised expert system descriptions.

pants). These were "build at Carnegie Mellon University" and, "held a large amount of knowledge." Four of the five features in the original human expert description (see Table 1) met the same recall criterion. These were "received an undergraduate degree," "experience after obtaining the degree," "experience in a top consulting firm," "promoted to partner." We used these results to build two new expert system descriptions as shown in Table 6.

The new descriptions incorporated the six features recalled to criterion by the participants in the pilot. The descriptions differ only in the sentences linking the expert system to the human expert (shown in boldface in Table 6). In the first description, called the Knowledge-linked condition, the expert system was portrayed simply as based on the knowledge of the human expert, but no mention of the comparative performance level was provided about the system. In the second description, called the Performance-linked description, the expert system was described in terms of its comparative performance with the human expert. Experiment 4 attempted to increase the trust in the expert system's advice by influencing confidence using these two description manipulations.

Method

Participants. The participants were sixty-three undergraduate students in introductory organizational behavior and marketing courses at Carnegie Mellon University. None of them participated in the prior experiments.

Materials and Apparatus. The stimuli for the experiment consisted of the same ten financial management decision problems and computing apparatus described in Experiment 1. However, the two revised expert system descriptions from the pilot study served as the experimental manipulation between groups.

Design and Procedure. Experiment 4 followed the same procedure as described for Experiment 1, and each participant was randomly assigned to one of two conditions reflecting the two (revised) descriptions of the expert system source of advice: the Knowledge-linked description and the Performance-linked description.

Hypotheses

For the Knowledge-linked condition, the description of the expert system was directly associated with a human expert's ability by asserting that the expert system's source of knowledge was the human expert (as defined in the human expert condition). This follows the common practice of describing expert systems as decision aids based on the knowledge "acquired from human experts." We expected the Knowledge-linked condition to have no significant impact in any of the four performance attribution ratings (H7a). Although this hypothesis is phrased in terms of all four causal factors, the primary relevant factor is ability. The prior results indicated that participants perceived the performance of the expert system and the human expert as being essentially equivalent in terms of ability (Experiment 1) and attribute much of this equivalence to knowledge (Experiment 2). Furthermore, as performance attributions should not change, confidence ratings should not change (H7b).

For the Performance-linked condition, the description of the expert system was comparatively associated with human expert effort by asserting that its performance was higher than the performance of the human expert. In a sense, the effect of this association is defined as a constrained residual internal factor. That is, if there are two internal causal factors which are used to explain performance variations, and one (ability) is held constant, then any reported increase in performance must be attributed to the remaining factor (effort). Consequently, we anticipated a significant increase in the effort attribution ratings for the new expert system description over the original ratings (H8a). In addition, this would directly account for subsequent increases in confidence (H8b). Experiment 1 indicated that participants were more confident in human experts than in expert systems while Experiment 2 found that the interpretation of effort accounted for the fundamental difference between human experts and expert systems in terms of confidence. Thus, if the manipulation can successfully exploit the association between increased performance and effort, then confidence in the expert system must increase.

As no source pedigree effect on agreement was detected in Experiment 1, we anticipated similar findings here (H7c and 8c).

Summarizing, the hypotheses for Experiment 4 are:

H7a. Knowledge-linked descriptions will not change any performance attribution ratings of the expert system's advice over the original description.

H7b. Knowledge-linked descriptions will not increase the confidence ratings of the expert system's advice over the original description.

H7c. Knowledge-linked descriptions will not change the agreement ratings of the expert system's advice over the original description.

H8a. Performance-linked descriptions will increase the effort attribution ratings of the expert system's advice over the original description.

H8b. Performance-linked descriptions will increase the confidence ratings of the expert system's advice over the original description.

H8c. Performance-linked description will not change the agreement ratings of the expert system's advice over the original description.

Results

Agreement Ratings. No statistically significant differences in agreement ratings were found between the original expert system and the Knowledge-linked condition, supporting H7c. When comparing the agreement ratings of the Performance-linked description to the original expert system and human expert descriptions of Experiment 1, there were statistically significant main effects for Pedigree Source ($F(2,88) = 5.65$, $p < .01$) and for Trial ($T_o^2 = 2.08$, $p < .001$), but no Pedigree Source by Trial interaction. H8c was not supported, as participants provided significantly higher agreement ratings for the advice from the Performance-linked description ($\underline{M} = 4.63$, $\underline{sd} = 1.03$) than for the advice provided by the original expert system ($M = 4.42$, $\underline{sd} = 1.09$; Newman-Keuls, p<.05). Participants also had higher agreement ratings than for the human expert ($\underline{M} = 4.23$, $\underline{sd} = 1.21$; Newman-Keuls, p<.01).

Confidence Ratings. Confidence in the Knowledge-linked expert system description ($\underline{M} = 2.56$, $\underline{sd} = 0.69$) was not significantly different from the confidence obtained with the original expert system description ($\underline{M} = 2.53$, $\underline{sd} = 0.63$) supporting H7b. Confidence in the Performance-linked expert system description ($\underline{M} = 2.70$, $\underline{sd} = 0.59$) was higher than that obtained with the expert system originally described ($\underline{M} = 2.53$, $\underline{sd} = 0.63$, Newman-Keuls, p<.01) supporting H8b. These confidence ratings were still significantly lower than those obtained with the source of advice described as a human expert ($\underline{M} = 2.96$, $\underline{sd} = 0.56$, Newman-Keuls, p<.01). Thus, even though participants reported having less confidence in the Performance-linked expert system than in the human expert, they still reported agreeing more with the

Performance-linked expert system.

Performance Attributions. For the Knowledge-linked condition, none of the four performance attribution factors was rated significantly different from those obtained under the original expert system description (Experiment 1), supporting H7a.

Paralleling the results of Experiment 1, no statistically significant main effects were found for attributional ratings of ability, task difficulty, and luck. There was, however, a statistically significant overall effect of Source Pedigree on ratings of effort (F(3 119) = 10.73, p < .001) as well as a statistically significant overall effect of Trial on effort (T_o^2 = 0.112, p < .01). The results differed from Experiment 1 in that there was a statistically significant Source Pedigree by Trial interaction (T_o^2 = 0.110, p < .05).

Figure 4 shows the effort attributions for four sources of advice. The performance of the Performance-linked expert system was attributed to effort ($\underline{M}$ = 2.27, $\underline{sd}$ = 0.54) to a greater extent than was the performance of the expert system in Experiment 1 ($\underline{M}$ = 1.96, $\underline{sd}$ = 0.51) Newman-Keuls, p<.01), supporting H8a. Effort attributions for the two expert system descriptions remained flat across trials while the effort attributions for the two human sources increased across trials (explaining the interaction between Source Pedigree and Trial).

Discussion

The manipulation of expert system descriptions, devised to link the ability of human experts to that of the expert system through the association of knowledge (Knowledge-linked), did not change any of the performance attributions about the expert system, nor agreement or confidence ratings. Participants seemed insensitive to how the knowledge for the expert system was acquired. In retrospect, this is not perhaps surprising considering the ability attribution results from Experiment 1 (no source pedigree differences) and the interpretations of these attributions revealed in Experiment 2 (knowledge, in part, was the basis for ability for both human expert and expert systems). In fact, the Knowledge-linked expert system description can be seen as a control for the expert system description devised to relate the effort of human experts to the expert system through the comparative association of performance (Performance-linked), since the only difference between them was one sentence linking the descriptions of the human expert and the expert system.

The effect of this sentence was dramatic. Participants significantly increased their confidence in the expert system over the original description. This resulted from a significant increase in the effort attributed to the expert system. However, the confidence remained significantly lower than that placed in the human expert. Thus it was possible to alter the confidence in

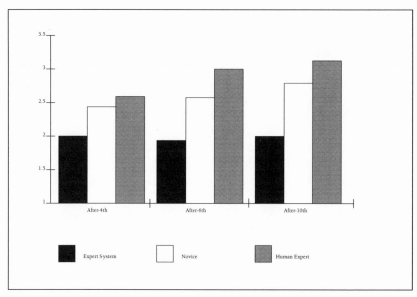

Figure 4. Effort attribution ratings for Experiment 4.

the source of advice from an expert system, but not possible to raise the confidence all the way to the level of human experts. In addition, the Pedigree Source by Trial interaction suggested that additional evidence (through direct experience with the source) can increase the performance factor attributable to effort over time for the human expert, but not for the computer. This indicates that the perception of confidence (via effort) for the computer can be initially increased, but not subsequently increased through additional information. On the other hand, additional interactions with a human expert's advice does result in increased attributions of effort over trials. The initial characterization of an expert system was critical, as it seems to have determined participants' fundamental level of confidence (and subsequently trust) in the advice obtained.

From Experiment 4, an interesting paradox emerged from the confidence and agreement results of the Performance-linked expert system and the human expert. Participants had the highest confidence in a source described as a "human expert," even when a source called an "expert system" was described as performing consistently *better* than the human expert. At the same time, confidence in a source described as an "expert system" did increase as a result of linking the characterization of the expert system to a human expert in terms of performance. Adding to the paradox, participants actually agreed more with the advice of the Performance-linked expert system description than with the human expert, even though they had less confidence in that same source!

The apparent paradox may be resolved by presenting the results in terms of the attributional process required for agreement and confidence judgments. Recall that *agreement* measured the *predictability* dimension of trust while *confidence* in the source reflected the *dependability* dimension of trust. As predictability is contingent on consistent situational behavior over time (in a stable environment), it is possible that agreement levels are higher because expert systems are believed to be better suited in the application of expert knowledge in a given situation and to be less prone to judgment error in the generation of specific advice. Furthermore, the Performance-linked description explicitly states that the expert system performs better than the human expert.

On the other hand, dependability judgments are based on internal characteristics that go beyond recurring situational behaviors. People may not build the same attributions of dependability that are generated when evaluating diagnostic evidence from a human expert because their fundamental characterizations of key attributes underlying the dependability construct for "expert systems" are different from that of "human experts" or, perhaps, even "humans." This is supported by examining the average differences in effort attributions. The average difference in effort attributions between the human expert and the human novice ($\underline{M}_{diff} = .32$) was equivalent in terms of absolute magnitude to the mean difference between the Performance-linked expert system and the original expert system description ($\underline{M}_{diff} = .31$). As previously suggested, these differences may be caused by the interpretation of effort ratings as a surrogate of expertise. On the other hand, differences between the two human descriptions and the two expert systems descriptions are likely to be accounted for by the interpretation of effort as an "exclusively human" capability.

General Discussion and Conclusion

The overall purpose of this series of studies was to investigate the nature of trust in expert system advice. Specifically, we explored whether characterizing advice as coming from a human or an expert system would result in any substantial differences in perceptions or judgment by the users; that is, we searched for a Turing Effect regarding trust. As bases for comparison, we included characterizations of human experts and human novices.

Trust is a multidimensional concept which we regard as comprising predictability, dependability, and faith. The focus in this research was on the first two dimensions. Predictability reflects the behavioral consistency of the source on specific situational events and does not rely on general attributions toward the source. This was measured by agreement with the advice presented by the source. Dependability, on the other hand, reflects particular dispositional attributions toward the source itself, rather than the behaviors in specific situations. This was measured by assessing the confidence in the source. In addition, four causal factors underlying performance were assessed: two factors reflecting internal attributions of the source (ability, effort) and two factors reflecting external attributions of the environment (task difficulty, luck). Confidence in the source was believed to be affected by the two internal attributions.

Was the Turing Effect demonstrated? Without question, participants reacted differently to sources of advice characterized as computers. In Experiment 1, participants were less confident in advice from an expert system than advice from a human expert, and rated effort as contributing less to the performance of the expert system than to the performance of either the human expert or novice. In Experiment 2, participants characterized expert systems' ability differently than those of human experts. Specifically, participants indicated that human experts can exert increased and significant effort toward a problem, but an expert system cannot "exert effort." In Experiment 4, after a manipulation of the description, participants actually agreed more with the advice presented by the Performance-linked expert system than that presented by the human expert (in contrast to Experiment 1, where there was no difference). However, these participants had lower confidence in the expert system than the human expert.

What could account for the Turing Effect? The results of Experiments 2, 3 and 4 indicate that confidence in the source is based on attributional processes, while agreement with the source comes from evaluating situation-specific behaviors. Participants view the internal attributions (contributing to performance, and thus confidence) differently for computers and human experts (and, perhaps, humans in general). Therefore, these differences in attributions could account for the Turing Effect.

What are the implications? First, it is important to recognize the possibility that characterizing a source as an expert system has effects that can be fundamentally different from those of a source characterized as a human. Second, Experiment 4 demonstrated that exploiting specific attributions can lead to changes in trust. Thus, differences in trust (as confidence and agreement) exist, and manipulations may be performed to affect those differences. Consequently, a better understanding of how users generate attributions may help us in the design and implementation of computer-based tools so the output of these tools are actually integrated into the users' problem solving processes.

However, more research is needed to obtain evidence of a causal link between dependability (confidence) judgments and the integration of advice in decision making and problem solving. Research in interpersonal trust and source credibility has conclusively shown a strong link between causal attribution and behavior (Fincham and Bradbury 1987), but it is possible that these results do not hold for the interaction between humans and computers.

A final note can be offered regarding explanations. This research was not on explanations per se, but in Experiment 3 we demonstrated that some form of explanation (either rules or prose) did significantly affect the users' agreement with the advice presented. But it did not affect confidence in the source of advice or the attribution ratings. At least in our laboratory setting, the simple forms of explanations we used did not change the attribution process by which dependability judgments were generated. In fact, these results contradict the claim made by designers of explanation capabilities that explanations are supposed to increase trust (i.e., dependability). Perhaps stronger effects could be gained when examining the value of explanation capabilities (and forms) when dealing with more complex problems. However, results from an extensive field study by Leonard-Barton (1987) suggest that "dispositions" toward expert systems, obtained through experience or formed by "rumor," play an important role in electing to use the technology.

Obviously these results may not be generalizable to other work settings, so further controlled experiments as well as field studies are needed to explicate the conditions under which these conclusions apply. In our experiments, the domain knowledge and experience of the participants was held constant and low, and the problems were relatively simple. The process of trust formation may differ for more knowledgeable participants solving more complex problems. But there seems to be an agreement that trust changes behavior (at least in managerial situations). For example, Mintzberg (1990) stated that managers often approve proposals based mainly on interpersonal trust: "One common solution to approving projects is to pick the person instead of the proposal. That is, the manager authorizes those projects presented by people whose judgments he or she trusts (p. 172)."

As organizations continue to rely on computer-based decision aids, more critical decisions made by humans will be influenced by computer systems. As information superhighways, on-ramps, frontage roads and traffic jams grow, computer-based resources will be made available to increasing numbers of discretionary users similar to (and even less sophisticated than) the participants in this study. If our empirical results hold, and trust predicts the likelihood of advice being taken into account, then user acceptance of computer-based recommendations is dependent not just on the specifics of the justification of the advice supplied, but also on the user's attributions about the internal characteristics of the systems supplying that advice. It is to the exploration and manipulation of such internal attributions that attention should now be paid, to generate concrete and specific recommendations for the successful development and deployment of the types of computer systems Turing envisioned.

Acknowledgments

The authors thank Mark Fichman for his help and guidance. We also thank

Renee Beauclair, Paul Goodman and Laurie Weingart for their comments, and Lester Diamond, Debbie Fenner and Brian Huguenard for data collection. Finally, we thank the editors of this volume for their detailed review and suggestions. We are especially grateful to Robert Hoffman for his advice and careful editing.

Note

There is a renewed interest in the Turing test with the establishment of the Loebner Prize (a cash award reportedly of $100,000) to the author of the program that solves a version of the test (Epstein 1992). The Loebner Prize, as well as the Turing test itself, remain controversial (Loebner 1994; Shieber 1994 a,b).

References

Adler, P.S. (1989). When knowledge is the critical resource, knowledge management is the critical task. *IEEE Transactions on Engineering Management, 36(2)*, 87-94.

Alavi, M. (1984). An assessment of the prototyping approach to information systems development. *Communications of the ACM, 27*, 556-563.

Alavi, M. & Henderson, J.C. (1981). An evolutionary strategy for implementing a decision support system. *Management Science, 27*, 1309-1323.

Anderson, N.S. & Reitman-Olson, J. (Eds.). (1985). *Methods for Designing Software to Fit Human Needs and Capabilities*. Washington, DC: The National Academy of Sciences/National Research Council Committee on Human Factors.

Baker, M.J. & Churchill, G.A. (1977). The impact of physically attractive models on advertising evaluations. *Journal of Marketing Research, 14*, 538-555.

Bannister, B.D. (1986). Performance outcome feedback and attributional feedback: Interactive effects on recipient responses. *Journal of Applied Psychology, 71*, 203-210.

Birnbaum, M.H. & Mellers, B.A. (1983). Bayesian inference: Combining base rates with opinions of sources who vary in credibility. *Journal of Personality and Social Psychology, 45*, 792-804.

Birnbaum, M.H. & Stegner, S.E. (1979). Source credibility in social judgment: Bias, expertise, and the judge's point of view. *Journal of Personality and Social Psychology, XX*, XX-XX.

Brock, T.C. (1965). Communicator-recipient similarity and decision change. *Journal of Personality and Social Psychology, 1*, 650-654.

Buchanan, B.G. & Shortliffe, E.H. (1984). *Rule-Based Expert Systems: The MYCIN Experiments of the Stanford Heuristic Programming Project*. Reading, MA: Addison-Wesley.

Chaiken, S. (1975). Communicator physical attractiveness and persuasion. *Journal of Personality and Social Psychology, 37*, 1387-1397.

Chandrasekaran, B., Tanner, M.C. & Josephson, J.R. (1988). Explanation: The role of control strategies and deep models. In J.A. Hendler (Ed.), *Expert Systems: The User Interface*. Norwood, NJ: Ablex.

Cole, I.W.L. & Grizzle, I.E. (1966). Application of multivariate analysis of variance to repeated measures experiments. *Biometrics, 22*, 810-828.

Davis, F.D., Bagozzi, R.P. & Warshaw, P.R. (1989). User acceptance of computer technology: A comparison of two theoretical models. *Management Science, 35,* 982-1003.

DeSanctis, G. (1983). Expectancy theory as an explanation of voluntary use of a decision support system. *Psychological Reports, 52,* 247-260.

Deutsch, M. (1973). *The Resolution of Conflict: Constructive and Destructive Processes.* New Haven, CT: Yale University Press.

Devine, P.G. & Ostrom, T.M. (1985). Cognitive mediation of inconsistency discounting. *Journal of Personality and Social Psychology, 49,* 5-21.

Dion, K.K. & Stein, S. (1978). Physical attractiveness and interpersonal influences. *Journal of Experimental Social Psychology, 14,* 97-108.

Eagly, A.H. & Chaiken, S. (1975). An attribution analysis of the effect of communicator characteristics on opinion change: The case of communicator attractiveness. *Journal of Personality and Social Psychology, 32,* 136-144.

Earley, P.C. (1988). Computer-generated performance feedback in the magazine subscription industry. *Organizational Behavior and Human Decision Processes, 41,* 50-64.

Elig, T.W. & Frieze, I.H. (1979). Measuring casual attributions for success and failure. *Journal of Personality and Social Psychology, 37,* 621-634.

Ellis, C. (Ed.). (1989). Explanation in intelligent systems. In *Expert Knowledge and Explanation.* Chichester, England: Ellis Horwood.

Epstein, R. (1992). Can machines think? *AI Magazine, 13(2),* 80–95.

Fincham, F.D. & Bradbury, T.H. (1987). The impact of attributions in marriage: A longitudinal analysis. *Journal of Personality and Social Psychology, 53,* 510–517.

Frieze, I.H. (1976). Causal attributions and information seeking to explain success and failure. *Journal of Research in Personality, 10,* 293-305.

Gould, J.D. & Lewis, C. (1985). Designing for usability—Key principles and what designers think. *Communications of the ACM, 28,* 300-311.

Haeckel, S.H. & Nolan, R.L. (1993). Managing by wire. *Harvard Business Review, Sep.-Oct.,* 122-132.

Hovland, C.I., Janis, I.L. & Kelley, H.H. (1953). *Communication and Persuasion.* New Haven, CT: Yale University Press.

Hovland, C.I. & Weiss, W. (1951). The influence of source credibility on communication effectiveness. *Public Opinion Quarterly, 15,* 635-650.

Keen, P.G.W. (1991). *Shaping the Future.* Boston, MA: Harvard Business School Press.

Kelley, H.H. (1967). Attribution theory in social psychology. In D. Levine (Ed.), *Nebraska symposium on motivation* (Vol. 15). Lincoln, NE: University of Nebraska Press.

Langlotz, C.P. & Shortliffe, E.H. (1989). The critiquing approach to automated advice and explanation: Rationale and examples. In C. Ellis (Ed.), *Expert Knowledge and Explanation.* Chichester, England: Ellis Horwood.

LaTour, S.A. & Miniard, P.W. (1983). The misuse of repeated measure analysis in marketing research. *Journal of Marketing Research, Vol. XX,* 45-57.

Leonard-Barton, D. (1987). The case for integrative innovation: An expert system at Digital. *Sloan Management Review, 29,* 7-19.

Loebner, H. (1994). In response. *Communications of the ACM, 37(6),* 79-82.

McGinnies, E. & Ward, C.D. (1974). Persuasibility as a function of source credibility and locus of control: Five cross-cultural experiments. *Journal of Personality, 8,* 360-371.

Meister, D. (1985). *Behavioral Analysis and Measurement Methods.* New York: Wiley.

Mills, J. & Aronson, E. (1965). Opinion change as a function of the communicator's attractiveness and desire to influence. *Journal of Personality and Social Psychology, 1,* 173-177.

Mintzberg, H. (1990). The manager's job: Folklore and fact. *Harvard Business Review, March-April,* 163-176.

Muir, B.M. (1987). Trust between humans and machines, and the design of decision aids. *International Journal of Man-Machine Studies, 27,* 527-539.

Patzer, G.L. (1983). Source credibility as a function of communicator physical attractiveness. *Journal of Business Research, 11,* 229-241.

Quinn, J.B. (1992). *Intelligent Enterprise.* New York: Free Press.

Reeder, G.D. & Brewer, M.B. (1979). A schematic model of dispositional attribution in interpersonal perception. *Psychological Review, 86(1),* 61-79.

Rempel, J.K., Holmes, J.G. & Zanna, M.P. (1985). Trust in close relationships. *Journal of Personality and Social Psychology, 49(1),* 95-112.

Robey, D. (1979). User attitudes and management information systems use. *Academy of Management Journal, 22,* 527-538.

Rotter, J.B. (1980). Interpersonal trust, trustworthiness, and gullibility. *American Psychologist, 35,* 1-7.

Scanzoni, J. (1979). Social exchange and behavioral interdependence. In R.L. Burgess & T.L. Huston (Eds.), *Social Exchange in Developing Relationships.* New York: Academic Press.

Shieber, S. (1994a). Lessons form a restricted Turing test. *Communications of the ACM, 37(6),* 70-78.

Shieber, S. (1994b). On Loebner's lessons. *Communications of the ACM, 37(6),* 83.

Sternthal, B., Dholakia, R. & Leavitt, C. (1978). The persuasive effect of source credibility: Tests of cognitive response. *Journal of Consumer Research, 4,* 252-260.

Swartout, W.R. (1983). XPLAIN: A system for creating and explaining expert consulting programs. *Artificial Intelligence, 21,* 285-325.

Turing, A.M. (1950). Computing machinery and intelligence. *Mind, 59,* 433-460.

Weiner, B. (1986). *An Attributional Theory of Motivation and Emotion.* New York: Springer-Verlag.

Weiner, B., Frieze, I., Kukla, A., Reed, L., Rest, S. & Rosenbaum, R. (1971). *Perceiving the Causes of Success and Failure.* Morristown, NJ: General Learning Press.

Wick, M.R. & Slagle, J.R. (1989). An explanation facility for today's expert systems. *IEEE Expert, 4(1),* 26-36.

Woods, D.D., Roth, E.M. & Bennett, K. (1987). Exploration in joint human-machine cognitive systems. In W. Zachary & S. Robertson (Eds.), *Cognition, Computing and Cooperation.* Norwood, NJ: Ablex.

CHAPTER 19

Interpreting Generic Structures: Expert Systems, Expertise and Context

Kieron O'Hara & Nigel Shadbolt

Circumstances forced him to shut up his library at home for the time being. He apparently submitted to his fate, but in fact he outwitted it. He would not yield an inch of ground in this matter of learning. He bought what he needed and in a few weeks would resume his work; his plan of campaign was largely conceived and well-adapted to the peculiar circumstances, he was not to be subdued; in freedom he spread his wise wings; with each glorious day of independence he grew in stature, and this interim collection of a small new library comprising a few thousand volumes was reward enough for his pains. He was even afraid that the collection might grow too big. Every night he slept in a different hotel. How was he to carry away the increasing burden? But he had an indestructible memory and could carry the entire new library in his head. (Elias Canetti, *Auto da Fé*)

Introduction

In this chapter, we wish to examine the role that expert systems can play in the study and expression of expertise. In particular, we wish to examine the extent to which such systems can contribute to this study without recourse to a simplistic mechanistic account of expertise. In this way we hope to clarify the relationship between the practice of *knowledge engineering* (i.e., building expert systems) and the study of intelligence and expertise. We will focus on the problem of understanding experts *in their context:* can expert systems help in the study of the operation of expertise in its context?

Clancey has called for a distinction to be made between psychology and the development of expert systems.

I draw a distinction between knowledge engineering and the study of intelligence and believe that evaluation of research, and hence progress, hinges on clearly committing to one or the other. It is fine to aim for both, but the respective contributions must be separated out (1991, p. 359).

We hope to provide some evidence for thinking that this distinction is not always as straightforward as Clancey suggests; a knowledge engineer should always be clear about his intentions and motivations, of course, but by building systems he will inevitably learn something about intelligence and expertise.

In this introductory section, we will set out the problems that are likely to be encountered by those who advocate the use of expert systems to study expertise, particularly in the light of recent innovations in the field of model-based expert system development that seem to abstract away from context. In the second section, we will examine some influential development methodologies to show how they are evolving to cope with these problems. In the light of this evolution, the final section will sketch the relationship between expert systems, expertise and context.

We begin with a brief discussion first of context, and second of the relationship between expert systems and expertise.

Context

There is a neglected problem with the concept of context, especially in relation to the evaluation of expert systems as psychological models. It is impossible to state *a priori* what the effects of context may be on any particular system. A builds a system. B tells her that her system is fatally flawed, because essential aspects of the environment are not, and cannot be, represented. "Ah," says A, laudably eager to learn, "do tell me what these effects are, that I might incorporate knowledge that will ease your mind." "Can't do that," replies B, "because if I can tell you how context will affect your system, then that would imply that such effects are representable. However," (waving a paper by Brooks) "it says here that such effects are *not* representable, so that, I'm afraid, is that. Stop trying to build geological prospectors and liver diagnosticians, and start on moths and earwigs."

The reason that our friend B doesn't like A's system is one factor of context, which is its *holism*. Context comes all of a piece; you can't simply put some of it into your machine and hope that that does the trick. But context has another interesting property that B, we will claim, has neglected, and that is its *ubiquity*. Nothing is context-free; every action has a purpose. One upshot of this is that it is impossible to say exactly what a context will *do* to a system; but a further corollary is that it is relatively difficult to establish when context is neglected to a dangerous degree.

The context in which a machine is built is at least as important as the context in which the expertise operates as a factor for evaluating its psychological import. We will complete our scene-setting remarks with a brief discussion of this issue.

Expertise

Intuitively, expert systems, by expressing the knowledge in a domain, provide a handle for the study of expertise because they thereby express *what an expert knows.* However, the relationship between an expert system and the expertise is not as simple as some commentators have thought (e.g., Slatter 1987); the "contents" of the expertise cannot simply be "read off" from the structure of the knowledge base. There are two reasons why greater complexity than this must be expected.

Firstly, expert systems are typically built to solve particular problems, and consequently, their representation of the expertise will be restricted or biased towards those particular requirements. For example, one might construct an expert system as a tool for training students; in that event, a premium will be placed on the system's careful explanation and justification of its problem-solving steps. The final structure and content of a system will depend on a complex process of negotiation between the client, the expert and the knowledge engineer who is responsible for the system's development. For this reason, any expert system's expression of expertise will necessarily be restricted to a particular frame of reference (Clancey 1991)—indeed, by an extension of the argument, a similar cavil will apply to *any* expression or representation of expertise. Hence, when expert systems are used to study expertise, due weight must be placed on the frame of reference of the system in question.

The second reason for the nontriviality of the relationship between expert systems and expertise is that expertise does not operate in a vacuum. An expert is characterized as much by her *constituency* (i.e., a group of people who will defer to her judgment in relevant matters) as by her knowledge. As such, her expertise must function in contexts in which her constituency is interested. Hence, much expert knowledge consists in functional, context-dependent abstractions (Agnew, Ford and Hayes 1994).

For both reasons, it will not be enough simply to postulate some cognitive mechanism isomorphic to the computational mechanism (at some specified level of abstraction). Sensitivity to context (both the context of the system itself, and the context of the expertise) will also be required.

However, a recent innovation in expert system development methodologies has been the construction of *libraries* of models of expert problem-solving intended to serve both as ready-made abstract descriptions of the expertise, and also as organizational principles for expert system development. The use of these libraries is becoming increasingly widespread, and it is arguable that models from such libraries can be seen as explanatory of expertise (Shadbolt and O'Hara this volume). The suspicion must be that prefabricated models of expert problem-solving, developed and represented free of context, are bound to fail precisely because of their neglect of context.

The Evolution of Modeling Methodologies

Our strategy for addressing the question of context will be to examine a few prominent examples of expert system development methodologies in order to see whether the suspicion that they neglect context, canvassed above, is well-founded. The issue is how context-independent libraries can deal with context; problems have been encountered, but they have been addressed to some extent. Our task in this section will be to measure that extent. Following brief discussions of generic tasks, the KADS-II library, and generalized directive models, we shall move on to discuss this issue in relation to architectural considerations.

Chandrasekaran's Generic Tasks

We begin with the generic task (GT) method as developed by Chandrasekaran and his colleagues. The original conception of GTs (Chandrasekaran 1983) underwent quite substantial evolution before it reached its current form (Chandrasekaran and Johnson 1993). It is our contention that that evolution was to a large extent necessary to ensure that the GT library was able to cope with contextual variation.

The 1980s conception consisted of a library of tasks that could be used to combine both conceptual modeling and system design. There were six such tasks: Taxonomic Classification; State Abstraction (given a change in a state of a system, predict further expected changes); Knowledge-Directed Information Passing (given attributes of a datum, predict attributes of other data); Object Synthesis (design an object satisfying specifications); Hypothesis Matching (decide whether a hypothesis explains a set of data); and Abductive Assembly of Explanatory Hypotheses (construct the best composite explanatory hypothesis for a set of data). Each of these six GTs contained a specification of the type of problems to which they should be applied, a specification of the forms of knowledge which should be acquired, and a set of control structures for solving the problem. As an example, Figure 1 gives the specification of object synthesis.

The other GTs shared this form. They could be used in model-based expert system development in the following manner (this is a simplified account). To begin with, the expertise should be modeled. After preliminary knowledge acquisition (KA) to establish a general view of the problem-solving that the expert performs, the problem-solving would be matched against the *task specification,* which, as can be seen from the example of Figure 1, is a

---

Object Synthesis (Design) by Plan Selection and Refinement

Task Specification
Design an object satisfying specifications (object in an abstract sense: they can be plans, programs, etc.).

Forms of knowledge
Object structure is known at some level of abstraction, and pre-compiled plans are available which can make choices of components, and have lists of concepts to call upon for 'refining' the design at that level of abstraction.

Organization of knowledge
Concepts corresponding to "components" organized in a hierarchy mirroring the object structure. Each concept has plans which can be used to make commitments for some "dimensions" of the component.

Control Regime
Top down in general. The following is done recursively until a complete design is worked out: a specialist corresponding to a component of the object is called, the specialist chooses a plan based on some specification, instantiates and executes some part of the plan which suggests further specialists to call to set other details of the design. Plan failures are passed up until appropriate changes are made by higher level specialists, so that specialists who failed may succeed on a retry.

Goal Types
E.g., Choose plan, execute <plan element>, refine <plan>, redesign (modify) <partial design> to respond to failure of <subplan> S, select alternative plan, etc.

Example use
Expert design tasks, synthesis of everyday plans of action.

Figure 1. The form of a generic task (after Brown and Chandrasekaran 1985)

relatively informal sentence about the type of problem-solving to be modeled.[1] The problem-solving must be an instance of the problem-solving type mentioned in the task specification.

Having matched the problem-solving type against this specification, the relevant GT would be selected from the library, and used to drive the remainder of the system development. Because the forms and organization of knowledge are given in the library (cf. Figure 1), this can help KA greatly; the value of modeling from the perspective of KA is that the model should tell the knowledge engineer what *types* of knowledge to look for and expect. Finally, when the knowledge engineer comes to design the system, a control regime and goal types are specified in the GT. This helps the processes of design and implementation. In effect, then, GTs partially collapse the conceptual modeling and design phases of expert system development. Selecting a model will automatically give hints on how to design the system itself.

So, using GTs can provide assistance in moving from the modeling of the expertise through to system implementation. To see how context might queer the pitch, consider that at the modeling stage, it is the matching of the task specification against the knowledge engineer's conception of the expert's problem-solving that does the work—he gets the forms of knowledge and control structures for free. The point is that how some problem-solving is *regarded* or *interpreted* will have ramifications on how the problem is solved by the target system. But how the problem is interpreted will depend, among other things, on contextual matters.

For example, a designer may be doing some problem-solving that can be characterized as object synthesis (i.e., design) under the definition in Figure 1. But it could equally well be characterized as classification, and indeed it may be more efficient to solve the problem artificially by using (the GT) Taxonomic Classification instead of (the GT) Object Synthesis. Nevertheless, the pressure to characterize what someone who is called a *designer* does as *design* may outweigh other pressures on the characterization of the problem-solving. In this way the expert's constituency (a crucial aspect of the context of expertise) can influence the makeup of a system. Allemang and Rothenfluh (1992) provide empirical confirmation of the possibility of different interpretations of the same problem-solving in terms of GTs—in their work six respondents modeled a standard room allocation problem in a variety of ways, ranging from design to abductive assembly.

Hence, the most efficient GT for an application will not necessarily be selected. Alternatively, if the knowledge engineer chooses his GT on the basis of efficiency, that would imply that he has already acquired enough knowledge about the domain to make a sensible choice (i.e., has already done substantial KA), and hence the generic task, rather than directing knowledge acquisition, has appeared long after KA has commenced.

The root cause of this difficulty is the functional ambiguity of the concept of a GT. A GT is made up of a specification of a problem-solving type together with a weak specification of forms of the associated knowledge and control structures. In this way, the selection of a model can be seen as both an interpretative classification step (a decision to see the problem-solving as an instance of some particular type), and as a commitment to use particular mechanisms for the solution of the problem. Difficulties may emerge once such a dual modeling methodology is applied in a particular context because that context may well dictate that idiosyncratic computational methods are appropriate for various reasons.

If the GT is not used to drive KA, then these context-dependent reasons can be discovered and an efficient system built, but in that event, the GT would not have been fully exploited in the knowledge modeling process. On the other hand, if the use of the GT to drive KA is maximized, then it may be selected from the library at too early a point in the modeling process to take the idiosyncrasies of context into account (i.e., at a point at which the problem-solving is only abstractly characterized by the knowledge engineer). The result is that the GT which is appropriate as an interpretative classification of the problem-solving may well turn out to be inappropriate as even a rough system design.

In response to these (and other) problems, Chandrasekaran altered his conception of generic tasks as Platonic characterizations of problem-solving types (1983), and moved to the idea of a GT as a form of task analysis (1990). In this view, each GT became an umbrella covering a series of possible methods or configurations of methods, hierarchically organized for ease of navigation. So, for example, in Object Synthesis (design), instead of the single method proposed in the early GT shown in Figure 1, a suite of methods was made available. This approach suggested a number of decompositions of design into subtasks (e.g., *propose* a design—*critique* the design on the basis of specifications/constraints—*modify* the original proposal on the basis of the critique). Associated with each subtask was a family of methods (which might involve further decomposition of the subtask into subsubtasks, etc.).

In the 1980s formulation of GTs, there was a danger that a problem could be handled badly by a system, not because the problem was misidentified, but because the method strongly associated with the identification was inappropriate. Under Chandrasekaran's 1990s formulation, this danger receded dramatically (O'Hara and Shadbolt 1993b). The KA step of identifying the nature of the problem-solving in the domain, and the design step of aligning methods for the solution of the problem, were now separated.

From KADS-I to KADS-II

Our second case study of a model-based methodology evolving over time in response to contextual pressures is of the KADS methodology (Tansley and Hayball 1993). The KADS methodology is the outcome of two projects, KADS-I and its successor KADS-II. Both KADS projects had the aim of developing a complete methodology for developing expert systems; therefore each project has important and interesting things to say about more areas than just modeling (e.g., project management, software maintenance). Our interest here, however, is with modeling; we want to indicate how the evolution of the KADS methodology from KADS-I to KADS-II has paralleled the evolution in generic tasks. In particular, we want to show how pressures from contextual variation have been neutralized to some extent by the later methodology. We will focus on the differences in approach between KADS-I and KADS-II with respect to a single task, assessment.

The KADS-I library contained a single model for assessment (Breuker, Wielinga, van Someren, de Hoog, Schreiber, de Greef, Bredeweg, Wielemaker, Billault, Davoodi and Hayward 1987, p. 63), the inference structure of which we see in Figure 2. There were various drawbacks to this approach of only having a single model; reviews (Löckenhoff and Valente 1993; Valente

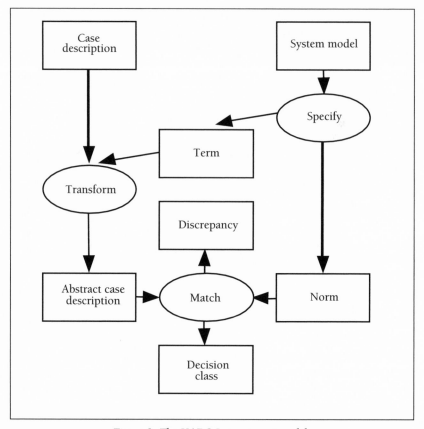

Figure 2. The KADS-I assessment model.

and Löckenhoff 1993) expressed concern both about the fact that there was only a single model (which therefore tended to be a relatively blunt instrument), and also that the particular model seemed to have important faults (e.g., some of the names of the roles were regarded as misleading).

For our purposes, what is germane about this critique of KADS-I models is the way that problems dealing with context were perceived to be the cause of trouble. This happened in three related ways. Firstly, like the early GTs, KADS-I interpretation models had an irredeemably dual nature; a description of the expertise and a rough system design. The system design was specified less exactly in KADS-I than it was in the early generic tasks,[2] but, nevertheless, similar difficulties presented themselves (O'Hara and Shadbolt 1993a). Secondly, the single abstract model had difficulty describing the particulars of an actual context, again, as with GTs. Thirdly, there was an ontological difficulty, in that the interpretation model is at such a level that it could only name the problem-solving roles that have been identified. But that is merely to say that some knowledge would play a particular role in the problem-solving without necessarily providing any guidance about how this would be done. The casting manager does not direct the play.

The response in KADS-II to these difficulties was the creation of a library with 105 models for assessment (Löckenhoff and Valente 1993). The key to such a large library was the hierarchical organization. The KADS-II analysis divided assessment into three lines of reasoning: abstraction of the case description, specification of a norm from a system model, and matching the norm against the abstract description. With this tripartite structure, the library contained various models of plausible ways of representing abstraction, specification and matching, which in combination produced the 105 models. The knowledge engineer would have to make at most four selections of modeling components to get a complete assessment model. The complexity of choosing a model from the library has increased, but the gain is increased representational fidelity.

This is a definite response to problems associated with the context of an application. Instead of a single model closely tied to methods designed to cover a wide variety of possible situations, we are given 100 models, and an indexing mechanism to aid navigation. The christening of some problem-solving as a type "assessment" no longer necessarily results in the inappropriateness of the model as before. Of course, the difficulties associated with insensitivity to context have not been definitively solved by this manoeuvre. A balance has to be struck between the size of the library and the accuracy of its models' representations of expertise. However, the likelihood of contextual insensitivity causing difficulties has been substantially reduced as a result of the evolution of KADS-II from KADS-I.

Generalized Directive Models

The third example of a model-based approach that we shall consider is the Generalized Directive Model (GDM) approach (Motta, O'Hara, Shadbolt, Stutt and Zdrahal 1996). GDMs are not based on a library, but a grammar; models are not stored and selected, but instead are constructed.

Like models from KADS-I and KADS-II, GDMs contain inference structures expressed as connections between roles and inference steps (e.g., the structure shown in Figure 2 can be represented as a GDM). Unlike KADS, there is no control structure. The key notion in the GDM grammar is that any inference step can be seen as an abstract specification of an inference in problem-solving. Since the specification is abstract, the inference step can be replaced with less abstract (and therefore potentially more complex) inference steps. This replacement operation is called *rewriting*. It is these rewrites that are governed by the GDM grammar. Figure 3 shows a set of possible

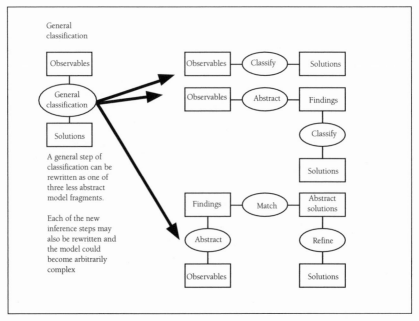

Figure 3. An example GDM rewrite rule: three possible
rewrites of a general classification step.

rewrites—a general classification step can be rewritten as simple classification, abstract-and-classify, or heuristic classification.

Figure 4 shows how the increasingly more specific series of GDMs can be used to direct knowledge acquisition. A step of model refinement will make the model less abstract, and may uncover new roles for knowledge to play. These roles will need to be filled, which is the task of domain KA. The increased knowledge of the problem-solving in the domain that results may then suggest a further rewrite of the GDM, and so on. Episodes of GDM refinement are interleaved with episodes of knowledge acquisition.

Each change that is made to the model is very slight, and hence the transition from one model to the next is relatively straightforward. The course of system development using GDMs might perhaps best be seen as in Figure 5. The use of GDMs is presented in (Motta, O'Hara and Shadbolt 1994) and (Motta *et al.* 1996).

There is, of course, a similarity between GDMs and the model libraries of KADS-II. In particular, the top-down development processes and hierarchical arrangement of the models are shared by the two approaches. But note the advantages of the GDM approach.

Firstly, the process of model selection and development does not have to begin with model identification. Recall the trouble caused by having to as-

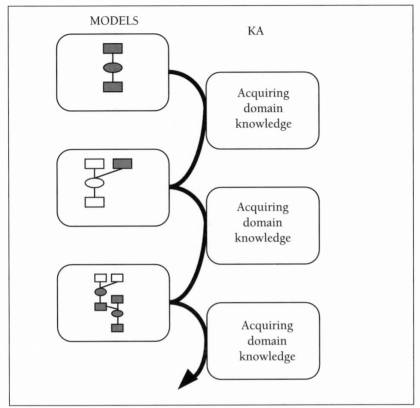

MODELS

KA

Acquiring domain knowledge

Acquiring domain knowledge

Acquiring domain knowledge

*Figure 4. Episodes of model refinement interleave
with episodes of knowledge acquisition.*

similate a problem-solving type with a mechanism for solving a problem. To
call a problem "assessment" may be perfectly reasonable, except that it can
then force a knowledge engineer to commit to a certain class of mechanisms,
mechanisms that may not be the most efficient for the case at hand (O'Hara
and Shadbolt 1996). KADS-II preserves the importance of model
identification—to gain access to the assessment library, one must have decided that the problem-solving is of the assessment type. Whereas with GDMs,
no model identification is required. The process needs only information,
gleaned from the domain, to secure a rewrite. A corollary of this is that a
number of models constructible in the library may not be of any known
type. Hence idiosyncratic domains (i.e., domains where the problem-solving
is unusual, and departs from standard, generic or well-known accounts of
problem-solving) are much more likely to get a reasonable representation
using GDMs.

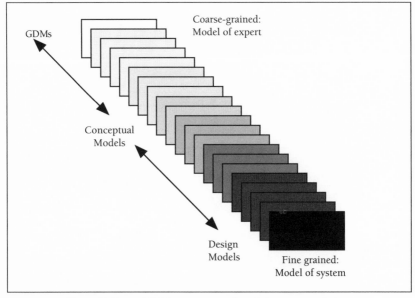

Figure 5. From GDM to conceptual model to system design.

Secondly, the GDM grammar is a neater way of storing information. The KADS-II library of assessment models has 105 possible models in it. Large fragments of each model have to be represented and stored. Whereas in the VITAL GDM grammar, a relatively small number of rewrite rules and model components have to be stored—but the library actually (thanks to recursive rules) contains infinitely many models!

Thirdly, the VITAL GDM grammar provides (at most stages of model development) a greater variety of options. The number of options available in KADS-II seems to be roughly between three and six at any time; in a GDM of moderate complexity (e.g., with two inference steps with available rewrites), one might expect ten or fifteen possible rewrites. However, these rewrites are sufficiently grouped and organized to render the choice manageable (Motta *et al.* 1996). Further, the analysis can be deeper than in KADS-II. The KADS-II assessment library permits each of the three components of assessment to be "rewritten" once (giving a maximum of three transformations), whereas even the simple example described by Motta, O'Hara and Shadbolt (1994) has eight rewrites.

Context and the Evolution of Model-Based Development Methodologies

Both generalized directive models and KADS-II are attempts to beef up the model-based approach to expert system development in the face of a mismatch between relatively monolithic model libraries and a complex and dynamic world. Both advocate the solution of having more models available, introducing a trade-off between the increase in the ability to represent idiosyncratic domains and the increase in the memory required to store the new models. Both methodologies involve the composition of models out of components. The generic task methodology is more concerned with the computational methods to be used by the target system, but even there there is a new interest with the decomposition of the task and the furnishing of a range of methods for the subtasks.

How does this impinge on the question of context? We can perhaps best illustrate this with a specific example. Recall the KADS-I assessment model from Figure 2. Depicted in that figure is a general form of the assessment task: a case description, suitably abstracted, is matched against norms generated from a system model, and any discrepancies noted. As a generalized description of assessment, this is fine. However, in particular contexts, problem-solving may diverge to some extent from the model.

For example, let us consider the "transform" inference. In the general KADS model, this inference takes a case description and a term as input, and creates an abstract case description as output. The inference is intended to take a raw description of the object to be assessed, and convert that description into usable form (the reason that a term has to be imported from the system model is that it is impossible to create the abstract case description until the terms in which it has to be described are known).

All that is a good general description of one process involved in assessment, and most would recognize it at a suitably high level of description. The problem arises when the model is applied to a specific case. In that event, the variation of assessment across contexts can cause trouble. One such situation is where the case description did not need to be transformed at all—the raw data were perfectly adequate for the assessment task. Another is when the inference may be described in more specific vocabulary than "transform"—the data may be better described as computed, or abstracted. Thirdly, extra types of knowledge could be used—for instance, information (unrelated to the system model) might have to be used to determine how the case is to be described, depending on whether the user of the output information is a human or artificial agent. A fourth situation might involve extra problem-solving steps (i.e., the insertion of an extra oval into the diagram)—one possibility here would be if the transformation process involved the construction of a case frame, whose slots would contain the important information about the case. A fifth situation might be that only certain inputs to the transformation step were required—such as when the term that is input is not needed because in the particular problem-solving context the terms in which the case description need to be presented are understood. See Figure 6 for problem-solving models based on these five situations.

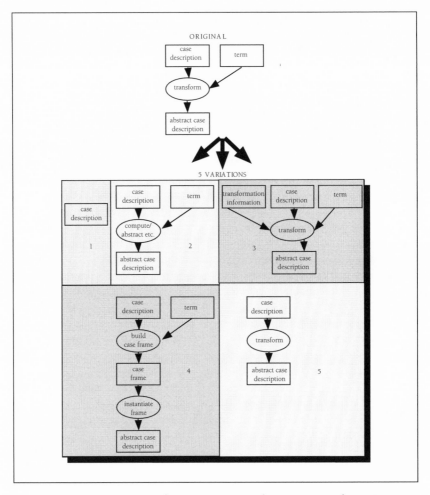

Figure 6. Five variations from a generic case description transformation.

The model needs to fit the specific problem-solving situation in order to be useful. When the model must be varied there are two strategies. The first is to pretend that the model really fits the problem-solving. In this case, the roles and inferences of the model may be misleading, and may set up unrealistic demands for knowledge that doesn't exist. Alternatively it may be that knowledge that is vital to the problem-solving is not asked for in knowledge acquisition.

The second strategy is to reconfigure the model so that it does fit in with the problem-solving. This is obviously the better solution. However, it may involve a measure of hand-crafting that is so labor-intensive that the gain to be made from using a generic library all but disappears.

A way around this dilemma is to include more models in the model library, to make sure that as many situations as possible are covered by the generic library. Indeed, this is analogous to one way that experts themselves handle complexity (Feltovich, Johnson, Moller and Swanson 1984, pp. 313-314). Such a strategy will be expensive in storage space, unless, as KADS-II, GTs and GDMs have discovered, decompositional factors can be exploited. A coarse-grained description of the problem-solving can be replaced by a range of finer-grained descriptions—this is the basic intuition behind the improvements described above.

This solution leads to another aspect of contextual relativity, which is addressed by GDMs in particular. Any problem-solving may be described at a number of levels, from a simple sentence which leaves all the details out (e.g., "she assesses the situation"), right down to a detailed description of the neuronal activity of the expert as she exercises her expertise. Of course, knowledge engineers require some level of description between the two. However, which level of description they actually need depends, among other things, on what the project itself requires. GDMs get more fine-grained as they are rewritten, and the rewriting stops when the knowledge engineer decides to stop. Hence the knowledge engineer has the capacity to create a model that is exactly as fine-grained as required by the project he is working on.

We have now seen how three particular views of model-based development have attempted to cope with contextual idiosyncrasy while trying to avoid paying for the attempt in time and memory. Up until now we have mainly been concerned with conceptual modeling and have concentrated on that subject. As a final example, we shall look at attempts to implement such models.

Architectures for Supporting Problem-Solving Models

Some of the earliest attempts to implement models originated in generic task research (Chandrasekaran and Johnson 1993). The aim was to construct method-specific shells that provided computational support for the implementation and execution of methods. Each GT had a clear characterization in terms of the types of knowledge needed and an associated control regime. Moreover, the early view was that a one-to-one mapping could be determined between task and method. Perhaps then for each GT a particular shell could be built.

The earliest such was CSRL (Bylander and Mittal 1986)—a language that allowed the knowledge engineer to encode classification hierarchies and reason about them using the method of "establish-and-refine." This was quickly followed by DSPL (Brown and Chandrasekaran 1989), a language and control regime that supported the implementation of routine design problem-solvers. Punch (1989), and many others extended the coverage of GTs by such method-specific shells.

An interesting extension to GT support can be found in the JIGSAW system (Pugh 1993). The system is based on a distributed architecture in which individual knowledge acquisition modules are responsible for eliciting knowledge about particular GTs. A degree of opportunism within the architecture allows the system to be reasonably flexible with regard to the KA modules that are invoked in any particular context. The GTs supported by the system can run the gamut of activity from elicitation through to code generation.

A feature of systems such as TIPS (Punch 1989) is that they attempt the selection of an appropriate method at run-time. Some proponents of expert system methodologies would argue that dynamic reconfiguration is neither possible nor desirable. For example, many KADS users place the emphasis on determining the appropriate model of problem-solving at design-time and not at run-time. The cost of the greater flexibility inherent in run-time configurability is that a substantial meta-reasoning activity must occur—namely, planning the selection and customization of GT methods.

Attempts to implement GTs show great variation in the granularity of method selection. Moreover, it is one thing to determine which of a number of detailed methods to select for a subtask such as "Propose" in Object Synthesis; it is quite another to decide which top level task is best for dealing with a goal in problem-solving. Indeed, Chandrasekaran's own view on the mapping between tasks and methods has evolved considerably beyond what was instantiated in the shells we have discussed so far.

> The task structure is meant to be an analytic tool. We do not mean to imply that the implementation of a system must have a one-to-one correspondence to the task structure, but that the system that performs diagnosis or design can be viewed as using some of the methods and subtasks. In particular, the task structure does not fix the order of subtasks or dictate that a single method must be used to achieve each task. It is also not meant to correspond to a procedure-call hierarchy, although that is one way directly to implement a task structure. The task structure simply provides the vocabulary to use in describing how systems performing the task work (Chandrasekaran and Johnson 1993, pp. 249-50).

This is not dissimilar to attempts to operationalize problem-solving component libraries. For example, in the ACKnowledge project, the KADS approach was operationalized using a GDM notation (Terpstra, van Heijst, Shadbolt and Wielinga 1993). Here there was a clear commitment to the early operationalization of conceptual models, moving away from the strict separation of conceptual and design modeling espoused by some KADS researchers. The idea was to exploit the structure-preserving aspects of mapping conceptual models into design and implementation modules. There might be methods to optimize aspects of the implementation, but this should not do substantial violence to the structures first discerned in the conceptual modeling activity.

In ACKnowledge this process was supported by associating domain level knowledge bases with the components of GDMs. A control flow was imposed on the GDM structure. This control information was used by a met-alevel interpreter that traversed the GDM structure and made calls down to the domain layer knowledge bases associated with the problem-solving model. Inference engines at the domain layer supplied requested information. In this way the problem-solving structures were animated and the conceptual models could be operationalized.

What all of these operationalizations lack is any capability to modify the model of problem-solving in response to the system's experience of problem-solving. One way to address this problem has been to characterize GTs within the SOAR architecture (Laird, Newell and Rosenbloom 1987), a system based on formulating problem-solving activity as a heuristic search in a set of problem states called a problem space.

Recent attempts to characterize GTs within SOAR have produced systematic accounts of how generic methods could be realized in the problem spaces of SOAR, and be seen to emerge from the chunking or learning mechanisms of SOAR (Johnson 1991). In general, the issue of the ontogenesis of problem-solving types has received little attention. Whatever criticisms one might level at SOAR, it seems to offer a general purpose architecture for a collection of weak methods, and as such could act as a vehicle within which to characterize what might be called a "content theory for tasks." Moreover, the learning process might lead to precisely the sort of strengthening of weak methods that characterizes task specific skilled behavior.

The SOAR approach to GTs has the additional attractive feature that one can leave the encoding of methods more or less underspecified and the system can still solve problems. It is a moot point whether the programming of methods in SOAR renders an understanding of GTs completely explicit. One may be moving the problem one stage back into the artful encoding of problem spaces.

Notwithstanding, the approach of using a unified architecture as both a specification and run-time implementation platform is a promising one. There is no reason to suppose that GTs are privileged from the point of view of SOAR, and we are currently investigating the implementation of GDM structures within SOAR. It would be interesting to see if the generalizations and specializations characteristic of GDMs are an emergent feature of SOAR learning methods.

The work discussed in this section has shown that the modeling approaches in expert system development have responded to the need to deal with environmental influences by adjusting generic libraries to create libraries of idiosyncratic models that are more likely to do justice to the multiplicity of real-world situations with which such a methodology might be expected to cope. This should not be seen, we think, as an inglorious retreat from a silly position. It is reasonable, having dreamt up an approach, to test it to the limits and modify it accordingly. However, the question is: can we be sure that these approaches have adjusted far enough? Is it possible for any such library-based approach to be responsive enough to the vagaries of circumstance? Worlds are complex; libraries are not (if they are to remain cheap on memory). If the outside world in its totality cannot be written into these libraries, perhaps they will always be missing something. This is the charge that we need to investigate.

The Contextual Representation of Context

One problem with the evaluation of expert systems as psychological models is the fact that expert systems—indeed, most AI systems generally—are really built to complement human capacities, not to emulate them. It is rare for any machine to be built and widely used without some gain in either labor or time. Ignoring this point can lead to misrepresentation of AI systems which purport to be of psychological importance, in the following way. The only criterion for intelligence that has widespread support is passing the Turing test (Turing 1950), where a machine and a human compete to convince a jury, through their answers to the jury's questions, that they are the human. This is a limited test from the AI point of view, since most AI systems simply will not aim for the ability to be convincing imitation humans in arbitrary circumstances. Of course, Turing himself was clear that his test provides a sufficient though not necessary condition of intelligence, as Ken Ford has reminded us. Nevertheless the lack of any widely accepted alternative does have the effect of making the Turing test the "only game in town," and therefore a de facto necessary and sufficient condition (Hauser 1993).

This point develops into the worry that, if intelligence is as human-centered as the Turing test implies, then models of intelligence, if they are to be of psychological import, should be equally so. Therefore, if machines that are based on such models fail to be sufficiently "human-like," then their psychological import should be correspondingly downplayed. This worry seems to be behind Clancey's (1992) suggestion that we should "view a *domain expert as an informant* about some system in the world (therefore knowledge acquisition is primarily concerned with modeling some system in the expert's world, in contrast with modeling his mental processes)" (p. 6, his emphasis).

So we now have two worries to address. One is the point that it seems impossible to anticipate and represent the full context of a system as, for example, a smallish set of sentences describing the environment in which a system finds itself, since contextual effects seem to be ubiquitous and unpredictable.

Even if it were possible in theory, it seems that such representation of them could involve such a massive overhead in memory and processing time as effectively to rule out the functioning of such systems in real time (recall our example from above; and the large variation possible within one particular process of the task of assessment). The second worry is that expert systems may fail to be sufficiently imitative of humans to be of psychological import.

These worries coalesce when we consider that one aspect of human performance is its ability to move across contexts productively. This is, on the face of it, an astounding ability. There is certainly no obvious route to the reproduction of such an ability in machines. Brooks (1991a) wants to build machines that can live in "a dynamic people-populated world" but explicitly trades that off against a high level of intelligence (p. 225). The two worries combine in the following way: since humans can move across contexts, then if expert systems are to be of psychological import, they must also be able to move across contexts (the second worry); however, context is very difficult to represent (the first worry); therefore expert systems will not be of psychological import. We need to defuse this combination of worries.

To do that, we might contrast the notion of context with the notion of a system's (animal's) *ecological niche* (which we can view as the set of contexts in which the system or animal can operate successfully). The set of contexts which makes up an ecological niche may vary, but will always remain bounded. So, although humans can operate in a number of different contexts, there is a large number of contexts in which they *cannot* operate, such as absolute zero, or the Marianas Trench. Human ingenuity certainly means that insulation against hostile environments is a real possibility; so, for example, humans can operate on the surface of the moon only by insulating themselves in tightly controlled environments (lunar modules, space suits) in such a way that they could be any place—back on Earth, for instance. What seems, from our human point of view, to be an astonishing range of contexts may well, from outside our ecological niche, not look particularly wide at all. Part of the success of humankind is based on the forcing of a number of environments to be within the human ecological niche; what, at first blush, looks like a triumph of human adaptation in fact is more plausibly seen as a triumph of human technology. In particular, expertise is highly sensitive to context (Agnew, Ford, and Hayes 1994), and may disappear even with minor contextual shifts.

An expert system will be tailored to a role in an organization. In other words, an expert system would be devised explicitly to operate in a limited number of contexts, and should be well adapted to those contexts (assuming the system is well-crafted). Those contexts will constrain both how the system is used (how it interfaces with other branches of the organization), and what assumptions are made about the world (e.g., what forms the data upon which it operates are assumed to take). Of course, take it out of those contexts, and it fails (just as if the deep sea diver's oxygen pipe is severed, he will fail too). The expert system will have its own ecological niche (defined by its user requirements), and it would not be expected to function well beyond that. Adaptation to an ecological niche carries with it the implicit suggestion that such adaptation will be to a bounded set of contexts.

Put another way, context (at least, every single discernible element of the context) does not have to be represented by a symbolic system explicitly, because that system itself has a context that determines the interpretation and import of much of its output.

Because context is ubiquitous, everything has one. Those who represent symbolic AI as a way of getting context-free or context-independent accounts of intelligence are clearly missing the point, and against such a position Brooks (1991b) and Clancey (1991) are right to rail. A system has a context that will include the method for the system's use, the place of the system in its host corporation, the way it actually gets used. This context need not be represented; the system will either be adapted to it or not. If it is adapted, then it will run smoothly in it. We have a continuum here; what is usually called a situated system can (in theory) cope with contexts and commands that a symbolic system cannot, and vice versa. But it does not follow from that that the symbolic system has (or is intended to have) no context. As Agnew et al. (1994) put it, it's turtles (= levels of representation) all the way down. None of this entails that no levels of representation can be privileged in a particular context. Some people require a logicist explanation of some psychological intentional faculty (perhaps because they want to build a system that does the same job using Prolog), others want a neuroscientific explanation (prior to brain surgery), still others want to develop something that can behave interestingly in various common environments. But the idea that any one of these types of explanation is in any way basic or prior is just false, it seems to us.

What this discussion boils down to in relation to model-based expert system development is that the libraries of models that have been developed as part of expert system research over the last ten years or so should be seen as descriptive of expertise *in context* (cf. Shadbolt and O'Hara, this volume). They are designed for a specific use, and are tailored for that use. Of course, in a sense, the libraries are context-free, in that they can be transplanted into a range of contexts or domains. But the extent of that range is implicitly specified by the methodological principles underlying the use of the libraries, and hence contextual limitations are implicit. It cannot, for example, be claimed that a set of universals of problem-solving behavior have been discovered. Still less can it be claimed that we have a set of tangible, in-the-head structures with a direct causal relation to behavior. But what we *can* claim is that, given that libraries of models are an effective solution to the knowledge engineering problem, no better description of expertise is available for knowledge engineering, and further that counterarguments about the supposed neglect of context miss their mark.

We have been critically examining Clancey's claim about the desirability of the distinction between knowledge engineering and the study of intelligence (1991) by looking at the evolution of model-based expert system development methodologies in the face of the need for sensitivity to expert context. On the assumption that expertise is highly context dependent (Agnew et al. 1994), one would expect that these approaches would have become more effective as they became more context sensitive, and this seems to have been the case (e.g., Chandrasekaran and Johnson 1993)—though much more evaluation remains to be done before it is thoroughly confirmed. The question now is: how firm need the knowledge engineering/psychology distinction be?

Relativists, such as Clancey, and Agnew et al., lay great stress on the ways in which expertise should be seen as a situated capacity or set of capacities. This jars with the apparent claim by a conceptual model that the expertise is an isomorphic structure in the expert's head (e.g., Slatter 1987). But we have argued that the reason that a conceptual model can make such a precise claim about the structures involved in expertise is that the context—which includes the context of use and the assumptions made about the data—is held fixed. The cognitive flexibility of experts, and the context-relative effectiveness of the expertise are simply ignored by the conceptual model, which models the operation of expertise in a narrow range of contexts determined by the user requirements.

It is a widely held assumption of cognitive science that intelligence is symbol manipulation. Symbols require interpretations (Clancey 1991, p. 389n.). Interpretations are imposed, not intrinsic to symbol tokens (Dennett 1987). Interpretations of symbols depend in part on environmental (Putnam 1975) and social (Burge 1986) factors. Hence it surely follows that cognitive psychology will be as plagued with the same "frame of reference problem" as is knowledge engineering (Clancey 1991).

The way that most expert systems cope with the problem of the frame of reference is by holding it constant. Of course, there will be many reasons why a psychologist might want more than a model of expertise-in-fixed-context. But equally, knowledge engineering can furnish psychology with an explanation of the operation of the expertise in a smallish set of contexts (to reiterate: both the context of use of an expert system, and the world-contexts in which the system can be successfully applied).

The cognitive psychologist studying expertise may want to extend that range of contexts, but surely the conceptual model is likely to provide important input to the psychological study. If the psychologist does want to extend the range, then he will have to find some route round the frame of reference problem. No doubt there are a number of possibilities, but it is not obvious that the solution chosen should necessarily be privileged over the characteristic knowledge engineering solution.

Our conclusion must be that models of expertise (conceptual models) for expert system development can be explanatory contributions to psychology, as can the expert systems developed from them (assuming that the expert system preserves sufficient aspects of the model's structure). Not only that, but our previous discussion shows that—within the model-based paradigm, at least—knowledge engineering purposes are served more effectively if the generic libraries of models are more flexible, and therefore psychologically more plausible (cf. also O'Hara and Shadbolt 1993a).

From the point of view both of psychology and knowledge engineering, surely greater progress can be made in collaboration than isolation. Clancey's suggestion (1991, p. 359) that the two disciplines be clearly distinct seems too strong. Of course, as he counsels, one should be clear when one's aims are broadly engineering-based and when they are broadly psychological. But in this chapter we hope we have given grounds for thinking that there is a very large gray area between the two, and that separating out the respective contributions of psychology and knowledge engineering may be easier said than done.

Acknowledgments

This chapter was first presented (under the title "Interpreting Generic Task Structures") at the Third International Workshop on Human and Machine Cognition, Seaside, Florida, May 13-15, 1993. The discussions at that workshop, both of our own paper and in other sessions, have enabled us to generalize the arguments, which were originally concerned exclusively with Chandrasekaran's GTs (hence we have dropped the work *task* from the title). We would like to thank the participants at the workshop whose contributions have aided us in this way. The editorial criticisms of Ken Ford, Paul Feltovich and Robert Hoffman, which forced us to clarify our ideas, have greatly improved the chapter.

Notes

1. Actually, since most problem-solving is too complex to be represented by a single GT, in the general case, a *group* of GTs would be assembled to model the expertise.

2. Unlike GTs, the KADS approach makes a clear separation between conceptual modeling and design. Nevertheless, as Valente and Löckenhoff (1993) say, the definition of assessment is so closely mixed in with the method for performing assessment as to make it impossible to dissociate the two. The result is that the choice of assessment as the basis for the conceptual model strongly implies that a particular method for the performance of assessment will be enshrined in the system design, and therefore KADS models can inherit all the problems of duality that we discerned in GTs.

References

Agnew, N.M., Ford, K.M. & Hayes, P.J. (1994). Expertise in context: Personally constructed, socially selected and reality-relevant? *International Journal of Expert Systems*, 7, 65-88.

Allemang, D. & Rothenfluh, T.E. (1992). Acquiring knowledge of knowledge acquisition: a self-study of generic tasks. In T. Wetter, K.-D. Althoff, J. Boose, B.R. Gaines, M. Linster & F. Schmalhofer (Eds.), *Current Developments in Knowledge Acquisition—EKAW'92* (pp. 353-372). Berlin: Springer-Verlag.

Breuker, J., Wielinga, B.J., van Someren, M., de Hoog, R., Schreiber, G., de Greef, P., Bredeweg, B., Wielemaker, J., Billault, J.-P., Davoodi, M. & Hayward, S. (1987). *Model driven knowledge acquisition: interpretation models* (KADS project deliverable A1). Amsterdam: Dept. of Social Science Informatics, University of Amsterdam.

Brooks, R.A. (1991a). How to build complete creatures rather than isolated cognitive simulators. In K. VanLehn (Ed.), *Architectures for Intelligence* (pp. 225-239). Hillsdale, NJ: Lawrence Erlbaum.

Brooks, R.A. (1991b). Intelligence without representation. *Artificial Intelligence, 47*, 139-159.

Brown, D.C. & Chandrasekaran, B. (1985). Expert systems for a class of mechanical design activity. In J.S. Gero (Ed.), *Knowledge Engineering in Computer-Aided Design* (pp. 259-282). New York: North-Holland.

Brown, D.C. & Chandrasekaran, B. (1989). *Design Problem Solving: Knowledge Structures and Control Strategies*. San Mateo, CA: Morgan Kaufman.

Burge, T. (1986). Individualism and psychology. *Philosophical Review, 95*, 3-45.

Bylander, T. & Mittal, S. (1986). CSRL: A language for classificatory problem solving. *AI Magazine, 7(3)*, 66-77.

Chandrasekaran, B. (1983). Towards a taxonomy of problem solving types. *AI Magazine, 4(1)*, 9-17.

Chandrasekaran, B. (1990). Design problem solving: A task analysis. *AI Magazine, 11(4)*, 59-71.

Chandrasekaran, B. & Johnson, T.R. (1993). Generic tasks and task structures: history, critique and new directions. In J.-M. David, J.-P. Krivine & R. Simmons (Eds.), *Second Generation Expert Systems* (pp. 232-272). Berlin: Springer-Verlag.

Clancey, W.J. (1991). The frame of reference problem in the design of intelligent machines. In K. VanLehn (Ed.), *Architectures for Intelligence* (pp. 357-423). Hillsdale, NJ: Lawrence Erlbaum.

Clancey, W.J. (1992). Model construction operators. *Artificial Intelligence, 53*, 1-115.

Dennett, D.C. (1987). *The Intentional Stance*. Cambridge, MA: MIT Press.

Feltovich, P.J., Johnson, P.E., Moller, J.H. & Swanson, D.B. (1984). LCS: the role and development of medical knowledge in diagnostic expertise. In W.J. Clancey & E.H. Shortliffe (Eds.), *Readings in Medical Artificial Intelligence: The First Decade* (pp. 275-319). Reading, MA: Addison Wesley.

Hauser, L. (1993). Reaping the whirlwind: reply to Harnad's other bodies, other minds. *Minds and Machines, 3*, 219-237.

Johnson, T.R. (1991). *Generic tasks in the problem-space paradigm: building flexible knowledge systems while using task-level constraints*. Ph.D. thesis. Columbus, Ohio:

Ohio State University.

Laird, J.E., Newell, A. & Rosenbloom, R.S. (1987). SOAR: an architecture for general intelligence. *Artificial Intelligence, 33,* 1-64.

Löckenhoff, C. & Valente, A. (1993). A library of assessment modeling components. In *Proceedings of the 3rd KADS Meeting* (pp. 289-303). Munich: Siemens AG.

Motta, E., O'Hara, K. & Shadbolt, N. (1994). Grounding GDMs: a structured case study. *International Journal of Human-Computer Studies, 40,* 315-347.

Motta, E., O'Hara, K., Shadbolt, N., Stutt, A. & Zdrahal, Z. (1996). Solving VT in VITAL: A Study in Model Construction and Knowledge Reuse. *International Journal of Human-Computer Studies, 44,* 333-371.

O'Hara, K. & Shadbolt, N. (1993a). AI models as a variety of psychological explanation. In *Proceedings of IJCAI-93,* Vol. 1, (pp. 188-193). San Mateo, CA: Morgan Kaufman.

O'Hara, K. & Shadbolt, N. (1993b). Locating generic tasks. *Knowledge Acquisition, 5,* 449-481.

O'Hara, K. & Shadbolt, N. (1996). The thin end of the wedge: Efficiency and the generalized directive model methodology. In N. Shadbolt, K. O'Hara & G. Schreiber (Eds.), *Advances in Knowledge Acquisition* (pp. 33-47). Berlin: Springer-Verlag.

Pugh, D. (1993). *Knowledge acquisition for generic tasks: a distributed architecture.* Ph.D. thesis. Aberystwyth: University of Wales, Aberystwyth.

Punch, W.F. (1989). *A diagnosis system using a task integrated problem solving architecture (TIPS).* Ph.D. thesis. Columbus, OH: Ohio State University.

Putnam, H. (1975). The meaning of 'meaning.' In *Mind, Language and Reality: Philosophical Papers,* Vol. 2, (pp. 215-271). Cambridge: Cambridge University Press.

Shadbolt, N. & O'Hara, K. (1996). Model-based expert systems and the explanation of expertise. In P.J. Feltovich, K.M. Ford, & R.R. Hoffman (Eds.), *Expertise in Context* (pp. 315-337). Menlo Park, CA: AAAI/MIT Press.

Slatter, P.E. (1987). *Building Expert Systems: Cognitive Emulation.* Chichester: Ellis Horwood.

Tansley, D.S.W. & Hayball, C.C. (1993). *Knowledge-Based Systems Analysis and Design: A KADS Developer's Handbook.* New York: Prentice-Hall.

Terpstra, P., van Heijst, G., Shadbolt, N. & Wielinga, B. (1993). Knowledge acquisition process support through generalized directive models. In J.-M. David, J.-P. Krivine & R. Simmons (Eds.), *Second Generation Expert Systems* (pp. 428-454). Berlin: Springer-Verlag.

Turing, A.M. (1950). Computing machinery and intelligence. *Mind, 59,* 433-460.

Valente, A. & Löckenhoff, C. (1993). Organization as guidance: a library of assessment models. In *Proceedings (Complement) of the 7th European Knowledge Acquisition Workshop* (pp. 243-262). Toulouse.

Pushing the Envelope

CHAPTER 20

An Argument for the Uncomputability of Infinitary Mathematical Expertise

Selmer Bringsjord

Introduction

Some human expertise is clearly computable. For example, suppose Cal is expert at taking arbitrary natural numbers, n and $m,$ and quickly returning the sum $n + m$. All of us could probably sit down and promptly build a (trivial!) expert system which captures Cal's expertise. Of course, to the majority of people involved in the study of expertise from a computational perspective, 'expertise' tends to refer to domains such as medical diagnosis, aircraft piloting, auditing, etc. Human experts in these domains tend to make Cal look a bit limited, to put it mildly. On the other hand, Cal does appear to share a certain feature with diagnosticians, pilots, and auditors. His expertise, like theirs, can apparently be captured, at least to a significant degree, by present-day expert system technology—technology which is based on computation, and as such is based, in turn, on finitary logic, first-order logic to be exact. (The computation-logic equivalence was proved by those—e.g., Alonzo Church and Alan Turing—who gave us computation. I review the equivalence below.) But what if we try to cast a broader, braver net in an attempt to catch varieties of expertise out there in the real world which don't, at least at first glance, look like they *can* be rendered in computational terms? Specifically, what about expertise in domains that from the outset put a premium on "infinitary" expertise? Are these domains also capturable by computation? In this chapter I focus on certain types of expertise in the domain of mathematical logic. I argue that even elementary expertise in this domain is indeed uncomputable. I end by discussing briefly the implications of this argument for the practice of artificial intelligence (AI) and expert systems.

Though the argument stands or falls on its own merits, it may be helpful if we contextualize things a bit. Accordingly, let me explain at the outset that by my lights there is a genuine difference between truly understanding an infinitary concept and not understanding it. I'm concerned herein with those experts who truly understand infinitary concepts (I give some key examples below). I imagine that the understanding achieved by experts in many fields differs from my dim understanding in *kind*.[1] I think students often become aware that the researchers they study (in the area of mathematics, physics, etc.) have a different understanding in kind than they do. This chapter is an attempt to put in precise, concrete terms the notion that mathematical expertise can be quite a "different beast"—that it's possible to obtain a level of mathematical understanding which is uncomputable.

The plan of this chapter is as follows. I'll first discuss the "cognition is computation" view at the heart of computational approaches to expertise, and review the reasons why this view implies that expertise as computation is at bottom expertise as deduction in first-order logic. (Nowhere do I affirm the radically different and controversial view that logic is the only, or even the preferred, tool for analyzing cognition or expertise.) In the next section, I isolate and explicate one aspect of elementary logical expertise (expertise with the infinitary system $\mathcal{L}_{\omega_1 \omega}$) which can serve as a paradigmatic instance of the sort of infinitary expertise one regularly sees in the domain of logic and mathematics. I then present the argument that the expertise explained in the third section, in light of the mathematical facts presented in the second section, is uncomputable, and hence is not capturable by standard conceptions of expertise and correlative expert system technology. The next section is a dialectic arising from objections to the argument of the previous section. Finally, I present an encapsulated version of what I see as the implications of my argument for the practice of AI and expert systems. This chapter is aimed at an audience of individuals who are familiar with some basic concepts of logic, and builds gradually on that familiarity.

Expertise as Computation in First-Order Logic

The view that cognition—and, therefore, expertise—is computation needs little introduction. Propelled by the writings of numerous thinkers (e.g., Barr 1983; Bringsjord 1992; Dietrich 1990; Fetzer 1994; Harnad 1991; Haugeland 1981; Hofstadter 1985; Johnson-Laird 1988; Newell 1980; Searle 1980; Simon 1980, 1981), this view (called computationalism) energizes AI, cognitive science and expert systems. The view has also touched nearly every major college and university in the world; even the popular media have, on a global scale, preached the computational conception of mind. Of course, this

conception is as protean as it is pandemic; the cognition-is-computation slo-
gan competes for equal time with a number of others. For example, for
starters we have "Thinking is computing," "People are computers (perhaps
with sensors and effectors)," "People are Turing machines (perhaps with sensors and effectors)," "People are finite state automata (perhaps with sensors
and effectors)," "People are neural nets (perhaps with sensors and effectors),"
and "Cognition is the computation of Turing-computable functions."

There are differences, and in some cases significant differences, between
these sorts of locutions. But surely there is a great and undeniable commonality in them—a commonality captured, for example, by Haugeland:

> What are minds? What is thinking? What sets people apart, in all the known
> universe? Such questions have tantalized philosophers for millennia, but…scant
> progress could be claimed…until recently. For the current generation has seen a
> sudden and brilliant flowering in the philosophy/science of the mind; by now
> not only psychology but also a host of related disciplines are in the throes of a
> great intellectual revolution. And the epitome of the entire drama is artificial in-
> telligence, the exciting new effort to make computers think. The fundamental
> goal of this research is not merely to mimic intelligence or produce some clever
> fake. Not at all. AI wants only the genuine article: machines with minds, in the
> full and literal sense. This is not science fiction, but real science, based on a the-
> oretical conception as deep as it is daring: namely, *we are, at root, computers our-
> selves* (1981, p. 2; italics his).

This conveys the core spirit of computationalism, which wavers not a bit
in the face of questions about whether sensors and effectors are necessary, or
where in the Chomsky Hierarchy from finite state automata to Turing Machines people fall. Nonetheless, it will facilitate matters if we have a rather
more focussed version of the doctrine on the table. Accordingly, we will employ the distilled view that computationalism amounts to the following: People (or minds, or brains) are computers. Computers, in turn, are essentially
Turing Machines (or other equivalent automata). Hence, the boundaries of
computability define the boundaries of cognition.

Computationalism immediately implies that cognition, and hence expertise, is deduction in first-order logic. This implication is based on well-
known theorems (e.g., the undecidability of first-order logic; cf. Boolos and
Jeffrey 1980; Ebbinghaus, Flum and Thomas 1984) which show that for
every computation there is an equivalent deduction in first-order logic. So
that there is no misunderstanding here, I will review the relevant facts.

Computationalism relies upon automata like Turing Machines (TMs) and
other equivalent formalisms to render the concept of computation sufficiently rigorous for relevant science and engineering pursuits. But what's a Turing
Machine? Put intuitively, TMs include a two-way infinite tape divided into
squares, a read/write head for writing and erasing symbols (from some finite,
fixed alphabet) on and off this tape, a finite control unit which at any step in

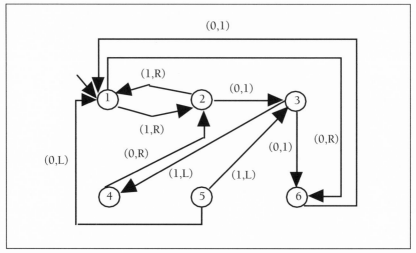

Figure 1. Gordon's 19 in 186.

a computation is in one particular state from among a finite number of possible states, and a set of instructions (a "program") telling the machine what to do, depending upon what state its in and what (if anything) is written on the square currently scanned by its head.

There are many readily understandable ways to capture the full set-theoretic description of TMs. One such method is the state diagram approach, which is used in figure 1. This TM, dubbed "Gordon's 19 in 186," is designed to start on a 0-filled infinite tape and produce, after 186 steps, 19 1's. (This machine, and many others, all ready to be run in *Turing's World*™, are available from my web site, http://www.rpi.edu/~brings, under my course *Computability and Logic*.)

Let us hand simulate an initial segment of the computation of Gordon's TM—we label the machine G—so that we completely fix the core mathematical concepts. The alphabet used is simply {0, 1}. The initial state of G is 1 (represented by the node labelled 1), and at the outset we'll assume that the tape is filled with 0's. The first thing G does is check to see what symbol it finds under its read/write head. In this case it initially finds a 0, so the arc labelled with (0, R) is taken, which means that the head moves one square to the right and the machine enters state 6. At this point, since there is another 0 found beneath the head, the 0 is changed to a 1, and the machine reenters state 1. It now finds a 1, and hence takes the arc labelled (1, R) to state 2 (i.e., the machine moves its head one square to the right, and then enters state 2)—etc. The machine's activity can be perfectly captured by a catalogue of its configurations from start to finish (figure 2).

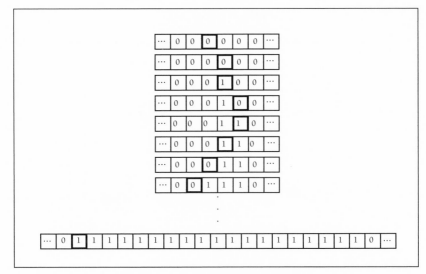

Figure 2. Catalog of Gordon's TM.

If this is your first exposure to TMs, you will doubtless be struck by how primitive and unassuming they are. But the surprising thing is that TMs apparently capture computation *in all its guises*. More precisely, whatever can be accomplished by way of an algorithm, by way of a programmed super-computer, by way of a neural network, a cellular automaton, etc.—whatever can be accomplished by any of these can be accomplished by a TM (Bringsjord 1991). Furthermore, we know that adding capabilities to our TMs doesn't give them any additional power. For example, if we give a TM *two* tapes rather than one, nothing that was impossible for the one-tape machine becomes doable for the two-tape creature.[2]

The next ingredient we need in order to appreciate the fact that computation is equivalent to deduction in first-order logic is a quick review of first-order logic itself: Given an alphabet (of variables $x, y, \ldots$, constants $c_1, c_2, \ldots$, n-ary relation symbols $R, G, \ldots$, functors $f_1, f_2, \ldots$, quantifiers $\forall, \exists$, and the familiar truth-functional connectives $(\neg, \vee, \wedge, \rightarrow, \leftrightarrow)$ one uses standard formation rules (e.g., if ϕ and ψ are well-formed formulas, then $\phi \wedge \psi$ is a wff as well) to build "atomic" formulas, and then more complicated "molecular" formulas. Sets of these formulas (say Φ), given certain rules of inference (e.g., modus ponens: from ϕ and $\phi \rightarrow \psi$ infer to ψ), can lead to individual formulas (say ϕ); such a situation is expressed by meta-expressions like $\Phi \vdash \phi$. First-order logic, like all logical systems, includes a semantic side which systematically provides meaning for formulas involved. In first-order logic, formulas are said to be true (or false) on an interpretation, often written as $\mathcal{I}$

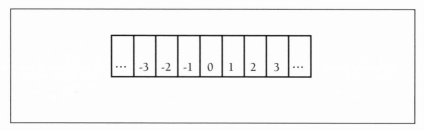

Figure 3. Numbered TM Tape.

⊨ φ. (This is often read, "𝒯 satisfies, or models, φ.") For example, the formula ∀x∃yGyx might mean, on the standard interpretation 𝓡 for arithmetic, that for every natural number *n*, there is a natural number *m* such that *m* > *n*. In this case, the domain of 𝓡 is **N**, the natural numbers, and *G* is the binary relation > ⊂ **N** × **N**, i.e., > is a set of ordered pairs (*i*, *j*) where *i*, *j* ∈ **N** and *i* is greater than *j*.

In order to concretize things a bit, consider an expert system designed to play the role of a guidance counselor in advising a high school student about which colleges to apply to (I have such a system under development at Rensselaer). Suppose that we want a rule in such a system which says "If a student has low SATs, and a low GPA, then none of the top twenty-five national universities ought to be applied to by this student." Assume that we have the following interpreted predicates: *Sx* iff *x* is a student, *L*$_s$*x* for *x* has low SATs, *L*$_g$*x* for *x* has a low GPA, *Tx* for *x* is a top twenty-five national university, *Axy* for *x* ought to apply to *y*. Then the rule in question, in first-order logic, becomes

$$\forall x \forall y [(Sx \wedge L_s x \wedge L_g x \wedge Ty) \rightarrow Axy].$$

Let's suppose, in addition, that Steve is a student denoted by the constant *s* in the system, and that he, alas, has low SATs and a low GPA. Assume also that *v* is a constant denoting Vanderbilt University (which happens to be a top twenty-five national university according the *U.S. News'* annual rankings). These facts are represented in the system by

$$Ss \wedge L_s s \wedge L_g s$$

and

$$Tv.$$

Let's label these three facts, in the order in which they were presented, (1), (2), and (3). Our expert system, based as it is on first-order logic, can verify

$$\{(1), (2), (3)\} \vdash \neg Asv,$$

that is, it can deduce that Steve ought not to apply to Vanderbilt.

The point of this example is to ground my encapsulated presentation of first-order logic. My point is *not* that the practice of AI and expert systems is married only to first-order logic. While as a matter of fact all expert system technology with which I'm familiar is first-order logic in action, I have no need here of such a claim. I gladly concede here for the sake of argument that there may be a way of doing AI and expert systems which (unlike the use of probabilistic inference, frames, scripts, forward- and backward-chaining, neural nets, etc.) really does depart from first-order logic *qua* tool. In order to articulate my argument I need only the unassailable fact that computation and first-order deduction are equivalent and wholly interchangeable.[3] In order to make this fact clear for readers who may be unfamiliar with it, I return to the TM of figure 1.

It is possible to recast every aspect of the TM "Gordon's 19 in 186" (called G earlier) as an assertion in first-order logic (Boolos and Jeffrey 1980). We know that this machine, upon starting on a blank tape, will halt with its head over the leftmost 1 of a string of 19 1's on an otherwise blank tape. What we would like is a set Γ of first-order formulas and an individual formula ϕ such that $\Gamma \vdash \phi$ if and only if Gordon's machine operates exactly as we know it does. In order to obtain this recasting of G, let us imagine that the squares of the tape upon which TMs operate are numbered in parallel with the integers (figure 3). Next, let's assume that time works the same way: TMs perform exactly one operation at each "click of the clock," and there is a 0 moment at which the action starts (in this case, with G scanning square 0), with each action taking one more click, time marching on in step with the positive integers.

Now let us fix a first-order language, and interpret it: Let variables range over the integers; let 0 denote (naturally enough) the integer of that name; and let s denote the successor function defined according to tradition $[s(n) = n + 1]$. What we need now are three relation symbols (predicates):

- $Q_i tx$ if and only if at time t the TM in question is in state i scanning square number x;
- $S_j tx$ if and only if at time t the symbol j is in square number x; and
- $x < y$ if and only if x is less than y.

With the machinery now at our disposal, let us focus on one arc in "Gordon's 19 in 186," namely the one corresponding to the quadruple (1 0 R 6). The general form of such an arc is $(ijRm)$. We're now able to capture such an arc completely in first-order logic. Let me express it first in English:

> If the machine is in state i at time t and is then scanning square number x on which symbol j occurs, then at time $t+1$ the machine is in state m scanning square number $x+1$, and for every square y, whatever was written there at time t is still written there at $t+1$.

In first-order logic, using our machinery, this becomes

$$\forall t \forall x \forall y \{(Q_i tx \land S_j tx) \rightarrow (Q_m s(t)s(x) \land (S_0 ty \rightarrow S_0 s(t)y) \land \ldots \land (S_r ty \rightarrow S_r s(t)y))\}.$$

In the case of G, the tuple (0 0 R 5) becomes

$\forall t \forall x \forall y \{(Q_0 tx \land S_0 tx) \to (Q_5 s(t)s(x) \land (S_0 ty \to S_0 s(t)y) \land \ldots \land (S_1 ty \to S_1 s(t)y))\}.$

This of course isn't the place to present all the details (I am covering the minimal number required for accurate exposition). Suffice it to say that every aspect of a given computation (or set or sequence of computations) can be captured according to the procedure I have adumbrated. The upshot of this is that computation is provably equivalent to deduction in appropriately configured first-order logic. Under the assumption of computationalism, it follows that expertise, one form or type of cognition, is in turn also provably equivalent to deduction in appropriately configured first-order logic. This fact has nothing to do with methodological issues involving the use of first-order logic to represent knowledge, expertise, reasoning etc. It is a brute fact that many practitioners in AI and expert systems, for weal or woe, reject first-order logic (and *a fortiori* other more powerful logics) as a tool for reaching their scientific and engineering objectives.[4]

We turn now to an account of the logical expertise I claim is beyond computation.

Sharpening Infinitary Expertise

Mathematical logic deals with infinite concepts from the outset; such concepts permeate the field. For example, a first course in mathematical logic often begins with Cantor's famous theorem that there are sets (e.g., the reals, or the power set of the set of natural numbers) which are "larger" than the infinite set of natural numbers. But for our purposes herein we need to bring "infinitary" expertise into sharp focus, otherwise the argument of this chapter will be vague. If this argument is to have any force, it can't be based simply on a hand-wavy reference to all of the infinitary aspects of logic.

The best way I know of to make the notion of infinitary expertise explicit is to isolate those systems studied by logicians that are by definition infinitary. I will focus here specifically on one infinitary system, the "smallest" and simplest one I know of, viz., $\mathcal{L}_{\omega_1 \omega}$. The nice thing about this system is that it builds naturally upon first-order logic, which I have already discussed. In fact, one way to motivate the study of $\mathcal{L}_{\omega_1 \omega}$ is to consider the fact that most mathematical concepts cannot be expressed in first-order logic (a system traditionally denoted by $\mathcal{L}_1$). (For a list of some of those ordinary mathematical concepts beyond the reach of first-order logic, see Keisler 1971.) Two such concepts are that of a "finite world (model)," and "ordinary arithmetic." Let us look at these two concepts, and the inability of $\mathcal{L}_1$ to capture them, in turn.

In order to understand that it is not possible to capture the ordinary notion of finitude in first-order logic, consider the $\mathcal{L}_1$-sentence,

$\psi_{\geq 2} = \exists x \exists y \, x \neq y.$

Any interpretation on which $\psi_{\geq 2}$ is true must have a domain that contains at least two elements, since $\psi_{\geq 2}$ "says" that there exist two distinct things x and y. Put in terms of the standard notation reviewed above, this becomes $\mathcal{T} \models \psi_{\geq 2}$ if and only if $\mathcal{T}$'s domain contains at least two elements. The technique here can be generalized. The sentence

$$\psi_{\geq 3} = \exists x \exists y \exists z\, x \neq y \wedge x \neq z \wedge y \neq z$$

can only be true in a world with an at-least-three-element domain. The same trick can be carried out for four, five, six, and so on. Now suppose that we collect together the set of all such formulas, with n getting larger and larger forever. Formally, this set—call it 'Ω'—is $\{\psi_n : n \geq 2\}$. Since any interpretation on which all of the members of Ω is true must be an interpretation with at least 2 members, 3 members, 4 members, *ad infinitum*, it follows that such an interpretation must be infinite. So we have assembled a recipe for expressing, in first-order logic, the notion of infinitude. However, and this is the present point, *there is no set of first-order formulas which can express the concept of finitude*. (There is no set of first-order formulas such that any interpretation which models this set must be finite.)

Now to the second limitation of first-order logic, namely that it cannot capture ordinary arithmetic. In arithmetic, the domain is the set **N** of natural numbers $\{0, 1, 2, 3, \ldots\}$ and the operators include the successor function (seen above when I discussed the equivalence of computation and first-order logic), addition, subtraction, multiplication, etc. Constants consist of names for the first two natural numbers, 0 and 1. Using these constructs, it's possible to axiomatize all of arithmetic by way of the following three statements (Peano's axioms):

P1   0 is not the value of the successor function (i.e., there is no way to add 1 to a natural number and get back 0).

P2   The successor function is one-to-one (i.e., if you plug two distinct natural numbers in as input, you get back as value two different natural numbers).

P3   For every subset X of the set **N** of natural numbers, if zero is in X, and if the successor of n is in X whenever n is X, then X is **N** itself.

In other words, all truths of arithmetic, from those we learned starting in kindergarten to those which call for Crays, can be derived from P1-P3 using deductive inference. However, there is a small problem: axiom P3 cannot be expressed in first-order logic!

Because $\mathcal{L}_1$ is so limited, logicians have studied systems like $\mathcal{L}_{\omega 1 \omega}$, which I now proceed to define. As we shall see, it turns out that the two limits on first-order logic just isolated can be handled easily by $\mathcal{L}_{\omega 1 \omega}$.

The basic idea behind $\mathcal{L}_{\omega 1 \omega}$ is straightforward. This system allows for infinite disjunctions and conjunctions,[5] where these disjunctions and conjunctions are no longer than the size of the set of natural numbers (let's use ω to denote the size of the set of natural numbers).[6] This fundamental idea is effortlessly regimented: First we simply add to the customary alphabet for first-order logic the prefix symbols $\vee$ and $\wedge$. To the ordinary formation rules for building grammatically correct first-order formulas, we add

- If Φ is a set of well-formed formulas $\{\phi_1, \phi_2, \ldots\}$ no larger than ω, then $\vee\Phi$ ($\wedge\Phi$) is also a well-formed formula, viz., the disjunction (conjunction) of the formulas in Φ.

The notion of when an infinite formula is true is fixed by extending the notion of truth in ordinary first-order logic:

- A possibly infinite disjunction, $\vee\Phi$, is true on an interpretation $\mathcal{I}$ (written $\mathcal{I} \models \vee\Phi$) if and only if there is a formula ϕ in Φ which is true on $\mathcal{I}$.

- A possibly infinite conjunction, $\wedge\Phi$, is true on an interpretation $\mathcal{I}$ (written $\mathcal{I} \models \wedge\Phi$) if and only if every formula ϕ in Φ is true on $\mathcal{I}$.

Proofs (i.e., derivations) in $\mathcal{L}_{\omega_1\omega}$ can, as the relevant literature states, be "infinitely long" (Ebbinghaus, *et al.* 1984). This is because in addition to classical cornerstones like *modus ponens*,

from $\phi \rightarrow \psi$ and ϕ infer to ψ,

$\mathcal{L}_{\omega_1\omega}$ allows rules of inference like

from $\phi \rightarrow \psi$ for all $\psi \in \Phi$, infer to $\phi \rightarrow \wedge\Phi$.

This rule says that if in a derivation you have an infinite list of if-thens (i.e., formulas of the form $\phi \rightarrow \psi$) where each consequent (ψ) in each if-then is an element of some infinite set Φ, then you can infer to an if-then whose consequent is the infinite conjunction obtained by conjoining all the elements of Φ. It may be worth pausing a bit to create a picture of the sort of derivation which is here permitted: Suppose that Γ is an infinite set of the same size as $\mathbf{N}$, the natural numbers. So Γ is $\{\delta_1, \delta_2, \ldots, \delta_n, \delta_{n+1}, \delta_{n+2}, \ldots\}$. Then here is one possible picture of an infinite derivation:

$$\phi \rightarrow \delta_1$$
$$\phi \rightarrow \delta_2$$
$$\phi \rightarrow \delta_3$$
$$\ldots$$
$$\phi \rightarrow \delta_n$$
$$\phi \rightarrow \delta_{n+1}$$
$$\ldots$$
$$\phi \rightarrow \delta_1 \wedge \phi \rightarrow \delta_2 \wedge \phi \rightarrow \delta_3 \wedge \ldots \wedge \phi \rightarrow \delta_n \wedge \phi \rightarrow \delta_{n+1} \cdots$$

It should be clear from this that derivations in $\mathcal{L}_{\omega_1\omega}$ can be infinitely long.

Now, let's return to the two limitations we saw in the case of first-order logic in order to see how $\mathcal{L}_{\omega_1\omega}$ surmounts them. The first limitation was that the concept of finitude couldn't be captured by any set of $\mathcal{L}_1$ formulas, let alone by one such formula. But here is one simple formula in $\mathcal{L}_{\omega_1\omega}$ which is such that any interpretation that satisfies it is finite:

$$\bigvee_{n<\omega} \exists x_1 \ldots \exists x_n \forall y (y = x_1 \vee \ldots \vee y = x_n).$$

I think it's worth pausing to make sure we understand this formula (and thereby understand some of the power of $\mathcal{L}_{\omega 1 \omega}$). This formula is an infinite disjunction; each disjunct has a different value for n. One such disjunct is

$$\exists x_1 \exists x_2 \forall y (y = x_1 \vee y = x_2),$$

which says, informally, that there exist at most two things x_1 and x_2 with which everything in the domain is identical, or there are at most two things in the domain. Obviously, any interpretation which satisfies this formula is finite, since it can at most have a two-element domain. Another disjunct in the infinite disjunction is the one generated by setting n to 4, that is,

$$\exists x_1 \exists x_2 \exists x_3 \exists x_4 \forall y (y = x_1 \vee y = x_2 \vee y = x_3 \vee y = x_4),$$

which says that there are at most four things. Here again, any interpretation which satisfies this formula is finite. But how do we go the other direction? How do we ensure that any interpretation which is finite satisfies the selected formula? This is where the infinite disjunction does its job. Notice that every finite domain will have a certain size k, where k is some natural number. This domain will make true the disjunct in the infinite disjunction where $n = k$; and since a disjunction, no matter how big, is true if but one of its disjuncts is true, this k-sized domain will make the entire infinite disjunction true.

The second limitation on first-order logic I isolated above was that arithmetic cannot be formalized in this system, because the third of Peano's axioms cannot be formalized in it. The situation is remedied in $\mathcal{L}_{\omega 1 \omega}$, because, where $s(n)$ gives the successor of n, we can supplant P3 with the infinite formula

$$\forall x (x = 0 \vee x = s(0) \vee x = s(s(0)) \vee \ldots).$$

This formula says that everything in the domain is either 0, or the successor of 0, or the successor of the successor of 0, and so on. In other words, the domain in question is **N**, the set of natural numbers, exactly as we want it to be.

I end this section by noting and explaining one simple, compelling reason why mathematical expertise concerning $\mathcal{L}_{\omega 1 \omega}$ cannot be recast as expertise concerning ordinary first-order logic: The expertise in question, as we have just witnessed, includes representing both the finitude of interpretations and Peano arithmetic in $\mathcal{L}_{\omega 1 \omega}$. So, if this expertise *could* be recast in first-order logic, it would follow that the two limitations on first-order logic we noted above would not in fact be limitations, for the recasting of the expertise here would constitute a rendering in first-order logic of precisely that which we know, on independent and indisputable grounds, to be beyond the reach of first-order logic.

We turn now to the argument at the heart of my case.

The Argument from Infinitary Expertise

Because I have taken pains to set the stage, articulating the argument is now easy and direct:

1. All expertise is computable. [assumption for contradiction]

2. For every case of expertise E there exists a Turing Machine (or other equivalent creature) M such that some computation C of M is such that $E = C$. [from 1]

3. For every computation C of every TM M there is an equivalent deduction D in some instantiation of the first-order system $\mathfrak{L}_I$. [from the second section]

4. For every case of expertise E there exists a deduction D in some instantiation of the first-order system $\mathfrak{L}_I$ such that $E = D$. [from 2, 3; universal instantiation, hypothetical syllogism, universal generalization]

5. There exists a case E^* of expertise—viz., expertise with $\mathfrak{L}_{\omega_1\omega}$—which is such that for every deduction D in some instantiation of the first-order system $\mathfrak{L}_I$, $E^* \neq D$. [from the third section]

6. It's not the case that all expertise is computable. [*reductio ad absurdum*, 4, 5 contradictory]

This argument is valid in the sense that the inferences are correct. This is so because the reasoning in question can be completely formalized using natural deduction rules.

We turn now to objections.

Dialectic

There are a number of objections which have been raised against this argument. I counter some of them in this section.

Objection 1: It All Hinges on Prior Beliefs

The first objection I consider seeks to reject the entire enterprise of ascertaining whether computationalism (and computationalist approaches to expertise) is true or false: "As an argument that human thinking is beyond the bounds of computation, your argument, Bringsjord, is convincing if, but only if, one already accepts that humans are capable of noncomputable feats. But if one starts by believing the opposite, then the argument seems fallacious. If you believe that people are supermechanistic, the argument may support your belief, but if you believe that they can only compute, it becomes vacuous."

The astonishing thing about this objection is that it itself commits the fallacy of *petitio principii* (begging the question). In this chapter I have put on the table a rigorous case for rejecting computationalism. When someone puts on the table a rigorous, sustained case for not-p, it begs the question to say, "I believe p, so your argument is no good." Interestingly enough, the only reason I, and others like me, reject (or recast) computationalism is that we understand and are moved by arguments like the one I've just given! Before I learned a thing or two about the math underlying what I was doing when trying to get a computer to do snazzy, intelligent things, I was not only a computationalist, I was a rabid, evangelistic computationalist.

Another problem with this objection is that it seems to require that my argument (and presumably others like it) be *convincing*. But there's a big difference between a convincing argument and a sound argument. Many proofs in the history of mathematics were for years after their publication almost universally rejected because acceptance necessitated a realignment of one's beliefs (Cantor's Theorem, mentioned above, is a perfect case in point). I can certainly see why a computationalist, a true believer, would be disinclined to accept my argument. But such inclinations count for nothing in open-minded debate; logic, emotionless logic, counts for everything. If my argument is to be rejected, then we must be informed as to which premise(s) is (are) false, since the inferences therein are certifiable in accordance with principles affirmed by all computationalists.

On the other hand, the present objection at least has the virtue of being falsifiable. This is so because if some thinkers *are* convinced (or even *partly* convinced) by the argument, the objection here evaporates. And, fortunately (as I see it), many people have been convinced by the argument (and others that preceded it, such as those seen in Bringsjord 1992) that computationalism, as it stands, is inadequate. If you are not yet convinced, wait. You may resist because you affirm one or more of the objections I refute below.

Objection 2: It's All Just Manipulation of Finite Strings

The second objection marks a reaction which I've heard from many; it begins as follows: "Your argument, Bringsjord, does not include a specification of what is meant by the terms 'finite,' 'infinite,' and 'infinitary.' Clearly, humans cannot actually manipulate an infinite expression, so to have 'infinitary expertise' with $\mathcal{L}_{\omega_1\omega}$ must mean to have expertise with the manipulation of finite strings used to represent hypothesized infinite expressions. For example, look at the formula which you made so much of above, viz.,

$$\vee_{n<\omega}\exists x_1...\exists x_n\forall y(y = x_1 \vee...\vee y = x_n).$$

You will notice that this formula is a finite string: it fits nicely on one line. And of course we all know that Turing Machines (and the like) have no trouble manipulating finite strings; that, after all, is the essence of what they do."

The first thing that needs to be said in reply to this objection is that with regard to terminology I'm wholly innocent: I've used the terms 'finite,' 'infinite,' and 'infinitary' exactly as they are used in logic and mathematics. Text after text, and article after article, say that $\mathcal{L}_{\omega 1 \omega}$ allows for infinite disjunctions and conjunctions; and these creatures are referred to by way of the sorts of finite strings which this objection features. Recall, as well, that I earlier quoted a standard text saying that $\mathcal{L}_{\omega 1 \omega}$ allows for "infinite derivations" (a picture for which I offered). And of course it's not just the study of infinitary logic which gives rise to this way of speaking. Turing Machines are said to have *infinite* tapes; there is said to be an *infinite* number of natural numbers; first-order logic is said to have an *infinite* supply of variables; π is said to have an *infinite* decimal expansion; there is said to be an *infinite* number of real numbers in the interval [0, 1] (a level of *infinity* greater than that of the natural numbers); certain computing machines are said to be allowed to run for an *infinite* amount of time, and so on, *ad infinitum*. What I have done is to bring the sort of expertise which is based on this way of speaking and thinking into sharp focus by narrowing things down to $\mathcal{L}_{\omega 1 \omega}$. But I have in no way employed idiosyncratic nomenclature. Quite the contrary. My terminology, whether it pertains to logic or computation, is herein entirely "off the shelf."

But of course Objection 2 is more than a complaint that certain key terms are ambiguous. The meat of the objection is that experts with $\mathcal{L}_{\omega 1 \omega}$ are simply manipulating finite expressions, and such manipulation is not at all beyond computation.

The first thing worth noting about this aspect of Objection 2 is that it reflects an attitude that seems to be exactly analogous to Hilbert's (1926) failed finitistic program for mathematics. Hilbert observed that mathematical proofs were invariably presented as finite strings on finite pieces of paper, and he hit upon an idea: proofs were to be entirely mechanical, step-by-step *finite* strings; and all problems in mathematics could be solved by such finitary methods. Demonstrations of consistency were to involve only finite procedures making reference to but a finite number of properties possessed by formulas, and procedures that employed only a finite number of operations over these formulas.

But as we all know by now, Gödel obliterated Hilbert's program. He proved that human mathematical expertise is *not* always limited to Hilbertian reasoning. Some form of infinitistic reasoning must be employed for some proofs of formulas about **N**, the natural numbers—formulas which expert mathematicians and logicians can see to be true. A bit more specifically, Gödel found a sentence of the form $\forall x \phi(x)$ about the natural numbers (i.e., a formula that says that every natural number has a certain property ϕ) which couldn't be proved by finite means, even though each of $\phi(0), \phi(1), \phi(2), \ldots, \phi(n), \phi(n+1), \ldots$ (where each of these formulas says that a particular natural number has the property ϕ) *is* provable by a finite proof from the first-order version of the axioms characterizing the natural numbers. Gödel found a formula which expressed a truth about the natural numbers which couldn't be proved by finite means. What was the reaction? Interestingly enough, many suggested that first-order formalizations of arithmetic be replaced by formalizations in $\mathcal{L}_{\omega 1 \omega}$.

So Objection 2, it seems, is an attempt to exhume Hilbert's program. But I can nonetheless imagine how one might endeavor to sustain it:

Objection 3: It All Flies in the Face of Finitism

"Bringsjord, there is, I concede, an analogy between my position and Hilbert's, but it's far from a perfect analogy. The fact remains that it's evident to me that no human activity can involve the deployment of infinite things, since infinite things cannot actually exist in this universe. You seem to be assuming what seems to me to be ridiculous, namely that the mathematical expertise in question is skill with infinite mental objects. Do you really believe that when a *human* logician thinks about $\mathcal{L}_{\omega 1 \omega}$, he or she actually has the infinitary concepts referred to by the finite strings in mind? Do you really believe, more generally, that when a mathematician thinks of the integers, he or she has an infinite set literally in mind? If this is your position, Bringsjord, you should state it clearly, and preferably defend it against some obvious objections (e.g., that our brains are finite and can only pass through finitely many states, it would seem)."

In response, let me first state the view underlying my argument: Expert mathematicians routinely use finite strings to denote infinite objects which they genuinely conceive of, ponder, reflect upon, reason about, manipulate, and so on. Since such activity is genuine, it cannot be recast as activity in finitary first-order logic, for the reasons given in the third section. I take it that my view is "motherhood and apple pie," but more about that when we see in detail why Objection 3 fails. Overall, the reason it fails is that it affirms a version of a finitistic philosophy of mathematics. The problem with such an affirmation, in the present dialectic, is three-fold:

1 Anyone who rejects finitistic mathematics will not regard Objection 3 to have any force, and most (for reasons discussed below) reject it;

2 The version of finitism suggested here, according to which the denial of this doctrine entails that infinite objects must somehow "fit inside" the brain, is preposterous;

3 Finitism, as Bertrand Russell and others noted long ago, is highly implausible, in large part because it cannot do justice to even a small part of the ontology that underlies mathematics *as it is practiced in the real world by real mathematicians.*

I consider these problems in order.

Problem 1. Suppose that I concede for the sake of argument that a finitistic philosophy of mathematics entails that my Premise 5 in the argument is false. (This is the only premise which seems to be vulnerable to Objection 3.)

Since proponents of such a view are in the minority (amongst philosophers and mathematicians, anyway), why should this worry me?

In order to make the point more than a rhetorical one, it may help to consider an analogous exchange, one involving the issue of defining computation. John Searle (1992) believes that 'computation' is a meaningless term from the standpoint of science, because he thinks it can be shown that every physical object can be said to be engaged in computation at any time. This view of Searle's is not one that most affirm, though a number of thinkers do. (Putnam 1988, one of the founders of computation, agrees with Searle. I think Searle does a good job of defending the view, but I'm not one of those who affirm it; see Bringsjord 1994). Now suppose that Smith offers a careful argument purporting to show that AI and cognitive science can succeed in creating computer programs having an ability to process visual images. In reply to Smith, Jones, armed with Searle's view, says, "Your argument doesn't convince *me*. After all, central to your argument is the concept of computation, and I think this concept is laughably vague—so vague that it's not suitable for use in scientific discourse." The point, of course, is that this objection is anemic. In light of the fact that most reject the underlying Searlean view, this objection must include a separate defense of this view. The same thing goes for a finitistic view of mathematics as an objection to my argument: we need to see a careful (if not a victorious) argument for this view. Absent that, the objection is but a curiosity.

Problem 2. The second problem with Objection 3 runs as follows. Suppose that I think about the planet Jupiter, its size, color, distance from Earth, and many other properties it has. Does it follow that Jupiter in some sense fits inside my finite brain? I doubt it. Suppose that I'm a theoretical physicist who thinks about the entire universe (as certain such physicists do). Does it follow that the universe is somehow inside a brain that is after all smaller than a basketball? (Perhaps it's worth noting that a number of physicists regard the universe to itself be infinite.) Hardly. The problem is that Objection 3 is based on a clear *non sequitur*: it doesn't follow from the fact that a human conceives of (or thinks about, etc.) *a* that *a* must in any nonmetaphorical sense fit inside this human's brain. What a human presumably *does* need in order to conceive of *a* is some sort of *representation* of *a*. And I see no reason why a human can't have a representation scheme by virtue of which he or she conceives of infinite objects. Indeed, such a view is the dominant one in classical mathematics, and it's the one I affirmed above.

Moreover, this second problem with Objection 3 can be put in the form of a rather simple *reductio*. Suppose for the sake of argument that the fact that the brain is finite does rule out a human's ability to genuinely conceive of and think about an infinite object like the set Z of integers. Since the brain is finite, it follows that it is of size k, and is able to pass through only $f(k)$ states, where both k and $f(k)$ are themselves positive integers. (What it means for something to be finite is that it is of a size that corresponds to some integer.) So, if Objection 3 succeeds, it does so because things like Z are a heck of a lot bigger than either k or $f(k)$—too big, so the story here goes, for a brain of this size to genuinely conceive of them. But suppose that there be some object which is known to be finite, but which is also known to be larger than k and $f(k)$. (If you're looking for examples, the field of complexity theory within computer science will provide an endless source.) We are forced to conclude that this object, say the perfect winning strategy for chess—which can be coded in the form of a *finite* state automaton guaranteed to dwarf k and $f(k)$—cannot be conceived of by a human with a brain of the size assumed here; but that is absurd. (Just ask those who think about such objects for a living.)

Problem 3. The third problem is that finitism is generally thought to be untenable. Bertrand Russell, in his famous essay "The Limits of Empiricism" (1936), fatally lampooned it long ago; anyone embracing finitistic attitudes toward mathematics is obliged to start by derailing Russell's biting observations. There isn't space to discuss Russell's essay here. I will say only that Russell was no wild-eyed dualist. He calmly asserted, over and over, that he was capable of routinely doing that which I claim herein expert mathematicians routinely do. In fact, Russell (and others, e.g., Weyl 1949) claimed that they could conceive of infinite objects provably "larger" than the objects at the heart of $\mathcal{L}_{\omega_1\omega}$. For example, one of the finitists of Russell's day, Ambrose, claimed that it wasn't possible for a human to know that there are not three consecutive 7's in the expansion of π. Russell replied—and this is the reply he would no doubt make to those who make Ambrose's finitistic claim about, say, the infinite derivations which are part of $\mathcal{L}_{\omega_1\omega}$—that it is only *medically* impossible to carry out the expansion in order to check for the three 7's. Russell said that he could easily imagine an Omniscient Diety, and such a being could not only know the answer, but could share it with a human. Russell also claimed that he could imagine an infinite number of operations taking place in a finite amount of time (1936, p. 144).

At any rate, the fundamental point, and the one Russell made, is that when a mathematician uses the existential quantifier $\exists$ to assert the existence of some infinite set (as, for example, when such a person proves in axiomatic set theory that there exists a set which we call the integers), this isn't an assertion, *contra* Objection 3, which merely amounts to the claim that there exists a finite string inscribed on pieces of paper which mathematicians use.

Objection 4: "Reasoning About" vs. "Reasoning With"

"Though you offered it merely for the record, Bringsjord, and not as part of your argumentation, your statement that

Expert mathematicians routinely use finite strings to point to infinite objects which they genuinely conceive of, ponder, reflect upon, reason about, manipulate, and so on. Since such activity is genuine, it cannot be recast as activity in finitary first-order logic….

reflects your fundamental error. Notice that you slip from 'conceive of, reflect upon, reason about' (with which I have no problem) to 'manipulate.' Here you switch from describing infinite sentences to somehow *using* them. That's precisely your mistake."

The objection continues: "However, I confess that I am puzzled by your 'second problem' to Objection 3. There you seem to be quite happy with the idea that we can use a finite representation to describe or refer to something infinite. I heartily agree. But now we seem to have switched horses. I thought you were denying this—via a claim that human mathematicians are using $\mathfrak{L}_{\omega1\omega}$. Surely it is quite possible that a human expert mathematician uses some finite mental representation to reason *about* $\mathfrak{L}_{\omega1\omega}$. Not even you, Bringsjord, can be reasoning *with* $\mathfrak{L}_{\omega1\omega}$: it can't be a proper description of your language of thought."

This objection is better than its predecessors, but it too ultimately fails. I readily admit that sometimes mathematicians (and, for that matter, nonmathematicians) merely reason *with* a finite representation and reasoning system. (I suppose the paradigmatic case of this would be the carrying out of derivations in some natural deduction system for $\mathfrak{L}_{I}$.) But it doesn't follow from this fact that my argument founders on the distinction at the heart of Objection 4. The key is that I have chosen $\mathfrak{L}_{\omega1\omega}$ for good reason. Some of the reasoning *about* this logical system is clearly reasoning with a representation and reasoning system having *at least* the infinitary grade of $\mathfrak{L}_{\omega1\omega}$. In order to see this we have but to look at what goes on when a relevant theorem about $\mathfrak{L}_{\omega1\omega}$ is pondered and proven. Take, for example, the following simple theorem, which I have often asked my students learning about $\mathfrak{L}_{\omega1\omega}$ to prove:

> *Scott's Isomorphism Theorem.* Let $\mathfrak{I}$ be an interpretation for $\mathfrak{L}_{I}$. Then there is a sentence ϕ of $\mathfrak{L}_{\omega1\omega}$ such that for all countable interpretations $\mathfrak{I}^*$ for $\mathfrak{L}_{I}$, $\mathfrak{I}^* \models \phi$ iff $\mathfrak{I}^*$ is isomorphic to $\mathfrak{I}$.

Intuitively, this theorem says that a single infinitary sentence can perfectly characterize a countable interpretation for $\mathfrak{L}_{I}$. The customary proof involves (among other things) constructing infinitely long conjunctions (*outside of* $\mathfrak{L}_{\omega1\omega}$), each conjunct of which is an atomic formula capturing a truth about the elements in the domain of $\mathfrak{I}$. For example, if the domain of $\mathfrak{I}$ is $\mathbf{N}$, the natural numbers, and $\mathfrak{I}$ includes > (ordinary greater than), then the following are elements of >: (3,2), (4,3), (5,4),…. Hence, if we are to capture $\mathfrak{I}$, there must be an atomic formula corresponding to each such fact, and the conjunction of these formulas (which is still only a part of the construction at the heart of Scott's Theorem) becomes (with the relation symbol G interpreted as >, and c_i as constants):

$Gc_3c_2 \land Gc_4c_3 \land Gc_5c_4 \land \ldots,$

or, in the notation for infinitely long conjunctions in $\mathcal{L}_{\omega_1\omega}$,

$\land \{Gc_ic_j : c_i, c_j \text{ are constants } \& \; \mathcal{T} \models Gc_ic_j\}.$

The point is that, *contra* Objection 4, the sort of mathematical expertise needed for carrying out such proofs requires that one reason *with* a "language of thought" that parallels $\mathcal{L}_{\omega_1\omega}$ itself.

Where From Here?

My principal concern has been to evaluate the philosophical, logical and mathematical status of the computational approach to expertise and expert systems. As I've tried to show, this approach, when confronted with mathematical expertise, is bound to fail. At bottom, this is because mathematicians and logicians, from the moment they step on the job, must directly contemplate, reason about, manipulate, represent...*cognize* infinitude. (The expertise enjoyed by mathematicians in "real life" goes well beyond what I've put on display.) If I'm right, where does this leave us? What are the consequences of what we've uncovered for the practitioners involved? Though such questions in many ways take me outside my own expertise, I'll venture a brief answer, in the form of a three-point homily.

First, I think AI and the narrower study of (and attempt to replicate) expertise needs to be careful not to inadvertently cultivate a warranted perception that certain domains have been conveniently left aside. Even a good many laypeople know that medical diagnosis, for example, has been significantly rendered in computational terms. And beginning students of AI and expertise can doubtless guess that attempts to analyze and replicate the expertise of, say, auditors and accountants will meet with considerable success. But of course AI has been dogged by accusations that it loves "toy worlds." This accusation will persist as long as the study of expertise fails to grapple with expertise that is at least ostensibly beyond computation. The antidote to the lingering "toy world" concern, with respect to expertise and expert systems, is to tackle head-on some domain which many hold to be impenetrable from the standpoint of AI and computation. Why not inaugurate a project centered around the attempt to represent the reasoning performed by expert mathematicians in connection with some specific problem? Such a project would do much to dispel the perception that AI is risk-averse and timid.

Second, it's important to realize that the view I have advocated herein can be the prolegomenon to a more sophisticated science of expertise and the mind. Just because some species of expertise is uncomputable doesn't mean that it will resist scientific analysis (a point noted by the likes of Douglas

Hofstader, Peter Kugel, Roger Penrose, Hao Wang and Kurt Gödel, to name a few). After all, computer science includes an entire subfield devoted to the rigorous study of uncomputability. We know that there are grades of uncomputability, we know much about the relationships between these grades, we know how uncomputability relates to computability, and so on. Uncomputability theory, mathematically speaking, is no different than any other mature branch of classical mathematics. So, why can't uncomputability theory be linked to work in psychology devoted to the scientific analysis of the uncomputable side of human expertise? (That it can be so linked is the view developed and championed in Bringsjord and Zenzen 1997.) One of the interesting properties of AI research is that people have come to expect that it invariably have *two* sides, a scientific side, and an implementation side. The basic idea is that the scientific side, which can be quite theoretical, ought to be translated into working computer programs. I think this idea, as a general policy, is wrongheaded. Why is it that the physicist can be profitably occupied with theories that can't be implemented, while the AI researcher labors under the onerous expectation that those aspects of the mind which admit of scientific explanation must also admit of direct replication in the form of computer programs? In short, perhaps we can come to understand mathematical expertise scientifically, while at the same time acknowledging that we can't (yet?) give such expertise to computers.

Finally, the third point in my sermon. Suppose that I'm correct; suppose that mathematical expertise is uncomputable, and that therefore it is expertise which no TM-equivalent computer can have. From this is doesn't follow that no system can *appear* to have such expertise. There are some well-known uncomputable functions which many are doing their best to "solve." (My favorite line of such research is the attack on the uncomputable "busy beaver" function; Marxen and Buntrock 1990.) AI, as far as I can see, has never settled the fundamental clash between those who, like Turing, aim at engineering a device whose behavior is indistinguishable from ours, and those who seek not only to create the behavior but also the underlying conscious states which we enjoy. Nothing I have said herein precludes success in the attempt to engineer a computational system which *appears* to have infinitary expertise. What I purport to have shown, or at least made plausible, is that no such system can *in fact* enjoy such expertise. I don't know the limits of an approach which resigns itself to engineering behavior only, no one does, but it seems to me to be an exciting avenue for future research. It is the avenue, indeed the creed, which I happily follow (Bringsjord and Ferrucci 1997).

Acknowledgments

I'm indebted to many who reacted to written and nuncupative ancestors of this paper, including: David Israel, Michael Zenzen, Jim Fahey, Drew McDermott,

Paul Feltovich, Bob Hoffman, Ken Ford, Marvin Minsky, Saul Traiger, Jim Moor, Stevan Harnad, Pat Hayes, Larry Taylor, Jim Fetzer, and a number of anonymous referees. I'm also indebted to Clark Glymour, whose elementary but esemplastic *Thinking Things Through* (1992, MIT Press) presents some of the background material presupposed herein in a most inspiring way.

Notes

1. A nice paper on this issue is Hoffman and Klein (1993), wherein (put roughly) the authors argue for the view that experts simply "see" things novices don't.

2. The interested reader can consult an octet of books I find useful: For broad coverage of the basic material, see Lewis and Papadimitriou (1981), Ebbinghaus, Flum *et al.* (1984), Boolos and Jeffrey (1980), and Hopcroft and Ullman (1979). For a nice comprehensive discussion of computability theory that includes succinct coverage of uncomputability, including the Arithmetic Hierarchy, see Davis and Weyuker (1983) and the difficult but rewarding Soare (1980). Partee (1990) contains a very nice discussion of the Chomsky Hierarchy. And, of course, there's always the classic Rogers (1967).

3. Of course, whether two formalisms are interchangeable in *practice* is a different question. It is well-known that an abacus (under the assumption that it can be expanded upon demand) is equivalent in power to a digital computer, but someone unskilled in the use of the ancient device certainly could not exchange it for a Macintosh.

4. But note the central role logic plays in AI and expert systems: (Russell and Norvig 1995.)

5. Of course, even finitary logics have underlying alphabets that are infinite in size (the propositional calculus comes with an infinite supply of propositional variables. $\mathcal{L}_{\omega_1\omega}$, however, allows for formulas of infinite length—and hence allows for infinitely long derivations.

6. This chapter is aimed at a multidisciplinary audience assumed to have familiarity with but the rudiments of AI and expert systems. So this isn't the place to baptize readers into the world of cardinal numbers. Hence I leave the size implications of the subscripts in $\mathcal{L}_{\omega_1\omega}$, and other related niceties, such as the precise meaning of ω, to the side. For a comprehensive array of the possibilities arising from varying the subscripts, see (Dickmann 1975).

References

Barr, A. (1983). Artificial intelligence: Cognition as computation. In F. Machlup (Ed.), *The Study of Information: Interdisciplinary Messages* (pp. 237-262). New York: Wiley-Interscience.

Barwise, J. & Etchemendy, J. (1993). *Turing's World 3.0.* Stanford, CA: CSLI Publications.

Bringsjord, S. (1995). Could, how could we tell if, and why should—androids have inner lives. In K.M. Ford, C. Glymour & P.J. Hayes (Eds.), *Android Epistemology* (pp. 93-121). Menlo Park, CA: AAAI/MIT Press.

Bringsjord, S. (1994). Computation, among other things, is beneath us. *Minds and*

Machines, 4, 69-488.

Bringsjord, S. (1992). *What Robot's Can and Can't Be.* Dordrecht. The Netherlands: Kluwer.

Bringsjord, S. (1991). Is the connectionist-logicist clash one of AI's wonderful red herrings? *Journal of Experimental and Artificial Intelligence, 3,* 319-349.

Bringsjord, S. & Ferrucci, D. (1997). *Artificial Intelligence, Literary Creativity, and Story Generation: The State of the Art.* Hillsdale, NJ: Lawrence Erlbaum.

Bringsjord, S. & Zenzen, M. (1997). *In Defense of Uncomputable Cognition,* Dordrecht, The Netherlands: Kluwer.

Bringsjord, S & Zenzen, M. (1991). In defense of hyper-logicist AI. *IJCAI '91* (pp. 1066-1072). Mountain View, CA: Morgan Kaufmann.

Boolos, G.S. & Jeffrey, R.C. (1980). *Computability and Logic.* Cambridge, UK: Cambridge University Press.

Davis, M. & E. Weyuker (1983). *Computability, Complexity, and Languages: Fundamentals of Theoretical Computer Science.* New York: Academic Press.

Dickmann, M.A. (1975). *Large Infinitary Languages.* Amsterdam, The Netherlands: North-Holland.

Dietrich, E. (1990). Computationalism. *Social Epistemology, 4,* 135-154.

Ebbinghaus, H.D., Flum, J. & Thomas, W. (1984). *Mathematical Logic.* New York: Springer-Verlag.

Fetzer, J. (1994). Mental algorithms: Are minds computational systems? *Pragmatics and Cognition, 2,* 1-29.

Harnad, S. (1991). Other bodies, other minds: A machine incarnation of an old philosophical problem. *Minds and Machines, 1,* 43-54.

Haugeland, J. (1981). *Artificial Intelligence: The Very Idea.* Cambridge, MA: MIT Press.

Hilbert, D. (1926). On the infinite. *Math. Annalen, 95,* 161-190. [Trans. in Van Heijenoort, 1967.]

Hoffman, R.R. & Klein, G.A. (1993). Seeing the invisible: Perceptual-cognitive aspects of expertise. In M. Rabonowitz (Ed.), *Cognitive Science Foundations of Instruction.* Hillsdale, NJ: Lawrence Erlbaum.

Hofstadter, D.R. (1985). Waking up from the Boolean dream (Chap. 26, pp. 631-665), in *Metamagical Themas: Questing for the Essence of Mind and Pattern.* New York: Bantam.

Hopcroft, J.E. & Ullman, J.D. (1979). *Introduction to Automata Theory, Languages and Computation.* Reading, MA: Addison-Wesley.

Johnson-Laird, P. (1988). *The Computer and the Mind.* Cambridge, MA: Harvard University Press.

Keisler, H.J. (1971). *Model Theory for Infinitary Logic.* Amsterdam, The Netherlands: North-Holland.

Lewis, H. & Papadimitriou, C. (1981). *Elements of the Theory of Computation.* Englewood Cliffs, NJ: Prentice-Hall.

Marxen, H. & Buntrock, J. (1990). Attacking the Busy Beaver 5. *Bulletin of the European Association for Theoretical Computer Science, 40,* 247-251.

Maudlin, T. (1989). Computation and consciousness. *Journal of Philosophy, 84,* 407-432.

Newell, A. (1980). Physical symbol systems. *Cognitive Science, 4,* 135-183.

Partee, B., Meulen, A. & Wall, R. (1990). *Mathematical Methods in Linguistics.* Dordrecht, The Netherlands: Kluwer Academic.

Putnam, H. (1988). *Representation and Reality.* Cambridge, MA: MIT Press.

Rado, T. (1963). On non-computable functions. *Bell System Technical Journal, 41,* 877-884.

Rogers, H. (1967). *Theory of Recursive Functions and Effective Computability.* New York: McGraw-Hill.

Russell, B. (1936). The limits of empiricism. *Proceedings of the Aristotelian Society,* XXXVI, 131-150.

Russell, S. & Norvig, P. (1995). *Artificial Intelligence: A Modern Approach.* Englewood Cliffs, NJ: Prentice-Hall.

Searle, J. (1992). *The Rediscovery of the Mind.* Cambridge, MA: MIT Press.

Searle, J. (1980). Minds, brains and programs. *Behavioral and Brain Sciences, 3,* 417-424.

Simon, H. (1981). Study of human intelligence by creating artificial intelligence. *American Scientist, 69.3,* 300-309.

Simon, H. (1980). Cognitive science: The newest science of the artificial. *Cognitive Science, 4,* 33-56.

Soare, R. (1980). *Recursively Enumerable Sets and Degrees.* New York: Springer-Verlag.

Van Heijenoort, J. (Ed.). (1967). *From Frege to Gödel.* Amsterdam, The Netherlands: North-Holland.

Weyl, H. (1949). *Philosophy of Mathematics and Natural Science* Princeton, NJ: Princeton University Press.

CHAPTER 21

Expertise and Context in Uncertain Inference

Henry E. Kyburg, Jr.

Introduction

One form of expertise on which we all depend is that which is displayed by statisticians. They are the experts on whom we ordinary mortals depend in a wide variety of contexts. Their expertise is often said to depend on the development of mature statistical judgment. While not all statisticians agree all the time—there is a sharp split between 'Bayesian' and 'classical' statisticians, for example, which affects a significant number of conclusions—what the statistician often seems to be trying to capture and formalize is a refined version of ordinary induction: it is reasonable to suppose that populations will be like the samples drawn from them, or even more simply, as denied by David Hume (1949), it is reasonable to suppose that the future will be like the past. Hume argued that there was nothing rational about this, and that in fact it just represented a human habit that we can't suppress, like falling in love.

Induction, another name for this issue, has a somewhat long and dismal history in philosophy. As a general problem (or rather a set of general problems, for there is no one problem that all writers have had in mind) few writers even claim to have solved the problem of explaining why induction is rational. On the other hand, in relatively simple situations, statistics seems to have relatively straight forward-answers to inductive questions: it is rational to believe that smoking affects longevity, because the statistical evidence is very strong?

Is this really the case? Can we suppose that at least in some simple cases this form of expertise—'mature statistical judgment'—be formalized and captured by a set of rules that could be embodied in a computer program?

Note that this is *not* the question of whether or not one can have a computer program that can embody the mathematics of statistical inference. That is a different question, and one that has been answered by a number of very fine computer programs that are available. We are concerned here with the application of these mathematical techniques to real situations in the real world, or, equally, with the application of statistical knowledge to decision making in the real world.

Of course, as statisticians have been telling philosophers for a long time, the soundness of statistical argument can depend heavily on context. Thus if we are to formalize statistical expertise, we must have a feasible way of taking account of the context in which that expertise is to be applied. In what follows we will argue that what is needed in the way of context can be captured by a set of statements comprising the relevant background knowledge in a particular case. Even the reference to 'relevance' need not be question-begging, since the standards of relevance are built into our way of analyzing statistical uncertainty.

The organization of this chapter is as follows. I will first discuss an example of the kind of inference I have in mind. Next, I will provide a framework in which such inferences can be formalized. The third section (Partial Entailment) develops an abstract definition of 'partial entailment'—a formal counterpart of the inductive relation, and the fourth section establishes a theorem applying this definition to a particular kind of statistical inference. The Main Theorem and Prior Distributions sections compare this approach to the Bayesian approach to the same problem, in particular examining the questions of prior probabilities and conditionalization. The Acceptance section deals with the (nonmonotonic) acceptance of inductive conclusions, and the Back to Earth section discusses the bearing of these technical matters on down to earth problems of empirical inference.

An Example

As a general guide for our future behavior and decisions, we may be interested in knowing the proportion of members of a certain population of women who marry before the age of 18. We obtain a random sample of 100 members of that population, observe that 17% of our sample get married before 18, and infer with .95 confidence that between 15.5% and 18.5% of the whole population satisfy this condition. This inference is based upon an experimental design that is characterized by a 0.95 confidence interval. We here ignore two very knotty problems: the problem of understanding what a 'random sample' is, and the related problem of secular trends: perhaps the proportion is changing over time.

The classical statistical analysis of this inference is that we have a method of generating intervals from samples which is such that the intervals cover the true value about 95% of the time. We have applied this method to this particular case, and there, as far as classical statistics goes, is the end of the matter. We cannot say that there is a high probability that from 15.5% to 18.5% of the population marry before 18; from a classical perspective, this probability can only be 0 or 1. But we can characterize our *procedure* with the number 0.95; .95 is the probability that the procedure will in general issue in a correct interval.

This seems like an instance of uncertain inference. It concerns uncertainty in two ways: To know that between 15.5% and 18.5% of women in that population marry before 18 gives us a handle on some of the uncertainties involving the marital state of specific women or groups of women. This is why insurance companies (who only insure specific women or groups of women) are interested in such statistical facts. But the statistical conclusion itself is uncertain. More precisely, this bit of knowledge embodies vagueness concerning the proportion in question ("between 15.5% and 18.5%") as well as uncertainty concerning particular individuals: knowing of an individual only that she belongs to this population, it is natural to use the interval $[0.155, 0.185]$ to characterize our uncertainty concerning her age of marriage. And the inference itself is uncertain, since even if the sample is random (whatever that means), there is a chance that it is misleading.

Suppose alternatively that we obtain the interval from a consulted expert: We ask for her estimate of the proportion of women who marry before age 18; we are told "17%." We reasonably say "Surely you don't mean to tell us that it is *exactly* 17%?" The expert responds, "No, of course not, but I'm very sure that it is between 15.5% and 18.5%." "How do you know?" We would not accept "intuition" as an answer. We would accept evidence of the sort just cited as an answer. There are various other grounds that we would accept as justification for that answer, but the idea of asking for objective grounds is an appealing one.

Combinatorial semantics (Kyburg, forthcoming) gives us a way of looking at uncertain inference or partial entailment. The following sections will show that the confidence interval analysis does correspond to a partial entailment that can be shown to hold under circumstances like those of the example. Characterizing those circumstances precisely, and even more important, being able to say when they do not obtain, is exactly to be able to specify the context in which this fragment of statistical expertise may reasonably be applied.

The Language L

Following Bacchus (1991) or Halpern (1990), I take the language L to be a two-sorted first order language. A two-sorted language is one with two classes of variables and terms, and, correspondingly, two domains in its semantic interpretation. One of the sorts concerns mathematics; in each model it receives the standard interpretation: mathematical variables take their values in the real numbers, and mathematical constants denote just the real numbers you would expect them to. The other part of the language is empirical, and is the only part we will model explicitly. Model structures have the standard form M = $\langle D, I \rangle$; we take D to be a finite domain in which the object variables of our language take values; I is an interpretation function for the empirical part of our language.

As in (Kyburg, forthcoming), I introduce only one syntactic novelty, the variable binding operator "%." Intuitively, "%(ϕ,φ,p,q)" says that the proportion of φ that are ϕ lies between p and q, where p and q are *rigid* or *standard* real number designators. The conclusion of our example would be expressed: "%(Married-before-18(x),woman-of-pop(x),.155,.185)."

We are obliged to impose some constraints on ϕ and φ to avoid philosophical puzzles. For example "(is-examined-before-2000(x) & is-blue(x)) ∨ (is-examined-after-2000(x) & is-green(x))" is a poor candidate for ϕ, and "is-toss-that-lands-heads(x) ∨ is-result-of-next-toss(x)" is a poor candidate for φ.[1] Since these formulas are a bother in a number of contexts, I shall here simply suppose that the syntax of the language restricts the formulas that can appear in the first and second places of the "%" operator. Neither they nor singleton predicates (x = john) will be allowed to occur in well formed formulas of the form "%(ϕ,φ,p,q)." One way of characterizing the acceptable predicates of the two kinds is suggested in Kyburg (1983). Here I shall simply require that ϕ belong to the specified set of open formulas T ('T' is for target) and that φ belong to the specified set of open formulas R ('R' is for reference).

The sentence "%(ϕ,φ,p,q)" is true in a model if and only if ϕ and φ have the same free object variables and no other variables, ϕ is in T, φ is in R, p and q are rigid real number designators, and the ratio of the cardinality of the satisfaction set of ϕ & φ, to the cardinality of the satisfaction set of φ lies in the closed interval $[p,q]$. If ϕ contains k free object variables, and no free mathematical variables, the *satisfaction set* of ϕ, $SS_M(\phi)$, in a model M = $\langle D, I \rangle$ is the set of k-tuples in D^k such that those objects, in that order, satisfy ϕ under the interpretation I.

Partial Entailment

Conventionally, we say that the set of formulas Γ entails the formula S when every model that makes Γ true, also makes S true. Here we will say that the set of formulas Γ *partially entails, to the degree [p,q]* the formula S, when there is a set of formulas Δ maximally informative about S that is entailed by Γ, and S is true in a proportion of those models that lies between p and q. A crucial phrase is "maximally informative about S." It is possible for us to try to take into account so much of our knowledge about S that our knowledge cancels itself out. Thus we know of the highly specific set $\{x{:}x$ is the next toss of coin $c\}$ that either 100% of that set are tosses that land heads, or 100% of that set are tosses that land tails. We don't know which. If we make use of the most specific knowledge we have, all we can say is that the chance is between 0 and 1. But if we look at only the maximally informative knowledge we have, we can consider the fact that about 50% of coin tosses land heads, and use that *general* knowledge as a basis for our belief.

The following definitions (D-1 to D-4) seek to capture the balance between knowing too little that is relevant to S and knowing too much that is relevant to S. D-1 through D-3 lead up to D-4, the definition of partial entailment.

The *model ratio* of ϕ to φ in the model M with domain D—$r_{M_D}(\phi,\varphi)$—is the ratio of the cardinality of the satisfaction set of ϕ to that of the satisfaction set of φ, provided that the latter is not zero, ϕ is in T , and φ is in R; otherwise let it be zero:

D-1 $r_{M_D}(\phi,\varphi) = \left|SS_M(\phi \wedge \varphi)\right| \, / \, \left|SS_M(\phi)\right|$

For real p let $[r_{M_p}(\phi,\varphi) = p]$ be the set of models with domain D in which $r_{M_p}(\phi,\varphi)$ has the value p. These sets constitute a partition of any set of models of domain D. The set $[r_{M_p}(\phi,\varphi) = 0]$ includes all those models in which $SS_M(\varphi)$ is empty, as well as those in which $SS_M(\phi)$ is empty.

Next define what it is for a set of sentences to give support of degree $[p,q]$ to a sentence S. We use "$M_D(S)$" to denote the set of models with domain D in which S holds.

D-2 $\Delta \; sup \; S[p,q] \; iff$

$$(\exists\alpha,\phi,\varphi)\left(\begin{array}{l} \Delta \vDash "\%(\phi(x),\varphi(x),p,q) \wedge \varphi(\alpha) \wedge S \equiv \phi(\alpha)" \wedge \neg\varnothing \vDash "\%(\phi(x),\varphi(x),p,q)" \wedge \\ p = \mathrm{glb}\{r_{M(\Delta)}(\phi,\varphi)\} \wedge q = \mathrm{lub}\{r_{M(\Delta)}(\phi,\varphi)\} \wedge \\ (\forall D)(x)\big(\big[r_{M_D(\Delta)}(\phi,\varphi) = x\big] \neq \varnothing \supset x \times \big[r_{M_D(\Delta)}(\phi,\varphi) = x\big]\big) = \big[r_{M_D(\Delta)}(\phi,\varphi) = x\big] \cap M_D(S)\big) \end{array}\right)$$

Some comments are (obviously) in order.

The quantification over terms of L—$(\exists\alpha,\phi,\varphi)$—is designed to focus our attention on statistical knowledge. The final quantification over every domain D captures the fact that whatever the size of our domain, the proportion of models in which the model ratio has the value x, in which S is also true, is x times the proportion of models in which the model ratio is x. In other words, the proportion of models in which S is true is bounded by our approximate statistical knowledge.

Note that if $\Delta \; sup \; S[p,q]$ then $\Delta \; sup \; S[p',q']$ whenever p' is less than p and q' is greater than q. All that is required is that for each such pair the model ratio in each of the corresponding equivalence classes must be the proportion of those equivalence classes in which S is true.

The next definition is what allows us to disregard information that is merely unhelpful; we say that a more informative set of data Δ is *sharper* than a less informative set of data Δ' with respect to a sentence S, if it shrinks the range of the model ratios relevant to the truth of S. More precisely:

D-3 Δ *sharper* Δ' *wrt S iff*

$$(\forall \alpha, \phi, \varphi, r, s) \left(\begin{array}{l} \Delta' \vDash "\%(\phi(x),\varphi(x),r,s) \wedge \varphi(\alpha) \wedge S \equiv \phi(\alpha)" \wedge \\ \neg \Delta \vDash "\%(\phi(x),\varphi(x),r,s) \wedge \varphi(\alpha) \wedge S \equiv \phi(\alpha)" \supset (\forall p, q)(\Delta \sup S[p,q] \supset \\ \mathrm{glb}\{r_M(\phi,\varphi) : M \in M(\Delta')\} \le p) \wedge \mathrm{lub}\{r_M(\phi,\varphi) : M \in M(\Delta')\} \ge q) \end{array} \right)$$

In other words, if Δ is sharper than Δ' then by expanding our considerations to take account of the larger body of knowledge Δ', we only *lose* precision; we learn nothing new about S.

Finally we come to the definition of partial entailment. We will say that a total body of knowledge Γ partially entails S to a degree measured by the *interval [p,q]* just in case there is a set of statements Δ entailed by Γ such that p and q are the upper and lower bounds of the intervals representing the support that Δ gives to S, and if Δ' is any stronger set of sentences, then its effect will be merely to broaden the bounds—i.e., Δ will sharpen Δ'. Δ' will be less informative about S than is Δ.

D-4 $\Gamma \vDash_{[p,q]} S$ *iff*

$$(\exists \Delta) \left(\begin{array}{l} \Gamma \vDash \Delta \wedge \\ p = \min\{t : (\exists u)(\Delta \sup S[t,u])\} \wedge q = \max\{u : (\exists t)(\Delta \sup S[t,u])\} \wedge \\ (\forall \Delta')(\Gamma \vDash \Delta' \wedge \Delta' \vDash \Delta \supset \Delta \textit{ sharper } \Delta' \textit{ wrt } S) \end{array} \right)$$

To see how a more complete database can be *less* informative about S, let us consider a database about death rates among 50 year old males in the city of Rochester and in the United States as a whole. This database might include (as a result of statistical inference from the data) such statements as

"%(L(x),M(x)&US(x),0.945,0.965)" and

"%(L(x),M(x)&US(x) &Roch(x),0.930,0.975),"

where "L(x)" means that x lives for one more year; "M(x)" means that x is male, "US(x)" means that x lives in the United States, and "Roch(x)" means that x lives in Rochester. Knowledge of mortality is based on a larger sample from the United States than from Rochester, and that is why the interval in the first statement is narrower than that in the second statement.

Now add to the database information about the individual j: "M(j)&US(j)&Roch(j)" and you can see that taking account of the fact that "Roch(j)" is entailed by the database does *not* contribute to the informativeness of what we can say about "L(j);" you would be led to the less informative interval [0.930,0.985] instead of the interval [0.9454,0.965].

I have represented the force of a partial entailment by an interval, and yet in a given finite domain D, the proportion of models of a set of sentences Δ in which a sentence S is true is precisely determined. In principle, it could be calculated for any domain of given cardinality: the number of interpretations of a primitive constant is the cardinality of the domain; the number of interpretations of a primitive one-place predicate is 2 to the cardinality of the domain, etc. Calculate the number of models that render Δ and S true. Divide by the number of models that make D true. For a reasonably rich language and a reasonably large domain, the task would be formidable. More important, while we can reasonably put some finite bound on the size of the domain that represents *our* world, it is not reasonable to suppose that we know exactly how big that world is. Furthermore, since the proportion of models of Δ also satisfying S may vary with $|D|$ (consider the statement "There are an even number of distinct things."), and there are many cases—the actuarial case, the anthropological case—in which we can impose bounds on this proportion without knowing the cardinality of D, it appears more fruitful to examine bounds themselves.

In the following section I will examine the details of an important kind of partial entailment—one that represents a direct and simple generalization of the anthropological inference that was described in the Language L Section.

Main Theorem

If 17% of a suitable sample of women in the society you are studying are married by the age of 18, it is natural for you to infer that *about* 17% of women in that society, as it now exists, are married by the age of 18. Of course you will admit that the conclusion of this inference could be in error, but that's *not very likely*. The main theorem concerns the replacement of the vague phrases 'about' and 'not very likely' with bounds. Specifically, if the evidence consists of a sample of 100 women, of whom 17 were married by the age of 18, this evidence partially entails, to at least the degree [0.95, 1.00] the conclusion that between 15.5% and 18.5% of the women in this society, as it now exists, marry by the age of 18.

THEOREM

For positive ε and δ, we can find a natural number j such that

$$S_j \models_{[1-\gamma, 1]} \text{"%}\left(P(x), Q(x), \frac{i}{j} - \varepsilon, \frac{i}{j} + \varepsilon\right)\text{"}$$

where S_j is a set of j statements of the form '$Q(a_k) \& \pm P(a_k)$' in which $\pm$ is replaced by nothing in i instances, and by "$\neg$" in $j - i$ instances, and the a_k are distinct individual constants of our language, say $a_1,...,a_j$, and γ is less than δ.

The proof of this theorem will show how statistical expertise bears on uncertain inference in a general way, and how the parameters of a context can be represented.

Partition the set of models into equivalence classes $[r]$ according to the value of r_M. Note that $[0]$ and $[1]$ are non-empty, and that if $|D|$ is even and large, $[1/2]$ is relatively large.

Let m be a model in the equivalence class $[r]$, for some rational number r. The relative frequency of P in Q in the model m has the value r. We now show that a certain sentence of our language L is true in m.

Consider Q^j— the set of j-membered sequences of Q's. For any $y \in Q^j$, let $rf(y)$ be the proportion of P's in the sequence y. In any model, given any assignment in the interpretation of Q to the variable y, '$rf(y) = s$' is true for exactly one rational number s. The expression "rf" is a perfectly good function, and is definable in a language with modest mathematical paraphernalia.

Let $r(P,Q)$ be the mathematical term "$|\{z:Q(z)\ \&\ P(z)\}|\ /\ |\{z:Q(z)\}|$." It has one value in each model, if we understand it to have the value 0 in models where there aren't any Q's. Note that it has different values in different models—it is *not* a rigid designator. But in each model it does designate some rational number.

Consider the sentence

$$"\%\left(\left\{y : |rf(y) - r(P,Q)| \leq \frac{k}{2\sqrt{j}}\right\}, Q^j, 1 - \frac{1}{k^2}, 1\right)" \tag{1}$$

This sentence says that the proportion of j-membered sequences of Q's that have the property that the difference between the fraction of P's in the sequence and the fraction of P's among Q's in general is no greater than $\frac{k}{2\sqrt{j}}$ itself at least $1 - \frac{1}{k^2}$.

First, observe that (1) is true in the model m. The random quantity (or random "variable") rf has a distribution in Q^j that has a mean of r, and a variance of $r(1-r)/j$ in this model. It follows from Tchebycheff's inequality that

$$"\%\left(\left\{y : |rf(y) - r(P,Q)| \leq \frac{k\sqrt{r(1-r)}}{\sqrt{j}}\right\}, Q^j, 1 - \frac{1}{k^2}, 1\right)"$$

is true in m. Since $[r(1-r)/j]^{1/2} \leq 1/2\sqrt{j}$, (1) is also true in m.

Next observe that (1) is true in each of the models in the equivalence class $[r]$; the choice of m from that set was arbitrary.

Third, note that (1) is true in all of the models in which the interpretation of Q^j is nonempty—and of course that includes the models in which the evidence statement S_j is true. Although the sentence (1) changes its "meaning" from one equivalence class [r] to another equivalence class [r′], it does not change its truth value.

Formula (1) is true in every model of every equivalence class: it is true in all models of our language, regardless of the size of our domain.

Let Γ be S_j. Take Δ to be $\{$"$Q(a_1)$ $\&\ldots\&$ $Q(aj)$"$\}$. It will now be shown that the proportion of models of Δ in which

$$"\left| rf\!\left(a_1,\cdots a_j\right) - \mathbf{R}(P,Q) \right| \leq \frac{k}{2\sqrt{j}}"\tag{2}$$

is true is at least $1-\dfrac{1}{k^2}$.

To make Δ true in a model, we must assign j objects to $a_1,\ldots,a_j$. Since each such assignment must pick out an element of Q^j, and since disregarding j-tuples with repetitions can't decrease the proportion that satisfy (2), the proportion of models of Δ that satisfy (2) lies in the interval

$$\left[1-\frac{1}{k^2},\ 1\right].$$

In fact, of course, it lies in some smaller interval, but that does not undermine the theorem.

It remains to be shown that no more complete utilization of our knowledge can lead to a conflicting result—this is the question of context, since context is determined by what *else* we know. We need to show, according to D-4, that if $S_j \models \Delta'$ and $\Delta' \models \Delta$ then Δ is *sharper than* Δ' with respect to (2). This requires that if there are α, ϕ, φ, r, and s such that Δ' entails

$$"\left(\left| rf\!\left(a_1,\cdots a_j\right) - \mathbf{R}(P,Q) \right| \leq \frac{k}{2\sqrt{j}} \equiv \phi(\alpha) \right) \wedge\ \varphi(\alpha) \wedge\ \%(\phi(\alpha),\varphi(\alpha),r,s)"$$

but Δ does not entail this sentence, then there are models of Δ' in which the relevant ratio of satisfaction sets is less than $1-1/k^2$ and models in which the ratio is at least 1.

What are the candidates for Δ'? The conjunction of Δ with one or more of the sentences in S_j having the form '$P(a_k)$' or the form '$\neg P(a_k)$'.[2] Suppose that in fact it consists of j' such sentences, of which i' are un-negated. Let the remaining terms be $b_1,\ldots,b_{j-j'}$. Γ implies the equivalence of (2) and

$$\frac{j}{j-j'}\left(\mathbf{R}(P,Q) - \frac{i'}{j} - \frac{k}{2\sqrt{j}} \right) \leq f_{j-j'}(\langle b_1,\ldots b_{j-j'}\rangle) \leq \frac{j}{j-j'}\left(\mathbf{R}(P,Q) - \frac{i'}{j} + \frac{k}{2\sqrt{j}} \right)\tag{3}$$

The quantity $f(y_1,\ldots,y_{j-j'})$ is defined on $Q^{j-j'}$ and has a mean of $r = \mathrm{R}(P,Q)$ and a variance of $(r(1-r))/(j-j')$ in the models belonging to the equivalence class $[r]$. The distribution of this quantity has a maximum at $\mathrm{R}(P,Q)$, and decreases in either direction: it is approximately normal with the stated mean and variance.

To exhibit a model in which the proportion of members of $Q^{j-j'}$ is less than $1 - 1/k^2$ choose an equivalence class $[r]$ where $|r - i'/j'|$ is large. The frequency with which members of $Q^{j-j'}$ satisfy (4), must be less than the frequency with which members of $Q^{j-j'}$ satisfy a symmetrical constraint. (To exhibit a model in which the proportion of members of Q^j is at least 1 is trivial: choose a model in which $R(P,Q)$ is just i'/j'.)

$$\frac{j}{j-j'}\left(\mathbf{R}(P,Q)-\frac{k}{2\sqrt{j}}\right)+\frac{j'}{j-j'}(\frac{i'}{j'}) \leq f(y_1,...y_{j-j'}) \leq \frac{j}{j-j'}\left(\mathbf{R}(P,Q)+\frac{k}{2\sqrt{j}}\right)+\frac{j'}{j-j'}(\frac{i'}{j'})$$

$$(4)$$

We are thus taking α to be the sequence of $j - j'$ terms for which it is not recorded in Δ' whether or not they are P's. The reference class j is $Q^{j-j'}$. The target class ϕ is the set of $j-j'$ termed sequences y in $Q^{j-j'}$ satisfying (4). But clearly there are less of these than there are of members of Q^j that satisfy (2).

We now have

$$S_j \vDash [1-\gamma,1] \text{ "} \left| f(\langle a_1,...,a_j \rangle) - \mathbf{R}(P,Q) \right| \leq \frac{k}{2\sqrt{j}} \text{"}$$

for some γ smaller than $1/k^2$. But note that S_j entails that

$$\text{"}\%\left(P(x),Q(x),\frac{i}{j}-\frac{k}{2\sqrt{j}},\frac{i}{j}+\frac{k}{2\sqrt{j}} \right) \equiv \left| f(\langle a_1,...,a_j \rangle) - \mathbf{R}(P,Q) \right| \leq \frac{k}{2\sqrt{j}} \text{"}$$

and so we have

$$S_j \vDash [1-\gamma,1] \text{ "}\%\left(P(x),Q(x),\frac{i}{j}-\frac{k}{2\sqrt{j}},\frac{i}{j}+\frac{k}{2\sqrt{j}} \right)\text{"}$$

for some γ smaller than $1/k^2$. Taking $k = 1/\delta$ and $j = 1/4\varepsilon^2\delta$ yields the result: in the context we have described, the support or partial entailment provided by the sample for the generalization

$$\text{"}\%\left(P(x),Q(x),\frac{i}{j}+\varepsilon,\frac{i}{j}-\varepsilon \right)\text{"} \text{ is at least } 1-\delta.$$

Observe that no assumptions about sampling, about prior distributions, or any other empirical matter of fact have been made. The inference is non-monotonic, however, in the sense that if we had more knowledge, if Γ included more empirical knowledge than we have supposed, then it might be possible to find a Δ' that would undermine the theorem. For a simple example, imagine an enlarged Γ that included "%($P(x),Q(x),0.2,0.2$)", where 0.2 does not lie in $i / j \pm \varepsilon$

A question that comes to mind immediately is this. How does this result relate to the popular Bayesian approaches to uncertain inference? Is the interval that characterizes partial entailment an interval of subjective probabilities? If so, how have I managed to conceal the role of prior probabilities? These questions will be dealt with in the next section.

Prior Distributions

It is important to note that this result represented by the theorem just proved is completely independent of the measures or weights, if any, that one might imaginatively apply to models of our language. Various ways of assigning measures to models have been suggested, including the assignment of equal weights to each model [c† in Carnap (1950), 'random worlds' in Bacchus, Grove, Koller, and Halpern (1992), Grove, Koller, and Halpern (1992)], equal measures to statistical structure descriptions, which are then divided up among the models of a given structure [c* in Carnap (1950), 'random structures' in Bacchus, Grove, Koller, and Halpern (1992)] and more general parametric assignments in Hintikka (1966), and Carnap (1952, 1980). Since (1) is true in *all* models, the result just proved holds independently of whether weights are assigned to models, or, if so, what weights.

Since there is considerable controversy about what weights ought to be assigned to models, and no generally accepted procedure for resolving such disagreements, and no *grounds* for assigning one weight rather than another, it seems desirable to avoid assigning weights to them at all.

The lesson to be learned is that the application of statistical expertise need not depend on or reflect the assignment of weights to possible worlds or models. Partial entailment may thus be perfectly objective, in the sense that arbitrary *a priori* assignments of measures on models are not needed. This allows the context in which these arguments can be applied to be specified explicitly. The soundness of statistical argument need not be dependent on the 'intuitions' or 'statistical sense' of experts.

On the other hand, if one begins with subjective or assumed measures on models of the world, and updates these measures in the light of empirical evidence by means of conditionalization (the application of Bayes' theorem), then the resulting subjective degrees of belief may conflict with the theorem stated in the Main Theorem section. Let us see how this can be.

Conditionalization

In what contexts will the assignment of a prior measure to the models of our language L, followed by conditioning on the sentences S_j, lead to a result that is consistent with the result of the main Theorem? Roughly, when we adopt a measure like Carnap's c*, which assigns equal measures to structure descriptions. One then has an analog of LaPlace's example of $N + 1$ urns, each containing N black and white balls (P's and Q's) in each possible proportion. We can calculate a posterior distribution by means of Bayes' theorem, and find an interval $(i/j) \pm \varepsilon$ such that the posterior probability will be at least $1 - \delta$ that an urn with a composition falling in this interval has been chosen. This posterior probability will not be an interval, of course, but an exact number at least as great as $1 - \delta$.

It is also interesting to note, however, that there are prior distributions on the basis of which conditionalization on S_j will lead to a value for the probability of

$$"\%\left(P(x),Q(x),\frac{i}{j}-\varepsilon,\frac{i}{j}+\varepsilon\right)"$$

that is *not* greater than $1 - \delta$. In such cases there is clearly a conflict between conditionalization based on prior probabilities, on the one hand, and the results embodied in the main theorem on the other. In an extreme case, almost all models that satisfy the evidence statements (the data base) also satisfy the hypothesis, yet the measure of these models may be negligible, so that (following the Bayesian path) the agent would attribute a high posterior degree of belief to the denial of the hypothesis. For example, if we assign the same weight to each model (Carnap's c†), then regardless of the evidence, we should be practically certain that the frequency of A's among the unexamined B's is a half (where A and B are primitive predicates). This was already noted in Carnap (1950).

What lesson should we learn from this? It is that there can be significant conflict between objective statistical methods and the subjective approach to the modification of belief. Probabilistic expertise should conform to defensible statistical knowledge; if there is conflict between subjective opinion, as embodied in assumed measures on models of the language, and the straight-forward objective counting of models, it is subjective opinion that should give way.

On the other hand, when the *a priori* measures are derived from public and defensible statistics, there can be no question but that they should mold our conclusions. But this is built into the definitions given earlier. Those statistics—not 'assumed,' but warranted—can be taken as part of our background knowledge.

It is one thing to accept as highly supported on the basis of statistical evidence an item of statistical knowledge. It is another to base your degree of belief regarding the 'next instance' directly on the basis of statistical evidence. So far, the focus has been on the former, and it has been argued that partial entailment gives us a reasonable representation of nonmonotonic statistical inference. What does the semantics of partial entailment tell us about basing our beliefs concerning the next instance on statistical evidence?

The Predictive Inference

What can we say about the support that the prediction "$P(aj+1)$" may have, based on the evidence S_j and "$Q(aj+1)$"? (According to Carnap, 1950, this is the *only* thing that should interest us!) Given an assignment of prior probabilities over the models of the language, we can compute, in principle, the conditional probability of "$P(a_j+1)$" given S_j and $Q(a_j)$. On the LaPlacean assignment of equal probabilities to statistical structures, the conditional probability of "$P(a_j+1)$" is easy enough to compute in the present case: it is just $(i+1)/(j+2)$. This LaPlace's famous (infamous?) law of succession is the predecessor of similar laws proposed by Carnap (1950) and others.

What does the main theorem tell us? Nothing about a_j+1! If P is a primitive predicate and our body of evidence is empty, "$P(a_j+1)$" will be true in half of the models of L. If the language consists just of "P" and the single constant "a_j+1" then that's clear. It will be unchanged if another predicate Q, is added, or if further individual constants are added.

Now suppose we have added S_j to our knowledge base. Let N be the set of models satisfying S_j. Each such model in which "$P(a_j+1)$" is true can be paired with a similar model in which "$P(a_j+1)$" is false. Exactly half the models among those that satisfy S_j make "$P(a_j+1)$" true. How can we take advantage of the evidence?

What receives support on the view that is being presented is not a proposition concerning the next instance (or any particular sample) but the generalization concerning P's and Q's. What becomes acceptable as a basis for other claims is the general statement that the long run proportion of P's among Q's is bounded by an interval around i/j. The source of knowledge about the future—the next toss, the next n tosses—is general knowledge of the world, not (directly) observations of the past. Not only does this view support a theory of acceptance, but it demands one.

Acceptance

The object of the study of partial entailment is to account for uncertain *inference*. While "$P(a_j+1)$" can't be inferred from S_j even uncertainly (and one shouldn't want to if i were less than half of j!), a general statistical statement concerning P's and Q's can be inferred from S_j, because it is partially entailed by S_j. It is possible to become practically certain of long run statistics on the basis of direct statistical evidence, without prior probabilities and without empiricial assumptions, contrary to the claims of both classical and subjectivistic Bayesian statisticians.

Expert judgment may be based on statistical evidence, or indirect statistical evidence, even though that evidence is not explicit, or even conscious in the mind of the expert. Nevertheless expertise, to be worthy of the name, should be based on objective facts. What can be expected of the expert is general knowledge: precisely the sort of knowledge has just been shown to be objectively attainable.

There is one problem to be faced in accepting statistical statements on the basis of the fact that they hold in $1 - \delta$ of the models in which the evidence for them holds. It is that there are too many such statements; in particular, there are an infinite number of statements of the form $\%(\phi(x),\varphi(x),p,q)$ that hold in $1 - \delta$ of the models in which the data concerning ϕ and φ is true. In our anthropological example they might include %(Married,W-18,0.152,0.184) and %(Married,W-18,0.156,0.188) as well as %(Married,W-18,0.155,0.185). In classical statistics for confidence intervals, the problem is resolved by seeking only the *shortest* confidence intervals. That solution will work for here, too, but it will not solve all the problems. There are unresolved issues concerning more general kinds of statistical hypotheses.

More needs to be said about acceptance. Suppose that Γ partially entails S to at least the degree $1 - \delta$, and that in the context at hand, that is a high enough degree of partial entailment to warrant acceptance. Does that mean that S should be added to the set of sentences Γ? That leads to difficulties with nonmonotonicity. At that point Γ entails S in the full sense. But then how can the addition of more data to Γ lead to the rejection of S? This can be arranged through some bookkeeping, as in a truth maintenance system (see de Kleer 1990, for example), but for present purposes the simpler procedure of distinguishing between the sentences accepted into Γ as evidence and those accepted as "practically certain" relative to Γ will suffice.

What is the benefit of the added complexity of dealing with a distinct set of statements rendered practically certain by a set of evidence statements? It is the benefit of having a general empirical knowledge base that can be used as a basis for decision making without the need of calculation, and without the need of assessing prior probabilities. If statistical statements are accepted, they can be used as a basis for objective probability statements, which in turn will enter into decisions and into further inferences, as suggested in Kyburg (1983).

There are two ways here where the question of context enters. First, it is context that determines the value of δ. In some contexts a much higher value of delta would be permissible than in others. It may be that it is the consumer of expertise, rather than the expert, who should be the source of this parameter. One suggestion, proposed in (Kyburg 1988), is that the value of δ should depend on what is potentially at stake in the context at hand. The issue may therefore involve questions of value.

This also raises a question that is pervasive whenever "context" is called on: how fine grained should a "context" be? What principles should we adopt in individuating contexts? Even if the proposal of (Kyburg 1988) is adopted, that doesn't settle the question of how broadly a context should be construed. Are we to look at the stakes that might be involved in the next decision? Or at the stakes that might be involved in a long sequence of decisions?

On the other hand, there is a large domain in which context represents what is known, what should be taken into account in making inferences. Much of this is known, not to the expert, but to the consumer of expertise. This introduces a second role for context. It is the knowledge of the particular circumstances that individuate the immediate problem from all other problems. It is context that renders that problem unique.

I would claim that much of what is involved in playing the generality of expertise against the particularity of context is captured by the definitions just given. Partial entailment seeks to play context against generality—even in the acquisition of statistical truths.

Back to Earth

Let us return to the expert system or the probabilistic database that is intended to be applied to the real world. A major problem involved in representing expertise is the problem of the delicate interplay between generality and specificity. One issue is the source of the propositional measures or probabilities assigned to the alternatives we face. To base these measures on statistical facts requires two stages of inference. First we must be able to justify general statistical knowledge on the basis of statistical samples. This is what the theorem cited establishes: it shows that it is possible for evidence to partially entail, under the appropriate objective circumstances, statistical assertions concerning the general state of the world.

Second, knowing general statistical facts about the world, it is important to be able to apply those known statistics in the formation of beliefs about the specific instances that concern us. To apply actuarial expertise to John's expectation of survival for five years requires both bodies of statistical knowledge concerning people who are 'like' John in various ways, and in addition, it requires knowing how to relate general statistical knowledge to the specific instance that concerns us, the context of application.

The relation of partial entailment outlined here incorporates both components: the general and the particular. It provides a framework within which the claims of statistical generality and the claims of contextual specificity can be adjudicated. It is not hard to tell when some part Δ of our total knowledge supports the sentence S to a certain (interval-valued) degree. What is difficult is to know whether and how to combine several parts of our total knowledge to arrive at a measure of partial entailment. What is most difficult is to know when to stop: when does the knowledge we have already taken into account *sharpen* an attempt to take more knowledge into account. The discussion of the relation of partial entailment is intended to throw light on this question.

Notes

1. The former predicate is pronounced 'grue' in the philosophical literature and leads to the puzzle as to why we should not believe that practically all emeralds are grue; the latter predicate has no name, but is described in Kyburg (1961). It leads to the

problem of why the objects satisfying the second predicate do not comprise a plausible reference class for the occurrence of tails on the next toss. Pollock (1990) and others avoid these problems by restricting their attentions to "projectible" predicates. We would do this too, if people could agree on what makes a predicate projectible.

2. This is handwaving, of course. To present a fully formal proof requires first specifying the formulas that can appear in the first and second blanks of the statistical formulas '%(, , ,)'. A proposal in this regard may be found in Kyburg (1983).

References

Bacchus, F. (1991). *Representing and reasoning with probabilistic knowledge.* Cambridge: The MIT Press.

Bacchus, F., Grove, A., Koller, D., & Halpern, J. (1992). From statistics to beliefs. *AAAI 1992 Proceedings.*

Carnap, R. (1980). A basic system of inductive logic, Part II. In R. Jeffrey (Ed.), *Studies in Inductive Logic and Probability* (pp. 7-155). Berkeley: University of California Press.

Carnap, R. (1952). The continuum of inductive methods. Chicago: University of Chicago Press.

Carnap, R. (1950). *The Logical Foundations of Probability.* Chicago: University of Chicago Press.

de Kleer, J. (1986). An assumption based TMS. *Artificial Intelligence, 28,* 127-162.

Grove, A., Koller, D., & Halpern, J. (1992). Random worlds and maximum entropy. In *Seventh IEEE Symposium on Logic in Computer Science.*

Halpern, J. (1990). An analysis of first-order logics of probability. *Artificial Intelligence, 46,* 311-350.

Hintikka, J. (1966). A two-dimensional continuum of inductive methods. In Hintikka & Suppes (Eds.), *Aspects of Inductive Logic* (pp. 113-132). Amsterdam: North Holland.

Hume, D. (1949). *An Enquiry Concerning Human Understanding.* LaSalle, IL: Open Court.Kyburg, H. (forthcoming). Combinatorial semantics. To appear in *Computational Intelligence.*

Kyburg, H. (1988). Full belief. *Theory and Decision, 25,* 137-162.

Kyburg, H. (1983). The reference class. *Philosophy of Science, 50,* 374-397.

CHAPTER 22

Negative Expertise

Marvin Minsky

"An expert is one who does not have to think. He knows."
— *Frank Lloyd Wright*

Introduction

The inclination to think of knowledge in positive terms is expressed in the "rule-based expert systems" that emerged from research in AI. Virtually all of their knowledge is encoded as positive rules: "IF X happens, DO Y." But this misses much of expertise. Certainly, competence often requires one to know what one must do—but it also requires you to know what not to do. "IF you are close to a precipice, DON'T walk toward it." An expert must know both how to achieve goals and how to avoid disasters. Sometimes we can take positive measures against accident—but mostly we do it by avoiding actions that might cause trouble. This essay argues that much of human knowledge is negative. And the same applies to thinking, as well. In order to think effectively, we must "know" a good deal about what not to think! Otherwise, we get bad ideas—and also, take too long. This raises a number of theoretical issues.

Why Is Negative Knowledge Important?

The world is a dangerous place for life. For example, biologists tell us that most mutations are deleterious. This because each animal is already near a sort of local optimum (with regard to its local environment) in the space of mutational variants. And near the top of any hill, most steps go down.

But why is each animal close to a local peak? Simply because evolution itself is a learning machine that is engineered to climb hills. All existing animals had ancestors that avoided enough accidents to have descendants, and those ancestors were just the ones that acquired machinery that enabled them to learn to avoid poisons, diseases, predators, competitors, and other dangerous situations. Of course, we also evolved to learn positive goals and ways to achieve them; still, to the extent that our world offers more perils than opportunities, our topmost goal must be—don't get killed! There are many ways to avoid dangers. You can escape your enemies by destroying, controlling, or evading them. Perhaps our societies, cultures, and governments themselves originated in negative goals, namely, for protection against the most common causes of accidents.

The evolution of intelligence brought great new opportunities but also gave us great new ways to fail. As soon as we were capable of reasoning, we became susceptible to fallacies. As we extended the range of our plans, we fell prone to more intricate kinds of mistakes. As the arts of speech evolved, this increased the risk of infection by more bad ideas from other minds. The mental, as well as the physical world may also contain more bad than good. Of course, communication can also transmit ideas that give immunities to other, good and bad, ideas.

The brain has many specialized agencies. In the later chapters of *The Society of Mind* (Minsky 1986), I argue that these must use a variety of different representations. Some agencies might use script-like structures for representing sequential concepts and story-like exemplars. Others may use tree-like data-structures and/or semantic networks for hierarchical classifications and more complex structures; topographical arrangements for representing spatial and haptic situations; production-like collections of rules for efficient execution of procedures; and "trans-frame" like structures for reasoning about causality. A cursory glance at the index to a neurology book shows that the brain includes hundreds of anatomically distinct "regions" and bundles of fibres that interconnect them. Why should a brain have so many ways to do things? I think, because no single scheme will work for all the many kinds of problems that the world confronts us with. Each problem-solving strategy, each style of thinking, each knowledge-representation scheme works in certain areas, but fails in other domains. Consequently, for each body of knowledge we accumulate, we also need knowledge about when to use that knowledge-base and when to not.

Some of my colleagues have argued that the brain is not a suitable basis for such a discussion, because it was never really designed to think. Surely, they say, most of that complexity could be avoided when we design such machines from scratch. Surely, some of them maintain, we can construct a single uniform, consistent, and effective logical system to perform all kinds of commonsense reasoning. I doubt (Minsky 1991) this will be feasible, because consistency and effectiveness may well be incompatible. Other colleagues maintain that we should be able to construct large, uniform neural networks that can learn to do all that minds might need. I do not see much hope of this because I fear networks that are too interconnected would be prone to becoming paralyzed by oscillations or instabilities. How could we stabilize such systems? My answer is that one might have to provide a variety of alter- native subsystems, decoupled enough, that if each part should fail from time to time, the rest could continue to function so that the system will not all fail at once. This means that those parts must be suitably insulated from one an- other. There has been so little recognition of this problem in modern AI that perhaps we need a new term for it. Perhaps we need to breed researchers who can call themselves "Insulationists."

Of course, some insulationist functions already are encompassed by tradi- tional learning theories. Because the most popular forms of neural networks and fuzzy logic can reduce as well as increase their weights, they could, in principle, eliminate "detrimental" connections. But it is my feeling that although that sort of thing is formally possible, it is heuristically impractical. Instead, I maintain, effective systems will need to be provided with suitable architectures from the start. Perhaps we'll have to design each agency with appropriately engineered machinery to prevent our machines from getting stuck. For example, in Minsky (1986), we proposed that a typical agency might be built to incorporate Sey- mour Papert's suggestion that when an agency develops a serious internal conflict, it should be inhibited so that others can take over.

How Much Human Knowledge Is Negative?

We spend our lives at learning things, yet always find exceptions and mis- takes. Certainty seems always out of reach. Except in worlds we invent for ourselves (such as formal systems of logic and mathematics), we can never be sure our assumptions are right, and must expect eventually to make mistakes and entertain inconsistencies. To keep from being paralyzed, we have to take some risks. But we can reduce the chances of accidents by accumulating two complementary types of knowledge:

1) We search for "islands of consistency" within which commonsense rea- soning seems safe.

2) We also work to find and mark the unsafe boundaries of those islands.

Both as cultures and as individuals, we learn to avoid patterns of thought reputed to yield poor results. In civilized communities, appointed guardians post signs to warn about sharp turns, thin ice, and animals that bite. And so do our philosophers, when they report to us their paradox- discoveries—those tales of Liars who admit to lying, and Barbers who shave all who do not shave themselves. These precious lessons teach us about which thoughts we shouldn't think; they are the intellectual counterparts to

Freud's emotion-censors. It is interesting how frequently we find logically paradoxical nonsense to be funny, and when we examine what underlies jokes, we'll see why this is so. For when we look closely, we find that most jokes are concerned with taboos, injuries, and other ways of coming to harm—and logical absurdities can also potentially lead to harm.

I think we have neglected that second kind of knowledge noted above—knowledge concerned with how experts manage to discern and defend the margins of their islands of consistency. But it's so hard to study what minds do *not* think that this seems to have placed that subject beyond the bounds of behaviorist psychology. And introspective methods also fail because such processes are hidden from consciousness. Neil Agnew pointed out to me that this poses a problem for knowledge engineers—those who would encode an expert's expertise (Agnew, Brown and Lynch 1986). Presumably, experts have more effective censors than the rest of us—but we can't rely upon their introspection to detect the work of their inhibitory agencies. Worse, perhaps as Freud proposed, our censors actively resist their exposure. Still, sometimes outsiders can see that in ourselves which we cannot, by noticing such nuances of behavior as avoiding, forgetting, displaying of temper, rationalizing, or citing only positive instances.

How Can We Implement Negative Knowledge?

One way is to divide the mind into parts that can monitor one another. For example, imagine a brain that consists of two parts, A and B. Connect the A-brain's inputs and outputs to the real world—so it can sense what happens there. But don't connect the B-brain to the outer world at all; instead, connect it so that the A-brain is the B-brain's world! Then A can see and act upon what happens in the outside world. On the other hand, B can only "see" and influence what happens inside A. This could be enough to help block some kinds of bad patterns of thinking in A.

- If A is not making progress toward its goal, force it to review that goal.
- If A seems to be repeating itself, make it stop and try something else.
- If A does something B considers good, reinforce A's learning system.
- If A is occupied with too much detail, then make it take a higher level view.
- If A is not being specific enough, then make it focus on more details.
- If A appears to be making things worse, suppress it in favor of another agency.
- If A asks more than three "whys" in a row, shift to another agency.

This sort of thing could be a step toward a more "reflective" mind-society.

A B-brain could experiment with its A-brain, just as the A-brain can experiment with the real-world objects and people that surround it. And just as A can try to predict and control what happens outside, B can try to predict and control what A will do. And even though B may have no concept of what A's activities mean in relation to the outer world, it is still possible for B to be useful in the sort of way that a counselor or management consultant can assess a client's mental strategy without having to understand all the precise details of that client's profession.

Emotions and Negexpertise

Negative knowledge is involved in many of the forms of thinking that we term "emotional," notably those involved with humor, shame, fear, and aesthetic appreciation. This machinery includes a variety of suppressors, critics, and inhibitors, some of which can inhibit not merely actions but entire strategies of thought. Thus, once one begins to look for it, one finds examples of negative knowledge in many activities that we usually see as positive. In the earliest theories about AI, for example, we emphasized the importance of heuristics for generating efficient search trees. This can be done either by pruning initially larger trees or by suppressing those branches right from the start—that is, by not thinking of them in the first place. When you decide to leave a room, you don't even think of jumping out the window. Thus, a positive system forces us to generate and test, whereas a negative-base system could more efficiently shape the search space from the start. To do this efficiently, we would have to invent ways to compile each new search generator, perhaps on the basis of previously learned negative prototypes. To wait for inhibition during run time would consume more time.

This relates to what is commonly called creativity. It annoys me how frequently people suggest that the "secret" of making creative machines might lie in providing some sort of random or chaotic kind of search generator. Nonsense! Certainly, there must be a source of variation—but that can be supplied by all sorts of algorithmic generators. What distinguishes the performance of a "smart" or "creative" artist or problem-solver is *not* how *many* trials precede a success, but how *few*. So the secret lies not in disorderly search, but in preshaping the search space so as to reduce the numbers of useless attempts. Of course, that's not the whole story. In order to establish individuality, a creative modern artist must also generate some unconventional alternatives. Doing that may also involve unsuppressing some conventional censors. In any case, from the negative knowledge point of view, we might argue that often beauty is neither in the eye, nor even in the mind of the observer, but precisely the opposite: it may lie in the power to inactivate many of that observer's internal critics.

To explain this, let us consider the role of emotions in thought. It seems generally agreed upon that, on the whole, the positive emotions involve learning what to do, while the negative ones involve learning what not to do. But if so, then I suspect that many emotions which we normally see as "positive" are actually not. For example, it seems to me that much of our celebrated sense of Beauty may be negative, no matter that we see it as positive. For when possessed by that emotion, many people seem to me to have suspended much of their normal question-asking machinery. When a person says, "How perfectly beautiful this is," they seem also to be saying, "It is time to stop evaluating, selecting, and criticizing." They often regard as hostile all requests to explain why they like it.

Humor, too, is also usually seen as positive, no matter that the force of a joke is to say, "Don't even think about doing X," or "Don't take it seriously!" Most people are quite unaware that jokes are usually about things that one should not do, because they are prohibited, disgusting, or simply stupid.

Similarly, we tend to think of decision-making as positive. Yet the act of decision, which we often describe as an "act" of free will, is more of a Neg-Act by nature, because what seems consciously to be the moment of "making" the decision is actually the moment of terminating the process of considering alternatives.

Perhaps it is the feeling of Pleasure that we consider most positive of all. Yet once we start to see the mind as not one, but as a society of processes, then the most extreme pleasure can be seen instead as most negative. For it may mean merely that a certain process has seized control, and has managed to turn off most of the rest. Naturally, that makes it hard to think about anything else. Surely the most extreme form of the control of mental agencies can be seen in what we call mystical experience. For when this happens to a mind, it is like saying to oneself, "Now my problems are all solved. I know the Truth, and know that there is no need to question it, or seek confirming evidence. Stop thinking now, and let all Critics cease."

We normally think of beauty, humor, pleasure, and decisiveness as positive. Iis it then paradoxical to claim the opposite? No, not at all—because we are dealing with things complex enough to constitute "double negatives." Putting something in a folder labeled "negative" can't keep it there, because we then can re-enclose it in a second sign-changing shell! Thus pleasure can seem positive to the agency now in control—no matter that your other agencies are suffering under its yoke. Thus, enjoying something very much can mean that you have engaged machinery that 1) makes you think yet more about that something, and 2) prevents, discourages, or dissuades you from thinking of other things.

Conclusion

We tend to think of knowledge in positive terms—and of experts as people who know what to do. But a "negative" way to seem competent is, simply, never to make mistakes. How much of what we learn to do—and learn to think—is of this other variety? How much of human competence is knowing methods for solving problems, and how much of it is knowing how to intercept and interdict unproductive lines of thought? It is hard to assess the importance of these, experimentally, because knowledge about what not to do never appears in behavior. And it is also difficult to assess them psychologically, because many of the feelings and judgments that we traditionally regard as positive may result from forms of censorship of other ideas, inhibition of competing activities, or suppression of more ambitious goals. Is it possible that the importance of this subject itself tends rarely to be recognized precisely because of the mass of inhibitory machinery that constitutes it?

Could it be that our accumulations of counterexamples are larger and more powerful than our collections of instances and examples? Could it be that we learn more from negative rather than from positive reinforcement? Our hedonistic culture holds that learning works best when it seems pleasant and enjoyable—but that discounts the value of experiencing frustrations, failures, and disappointments, either in actuality or in the vicarious forms of forewarnings and admonishments.

Note

Several paragraphs of this text are adapted from sections of *The Society of Mind.*

References

Agnew, N., Brown, J.L. & Lynch, J.G. (1986). Extending the reach of knowledge engineering. *Future Computing Systems, 1*, 115–141.

Minsky, M. (1986). *The Society of Mind.* New York: Simon and Schuster.

Minsky, M. (1991). *The Society of Mind:* A response to four reviews. *Artificial Intelligence, 48*(April), 371–396.

CHAPTER 23

Context, Cognition, and the Future of Intelligent Infostructures

Alain T. Rappaport

Introduction

With the arrival of interactive technologies, nomadic computing devices, wireless communications, multimedia clients and servers, high-performance computing and networking, internetworking and other major technological trends comes a new organizational revolution. It entails the decentralization of management, production and distribution, just-in-time adaptations, and rapid customization of goods. Arguably the most important of those goods has become information itself. It is this age's raw material, processed by human or artificial mills. Organizations, companies and individuals increasingly access, use, process, interpret or create knowledge, locally and globally, using digital information infrastructures. By definition, infrastructures are basic frameworks providing the necessary resources for given activities. Beyond providing information at the fingertips of people, information infrastructures, also called "infostructures" in this chapter, should ultimately be intelligent and enhance decision-making, problem-solving, design, and other knowledge-based activities by participating in extending the human thought processes these activities entail. The goal of this chapter is to expose some principles that the author believes will be involved in designing and building intelligent interactive information infrastructures. It is also to highlight the multidisciplinary nature of this endeavor.

Endowing information infrastructures with the characteristic of being intelligent consists in establishing a form of "cognitive resonance" between them and the minds of their users. In the latter, internal and external factors influencing thoughts constitute the "context" of those thoughts. Etymologically, the term "context" comes from the past participle form in Latin of *contexere*, to weave together (Merriam-Webster 1993). Capturing this context plays a central role in the idea of cognitive resonance. In the first part of this chapter, I address the view of cognition as a complex system, highly interactive, where such a "weaving together" of inputs contributes significantly to defining the course of human thoughts and reasoning. The cognitive resonance should then be attained by making the intelligent infostructures actively participate in the construction of the context. After characterizing the function of context definition as an active cognitive process, I will focus on the technology background necessary to implement artificial agents that would act as cognitive extensions and support human contextualization. The general properties of these agents are addressed. The last section emphasizes the need to take cognitive neuroscience research into account when it comes to designing intelligent agents. New research and perspectives should be important sources of information to derive principles of agent construction. Furthermore, only in this fashion is it possible to extend the view of cognitively relevant agents beyond the classical information-processing paradigm into a new perspective that takes into account the biological, cognitive, behavioral, and social levels of human activities.

Cognition, Representations and Complex Systems

The cognitive mind is grounded in a set of biological structures that interact with one another and with the external world. Having to take these interactions into account prevents us from building any deductive theory of the mind, where an understanding of cognition would result from the sum of the subsystems it involves. Indeed, each functional subsystem does not depend only upon its relations to the others but also on the properties of the whole. Building a bottom-up architecture would require having understood the whole and how the whole is taken into account in each component, an impossible proposition. It is this basic interdependence between the parts and the whole that makes cognition a complex system. This circularity presents a fundamental challenge in the formalization of artificial systems. One answer to this challenge is to build systems that are extensions to the human mind, that is, enhance the value of its functional properties and contribute to a positive change in the emerging intelligent behavior.

Recently, proponents of the "situated cognition" view in artificial intelligence have correctly stated that no mental process can be described outside the mind's rich interactions with the environment (Clancey 1994). However, among the consequences inferred by the more extreme believers, one finds that no representation really exists in the mind, that, to understand human thoughts their full context must be considered, and hence that no symbolic representation can be the basis of artificial reasoning systems or of a theory of high-level cognition, a position that has already been debated (Hayes *et al.* 1994). At first glance, to deny the notion of explicit representation seems akin to saying that, for example, a text can be given virtually any interpretation based on the reader's context or theory. Adopting this perspective leads to a view of systems, including humans, allowing for any arbitrary interpretation of reality, opening the door, in passing, to rather dangerous social, historical, and political positions (Lehman 1991). It denies the existence of some form of irreversibility in the creation and evolution of meaning. Such a capacity for *ad-libitum* interpretations of meaning makes it difficult to envision conceiving any type of intelligent systems in a representation-free approach. In effect, whatever such systems would be doing would be the subject of endless and recursive argument. A text is one representation of its author's thoughts and knowledge, which will in turn be interpreted, to a certain extent only, by the reader. Representations are not separate from knowledge, they are simply one of its facets or forms. While the knowledge content of the mind may be deeply rooted in neuropsychological mechanisms involving both intellectual and emotional circuits of the brain, it is likely shaped by additional processes, such as categorization and generalization, into representations useful for communication. Thus, representations are viewed here as expressions of knowledge, the results of a constructive process coding at a higher level the more elementary mechanisms of thoughts. Speech, text, facial expressions, body languages, and certainly other unexplored internal states of the mind all contribute to the representational level. Context and representations are interdependent; their interactions determine both continuity and changes in behavior.

Whether they are symbolic, as with the use of rules, logics and plans, or neuromimetic, as with the use of neural networks, representations in artificial systems do not have to be either complete or clear; in fact, they are more likely to be partial, subjective and ill-defined. They may also exist for a very limited or extended period of time. Although such limitations and boundaries on one hand seem to impinge upon the realm of possibilities, on the other hand they focus the mind on a universe of comprehensible avenues for thinking; that representations are both limiting and directive is an important trade-off at the origin of the intelligence phenomenon. Much as limited resources constitute an invariant property of cognition, one can venture to suggest that representations are actual emerging properties of the mind as a complex system.

Consider the original theory of complex systems in the field of chemistry. A "bifurcation" in a chemical system is "simply the appearance of a new solution of the equations for some critical value" based on the presence of "fluctuations" at the same or other levels of scale (Prigogine 1980). Put differently, some external factors will force the system to reach a new nonequilibrium stable state. Let us assume, by analogy, that the chemical system in question is now a human thought process, such as a problem-solving or decision-making activity, and that the fluctuations constitute the context in which it is taking place. The intervention of this context would generate new solutions characterized by the reaching of some new state leading to new actions. These solutions are then the equivalent of bifurcation points in the chemical system. Between such bifurcation points, complex chemical systems tend to follow deterministic laws, while in the neighborhood of bifurcation points they follow what appears to be a mix of both deterministic and probabilistic laws. The probabilistic laws are imposed by the uncertainty relating to the state of the environment, the surrounding, or the whole that generates the fluctuations. Thus, by pushing the analogy with cognition further, the mind may follow at times more deterministic paths, based, for example, on learned strategies or well defined problem-solving techniques, while at other times it follows less predictable avenues based on the presence of contextual information. It is quite likely that both types of mechanisms are constantly at play in human activities, with one being more prevalent than the other at times. From these considerations, one can infer that the very introduction of contextual information in an otherwise closed system turns it into a complex one. Since complexity in the physical sense is related to a form of continuing constructivism, the context is thus not only necessary to make sense of our actions relative to the environment, but it may also be the source of subjectivity, imaginary attitudes and creativity. Capturing it somehow is understandably critical to make progress towards the goal of cognitively resonant systems.

Interestingly, some early theoretical work in economics and artificial intelligence relates well to the complex system approach. The "bounded rationality" theory (Simon 1982) states that people reach satisfying rather than optimized solutions in their reasoning processes. In the complex system framework, these "good enough solutions" would be depicted as bifurcations. Conversely, because bifurcations are the result of cross-influences among different levels of scale (the whole and the individual), if cognition is a complex system, it is most likely to work in the same fashion, as a continuum of new, good enough and nonoptimized solutions based on the context of the time. Furthermore, satisfying solutions serve the individual because they do take into account the interactions between the personal and societal levels. By the same reasoning, they also serve society. This fact would suggest that a type of bounded rationality, just as the notion of representation, may be an evolutionary trait of cognition, an emerging property of the mind as a complex system, helping the brain manage the myriad of reality's facets and make decisions.

The complex system approach offers significant opportunities to formalize and build better adapted systems, context-dependent, implementable in a variety of ways, symbolic or nonsymbolic, on top of new computing infrastructures. In the next section, we explore further the role of the context in artificial systems and postulate that contextual mechanisms may be active mental processes intermixed with others.

Context-Scoping

Decision-making in everyday professional activities like medicine, law, management, design, and many others, involves an astonishing number of facts, considerations, theories, or beliefs. In such information-intensive environments, it is quite amazing that humans do make decisions and do solve problems. These processes do occur because there exists, as suggested earlier, a fundamental ability to reduce the overwhelming amount of information into a manageable limited set from which actions are then derived, and, in addition, significant order or structure is already present in the environment. The reduced set of information is established according to certain criteria which make up the context of the reasoning process. The real-time and interactive definition of these criteria is what we call the function of "context-scoping." In short, context-scoping is a dialog and communication with internal and external representations resulting in the identification of the relevant dimensions to deal with a particular situation. It allows to define the relative role of the parts and of the whole of any given situation. Internally, this may be using partial mental images from memory, intuitions (as acquired anticipatory knowledge), emotions (as functional links between the body and the mental level) or a system of beliefs about, for instance, the domain, other individuals or other artificial agents. Externally, it may be through direct interactions with other individuals or agents, or with the physical environment.

This function is intimately related to problem solving and decision making and its importance for a complex system makes the context the result of an active mental process rather than just the instantiation of a static enumeration of criteria. Context-scoping may be different for each individual and thus could explain why two individuals, even experts in their field, may disagree on apparently simple problems based on their experience, beliefs, or emotions, all differences which account for the relativity of the notion of expertise in real-world settings.

Decision-making is the task of choosing between different possible alternatives at a given time. The mechanisms by which humans estimate the likelihood of events in decision-making generally do not follow standard computational or mathematical models (Kahneman and Tversky 1982). Rather, they are based on a set of intuitions, perceptions, past experiences, and even emotional responses which constitute the context of the situation. The context-scoping phase is thus a critical phase, so much so that, once done and the criteria identified, the actual decision-making may be reduced to its simplest form. Problem-solving is a different task from decision-making. It is that of defining the steps that will lead to a particular goal, measuring distances to this goal and establishing subgoals. Humans rarely solve puzzle-like problems with formally optimal solutions; instead they must satisfy themselves of the quality of their reasoning steps in ill-defined problem spaces by reaching the good enough solutions mentioned above. They "feel" the progress they are making towards the goal, more than they can actually measure it since there is no ideal metric (or only an ill-defined one) to measure the distance between subgoals. People attain this sense of progress when reaching a satisfying situation, which, as discussed above, is based on matching the current situation to contextual information, internal and external. Integrating context-scoping with decision-making and problem-solving, as well as other functions such as planning, should lead to systems more fit for the real world. It may be that context-scoping is an invariant property of formalisms applicable to real-world problems, involving higher level and executive functions which filter, select and analyze information prior to engaging in more structured problem-solving activities. At times, these functions may even become sufficient in themselves to decide and act. Thus, activities such as context-scoping, problem-solving or decision-making are part of a continuum of functions that all have their relative and complementary importance.

Among professional activities, medicine has always been a favorite field of inspiration and application for building intelligent systems. The actual practice of clinical medicine is still as much an art as a science, and a reason for this is the extraordinarily large variety of contexts in which to apply the wide body of accepted medical knowledge. Consider the following situation. Economically strained medical care environments foster the use in medical practice of studies called "outcome research." These consist in evaluating the price-performance of certain procedures based on large population studies. Such results, when applied to an individual case, can be at odds with the idiosyncrasies of a given case, thus creating a tension in making the proper decision. The physician has the difficult task of determining the context of the individual case in terms of patient information, timing, economic factors, social dimensions and so on (Feltovitch et al. 1992; Tanenbaum 1993). For example, a physician may have to consider the social situation of the patient before choosing a treatment (if the drug needs to be taken very regularly, can the patient's life pattern allow for this schedule?), or complex contra-indications due to drug interactions or other conditions. Figuring out the "right" attitude from this context may be very difficult. A key activity in this process is to identify the very criteria that will be involved in the decision-making (i.e., context-scoping).

The richness of medical cases represents a challenge not only for the formalization but also for the educational transfer of medical knowledge (Kassirer 1995). The same process of context-scoping is necessary in other professional activities like designing new products, marketing, managing virtual organizations or policy-making. The latter are typically highly context-sensitive, involving large amounts of informal information at different levels of scale. Whatever common knowledge is accepted by the community, there are personal, social, economic, and technical fluctuations or contexts, which, superimposed on an otherwise commonly accepted and standardized body of knowledge, allow for the generation of new and creative solutions.

The question is how to build artificial agents that would help support this form of real-world contextualization. The challenge raised by the importance of the context is as much in the interaction between the system and its environment (including the user) as in the actual AI methodologies, which have been shown to be possibly of a very different nature (symbolic or not) and just as effective for the same problem (Vera and Simon 1993). The answer suggested in this chapter is to build systems based on a better understanding of the informal and personalized knowledge-processing activities involved in human context-scoping. This process will involve, for example, multi-media repositories with content-based search mechanisms, and informally structured databases and software agents with minimal "theories of mind" in them. Before engaging further in the discussion of agents and other knowledge vehicles, it is essential to mention that none of these systems could be built without the proper technology infrastructure. This foundation is provided by a far-reaching phenomenon in progress world-wide, namely the "digital convergence." Contrary to previous computing paradigms, this one is based on *interactivity* and extends its capabilities into virtually all aspects of life, from home to business, from professional activities to education and entertainment. It constitutes a veritable petri-dish for the new generation of intelligent systems.

The Digital Convergence

The technological convergence of computing, media, telecommunications, and consumer electronics and the rise of the information highway are irreversible trends bundled in one phrase: the digital convergence. The last few years have seen a fundamental shift in computing paradigms, from monolithic systems made of proprietary and closed operating systems and applications to decentralized, personalized, networked enterprise-wide architectures. Client-server computing, multimedia, distributed and collaborative systems are forms of computing representative of this new wave. Downsizing, forward engineering, re-engineering (Hammer and Champy 1993) or aligning information technology to business requirements are examples of effective management philosophies. The designs of applications for business, education, entertainment, health care and other fields encompass new functionalities such as broadband, wireless, multimedia and interactive technologies.

Services like distance learning, digital libraries, interactive handbooks, telemedicine, or electronic shopping and banking are being actively developed and deployed. Internetworking links children and adults, students and professionals, universities, governments, organizations, and companies by way of a network of networks, without borders and provides them with instant access to one another's sources of information. The world-wide web (Berners-Lee 1994) transports text, sound, video, applets, and images across all layers of society and cultures; yet, today it is giving only a hint of what lies ahead. Underlying these infrastructures are new software engineering methodologies, most notably object-oriented programming, component-based software, and business modeling tools.

Images, text, and videos do support cognition by themselves. For example, the physician mentioned earlier could request a small video clip of one or several experts on a particular aspect of the situation he/she is facing, and from there decide. In an existing testbed, a teacher can, using an available broadband infrastructure, summarize a day in school on a dedicated television channel that the parents have access to from home, and vice-versa where the parents input information about their child. This simple example requires no specifically intelligent technology: the video infrastructure allows the teacher to transfer the context of the child's school day into the home where then relevant comments, discussions, or other activities can take place. Consider as well a design process during which the critical steps and decisions are somehow recorded by means including images, virtual documents and videos. The latter would then allow designers and engineers to later understand design decisions in their formal, but also, and most importantly, their informal contexts. Such context-inclusive corporate memories would have considerably more value for supporting the on-going business, technical, and educational efforts of firms. In the above applications, the interactive digital infrastructure acts as a vehicle for the preservation and future use of contextual information.

However, despite their rich data types and powerful interconnectivity, digital infostructures by themselves are amorphous. The challenge ahead is to turn them into intelligent ones that act as an extensions of their users' mind, much like a car acts as a powerful extension of our own biological motor system. The following section focuses on how some forms of "agents" could establish the beginning of a cognitive resonance between these infostructures and their users.

Somewhat-Minded Agents

As explained earlier, context-scoping is an active process, based on interactions with the external and internal world. The digital convergence phenomenon has (or will have) the property of being interactive, meaning it will communicate in two directions, to and from each participant or "agent." An agent is an entity that somehow transforms or processes the information and is to a certain degree "minded" in that it embodies *some* theory of mind. On one side of the spectrum, humans are fully minded agents. In scoping out context, they interact with their internal world (e.g., memory, feelings), with one or several other agents (e.g., knowing their beliefs, understanding their intents), and with other aspects of the environment. Towards the opposite side of the spectrum, a software agent consisting of just a mere video clip object is a most simple form of knowledge-containing agent. More sophisticated agents with a minimal theory of mind may be endowed with some representation levels for concepts such as beliefs and intentions. These software agents are what we call "somewhat-minded agents" in that they have some theory of mind in their own constructs. They are not designed to be themselves cognitive agents in the image of human cognition, but to subserve the human user's cognition by extending its capabilities. They are envisioned to communicate between them and collectively constitute a type of society with resulting social attitudes and choices. As a society, these somewhat-minded agents should form a complex system as well.

Agents are traditionally delegated and entrusted with tasks like classification, planning or scheduling, although there are now several definitions and approaches (Bradshaw 1997). Some are designed to learn about regularities in human-machine interfaces. In the majority of cases, the agent is a passive entity receiving requests, carrying out tasks, and then returning some result. For example, an entertainment selection agent has knowledge that is based on past user-system interactions or social filtering (Maes 1994). The category of agent that can support context-scoping is more interventionist and interactive than it is a passive executant. These agents raise questions; they try to discern the intellectual and emotional context of the user's request at this time; they confront opinions and beliefs. They could embody organizational knowledge and thus expose possible decision criteria of that nature. They may be aware of strategic directions and inclinations. They may know of the invariant properties of the domain and check against those. They could learn by instruction, by analogy, by doing, or by induction or abduction, using additional computational resources such as multi-dimensional analysis, statistical techniques and so on.

The following general concepts are proposed for a discussion of internal mechanisms of somewhat-minded agents. This is not an exhaustive list, but it highlights some of the key capabilities necessary to perform their function in a space of informal and personalized knowledge.

- Their objectives are to support the construction of a local rationality for decision-making or problem-solving. In doing so, they help define the criteria (context-scoping) involved in the user's activity and have access to the necessary resources.

- They must be able to deal with incomplete information, which implies avoiding information-intensive techniques in their design (such as decision-theoretic algorithms), in favor of more compiled and efficient forms of knowledge. However, their computational methods could also evolve from weak, or domain-independent, to strong, or domain-specific, methods by learning.
- They should use personalized default theories and nonmonotonic logical languages. Their functioning is thus not necessarily deducible by others. In other terms, they would have their own personal logics, evolving with both time and additional knowledge. However, common representations and channels of communication should emerge from dealing with common constraints at the domain, social, or cultural levels.
- They can live with inconsistencies. In other words, their purpose is more argumentative than conclusive. Hence, they can provide multiple potential solutions to the same situation.
- They have personalized conflict resolution mechanisms. Thus, two somewhat-minded agents may not use the same method to choose, for instance, between two contradictory conclusions, raised by their own reasoning or that of others.
- They can use social choices based on multi-agent cooperations. These choices may contribute to their own individual choices.
- It must be possible to invoke them in an event-driven and opportunistic manner.

Hence, somewhat-minded agents are envisioned to be simple and as little computationally intensive as possible. The main reason for simplicity is that they need to be custom-made, and simplicity is a strong incentive for actually building and maintaining them. The simplicity could reside at the development tools level. Another way to describe these agents is as extensions of human short-term memory and attentional processes, or additional resources for determining the context of the situation and the direction to take from a particular bifurcation point. Different approaches may already be relevant to such constructions, from nonmonotonic logics (Doyle 1982; Ford 1994) to primitives better adapted than, for example, probabilistic or pattern-matching based reasoning, to capturing knowledge from compiled, agenda-based reasoning (Rappaport 1988). Regarding beliefs, even an elementary representation based on distributed objects with "belief models" may constitute a type of early implementation (Nagao and Takeuchi 1994). Regarding collective information, methods performing consensus or statistical analysis may be attached to a somewhat-minded agent to generate social choices. Incidental learning agents can help present motivating information (Boy 1995). Other fields of study such as story telling systems are relevant as well. The design and implementation of technologies such as somewhat-minded agents are rather creative processes, forcing students of artificial intelligence and software engineering to leave behind the rather comfortable setting of well-bound problem spaces and formal logic, ill-adapted to representing the real-world.

These kinds of design characteristics should eventually be translated into actual enabling technologies. Recent progress in software and networking environments (Berners-Lee 1994; Microsoft 1994; Sun Microsystems 1995) provides the fertile ground for such realizations. The general trend heads towards the customization or personalization of software solutions, the on-demand construction of applications, and the management of common and individual software semantics on distributed and interactive infrastructures. All in all, it is becoming possible, in this software context, to perform a "casual integration" of knowledgeable or somewhat-minded agents in new digital infrastructures. The next section explores another fundamental dimension to take into account in the design of somewhat-minded agents and related technologies, namely the rapidly evolving understanding of the biological underpinnings of human cognitive and emotional functions.

The Cognitive Convergence

Cognitive science has evolved considerably in the past few years. The emerging paradigm of cognition is based on data, theories and models coming from psychology, neuroscience, cognitive science, medical sciences, social sciences and other related fields. These data converge towards a view of the human brain as a complex system, distributed, dependent on its internal structure and functions, the external world and the body, and where timing of interactions, approximations of concepts and adaptation to change are as important as the physical wiring. In short, the "cognitive convergence" yields a view of the mind as an open system acting in context rather than that of a well-programmed and closed black box. The purpose of this section is to highlight through some examples the importance of taking cognitive neuroscience into consideration for the design of agents, since it provides us with fundamental insights into the functioning of the mind.

The large majority of cognitive neuroscience results clearly confirm the nature of the mind as a unique property of the brain's biological structures. The complexity of the neural code and the vast individual variations make each brain unique. Recently however, several approaches, such as dispositional representations (Damasio 1994), representational redescriptions (Karmiloff-Smith 1995), and studies such as those on cortical representations do tend to support the notion of representations in the brain. For example, there are populations of neurons coding for given parameters of central nervous system functions such as hand movement (Schwartz 1994). The notion of representation in this case emerges from the finding that a population vector obtained by spatial transformation of the measured neuronal activity does precede the actual movement in well-defined circumstances. The representation thus acts as a predictive mechanism. Whether similar mechanisms are at play in higher-level functions is an interesting question. In the remainder of this section I mention other results which can be related to the question of designing intelligent infostructures as extensions of cognition.

Consider the following experiment on cognitive deficits in autistic children (Frith 1991). It involved the use of a puppet show with two characters, Sally and Ann, hence the name "Sally-Ann experiment." There are also three objects on the stage: a marble, a box and a basket. Ann watches Sally put the marble in the box. Then Ann leaves and while she is away, Sally moves the marble from the box to the basket. Ann comes back. At this point, each child is asked to say where Ann is going to look for the marble. Normal children (at four years of age), or even those with lower intellectual capacities such as Down's syndrome children (age five or six years), will correctly say that Ann should be expected to look for the marble in the box, while autistic children of a mean age of nine years will generally say it will be sought in the basket. One possible interpretation of this result is that there exists a cognitive breakdown in autistic children defined as an inability to generate and store higher-order knowledge, that is, knowledge about beliefs rather than facts (first-order knowledge). These children cannot conceptualize the false belief of Ann; there is no construction of mental models of other beings. The experiment lends support to a theory of separate representation and processing of higher-order knowledge in the brain, which does not imply a specific location. A representational deficit could contribute significantly to explain the communication disorders of autism and the acultural behavior of autistic children (Tomasello *et al.* 1993). Indeed, without mental models of others, it is not possible to communicate with them on this higher-order level.

The Sally-Ann experiment points to an apparently well-defined deficit. Would the same deficit in an artificial agent generate the same type of overall breakdown? If agents and other structures cannot build even a very elementary theory of mind, can they contribute to an adaptive, culturally-relevant infostructure? If such elementary mental models are necessary for effective communication, imagination, and socialization attitudes, interactions with an agent lacking this property might be ineffective. Imagine, for example, that the marble is now a document modified by Sally during a teleconference session while Ann is out of the room for a moment. When Ann comes back into the session, an agent at Ann's service only aware of the document's contents but not of her absence could not do much to help Ann. It would need to detect a contradiction between Ann's beliefs about the document and its new form. This example is a straightforward transposition, but scenarios abound where agents with some beliefs would be much more powerful than agents with none. To summarize, this research on autistic children highlights how a specific deficit may be sufficient to trigger general communication and socialization problems, a result that may be of important value to design somewhat-minded agents. As it turns out, it also appears that autism is not only related to a theory of mind problem but also to an inability to integrate contextual information as part of the normal information-processing functions. This particular deficit points to problems in executive functions which cover a wide range of cognitive abilities and will certainly be the focus of further research (Happé 1995). The latter could shed new light on the biological basis of context-scoping functions, and help refine computational extensions of the latter.

On another front, the use of noninvasive imaging techniques, although still in its infancy, has opened up a new era in the study of human cognitive functions. Tools such as functional magnetic resonance imaging (fMRI) allow researchers to investigate the relations between certain tasks and the activation of specific cortical or other brain areas (Sergent 1994), to verify models of attentional mechanisms (Posner and Dehaene 1994), explore visual imagery (Roland and Gulyás 1994) or to investigate the critical spatio-temporal properties of brain activity (Heinze *et al.* 1994). For example, the involvement of the prefrontal cortex in human working memory can be confirmed by fMRI studies (D'Esposito *et al.* 1995). The same study shows that different subregions of the prefrontal cortex are activated in various individuals, indicating that the underlying cognitive system is distributed and variable. How are all those studies relevant? Briefly stated, we may learn which functions, types of memories, and emotional circuits are involved in a given type of activity. By studying the relative activation of regions during mental or physical activities, we can learn about the role of motor or perceptual functional areas in the conceptualization of the same functions, providing new insights on human-computer interactions. Understanding how we perceive high level emotional cues can lead down the path of new revolutionary interfaces or computer-generated metaphors; while establishing neurological processes, such as the relations between declarative and emotional learning in the brain (Bechara *et al.* 1995), helps understand the way we interact with the world and categorize information. Conversely, the use of digital technologies might help understand and correct human dysfunctions. For example, the use of parametrized speech-processing techniques included in a computer "game" environment might be able to ameliorate both temporal processing deficits (Merzenich *et al.* 1996) and language comprehension (Tallal *et al.* 1996) in language-learning impaired children. As results of this type become confirmed and new developments in interactive systems take them into account, it is possible to foresee the emergence of a better resonance between human and machines in their interactions.

Studies have shown that there may be a normative perception of beauty in humans and that certain cues are fundamental in perceiving emotional states of mind. For example, highly attractive facial characteristics appear to differ from those of an average composite (Perrett *et al.* 1994). Thus, perception of beauty seems driven by patterns of preferences, or representations, which are quite specific. Such results could have consequences in user interface design or in visually representing an emotional context by modulating facial traits, between average and attractive, or other characteristics where the same difference effect with averageness may apply. As another example, it appears that when performing an apparently complex task such as steering a car along a curve, the brain uses in fact a very simple cue, namely the tangent from the car to the inside edge of the road, to which the eyes keep coming back (Land 1994). The strategy used is thus one of higher predictability based on finding the invariants of the perceptual array. The visual context is reduced to a minimum, and the brain can thus time-share with other activities. This result is naturally of importance for those building autonomous vehicles, but it also raises interesting questions in the world of somewhat-minded agents which, if they do not need to follow curves like a car, how do they navigate in complex information spaces? Could somewhat-minded agents (which we could call "smagents") learn to detect invariants to keep certain tasks easy while having time to process other important functions? Are there individual and social invariants that can be represented and help build smagents that can discern interesting traits and criteria? Could smagents carry out some of these "tricks" on large amounts of information, thereby pushing the envelope of their ability to extend our own capacities? Can such capabilities be customized or personalized by designing individual logical languages?

Perhaps one of the most significant recent outcomes in neuroscience has been the verification at the biological level of the importance of the first three years of life in the formation of the mind. These years constitute the period when the post-natal circuitry of the brain is selectively established, in a manner highly dependent upon the interactions with the external world. The resulting structure then has a life-long influence. While the enhanced cortical plasticity at an early age allows for the formation of key cognitive categories, adult cortical plasticity is mostly limited to modulatory functions of already assembled circuits (Singer 1995). This theory is the emerging synthesis resulting from a number of different scientific studies over the past decade and should have implications reaching well beyond the scientific community (Carnegie Corporation 1994). It re-emphasizes both the unique biological nature of human cognition and its continuous dependence upon the environment, or to put it differently, the context.

A Multi-Disciplinary Effort

The element of circularity between the individuals and their social and physical environments is a cornerstone of behavior and intelligence. As further illustrations, it has been suggested that a society with a certain justice system implies some sense of that same justice in its individuals (Rawles 1971), or that a society aware of and concerned with long-term social costs can better define the value of individual transactions and therefore better plan the future (Coase 1991). Problems such as that of social and individual choices (Arrow 1951) also concern the relation between scale levels and are relevant to agent behaviors. These types of contingencies show how information and knowledge flow among levels of scale—and how decisions we make every day result from a tension between our relative personal knowledge or expertise in a field and the local and global contexts of the situations attended to. People reason analytically, intuitively and even emotionally, using personal, professional, and social arguments. Intelligent infostructures as conceived of in this chapter should extend these different dimensions of human behavior.

The question we have been addressing in this chapter is not how to build systems that resemble humans; rather, it is to build cognitive extensions of ourselves and to improve the means by which we can leverage our intellectual, perceptual and emotional abilities using digital infostructures. Nor is the goal to normalize and standardize means of interactivity between humans and machines. On the contrary, these future intelligent infostructures, armed with higher-level knowledge and human-based interactions, can be viewed as instruments to refine our own capacity to learn and associate contextual information. They should contribute to individual creativity, imagination and initiative. The ability to represent logics of different types that live with inconsistencies, to integrate contextual information from different levels of scale in order to find good enough solutions or to implement even a very minimal theory of mind in software agents, are all powerful seeds towards more cognitively resonant intelligent infostructures.

Clearly, designing and building future intelligent information infrastructures is a multi-disciplinary effort. It lies at the cross-roads of artificial intelligence, computer science, digital technologies, and cognitive neuroscience, and will without a doubt overlap with other disciplines such as economics, social sciences and education. The outcome should be new and significant means to enable the future.

Acknowledgments

Many thanks to the editors for their critical comments.

References

Arrow, K.J. (1951). *Social Choice and Individual Values*. New Haven, CT: Yale University Press.

Berners-Lee, T. (1994). The World-Wide Web. *Communications of the ACM, 37*, 76-82.

Bechara, A., Tranel D., Damasio H., Adolphs, R., Rockland, C. & Damasio, A.R. (1995). Double dissociation of conditioning and declarative knowledge relative to the amygdala and hippocampus in humans. *Science, 269*, 5227:1115-1118.

Boy, G. (1995). Agent-oriented interaction in computer-supported networks for teachers. *Proceedings of the 9th Banff Knowledge Acquisition for Knowledge-Based Systems Workshop*. Banff: Canada.

Bradshaw, J.M. (1997). *Software Agents*. Menlo Park, CA: AAAI Press/The MIT Press.

Carnegie Corporation of New York (1994). *Starting Points: Meeting the Needs of Our Youngest Children*. New York: Carnegie Corporation of New York.

Clancey, W.J. (1993). Situated action: a neuropsychological interpretation. *Cognitive Science, 17*, 87-116.

Coase, R.H. (1989). *The Firm, the Market and the Law*. Chicago: University of Chicago Press.

Damasio, A. (1994). *Descartes' Error: Emotion, Reason and the Human Brain*. New York: Grosset-Putnam.

D'Esposito, M., Detre, J.A., Alsop, D.C., Shin, R.K., Atlas, S. & Grossman, M. (1995). The neural basis of the central executive system of working memory. *Nature, 378*, 279-281.

Doyle, J. (1982). *Some theories of reasoned assumptions: An essay in rational psychology*. Pittsburgh: Department of Computer Science, Carnegie-Mellon University.

Feltovich, P.J., Coulson, R.L., Spiro, R.J. & Dawson-Saunders, B.K. (1992). Knowledge application and transfer for complex tasks in ill-structured domains: Implications for instruction and testing in biomedicine. In D. Evans & V. Patel (Eds.), *Advanced Models of Cognition for Medical Training and Practice*. Berlin: Springer-Verlag.

Ford, K. (1994). Personal communication on "soft logics."

Frith, U., Morton, J. & Leslie, A.M. (1991). The cognitive basis of a biological disorder: Autism. *Trends in Neuroscience, 14*, 10:433-438.

Hayes, P.J., Ford, K.M. & Agnew, N. (1994). On babies and bathwater: A cautionary tale. *AI Magazine, 15*, 15-26.

Heinze, H.J., Mangun, G.R., Burchert, W., Hinrichs, H., Scholz, M., Münte, T.F., Gös, A., Scherg, M., Johannes, S., Hundeshagen, H., Gazzaniga, M.S. & Hillyard, S.A. (1994). Combined spatial and temporal imaging of brain activity during visual selective attention in humans. *Nature, 372*, 543-546.

Hammer, M. & Champy, J. (1993). *Reengineering the Corporation: A Manifesto for Business Revolution*. New York: Harper Business.

Happé, F. (1995). *Autism*. Cambridge, MA: Harvard University Press.

Kahneman, D. & Tversky, A. (1982). Subjective probability: A judgment for representativeness. In D. Kahneman & A. Tversky (Eds.), *Judgment Under Uncertainty: Heuristics and Biaises* (pp. 32-47). Cambridge: Cambridge University Press.

Karmiloff-Smith, A. (1995). *Beyond Modularity. A Developmental Perspective on Cognitive Science*. Cambridge, MA: MIT Press.

Kassirer, J.P. (1995). Teaching problem-solving—how are we doing? *New England Journal of Medicine, 332,* 22:1507-1509.

Land, M.F. & Lee, D.N. (1994). Where we look when we steer. *Nature, 369,* 742-744.

Lehman, D. (1991). *Signs of the Times: Deconstruction and the Fall of Paul de Man.* New York: Simon and Schuster.

Mayes, P. (1994). Agents that reduce work and information overload. *Communications of the ACM, 37,* 31-40.

Merzenich, M.M., Jenkins, W.M., Johnston, P., Schreiner, C., Miller, S. & Tallal, P. (1996). Temporal processing deficits of language-learning impaired children ameliorated by training. *Science, 271,* 77-81.

Merriam-Webster. (1993). *Merriam-Webster's Collegiate Dictionary.* Springfield, MA: Merriam-Webster.

Microsoft. (1994). *OLE: Component Software Solutions,* Report 098-56457.

Nagao, K. & Takeuchi, A. (1994). Social interaction: Multimodal conversation with social agents. *Proceedings of the Twelfth National Conference on Artificial Intelligence, 1,* 22-28. Menlo Park, CA: AAAI Press / The MIT Press.

Perrett, D.I., May, K.A. & Yoshikawa, S. (1994). Facial shape and judgement of female attractiveness. *Nature, 368,* 239-241.

Posner, M. & Dehaene, S. (1994). Attentional networks. *Trends in Neuroscience, 17,* 75-79.

Prigogine, I. (1980). *From Being to Becoming: Time and Complexity in the Physical Sciences.* New York: W.H. Freeman.

Rappaport, A.T. (1988). Cognitive primitives. *International Journal of Man-Machine Studies, 29,* 733-747.

Rawls, J. (1971). *A Theory of Justice.* Cambridge, MA: Harvard University Press.

Roland, P.E. & Guylás, B. (1994). Visual imagery and visual representation. *Trends in Neuroscience, 17,* 281-287.

Schwartz, A.B. (1994). Direct cortical representation of drawing. *Science, 265,* 540-542.

Sergent, J. (1994). Brain-imaging studies of cognitive functions. *Trends in Neuroscience, 17,* 221-227.

Simon, H.A. (1982). *Models of Bounded Rationality: Behavioral Economics and Business Organization.* Cambridge, MA: MIT Press.

Singer, W. (1995). Development and plasticity of cortical processing architectures. *Science, 270,* 758-764.

Sun Microsystems. (1995). *The Java language.* White paper. Mountain View, CA: Sun Microsystems.

Tallal, P., Miller, S., Bedi, G., Byma, G., Wang, X., Nagarajan, C., Schreiner, C., Jenkins, W.M. & Merzenich, M.M. (1996). Language comprehension in language-learning impaired children improved with acoustically modified speech. *Science, 271,* 81-84.

Tanenbaum, S.J. (1993). What physicians know. *New England Journal of Medicine, 329,* 17: 1268-70.

Tomasello, M., Kruger, A.C. & Ratner, H.H. (1993). Cultural learning. *Behavior and Brain Sciences, 16,* 495-510.

Vera, A.H. & Simon, H.A. (1993). Situated action: A symbolic interpretation. *Cognitive Science, 17,* 7-48.

Recapitulation & Synthesis

CHAPTER 24

A General Framework for Conceiving of Expertise and Expert Systems in Context

Robert R. Hoffman, Paul J. Feltovich & Kenneth M. Ford

Introduction

In this chapter we present a general framework for the issues and themes raised in the other chapters of this volume. [Author(s) references are for this volume unless otherwise annotated.] The justification for a framework goes well beyond the need to be coherent in presenting a retrospective analysis of the chapters. The issues raised in the volume are broad in scope; therefore the general framework we offer is correspondingly broad in its potential applicability. In this volume we find an expression of some of the perennial issues in cognitive psychology, sociology of scientific knowledge, and artificial intelligence (AI). Issues concern, among other things, the nature of knowledge, the nature of context, and the limitations and prospects of knowledge-based systems. One theme that makes this volume an interdisciplinary microcosm involves what could be collectively called "contextualist" approaches to expertise and expert systems. A second theme is methodology in the analysis of expertise and in the development of expert systems.

After briefly discussing the themes and issues, we present the framework in an attempt to organize and illuminate them. The framework builds upon Jenkins' (1979) "tetrahedral model" of learning. We elaborate upon this model, making it applicable to the cognitive psychology of expertise, and then expanding it and integrating it with the concerns of AI and expert system researchers. Along the way, we show how each chapter in this volume—the approach of the authors, their research or system development efforts, the issues raised, etc.—can be regarded as falling into one or another variation on the expanded tetrahedral model.

Why Seek a General Framework?

This question needs to be addressed from three perspectives, the psychological, the sociological, and the computational. The perspectives involve history: What has been accomplished in a field and how the accomplishments have led to recent debates and fresh ideas.

The Background in Psychology

For some years cognitive psychologists have been conducting research on various aspects of expertise—expert-novice differences, training, memory and categorization, problem solving, perceptual skill, heuristics and biases, and so on. Expertise has been studied in domains as diverse as chess playing (a favorite), piano playing, computer programming, livestock judging, and the classification of archaeological artifacts (see Chi, Glaser and Farr 1988; Ericsson and Smith 1991; Hoffman 1992).

Expertise has been conceived as being a matter of:

* knowledge (e.g., knowledge extent and organization),
* special reasoning processes (e.g., domain-bound heuristics),
* development (e.g., expert-novice differences, life-span development),
* intelligence (e.g., measures of individual differences in ability and creativity; see Ericsson and Charness),
* practice and skilled performance (e.g., automaticity; see Ericsson and Charness).

Most recently, expertise has been conceived as a prototype-like concept that combines all of these features and phenomena to varying degrees in various domains at various times (see Sternberg). Even physiology and motor skills have come under the cognitivist's microscope, especially in performance domains (music, dancing, typing; see Ericsson and Charness). The progression toward expertise can entail considerable physiological adaptation. It can also involve very subtle adaptations, such as the diamond-cutter's coordination of breath pauses with taps of the mallet that must be precise down to the millimeter (Kaplan 1936).

Representing and summarizing some of the best research on the cognition of experts is the chapter by Patel and Ramoni focusing on the domain of medical diagnosis. They used a task in which experts have to explain their diagnoses and a data analysis method using graphs of causal relations and reasoning sequences. Patel and her colleagues replicated for this domain the finding that experts possess extensive and highly-organized declarative knowledge. One of their specific results is pertinent to expert systems engineering. This involves the relative contributions of forward, backward, and causal reasoning, and especially the ways in which uncertainty can trigger a re-evaluation of nonsalient cues and a shift in reasoning (from forward to backward and vice versa), on the one hand, or can relate to errors and inaccuracies in diagnosis, on the other.

Feltovich, Spiro and Coulson carry this sort of research a step further by looking at the ways in which reasoning sequences can be either flexible or inflexible. Based on numerous experiments in which expert and trainee physicians reason about clinical cases, Feltovich et al. have amassed a number of observations showing that when confronted with "garden-path" or misleading cases, experts, and especially trainees, tend to oversimplify their explanations, restrict the scope of explanatory principles, regard continuous phenomena as discrete and dynamic phenomena as static, and so on. The characteristics of cases or situations in which inflexibility is likely to appear suggest ways in which training might instill flexibility and overcome rigidity.

Cognitive research on expertise sometimes involves taking a basic phenomenon from the psychology laboratory and investigating its manifestation in the case of expertise. Illustrating this is the series of experiments reported by Seifert, Patalano, Hammond and Converse that bear on classical findings involving "encoding specificity" (Tulving and Thompson 1973). College students (experts in dormitory behavior) were presented with a problem involving the search of a friend's dormitory room, and a set of situations and goals (e.g., putting back a poster that accidentally falls off the wall, taking off a ring belonging to your friend that you slipped on your finger). Problem situations also included reference to a number of objects encountered in the search of the dorm room (e.g., a jar of Vaseline under the sink, a roll of tape). After reading descriptions of the problems, some of the participants had to generate plans with the aid of hints ("If you could only lubricate your finger … If you only had some Vaseline, you could…"). The participants were next given a memory task in which they were presented descriptions of objects that might relate to the goals (e.g., a jar of Vaseline, a roll of tape) or that might not (e.g., a comb). Participants were asked if any of the goals came to mind.

As one might expect, reminding was facilitated by the plan generation condition—even by objects that fit the suggested plan but that had not been mentioned in the problem statement or given as hints in the plan generation phase (e.g., "butter" rather than "Vaseline"). Objects that could satisfy the goal by some other plan (e.g., "ice cubes") were less effective reminders of the goals. As a problem situation is encountered and plans are generated, the elements of the situation are likely to be encoded in memory in terms of the type of plan. This result can be taken as a demonstration of encoding specificity. Preplanning needs to be balanced with the unpredictability of situations (see Feltovich, Spiro and Coulson). Hence, "predictive encoding" is not entirely specific to the preplan but is specific to the *type* of preplan, thus allowing for the recognition of opportunities.

The chapter by Zeitz reviews much of the work on the cognition of experts in the paradigm of studies of the development of expertise and expert-novice differences. Beginning with the established finding that experts reason at a conceptual level, she argues that experts' problem solving involves representations that integrate abstract concepts with the more literal or specific features of particular problems, forming an "intermediate" level of abstraction. She then pursues the fundamental question of how abstract and intermediate-level conceptualization play a functional role in problem solving (organization and integration of information, facilitation of memory retrieval, perception of relations and analogies, etc.) and why abstract and intermediate-level representations can sometimes detract from effective problem solving (e.g., automaticity can lead to inflexibility, false recognition errors, etc.) (see also Feltovich et al. and Patel and Ramoni). This feeds into practical educational issues, that is, the question of how to facilitate the novice's acquisition of intermediate-level problem representations.

Ignorance is Blitz

As Sternberg points out, much of the psychological work, including most of the developmental work, has not touched on (let alone grappled with) issues that fall more in the social realm—the social psychology and sociology of expertise, the social construction of expertise, the role of expertise in successful technological innovation, and so on. One reason is simple—cognitive psychologists have been interested in studying cognition. Among the heroes are Adriaan De Groot (1965) for his classic studies of expertise in chess. Also, Karl Duncker's (1945) model of problem solving (see Newell 1985) is echoed in modern psychological theories and AI systems in which there is a cycle involving hypothesis (or mental model) formation, hypothesis testing, and hypothesis refinement. Stern and Luger describe an expert system for semiconductor failure analysis that involves this cycle (with some flourishes).

In the bulk of the cognitive research on expertise, the implicit belief has been that the social aspects can usually be safely ignored when one is conducting experiments. For example, a study that probes the memory organization of expert physicists can measure such things as recall, recognition or reaction time; it can use such methods as protocol analysis; and it needs to control or manipulate such variables as skill, experience level and problem type. At least at the outset, such research can safely (one hopes) ignore questions having to do with such factors as social, motivational, emotional, and individual difference influences in the community of physicists. It can also safely ignore the problem of operationally defining expertise and specifying landmarks along the continuum of expertise, since experts in many significant domains can readily be found (e.g., physics professors, chess Masters, operational forecasters, fighter pilots, radiologists, etc.).

The Fresh Perspectives from Sociology, Ethnomethodology and Ergonomics

Contrasting with the cognitive approach have been studies of expertise in the manner of cognitive anthropology, so-called "everyday cognition" or "cognition in the wild" (Hutchins 1995; Lave 1988; Scribner 1984; Suchman 1993), spanning domains ranging from ship navigation to farming in Peru. The work has reinforced some hypotheses about expertise:

- Knowledge and skill are highly domain-bound (e.g., boat builders in the Paulawat Islands use the canoe as their basic unit for measuring volume; dairy inventory workers use the "case stack" as a unit for counting, etc.).

- Even so-called experts can be rigid, but the most proficient reasoning is very flexible, even in domains where the outsider might expect to find just routine tasks and procedures (e.g., wholesale delivery, warehouse inventory management, office clerking, and product assembly, etc.).

- There are individual differences in reasoning style and interpersonal social skills, and these play a significant role in the exercise of expertise.

Fitting the spirit of "everyday cognition" is the considerable amount of research that places itself under the new banner of Naturalistic Decision Making (NDM; see Zsambok and Klein, in press). These investigations have focused on domains such as military command and control, fire fighting, clinical nursing, design engineering, computer programming, and business management (see Shalin, Geddes, Bertram, Szczepkowski and DuBois). NDM research has made significant contributions to our understanding of the nature of expertise, especially the role of perceptual skill as opposed to declarative knowledge, and the importance of situational assessment in many domains of expertise.

While the main historical roots of NDM are in human factors psychology and the specialization calling itself Judgment and Decision Making (as one might expect, given the sorts of domains that have been studied), the NDM researchers seem to have come around to a contextualist viewpoint. The research has generated ideas about how to generate effective knowledge elicitation methods for any given domain, ideas about how to make decision aids and information processing systems more usable in operational contexts, and has led to a deeper appreciation of the need to develop methods for the study of team performance rather than the performance of individuals.

Dovetailing with the studies of cognition in the wild is the discipline calling itself the sociology of scientific knowledge (e.g., Collins; Fleck and Williams 1996; Knorr-Cetina 1981; Knorr-Cetina and Mulkay 1983). This work has involved detailed analyses of science as it is practiced (e.g., the history of the development of new lasers and of gravity wave detectors). The research has shown ways in which scientific reasoning deviates from normative (e.g., hypothetico-deductive) methods, the role of social consensus in decisions about what makes for proper practice, problems in the attempt to transmit skill in the construction of apparatus from one laboratory to another, and apparent failures in science or in the attempt to apply new technology. (For an alternative interpretation of these findings, see Agnew, Ford and Hayes.)

In this approach, cognitive variables are not directly investigated in ways characteristic of the psychology laboratory. Indeed, cognitive variables are not even singled out as being somehow uniquely (or solely) cognitive in nature. Rather, they are regarded as part of a complex and dynamic mix which includes social, cultural, and historical aspects…but these aspects too are not regarded as "isolated" variables or "factors" (see Collins).

This work has led some scholars to an appreciation of how skilled action depends upon its broader context, the ways in which expertise relates to power politics, the ways it may or may not give rise to successful technological innovation, the ways in which expertise may or may not relate to effective social policy-making, and the implications of all this for such things as the management of technological change.

The Background in AI

In the field of AI, systems developers have for some years gone about eliciting knowledge from experts, and then implementing representations of the knowledge as "expert systems." Some of the landmarks in that work are described in Shadbolt and O'Hara. In the years since the seminal work, the AI community has developed an appreciation of many issues, including:

- What it means to explain. A print-out of cryptic rule sequences is not very explanatory (see Alty 1987; Clancey 1983; Ford, Cañas and Adams-Webber 1991; Shadbolt and O'Hara).
- What it means for a system to be usable and to provide good explanations—it must be domain- and context-specific, if not task-specific (Bobrow, Mittal and Stefik 1989; Collins; Shadbolt and O'Hara). Hence, "good" expert systems often are not transportable things (see Agnew *et al.*); they each have their "ecological niche" (see O'Hara and Shadbolt).
- What it means to use a system effectively—the actions that are needed to repair or overcome system limitations, people's unwarranted attributions of system capability, etc. (See Collins; Lerch, Prietula and Kulik.)
- What it takes to acquire the knowledge of experts. It can take more effort to elicit expert knowledge than to actually build an expert system. Background domain knowledge must be extracted from texts, documents, etc. Next, experts must be interviewed, and so on. This led to a major frustration of knowledge engineers, the so-called knowledge acquisition bottleneck (see Cullen and Bryman 1988; Hoffman 1987).

Also spanning the first generation of expert systems work there have been vigorous challenges to the enterprise, cast in terms of possible differences of human and computer capabilities (see Bringsjord; Collins) and in terms of challenges about new positive directions (see Minsky; Rappaport). Debate continues on the theoretical foundations of AI, including the validity of the symbol system hypothesis (e.g., Davis 1989; Dreyfus 1993; Vera and Simon 1993). Some feel that many of the debates are silly (see Hayes and Ford 1995a), but in any event one hopes that the challenges will ultimately lead to new approaches and ideas (see Rappaport; Reddy 1988).

Unfortunately, the challenges to AI and the frustrations of knowledge engineers led to a cottage industry criticizing expert systems for being inherently brittle and fragile, user-unfriendly, devilishly intent on replacing experts, distastefully symbolic, disembodied (whatever that means), reductionist (that's always naughty), and even emblematic of the fundamental errors of Western Thought. There is one kernel of wheat that can be de-chaffed from these criticisms—the lack of appreciation of the socially situated and personally constructed nature of expertise. If, as we suggested above, the psychological research on expertise has largely ignored the social aspects of expertise, the knowledge engineering community (with a few notable exceptions) has, until recently, been pleased to follow suit.

Fresh Perspectives in AI

Lately, however, the field of AI has been infused with ideas from "pragmatic constructivism" (Ford and Adams-Webber 1992; Ford, Bradshaw, Adams-Webber and Agnew 1993) and from what is known as the "situated cognition" view (see Clancey). These outlooks have been motivated by empirical findings and by practical issues arising in AI, the things that expert systems engineers had learned the hard way (Bobrow, Mittal and Stefik 1986). First-generation expert system technology seemed to be useful only when applied in highly restricted domains for highly specific tasks (Alty 1987). Some systems were fragile or brittle not because of some mysterious or fundamental shortcoming associated with their symbolic or computational natures (as many have mistakenly claimed). Rather, the systems often had limitations that were due to the fact that expertise is itself often brittle and fragile (Agnew et al.). In addition, it came to be recognized that systems needed to be designed so as to fit with the social-interactional aspects of collaborative work (Greenbaum and Kyng 1991; Suchman 1991).

From the pragmatic constructivists, the knowledge acquisition community has adopted the notion that the knowledge acquisition process is best understood as a modeling activity in which the knowledge engineer and domain expert collaborate to produce a functional (though fallible) model of the latter's domain of expertise (Ford and Adams-Webber 1992; Ford and Bradshaw 1993; Gammack and Anderson 1990; Hoffman 1994; LaFrance; Shadbolt and O'Hara; O'Hara and Shadbolt).

Shadbolt and O'Hara, and O'Hara and Shadbolt, describe the process of this modelling, called "knowledge acquisition." In computer terminology this means knowledge elicitation plus instantiation or implementation. Expert knowledge is not just extracted and then programmed as a set of symbolic rules. Rather, knowledge acquisition begins with an analysis of requirements and documentation of tasks or procedures. This supports the construction of an initial conceptual model of the domain. This initial model is then assessed by experts and progressively refined, as described next.

In many modern expert systems development projects, the so-called second generation of expert systems work, the second phase of modeling is supported by computer systems that serve as "toolkits" to assist the process of knowledge acquisition. Using an automated knowledge acquisition system, input data can go more or less directly into an instantiated form. O'Hara and Shadbolt describe many of these shells, which go by acronyms such as CSRL, JIGSAW, TIPS, KADS, SOAR, and VITAL.

The next stage is to go from the conceptual model to a design model, that is, a design for a system architecture that would implement expert reasoning. Typically, the system includes representations of domain concepts, a rule base of inferences, and schemes for heuristic classification that relate problem representations to goals. Shadbolt and O'Hara discuss some of the advantages of the modeling approach, including: efficiency in knowledge elicitation, support for system evaluation, usefulness of models in training, and potential long-term savings as compared with the "rapid prototyping" approach.

The pragmatic constructivist view has also arisen from studies of computer supported cooperative work. For example, Robinson and Bannon argued that:

> The process of interpretation and reinterpretation is central…to analysis, design and implementation. The passing of work between different semantic communities, each with their own ontologies, epistemologies, and conventions, each interpreting and recontextualizing the products of other communities, generates a phenomenon we term ontological drift…. If this is not taken into account in the design dialogues, the final outcome may come as a nasty surprise to all concerned. If it is taken into account, expectations of the nature and results of the design process may change considerably (1991, p. 231).

There has developed a consensus that expert systems are not emulations of expertise, but tools to support experts as they go about their familiar tasks. To do that, they must to some extent be models of the domain and setting as well as models of expert reasoning. But they are not emulations of expertise, let alone substitutes for it.

In addition to the pragmatic constructivist view, that expertise is personally constructed and socially situated, a second and more radical point of view has arisen, called "situated cognition" (e.g., Clancey 1993; Norman 1993). Both the pragmatic constructivists and the situated cognition communities hold that expertise can only be understood relative to its broader social contexts, and emphasize that expert systems can be effective only if they achieve an adequate goodness of fit to their context. However, those researchers who are "very situated," so to speak, have advocated some radical assumptions which amount to an attack on the basic idea of knowledge representation. This radicalism has led some in the AI community to claim that they have "thrown out the baby with the bathwater" (Hayes, Ford and Agnew 1994, p. 15).

Constructivists and advocates of the situated cognition view would largely agree that expertise is a kind of interaction or role. However, constructivists contend that in some domains expertise is closely linked with knowledge, while in others they are more distinct. In other words, unlike the radical situated cognition view, constructivism still puts knowledge in heads, as well as in contexts. Constructivists would not deny that knowledge can reside in groups or cultures to the extent that groups and cultures are complex interactions and constructions of individuals. Knowledge and expertise are not the same, and many of the recent debates stem from the assumption that they are.

The Upshot

So now we have a formidable body of cognitive research and various models of cognition from the psychologists, but we also have new approaches to expert systems and new inputs from sociologists. In a sense, the AI and sociology of science communities have a jump on psychology—context of a sort must by definition be taken into account in systems that do things. But the fresh views go well beyond that by placing all expert systems squarely in their social context. However, the new models and approaches have not been pulled together to provide any sort of satisfying big picture. All we seem to have is a bunch of "-isms." Underlying the -isms there seems to be some polarities or dimensions, and perhaps a general framework can be found that might suggest a middle ground between the extremes. The task of finding that middle ground can be commenced by considering two questions: What is knowledge? and What is context?

Knowledge and Metaphor

A traditional assumption has been that expertise is a phenomenon best accounted for in terms of the quantity, quality and organization of the domain-specific knowledge that is possessed by experts. Under this assumption, the concepts denoted by the terms "true knowledge" and "expertise" are believed to be highly related, that is, expert knowledge is based on deep reflection, allowing experts to do well because they know more, know better, and know in a more usable way. This has been a dominant view in the psychological study of expertise. This perspective leads the knowledge engineer to regard the system under study to be the expert, rather than an expert-in-context.

In contrast, in some circles, it has become fashionable to deny the existence of representations in the head and the idea that individuals possess knowledge at all. Not only is the idea of representation seen as misleading and false, but even the notion of knowledge itself is deeply suspect. Knowledge and meaning are seen as extra-personal and located in the community rather than within people.

Where's the Beef?

We approach the question "What is expertise?" by asking where it resides. As we have seen, expertise is perceived to be "located" in different "severences" (dangerous language with all this talk of heads) by different researchers. Some construe expertise as facts residing in the head of the expert and see knowledge acquisition as a sort of cognitive mining operation. In bold contrast, others have recently proclaimed that knowledge is not to be found in the expert at all! We argue that when construing expertise, it is important to transcend individual heads, but it is equally important not to lose them altogether.

Consider, as an example, a story about a plumber as told by Hayes *et al.* (1994). An expert plumber and a customer who knows nothing about plumbing are together in a kitchen discussing the problem at hand. Now imagine that the plumber is called away to perform an emergency repair. *Where* is the expertise? It seems obvious that the expertise is at least partly inside the plumber's head bone. Where else could it be? As Hayes *et al.* wryly note,

> It seems clear that the plumber's knowledge of plumbing is firmly attached to the plumber. Perhaps some kind of invisible mental leash would explain its attachment to him, but we suggest that a simpler and more plausible theory of this phenomenon might be that the plumber's knowledge of plumbing is in his head, and therefore moves with him, much as his kidneys and his toenails do (p. 20).

On the other hand, one might point out that the plumber is one who has been selected by numerous chaotic and systematic forces, ranging from happenstance, to individual choice and preference, to the formalities of a guild system of apprenticeship and licensing (Agnew *et al.*). The trade of plumbing has been shaped by a community of practice and built upon centuries of trial and error. Proficiency cannot be meaningfully or fully described without taking that history into account. The description of expertise can not be separated, let alone completely separated, from the description of the tools, the training and the culture of plumbing. The plumber's expertise has meaning only by virtue of its role in a society of which he is part. In a sense, then, the expertise lies "in the world." Where else could it be?

The Middle Path

The answer, of course, lies between the contrasting views, each with its own particular admixture of features that can be regarded as either necessary or sufficient to a definition of expertise (Greeno and Moore 1993).

Our view is that while there are things in the head we call representations, any account of the meaning of these things (and hence any account of why they should be regarded as representations) must be inherently social. Notice the difference between this position (which regards the meanings of mental representations as necessarily socially-determined) and the more extreme (situated cognition) view which holds that the representational tokens themselves aren't in the head, that representational tokens can only have an external, social existence, or even that there isn't any representation at all.

If, as has been claimed (Agnew et al.), "expert" is best understood as a role that some are chosen to play as the result of a constituency selection, then "expertise" can be considered the knowledge that accounts for that selection (often having connection only to a social reality). In this view, although individuals' expertise is indeed in their heads, the meaning of the expertise does not reside in the individuals, but rather arises in a dynamic interaction matrix involving the individual and his physical/cultural domain. Thus, when studying expertise, the minimum unit of analysis is the "expert-in-context."

The expert's constructions or procedures (i.e., mental models) may be more or less valid in a scientific sense; but they do need to be functional in helping the constituencies manage their uncertainty (as, for example, "invalid" past medical practice seen from the vantage of current belief).

This view of expertise suggests that knowledge engineers should focus on modeling the functional (but fallible) interactions between the expert and his social/physical context (see Stein). In particular, they should be looking for what constitutes a functional solution not only in terms of formal domain content, but also in terms of knowledge that can help explain this expert's selection by the constituency network. There is often a great deal of highly functional, if fallible, expertise located in the goodness of fit between the selected expert and the practical needs of their constituencies.

The Role of Metaphor in the Definition of Knowledge

The notion that "knowledge is in the head" is often expressed in terms of the usual metaphors for knowledge and memory. Similarly, the view that "knowledge is in the social context" is adorned by another particular set of metaphors (i.e., knowledge is soup-like; it is an activity, an on-going social construction; without society and history it would not exist; it can be conceived of as being like a process of natural selection, etc.).

There can be little doubt that nonliteral expression is pervasive in natural language (Pollio, Barlow, Fine and Pollio 1977; Reddy 1979; Rhodes and

Lawler 1981). It has been argued that word origins, conceptualizations, and definitions of all abstract concepts depend on metaphor (Becker 1975; Lakoff and Johnson 1980). (Even definitions of metaphor rely on metaphors; see Nemetz 1958.) It comes as little surprise that metaphor is rampant in the terminology and concepts in diverse domains of expertise (Hoffman 1992; Voss, Kennet, Wiley and Schooler 1992; Weitzenfeld, Riedl, Chubb and Freeman 1992). Metaphor is indubitably rampant, and useful if not necessary, in physical science (Black 1962; Boyd 1979; Gentner and Jeziorski 1993; Hesse 1993; Kuhn 1993), cognitive science (Leary 1990; Roediger 1980; Valle and von Eckartsberg 1981), and AI (Hoffman, Cochran and Nead 1990).

A salient example of metaphor in AI is to be found in the chapter by Hexmoor and Shapiro in their approach to developing systems that learn from experience. They describe their systems in terms of automaticities that become the "unconscious habits of intelligent agents." As with any scientific metaphor, this metaphor might ultimately result in advances if it is pushed and refined (see Hoffman 1980). But it is perhaps too easy to see Hexmoor and Shapiro's language as a misuse of scientific metaphor, implying as it does that the problems of building conscious computers have been settled. Meanwhile, Hexmoor and Shapiro are busy building unconscious intelligent computers.

Our main point here is that the abstract concept of "knowledge" cannot be defined or even discussed without using metaphor (Regoczei and Hirst 1992).

Having a palette of alternative metaphors for describing knowledge is really a quite good situation in which to be. The metaphors provide a means of organizing the literature on knowledge elicitation and acquisition ("mining," "capture," "extraction," "construction," etc.) by parsing the various methodologies that are entailed by the metaphors (LaFrance 1992; Spiro, Feltovich, Coulson and Anderson 1989). This allows one to compare the relative strengths of methodologies (those aspects of expertise that a given metaphor makes salient) and specify their assumptions and weaknesses or points of breakdown (those aspects of a given metaphor that it ignores, de-emphasizes or even just plain misrepresents). The definitions can thereby be refined and new creative approaches can more easily be generated—including the search for a middle path of "and" rather than "or" (as pursued in Agnew et al.; Greeno and Moore 1993).

Pushing us along that middle path is the second question, "What is Context?"

Into the Soup: What is "Context"?

Differences in domains of knowledge or practice are easy to single out. The important question is whether a domain difference can have effects on the mind and/or on the exercise of expertise. If expert systems are to be more useful, and perhaps tightly coupled to their context of use, then cognitive scientists and computer scientists need to get a serious handle on domain variations and differences if they are to create systems that are useful and also potentially transportable.

Domain Types

In the study of expertise (psychology, AI, etc.) there is a distinction between types of domains, one of which Hoffman (1987; Hoffman, Shadbolt, Burton and Klein 1995) has referred to as "significant"—domains such as aircraft piloting, medical diagnosis, electronics troubleshooting, etc.—domains that are important to business, government, or society at large. The contrast is with other domains that are regarded with raised eyebrows when someone asserts that the domain includes people who are experts—snake oil salesmen, TV evangelists, witch doctors, etc. (For a discussion of these contrasting types of domains or levels of expertise, see Agnew *et al.*)

This dimension of "significance" is somewhat slippery—TV evangelism is very important to a lot of people, TV evangelists can be very good at what they do and know lots of domain-relevant things. Another way of categorizing domains involves the fact that expertise in some domains is largely if not entirely a matter of social consensus or attribution. Within many organizations, certain people are known to be the best ones to consult about particular types of problems (see Stein). Not only is expertise defined and shaped by internal social factors (organizational history and interpersonal relations, professional credentials and licensing, etc.), but also by society at large, including political and economic forces.

Purpose also has a considerable effect on the practice of expertise. For instance, in the domain of "terrain analysis" using aerial photographs, the expert does not just determine that a particular coverage shows rolling hills with underlying interbedded limestone. Rather, the analysis has particular purposes (e.g., resource management, military trafficability, etc.). Purpose shapes the familiar task procedures, goals, and products.

There are many open questions about the effects of domains on cognition and skill. In the tasks that are familiar in any given domain, there will be required some mixture of categorization skill, planning skill, perceptual skill, world knowledge as well as domain-specific knowledge, flexibility in reasoning, creativity in generating new methods to handle tough cases, etc. (Feltovich *et al.*; Weilinga and Breuker 1986). The mixture is determined by a number of factors—the lawful regularities and facts in the world itself, the education and training procedures, the shape of the familiar tasks, and the frequency of rare or "tough" (nonschematic) cases.

Surely, both AI researchers and cognitive psychologists would agree that if we are to get a good handle on expertise, for whatever purposes, we need to look at a great variety of domains, domain types, problem types, and so forth. Both AI researchers and cognitive scientists can look at what's been done in their field and say, *"Hey, you've been ignoring this or that aspect of context, and this or that aspect turns out to be really important."* The situated cognition criticism of AI might be a case in point (see Agnew *et al.*; Clancey; Hayes *et al.* 1994). Also, cognitive psychologists who have studied expertise (e.g., chess, mechanics problem solving, etc.) have yet to look in detail at social factors. Both computer scientists and cognitive scientists need the input of social scientists—what are the important social or contextual variables, and what are the invariants that underlie the relativities? How can one go from a knowledge of the relativities and invariants to the creation of systems that people can use?

Is that all there is to it?

Contextualism

We know that constructivists and situationalists would agree with us that there *is* more to it, that the concept of context is somehow very important at many principled levels other than the level of *"Oh, hey, what have you not bothered to look at or take into account?"*

The principles of the general philosophy of contextualism (Gillespie 1992; Hoffman and Nead 1983; Jenkins 1974; Pepper 1942) may offer some help:

- One cannot have any "text" without its having multiple contexts, some of which are almost of necessity going to be implicit.
- At a minimum, a context includes: (a) the analyst's purposes and goals, (b) the analyst's views, assumptions, and theories, and (c) the analyst's methods.
- The above will influence the appropriate level or "grain" of analysis for any given purpose. Stated another way, the act of selecting a particular text both presupposes and expresses certain units of analysis.
- The units of analysis, in turn, point to the components of the available data that are regarded as meaningful. A change in context may necessitate a change in the units of analysis. There are no ultimate units of analysis for anything.

That is why the concept of "context" is important. There are multiple yet partially-overlapping perspectives that can be taken on expertise. And each may be legitimate for its particular purposes. And each may be legitimate for other purposes, but generalizability is an empirical and pragmatic question, not something that can be decided a priori on theoretical or philosophical grounds.

In other words, it is not only appropriate to integrate contrasting views, it is necessary. This leads us to the general framework we wish to present.

Finding Orderliness in the Knowledge Soup:
The Tetrahedron Model

The framework is best laid out by following the path of its historical development. The first brick in this yellow road was laid by James J. Jenkins in some seminal papers on the psychology of learning. These were a part of the "cognitive revolution," in which he played a major role.

Historical Background on the Tetrahedron Model

Jenkins' early work on learning was in the semibehaviorist paradigm of "verbal learning and verbal behavior." The research concerned topics in the associative mediational theory of memory, and utilized such methods as paired-associate learning of lists of words, syllables, or other types of verbal stimuli. Key variables were such things as word association frequency norms, word concreteness, etc. The research clearly suggested that the learner contributes to the learning process (i.e., learning is not just the stapling together of stimuli and responses). For example, in the free recall of lists of words, recall shows clusters in which the words are reordered by individuals into categories (Bousfield 1953; Tulving 1962).

As the research of that era continued, it became clear that words were not "the" fundamental units of language, that words could be related on a number of semantic dimensions (and not just frequency), and that mental structures were not mere chains of automatically-produced associations (Jenkins 1974). Coincidental with these developments was the advent of Chomsky's theory of language, which in some respects was a death knell for the neobehaviorist associationistic theory of language.

Jenkins' search for a more satisfying theory of learning was stimulated by research showing a strong interaction between task performance and the nature of the acquisition task (a learning task, not to be confused with "knowledge acquisition" as used in AI). For example, in a free recall task the subject could be shown a list of words and asked to rate each word as "pleasant" or "unpleasant." Alternatively, the subject could be asked to determine if each word was spelled with an "e." After that, the participant was given a "surprise" (or incidental) recall task, and it turned out that the orienting or acquisition task had a significant effect on clustering in free recall: if the acquisition task focused the participants on word meaning, free recall clustering would occur. Alternatively, if the acquisition task focused the participant on formal aspects of the words (e.g., spelling), there was not only little semantic clustering but also less recall overall. Indeed, providing the right sorts of semantic-level orienting tasks could result in incidental recall that was superior to recall when the participants were given no orienting tasks but were informed in advance that their memory would be tested in a subsequent task (for reviews of this body of work see Bransford 1979; Sternberg 1996, Chap. 8).

Numerous results were added to the mix by researchers who demonstrated interactions between subject variables, task variables, and performance measures in learning experiments. Memory effects, even some hallowed ones like primacy and recency in short-term memory, could be made to come and go. New research put nails in the coffin of the "modal model" of memory (Atkinson and Shiffrin 1968), which distinguished short-term and long-term memory. Phenomena such as encoding specificity supported a "levels of processing" approach (see Cermak and Craik 1979).

Neofunctionalism

All this led Jenkins to take a functionalist approach and conceive learning experiments not in terms of any grand model of the mind, but in terms of the more concrete particulars of experimental design (Jenkins 1979). This was expressed as a "tetrahedron" model, a heuristic for classifying experiments, reproduced in figure 1a.

The beauty of this model was that it captured not only the main effects of each of the four key variables, but also the interactions of the variables (the lines) and the three-way interactions of the variables (the planes). Depending upon the specifics of one's experiment and the focus of one's interest, any of the main effects or interactions could combine to determine the results. Complex interactions are the rule rather than the exception. The general thrust of the tetrahedron is that models of learning that stem from experiments of a given type on some particular phenomenon are more likely to be models of the task rather than models of the head. Memory is not one single, simple box in a flow diagram. Rather, it is extremely context-sensitive, complex, flexible and dynamic.

In the years since the introduction of the tetrahedron model and the advent of the contextualist, ecological, and neofunctionalist approaches to memory research (see Gillespie 1992; Hoffman and Deffenbacher 1993; Hoffman and Palermo 1991), variants on the tetrahedral model have appeared. One of these, which we discuss next, has referred specifically to expertise (see also Feltovich, Coulson, Spiro and Dawson-Saunders 1992; Prietula, Feltovich and Marchak 1989).

Finding Orderliness in the Soup: The PEST Model of Expert Cognition

Honeck and Temple (1992) offered a variation on the tetrahedron, depicted in figure 1b. This variation arose from the background of psycholinguistic research on metaphor and, in particular, the suggestion that people (in general) would be more likely to use creative metaphor in the problem solving pro-

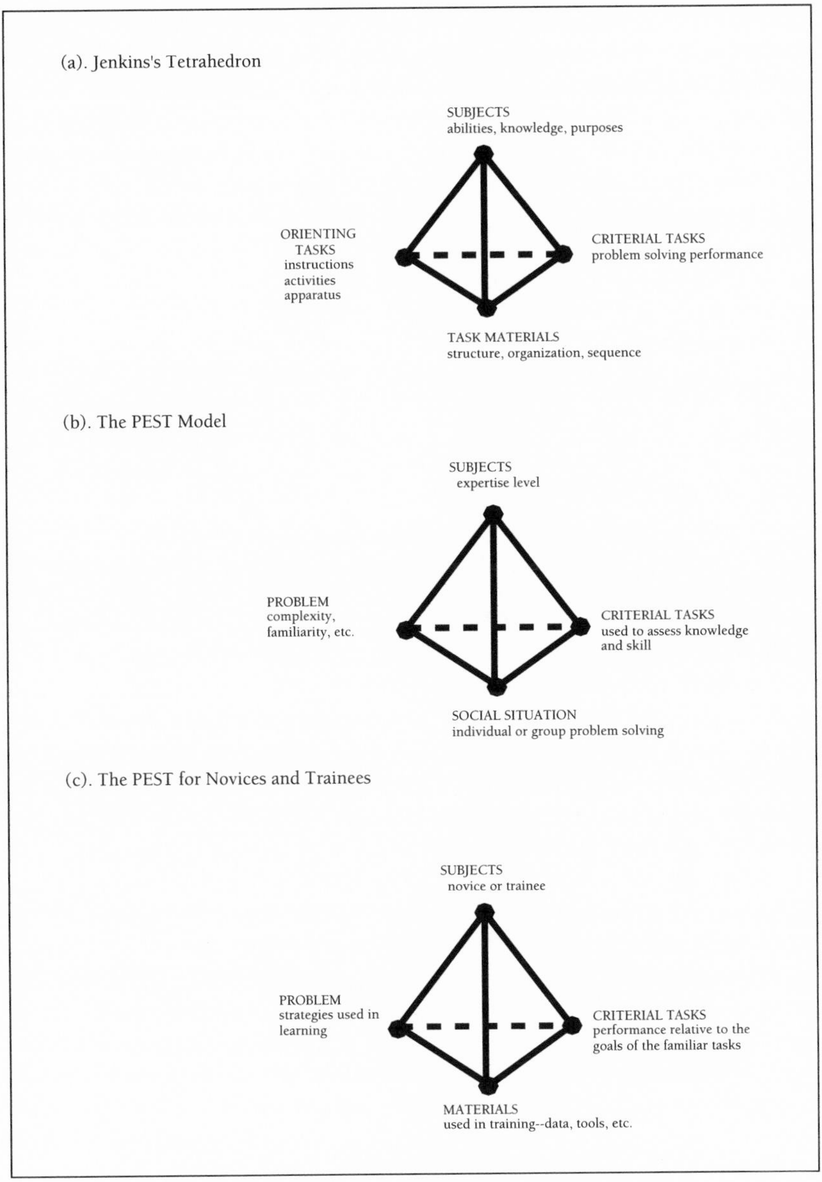

(a). Jenkins's Tetrahedron

SUBJECTS
abilities, knowledge, purposes

ORIENTING
TASKS
instructions
activities
apparatus

CRITERIAL TASKS
problem solving performance

TASK MATERIALS
structure, organization, sequence

(b). The PEST Model

SUBJECTS
expertise level

PROBLEM
complexity,
familiarity, etc.

CRITERIAL TASKS
used to assess knowledge
and skill

SOCIAL SITUATION
individual or group problem solving

(c). The PEST for Novices and Trainees

SUBJECTS
novice or trainee

PROBLEM
strategies used in
learning

CRITERIAL TASKS
performance relative to the
goals of the familiar tasks

MATERIALS
used in training--data, tools, etc.

Figure 1.

(a). The Jenkins (1979) tetrahedron model for learning research showing the main variables and their interactions.

(b). The Honeck and Temple (1992) PEST model of cognitive research on expertise, an instantiation of the Jenkins tetrahedron.

(c). The PEST model instantiated for novices and trainees.

cess when they encountered an unfamiliar or unusual problem that could not be solved by the usual methods or modes of thinking. To conceptualize the role of metaphor in the cognition of experts, Honeck and Temple offered a variant of Jenkins' tetrahedron, which they called PEST, referring to four of the main variables in cognitive research on expertise:

1. The features of the *Problem* (complexity, familiarity, etc.).
2. The *Expertise* level of the research participants.
3. The social *Situation* (e.g., an individual working alone, experts working in groups, etc.).
4. The *Task* used to elicit knowledge (e.g., think-aloud protocols, conceptual graphing, etc.).

Here, Honeck and Temple created a variation in which the tetrahedron variable of *Subjects* is be instantiated in terms of the ability level attributed to experts, and the other three variables are instantiated in ways particular to cognitive research.[1]

Examples of Research Captured by the PEST Model

The research on medical diagnosis summarized by Feltovich et al. and by Patel and Ramoni illustrates the manipulation of two of the variables in the PEST model—*Subject* variables (i.e., cardiologists, endocrinologists, residents, medical students, etc.), and *Problem* variables (cardiology problems of varying complexity and rarity; the extent of the information that is made available)—in order to reveal evidence about the reasoning strategies used in the criterial (diagnosis) task and reasoning biases that might occur.

In figure 1c, the *Experience* level is specified as novice or trainee, and there are correlated specifications on the other variables. PEST would allow integration of the research on expert-novice differences, research on cognitive development, research on teaching and training, etc. (as summarized in Zeitz). Here we see that the PEST, like Jenkins' original tetrahedron, serves a heuristic function by embracing the approaches taken in a number of bodies of research. It continually reminds one of the difficulty in operationalizing expertise, the difficulty in defining levels of expertise, and the potential influences of the knowledge elicitation task on the knowledge that is elicited (e.g., task demand characteristics).

Variations: The PEST Model Re-interpreted for the Practice of Expertise

Somewhere along the way, Jenkins's tetrahedral model came to be referred to, affectionately, as "Jenkins' kite," and in planning this volume it dawned on us that there is more, much more, to flying a kite than just the kite itself. There is the main driving force (the wind), and there are also controlling and stabilizing mechanisms (the kite string and the tail). This suggested some possible elaborations and refinements of the PEST.

The TEMPEST Model

Cognitive psychologists have focused on the kite (figures 1a, b, and c)—the interacting factors believed to be the primary determinants and measures of cognition and skill. In contrast, sociologists and advocates of the situated view focus on the wind, the tail, and the string—the driving, stabilizing and controlling forces that are external to the individual.

In the model shown in figure 2, the focus is on experts going about familiar or usual problem solving tasks. With regard to the kite itself, the focus of the *Subject* variable is on the background of the expert's experience, knowledge and skills. Jenkins' *Orienting task* variable is instantiated as the strategic component to problem solving; the *Criterial task* variable is instantiated as the goals of experts in conducting their familiar tasks; and the *Materials* variable is instantiated in terms of the data and tools used in the expert's familiar tasks.

Going beyond the kite itself (the PEST), the elaborated model in figure 2 incorporates dynamic interactions. Thus, a change in any one of the variables (e.g., societal needs, personal motives, professional standards, etc.) may necessitate some accommodation in the other variables (e.g., if you cut one inch off the tail it may not matter until the wind speed changes drastically). For ease of exposition, in what follows we refer to the elaborated and modified PEST model as the TEMPEST model.

Examples of Research Encompassed by the TEMPEST Model

The chapter by Stein presents an empirical investigation of the driving, controlling and stabilizing forces. The practical goal of the research was to develop methods for going into organizations and identifying the experts. The method involved having members of an organization describe one another on a number of scales that tapped into accessibility, cooperation and leadership (e.g., "To what degree do you trust X's judgments?," "From whom do you seek information about such-and-such a problem type?"). Multidimensional scaling proved itself useful and relatively efficient in determining the "centrality" of members of an organization and specifying their particular knowledge of subdomains or problem types.

Stein's method and results should be somewhat satisfying to situationalists and constructivists, representing an empirical attempt, a successful one, at defining expertise precisely in terms of social constituency. One *can* build a representation of the social network that identifies the experts, semi-experts, and nonexperts within an organization. Stein's work should also be satisfying

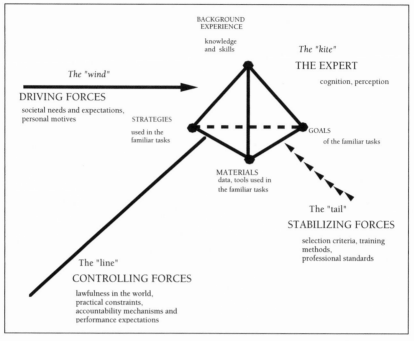

Figure 2. The TEMPEST model, which incorporates a
number of contextual variables and constraints.

to knowledge engineers—using results from a mail-in questionnaire, for example, one could build a social network graph and identify candidate participants for knowledge acquisition procedures.

The chapter by Shalin et al. shows clearly how the components of expertise in the PEST kite can be investigated together with the contextual variables that TEMPEST adds on (and that Stein investigated). Shalin et al. begin with a contrast between traditional laboratory context (contrived materials and tasks) and the observational studies of the everyday cognition paradigm (interviews, observations in the real task environment). They also describe the sorts of different findings and theories that have stemmed from these two alternative approaches (mental manipulation of symbol structures versus flexibility and sensitivity to the dynamics of operational environments).

As a part of a system development project, Shalin et al. conducted research in three task domains: on-foot land navigation, the piloting of commercial aircraft, and medical intensive care. All these domains involve situational awareness, performance under time pressure, sensitivity to feedback, and perceptual skill—the factors explored more in NDM research than in traditional cognitive research.

Experts' activities (in simulations, training exercises or real events) were recorded (on audio and/or video), and the protocols were analyzed using conceptual graphs (showing such things as plans and goals) and a number of performance measures. In all three domains, Shalin et al. found a significant reliance on certain "accepted," or frequently-utilized, and hence routine, methods. Although the transcripts often included cases of explicit discussion and comparative evaluation of alternative methods, as well as experts' commentaries on the performance of other experts, the accepted methods were not always referred to explicitly. As a part of their shared knowledge, the experts assumed the applicability of one or two particular methods for a given scenario.

The findings led Shalin et al. to a discussion of the importance of what TEMPEST calls:

- The kite (the expert engaged in a task)—especially goals, strategies and skills.
- The line (the controlling forces)—the ways in which reliance on accepted methods helps to reduce risk, supports situational awareness (through the generation of expectations), and supports the interweaving of multiple methods serving different yet simultaneous goals.
- The wind (the driving forces)—in this case, the societal expectations that lead to the development and refinement of effective methods.
- The tail (the stabilizing forces)—in this case, the training methods that lead to the inculcation of accepted methods.

The implication for expert systems or decision support systems is a hopeful prospect. Even for domains involving dynamic task situations and time pressure, many reasoning strategies can be supported by available technology, precisely *because* they are routine or "accepted." However, there is also a challenge. It will be necessary for the system to support the perception and recognition of conceptual and relational similarity—in order to access appropriate methods and goals. Once a method has been chosen and applied, it will be necessary to represent and process temporal information and expectations.

What Shalin et al. have done is take one possible cut on undoing a confound. While the everyday cognition research has demonstrated the great sensitivity of expertise to context, the results of Shalin et al. emphasize the reliance on routine methods. While the traditional cognitive research on expertise has revealed the consistencies in expert knowledge and performance, the results of Shalin et al. emphasize the importance of flexibility, the importance of event cognition, and the importance of perceptual skill (see also Feltovich et al.).

As one next step along the middle path, the TEMPEST model need not be restricted to the expertise as an accomplishment—the driving forces, cognition, controlling forces, and stabilizing forces can all be interpreted for the context of development and training.

Variations: The Model Re-interpreted for the Development of Expertise

By taking the PEST model for novices and trainees (figure 1c) and inserting it into figure 2, one has the TEMPEST model as interpreted for the context of development and training. The focus of the *Strategies* variable is on learning strategies; the controlling forces include the educational system; the stabilizing forces include selection criteria, criteria for progress, and so forth.

Research that clearly illustrates this variant on the TEMPEST model is that by Patel and Ramoni on the changes that occur in diagnostic reasoning strategy as a function of education across the years of medical school and residency. As this research shows, the path to expertise does not always involve simply getting more of what you already have (i.e., knowledge). For example, while the more advanced medical students do possess more knowledge they can tap, and do form more appropriate problem representations of causal relations, they do not always systematically evaluate, elaborate, or refine the multiple hypotheses that they generate. Nor are they very adept at forward reasoning, going from patient information directly to a diagnosis.

Variations: The Model Re-interpreted for Knowledge Elicitation

Figure 3 shows the TEMPEST model as interpreted for knowledge elicitation and knowledge acquisition. Here the focus is not on experts conducting their typical or familiar tasks, but on experts supporting knowledge engineering or cognitive research. Thus, the *Strategies* variable focuses on strategies as induced by the knowledge acquisition task—reflecting the notion that knowledge acquisition is modeling or creative construction, rather than extraction.

Two Kites

The TEMPEST model in figure 3 has two kites strung together, a type of kite one sometimes sees. The second kite represents the expert system. The arrows in figure 3 that denote the mappings go from the Expert kite to the System kite, intended to suggest that expert systems (the knowledge bases and inference engines) can be based on empirical evidence specifying the knowledge and reasoning of the human expert.

The relationship between expertise and expert systems, especially second-generation expert systems, is not trivial (O'Hara and Shadbolt). The dashing of the mapping arrows is intended to reinforce a particular nontriviality—the fact that the mappings are partial, and sometimes tenuous. The discussion by Feltovich et al. reminds us that the mapping is partial, by a cautionary tale

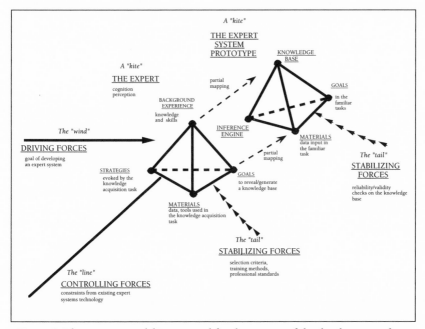

Figure 3. The TEMPEST model interpreted for the context of the development of expert systems (knowledge elicitation, knowledge acquisition), and the evaluation of systems (verification and validation of the knowledge base and inference engine).

from research that has demonstrated the "reductive bias"—which occurs when the researcher misconceives or overly simplifies the domain, creates artificial distinctions, or misinterprets domain concept-terms that happen also to be everyday terms.

Illustrations of the Kite-to-Kite Mapping

Illustrating the mapping direction depicted in figure 3 is the research summarized by Patel and Ramoni showing the relative contributions of forward and backward reasoning in various medical diagnosis tasks. Such findings can inform the development of knowledge representations for expert systems. Expert reasoning is not always "deep" nor is it always "causal," it is sometimes data-driven. A number of examples of the use of (psychological) models in the development of expert systems are presented in Shadbolt and O'Hara.

The chapters by Hexmoor and Shapiro, and Stern and Luger, also illustrate the mapping, but go beyond the generation of ideas about how one might build systems to the step of actually trying to build them. Hexmoor and Shapiro do this in their game-playing and robotic systems that learn from experience (learning "enriches conscious knowledge"). In addition, highly-practiced skills can become "automatic" (i.e., migrate across levels of repre-sentation) and become inaccessible by the interface—modeling the shift from declarative to procedural knowledge (as in Anderson 1983) that is believed to characterize human skill acquisition.

The work reported by Stern and Luger also carries the mapping all the way to implementation. But their system development efforts are based on empirical studies of expert behavior and performance, not just general psy-chological considerations. In developing an expert system for the analysis of semiconductor failures, they began with the notion of a memory schema, in-stantiated as a frame-like representation. The schemas use hypotheses to guide search (slots can refer to other frames) through a causal chain of semi-conductor evaluation, and thereby support the process of explaining semi-conductor performance ("failure modes") and explaining the results of diag-nostic tests. At the same time, the search is guided by practical constraints (e.g., certain tests can destroy the semiconductor).

Based on five years of analysis of the verbal protocols of five experts solv-ing problems in "the field," Stern and Luger developed a number of modules for an expert system (one thing at a time—diodes, transistors, etc.). Each module includes schemas for a number of "failure mechanisms," based on heuristic classification, or the association of sets of symptoms with causes. Heuristic classification rules involve associations that stem from accumulated experience and do not *necessarily* involve causal relations. The goal in prob-lem solving in the Stern and Luger system is to link failure mechanisms to "failure modes," which explicitly explain the part's behavior in terms of the causal principles of semiconductor physics.

It is interesting to note that Stern and Luger discovered a nice context ef-fect in their work. Experts who worked in the context of manufacturing tended to produce many more protocol statements oriented toward process control than experts who worked in the commercial context (end-users).

Switching the Direction of the Kite-to-Kite Mapping

The kite-to-kite mapping arrows depicted in figure 3 can go in the other di-rection, from the expert system back toward the expert. That is, the failure or success of some clever system architecture or AI approach might suggest a re-examination of human expertise or its relation to expert systems. O'Hara and Shadbolt pursue the question of whether expert systems "explain" expertise: Can knowledge engineering assist in the understanding of the cognition of expertise in context? The ways in which second-generation expert systems represent context might suggest ways in which cognitive models of expertise could be refined.

One AI strategy for modeling expertise has involved the notion that there are "generic tasks" that cut across domains (e.g., diagnosis, planning, classification, explanation, etc.; Chandrasekaran 1983). Each task is regarded as requiring its own flow diagram. Modeling, or expert system development, would involve identifying the task or tasks used in a domain and then using the appropriate task model(s) "off the shelf." One feature of the work constituting second-generation expert systems is that the generic task theory has been refined considerably.

The refinement has hinged on the experience of system developers: The generic task theory was insensitive to (guess what) context. It lacked a mechanism for a functional specification of tasks. The original generic task theory came to be regarded as an approach to task analysis rather than as a Platonic scheme for classifying expertise. Both the refined generic task theory, and the KADS and VITAL methodologies developed in Europe (see Breuker et al. 1983), involve representing each generic task with a suite of models (there are over 100 models in KADS-II), the choice among models being dictated by domain-dependent contextual nuances that are pursued in a top-down analysis (Chandrasekaran 1990; Feltovich et al.).[2]

This work, stemming from the hard-learned lesson of the necessity of incorporating context, has led to some back-peddling from the notion that expert systems must be simulations of a human expert. In contrast, they are thought of as tools or decision aids that, in order to work effectively, must to some extent model expertise-in-context. As model libraries have grown, the systems that rely on them have become more flexible, and in this sense the second-generation approaches to knowledge acquisition and modeling serve as better approximations to human expertise.

The research reported by Seifert et al. also illustrates the re-examination of expertise based on the experience of expert system developers, but their re-examination goes beyond theoretical analysis (as in O'Hara and Shadbolt) to experimental work with experts.

AI work on planning and case-based reasoning involves mechanisms for storing plans, for retrieving stored plans, for modifying plans, for predicting outcomes assuming successful plan execution, for blackboarding input information as situations and events unfold, for recognizing opportunities, for suspending and shifting between goals, for repairing and refining plans that fail, and for predicting future plan failures (Hammond 1989). Many of the mechanisms are aimed at dealing with the tough problem of how to allow for "smart indexing" or meaning-based plan retrieval—plans may not be stored according to features of new or on-going situations. Mechanisms that have been instantiated in AI systems are based on hard-gained experience at trying to build effective planning systems in diverse domains (Sezechwan cooking, route planning for pick-up and delivery, etc.). Furthermore, the ideas from AI can be used to generate a great many specific hypotheses about human problem solving.

An example is one of hypotheses that Seifert et al. explored, that objects related to a goal may not serve as effective memory cues unless at the time of goal suspension one was considering a plan in which the object might play a role. For example, you find yourself locked in a room, and upon failing to find a key, you suspend the goal of getting out. Moments later you might notice a credit card but might not think back to your escape goal unless you had considered a plan involving slipping the lock rather than finding the key.

Their psychological research on opportunistic reasoning motivated the development of a system in which goal suspension triggers a process in which activation can pass up ISA links. With this mechanism, new input data can trigger opportunistic recognition even though the input data do not exactly match the specific features stored along with plans. The ultimate goal of their work, shared by many in AI, is to develop systems that intelligently mix pre- planning with adaptive adjustment to dynamic context (situation assessment), and their approach to the goal is to pursue questions and issues using psychological experimentation, arm in arm with system development projects.

Variations: The Model Re-interpreted for the Evaluation of Expert Systems

Figure 4 shows the TEMPEST model as interpreted for the context of using a working information processing system (expert system, decision aid, workstation system, etc.). The driving force comes from the organization that needs and uses the system. One focus can be on the reliability, validity, and efficiency (the performance) of the operational system, including comparisons with the performance of human experts. Such evaluation research serves a stabilizing function for the second kite.

Examples of Research Embraced by this Variant on the TEMPEST Model

The chapter by Hayes is an example of the instantiation of TEMPEST represented in figure 4. Her research relied on two variants on an expert system for the generation of plans to manufacture metal parts using machine tools. A set of machining problems was processed by the two expert systems and also presented to human experts (with different degrees of experience).[3] All the machining task solutions, both human- and system-generated, were next presented to two highly-experienced machinists, who served as judges and evaluated each of the plans on dimensions such as efficiency and feasibility.

In this type of experiment, the mapping of the *Materials* variable on the expert kite with the *Materials* variable on the system kite is not partial—the problems presented to human and system are exactly the same. Nor is the *Goal-Goal* mapping partial. The mapping of the *Strategy* and *Knowledge* variables is open to question (i.e., the success of the system). By including experience level as a variable describing the participant experts (the tail on the ex-

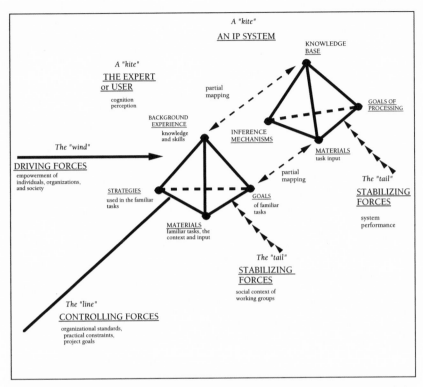

4. *The TEMPEST model interpreted for the context of information processing (IP) systems (including expert systems, decision aids, or workstation systems) in-use.*

pert kite), Hayes was able to gauge the "expertise level" of the two expert systems (i.e., build a tail for the system kite), here using human expertise itself as a metric, a metric with some surprising twists.

The figure 4 version of the TEMPEST model can be taken beyond the evaluation of systems to a broader analysis.

More AI Issues

In addition to psychological issues, there are important computational and logical issues that arise when one moves beyond talking about the nature of expertise into the realm of implementation. Just as our understanding of the nature of human expertise has shifted over time, so too has there been a continuous evolution of approaches and methods for the physical realization of machine reasoners that model or embody sufficient knowledge that their performance might be called expert.

The chapter by Miller and Perlis presents a new idea about how AI might deal with the problem of default reasoning—the fact that people reason on the basis of incomplete information. Specifically, one may not know the exact features or values for some new concept or instance, but if one knows the category into which the concept or instance falls, one can make "default" assumptions about the concept's features or slot values, assigning to the concept the "typical" values as specified in the category (e.g., "If this is a cardinal, it must be red, since cardinals are typically red").

This topic leads one to consider some aspects of expert reasoning that cognitive psychology is just beginning to investigate.[4] Experts (as opposed to novices) may possess more default rules; experts' default rules may span a range of generality-specificity (novices' defaults may tend to be just specific ones); experts may possess more default denial rules to allow them to avoid mistakes; experts are better prepared to deal with exceptions to defaults, etc. (see Feltovich, Johnson, Moller and Swanson 1984; Feltovich et al.).

One approach to default reasoning in AI is to rely on simple inheritance across an associative net or hierarchy. Difficulty arises when default assignments have to be denied or negated. In the mechanisms of standard default logic, the denial of a default assignment actually negates two things at once—the inference itself and the assertion that the concept in question possesses a value on some variable that is the same as the typicality specification in its category (some cardinals are brown, and there are albino cardinals).

Miller and Perlis suggest that default negation can be broken up, separating the negation of defaults about the *range* of possible values of a variable (~["Cardinals are typically red"]) from the negation of the *inference* itself (~["If this is a cardinal, it must be red"]). Using this mechanism, one can specify the conditions under which a default can be denied. Through this mechanism Miller and Perlis propose to deal effectively with default management in all (nonmonotonic) formalisms. This is a hopeful prospect for the coupling of the two kites of figure 4.

Like the chapter by Miller and Perlis, Kyburg's chapter presents a hopeful prospect involving the couplings between the two kites. At a practical level, Kyburg's discussion centers on the problems of reasoning by rules which incorporate uncertainty or probability. Kyburg asks whether statistical inference is the sort of expertise that can be captured with available technology and representation systems, but his discussion does not focus on the tenuousness of the partial mappings of the two kites. To the contrary, he argues that it is possible to restore some certainty (reasoning has a specifiable logical structure) through the incorporation of context. Although some aspects of classical statistical inference have been instantiated in computer systems, Kyburg argues that what is needed to achieve expert performance in statistical induction is the incorporation of the rich background knowledge needed for each context in which statistical induction is to be made.

Some mental processes play a critical role in human reasoning but are largely or entirely neglected in AI models of proficient reasoning. The chapter by Minsky is a "call to arms" for more psychological research and AI effort on the role of emotion in reasoning. Minsky is especially concerned with the fact that much knowledge consists of what *not* to do and how to avoid mistakes—so-called negative expertise. In these cases, the links between the kites are not tenuous; they are not yet existent (but see Miller and Perlis). In considering the role of experience in the acquisition of knowledge and expertise, rarely is much thought given, in either psychology or AI, to the possibility that failure and frustration may play a role that is just as important as the accumulation of successful experience. Minsky offers a cautionary tale about a major gap in research on expertise—rarely if ever does a cognitive experiment or a knowledge elicitation project involve the assessment of negative knowledge.

We included Selmer Bringsjord's essay in this volume for its value as a clear example of the obscure use of logic in supporting a claim about the impossibility of AI and the singularity of humans. Bringsjord contends that expert reasoning about mathematical concepts of infinity cannot be captured in any sort of available computational method, for to do so would presuppose that a formal logic can generate another logic that is more powerful than itself. According to the TEMPEST model in figure 4, Bringsjord's argument is that the kite representing human expertise embodies something infinite (infinitary logics)—thus making it impossible to use computer system (the other kite) as a model of expertise because of its finite nature.

Variations: The Model Re-interpreted for Expert Systems In-use

Figure 4 also depicts the TEMPEST model as interpreted for the context of systems in use. Here there is more of a focus on the social aspects of expert systems and the practices of actual working groups. This is the TEMPEST expression of many of the central concerns of those who advocate the situated cognition view.

Examples of Research Encompassed by this Variant on the TEMPEST Model

The chapter by Lerch, Prietula and Kulik gets directly at the controlling forces, the stabilizing forces and the psychology of the user, as depicted in figure 4—but with a twist. What happens when the user attributes too much capability or competence to the system and fails to bring to bear the controls and stabilizations that would be appropriate from an objective (or even rationalist) point of view?

The topic of trust in expert and AI systems and the related issues of accountability, legality, etc. are becoming evermore salient (LaFrance, in press;

Perrolle 1988; Will 1991). Lerch et al. approach this issue using a clever technique based on the Turing Test. Rather than having people (here, college students) guess if information is the output of a computer or a human, the participants are *told* that certain advice (in the domain of financial management) is from either a person or a computer, and their task is to gauge the difficulty of each problem, their trust in the advice (credibility, dependability, agreement with the participant's own judgment, confidence in the correctness of the advice) and the performance of the human or computer (ability shown, effort taken). The experimental method takes into account the degree of each participant's experience with computer systems.

This technique and experimental design could be considered a broadly useful paradigm in the empirical exploration of trust issues. As their results show, Lerch et al. were able to explore many, and specific, hypotheses concerning issues of trust and attribution. The results take us a step toward some understanding of the boundary conditions of trust. That is, depending on how the source of advice is described, people can agree more with the computer-generated advice than with the expert-generated advice, and yet they may express lower confidence in the computer than in the human. Going out of one's way to tell people that the knowledge base of an expert system comes from detailed analyses of actual experts can increase people's willingness to trust the advice that the expert system provides, but they will not necessarily trust it as much as the advice from a human expert—even when they are explicitly told that the expert system performs better than the human.

This research not only mitigates certain social concerns (e.g., do people really place too much trust in computers?), but also relates directly to systems development. A better understanding of how users generate attributions can support designs that fit the user's reasoning about the system output. This may be critical as more and more decision-aiding systems are developed, become operational, and are used in organizational settings.

As we illustrated above with the kite-to-kite partial mappings (Bringsjord; Kyburg), the TEMPEST model in figure 4 can also be taken to a broader level with regard to the controlling and stabilizing forces.

Upping the Stakes

The chapters by Shadbolt and O'Hara, and O'Hara and Shadbolt, discuss the prospects for AI by envisioning the compilation of "libraries" of conceptual models that can be accessed and applied as modules in expert system development projects or in training programs, even in domains other than those in which a particular model was created. This is not the future; this is to some extent now (see Breuker *et al.* 1987; Weilinga and Breuker 1986).

Looking to the future, the chapter by Rappaport discusses the prospects of AI in a particular vision about "info-structures." Rappaport begins with the contextualist notion that information is a social commodity, always flowing not only among individuals but also between levels of scale or context (similar to the observations made by the situationalists). Rappaport envisions technology to empower individuals, groups, and society by supporting the cross-domain and cross-context sharing and use of information and knowledge (software, images, inference engines). This must include knowledge about context. Of the many challenges implicit in Rappaport's vision, one is to deal with the tension between the knowledge and personal beliefs of individuals (experts) and the local and global contexts of the situations to which expertise might be applied.

Agreements and Prospects

We have no doubt that other variations on the TEMPEST model are possible. This framework does not directly specify a research program that would satisfy the hard-core experimental psychologist, nor does it specify what people who build expert systems should do, or do differently from what they do now. The TEMPEST model and the research it embraces are suggestive of what cognitive scientists and systems developers might do. We regard the framework as valuable primarily because it affords a sense of overall organization, lending some coherence to the topic of expertise. We regard it as potentially useful because it suggests how one can cut through the "either-or" debates and lay waste at least some of the straw men. Most of the issues that are important to the authors of chapters in this volume have their place in the TEMPEST framework.

Upon what, then, do the contributors to this volume agree—or rather, upon what would we like them to *seem* to agree?

- We agree that it is both possible and necessary to study expertise in the sense of cognitive phenomena, and that the phenomena are palpable even though multifaceted, process-like and flexible.
- We all agree that one should be careful in assuming that a computer representation is a veridical simulation of human expertise. Beyond that, we agree that AI is positioned to evolve beyond the assumption that intelligence in computers must have the human as its sole benchmark (see Hayes and Ford 1995b).
- We agree that context is necessary in defining knowledge and reasoning. More importantly, we agree that social factors are not "mere" context for cognitive factors.
- We agree that in cognition, both human and machine, there is a valuable place for both the routinized or standard, as well as the novel and constructive.

- We agree that the interdisciplinary study of expertise is mature enough to take laboratory methods (the cognitive science paradigms) "into the wild."
- We agree that the exercise of expertise, just as any human endeavor, involves complex and dynamic nestings of acts, actions and social situations.
- We agree that the appellation of "expert" can be usefully understood as a constituency selection—a social attribution. This is not to argue that experts don't know anything, or that the knowledge claims of experts are untrue, but is only a recognition that "expert" is a role that some are chosen to play" (Agnew et al., p. 220).
- We agree that expert systems can be and will be advanced significantly, but not if there is reliance solely on the notions of decontextualized knowledge.
- We agree that empirical methods can be used to study effectively the sorts of questions and issues raised by the contextualist and situationalist points of view.

Our own view is that the empirical approach is the most important and useful way to address questions of expertise and knowledge. We share the view of McCarthy (1983) and Newell and Simon (1976), that computer science, particularly AI, is also best practiced as an empirical enquiry.

Science (writ large) is fallible, and we wonder who would think otherwise, given that science is practiced by humans. As Collins and other critics of science have noted, the process by which scientists' opinions evolve is complex and error-prone, subject to many of the same pressures as other social trends. But it is ridiculous, in our view, to move from this fact to the claim that scientific results are on a par with agreements about politics, or styles of art. If that were the case how could someone ever determine that a scientist had made an "error"? Science is unique in that it has institutionalized the process of experimental disconfirmation. Its own methods are self-applicable and lead to self-improvement. As Ford, Hayes and Barnes (1995) have noted, "Even if no single scientist operated according to the proper 'scientific method'...the overall result is to produce theories which the hidden-hand editor of reality has grasped as firmly as it can be made to" (p. 45).

Notes

1. With regard to its original motivation, the PEST model suggested some new and interesting lines of research on metaphor and creative problem solving. Whether novel metaphor production increases or decreases with expertise should depend on the familiarity of the problems that are encountered. As expertise grows and problems become familiar, metaphor use should become less frequent and more entrenched. Un-

familiar problems should motivate the use of new metaphors or the novel use of old metaphors (Honeck and Temple, p. 240).

2. Another approach is to store just a few models for each task but append a set of re-write rules, as in the VITAL methodology for knowledge acquisition. See O'Hara and Shadbolt.

3. Like other "significant" domains, mastery in machining can take upwards of ten years to achieve.

4. Reasoning about concept and category formation, including reasoning about the negation of feature assignments, has been extensively studied in the traditional learning laboratory, and a great many models of category structure have been proposed (exemplar models, prototype models, network models, feature similarity theories, etc.), but this work focuses on common knowledge (college students as participants) and not on expertise per se. For an exception, see Tanaka and Taylor (1991). For a review, see Estes (1994).

References

Agnew, N.M., Ford, K.M. & Hayes, P.J. (this volume). Expertise in context: Personally constructed, socially selected, and reality-relevant?

Alty, J.L. (1987). The limitations of rule based expert systems. In J. Kriz (Ed.), *Knowledge-Based Systems in Industry* (pp. 17-22). Chichester, England: Ellis Horwood.

Anderson, J.A. (1983). *The Architecture of Cognition.* Cambridge, MA: Harvard University Press.

Atkinson, R.C. & Shiffrin, R.M. (1968). Human memory: A proposed system and its control processes. In K.W. Spence & J.T. Spence (Eds.), *The Psychology of Learning and Motivation, Vol. 2: Advances in Research and Theory* (pp. 742-775). New York: Academic Press.

Becker, J.D. (1975). *The phrasal lexicon* (Rep. No. 3081). Cambridge, MA: Bolt, Beranek and Newman.

Black, M. (1962). *Models and Metaphors.* Ithaca, NY: Cornell University Press.

Bobrow, D.G., Mittal, S. & Stefik, M.J. (1989). Expert systems: Perils and promise. *Communications of the ACM, 29,* 880-894.

Bousfield, W.A. (1953). The occurrence of clustering in the recall of randomly arranged associates. *Journal of General Psychology, 49,* 229-240.

Boyd, R. (1993). Metaphor and theory change: What is a "metaphor" a metaphor for? In A. Ortony (Ed.), *Metaphor and Thought* (2nd ed.) (pp. 481-532). Cambridge, England: Cambridge University Press.

Bransford, J.D. (1979). *Human Cognition.* Belmont, CA: Wadsworth.

Breuker, J., Weilinga, B.J., van Sommeren, M., de Hoog, R., Schreiber, G., deGreef, P., Bredeweg, B., Wielemaker, J., Billaut, J.-P., Davoodi, M. & Hayward, S. (1987). *Model-driven knowledge acquisition: Interpretation models.* Amsterdam: Dept. of Social Science Informatics, University of Amsterdam.

Bringsjord, S. (this volume). An argument for the uncomputability of infinitary mathematical expertise.

Cermak, L.S. & Craik, F.I.M. (Eds.). (1979). *Levels of Processing in Human Memory.*

Hillsdale, NJ: Lawrence Erlbaum.

Chandrasekaran, B. (1983). Towards a taxonomy of problem solving types. *The AI Magazine, 4(1)*, 9-17.

Chandrasekaran, B. (1990). Design problem solving: A task analysis. *The AI Magazine, 11(4)*, 59-71.

Chi, M.T.H., Glaser, R. & Farr, M.L. (Eds.). (1988). *The Nature of Expertise*. Hillsdale, NJ: Lawrence Erlbaum.

Clancey, W.J. (this volume). The conceptual nature of knowledge, situations, and activity.

Clancey, W.J. (1993). Situated action: A neuropsychological interpretation response to Vera and Simon. *Cognitive Science, 17*, 77-86.

Clancey, W.J. (1983). The epistemology of a rule-based expert system: A framework for explanation. *Artificial Intelligence, 20*, 215-251.

Collins, H.M. (this volume). RAT-tale: Sociology's contribution to understanding human and machine cognition.

Cullen, J. & Bryman, A. (1988). The knowledge acquisition bottleneck: Time for reassessment? *Expert Systems, 5*, 216-225.

Davis, R. (1989). Expert systems: How far can they go? *The AI Magazine, 9(1)*, 61-67.

De Groot, A.D. (1965). *Thought and Choice in Chess*. The Hague: Mouton.

Duncker, K. (1945). On problem solving (L.S. Lees, trans.). *Psychological Monographs, 58*, 1-113 (Whole No. 270).

Ericsson, K.A. & Charness, N. (this volume). Cognitive and developmental factors in expert performance.

Ericsson, K.A. & Smith, J. (Eds.). (1991). *Toward a General Theory of Expertise*. Cambridge: Cambridge University Press.

Estes, W.K. (1994). *Classification and Cognition*. Oxford: Oxford University Press.

Feltovich, P.J., Coulson, R.L., Spiro, R.J. & Dawson-Saunders, B.K. (1992). Knowledge acquisition and transfer for complex tasks in ill-structured domains: Implications for instruction and testing in biomedicine. In D.A. Evans & V.L. Patel (Eds.), *Advances in Models of Cognition for Medical Training* (pp. 213-244). Berlin: Springer Verlag.

Feltovich, P.J., Johnson, P.E., Moller, J.H. & Swanson, D.B. (1984). LCS: The role and development of medical knowledge in diagnostic expertise. In W.J. Clancey & E.G. Shortliffe (Eds.), *Readings in Medical Artificial Intelligence: The First Decade* (pp. 275-319). Reading, MA: Addison Wesley.

Feltovich, P.J., Spiro, R.J. & Coulson, R.L. (this volume). Issues of expert flexibility in contexts characterized by complexity and change.

Fleck, J. & Williams, R. (1996). *Exploring Expertise*. Edinburgh: University of Edinburgh Press.

Ford, K.M. & Adams-Webber, J.R. (1992). Knowledge acquisition and constructive epistemology. In R.R. Hoffman (Ed.), *The Psychology of Expertise: Cognitive Research and Empirical AI* (pp. 121-136). New York: Springer-Verlag.

Ford, K.M. & Bradshaw, J.M. (Eds.). (1993). *Knowledge Acquisition as Modeling*. New York: Wiley.

Ford, K.M., Cañas, A.J. & Adams-Webber, J.A. (1991). Explanation as a knowledge acquisition issue. In M. Fishman (Ed.), *Proceedings of Fourth Florida Artificial Intelligence Research Symposium* (pp. 185-191). St. Petersburg, FL: Florida AI Research Society.

Ford, K.M., Hayes, P.J. & Barnes, W.G.W. (1995). About artificial criticism: A reply to Harry Collins. [Reader Response, Phi Kappa Phi Journal.] *National Forum, 75(1),* 44-46.

Gammack, J.G. & Anderson, A. (1990, Feb.). Constructive interaction in knowledge engineering. *Expert Systems, 7(1),* 19-26.

Gentner, D. & Jeziorski, M. (1993). The shift from metaphor to analogy in western science. In A. Ortony (Ed.), *Metaphor and Thought* (2nd ed.) (pp. 447-480). Cambridge, England: Cambridge University Press.

Gillespie, D. (1992). *The Mind's Eye: Contextualism in Cognitive Psychology.* Carbondale: Southern Illinois University.

Greenbaum, J. & Kyng, M. (Eds.). (1991). *Design at Work: Cooperative Design of Computer Systems.* Hillsdale, NJ: Erlbaum.

Greeno, J.G. & Moore, J.L. (1993). Situativity and symbols: Response to Vera and Simon. *Cognitive Science, 17,* 49-60.

Hammond, K. (1989). *Case-Based Planning: Viewing Planning as a Memory Task.* San Diego: Academic Press.

Hayes, C.C. (this volume). A study of solution quality in expert and knowledge-based system reasoning.

Hayes, P.J. & Ford, K.M. (1995a). The Simon Newcomb Awards. *The AI Magazine, 16(1),* 11-13.

Hayes, P.J. & Ford, K.M. (1995b). Turing Test considered harmful. In C.S. Mellish (Ed.), *Proceedings of the 14th International Joint Conference in Artificial Intelligence* (pp. 972-977). San Mateo, CA: Morgan Kaufman.

Hayes, P.J., Ford, K.M. & Agnew, N. (1994). On babies and bathwater: A cautionary tale. *The AI Magazine, 15(4),* 15-26.

Hesse, M.B. (1966). *Models and Analogies in Science.* Notre Dame, IN: University of Notre Dame Press.

Hexmoor, H. & Shapiro, S.C. (this volume). Integrating skill and knowledge in expert agents.

Hoffman, R.R. (1994). Constructivism versus realism or constructivism and realism? *Journal of Experimental and Theoretical Artificial Intelligence, 6,* 431-435.

Hoffman, R.R. (Ed.). (1992). Metaphor and expertise: A special issue of *Metaphor and Symbolic Activity, 3.*

Hoffman, R.R. (1987). The problem of extracting the knowledge of experts from the perspective of experimental psychology. *The AI Magazine, 8(2),* 53-66.

Hoffman, R.R. (1980). Metaphor in science. In R.P. Honeck & R.R. Hoffman (Eds.), *Cognition and Figurative Language* (pp. 393-424). Hillsdale, NJ: Erlbaum.

Hoffman, R.R., Cochran, E.A. & Nead, J.M. (1990). Cognitive metaphors in the history of experimental psychology. In D. Leary (Ed.), *Metaphors in the History of Psychology* (pp. 173-229). Cambridge, England: Cambridge University Press.

Hoffman, R.R. & Deffenbacher, K.A. (1993). An analysis of the relations between basic and applied psychology. *Ecological Psychology, 5,* 315-352.

Hoffman, R.R. & Nead, J.M. (1983). General contextualism, ecological science, and cognitive research. *Journal of Mind and Behavior, 4,* 507-560.

Hoffman, R.R. & Palermo, D.S. (Eds.). (1991). *Cognition and the Symbolic Processes: Applied and Ecological Perspectives.* Hillsdale, NJ: Erlbaum.

Hoffman, R.R., Shadbolt, N.R., Burton, A.M. & Klein, G. (1995). Eliciting knowledge from experts: A methodological analysis. *Organizational Behavior and Human Decision Processes, 62,* 129-158.

Honeck, R.P. & Temple, J.G. (1992). Metaphor, expertise, and a PEST. *Metaphor and Symbolic Activity, 7,* 237-252.

Hutchins, E. (1995). *Cognition in the Wild.* Cambridge, MA: The MIT Press.

Jenkins, J.J. (1979). Four points to remember: A tetrahedral model of memory experiments. In L.S. Cermak & F.I.M. Craik (Eds.), *Levels of Processing in Human Memory* (pp. 429-446). Hillsdale, NJ: Erlbaum.

Jenkins, J.J. (1974). Remember that old theory of memory? Well, forget it! *American Psychologist, 29,* 785-795.

Kaplan, L. (1936). Cutting the Jonker diamond. *Natural History, 38,* 227-236.

Knorr-Cetina, K.D. (1981). *The Manufacture of Knowledge.* Oxford: Pergamon.

Knorr-Cetina, K.D. & Mulkay, M. (1983). *Science Observed.* Berkeley Hills, CA: Sage.

Kuhn, T.S. (1993). Metaphor in science. In A. Ortony (Ed.), *Metaphor and Thought* (2nd ed.) (pp. 533-542). Cambridge, England: Cambridge University Press.

Kyburg, H.E. (this volume). Expertise and context in uncertain inference.

LaFrance, M. (in press). Why we trust computers too much. *Technology Studies.*

LaFrance, M. (this volume). Metaphors for expertise: How knowledge engineers picture human expertise.

LaFrance, M. (1992). Excavation, capture, collection, and creation: Computer scientists' metaphors for eliciting human expertise. *Metaphor and Symbolic Activity, 7,* 135-156.

Lakoff, G. & Johnson, M. (1980). The metaphorical structure of human conceptualization. *Cognitive Science, 4,* 195-208.

Lave, J. (1988). *Cognition in Practice.* Cambridge, England: Cambridge University Press.

Leary, D. (Ed.). (1990). *Metaphors in the History of Psychology.* Cambridge, England: Cambridge University Press.

Lerch, F.J., Prietula, M.J. & Kulik, C.T. (this volume). The Turing effect: The nature of trust in expert systems advice.

McCarthy, J. (1983). President's Quarterly Message. *The AI Magazine, 4(4),* 5.

Miller, M. & Perlis, D. (this volume). Toward automated expert reasoning and expert-novice communication.

Minsky, M. (this volume). Negative expertise.

Nemetz, A. (1958). Metaphor: The Daedalus of discourse. *Thought, 33,* 417-442.

Newell, A. (1985). Duncker on thinking: An inquiry into progress in cognition. In S. Koch & D.E. Leary (Eds.), *A Century of Psychology as a Science* (pp. 392-419). Englewood Cliffs, NJ: Prentice Hall.

Newell, A. & Simon, H.A. (1976). Computer science as an empirical inquiry: Symbols and search. *Communications of the ACM, 19(3),* 113-126. Reprinted in G. Luger

(Ed.), (1995), *Computation and Intelligence* (pp. 91-119). Cambridge, MA: AAAI/MIT Press.

Norman, D.A. (Ed.) (1993). Special issue: Situated action. *Cognitive Science, 17,* 1-133.

O'Hara, K. & Shadbolt, N. (this volume). Interpreting generic structures: Expert systems, expertise, and context.

Patel, V.L. & Ramoni, M.F. (this volume). Cognitive models of directional inference in expert medical reasoning.

Pepper, S.C. (1942). *World Hypotheses.* Berkeley: University of California Press.

Perrolle, J. (1988). The social impact of computing: Ideological themes and research issues. *Social Science Computer Review, 6,* 469-480.

Pollio, H.R., Barlow, J.M., Fine, H.J. & Pollio, M.R. (1977). *Psychology and the Poetics of Growth: Figurative Language in Psychology, Psychotherapy and Education.* Hillsdale, NJ: Erlbaum.

Prietula, M.J., Feltovich, P.J. & Marchak, F. (1989). A heuristic framework for assessing factors influencing knowledge acquisition. In D. Blanning & D. King (Eds.), *Proceedings of the 22nd Hawaii International Conference on Systems Science, Vol. 3: Decision Support and Knowledge-Based Systems* (pp. 419-426). New York: IEEE.

Rappaport, A.T. (this volume). Context, cognition, and intelligent interactive information infrastructures.

Reddy, M. (1979). The conduit metaphor: A case of frame conflict in our language about language. In A. Ortony (Ed.), *Metaphor and Thought* (pp. 284-324). Cambridge: Cambridge University Press.

Reddy, R. (1988). Foundations and grand challenges of artificial intelligence. *The AI Magazine, 9(4),* 9-21.

Regoczei, S.B. & Hirst, G. (1992). Knowledge and knowledge acquisition in the computational context. In R.R. Hoffman (Ed.), *The Psychology of Expertise: Cognitive Research and Empirical AI* (pp. 12-25). New York: Springer-Verlag.

Rhodes, R.A. & Lawler, J.M. (1981). Athematic metaphors. *Papers from the Seventeenth Regional Meeting of the Chicago Linguistic Society* (pp. 318-342). Chicago: The Chicago Linguistic Society.

Robinson, M. & Bannon, L. (1991). Questioning representations. In L. Bannon, M. Robinson & K. Schmidt (Eds.), *Proceedings of the Second European Conference on Computer Supported Cooperative Work* (pp. 219-233). Amsterdam: North Holland.

Roediger, H.L. (1980). Memory metaphors in cognitive psychology. *Memory & Cognition, 8,* 231-246.

Scribner. S. (1984). Studying working intelligence. In B. Rogoff & J. Lave (Eds.), *Everyday Cognition: Its Development in Social Context* (pp. 9-40). Cambridge, MA: Harvard University Press.

Seifert, C.M., Patalano, A.L., Hammond, K.J. & Converse, T.M. (this volume). Experience and expertise: The role of memory in planning for opportunities.

Shadbolt, N. & O'Hara, K. (this volume). Model-based expert systems and the explanation of expertise.

Shalin, V.L., Geddes, N.D., Bertram, D., Szczepkowski, M.A. & DuBois, D. (this volume). Expertise in dynamic, physical task domains.

Spiro, R.J., Feltovich, P.J., Coulson, R.L. & Anderson, D.K. (1989). Multiple analogies for complex concepts: Antidotes for analogy-induced misconception in advanced knowledge acquisition. In S. Vosniadou & A. Ortony (Eds.), *Similarity and Analogical Reasoning* (pp. 498-531). Cambridge: Cambridge University Press.

Stein, E.W. (this volume). A look at expertise from a social perspective.

Stern, C.R. & Luger, G.F. (this volume). Abduction and abstraction in diagnosis: A schema based account.

Sternberg, R.J. (this volume). Cognitive conceptions of expertise.

Sternberg, R.J. (1996). *Cognitive Psychology.* New York: Harcourt Brace.

Suchman, L. (1993). Response to Vera and Simon's "Situation action." *Cognitive Science, 17,* 71-76.

Suchman, L.A. & Trigg, R.H. (1991). Understanding practice: Video as a medium for reflection and design. In J. Greenbaum & M. Kyng (Eds.), *Design at Work: Cooperative Design of Computer Systems* (pp. 65-89). Hillsdale, NJ: Erlbaum.

Tanaka, J. W. & Taylor, M. (1991). Object categories and expertise: Is the basic level in the eye of the beholder? *Cognitive Psychology, 23,* 457-482.

Tulving, E. & Thompson, D.M. (1973). Encoding specificity and retrieval processes in episodic memory. *Psychological Review, 80,* 352-373.

Valle, R.S. & von Eckartsberg, R. (Eds.). (1981). *Metaphors of Consciousness.* New York: Plenum.

Vera, A.H. & Simon, H.A. (1993). Situated action: A symbolic interpretation. *Cognitive Science, 17,* 7-48.

Voss, J.F., Kennet, J., Wiley, J. & Schooler, T.Y.E. (1992). Experts at debate: The use of metaphor in the U.S. Senate debate on the Gulf Crisis. *Metaphor and Symbolic Activity, 7,* 197-214.

Weilinga, B.J. & Breuker, J.A. (1986). Models of expertise. In L. Steels (Ed.), *Proceedings of the 7th European Conference on Artificial Intelligence* (pp. 306-318). Brighton, UK: European Conferences on Artificial Intelligence.

Weitzenfeld, J., Riedl, T., Chubb, C. & Freeman, J. (1992). The use of cross-domain language by expert system developers. *Metaphor and Symbolic Activity, 3,* 185-195.

Will, R.P. (1991). True and false dependency on technology: Evaluation with an expert system. *Computers in Human Behavior, 7,* 171-183.

Zeitz, C.M. (this volume). Some concrete advantages of abstraction: How experts' representations facilitate reasoning.

Zsambok, C. & Klein, G. (Eds.). (in press). *Naturalistic Decision Making.* Hillsdale, NJ: Erlbaum.

Index

Composed in Berkeley, Berkeley Book, &
Berkeley Oldstyle digital fonts by
Adobe Systems, Inc.
The Berkeley family of fonts
were originally designed
in 1938 by Frederic W. Goudy
for the University of California Press.
These ITC fonts were redrawn
in 1983 by Tony Stan.

Printed and bound by
Braun-Brumfield, Inc.
Ann Arbor Michigan